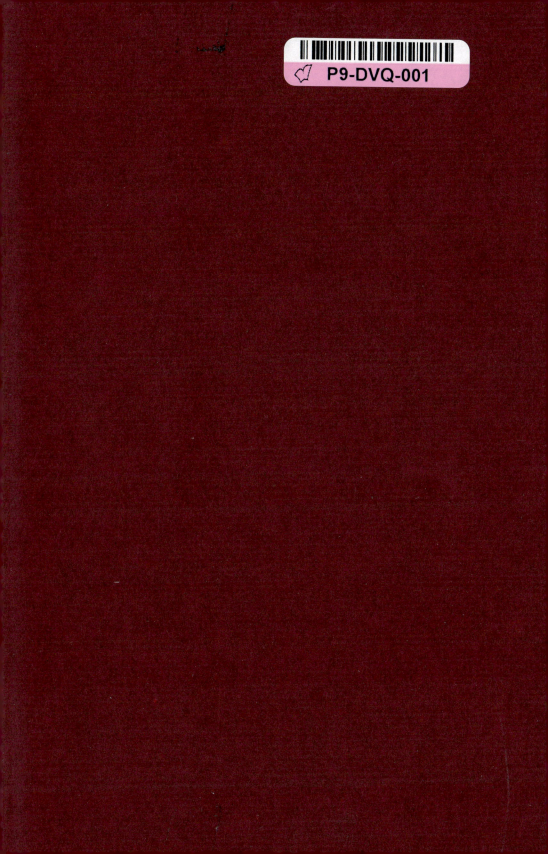

THE PHILOSOPHY
OF JUDAISM

THE PHILOSOPHY OF JUDAISM

The History of Jewish Philosophy
from Biblical Times to Franz Rosenzweig

by

Julius Guttmann

translated by

David W. Silverman

JASON ARONSON INC.
Northvale, New Jersey
London

Previous edition of this book was entitled *Philosophies of Judaism* (copyright © 1964 by Holt, Rinehart and Winston, Inc., New York).

Copyright © 1988 by Jason Aronson Inc.

10   9   8   7   6   5   4   3   2   1

Jason Aronson Inc. gratefully acknowledges the Leo Baeck Institute for permission to reprint "Julius Guttmann-Philosopher of Judaism" by Fritz Bamberger, copyright © 1966 by The Leo Baeck Institute (Year Book V, pp. 3-31).

Library of Congress Cataloging-in-Publication Data

Guttmann, Julius, 1880–1950.
  The philosophy of Judaism.

    Translation of: Die Philosophie des Judentums.
    Bibliography: p.
    Includes index.
    1. Philosophy, Jewish—History.   I. Title.
B154.G813   1988   181′.06   88-26214
ISBN 0-87668-872-5

Manufactured in the United States of America. Jason Aronson Inc. offers books and cassettes. For information and catalog write to Jason Aronson Inc., 230 Livingston Street, Northvale, New Jersey 07647.

Contents

Introduction

Julius Guttmann — Philosopher of Judaism
by Fritz Bamberger

THE *Hochschule für die Wissenschaft des Judentums* in Berlin, the seminary for the training of liberal rabbis and modern Jewish scholars, was founded in 1869, opened in 1872, and closed in 1942 when Nazi edicts forced the cessation of teaching.[1] During most of that time, roughly the first half-century of its existence, the school had no chair of philosophy. The main reason for this severe shortcoming lay in the institution's chronic and most troublesome problem, its continual lack of funds. The founders of the *Hochschule* had desired to fortify its academic freedom by making it financially independent of the state and the Jewish *Gemeinden*. They had hoped for enlightened Jewish individuals to come forward with ample support, an expectation that never materialized. In the first twenty-five years the average annual expenditure for the salaries of the school's professors amounted to a pitiful 9,380 marks. Around the turn of the century, the faculty was down to one full-time and one part-time teacher. In 1904 the *Hochschule* received a gift of 100,000 marks, a sum towering impressively in its financial annals unaccustomed as they were to six-figure entries. The fund's income was barely sufficient to pay for the modest salary of one new professor.[2] At the beginning of World War I the faculty of the *Hochschule* numbered four men, as many (or as few) as it had when it began operating in 1872. Some progress, though, there was: of the faculty of 1872 only one member devoted all his time to teaching; in 1914 there were three. German Jewry has proudly, and correctly,

---

[1] For its early history see I. Elbogen, *Die Hochschule, ihre Entstehung und Entwicklung, in Festschrift zur Einweihung des eigenen Heimes,* Berlin, 1907, pp. 1–98.

[2] The donor, stipulating that the gift was to be used for a chair in honour of her late husband, Louis Simon, left to the discretion of the school whether to establish a professorship in History and Literature or one in Ethics and Religious Philosophy of Judaism. The decision was in favour of Jewish history; Ismar Elbogen became the chair's first (and last) occupant.

claimed modern *Wissenschaft des Judentums* as its offspring. However, obviously, it did not over-exert itself to keep the child alive.

Despite the fact that for many years the *Hochschule* did not have a chair of Jewish philosophy, philosophical instruction had not been entirely absent. A philosopher, Moritz Lazarus, the originator of a new psychological discipline, *Völkerpsychologie,* was among the prime movers of the new school. Another philosopher, Hayim Steinthal, a brother-in-law of Lazarus and his associate in the new field of comparative folk-psychology, was one of the four men appointed to its first faculty. Steinthal's assignment was the teaching of Comparative History of Religion, Biblical Exegesis, and Linguistics;[3] occasionally, however, he gave classes in "Philosophy of Religion," "The Development of the Religious Idea in the Bible," and "Ethics." In like manner, in later years other professors taught Jewish philosophy in addition to their main courses. The immensely gifted P. F. Frankl, a scholar particularly interested in the literature of the Karaites, who in 1877, when only 29 years old, had succeeded Abraham Geiger as rabbi of the Berlin Jewish Community, taught Jewish Literature and Homiletics as well as History of Medieval Jewish Philosophy. Frankl died in 1887 and six years later Martin Schreiner joined the faculty of the *Hochschule.* Officially he was to serve as successor of David Cassel, instructor in Jewish History (which had not been Schreiner's field); but from sheer necessity—there was no one else to teach them—he also took over Bible and Philosophy of Religion (*biblische Wissenschaften* and *die religionsphilosophischen Disciplinen*). His vast erudition was quoted to justify such an immense load. Schreiner, mercilessly driving himself, and his students as well, to stay on top of so vast and diverse an area of scholarship, eventually collapsed—"a noble mind o'erthrown"—leaving behind impressive unfinished drafts of works in virtually all the fields he had tackled. Before his breakdown in 1902, he had written extensively on the various schools of Islamic theology, their connections with Arabic philosophic movements, and the relations of medieval Jewish philosophy and Arabic thought. At the conservative rabbinical school in Breslau, the *Jüdisch-Theologisches Seminar,* Manuel Joël in the 1850's and 60's and later Saul Horovitz had pursued a similar line of studies investigating the Greek and Arabic "sources" of medieval Jewish philosophy.

It was against this approach in teaching Jewish philosophy, the pre-eminence of the Arabist scholar, and the lack of systematic

---

[3]The other teaching assignments were: History of Judaism and its Literature (Abraham Geiger); Jewish History and Literature, Semitic Linguistics and Biblical Exegesis (David Cassel); Talmudic Disciplines (Israel Lewy).

treatment and genuine philosophical analysis, that an angry protest
was building up. An eminent philosopher but an outsider to Jewish
academic learning, Hermann Cohen, Professor at the University of
Marburg and founder of the Neo-Kantian School in German
philosophy, stepped before the representatives of Jewish scholarship
and demanded that *systematic* philosophy and philosophers equipped to
teach it be given their place in the institutions of higher Jewish
theological learning. On January 6, 1904, he spoke before the
members of the *Gesellschaft zur Förderung der Wissenschaft des Judentums*
(Society for the Promotion of the Science of Judaism) to justify *Die
Errichtung von Lehrstühlen für Ethik und Religionsphilosophie an den
Jüdisch-Theologischen Lehranstalten* (The Establishment of Chairs
of Ethics and Philosophy of Religion at the Jewish-Theological
Seminaries).[4] The idea was not born from a sudden impulse. Traces
of it may already be found in Cohen's *Ein Bekenntnis in der Judenfrage* (A
Confession on the Jewish Problem) of 1880, a pamphlet written in
reply to Heinrich von Treitschke's racist anti-Semitism.[5] "The
scientific concept of religion" and an autonomous system of ethics
related to it are the ground and sufficient justification of Judaism,
Cohen declared, and both essential to an understanding of Jewish
religion. Almost two decades later, the work of a Jewish author,
Moritz Lazarus' *Ethik des Judentums* (Ethics of Judaism) (1898)
stirred Cohen into a broader presentation of his Jewish philosophic
position. Cohen subjected the book to a devastating critique,[6] a
critique so furiously overheated and so patently unfair that it provoked
an equally hot-headed retort by the author. Coupling Cohen's review
of his book with another review by an anti-Semitic writer, Lazarus
disposed of both in one sentence: "Both gentlemen may differ
considerably from one another, but when it comes to my book they are
decidedly *par nobile fratrum.*"[7] Cohen had indeed taken a stand which
made the breach between him and Lazarus irreconcilable. He accused
Lazarus of ignorance, plagiarism and playing up to the vulgar taste of
the masses. Disregarding the finely detailed descriptions of Jewish

---

[4]Hermann Cohen's *Jüdische Schriften, hrsg. von Bruno Strauss,* vol. 2, Berlin, 1924, pp. 108-125.

[5]ibid., pp.73-94.

[6]*Das Problem der jüdischen Sittenlehre; eine Kritik von Lazarus' Ethik des Judentums,* in *Monatsschrift für Geschichte und Wissenschaft des Judentums,* vol. 43, 1899, pp. 385-400, 433-449; reprinted in *Hermann Cohens Jüdische Schriften,* vol. 3, Berlin, 1924, pp. 1-35.

[7]See David Baumgardt, The Ethics of Lazarus and Steinthal, in Year Book II of the Leo Baeck Institute, London, 1957, pp. 213f., containing a defence of Lazarus against Cohen.

ethical attitudes with which Lazarus' book abounds,[8] blind to its author's psychological and aesthetic skill in defining and articulating the quality and tone of Jewish morality, Cohen slashed into Lazarus' basic concept of a Jewish *Volksseele*. To Lazarus this Jewish folk-soul was a living source of ethical judgment keeping it pure and ever-freshly flowing. To Cohen such a concept, grounded in history and psychology, negated the reliability and certitude of the ethical judgment. To Lazarus the ethical commandments, as well as the historical institutions of Judaism which include religion and its ceremonies, were expressions of the Jewish folk-soul. To Cohen, the Kantian, ethics was autonomous (which religion is not); its validity derived from the concept of law; as *reine Gesetzgebung* it was of the highest objective order.

Moritz Lazarus died in 1903. Ironically, Hermann Cohen became his successor on the Board of Trustees of the *Hochschule*. For thirty years the philosophical ideas of Lazarus and Steinthal and, preceding them, of Abraham Geiger had set the intellectual tone of the *Hochschule*. Where Lazarus and Steinthal cited the Jewish folk-soul, Geiger, taking his cue from Schelling's Philosophy of Revelation, had called upon an *Allgeist* (universal spirit) who intimately touches and reaches into the *Einzelgeist* (individual spirit). With the official appearance on the scene of Cohen the atmosphere changed. Kant took over.

When Cohen spoke in 1904 before the members of the *Gesellschaft zur Förderung der Wissenschaft des Judentums* he enlarged on a thought which had previously appeared in his critique of Lazarus. Emphasis on the material contents of Jewish ethics, Cohen said, is misleading and dangerous when the influence of the ethics of Judaism on culture is under discussion. The unique distinction of Judaism lies elsewhere, namely in the way ethics and the idea of God are related. The Jewish idea of God has for its exclusive content the ethicalness of man. From this stems the irreconcilable contrast between Judaism and Christianity. The essence of Judaism has no parallel in what Christians define as the essence of Christianity. The *philosophy* of Judaism is the essence of Judaism and only the philosopher can express that essence. S. L. Steinheim, Samuel Hirsch, and Salomon Formstecher showed the kind of genuinely philosophic impetus and systematic intent which are appropriate and necessary for a presentation of the thought-content of Judaism. The later scholars who dealt with philosophy in the framework of *Wissenschaft des Judentums* lacked these qualities. Science of

---

[8]In his later Jewish writings Cohen showed an eminent flair for the same kind of description.

Judaism began as *Altertumswissenschaft* (science of antiquity) and, like most other 19th-century scholarship in the humanities, it was conducted as a historical science. History, as emphasis and method, dominated also the study of Jewish philosophy. Scholars such as Munk and Jöel who followed this trend did important work. But, on the other hand, the fact that classic Jewish philosophy flourished in the Arab-Spanish period, and that therefore knowledge of Arabic was indispensable for the study of its main works written in that language, gave the "Arabists" too strong a hold on "philosophical" studies. The philologist superseded the philosopher. But only the philosopher can produce the systematic presentation *(systematischer Lehrvortrag)* of Jewish ethics and philosophy of religion which does justice to what is essential in Judaism. The universities certainly will not offer it to young Jewish theologians. Therefore, Cohen concluded, Jewish philosophers are needed to teach philosophy of Judaism in the Jewish theological seminaries.[9]

It is in this spirit that Cohen himself began teaching at the *Hochschule*. During the vacation period in March 1905 he gave a course, four hours a week, on Logic with Reference to Ethics and Philosophy of Religion, and in the next year one on Ethics with Reference to Philosophy of Religion. In addition, he conducted seminars on Plato, Kant, and The Foundation of Jewish Medieval Philosophy in Greek Philosophy. The *Gesellschaft zur Förderung der Wissenschaft des Judentums* was planning at about that time its *Grundriss der Gesamtwissenschaft des Judentums* (Systematic Encyclopedia of the Science of Judaism) and Cohen was eager to write the volume on Jewish philosophy of religion[10] because, as he wrote to Rabbi Leopold Lucas in 1904, "the plan is wholly in conformance with the therapeutic procedure which I am urging. We thereby declare the philosophy of religion as our actual centre of gravity *(unsern aktuellen Schwerpunkt)*. "[11] He regarded his lectures at the *Hochschule* as a "political activity,"[12] since giving philosophy of religion

---

[9]It is revealing that when his lecture before the *Gesellschaft* was published as a booklet Cohen retitled it *Ethik und Religionsphilosophie in ihrem Zusammenhang* (Ethics and Philosophy of Religion in their Connection) (Berlin, 1904).

[10]The volume appeared in 1919, after Cohen's death, under the title *Die Religion der Vernunft aus den Quellen des Judentums*. The editor of the second edition of 1928, Bruno Strauss, basing this change on Cohen's correspondence with the *Gesellschaft* (now in the Archives of the New York Leo Baeck Institute), used the correct title *Religion der Vernunft* etc.

[11]Hermann Cohen, *Briefe, Ausgrevählt und hrsg. von Bertha und Bruno Strauss,* Berlin, 1939, p. 73.

[12]Letter to August Stadler, February 2, 1905; ibid. p. 73.

central significance "will enforce for us the attention which is so far lacking, and without which we will remain powerless in our own camp."[13] He enjoyed his teaching "because I know that I have the duty and ability to instruct the Jewish circles philosophically and to orientate the Jewish theologians. That they receive so cheerfully my presentation which denies the autonomy of religion is certainly a remarkable symptom."[14]

To continue, and to continue more systematically, the self-imposed mission of enlightening "his Jews" was one of the main reasons for Cohen's settling in Berlin after becoming in 1912 an *emeritus* in Marburg. His lectures at the *Hochschule,* such as "Introduction to Philosophy," and his seminars on Maimonides' *Moreh Nevuchim* and on "The Concept of Religion in the System of Philosophy" did not draw the crowds Cohen had expected. Only a small élite audience of students and friends attended, among them Franz Rosenzweig who wrote in February 1914 that he had been advanced to the role of discussion leader.[15] Important as Cohen's influence on these few was, the rather irregular lectures of the old man could not fill the need for a full-time teacher of philosophy of which the *Hochschule* had become increasingly aware.[16] Cohen himself was urging such an appointment. Already in 1911, one year before Cohen's coming to Berlin, the school had entered into negotiations with Julius Guttmann, *Privatdozent* at the University of Breslau, who the year before had obtained the *venia legendi* in philosophy. But Guttmann had declined the offer.[17] In 1917, under strong prodding from Hermann Cohen and Ismar Elbogen, the *Hochschule* Board of Trustees renewed its offer. Guttmann, still an instructor, had been made a titular professor the year before; he also had received an offer from his *alma mater,* the *Jüdisch-Theologisches Seminar* at Breslau.[18] This time Guttmann accepted and, early in 1918,

---

[13]Letter to Leopold Lucas; ibid. p. 73.

[14]Letter to August Stadler; ibid. pp. 73f.

[15]Franz Rosenzweig, *Briefe,* Berlin, 1935, p. 83.

[16]The faculty had been working for years on a prescribed plan of studies to replace the notoriously loose curriculum which in fact existed mainly as "oral tradition." As late as 1922, at the celebration of the school's 50th anniversary, a student chorus lamented mockingly:

" . . . . *es ist nun an die funfzig Jahr,*
Dass unser Studienplan in Bearbeitung war."

[17]His business-like and to-the-point (*geschäftlich und nüchtern*) letter was resented by the Board as undeservedly brusque. (Letter of Guttmann to Ismar Elbogen, January 6, 1912; Archives of the Leo Baeck Institute, New York).

[18]Letter of Guttmann to Elbogen, October 14, 1917; Archives of the Leo Baeck Institute, New York. The position at the Breslau seminary was filled by Isaak Heinemann.

the *Hochschule* announced that Guttmann, "a very eminent talent," would occupy the chair of philosophy upon his discharge from military service. The appointee, anything but a soldierly type, was then a war-time private in the Prussian army, enduring philosophically the attentions of a sergeant who regarded him as ideally fitted for kitchen duty. In the spring of 1919 he began teaching in Berlin.

Julius Guttmann was then 39 years old. Born in Hildesheim and living in Breslau since 1892, he was the son of Jakob Guttmann, a leading figure in the German rabbinate and a prolific author of learned books and treatises on medieval Jewish philosophy and its relationship to Christian scholastic philosophy. His mother was the sister of Professor David Jacob Simonsen, at one time chief rabbi of Denmark, an orientalist and bibliophile whose Judaica and Hebraica collection of more than 100,000 volumes is now part of the Royal Library in Copenhagen. Upon his graduation from the *Johannes-Gymnasium* in Breslau, Julius Guttmann became a student at the University of Breslau and the *Jüdisch-Theologisches Seminar*. In 1903 he obtained his Ph.D. from the university, in 1906 the rabbinical degree from the seminary. For a few months he served as substitute preacher *(Hilfsprediger)* in Berlin, a role in which he was so unsuccessful that he was anxious to forget that episode. Attempts to obtain a rabbinical post in other cities also failed[19] and Guttmann turned to an academic career. From 1911–1919 he was a member of the philosophy department of the University of Breslau.

If one surveys Guttmann's philosophical writings during this period, one understands why Hermann Cohen, the Kantian, had shown so strong an interest in the Breslau *Privatdozent*. Guttman's doctoral dissertation (1903) was a treatise on Kant's concept of God,[20] an unexpected theme considering the composition of the university's philosophy department. His teachers in philosophy were Clemens Baeumker, Hermann Ebbinghaus, and Jacob Freudenthal. Baeumker was a Catholic historian of medieval philosophy, Ebbinghaus a psychologist, and Freudenthal, whose main interest was in Hellenism and Spinoza, usually had his students, especially those from the

---

[19]Years later, when his colleagues discussed a young man who had given a disastrous *Probepredigt* (the sermon preached by the candidate for a rabbinical position), Guttmann remarked that it appeared from the reports that the candidate had handled himself worse then he had at the time he appeared before the Jewish community of Kassel and no man could have done *that* badly.

[20]An enlarged version, *Kants Gottesbegriff in seiner positiven Entwicklung* (Kant's Concept of God in Its Positive Development), appeared in 1906 in *Ergänzungshefte der Kantstudien*.

Jüdisch-Theologisches Seminar, write their theses on one or the other of these subjects. But Guttmann's father was strongly drawn toward Kant's philosophy as a means for a philosophic interpretation of Judaism,[21] and his influence, often acknowledged by the son, may explain the topic of the dissertation. In 1905 Julius Guttmann wrote for the *Monatsschrift* an article on Hermann Cohen's *Ethik* endorsing it with only a few minor reservations and stressing its importance for a modern philosophic understanding of Jewish religion. In 1908 he published a lecture[22] in which he presented, though only sketchily, the relation between Kant and Judaism with the same kind of "idealization" which, for the same purpose, Cohen adopted two years later in a lecture, *Innere Beziehungen der Kantischen Philosophie zum Judentum* (Inner Relations of Kant's Philosophy to Judaism).[23] Guttmann concluded that "the religious consciousness of modern times finds its expression in Kant and that this new religious consciousness, as it began to appear in Protestantism, means a return to the ideas of Judaism." In the same vein, Cohen, in summing up, declared that the importance of Judaism lies in the teachings of the prophets, their ethics, universalism, and humanism—an importance which is generally acknowledged today and recognized also as vital to the further development of Protestantism. And finally, the theme of Guttmann's dissertation *pro venia legendi, Kants Begriff der objektiven Erkenntnis* (Kant's Concept of Objective Cognition) (1911), was not far removed from that of Cohen's early work *Kants Theorie der Erfahrung* (Kant's Theory of Experience) (1871).

Although Guttmann's main subject while he was a student at the University of Breslau was philosophy, his studies in economics were so extensive and showed so much promise that his teacher, Werner Sombart, urged him to become his assistant and teach economics. Only after considerable deliberation did Guttmann decide in favour of philosophy. Some of his early writings stem from his interest in economics. In 1907, he published an essay on "The Economic and Social Significance of the Jews in the Middle Ages."[24] Though it offered no new data and relied entirely on known material, it succeeded in demonstrating that economic history is useful in throwing

---

[21]See Julius Guttmann's introduction to his father's *Fest- und Sabbath-Predigten,* Frankfurt, 1926.

[22]*Kant und das Judentum,* Breslau, 1908 *(Schriften hrsg. von der Gesellschaft zur Förderung der Wissenschaft des Judentums).*

[23]*28. Bericht der Lehranstalt für die Wissenschaft des Judentums in Berlin,* 1910; also in *Jüdische Schriften,* vol. 1, Berlin, 1924, pp. 284–305.

[24]*Die wirtschaftliche und soziale Bedeutung der Juden im Mittelalter,* in *Monatsschrift für Geschichte und Wissenschaft des Judentums,* vol. 51, 1907, pp. 257–290.

light on the development of post-biblical Jewish religion. Guttmann pointed out that one may well recognize economic motivations as instrumental in shaping certain phases of the religious development of Judaism (without falling prey to the exaggerations and the absolutism of the economic interpretation of history) and nevertheless assert the preeminence of religious forces in that development. This thesis also underlay the detailed criticism by Guttmann of Werner Sombart's book, *Die Juden und das Wirtschaftsleben* (The Jews and Modern Capitalism).[25] For Sombart the spirit of Judaism was identical with the spirit of capitalism. As he saw it, the idea of divine reward and punishment, asceticism *within* the world, the close connection between religion and business, the arithmetic concept of sin, and, above all, the rationalization of life—all of them characteristic of Jewish religion— developed in the Jews traits that caused the rise of the capitalistic spirit and resulted in a permanent attraction toward capitalistic attitudes. Guttmann's review differs from most other Jewish critiques. The others focused on the author's obvious anti-Semitic leanings and dismissed his findings altogether as unscientific because of that taint. Guttmann, in an almost casual and genteel aside, disarmed Sombart's "private confessions" as sentiments without interest to the scholar and pro- ceeded to examine each of Sombart's points as if there were no anti-Jewish bias at all. The prevailing climate of economic conduct among Jews (*jüdische Wirtschaftsgesinnung*), its inherent values, and the economic methods which result are indeed identical with those of modern capitalism, Guttmann stated.[26] But, he asserted, no causal relationship exists between the teachings of Jewish religion and modern capitalism. Jewish religion and the Jews did not create capitalism. Jewish religion is not a hotbed of intellectualism, pragmatic or otherwise. The highly reflective character of the Jew which shows in some Jewish post-biblical literature did not derive from the precepts of Judaism, but rather was the result of its long history and the historical influences it underwent. The original core of Jewish life, which survived most strongly in Jewish family life, is characterized by naive simplicity, ethical pathos, and a patriarchalism moved by warm sentiment and not marked by analytically sharp rationalism which is the ground in which capitalism flourishes.

---

[25] *Die Juden und das Wirtschaftsleben*, in *Archiv für Sozialwissenschaft und Sozialpolitik*, vol. 36, 1913, pp. 149–212.

[26] It would be a thorough misunderstanding of Guttmann's character to say Guttmann *conceded*; apologetics were abhorrent to him. When the *Berliner Tageblatt* once reported one of his infrequent popular lectures the account read as if he had argued apologetically. Guttmann was distressed for days and tried to have it corrected.

Throughout his life, and particularly during his years at the Hebrew University, Guttmann enjoyed discussing problems of economics, especially theoretical and methodological ones. At times, in the middle of the twenties, he toyed with the notion of developing his thoughts on the relationship between the religious concept and the economic activities of the Jews into a book. But nothing ever came of it.

The *Hochschule für die Wissenschaft des Judentums* which Julius Guttmann joined in the spring of 1919 was in a state of change. In the fifty years of its existence it had primarily been a school for the training of rabbis. But that was not what its founders had intended. They had carefully avoided in the name any indication to that effect. They had stipulated that the courses be given "exclusively in the pure interest of the *Wissenschaft des Judentums,* its preservation, advancement and propagation," and they had hoped that the expressly scientific character of the school would attract many nontheological students. These expectations did not come true. The school did produce an imposing number of scholars, but for all practical purposes it remained a rabbinical seminary. The years after World War I brought somewhat of a change. A new type of student began to appear, not many of them — the student-body was never large — but enough to make themselves felt.

From its beginning the *Hochschule* had drawn the majority of its students from orthodox families. Some were the sons of rabbis, many the sons of Jewish teachers. Most came from small communities in Silesia, the Province of Posen, East Prussia, and Southern Germany in which the firm tradition of Jewish life had never faltered. The *Hochschule* had also relied on a steady influx of students from Eastern Europe, young men, slightly older than the average German student, who had gone through long years of traditional Jewish learning and were eager to expose the methods and tenets which the *yeshivoth* had taught them to the questioning of critical scholarship. The "new student" had neither shared the traditonalist climate of the small Jewish community, nor did he possess any sizeable fund of Jewish learning. In all probability, one of the Jewish youth-movements which had sprung up in recent years had made him aware of the Jewish problem. He had read, though not necessarily fully understood, Buber and later Rosenzweig, and he was bursting with questions and eager to acquire a Jewish philosophy. He was deeply emotive, penitently aware of his insufficiency of Jewish learning, and sincerely anxious to acquire it together with a firmly founded Jewish *Weltanschauung.* The difference between learning and *Weltanschauung* was not settled in his mind either.

He looked forward to a university education, but felt strongly that getting only a university education, as perhaps his family expected, was wrong from the Jewish point of view. Some of these post-war students were considering professional careers in the Jewish field, possibly the rabbinate, but all that would depend on the clarification of their Jewish problems and the answer to their personal *Lebensfragen* which they expected to get in the classrooms of the *Hochschule*. They did not get them there, at least not expressly. The *Hochschule* taught *Wissenschaft*. Teaching was strictly academic and there was rarely a professor who allowed "opinion" or *Tendenz* to colour his presentation. Even stronger was the reluctance to point out the effect which ways of scholarly interpretations and scientific facts might have in influencing personal attitudes of Jewish and religious life.

This conscious reticence to mix scholarship and personal views, indeed a passionate opposition to step beyond the realm of "pure scholarship," was nowhere more evident than in the classes of Julius Guttmann. The statement, made in different context in his important essay *Religion und Wissenschaft im mittelalterlichen und im modernen Denken* (Religion and Science in Medieval and Modern Thought),[27] "the more philosophy is filled with religious life, the less it knows of religion as a specific object of its work," was central to his teaching of Jewish philosophy. Putting it simply, much too simply: philosophy is the non-religious tool, working with scientific precision, to analyze religion which as such is not philosophical. Guttmann never wavered from this fundamental position. It explains the man and the scholar, and marked his attitude toward the philosophers of religion of his time. A *religious thinker* was no philosopher to him. A philosophy that produced or communicated religious ideas and values, he thought, was not philosophy. This conviction explains his feelings, ranging from suspicion to rejection, toward religious philosophers like Buber, Baeck, and Rosenzweig. Sometimes, privately, these feelings were expressed sharply. When Leo Baeck, his colleague at the *Hochschule*, accepted an invitation to lecture at Count Keyserling's *Schule der Weisheit* (School of Wisdom) at Darmstadt, Guttmann remarked: *Nun ist er auch unter die Säulenheiligen gegangen* ("Now, he too has joined the halo-wearers").

The student who came to his classes for inspiration or in search of a guide to the religious controversies of the day had to be disappointed. Guttmann's lectures lacked topicality. They were impersonally abstract

---

[27]In *Festschrift zum 50jahrigen Bestehen der Hochschule für die Wissenschaft des Judentums*, Berlin 1922, p. 147.

and difficult. The man standing behind the lectern, usually dressed in an old-fashioned, comfortably loose black or grey "swallow-tail," his figure already stooped when he was in his early forties, his head bent toward the right shoulder, almost resting on it, was no smooth orator. He spoke haltingly, though forcefully, in a strange staccato rhythm, moving his right arm deep down and up in pumping movements as though he were digging words and phrases from the ground. And all the while his face shone through the clearest and friendliest of eyes, particularly so when, after a long pause, a complicated sentence had exploded into its final phrase. It required a good deal of attention and a good deal of training — training in listening to Guttmann — to follow his lectures. They were carefully prepared though invariably delivered without a manuscript or notes. It was like watching the labour pains of thought. But after a while one realized and admired the clear, unbroken, and logical flow of ideas. He did not illustrate; he did not clarify by metaphors. His presentation progressed evenly without dramatic crescendos or ritardandos and without restful diversions. All his effort was put into the understanding of a philosophical position, and such understanding was sought in the precise interpretation merely of its philosophical thought-content. No attempt was made — one should rather say, any attempt was absent — to show the views of philosophers as influenced, ever so slightly or accidentally, by personal factors, difficulties, or doubts. Philosophical attitudes appeared to be shaped by their inner philosophical necessity. Never was there any mention of non-philosophical outside motivations that might have influenced a philosopher. And also totally absent in his lectures was the spectacle of one kind of *Ideengeschichte* which some of his contemporaries offered in their treatment of history of philosophy: ideas detached from the ground in which they had grown, fighting with and superseding one another, fusing, breaking up and germinating new ideas, all happening in a philosophic no-man's-land.

His interpretations were not shaped or coloured by his own predilections. One had a hard time finding any in his lectures, which lacked value-judgments and were dispassionate to the degree of coolness. His presentations were governed by an unbounded faithfulness to the philosopher or the text under discussion. The temperament of the interpreter did not enter into the analysis of a viewpoint or thought-sequence. He conscientiously was bent upon the discovery of the genuine meaning. As a consequence, it sometimes seemed to the student that all philosophers were right. In private discussion Guttmann was critical of books and systems. In his writings some such criticism appeared (though only reluctantly and after long deliberation which usually did not fully remove his uneasiness about it),[28] but in his classes he avoided it rigorously. There the only way to learn of which philosophers he was critical was to attempt a list of those whom he never mentioned.

All this partly explains why Guttmann had students, though never many, but no disciples. Disciples are partisans, and this teacher did not lead to, nor did his temperament tolerate, partisanship in his students. One could learn much from him, although putting it this way does not seem adequate. One could learn *under* him and, if one advanced sufficiently, *with* him, the prerequisites of scholarship, unprejudiced methodic and clear thinking, uncompromising standards of research (above all the necessity for first-hand knowledge of the sources[29]), and an unromantic ethical devotion to truth. His students have gone many different ways philosophically, but they agree that though he could not *form* a school, for them he *was* one.

Guttmann's scholarly character, unbending and not prone to change, also made itself felt when he took over the scientific directorship of the *Akademie für die Wissenschaft des Judentums* (Academy for the Science of Judaism). When in 1917 Franz Rosenzweig addressed his brochure *Zeit ist's* to Hermann Cohen and asked for the creation of a Jewish Academy as a *jüdischgeistige* organization, he wanted the new institution to be the instrument for the solution of a pressing educational problem. The Academy was to train not theologians, but teachers of religion — a cadre of young men thoroughly imbued with Jewish scholarship and going out into the Jewish communities to reform the superficial religious instruction and lead Jewish youth to the living sources of Jewish religion. Hermann Cohen, who a year later publicly joined Rosenzweig's appeal equally, "saw the Academy, as it shaped itself before his eyes, not just as a place for the training of scholars and

---

[28]In the late 20's Guttmann held a private seminar, attended by his wife, a few friends, and a few students, in his apartment. The group studied first Max Scheler's *Der Formalismus in der Ethik und die materiale Wertethik* and then parts of Franz Rosenzweig's *Der Stern der Erlösung*. Guttmann was urged to publish his criticisms. The Scheler study was never completed; his criticism of Rosenzweig, often thought through anew by Guttmann, appeared eventually (1951) as the conclusion of the Hebrew translation of *Die Philosophie des Judentums*.

[29]When from 1926 to 1933 Guttmann served as one of the supervising editors of the Academy edition of Moses Mendelssohn's Collected Works, he was not satisfied to merely look over what his department editors submitted. He felt he could judge and had the right to make suggestions only if he possessed a self-acquired knowledge of all the original sources. He was not loath to read extensively, even if it was only to examine a minor point.

research workers, but as something he had hoped and longed for, a means to intensify and renew the spirit of Judaism."[30] In 1919, Eugen Taeubler, the first director of the *Forschungs-Institut für die Wissenschaft des Judentums* (Research Institute for the Science of Judaism), announced an organizational plan for the Institute which he had drafted.[31] To the Academy and its Institute were no longer assigned the far-flung aims which had motivated Rosenzweig. The Academy's goal now was to raise, through the collective and individual scholarly efforts of its members, Jewish scholarship in extent and depth to the level of general scholarship—a level, it was maintained, which the Jewish scholar, except in a few individual instances, had not achieved. "Jewish science stands in the shadow. The Academy ought to become the lever to lift it up to the realm of general sciences and to bring it beyond its national-religious framework *(über den völkisch-religiösen Rahmen hinaus)* to that effectiveness in the whole of culture which its inner riches merit."[32]

This trend away from the Academy's original objectives became stronger when, in 1922, Guttmann took over the directorship of the Research Institute from Taeubler. Guttmann realized and acknowledged that the call for a reconstruction of Jewish science had not been issued for merely theoretical, scholarly interests. "Science of Judaism was wanted because Jewish life was wanted." With Rosenzweig it was a religious will which wanted to rebuild a dissolving "Jewish world" with the help of scholarship. Similarly Cohen, out of the innermost motives of his religious and philosophical idealism, regarded science as the "spiritual bulwark of continuous existence." Others were prompted by non-religious motivations, the inner clarification of Jewish consciousness *(jüdisches Bewusstsein)* or the idea of a spiritual representation of Judaism through a rejuvenated science of Judaism.[33]

Against all such ideas of "a life-connected and life-determining Jewish science" *(lebensverbundene und lebensbestimmende jüdische Wissenschaft)* Guttmann held that "only when science does full justice to *its own law* can it also fulfil the function which falls to it in the totality of

---

[30]Ernst Cassirer, as quoted by Selma Stern-Taeubler, *Eugen Taeubler and the Wissenschaft des Judentums,* in Year Book III of the Leo Baeck Institute, London, 1958, p. 50.

[31]*Korrespondenzblatt des Vereins zur Gründung und Erhaltung einer Akademie für die Wissenschaft des Judentums,* I, 1920, pp. 10–18.

[32]ibid., p. 18.

[33]*Die Akademie für die Wissenschaft des Judentums zu ihrem zehnjährigen Bestehen,* in *Festgabe zum zehnjährigen Bestehen der Akademie für die Wissenschaft des Judentums 1919–1929,* Berlin, 1929, p. 4; see also Guttmann, Franz Rosenzweig, in *Korrespondenzblatt,* 10, 1929, pp. 2f.

Jewish life. . . . Living science distinguishes itself from dead scholarship only in that its specialized work is governed by general viewpoints
and aims at a unified methodic goal. . . . Therefore the connection [of
science of Judaism] with the interests of Jewish life cannot by nature
always have the same degree of immediacy and closeness. All phenomena of Jewish life, all periods of Jewish history, all areas of Jewish
literature have their rightful place within the science of Judaism,
regardless of whether their relation to current Jewish interests is close
or remote. . . . The more conscientiously the Research Institute is
guided in the selection of its topics by the *inner needs* of Jewish science,
the more it will be able to contribute to the whole of Jewish life (*jüdische
Gesamtheit*)."[34] Once a student approached Guttmann and asked him
whether, since *Wissenschaft des Judentums* was *jüdisches Lernen,* it could not
well be of itself a sufficient and full form of Jewish life. Guttmann
replied that modern Jewish scholarship was not Jewish learning in the
traditional sense, that one could even imagine it being practised by a
non-Jew, and that the Jews who spent their day in *lernen* did not give
up praying.

It has been suggested that Guttmann's views on the relation
between the science of Judaism and the exigencies of Jewish life
problems, and his uncompromising differentiation between the *homo
philosophicus* and the *homo religiousus* might have been influenced by Max
Weber's postulate of the *Wertfreiheit* (freedom from value-judgments) of
science. Weber admonished the academic teacher to present scientifically acquired knowledge of *factual* relationships and to refrain from
playing the role of the seer or prophet. When Alfred Bonné, professor
at the Hebrew University, brought up this suggestion, Guttmann only
conceded that he agreed with Weber and had found support in him for
his position. Indeed, Guttmann did not need such an outside stimulus;
his views were the necessary concomitant of his own philosophical
tenets.

In his philosophical writings Guttmann never presented a systematic outline of these tenets. His writings,[35] mostly articles, with the one
exception of his book *The Philosophy of Judaism,* are on the *history* of
philosophy, and it is from these historical investigations that one has to
extract his methodic and systematic views. The best key to them is the
article on *Religion und Wissenschaft im mittelalterlichen und im modernen*

---

[34] *Bericht des wissenschaftlichen Vorstandes über das Jahr 1922/23,* in *Korrespondenzblatt,* V,
1924, pp. 46f.

[35] A bibliography of Guttmann's writings by Baruch Schochtman appeared in *Iyyun,*
vol. 2, no. 1, Jerusalem 1951, pp. 11–19; a supplement to it by Saul Esch, *ibid.,* no.
3, pp. 182–184.

Denken (Religion and Science in Medieval and Modern Thought) which he contributed to the *Festschrift* on the occasion of the 50th anniversary of the *Hochschule* (Berlin 1922). This article clearly reveals the pedigree of Guttmann's philosophical beliefs. Kant and Schleiermacher were his masters. Kant, said Guttmann, gave philosophy of religion its decisive turn. He liberated the philosophical analysis of religion from its most hampering burden, the identification of religious and metaphysical truth. The criticism of religion by the philosophers of the Enlightenment had already invalidated the historical proofs of religion. Thus, Guttmann stated, it was established, once for all, that religious truth can rest neither on metaphysical nor on historical knowledge. But Guttmann did not follow Kant in the latter's characterization of religious truth. According to Kant, the truth of religion is guaranteed by the validity of the ethical law which postulates the belief in the dominion of ethics over reality. Religious truth is a consequence of ethical truth and thus its contents can be deduced from ethical principles. Religion is moral religion. The religious act of faith remains the form in which the ethical demands a religious supplementation, but, said Guttmann, it never leads to the possession of genuine religious truth.[36] It is at this point, where in Kant the meaning of the religious is swallowed up by the ethical, that Guttmann left him — and Cohen — to turn to Schleiermacher.

In Guttmann's interpretation Schleiermacher fulfils the methodic aims of Kant's philosophy of religion. Schleiermacher's analysis of religion is in its ultimate methodic intent the application to religion of Kant's epistemological method. His religious philosophy is dominated by the thought that to religious experience belongs a specific certitude on which all religious conviction is founded. Religious consciousness is coupled with a particular truth — religious truth. This truth is not that of objective knowledge, but *personal* certitude, which though personal is trustworthy nevertheless. That certitude relates man to a world of religious truth which is an autonomous realm of objectivity. Religious objects possess a character of reality. To determine that character of reality is the ultimate goal of the analysis of religion.[37]

It is obvious that the Schleiermacher whom Guttmann interpreted and from whom he took a key point for his own programme of a philosophy of religion is not the complete Schleiermacher. Schleiermacher's "description" of religious reality did not come into Guttmann's focus. He did not, and as a religious Jew could not,

---

[36] *Religion und Wissenschaft*, pp. 205–207.
[37] ibid., pp. 207–210.

recognize God's immanency in the universe. The identification of God with the world was left unconsidered. And God was never regarded as the unity of man's personal life, as the One preserving and symbolizing that unity which, in worldly life, is constantly breaking up. Guttmann utilized selected aspects of Schleiermacher's philosophy; but in doing so he transformed Schleiermacher. He reinterpreted him in the light of Kant and thus eliminated the romantic Schleiermacher, the Schleiermacher who broke away from Kant to become an irrationalist with pantheistic leanings. Guttmann incorporated elements of Schleiermacher into Kant's epistemological criticism which thus was expanded to include a platform from which religion could be reached and maintained as an autonomous entity, not merely as an auxiliary supplement and postulate of ethics.

The position which Guttmann propounded in the essay of 1922 is distinctly different from that of his early writings in which he spoke more or less like an orthodox Kantian and follower of Cohen. The trend toward the new view is found for the first time, though still indecisive, in Guttmann's article *Das Verhältnis von Religion und Philosophie bei Jehuda Halevi* (The Relation between Religion and Philosophy in Yehuda Halevi), his contribution to the *Festschrift zu Israel Lewy's 70. Geburtstag* (Breslau 1911).[38] Most interpretations had presented Yehuda Halevi as an irrationalistic antagonist of all philosophy. Guttmann showed this was not so. In Halevi's *Kusari*, certitude flowing from an inner, specifically religious experience and certitude derived from philosophical proof are not mutually exclusive. Their identity, the identity of revealed and philosophical truth which most of the medieval philosophers asserted, was denied by Halevi. He made revelation autonomous. In the realm of religion he supplanted rational philosophy with a rational supernaturalism which, of course, is not acceptable to modern philosophy of religion. But on the way to that position, Guttmann emphasized, Halevi came in one respect close to the modern concept of religion. Declaring the immediate certitude of God and the individual's communion with God as the essence of piety, Halevi correctly described basic phenomena of religious life. Halevi was satisfied with the mere description. The modern philosopher, Guttmann pointed out, has to show the validity of religious belief beyond its mere existentiality. At the same time, he must recognize that the inner experience of man's communion with God is the source

---

[38]The importance of this early essay was recognized by Ephraim Shmueli in his article on Julius Guttmann, in *Chokhmath Yisrael be-ma'arav Eropa,* ed. Simon Federbusch, New York, 1958, pp. 148–165.

of knowledge which guarantees the reality of a living God as the surest possession of our consciousness.

This is neither Kant's nor Cohen's language. Yet, in his essay of 1911 Guttmann still regarded as incompatible the Kantian attempt to provide a philosophical foundation for religion (by assigning the religious convictions to the inventory of ethical truths) and Schleiermacher's concept of religion (which denied Kant's ethical postulation of religion and made the certitude of personal feeling the sole ground of a non-ethical religious reality). Guttmann realized, though, that the phenomena of religious life as Yehuda Halevi described them constitute its very essence. Even if the philosophical justification of religious belief were based on ethical reason, true religious life, as Guttmann concluded, is possible only "where the certitude of God seizes us with the full force of feeling and personal certitude is alive in us with immediacy. . . . Religious life cannot be produced by laying the foundations of religious truth ideationally."[39]

This strong, often reiterated insistence on the priority of personally experienced religious life over the philosophical and systematic construction of religion marks the difference between Guttmann and Cohen and other philosophers who followed Cohen. Guttmann never sounded like Paul Natorp and Benzion Kellermann. And differing from other interpreters of Cohen, Franz Rosenzweig foremost among them, Guttmann maintained that even the Cohen of the *Religion der Vernunft aus den Quellen des Judentums* (Religion of Reason Out of the Sources of Judaism), though he had modified the content of his God-idea, had not changed its methodic character.[40] The last chapter of Guttmann's great historical survey of the philosophy of Judaism, published in 1933, is devoted to an analysis of Cohen's philosophy of religion.[41] Here the choice of terminology and the direction of Guttmann's analysis make it perfectly clear where his and Cohen's ways separated. "For Cohen, God still remains idea in this last phase of his thinking."[42] For Guttmann, God was reality.

In his personal studies and in his lectures Guttmann tried to progress from the critical ascertainment of Cohen's shortcomings to a determination of where his own stand on the autonomy of religious

---

[39] *Das Verhältnis von Religion und Philosophie*, p. 358.

[40] A letter from Rosenzweig to Jakob Horovitz of April 1924 (Franz Rosenzweig, *Briefe*, Berlin, 1935, p. 499) indicates that Guttmann had read Rosenzweig's Introduction to the Academy edition of Cohen's *Jüdische Schriften* prior to publication and raised doubts about the decisive character of Cohen's "conversion."

[41] *Die Philosophie des Judentums*, pp. 345–362.

[42] ibid., p. 362.

experience would take him. It did not take him far. He was aware that others, in fact the most important contemporary philosophers of religion, had moved toward a new metaphysics or irrationalism in accord with the general philosophical trend of his day.[43] Conscientious personal scruples and strong philosophical doubts kept him apart from them. He was constitutionally too deeply rooted a philosopher of reason to even try their way. He was more attracted to the phenomenological school of Husserl and his disciples, and convinced that phenomenological analysis would be useful in describing religious experience and defining its general structure. The few indications in his published works and other casual references show that one of the main attractions of this method for him was — at least as he saw it — that it was not an outright denial of Kant's achievement, but rather the extension of Kant's *a priori* beyond the realm of mere form. Also in this approach to phenomenology Guttmann revealed himself as the philosopher of reason.

The various facets of Guttmann's philosophical personality and his rational *credo* from which they derive are reflected in his imposing historical work, *Die Philosophie des Judentums* (The Philosophy of Judaism, 1933). In one sense, though most of his writings deal with the history of philosophy, Guttmann was not genuinely a historian. The strongest interest of the historian, studying what time does to men, their ideas and their creations, and what men's ideas do to time, was markedly absent in Guttmann's history of Jewish philosophy covering the basic ideas of biblical religion, Jewish hellenistic philosophy, the ideas of Talmudic Judaism, the Jewish philosophy of the Middle Ages, and culminating in a review of the Jewish philosophers of modern times. Again, emphasis on method is strong in this book. Philosophy is charged with the task of *expressing* the idea-content *(Ideengehalt)* of religion, and even when Guttmann treats philosophers whose prime motivation was the justification of Jewish religion, he stresses their contribution in formulating philosophically the religious ideas. And because such philosophical formulation with the aim of expressing a specific truth is a function of reason, Guttmann's history of Jewish philosophy is fundamentally a history of rationalist Jewish philosophy.[44]

---

[43]See, for example, *Religion und Wissenschaft im mittelalterlichen und im modernen Denken*, p. 213.

[44]Gershom Scholem, *Julius Guttmann zum 70. Geburtstag*, in *Mitteilungsblatt des Irgun Olej Merkas Europa*, Tel Aviv, 1950, no. 15, characterized *Die Philosophie des Judentums* as "the for-a-long-time-to-come definitive presentation of rationalist Jewish philosophy." Stressing the rationalist character of Guttmann's philosophizing he said: "Even

In Jewish philosophy, Guttmann showed, two main approaches exist. Medieval philosophy did not separate religion and philosophy methodically, but equalized their respective contents. Modern philosophy, on the other hand, did separate those two realms of validity. In the process, medieval philosophers had to modify philosophy to accommodate religion and had to alter Jewish religious concepts to conform to Greek philosophy. Modern thinkers, Guttmann asserted, were better able to preserve the genuine meaning of Judaism.

Two years after the publication of Guttmann's *Die Philosophie des Judentums,* Leo Strauss subjected the book and its general philosophical approach to penetrating criticism.[45] Strauss, denying the superiority of modern over medieval Jewish philosophy, pointed out that attributing such a superiority to modern philosophy would imply giving up the belief in revelation as one of the central ideas of traditional Jewish religion. And, Strauss insisted, that belief was a central idea as a matter of historical fact. Indeed it was so central that it was the *conditio sine qua non* for all other religious ideas. Further, Strauss argued, Guttmann's presentation makes it appear that to the philosophers of the Middle Ages the primary purpose of revelation was the communication of *truths,* not the communication of the *Law.* Strauss recommended that the *historian* of Jewish medieval philosophy, at least for heuristical purposes, accept the superiority of medieval over modern philosophy and understand the medieval dichotomy of belief and knowledge correctly as that of law and philosophy. Only by discarding the modern concept of a "religious consciousness," and after a reinterpretation of the philosophical idea of the divine law in the light of its origins in Plato, would it become evident which philosophy, medieval or modern, was more capable of preserving the essence of Jewish religion.

Strauss' answer is implicit in his criticism. He recognized that Guttman's concept of philosophy of religion was strongly conditioned by Schleiermacher. He pointed out that it was in the tradition of Schleiermacher that Guttmann, like other modern philosophers, had replaced the medieval concept of belief—rationalistic or supernatural-

---

when in philosophical analyses he penetrated to the truly abysmal depths of religious thinking, Guttmann never allowed himself to luxuriate in an existentialist ecstasy or in mystical ambiguities, but rather carried clarity and light into these depths."

[45] *Der Streit der Alten und Neueren in der Philosophie des Judentums — Bemerkungen zu Julius Guttmann, Die Philosophie des Judentums,* in Leo Strauss, *Philosophie und Gesetz,* Berlin, 1935, pp. 30–67. Strauss was formerly a member, working under Guttmann, of the Research Institute of the Berlin *Akademie für die Wissenschaft des Judentums.*

istic, but in any case intellectualistic—with one built on the "innerness of the religious consciousness" *(Innerlichkeit des religiösen Bewusstseins).* Strauss rejected this concept. It should be emphasized however—and this did not come into the purview of Strauss' criticism—that Guttmann, rationalist that he was and remained, never followed Schleiermacher all the way. Having set the methodic scheme for a philosophy of religion, he was forever hesitant to fill it out. The systematic philosophy of religion which fused Kant and Schleiermacher, or, in Jewish terms, Maimonides and Yehuda Halevi, never emerged, probably because their fusion was an impossibility within a strictly rationalist scheme.

Guttmann was aware of the importance of Strauss' frontal attack. To answer it and the other essays in Strauss' book,[46] he wrote an article, *Philosophie der Religion oder Philosophie des Gesetzes?—eine Auseinandersetzung mit Leo Strausses Buch "Philosophie und Gesetz"* (Philosophy of Religion or Philosophy of the Law? A Critical Discussion of Leo Strauss' Book *Philosophy and Law*). The article was written when Guttmann was living in Jerusalem. It was to appear in the *Monatsschrift,* and when that became impossible after its expiration in 1939, Guttmann wrote twice to Ismar Elbogen in New York asking him to place it for publication in America: "To publish it in Hebrew serves little purpose." "Though the book appeared a number of years ago, it seems to me that a discussion of principles *(eine prinzipielle Auseinandersetzung)* is still justified."[47] The article never appeared and seemingly is lost.[48] This is all the more regrettable since philosophical controversy furnishes insights into a man's thinking and provides an illumination that a tightly written book, such as Guttmann's, does not offer. On the other hand, there is no doubt that Guttmann's views did not change. The Hebrew translation of his *Die Philosophie des Judentums*[49] which appeared one year after his death had been supervised by him. He had added to it a chapter on Nachman Krochmal[50]

---

[46] *Die gesetzliche Begründung der Philosophie* (The Founding on Law of Philosophy) and *Die philosophische Begründung des Gesetzes* (The Founding on Philosophy of the Law).

[47] Letters of November 18, 1940 and September 29, 1941; Archives of the Leo Baeck Institute, New York.

[48] A few years later, Guttmann wrote to Strauss that since the latter had changed his views regarding medieval philosophy, he would rather postpone publication of his answer until Strauss had sufficiently elaborated his new position. The bibliography of Guttmann's writings, mentioned p. 24 no. 35, lists only one manuscript volume found after his death containing five unpublished lectures from the years 1927—1932.

[49] *Ha-pilosofiyyah shel ha-yahaduth,* Jerusalem, 1951.

[50] In his letter of November 18, 1940 to Elbogen, Guttmann reported that he was

and a concluding chapter on Franz Rosenzweig, and had made corrections and small insertions throughout the book. None materially affected his interpretations of Jewish philosophers, nor his methodic concept of a philosophy of Jewish religion. His presentation and criticism of Rosenzweig's philosophy in fact served to underline the character of Guttmann's philosophical and religious personality.

Guttmann, to whom the object of a Jewish philosophy of religion was the idea-content of Judaism, criticized Rosenzweig for basing it on personal experience, and exaggerating whatever influences had been decisive in his life. He disapproved of Rosenzweig's using the language of Judaism to express personal experiences which had no general validity and which a Christian or non-religious thinker could as well express. In addition, Guttmann pointed out that Rosenzweig's philosophy often occupied itself with ideas and distinctions taken from Jewish dogmatic tradition, instead of dealing with ideas of primary religious experience. Concluding thus with a rejection of Rosenzweig's personalized Jewish philosophy, denying it validity as a construction of personal experiences though acknowledging its stimulating influences on a generation of Jews, Guttmann took his stand against existentialist philosophy. Setting idea against existence,[51] Guttmann objected, to use Rosenzweig's term, to "occasionalistic thinking" *(Gelegenheitsdenken)*.[52] Opposed to Rosenzweig's "apologetic thinking" in which nothing in Judaism is self-understood and which, as Rosenzweig pointed out, begins to operate "once the philosopher has been thrust to the boundaries of Judaism," Guttmann reaffirmed a philosophy of Judaism which is not "thinking inside Judaism" *(Denken im Judentum),* does not produce religious attitudes, but rather expresses and formulates the ideas of Judaism by the means of a rationalist philosophy.

Writing *Die Philosophie des Judentums* had been an arduous effort. A long book did not come easy to Guttmann. Without the constant prodding of his wife, Grete, he might never have accepted the

working on an anniversary article about Krochmal (published in 1941 in a Bialik memorial volume) and remarked: "I realize how little we know of his philosophical views in spite of what has been written about him."

[51]In 1944, Guttmann contributed a deep-reaching critical investigation of Heidegger's existentialist philosophy, *Eksistentziah ve-ideah* (Existence and Idea), to *Haguth, a Festschrift* on the occasion of Hugo Bergman's 60th birthday (pp. 153–173). An English translation appeared 1960 in vol. VI (pp. 9–40) of Scripta Hierosolymitana, Publications of the Hebrew University Jerusalem: Existence and Idea. Critical Observations on the Existentialist Philosophy.

[52]*Apologetisches Denken — Bemerkungen zu Brod und Baeck* (Apologetic Thinking — Annotations on Brod and Baeck), in *Zweistromland,* Berlin, 1926, p. 71f.

invitation from the publishing house of Ernst Reinhardt in Munich to write it. Certainly, without her it never would have been finished. "I am his catalyst," she once said. That probably was incorrect terminology. But she did continually prompt him to go on and overcome his over-conscientious doubts as to whether he was ready, and whether all the necessary preparatory work was done. Guttmann's handwriting was hard to read and often illegible. So he dictated the entire book to his wife who took it down in longhand.[53]

Guttmann married Grete Henschel shortly after he joined the faculty of the *Hochschule*. She had been a student of Eugen Kühnemann (of whom her husband did not think very much) at the University of Breslau and obtained the Ph.D. degree with a dissertation on Schiller's philosophy of history. It is difficult to imagine two more different people and it is difficult to think of a happier marriage. Grete Guttmann came from a well-to-do, liberal family, and her interest in religion can best be described as literary or intellectual. Julius Guttmann was pious and lived like an orthodox Jew although there was nothing ostentatious in his religious practices. Grete Guttmann showed an unending attraction for the bizarre, the daring, and the bohemian; her husband's tastes were conservative. Grete Guttmann had an immense capacity for people, any kind of people and especially people out-of-the-ordinary. She was the interested and sympathetic confidante to many a bohemian writer, artist, and professor who confessed to her his troubled life. The Guttmanns were twice in America, in 1924, when Julius Guttmann was a guest professor at the Jewish Institute of Religion in New York, and in 1930, when he taught at the Hebrew Union College in Cincinnati.[54] Both times, and particularly from her stay in New York, Grete Guttmann came back madly in love with America, its *élan vital*, and its wild contrasts. She loved Stephen S. Wise because he had taken her to dingy speak-easies and the jazz-joints of Harlem. Julius Guttmann shuddered when he remembered a lecture he gave before some club where he was preceded on the programme by a magician and followed by dancing. His wife enjoyed every minute of the affair, including her husband's uncomfortable bewilderment. Willingly, with a bit of embarrassment and a shy smile, Guttmann tolerated his wife's teasing gibes at his old-fashioned suits, shirts and ties, and only when she showed a mocking impatience with what she

---

[53]When the publisher acknowledged the manuscript he asked whether the invention of the typewriter had remained unknown to the Guttmann household.

[54]The Cincinnati school, which earlier in the twenties had approached Guttmann to become the successor of David Neumark, again offered him a professorship during his visit, but he declined.

regarded as too long a religious ritual or prayer did an angry flash from
his eyes call her to order.

On Saturday afternoons, friends and casual visitors would gather
in the Guttmann's comfortable apartment at 2 *Wullenweberstrasse* in the
Berlin *Hansa-Viertel.* After coffee and cake they would sit in the library
where Guttmann's and his father's books lined the walls from floor to
ceiling.[55] The talk would range from politics over literature and new
books to scholarly matters. There Guttmann, in public often shy or
professorially formal, would be at his freest and his humor at its most
genial. One could easily foretell a witticism in the making. The fingers
that tapped out a beat on his knees would tap faster, an impish smile
would appear on his face, and a sparkle in his eyes would indicate that
he was ready to tell his joke. His wit had bite. A writer who was built
like a heavy-weight, whose books were big and whose introductions to
books were usually longer than the writings they were to explain, was
called *der in jeder Beziehung breite.* Told of the many short-lived love
affairs of a philosopher who had just denounced neo-Aristotelianism he
remarked: *Auf dem Gebiet wenigstens ist er ein Peripatetiker geblieben.* When
a department store owner proposed to subsidize the *Akademie* but
demanded influence on its scholarly direction, he summarized the
offer: *Er wollte mich zu seinem philosophischen Rayonchef machen.*
Guttmann's contemporaries at the Breslau seminary never had forgotten his satirical essay, *Der Seminarist,* published in a student paper.
It began: *Der Seminarist ist ein Herdentier. Er tritt meistens in Rudeln auf und
ernährt sich von Barmizwa-Knaben. Im Herbst wird er oft von einer epidemischen
Krankheit befallen, der Festpredigt. Man hatte schon in alter Zeit Predigten; man
nannte sie Midraschim. Diese darf man abschreiben. Manche nennen auch die
neuere Predigt Midrasch.* —Guttmann was a chain smoker of cigars[56] and
on Sabbath afternoons, long before the holiday had ended, he would
carefully select his first cigar of the week, caress it affectionately, and
light it as soon as the *Havdalah* ceremony was over.

When Hitler came to power, Guttmann had less illusions about the
outcome than many others. In 1934 he left Berlin. America, which he
knew from his two visits, did not attract him. He accepted an invitation
from the Hebrew University and after a few months he decided to stay.
The decision to cut his ties with the *"Heimat"* and the *Hochshule,* "the
ideal of a Jewish scholarly institution," had been a difficult one, he

---

[55]Guttmann's books are now in the Library of The Hebrew University in Jerusalem.

[56]In Jerusalem he used to say: "What this country needs most is a good cigar." His
facetious translation of the Hebrew term *totzereth ha-aretz* (Made in Israel) was "the cigar
for the non-smoker."

wrote. But "hard times require hard decisions and I belong to the lucky ones who make this sacrifice for the sake of something positive."[57]

Guttmann had never been a political Zionist. The philosophic foundations of Zionism, especially as the German academic Zionists expounded them, were antagonistic to his philosophic tenets. He sensed a strong romantic undertone, the mystique of a *Volksgeist* which his rationalism could not take. Before the Hitler years he would concede that political Zionism was useful to restore de-judaized Jews to Judaism and once remarked that he did not need that crutch—a phrase he withdrew as too harsh the moment he had uttered it. Finally, he did not believe in the practicality of Zionism as the ultimate solution of the "Jewish problem." "That Palestine can receive sufficient numbers of Jews to lead to a solution of the political *Judenfrage* (Jewish question) lies outside the realm of possibility for the predictable future," he wrote as a conclusion in the article on Zionism which he contributed in 1931 to *Die Religion in Geschichte und Gegenwart* (Religion in History and the Present), a Protestant encyclopedia, adding "but the strong moral energies of the Zionist movement may well succeed in making her (Palestine) into a spiritual centre of Judaism which can carry new strength to the Jewish life of all countries."

Guttmann's attitudes toward Zionism had not been hastily formed. Neither were they preponderantly emotional. His scholarly make-up required scientific clarity and analysis in areas of personal belief. He never relented in his conviction that the scholar's responsibility was to separate scientific fact from value-judgment in public issues and that his public function was to create awareness of where the dividing line lay. However in doing so the scholar need not deprive himself or others of the right to value-conditioned decisions and opinions. Such was the purpose of the scholarly essay, *Der Begriff der Nation in seiner Anwendung auf die Juden* (The Concept of Nation in its Application to the Jews), which he published in 1914 in the anti-Zionist K.C.-Blätter.[58]

The question of whether or not the Jews were a nation was in those days, and had been since the rise of the Zionist movement, a matter of heated discussion. Instead of re-arguing the shop-worn and frozen arguments, Guttmann proposed a methodic examination of the question (*Fragestellung*) underlying the controversy. This controversy, he found, was primarily semantic; throughout, it depended too much on the definition of the word "nation." But the dictionary should not decide the future of the Jews, particularly when the term in question

---

[57]Letter to Elbogen, first half of 1935 (exact date illegible); Archives of the Leo Baeck Institute, New York.
[58]Vol. 4, pp. 69–79, 109–116.

was by nature so suspiciously vague. Further, there was dangerous basic ambiguity. Saying that the Jews are an exclusively religious group can mean that religious motives *factually* tie the Jews together. It can also mean that the *value* of Judaism, which justifies its continuance, rests exclusively on its religious aspects. The same ambiguity prevails in the arguments of the opposite camp which declares that the Jews are a national group. Judgments on what factually is, are interwoven with convictions of what ought to be. What are the facts, asked Guttmann.

Since the Dispersion, Jewish group consciousness *(Gemeinschaftsbewusstsein)* has consisted of more than mere awareness of the factual identical features which the group shares. The motivations which held the individual in the group became premises of its continuance and factors which determined its character. That these motivations were of a religious nature was, in Guttmann's opinion, indisputable. Biblical Judaism produced a universal concept of religion and fused it with a concept of a nationally determined group. In later Judaism the Jewish people lived on as a religious group consisting of members of the Jewish tribe *(Angehörige des jüdischen Stammes)*. Religious group consciousness merged with tribal consciousness *(Bewusstsein der Stammesgemeinschaft)*. The seclusion of the group and strong hostile pressure from the outside caused the expansion of Jewish group life beyond the religious realm. The religious community became a legal and cultural group with an autonomous intellectual and literary life. Separated from any political or territorial foundation, medieval Jewry possessed a life of its own which came close to that of a nation. Nevertheless, as Guttmann emphasized, the continued existence of Judaism depended on religious motives. A change was brought about by the Emancipation which created modern Jewry. More correctly, this change is due to two developments in the European world of which the Emancipation was only a consequence, namely the destruction of the feudal order of society and law by the modern state, and the secularization of culture. The group life *(Gemeinschaftsleben)* of the modern Jews is completely limited to the religious realm. Concurrently with the change in Jewish group life, the group consciousness of the modern Jew changed. No longer is it exclusively directed at the religious community *(Glaubensgemeinde)*. A family-like feeling of belonging exists, extending even to Jews of other countries; this feeling partly retains the group awareness of the tribe. Guttmann doubted that in the Diaspora this feeling, of itself, could provide sufficient support for the continuance of the group. An individual may remain in the group even if religion is meaningless to him because the religious life of the majority carries him along. But a group of individuals lacking a common concrete substance of life *(blosse Personalgemeinschaft ohne jeden sachlichen Lebensinhalt)* for any length of time is bound to fall apart. Jewish culture in the Diaspora also cannot replace the religious substance. What has been claimed as Jewish culture was, in Guttmann's opinion, an artistic and literary movement which has Jewish life and Jewish problems as its subject matter. Only a Jewish state can produce a Jewish culture. In the *Diaspora* the all-embracing unity of spirit and work cannot be realized.

Living among modern peoples the Jew shares with them their language and culture, but, Guttmann insisted, such natural participation is not assimilation *(Assimilantentum)*. The tribal memories *(Stammeserinnerung)* of the German Jew are not linked to Hermann of the Cherusci but to Judas Maccabaeus. However, the sources of his spiritual life *(geistiges Leben)* are in the history of the German spirit. And yet, Guttmann realized, though the German Jew has achieved a work communion *(Arbeitsgemeinschaft)* with the non-Jew, he has not achieved a life communion *(Lebensgemeinschaft)* in which he would fulfil his human and personal relations.[59] In the Middle Ages it was the Jewish *group* which felt the outside pressure, leaving the inner, personal life of the individual, who lived his narrow life within the group, relatively unaffected. Now, Guttmann pointed out, it is the individual which is driven into isolation. The spiritual communion *(geistige Gemeinschaft)* in cultural work has not led to a corresponding communion of the souls *(seelische Gemeinschaft)*. There is something problematic and unsatisfactory in the Jews' relations with non-Jews, Guttmann found and he asked, Is there hope that a quick elimination of anti-Semitism will remove it? In the long run, Guttmann thought, the antagonism will mellow. But one must remember, he cautioned, that structurally the Jewish group is not mere denomination *(Konfession)*, but a strong fusion of religious and tribal elements, and is bound to be affected not only by religious intolerance but by other antagonistic instincts.

Still, Guttmann felt, the strictly empirical analysis of the factual character of the Jewish group and its position in the modern world, as he presented it in his essay, does not of itself justify a decision in favour of either the nationalist or religious concept of modern Judaism. But neither need such a decision be based on the personal feelings of an individual. An objective decision can be arrived at, Guttmann be-

---

[59]In this connection Guttmann referred to the debate in the *Kunstwart* of 1912 "in which this conflict found passionate expression" though "the strong over-excitement, particularly of Goldstein, presented it far more glaringly and crassly than it really is." See Moritz Goldstein, German Jewry's Dilemma, The Story of a Provocative Essay, in Year Book II of the Leo Baeck Institute, London, 1957, pp. 236ff.

lieved. For such a decision one has to turn to ethics and philosophy of culture.

"The hope for a national Jewish future is founded . . . on a group feeling that concentrates entirely on Judaism and, therefore, must necessarily lead to the longing for a closed Jewish group life. Where this goal exists, the hope for a gradual improvement [of the position] of the Jews in the *Diaspora* cannot mean very much, and detaching oneself from the present cultural world for the sake of an untroubled, harmonious life in a Jewish commonwealth cannot appear as too difficult a decision. However only under the pressure of strictest necessity will he who feels himself a part of that world decide to take that step. So long as he sees hope for the improvement of the condition of Judaism in his homeland, be it only through slow and toilsome labour, he will gladly renounce the less strained life which is open to him elsewhere."[60] Guttmann concluded that the choice for West European Jewry is strictly between political Zionism and religious Judaism; Jewish cultural nationalism (*Kulturnationalismus*) in the midst of modern cultures is impossible.

This article of the young *Privatdozent*, strikingly different in content and tone from most other articles which appeared in the *K.C.-Blätter*, is important for two reasons. First, it throws light on what Guttmann termed his "religio-sociological view of Jewish history." Some of the ideas and distinctions occupied him for a long time,[61] others he dropped. Secondly, it is a significant personal document. Not because it dwells only on his personal convictions, since it does not; but rather because it reflects some of the deep layers of his personality. To him scholarship and scientific method were not professional tools that could be laid aside when one moved into current events and controversy.

---

[60]Note the similarity to Hermann Cohen's famous summing-up of the Zionist goal: *Die Kerle wollen glücklich sein* (The guys want to be happy).

[61]Guttmann's "religious group" concept, its application to the "Jewish group form" (*jüdische Gemeinschaftsform*) and the resulting form of "Jewish group consciousness" (*jüdisches Gemeinschaftsbewusstsein*) were thoroughly discussed at his seminar held at the Hochschule in 1926. See also Guttmann's article *Max Webers Soziologie des antiken Judentums* (Max Weber's Sociology of Ancient Judaism), in *Monatsschrift für Geschichte und Wissenschaft des Judentums*, vol. 69, 1925, pp. 195–223: "For the sociological analysis, the mutual relation between Jewish group life and Jewish religiosity becomes naturally its central problem. . . . The life form of Diaspora Judaism is wholly conditioned by religion" (p. 196). Compare further Guttmann's essay *Die Idee der religiösen Gemeinschaft im Judentum* (The Idea of the Religious Group in Judaism), in *Zum sechzigjährigen Bestehen der Hochschule für die Wissenschaft des Judentums (49. Bericht)*, Berlin, 1932, and his unpublished contribution to a volume dedicated to Oscar Wassermann, 1929 (from the Archives of the Leo Baeck Institute, New York).

Continually and methodically he tested and re-tested his views, and he did so particularly on the rare occasions when he spoke on problems that as such were not scholarly problems. On being subjected to scientific questioning they became scientific topics. Only to the extent that the scientific process could be applied did he treat of them. He was carefully cautious not to transgress from scientific fact into areas where opinion prevailed. Thus his discussions of current events often remained preliminary treatises on method. On the other hand, his scholarly caution did not lead to indecision. When he came forth with results, he stood on firm ground and defended them, if challenged, with unbending conviction.

Many of the historical vistas of Guttmann's article in the *K.C.-Blätter* reappear in a "popular" article, *Der Wiederaufbau Palästinas im Zusammenhang der jüdischen Geschichte* (The Reconstruction of Palestine in the Context of Jewish History), published in 1922.[62] Writing after the Balfour Declaration when the British Mandate had just begun to operate, Guttmann, aware of the momentous turn Jewish history had taken, presented his ideas on Jewish culture in the new Palestine. All Jews, including those who do not want to see their personal political status affected by a national change, must realize that the reconstruction of Palestine means a renewal of Jewish life everywhere, he wrote. In a "Judaism of unbroken unity" the Jewish spirit will be able to unfold unhampered and its creative life will become a source of strength on which Diaspora Judaism can draw. The position of religion in the new state will not be different from that in European countries, because the Jewish state will be a secular state, Guttmann predicted. But, for the first time, Jewish religion will have the opportunity to develop its potentialities in a modern society without being burdened, as it was in the Diaspora, with the responsibility for the survival of Judaism. That task will be taken over by the state. Religion will be able to regain its full influence by imbuing an autonomous and ethical culture with religious spirit. Even though the new Jewish community will not be a religious community, a vital Jewish religiosity can become central to Jewish development. The material elements from which the new culture will be built cannot be different from those in any European culture. In that respect the culture of the new land, Guttmann insisted, cannot be Jewish. "Only the shaping power of the spirit creating something of different and new value from materials which are taken over, can be Jewish." The strength of the religious idea in the new

---

[62] *Jahrbuch für jüdische Geschichte und Literatur*, v. 24, 1921–1922, pp. 63–89; reprinted in *Schriften des Keren Hajessod*, no. 10, Berlin, n.d.

Palestine will determine its influence on the Jewish Diaspora. Diaspora Judaism will remain a religious group. There is no room in it for a Jewish culture. But the Jewish spirit of the new land will speak to it as a living reality, and no longer merely through the medium of history. A genuine unity of the spirit can thus form in the total Jewish community and restore to it a distinctly Jewish imprint.

This author does not know how Guttmann felt when he measured the realities of life in Palestine and Israel against the expectations of his programme. But Guttmann was no utopian, rather a realist gifted with a patience that flowed from his knowledge of history. Neither was he a politician, though always a fascinated and sharp-eyed observer of politics with an acute sense for the possible and the impossible in the affairs of the world. Some who knew him only from afar considered him a *weltfremder* occupant of an academic ivory tower. That he was not. He regarded the Academe as his only business and vocation — which is something entirely different from being an academic recluse. Thus he had lived in Germany; thus he continued to live in Israel. The Hebrew University offered him opportunities of more varied kind than the *Hochschule,* as a theological school, could furnish. Guttmann became an active member of the University Senate, he served as a member of the Executive of the University and as Dean of its Faculty of the Humanities. That some in the University administration opposed the latter appointment because he was not an old-time Zionist hurt him long and deeply. His students were many and his influence on a considerable number of them was strong and lasting.

Guttmann's letters from Israel[63] complained that he was not able to concentrate on "the systematic projects close to my heart." There was the worry about his family in Europe; there were the illnesses of his wife. He planned to write a theology of Judaism, or at least to explore the premises of such an undertaking. No essays or manuscripts are left to indicate the direction this work would have taken except, perhaps, an abridged account of five lectures, and the discussion following them, which Guttmann delivered during the summer of 1943 at a seminar on religious education, organized by the *Chug-ha-dati* (Religious Circle), a group of Israeli scholars and educators interested in the discussion of theoretical and practical problems of religion.[64]

---

[63]See footnote 47, p. xxvii.

[64]*Al yesodoth ha-yahaduth,* in *Din ve-cheshbon al seminaryon le-chinnukh dati,* Jerusalem (1945), pp. 7–27, reprinted in *Dat u-mada,* a collection of essays of Guttmann published 1956 by the Magnes-Press of the Hebrew University. A not always precise English translation, The Principles of Judaism, appeared in "Conservative Judaism," vol. 14, 1959, pp. 1–23. The editor of the Hebrew lectures notes in the preface, p. 5, that the

The published version of the lectures is sketchy and the progression of the arguments, usually clear and faultless in Guttmann's writings, is uneven and full of jumps and breaks. Thus one only reluctantly draws inferences from these lectures as to Guttmann's theology of Judaism to which over the years he had given a great deal of preliminary thought. But one point can be safely made. Guttmann had once remarked that the meeting of philosophy and monotheistic religion produces philosophy of religion when the meeting takes place in the sphere of philosophy, and produces theology when the two meet in religion.[65] His theology, judging from the lectures, would have been such a philosophical theology, or, putting it in Guttmann's way, an attempt to give rational expression to the principles of religion in a form appropriate to today's intellectual positions.[66]

The lectures discuss to what extent Judaism has such fundamental principles.[67] They ask: what are the religious sources of these essential beliefs for the believing Jew—a new kind of believing Jew, to be sure, for he no longer necessarily accepts revelation as the source of religious conviction. They define the idea of the personal God who can be approached through ethical action as well as through immediate, personal communion. They discuss the religious commandments and the rituals which are necessary for the sanctification of life,[68] because no man is filled with religious ecstasy (hithlahavuth) all the time. And they conclude with a chapter on the distinctions between Judaism and Christianity.

Guttmann's purpose in establishing basic principles of Judaism was practical, not merely theoretical or systematic. The set of principles with which he dealt were from areas of religion which had been the target of doubt and attack. In a period of religious unrest he was desirous of defending the teachings of Judaism. But although in these lectures Guttmann did not want to be a philosopher who analyzes the phenomena of religion and their particular character of reality and truth, interestingly enough he could not help retaining the methodical

---

lectures appear abridged because the author intends to deal with the same subject in considerably enlarged form in a forthcoming book.

[65]*Religion und Wissenschaft im mittelalterlichen und im modernen Denken*, p. 148.

[66]Guttmann's article, *Die Normierung der Glaubensinhalte im Judentum* (approximately: The Codification of the Contents of Religious Belief in Judaism), in *Monatsschrift für Geschichte und Wissenschaft des Judentums*, vol. 71, 1927, pp. 241–255, touched upon the same problem.

[67]In this connection Guttmann made the astonishing remark that rituals are needed in Israel more than in the Diaspora, not to give to the life of the Israeli Jewish character—which it has *per se* —but to save it from emptiness.

[68]*Al yesodoth ha-yahaduth*, p. 15.

conscience of the philosopher. Asked in the question period how religious beliefs can be demonstrated to others, Guttmann answered that the only certainty in religion is personal certitude. The *homo religiosus,* deprived of recourse to a historical revelation which speaks to all men, can tell only of his personal beliefs. The religionist is unable to convince his fellowmen of the grounds of his religious devotion. The only way to bring religion to man is to convince him that without religion there would be a vacuum in his life. The values of the ethical and the emotional would stand powerless were it not for the unifying power of religion in which existence and value join. Religion is the sublime unity of that which is and that which ought to be.

Guttmann realized that, at this pivotal point of his argument, he had resorted to Kant's method of postulation. As a philosopher he had overcome that dubious procedure by joining Schleiermacher. As a theologian he felt compelled to withdraw from Schleiermacher and go back to Kant's discredited method again. Is it too dramatic to say that when he did so the religious intent collided with the philosophic method and that, as a result, both suffered? The "Theology of Judaism," which Guttmann never wrote, might have provided the answer. It would have shown whether the philosophy of religion which he had taught and which underlies his "Philosophy of Judaism" would stand up to confrontation with the principles established by a "Theology of Judaism."

Julius Guttmann's death, after painful illness, on May 19, 1950, left these questions unanswered. Another period of modern Jewish philosophic thought had come to its end. There was no one in sight equipped or willing to pose the questions as he had done. As Guttmann had well realized, philosophy *and* theology were going ways which he could not follow. And Kant and Schleiermacher or, for that matter, Maimonides and Yehuda Halevi, whom Guttmann wanted to fuse, stood as apart as ever.

I

Fundamentals and First Influences

1 The Basic Ideas of Biblical Religion

THE Jewish people did not begin to philosophize because of an irresistible urge to do so. They received philosophy from outside sources, and the history of Jewish philosophy is a history of the successive absorptions of foreign ideas which were then transformed and adapted according to specific Jewish points of view.

Such a process first took place during the Hellenistic period. Judaeo-Hellenistic philosophy is so thoroughly imbued with the Greek spirit, however, that it may be regarded, historically speaking, as merely a chapter in the development of Greek thought as a whole. It disappeared quickly without leaving behind any permanent impact upon Judaism.

Philosophy penetrated Jewish intellectual life a second time in the Middle Ages. It was Greek philosophy at second hand, for the philosophic revival took place within the orbit of Islamic culture and was heavily indebted to Islamic philosophy, which, in its turn, derived from Greek systems of thought. This time, however, the vitality of Jewish philosophy proved stronger than during the Hellenistic period. It persisted from the ninth century to the end of the Middle Ages, and some traces of it are still discernible as late as the middle of the seventeenth century. Nonetheless, it is true to say that throughout this time, Jewish philosophy remained closely bound to the non-Jewish sources from which it originated.

After Judaism had entered the intellectual world of modern Europe, modern Jewish thought remained indebted to contemporary trends of European philosophy. This applies not only to the contribution of Jewish thinkers to the philosophic labors of the European nations, but also to those systems of thought specifically concerned with the interpretation and justification of the Jewish religion. The former has its place in the general history of modern philosophy; its dependence on contemporary thought is consequently a truism. But even Jewish philosophy in the specific and

3

narrow sense of the term, like its Christian counterpart, operated within the framework, the methods, and the conceptual apparatus of modern European philosophy.

The peculiar character of Jewish existence in the Diaspora prevented the emergence of a Jewish philosophy in the sense in which we can speak of Greek, Roman, French, or German philosophy. Since the days of antiquity, Jewish philosophy was essentially a philosophy of Judaism. Even during the Middle Ages—which knew something like a total, all-embracing culture based on religion—philosophy rarely transcended its religious center. This religious orientation constitutes the distinctive character of Jewish philosophy, whether it was concerned with using philosophic ideas to establish or justify Jewish doctrines, or with reconciling the contradictions between religious truth and scientific truth. It is religious philosophy in a sense peculiar to the monotheistic revealed religions which, because of their claim to truth and by virtue of their spiritual depth, could confront philosophy as an autonomous spiritual power.

Armed with the authority of a supernatural revelation, religion lays claim to an unconditioned truth of its own, and thereby becomes a problem for philosophy. In order to determine the relationships between these two types of truth, philosophers have tried to clarify, from a methodological point of view, the distinctiveness of religion. This is a modern development; earlier periods did not attempt to differentiate between the methods of philosophy and religion, but sought to reconcile the contents of their teachings. Philosophy was thus made subservient to religion; and philosophical material borrowed from the outside was treated accordingly. In this respect the philosophy of Judaism, whatever the differences in content deriving from the specific doctrines and the concepts of authority of the religions concerned, is formally similar to that of Christianity and of Islam. Appearing for the first time in Jewish Hellenism, this type of philosophy, though not productive of original ideas, nevertheless proved of far-reaching significance and influence. From Jewish Hellenism it passed to Christianity, was transmitted to Islam, from whence it returned, in the Middle Ages, to Judaism.

This special character of Jewish philosophy may justify a short introductory description of its underlying assumptions, implicit in the Bible and the Talmud. We are not concerned here with a full evaluation of the religious motives of the Bible and Talmud, but rather with those of their conceptual elements that are relevant to an understanding of Jewish religious philosophy. In connection with this, and for the reasons already given, only the barest indications will be given concerning the place of Jewish-Hellenistic philosophy in the total context of the history of Judaism.

The distinctiveness of biblical religion is due to its ethical conception of the personality of God. The God of the prophets is exemplified by his moral will; he is demanding and commanding, promising and threatening, the absolutely free ruler of man and nature. This conception of God developed only slowly in the history of Israelite religion. Neither God's uniqueness and superiority over the forces of nature nor his character as pure will were to be found in its beginnings. Only after a long process of evolution did the God of Israel become the God of the world. It also took a long time before he could shed his primitive attributes as a nature God, making it possible to think of him in purely personal terms. Even in the primitive understanding of God, of course, we could point out those traits which anticipated later developments, but the final result was a completely novel and original creation whose substance was unpredictable on the basis of the earlier conception. This "prehistory" of the Jewish idea of God is beyond the scope of our present enquiry. We shall be concerned with the idea of God as it is already present in the earliest literary prophets of Israel, and which, in its essential characteristics, remained substantially the same despite obvious and inevitable variations in detail.[1]

This idea of God, not the fruit of philosophic speculation but the product of the immediacy of the religious consciousness, was stamped with its definitive character during the crisis which saw the destruction of the kingdoms of Israel and Judah. The destruction of Jerusalem and the exile of the nation were looked upon by the people as visitations of their own God, who became thereby a universal God: the kingdoms of the world were his tools, and he established the course of world history according to his will. Jewish monotheism grew out of this fundamental experience, and through it were established all those religious characteristics that were, in turn, transmitted to Christianity and Islam. The decisive feature of monotheism is that it is not grounded in an abstract idea of God, but in an intensely powerful divine will which rules history. This ethical voluntarism implies a thoroughly personalistic conception of God, and determines the specific character of the relationship between God and man. This relationship is an ethical-voluntaristic one between two moral personalities, between an "I" and a "Thou." As God imposes his will upon that of man, so man becomes aware of the nature of his relationship to God.

Communion with God is essentially a communion of moral wills. The meaning of "nearness" to God or "estrangement" from him is determined by this perspective. This purely formal determination still allows of great variety in the relations between God and man. For Amos, the relationship seems to have been determined by an acute sense of the "numinous" majesty and grandeur of God, whereas his immediate successor, Hosea, appears to have experienced the divine will primarily as a loving communion between God and his people. Whereas for Isaiah, the essential stance of man before God is humility before his awesome majesty, the Psalms testify to the feeling of closeness between God and man. Despite variations in its material forms of expression, the personalist character of this relationship remains the same throughout.

God's relationship to the world is conceived along the same lines. He is the Lord of the world, he directs it according to his will, and he realizes his purposes within it. His relationship to the world is not grounded in a natural force, but in the unconditioned freedom of his will. This conception empties all the ancient accounts of creation of their mythological content, and permeates them with its own spirit. The omnipotence of the divine will appears most clearly when the world itself is looked upon as nothing but the work of this will. The Creator-God is not a part of, or link in, the world; but God and world face each other as Creator and creature. This trait emerges with increasing distinctness in the course of the evolution of the biblical idea of creation. At first, creation was conceived of as a kind of "making," or "fashioning," by God; in the end, it is the Creator's word that calls the world into existence. The divine act of will is sufficient for bringing everything into being. The biblical idea of creation does not pretend to provide a theoretical explanation of the origin of the universe; it is the form in which the religious consciousness of the nature of the relationship between God and the world has become articulate.

The personalist character of biblical religion stands in the most radical contrast to another, basically impersonal, form of spiritual and universal religion, which underlies all mysticism and pantheism.

Whatever the significant differences between mysticism and pantheism, their general divergence from biblical religion becomes more evident as its radically different conception of the relationship between God and the world becomes apparent.[2] God is not conceived by them as a sovereign will ruling the universe, but as the hidden source from which all being emanates, or as the inner life-force which pulsates throughout the cosmos. This difference is not a matter of choosing either a theoretical or an imaginative representation of the idea of God, but is a matter of fundamental religious attitudes, as is convincingly demonstrated by the completely different relationship between God and man which mysticism and pantheism affirm.

Neither pantheism nor mysticism knows a personal, moral communion between God and man; in its place, there is union with the Godhead. It does not matter, for our present purpose, whether this union is experienced by man as an accomplished fact, or as the ultimate goal of his religious aspirations; whether it is envisaged as an essential identity of the self with the divine life of the universe, or as a merging of the soul in the mysterious divine ground of Being. The living relationship between persons is replaced by the extinction of personal individuality, which is felt to be the main barrier separating us from God.

Disregarding, for the moment, all mixed or transitional forms, our distinction between the two types of religion remains valid, even when they apparently use the same language. The *amor dei* of pantheism and the love of God of the mystic are as different in essence from the personalistic love of God (however enthusiastically the latter may experience the raptures of the divine presence) as is the mystic shudder before the hidden abyss of the divine being from the experience of the sublime majesty of the personal God.

The same distinction is again seen when we compare the respective relationships between God and the world in the various types of religion. Here, too, it is not just a matter of conflicting ideas, but of fundamentally contrasting religious attitudes. The transcendence of God as personal Creator is foreign to the doctrine of pantheism and mysticism because, according to the latter, the world is not subject to a sovereign divine will. This is too obvious to require further elaboration, particularly with regard to those views that conceive of God as the "inner life of things." Of greater interest is a comparison of the acosmism of the mystical notion of a divine "ground" of the world, with the transcendence predicated of God the Creator. In theoretical terms the difference is usually formulated by saying that for mysticism, the divine "ground," or source, does not create the world, but rather expels it from its own substance. In religious terms, this means that God is not conceived as the will which determines the world, but rather as a transcendent self-subsistent Being, completely withdrawn into itself. To elevate oneself to God, therefore, would mean separation from the world, that is, detaching the soul from the confusing multiplicity of the world and breaking through the barriers which the world places between the soul and God. In a way, the transcendence of God to the world is even more extreme here than in the notion of the personal Creator-God, who, despite his transcendence to the world, is still related to it, and, thereby, also confers upon it a measure of religious significance. Nonetheless, the relationship between God and the world, as envisaged by mysticism, is essentially characterized by a peculiar dialectic; however much the difference between God and the world may pervade the religious consciousness, the world is at the same time seen as the manifestation of God.

The radical distinction between God and the world is blurred even more by all those systems that consider the transition from one to the other as continuous and gradual, and posit an intermediary, suprasensual world between the Godhead and the world of the senses. Whereas the Creator-God stands over and against the world, his creation, the God of mysticism becomes the principle underlying the suprasensual world. Even the ascent of the soul to God is nothing more than the final completion of its way to the suprasensual or "intelligible" world. Such an interpretation helps us to account for one of the most significant phenomena in the history of religions: the differing attitudes of biblical religion and pantheistic-mystic religion toward polytheism. The latter could easily admit that alongside the oneness of the divine ground of all being, the multiplicity and variety of its manifestations should also be regarded as divine. There was no difficulty, therefore, in patiently tolerating the many gods of polytheistic religion. Personalist monotheism, however, can make no such concession. Even where it pictures a kind of celestial world inhabited by angels, neither the basic difference between God and his creation, nor the uniqueness of God himself is compromised.

Mysticism and pantheism did not cross the path of Jewish religion until after the close of the biblical period; we have compared the two only in order to better grasp the essential quality of biblical religion. Of more immediate historical significance is the battle which biblical religion waged against magic and myth.

The purging of magical and mythical elements which were embedded within biblical religion in its beginnings marks one of the most important achievements of biblical monotheism. This development was, from the nature of things, inevitable, because mythology and magic are possible only where the gods, in their actions and passions, are conceived as natural forces. The well-known observation that the characteristic quality of mythical thinking lies in its personification of natural forces is only half of the truth; the other half is the fact that even anthropomorphic personification is conceived completely in natural categories. As is well illustrated by the many creation myths and their mixture of natural processes and divine actions, the personal and the natural are commingled and undifferentiated. The same may be said also of the basis of magic, for magic, too, assumes that gods and demons are subject to some mysterious natural necessity.

In the voluntaristic religion of biblical monotheism, the personal was radically dissociated from its natural and material elements. It is true that the struggle against magic in the preprophetic age did not proceed on the assumption that magic was ineffectual, but rather that it was sinful to attempt by magic to coerce God. In spite of granting to magic a modicum of efficacy, this attitude bespeaks a religious consciousness for which magic and a genuine relationship between God and man had become incompatible. By its very nature this kind of religious consciousness ends by so exalting the notion of God that any thought of magical influence is completely excluded. To the extent that man realizes his relationship to God in its utmost purity, by complete submission to the divine will, he also realizes a spiritual conception of the divine personality which transcends all "natural" forms of existence. This specific conception of the nature of the divine will also gives a new significance to all other parts of the religious system. Thus, a miracle is essentially distinct from magic not only in that it is a completely free divine act, but more particularly in that it subserves the intelligible purposes of the divine will. In the same way, revelation is different from oracle and augury, for the secrets of the future are not unlocked by a mysterious causality, but are revealed by God himself for a specific purpose.

All the external similarities between prophetic and magical ecstasy notwithstanding, prophecy differs essentially from soothsaying.[3] An analogous transformation was accomplished in the sphere of cult and ritual. No doubt a great many of the cultic practices recorded in Scripture originally had magical significance. Although biblical monotheism retained these practices, it invested them with completely new meaning. Many old practices were supplied with an ethical content and even those which were not formally converted into commandments of the divine will, were at least deprived of the last trace of magic. Reality as a whole becomes related to the ethical content of the divine will and thereby susceptible to rational comprehension. True, Judaism was unable to withstand forever the periodic eruptions and invasions of magic. During the Hellenistic period as well as in the Middle Ages, magical practices and, in particular, astrology found their way into Jewish life,[4] but were never able to penetrate the inner sanctum of the religious relationship to God. The struggle against magic was continuously renewed during the peaks of the religious history of Israel.

The above considerations apply equally to the relationship of biblical monotheism and mythology. The myths of creation and of the flood are among the better-known examples of how biblical monotheism stamped with its own characteristic spirit the mythological legacy which it had received from its surroundings. At times mythological themes are used partly for purposes of poetic imagery. We are not now concerned with the question of whether traces of mythical thought have survived in the Bible. The point at issue here is this: religion is as different from myth as it is from magic, and the same force underlies its separation from them both. The idea of creation marks the point of cleavage between myth and religion, since it excludes any evolution or emanation by which the world proceeds naturally, as it were, from God, and posits the free will of God as sole cause of the world. Here too, the voluntaristic and personalist character of God forms a barrier against mythological intrusions, for over and against the voluntary and half-natural causality of the cosmogonic myths, it posits the absolute freedom of God in the act of creation. Nature has lost its divine quality; from the dwelling place of the divine it has itself become the work of God's hands.

This conception of nature dominates the story of creation found in the first chapter of the Book of Genesis. Nature here has a substantial life of its own, but is conceived as inanimate and subordinate to the purposes of God, which, as such, are foreign to it. Man himself, the end and purpose of creation, is not conceived solely as part of nature, but as standing over and against nature, as the image of God. This anthropocentric conception grants man the right to conquer the earth, and relegates astral "divinities" to the role of mere luminaries for the earth; it redirects all religious feeling from nature towards the transmundane God. Henceforth man sees himself as a being superior to the forces of nature, which in a natural religion would be considered as divine. The nature poetry of the Bible expresses the same attitude; nature is looked upon as a manifestation of the majesty of God; any kind of pantheistic feeling is quite alien to it. Nature remains the work of God's hands, and above the rest of creation there is always present the thought of man's superiority. This opposition between man and nature has, as yet, no metaphysical connotation. There is certainly no hint of an opposition between the world of the senses and a suprasensual world. Man is a creature of this world, and it is only his character as a person that raises him above things natural. This also explains why, in the later history of monotheism, periods of intense "personalistic" piety tended toward a mechanistic conception of nature; both a mechanistic science and a rejection of all metaphysics are in accord with a religiosity which promotes man's mastery over nature.

From its very beginnings Israelite religion viewed God as the Lord of history. Israel saw its history as rooted in a covenant between YHWH and his people Israel; the covenant was upheld by Israel through its observance of the divine commandments, and by God through the providence he extended to his people. The history of the people thus became the locus wherein God might be known. This historical conception was raised by the later prophets to the level of world history. The impending destruction of the Israelite state by the Near Eastern kingdoms was interpreted, as has already been noted, as an act of judgment of the God of Israel who uses great nations as tools for the accomplishment of his own ends. As God was transformed into the God of history, he likewise became the God of the universe. The divine perspective now embraced both past and future.

The consciousness of the prophets was primarily directed to the future. The destruction of the nation which they predicted would not seal the end of Israel but would be followed by a renewal, a new communion between God and Israel, and a new salvation. This future blessing, not the property of Israel alone, would be consummated in the kingdom of heaven in which all the nations would share. From this religious eschatology there emerges a unity of purpose which joins together the varied elements of the traditional past, embraces all nations, and turns them toward a common point to which all history is directed. The early history of the Israelites and the tribal legends of the patriarchs are combined with myths about the creation of the world and the first men, forming an historical picture which unfolds according to a divine plan. The resulting view of history, predicated as it is upon the uniqueness of the historical process,[5] unites past and future in one great vision. It is in the unique historical process and not in the unchanging being of nature that the revelation of God's will and the satisfaction of all religious aspirations are to be found. There, more than anywhere else, the contradiction between the biblical God and the God of mysticism dwelling within himself, beyond all time, becomes apparent. For biblical religion the world of time does not dissolve into empty nothingness; on the contrary, the moral activism of the Bible envisages the world as the scene of the realization of a divine order, which is an order of moral will and moral life.

Biblical religion is essentially historical in yet another sense. It sees its origin in an historical revelation, through which Israel became the people of God. Every subsequent revelation refers back to this parent revelation and bases itself upon it. The prophets do not claim to reveal something radically new, but merely seek to restore the ancient pristine faith of Israel. In the days of living prophecy this reference to an ancient faith certainly did not imply an explicit belief in a definite body of teaching communicated from outside, but rather expressed the faith that the truth given by God to the prophets was the same as that revealed to the patriarchs. Gradually, however, the reliance upon a definite historical event became stronger. Moses came to be thought of as the greatest of prophets "like unto whom there arose none in Israel." The revelation granted to him—which is the source of Israelite faith—is greater than any succeeding revelation. The decisive step in this direction was taken with the growth of a sacred literature ascribed to Mosaic authorship. Finally the whole Pentateuch was considered Mosaic writing. The text of the original revelation, as it was considered, was placed as a norm of the religious history of Israel; subsequent revelations could merely bear witness to it and confirm it. When prophecy itself ceased and became an inheritance from the past, the notion of historical revelation ruled supreme in religious life.

Religious truth was thought of as something historically "given"; development was possible only by reading new ideas back into the traditional faith. The importance of this type of religion (that is, the religion of historical revelation) lies in the fact that it created the supreme expression of religious truth. Biblical monotheism, denying the very existence of all the gods of polytheism, claimed for itself final and exclusive religious truth as given in the divine revelation. The combination of profundity of content with rigidity in conception made it possible for all religious life and thought to be subordinated to the law of this "given" religious truth. In this way Judaism became an example for Christianity and Islam. By developing the notion of "revealed truth" it also created what was to become later the main issue dividing religion and philosophy.

During the biblical period the fundamental notions of biblical faith, which we have described, received an additional development. The religious thought of the prophets, nourished by their awareness of a crisis within the life of Israel, was centered upon the relationship of God to the people as a whole. God had made a convenant with Israel as a people; the sin of the people had brought down God's punishment upon the nation; but it was to the same nation or to its remnant that God had promised a future redemption. The subject of religion was thus the nation. Even the historical universalism of the prophets adhered to this national, "political" view. Humanity, a concept created by the prophets, was a community of nations. The individual, for the moment, was secondary to the people.

The relationship of God to the individual, already found in preprophetic popular religion, was never denied by the prophets, though their religious pathos was mainly focused upon their concern with history. The problem of the individual, however, appears with the later prophets. Individual religiosity, too, was subjected to the prophetic view of the divine. The problem of individual moral responsibility, though it can hardly be considered to have been discovered by Jeremiah, was clarified by him, and even more by Ezekiel. Every man was responsible before God for his own deeds, and according to those deeds—not according to the merit or demerit of his ancestors—he would be judged. This notion of individual responsibility evolved together with that of individual retribution. Divine justice manifests itself in the individual too, and not only in the collectivity of the people, though, of course, the relation of individual destiny with that of the nation is never obliterated.

In post-exilic literature the individual aspect of religion gains in importance and outstrips the limited ambit of rewards and punishments. The idea of a loving relationship with God is extended to the individual, especially in the Psalms; the greatest happiness of the pious becomes the nearness of God. At the same time, the notion of divine retribution loses none of its significance, but becomes the starting point for the problem of theodicy.

Jeremiah asks the perennial question concerning the prosperity of the wicked and the adversity of the righteous, and post-exilic literature amply illustrates to what extent this problem exercised the minds of the post-exilic prophets and psalmists. It is this problem, too, which has made the Book of Job the earliest poetic expression of religious reflection in the Bible. We need not detail here the many and varied answers to this problem. Some held the opinion, despite all external evidence to the contrary, that suffering came as a result of sin; others considered the suffering of the righteous a means of purification for the soul. Deutero-Isaiah introduces the figure of the Servant of the Lord who suffers for the sake of the collective sin of the people. Finally, the Book of Job concludes with faith in the majestic and sublime God, who is above and beyond all human questioning.

It is noteworthy that the idea of a heavenly reward is never proposed as a possible solution to the problem. Apparently the belief in reward in the hereafter did not yet exist at the time; existence after death was thought of in terms of the popular ideas about a shadow life in *Sheol*—a Hades-like underworld. Nevertheless, there is little doubt that the problem of theodicy was the point at which beliefs about retribution could enter the Jewish religion. These beliefs appeared in two forms: the resurrection of the dead and the immortality of the soul. It is a matter of some doubt whether they were borrowed from others, and more particularly, whether belief in resurrection was taken over from Persian religion. Even if there was borrowing, it could only have taken place because the inner development of Judaism rendered it susceptible to influences of this kind. The emergence of these eschatological beliefs brought a change in religious perspective that was to prove of great consequence for future developments. The religious meaning of the world is no longer fulfilled within it, but in another sphere of existence. Alongside of the historical future towards which the prophets had directed their hopes, there exists a transcendent world of ultimate fulfillment. This certainly holds true of the belief in the immortality of the soul, whereas the notion of a resurrection of the body inserts itself into the historical perspective of prophetic religion.

The problem of theodicy is important not only for its contribution to the content of Jewish religion. Its significance, from a formal point of view, resides in the fact that it represents the first fruition of religious reflection in Judaism. Whereas prophecy had been the product of the immediacy of religious consciousness, we find here, for the first time, an intellectual wrestling with religious truth. Traces of this change are present in the later prophets. Ezekiel is something of the schoolmaster when he expounds his notion of individual responsibility[6] by means of the parable of the evil son born to a righteous man, and of the righteous son born to an evil man.

Reflection in its full sense, however, comes to the fore in the Book of Job. The dialogue form of Job is essential to its content. With the play of opinion being expressed through question and answer, the problem of divine justice becomes one that can be solved by thought. Thought pits the differing possibilities one against the other, and through the clash of opinion seeks for truth. However, this thought is not yet reflection concerning religion; it is the religious consciousness itself, which in its anguish calls to thought for aid. Divine justice becomes a problem for religious thought, which tries to solve it in a mighty struggle. Various forms of faith are arrayed against each other. It is characteristic of the book that the final answer is given in the form of a divine revelation. The struggle of faith comes to rest in the immediate certitude of divine majesty. The very fact that it is at this juncture that religious reflection reappears, emphasizes the distinctiveness of biblical religion.

Jewish thought is not oriented towards metaphysical questions. The sloughing off of mythological cosmogonies eliminated all potential starting points for the growth of metaphysics. The notion of a Creator provides no occasion for a theoretical interpretation of the world. This may well be part of the answer to the question: Why did Judaism not develop its own philosophic system? The first attempt at reflective thought was directed toward an understanding of those of God's acts which appeared dubious. For the monotheism of the prophets, the belief in the moral quality and purposive nature of the divine will was an absolute certainty which informed all aspects of religious life. It was the basis of their understanding of history. To interpret reality in terms of the purposiveness of the divine will, and to uphold this purposiveness in the face of the facts of experience—this was the task that necessarily followed from the basic assumptions of Jewish religion.

The form in which the problem of theodicy posed itself corresponded precisely to this context. It was not a reason for "suffering in general" that was sought. The question underlying the ancient story of the Garden of Eden—how suffering and death came into the world—was never taken up again. Not suffering in general, but rather the suffering of the righteous, causes us to doubt the justice of God and becomes a stumbling block. The Book of Job especially reveals to what extent everything revolves about this one question. Job does not revolt against the magnitude of his suffering. He would resign himself to it, if only he knew its reason. He is driven to rebellion because he suffers without cause, and because he feels himself the victim of God's despotism. He finds peace once again when he regains his belief in the meaningfulness of God's acts.

It may be said, therefore, that the first movements of reflection within Judaism took place within the sphere of religious meaning, and emerged from the immanent problems of biblical religion. Jewish religious speculation was to continue along that path. The premise underlying such thought is the notion that God's moral will is accessible to human comprehension. The theoretical question, whether ethics as such was independent of God or dependent upon him, was completely beyond the intellectual horizon of the prophets.[7] They were all the more conscious of the inner evidence of the moral claim as something proceeding from God. Every man apprehends intuitively what is good or evil. The intelligibility of moral obligation implied the rationality of the divine will. Hence God, too, in his actions conformed to moral standards and could be measured by them.[8] At the same time there existed also the opposite recognition that God was incomprehensible, and that his ways were higher than the ways of man, even as the heavens were higher than the earth. All this, however, did not detract from the belief in the moral reasonableness of the divine will. Only the Book of Job seems to question this principle when, as its sole answer to the doubts raised by humanity, it points to the impenetrable majesty of God. In spite of some signs apparently pointing to Moslem and Calvinist doctrines of the absolute and sovereign superiority of the divine over all ethical criteria, this is hardly the real intent of the Book of Job. The problem of theodicy is not settled for Job by saying that God is above all ethical criteria, but rather by the recognition of God's utter incomprehensibility paradoxically becoming a ground for trust in the meaningfulness of his providence, a providence of love and justice which is no less meaningful for remaining impenetrable to human understanding. Thus, even where biblical religion seems to verge most on an irrational conception of the divine will, it never relinquishes the basic conviction of an essential meaningfulness. Even the intelligibility of the divine will is merely limited, not nullified, by our deficient human understanding.

2 Jewish Hellenistic Philosophy

THE ideas outlined thus far supplied Judaism with the intellectual equipment necessary for its encounter with Greek culture. The full effect of the latter cannot detain us here, for the same reason that prevented, in the preceding chapter, a more detailed discussion of the relationships of biblical religion to Near Eastern and Oriental culture. We shall confine ourselves to the penetration of Greek philosophy into Judaism.

It has often been remarked that at least one scriptural book, the Book of Kohelet, clearly shows the influence of Greek philosophy. If this is the case, Greek philosophy must have made its influence felt in Palestine at the beginning of the second century B.C.E., for Kohelet cannot have been composed later than this date.[1] All efforts to find specific Greek doctrines in the Book of Kohelet, however, have yielded only vague analogies, from which the characteristic Greek flavor has been lost. Thus, Kohelet's complaint that there was nothing new under the sun, or that the thing that has been was that which shall be,[2] has been compared to the Greek doctrine of eternal cyclical return. What is missing from Kohelet, however, is precisely that specific philosophic turn which differentiates the Greek doctrine from the popular observation of the monotonous recurrence of all things. In the same way, Kohelet's observation that whether it is birth or death, war or peace, there is a season for all things,[3] differs from the Heraclitean notion of the relativity of opposites, just as a simple life observation differs from a philosophical doctrine. The actual parallels between Greek and Jewish thought in the Book of Kohelet are no proof of necessary connection with any definite philosophic school. They merely show the contact of Judaism with contemporary popular Greek thought.

Whatever our opinions may be concerning this matter, it is certain that Kohelet's thinking is far removed from and uninfluenced by any scientific philosophy. The Preacher's criticism of life's blessings does not rest, as with the Greek philosopher, upon a methodological principle, but upon immediate experience. He does not measure earthly goods against a philosophically conceived *summum bonum,* but convinces himself empirically of their worthlessness. Certain facts about life, its subjection to accidents, the inevitability of death which robs us of all our possessions, the manifest injustice in the distribution of goods, the insatiability of human desires, and the like, are sufficient to prove to him that all is vanity.[4] Also, his belief that man's reason is powerless is founded on similar observations and not on a thoroughgoing scientific skepticism. Theoretical doubts concerning the possibility of knowledge are altogether beyond Kohelet's horizon. The book, as a whole, breathes the certainty that we are capable of knowing the reality around us, though its meaning and inner articulation remain impenetrable.[5] The book's key concept, "Wisdom," thus seems to denote practical wisdom. The superiority of the wise man to the fool is due to his more penetrating overview of life, rather than to any scientific theorizing.[6] Moreover, the substance and occasional profundity of Kohelet's thought points in a direction which is very different from that of Greek speculation. The very first chapter, surely the most profound portion of the book, bespeaks a basic attitude toward life that is radically foreign to Greek philosophy. The eternal recurrence of natural events, which was what had suggested the idea of an eternal order, and thereby provided the mainstay of Greek philosophy, is, for Kohelet, the epitome of senselessness: vanity of vanities. The regularity of nature does not reveal to Kohelet the majesty of a divinely instituted natural law, but rather a meaningless monotony. If one adds to this Kohelet's fundamentally un-Grecian deprecation of knowledge, epigrammatically expressed in the phrase, "He that increaseth knowledge, increaseth sorrow,"[7] his distance from Greek turns of speculation is underscored.

Even more than from Greek philosophy, Kohelet deviates from Jewish religious feeling. He does, of course, uphold the Jewish faith in a God who determines man's fate, and he recommends submission to the will of God. It would doubtless be wrong to consider all statements to that effect as additions to the text of Kohelet, but it is apparent that they did not mean very much to the author, who offers them less as expressions of his personal opinion than as an inherited tradition of ideas. This submission to a divinely ordained fate does not, really, amount to very much more than a resignation to life as

it is. Kohelet's evaluation of life is independent of any religious presuppositions or criteria. His entire outlook is thus oriented to this
world and to the worldly happiness of the individual. Kohelet's religious sense does not extend much beyond this. Submission to the
will of God appears as an expression of worldly wisdom.[8] How far all
this is from the biblical outlook as a whole becomes evident where
the two seem to be most similar. Kohelet too, is aware that the righteous frequently suffer the fate of the wicked and vice versa, but to
him this is merely further confirmation of the fact that all is vanity.[9]

The tenor of the Book of Kohelet is skeptical. The author approaches life with a critical stance, trusting only his personal observations, believing only what his eyes can see. He wants to search out
all things that are done under heaven, to explore—systematically, as
it were—all the possibilities of life.[10] Though much of what he has to
say is reminiscent of the proverbial style of biblical wisdom literature (where, frequently enough, the religious mentality is displaced
by a more realistic appraisal of life) yet the spirit of the Book of
Kohelet is quite different from the rest of Scripture. The practical
realism of Proverbs is restricted to the ordinary concerns of daily life,
and remains subordinated to the authority of a self-evident religious
conception of life. Compared with its simple practical wisdom, Kohelet's radical criticism of life is something altogether new. This kind
of criticism is possible only in a world in which traditional ways of
life have lost their authority, and the individual is looking to himself
as the measure of things. In this somewhat broad sense Kohelet is
undoubtedly related to the individualism of the Greek enlightenment without which, indeed, it is unthinkable. Here and there (as
has already been indicated) some more specific points of contact with
Greek popular philosophy may exist; even reliance upon the pessimistic viewpoint of certain Greek philosophers cannot altogether be
excluded. As to genuine dependence of Kohelet on Greek philosophers, there is none. Just as the Preacher's own peculiar view is without a Greek exemplar, so the characteristic marks of Greek speculation are all missing.

The Palestinian Judaism which produced Kohelet does not seem
to have been deeply affected by Greek philosophy. Apocryphal literature contains few if any philosophic elements. As for Talmudic Judaism, the extent of its knowledge of Greek philosophic doctrines
and of its rapprochement to Greek thinking will be discussed in a
later chapter. Only for the Jews dwelling in the Diaspora did Greek

philosophy become an essential factor of spiritual life. To what extent skeptical and Epicurean criticism of religion became common among Jews cannot be determined from the sources available to us; what they do show is the extent to which Judaism had merged with the kind of philosophic religion that had developed especially in Neoplatonic and Stoic philosophy. The affinity of Jewish monotheism with the concept of God as developed by the philosophers had been recognized by both sides at an early date. Cleanthes—in his account of the meeting of his teacher Aristotle with a Jewish sage—as well as Theophrastus, describes the Jews as a kind of philosophic sect; Hecataeus and Strabo interpreted the Jewish idea of God in the spirit of Stoic pantheism.[11]

The Jews who lived within the orbit of Greek culture conceived of the relation of their religion to Greek philosophy along similar lines. They called their religion a philosophy, and in their apologetics sought to demonstrate the philosophic character of the Jewish idea of God and the humane nature of Jewish ethics.[12] They laid the foundations for the attempt to provide a philosophical form for the intellectual content of Judaism, clothing it in Greek modes of expression and using philosophical arguments in support of the ethical doctrines of the Bible. Not only the form but the content of Greek philosophy also invaded Judaism. The manner and extent of this penetration varied, ranging from the mere philosophical embellishment of Jewish ideas, to their replacement by Greek doctrines, and culminating in the radical philosophical sublimation undertaken by Philo.

An intermediate position is occupied by the Wisdom of Solomon. Despite the use of philosophic concepts, occasionally quoted verbatim from Greek sources, and the occurrence of a number of ideas that are essentially foreign to Judaism, the basic attitude of the book is thoroughly Jewish.[13] Its main themes are the comparison of the fate of the wicked with that of the righteous, the praise of wisdom and the exhortation to seek it, excursuses upon the role of wisdom, and the proofs on its behalf drawn from the history of Israel. All these clearly betray the influence of Scripture, the first two more especially that of Proverbs. Equally Jewish are the book's conception of a personal God who intervenes in the affairs of man to reward or punish, who reveals himself in miracles, and who demonstrates, through the history of Israel, his own power and the vanity of idols,[14] as well as the ethics rooted in such a belief. The mention of Plato's four cardinal virtues[15] gives the ethics of the book a vaguely philosophic coloring without determining its material content. Altogether, the Wisdom of Solomon is much given to using philosophic concepts in order to present or justify notions drawn entirely from the Bible. The ideal philosophical system for this exercise was provided by the Neoplatonic version of Stoicism, founded by Posidonius, which, in fact, underlies its philosophy.

Characteristically enough, the fullest and most detailed rendering of philosophic concepts can be found in the polemics against idolatry. Posidonius' argument is rendered in great detail and with scholastic thoroughness, but all this philosophy only serves as scientific support of the biblical rejection of idolatry.[16] The author uses philosophic and scientific concepts even in his accounts of the biblical miracles. The same holds true for wisdom, the central concept of the book, for which Greek philosophy supplies the formal description, rather than the material content. Wisdom is described with all the attributes of the Stoic *pneuma*.[17] Its source, however, is not in Stoicism, but in the Jewish wisdom literature. The latter was already familiar with the remarkable hypostasis of wisdom, and at least in this respect the author of the Wisdom of Solomon goes beyond the Book of Proverbs. The creative activity of God and his direct influence on the course of the world is emphasized to such an extent that not much weight can be attached to the utterances concerning wisdom's role in the creation and its miraculous influence,[18] especially as the forcefulness of these expressions is frequently matched by their vagueness. Evidently, the psychological and ethical value of the concept is more important to the author than its cosmic function; above all, wisdom is the principle that enlightens the spirit of man.[19] The precise nature of the relation between heavenly wisdom and man remains obscure. Occasional phrases call to mind the Stoic doctrine of the *pneuma* residing in every man's soul, but these do not agree very well with the prayers to God that he grant wisdom, or with the demand that princes should acquire it. The metaphysical status of wisdom remains doubtful, and only its ethical character is unequivocally clear. In accordance with Stoic ethics, wisdom becomes the fountainhead of the virtues in general.[20]

However, in spite of its recourse to Stoic doctrines, the ethics of the Wisdom of Solomon are essentially biblical. The fundamental ethical opposition is that between the righteous and the godless; the Stoic concept of wisdom is merely the form in which to clothe the ethical ideal of Judaism.[21] In some respects, however, Greek philosophy exerted a profound material influence. In place of the biblical doctrine of creation, we find the Platonic notion that God had created the world from formless matter. But the subject is hinted at with such brevity that it is impossible to form any opinion as to the extent and significance of this conception.[22] The relationship between body and soul is also conceived in Greek fashion. The doctrine of the immortality of the soul may, of course, derive either from Jewish or from Greek sources. The book's descriptions of the afterlife are partly indebted to Plato, partly of obviously Jewish origin. The notion that the soul is degraded by its entry into the body (ignoring, for the moment, the doctrine of the pre-existence of the soul, for which the evidence of the text is inconclusive)[23] is, however, definitely Platonic. This dualistic conception of man, which places body and soul in axiological opposition to each other, is important from more than a metaphysical viewpoint. It contains the elements of a religious ideal which was still foreign to biblical Judaism, which aimed at liberating the soul from the fetters of matter and preserving its pure spirituality. These conclusions are not actually drawn in the Wisdom of Solomon, but are clearly implicit.

A similar compromise between Greek and Jewish elements can be found in IV Maccabees. This book purports to be "a true philosophic discourse" and is composed according to the rules of Greek rhetoric. The introduction offers a philosophic disquisition on the subject of the rule of the intellect over the emotions, the like of which is not found in the other Book of Wisdom.[24] But here again it is the form of expression rather than the substance of the book that is influenced by philosophy. In its fundamental religious doctrines, which, of course, are not developed systematically within the book itself, IV Maccabees remains essentially and distinctively Jewish. Despite the occasional use of abstract terms borrowed from the language of the philosophical schools, the author has preserved the full and living concreteness of the biblical God. He is so unphilosophic as to ascribe to God pity for the sufferings of the righteous and anger over the prosperity of the wicked.[25] Belief in the immortality of the soul appears in the form of the doctrine that the righteous will join the heavenly choir of the patriarchs. The sufferings of the righteous are said to have atoning power.[26] Only the ethical teachings of the book, including their psychological presuppositions, are treated in a genuinely philosophical manner.

The principle common to all schools of Greek ethics, that reason should rule over the passions, could easily be considered the philosophical expression of the biblical demand of submission to the divine law. The high moral seriousness of the Stoic ethic could appear very close to that of the Bible. The book closely follows Stoic ethics, in spite of occasional deviations both in terminology and substance; for example, the Jewish martyrs are described as Stoic sages.[27] Even in this identification, in spite of a superficial reliance on Stoic concepts, the substance of the ethical ideal is determined by Judaism. But the book's mildness in dealing with the passions, its renunciation of the harsh Stoic demand to extirpate them, and its substitution of the precept to conquer and rule them need not necessarily be attributed to Jewish influence. Our author may very well be influenced by Peripatetic teaching or by the Middle Stoa, which had already mitigated the original Stoic rigor.[28] Even so, a specifically religious coloring, foreign to Stoicism in all its forms, is given to Stoic ethics. The "fear of the Lord" which, at first, takes the place of wisdom as one of the four cardinal virtues, eventually becomes their very source. Similarly reason, which is the basis of all virtues, is described as "pious reason."[29] In dealing with the question of whether reason is powerful enough to control the passions, the author clearly relies upon piety to give reason the necessary strength.[30] Reason receives its strength from piety that puts its trust in the Lord, and expresses itself both in the observance of the ritual laws given by God and in ethical conduct. The self-sufficiency of the Stoic sage is thus subordinated to the higher ideal of a piety founded in God himself. The ultimate impulse of ethics has changed.

The only literary representative of a thoroughgoing philosophic reconstruction of Judaism is Philo of Alexandria, who, however, alludes to several Jewish predecessors. For Philo, philosophy is not merely a convenient means for an exposition of his ideas, nor is the acceptance of philosophic doctrines limited to details only; Judaism as a whole is conceived as a philosophic doctrine inasmuch as it contains a complete system of philosophy. With the aid of the allegorical method evolved by the Stoics, Philo succeeded in preaching a philosophical reinterpretation of both the historical and the legal parts of the Pentateuch; he was sincerely convinced that he was not misrepresenting Judaism but revealing its deepest meaning. The extent to which he was rooted in Judaism is borne out by the literary form of his writings, most of which are commentaries on the Torah and probably originated from homilies delivered in the synagogue. The substance of his teaching also exhibits Jewish elements, though these

appear in the sentiments underlying it rather than in its conceptional content. But on the whole, Philo's system can only be understood in terms of its Greek presuppositions.

In the wake of Posidonius' synthesis of Platonic and Stoic doctrines, Philo reduces the whole of reality to two factors. The two ultimate principles in the world are the active divine cause and matter, which is the object of divine causality. The idea of a formless primal matter, which was mentioned in the Book of Wisdom only in passing, becomes one of the main pillars of Philo's system; the scriptural doctrine of creation gives way to the notion of the fashioning of the world out of formless matter.[31] Of course, the relationship between God and the world is not seen in terms of Stoic pantheism. Philo's God is not the Greek *pneuma* that fills the world; he stands over and against the world in absolue transcendence, and unlike the Stoic *pneuma* is conceived as absolutely immaterial. Quite rightly, the influence of the traditional Jewish idea of God has been detected in the Philonic emphasis on God's transcendence and spirituality. However, the effect of this influence seems to manifest itself more in Philo's rejection of Stoic materialism and pantheism than in the concept of a personal God, which, in fact, is completely missing.

Philo's sublimation of the concept of God is not fulfilled merely by ridding it of all anthropomorphic characteristics; actually the concept of God is elevated above all values and perfections conceivable to the human mind. God is above knowledge and virtue, above the good and the beautiful.[32] Since God is exalted above all that is knowable, only his bare existence is accessible to our intellect; in fact, Philo prefers to describe God as "He Who Is," or in even more abstract language, as "Being."[33] The direction in which Philo developed the concept of God had already been anticipated by Plato. But Philo went far beyond Plato, and for the first time gave to the notion of divine transcendence the radical twist of later negative theology. If God is also described as the sum of all perfection, this is but the reverse side of the same idea, and though this also seems to open the door again to the habit of predicating personal attributes to God— calling him Father and Creator, or speaking of his grace and goodness —this result was certainly not seriously intended by Philo.[34] Consistency was never Philo's strong point; if he occasionally seems to approach the biblical conception of a personal God, this may more safely be considered inconsistency rather than the essential nature of his teaching.

The endeavor to bridge the gap between God and the material

world gave birth to Philo's doctrine of intermediate beings, and in particular, to his doctrine of the logos. God does not act immediately upon the world, but through mediating powers emanated by him. The first among these is the logos. It is in the doctrine of the logos that we encounter the most famous and most difficult part of Philo's system. His concept of divine powers combines the Platonic doctrine of ideas, the Stoic *logoi spermatikoi* which permeate the cosmos, and Jewish angelogy. Accordingly, the logos corresponds to all three; it is the unity of ideas, the simple source of all cosmic powers, and the highest of the angels. This combination of Stoic, Platonic, and Jewish notions has resulted in a complicated mixture riddled with contradictions.[35] These contradictions concern the relationship of these intermediate beings to God. Sometimes they are thought of as powers inherent in God, and sometimes as effects proceeding from him and their mutual relations to each other; lastly, it is hard to decide whether they are personal or impersonal beings.

In spite of the incompleteness and lack of balance of this concept, its underlying intention has considerable historical importance. Such an attempt to bridge the gap between a highly sublimated idea of God and the world of the senses, by interposing a series of intermediate steps which would convert an absolute opposition into one of degrees, was original in Philo and was to be repeated time and again in the history of metaphysics. Plato's derivation of the *ideas* from the idea of the good is quite different and can hardly have influenced Philo. Although the substance of Philo's doctrine of the logos and the heavenly powers is borrowed from others, its function within his system is unique.

The value of Philo's doctrine is not restricted to the domain of metaphysics, but has relevance as well to religion. By making God the source of a supersensual world, it relates the opposites, God-cosmos and supersensual-sensual world, in a structured hierarchy. The imperfection of the world of the senses arises from the matter out of which it has been fashioned by the divine powers, which prevents these powers from becoming manifest in all their perfection.[36] The dualism of this conception is of special importance for understanding the nature of man. Through his body and the inferior parts of his soul, man belongs to the world of the senses; through his reason, however, which is an emanation from the divine logos, he belongs to the suprasensual world. To the superior part of his soul, man's body appears to be a prison house. It is the purpose of man, therefore, to

free himself from the chains of corporeality and to return to his heavenly source.[37] The general direction of Philo's ethics is thus clearly indicated. He follows the earlier, more rigorous, version of Stoic ethics,[38] but gives it an entirely different, religious accent. War is to be waged against the passions no longer in order that man may follow the laws of universal reason and become master of himself, but in order to liberate the soul from the fetters of sensuality and enable it to fulfill its heavenly destiny. Stoic ethics is thus interpreted (as it was already by Posidonius) in the spirit of the dualistic religious sensibility of Plato. In a strange but revealing paradox, Philo asserts, against Stoic determination, the idea of man's freedom, while maintaining at the same time that without the aid of God man is unable to do good by his own power.[39] The consciousness of man's moral freedom seems to be maintained against scientific determinism, but not in the face of the religious experience of man's impotence before God.

Philo's dualism is intended to lead us from earthly existence to a suprasensual world: liberation from the dominion of the senses means elevation to the realm of spirit. The same idea is expressed by the notion that the contemplative life is man's highest end.[40] However, the concept of contemplation (*theoria*) has lost the all-embracing character it had with Aristotle, and becomes restricted to the sphere of religion. Empirical knowledge is merely a preparation for the knowledge of God and has no value of its own.[41] Philo's scientific interest underscores this attitude since he uses Greek science exclusively for religious purposes. The result is equally significant for science and religion. By valuing science solely for its religious function, religion, in its turn, is made knowledge. The philosophic knowledge of God and the religious knowledge of God are now one. Religion may seem to become unduly intellectualized in this system, though this is certainly not Philo's intention. Next to and above the "scientific" knowledge of God there is an immediate intuition which requires no scientific preparation and which, in fact, is a deliberate repudiation of all theoretical knowledge.[42] At the same time that Philo praises the mystical knowledge of God, without noticing the contradiction he abandons scientific inquiry—which elsewhere he had highly praised—and actually argues against it in the manner of Greek skepticism.

However, Philo's religious ideal, for the sake of which philosophy is deprecated, is by no means the traditional Jewish one. The goal of

Philo's piety is as far from historical Judaism as is his speculative reconstruction of its religious ideas. The ideal of an ascent of the soul to the suprasensual world, culminating in a union with God, is alien to the ethical religion of Judaism and closer to the world of mysticism. Already, the purely philosophic notion of the soul's ascent to God harbors a mystical element which becomes dominant in Philo's preference of immediate intuition over and above the rational knowledge of God. Philo even interprets the concept of revelation mystically. For mysticism, revelation is not tied to any particular historical event; rather it is part of individual piety and renews itself therefore in every soul that has entered into true communion with God. Philo adopts this mystical concept of revelation and interprets biblical prophecy accordingly.[43] He exhibits the same combination of mystical and moral religion as Plato, and like the latter, conceives the aim of ethics as the imitation of God, by which man becomes similar, as far as possible, to his model.[44] The relationship to God thereby acquires an ethical character and Philo in fact does subscribe—although in Platonic formulations—to the ideal of Jewish religion and ethics. From this side of his religious consciousness, Philo is thus deeply anchored to Judaism. The relationship between man and God is conceived from a thoroughly Jewish point of view: humility, trust and obedience are the cardinal religious virtues.[45] Trustful submission to God is as important for him as the longing for mystical union with God. Philo probably did not realize the contradiction between the two ideals.

The two sides of Philo's religious consciousness are reflected also in his theological speculation. His concept of God, which is above and beyond all positive content, corresponds to the mystical. There is no doubt that, for Philo, this idea of God is the ultimately valid one; the personal traits occasionally attributed to God are, from a philosophic point of view, inconsequential lapses from consistency. However, what appears as mere inconsistency from a theoretical point of view, may well be an essential part in the religious context of Philo's thought. Despite the fact that the purely abstract idea of God logically excludes a personalistic conception, Philo seems unable to do without the latter when he wants to say what God really means for him.

In his doctrine of divine powers, the Jewish element in Philo again comes to the fore. When he attributes two main forces to the logos—goodness, the creative and merciful force, and power, the ruling and punishing force[46]—it is evident that the cosmological aspect of this notion is incidental to its ethical bearing. The mystical side of Philo's thought and feeling may well be the stronger, yet it is nevertheless true that for him Jewish piety is not merely an historic inheritance, but a personal possession, influencing the complexion of his system though not determining its basic structure.

This is illustrated once more by Philo's concept of revelation. We have already referred to his interpretation of historical revelation in mystical terms. Nevertheless, the special status of historical revelation is not lost in the process. Philo adheres to the Jewish concept of revelation and regards the Torah as the complete and absolute vehicle of God's truth, no less than any teacher of the Talmud.[47] The five books of Moses are for him the highest expression of the truth and contain everything that science can discover. The significance of the allegorical interpretation of Scripture was therefore, for Philo, different than the allegorical explanation of myths was for his Stoic predecessors. Philo's aim is to bring together the two forms of truth: human knowledge and divine revelation. But the very contrast between these two forms of truth is possible only upon the assumption of an historically revealed religion. Philo was the first systematically to attempt to unite them, and in this respect he certainly deserves the title of "the first theologian" bestowed upon him by historians of philosophy. He was the first to pose the basic problem that subsequently was of continual concern for the philosophy and theology of the monotheistic religions; this fact by itself, even more than the actual content of his teachings, gives him his importance in the history of religious thought.[48]

3 The Religious Ideas of Talmudic Judaism

JEWISH Hellenism was a transitory phenomenon in the development of Judaism. The dominant form of Jewish religion since the last centuries of antiquity—and the one that served as the foundation for the development of Judaism in the Middle Ages and modern times—was Talmudic Judaism, which developed in Palestine and Babylonia. Until the end of the first century of the Common Era, the most diverse religious tendencies flourished in Palestine, and many of the apocryphal books show the extent to which the Jews of Palestine were influenced by the religious syncretism of late antiquity. However, after the destruction of Second Temple by Titus (70 C.E.), all the religious currents that had competed with Pharasaic Talmudic Judaism quickly disappeared, and the latter achieved a unified form. The significance of the Talmud for coming generations resides mainly in religious law, which does not concern us here. The ritual, ceremonial, and legal provisions of the Talmud gave Jewish religious life its fixed and distinct form, which maintained itself until the end of the eighteenth century. The basic religious ideas of Judaism, on the other hand, were never given a similarly definitive form by the Talmud. The Talmud never attempts to formulate religious truths in fixed dogmatic expressions. The borderline between those binding doctrine and individual opinion is extremely fluid, and there is far greater variety between different generations and individuals than in the realm of religious law. The most diverse religious ideas were current between the last centuries B.C.E., when the development of the Talmud began to take place, and its final redaction at the end of the fifth century. Many of the foreign doctrines which had penetrated into Judaism during the syncretistic period reappeared in Talmudic literature. Many of them, however, like those fantastic eschatological descriptions which we have already seen in the apocryphal literature, should be considered simply as the free play of imaginative fancy or the product of popular faith, rather than as doctrine in the precise sense. It is possible, after all, to detect a common and permanent pattern of basic ideas which proved of the greatest importance for subsequent developments.

The faith of Talmudic Judaism rests completely on biblical foundations. Central to it are the simple and sublime ideas of the Bible concerning a transcendent God, the Torah as the embodiment of his moral demands, the moral nature of the relationship between God and man, the wisdom and justice of divine providence, the election of Israel, and the promise of the coming kingdom of God. No theoretical reflection diminishes the living reality of God. Even speculations concerning hypostases and other mediating agencies could not affect his immediate presence to the world or remove him to an unapproachable distance. God acts as much in the present as he did in the past. It is true that prophecy and the miraculous events of biblical times belong to the past, and that the salvation announced by the prophets belongs to the future—the "end of days." This distinction between the present, on the one hand, and the mighty revelations of God in the past and future, on the other, is a necessary corollary of the historical character of the Jewish concept of revelation, and the expectation of a future (historical) salvation. Similar causes operated in Christianity and in Islam and led to similar distinctions between the present and the time of revelation—that is, the past. But even if the present was devoid of historic revelation, men still felt the immediate presence of God in their lives. Every individual Jew knew himself under the same divine providence which had governed the lives of his ancestors, and through some chosen pious persons, even miracles would be wrought—though these could not, of course, be compared to those wrought by the prophets.[1] In order to express the consciousness of the presence of God, the religious imagination did not stop even before the most daring anthropomorphisms. In order to emphasize the value of the study of Torah, the Talmudic rabbis describe God himself as studying the Torah. The faith that the sufferings of Israel could not destroy the intimate bond between God and his people was expressed by saying that God not only lamented over the sorrows that he had brought upon Israel, but actually shared their exile.[2]

But the Talmudists clearly recognized the nature of the anthropomorphisms of their own religious fantasy, as well as those of the Bible. They pointed out how God revealed himself according to the varying historical situations, and how the prophetic utterances were influenced by the individual personality of each prophet; in fact, they even suggested that every Jew standing at Sinai saw God in a slightly different fashion.[3] These notions were never systematically developed; no attempts were made to distinguish between anthropomorphic forms of expression and the actual content of the idea of God, but their intention is quite clear. The idea of the personal and moral nature of God remains beyond all criticism, and provides the basic common core of the different concrete images.

The passionate violence of the religious ethos of the prophets had given place, in Talmudic times, to a quieter, more restrained, and in a way even sober piety, bound to history and tradition. However, the activist character of Jewish religion was preserved. Religious life was still centered on the divine "commands," in which God addressed himself to the human will, and showed the way of communion between man and God. Human destiny is conceived in different ways. Piety is not so much the mere observance of the divine commandments as the imitation of a divine model. The biblical commandment to be holy even as the Lord God is holy, and the injunction to walk in the ways of God, are interpreted as demands to imitate the divine qualities of love and mercy.[4] Love of God and faithful trust in him are considered the foundation of the right observance of the commandments. The spirit of rabbinic religion is thus elevated above mere submission or obedience of the will. Its religious activity is rooted in the inner certainty of community with God, yet its piety remains one of precept and duty. Consequently, much stress is laid on moral freedom: man's actions are his own, even in relation to the divine omnipotence. The Torah is the embodiment of the divine will, and the observance of its commandments is the task given to Israel by God. The universality of the divine commandment is established by the notion of an original, pre-Israelite revelation, addressed to all nations and containing the foundations of morals.[5]

However, the perfect divine revelation is the Torah given to Israel. As a divinely revealed law, all its parts—ritual as well as moral—are of equal validity, and equally constitute the religious duty of Israel. The idea of equal and unassailable validity—from a formal point of view—of all parts of the Torah follows as a logical consequence from the biblical notion of a divine legislation; at the same time the rabbis—from the material point of view—distinguished between central and marginal laws, between means and ends. The Talmud frequently interprets ceremonial and cultic items of the biblical legislation as means toward the ultimate moral ends of the divine law, subordinating the former to the latter in spite of their common divine origin.[6] Psychologically of course, it is only to be expected that sometimes one, and sometimes the other of these two facets comes to the fore; at times the observance of the commandments is permeated by ethical attitudes; at other times, the distinction between ethics and ritual becomes blurred.

The messianic promises of the prophets were the mainstay of the Jewish community. We need not concern ourselves here with the transformation of the relatively simple expectations of the prophets into the more complicated notions of the later eschatologies developing in the last centuries of the pre-Christian era, or with the differences between the more national and the more universalistic versions of the messianic ideal, or with the changing ideas about the imminence or distance of the messianic coming. All these, though of considerable consequence for later times, are largely irrelevant to our present theme. Throughout all these variations on the messianic theme, the historical character of the prophetic hope for the future is preserved intact. An expectation of an entirely different sort is found in the ideas of the resurrection of the dead and the immortality of the soul. In a way, the resurrection of the dead still links up with the expectations of an historical fulfillment. It will take place at the end of time, and the resurrected will take part in the miraculous events of that age. The individual hope for an eternal life was thus combined with the idea that past generations too, would share in the promise of the kingdom of God. The personal longing for eternal life is satisfied within the framework of collective historical eschatology.

These two elements are completely separated by the belief in the immortality of the soul. Frequently, the idea of immortality is overshadowed by that of resurrection. The Talmud, like the apocryphal literature, knows of a kind of intermediate state of the soul between death and resurrection; true retribution will be dispensed only after the resurrection of the body.[7] But along with it, we also find the faith in a retribution coming immediately after death, and in a life of blessedness for the soul in the beyond.[8] According to the latter view, the individual hope for the future has no connection whatsoever with history. "The world to come," the place of reward and punishment beyond, is distinct from the future "kingdom of God" even in its most eschatological form. "The world to come" does not succeed "this world" in time, but exists from eternity as a reality outside and above time, to which the soul ascends. This view faces a double opposition—on the one hand between the present reality of history and the future kingdom of God, and on the other, between life on earth and life beyond. The two orientations do not necessarily exclude each other. The original Jewish eschatology with its historical and collective hopes did not lose its power or intensity because of the belief in individual immortality, and the latter, as we have seen, could combine with the idea of the resurrection of the dead. Nevertheless, religious interpretation of the world had taken a new and decisive turn which provided starting points for the most diverse developments of Jewish thought in later periods.

The belief in another world, above and beyond time, led to a new evaluation of the present world. It was not enough that this world should find its perfection and fulfillment in a world to come, and that the wrongs of this earthly life should be made good there, but the ultimate end of man was shifted to the world to come. Our life in this world came to be conceived as a mere preparation, whether in terms of the resurrection of the dead or of the immortality of the soul. According to a well-known Talmudic saying, this world is like a vestibule in which man should prepare himself for entering the banquet hall of the world to come.[9] The blessedness of the world to come is understood as consisting of the pious enjoying the radiance of the presence of God.[10]

Nevertheless, this rabbinic view is very different from the dualistic contempt for the world of the senses exhibited, for example, by Philo, under Platonic influence. The Talmud emphatically repeats the biblical affirmation of this world and interprets the words of Genesis, "and God saw everything that He had made and behold it was very good," as referring to *both* worlds.[11] The good things of this world, including sensual pleasures, may be enjoyed simply and naturally; only in rare instances do we find any ascetic tendencies. Even more important is the fact that asceticism plays no role in the understanding of ethics. Although the moral act was understood as a preparation for the future world, it lacked the negative connotation of separation from the world of the senses. Its meaning was rather wholly positive: to serve God in this world, to fulfill his will, and to build a social order in accordance with his will. The religious value of moral action is maintained even in the face of eschatological communion with God, since fulfilling the will of God in this world is no less communion with God than the state of blessedness in the hereafter. The same Talmudic teacher who described this world as only a vestibule to the coming world, also said that although one hour of blessedness in the world to come was worth more than all the life of this world, yet one hour of repentance and good deeds in this world was worth more than all of the life of the world to come.

What has been said regarding the rabbinic view of the world applies as well to the idea of man. The Bible had ascribed a divine origin to the human spirit, but now we find an explicit dualism. The body and the soul are seen in sharp contrast. Because of his soul, which is destined for eternal life, man belongs to the superior world of the spirit; in his body, he belongs to the earth. Thanks to his soul, he resembles the angels; thanks to his body, a beast. Following the Stoics and Philo, the relationship of the soul to the body is compared to that of God to the world.[12] The idea of the pre-existence of the soul is also known to the Talmud.[13] Man's higher powers, such as his reason and moral consciousness, are attributed to the soul; his lower passions are assigned to the body. The corollary of man's intermediate position between the higher and lower worlds is that by observing the divine commandments, he can rise to the rank of the angels, but by transgressing them he descends to the level of the beasts.[14]

But this dualism is far from identifying evil with man's sensual nature. The body is not the ground of evil, and consequently man's moral task does not consist in his separation from the body. The warfare between good and evil is fought out *within* man's soul; it is there that good and evil impulses face each other.[15] They represent two directions of the human will, and man must choose between them. As the source of temptation, sensuality occasionally is identified with the "evil impulse," but in itself it is ethically indifferent and has its legitimate sphere of existence. In spite of the Talmudic praise of the virtue of frugality as practiced by the pious, sensuality —provided it is kept under control—is considered unobjectionable, and the body is regarded as an essential part of man's God-given nature. Even the evil impulse is a necessary part of human nature, and the Talmud voices the remarkable demand to love God with both of our impulses—the good and the evil.[16] Here again the end of ethics is seen not as separation from the world of the senses, but rather serving God within that world, with all available human powers. The body and the senses should be subordinate and subservient to the soul; they are not, of themselves, enemies of its heavenly destiny.

Nonetheless, the whole complex of ideas described so far—the belief in a spiritual world above the world of the senses, the eternal destiny of the soul, and the dualistic conception of man, could easily be turned in the direction of an ascetic contemplative religion; it did, in fact, provide the opening through which the Neoplatonic type of spirituality entered Judaism in the Middle Ages.

Along with these speculative developments, there emerged another, more formal, though no less significant phenomenon: the growth of theoretical reflection on the contents of religion. Inquiry into fundamental religious questions is no longer an expression of the religious consciousness itself, seeking an answer to its doubts and anxieties (as in the later prophets, or in the book of Job), but acquires an independent value. The basic religious ideas of the Bible, as well as the commandments of the Law, become objects of theoretical reflection. Particularly in regard to ethical questions, a high degree of abstraction was reached. Of particular interest is the attempt to reduce the entire content of the biblical commandments to one principle. The Talmud, like the gospels, seeks to determine the "major principle" of the Torah. One Talmudic master finds it in the commandment, "But thou shalt love thy neighbor as thyself" (Leviticus 19:18); another finds it in the sentence, "This is the book of the generations of Adam. In the day that God created man, in the likeness of God made He him" (Genesis 5:1). Similarly, a well-known legend has Hillel, the greatest of the Talmudic sages, declare that the rule, "That which is hateful unto thee, do not do unto thy neighbor," was the "entire Torah," and everything else was only a commentary on it.[17] By declaring love of one's neighbor to be the supreme ethical virtue, the Talmud does not make any material addition to the teaching of the Torah; the novelty lies in the theoretical formulations which describe the commandment of love as the greatest and most inclusive commandment of the Torah, or assert the whole Law to be merely a commentary on this superior ethical rule, to which both ethical and ritual laws are thus made subordinate. Elsewhere a comment on Leviticus 18:4, "Ye shall do my judgments and keep mine ordinances," emphasizes the difference between ethical and ritual commandments. These "judgments," which include the ethical commandments of the Torah, are defined as those laws that "ought to have been written" even if Scripture had not stated them.

The incomprehensibility of the ritual commandments is expressed in the saying that they were open to the objections of the "evil impulse and the nations of the world."[18] The idea of the intrinsic self-evidence of the ethical commandments which God gave to man is essentially a biblical heritage; it is merely the theoretical formulation that is new. The self-evidence of the moral law, implied by the Bible, is emphasized in obvious imitation of the Greek notion of an "unwritten law" in the pointed formulation that moral laws are laws that "ought to have been written down." True, according to the Talmud, the biblical laws which lack this intrinsic evidence possess the same unconditioned validity as the self-evident "judgments of the Lord." The Talmudic doctrine that the whole biblical law, by virtue of its divine origin, is equally and unconditionally authoritative—although material distinctions can be drawn between ethical and ceremonial precepts—appears here in its utmost clarity.

The doctrine of retribution is strongly emphasized and elaborated in considerable detail; yet the Talmud demands the disinterested observance of the divine commandments. It is not demand in itself, but the theoretical precision with which it is formulated, that is of immediate relevance to our theme. In the saying to which we have already referred—"Better is one hour of repentance and good deeds in this world than the entire life of the world to come, and better is one hour of blessedness in the world to come than all of the life of this world"—the religious pathos employs conceptual language. Elsewhere the same demand is stated in sober theoretical language.

In connection with the commandment to love God, the Talmud discusses the difference between those who serve God out of love, and those who serve him out of fear. The question is raised in the form of a casuistical problem, whether an observance of the Law because of a desire of reward or fear of retribution has any value at all. The decision is that observance of the Law, even for ulterior motives, was not devoid of value, for through it men could rise to a disinterested observance.[19] To this ideal of the observance of the commandments is added the study of the Law. The latter was not only a divine commandment in itself but also gave full scope to the desire for education. Discussing the primacy of "theory" (learning), over "practice" (the observance of the commandments), the Talmud solves the dilemma on one occasion by declaring that the study of the Law was equivalent to the observance of all the commandments, and on another by concluding that not theory but deeds were what mattered. Elsewhere a kind of compromise is reached: the dilemma is decided in favor of study, but the reason given is that "study leads to practice."[20]

Some of these ethical questions also led to theological discussions of dogmatic problems. Belief in the freedom of the human will, which in the Bible is an immediate religious certainty, becomes a doctrinal proposition in the Talmud. Talmudic predilection for pointed formulations produces the paradox: "Everything is in the hands of Heaven, with the exception of the fear of Heaven."[21] The difficulty of reconciling man's freedom with God's omniscience was fully realized, but was not resolved. Instead, the rabbis held fast to both horns of the dilemma: "Everything is foreseen, yet permission is given; the world is judged with mercy, yet the verdict is according to one's deeds."[22] The second half of this sentence refers to a question which greatly preoccupied the Talmudic sages. Once we realize that even the righteous are not free of sin, and that there is no wicked man who has not done some good, what is the line of division between the righteous and the wicked? The answer, though somewhat primitive, states that man is to be considered good or evil according to the preponderance of his good or evil deeds.[23] The biblical question "Why do the righteous suffer and the evil men prosper?" is treated in many and varied ways, and though faith in a future life dulled the point of this question to some extent, it did not solve it in principle. The meaning of human suffering remained a riddle. The Talmud stresses the purgative quality of suffering, and in some of its reflections on this subject it touches the most profound reaches of the religious consciousness.[24] But in addition to such levels of insight we also find a mechanical explanation: the sufferings of the righteous in this world are punishment for those sins they have committed, and the prosperity of the wicked represents a reward for the good deeds that they have done; ultimate retribution for both is left to the world to come.[25]

The rabbinic manner of thinking is seen in the form in which it is expressed. The terse and pithy formulations we have cited suggest its capacity for conceptual thinking. This appears at its best in those sentences and maxims in which the Talmudic masters enunciate with extraordinary concision fundamental religious and ethical doctrines. The art of coining such maxims was apparently cultivated in the schools of the Talmudic sages. One tractate of the Mishna—known as the *Sayings of the Fathers*—consists of a collection of sentences by some of the greatest Talmudic masters (some of which have already been quoted). Comparing these maxims with the proverbs or sayings in the biblical wisdom literature, one is immediately struck by the vast difference between them in regard to their subject matter, and perhaps even more, to their form of thought.

The Talmudic epigram is built on the pointed abstraction; its charm resides in its striking felicity and terseness of form. The epigram just quoted, concerning the relationship between divine providence and human freedom, may be taken as a complete theology in one sentence; in its power of compression it is not alone among rabbinic sayings. Even where the specific form of the epigram is not intended, rabbinic thought almost instinctively expresses itself in this way. The saying that certain precepts would have to be written down if they had not *already* been written down in the Torah, and the statement that everything is in the hand of God except the fear of God, are not less pungent than the maxims proper. A more precise formal analysis, which until now has never been attempted, would probably reveal, in addition to the characteristics described above, a whole series of typical forms of thought recurring again and again in rabbinic discussion of religious fundamentals.

These hints must suffice for our present purpose. They also enable us to recognize the limitations within which this type of thought moves. Its form of expression shows that the systematic treatment of religious problems is intended; it is satisfied with an individual maxim or comment on a scriptural verse, and at the utmost proceeds from there to the discussion of a particular question. This lack of system is characteristic of Talmudic discussions of theology. Problems are taken up one by one; there is never an attempt to combine isolated conclusions in a coherent framework. As our examples have shown, there are insights into the most basic problems of religion, with full awareness of their fundamental significance; but fundamentals are discussed in the same way as details, and no attempt is made to follow them systematically to their conclusions. The Talmud is content with the abstract statement that the love of one's neighbor was the supreme principle of the Torah, but it never attempts to trace the different moral laws to this supreme principle or to demonstrate concretely (apart from a few occasional examples) the moral purpose of the ceremonial law. The demand of completely disinterested worship of God does not in itself contradict the doctrine of retribution which occupies so important a place in Talmudic ethics; but the problems posed by the juxtaposition of these two ideas are never properly discussed.

All the most important ideas in connection with the problem of theodicy can be found in the Talmud; yet it is impossible to construct from them a systematic doctrine. This is especially true of the metaphysical aspects of theology. The Talmud repeatedly emphasizes that the anthropomorphic expressions of the Bible are only metaphors, but it never enquires into the criteria for delimiting metaphorical from literal utterances. We may therefore speak of a definite and consistent over-all religious viewpoint of the Talmud, but no correspondingly consistent and unified theoretical comprehension of the central questions of religion. What the Talmud has produced is not theology, but scattered theological reflections. This accounts for the sometimes strange coexistence of ideas; next to insights of the utmost profundity there are other pages which show a primitive thought wrestling laboriously with its problems. Lack of theoretical maturity is often found in conjunction with sharp and pointed conceptual formulations.

The difference between the righteous and the wicked man consists, as we have seen, in the preponderance of good over evil deeds. This atomistic conception of man characterizes not so much the moral view of the Talmud as the adequacy of its conceptual tools, which can measure the good or evil in man only according to the number of individual acts. Equally naive is the answer which tries to solve the profound question of theory versus practice by pronouncing in favor of the superiority of learning because it leads to practice. Rabbinic thought is struggling to master the content of religion, but seems still unable to grasp it in its wholeness and unity.

After what has been said, it is hardly necessary to point out that rabbinic Judaism was little affected by the scientific philosophy of the Greeks. Only the most popular forms of these Greek doctrines, in which they were spread among the masses, whether orally or in writing, seem to be echoed in the Talmud. Much in Talmudic ethics is reminiscent of Stoic popular philosophy. Both teach that everything that man possesses is borrowed from God, and therefore man should not complain if God demands the return of that which is properly his. Both consider the soul as a stranger in this world, praise the virtue of moderation as the true riches, and advise man to live every day as if it were his last.[26] Some of the rabbinic maxims which ask man to do his duty without thought of reward bear a strong formal resemblance to Stoic sayings. The dependence on Stoic models may be doubtful in the case of individual parallels. Stoic influence as such is beyond doubt. The comparison of the soul to God derives from Stoic metaphysics; the soul fills and vitalizes the body as God fills the world, and like God, it sees but cannot be seen.[27] The Talmud incorporates Platonic as well as Stoic ideas, which, divorced from their systematic context, were part and parcel of general Greek culture. The Talmud not only knows of the pre-existence of the soul, but also says that before birth the soul knew the entire Torah, forgetting it only at the moment of birth. Here the Torah takes the place of the Platonic Idea, as also in the saying that God looked at the Torah and from this model created the world. The invisibility of God is exemplified by the Platonic parable of the human eye which cannot bear to look even at the brightness of the sun.[28] The Talmud uses such ideas in order to rebut the arguments of Gentile opponents and Jewish skeptics. The admonition, "Know what to answer to an Epicurean," (the Epicurean is, for the rabbis, the typical freethinker)[29] proves that the knowledge of foreign ideas was promoted by apologetic considerations. However, since the attacks emanated from popular philosophy rather than from strictly scientific circles, popular Greek wisdom could suffice for their rebuttal.

Gnostic speculation exerted a profounder influence than philosophy on the Talmudic rabbis. Particularly in the first and the beginning of the second century, Gnosticism fascinated many of the leading teachers. Later the suspicions against this trend, which had been present from the very beginning, gained the upper hand, and the Mishnah pronounced an anathema on it: "Whosoever speculated on these four things, it were better for him if he had not come into the world—what is above? what is beneath? what was beforetime? and what will be hereafter?"[30] This hostility to Gnosticism, or at least to its more extreme forms, did not destroy it but definitely broke its power. From its very beginning Gnosticism was considered an esoteric doctrine that could be propagated only in the narrow circle of the elect. Naturally, Judaism had no room for its dualistic and antinomian doctrines.

In its teaching that the creation of the world and the biblical legislation were not the work of the supreme good God but rather of a hostile demiurge, Gnosticism meant to hit and destroy its hated enemy, Judaism. The Gnostic doctrine of the "two powers" consequently became the worst heresy in Jewish eyes.[31] Accordingly, Jewish Gnosticism was unable to accept the pessimistic Gnostic doctrine of matter as an essentially evil principle completely independent of God. After discarding these elements, Jewish thought nevertheless preserved a number of characteristic and decisive Gnostic traits. The two main subjects of Jewish esotericism—the "work of creation" (maaseh bereshit) and the "the work of the chariot" described by

Ezekiel (*maaseh merkabah*)[32] correspond to the central themes of Gnosticism. The world of the chariot—that is, the throne of glory and the angels surrounding it—corresponds to the highest spiritual sphere, the *pleroma* of the Gnostics. It is the terminus of the soul's mystical journey, the ascension to heaven, which is portrayed in similar terms by Jewish as well as non-Jewish Gnosticism.[33]

The doctrine of creation presents speculation concerning the origin of the world in the form of mystical interpretation of the biblical text. Gnostic ideas are adapted to the biblical notion of creation, but in such a way that the act of creation becomes merely the starting point of a highly mythological cosmogonic process. In the spirit of Gnostic metaphysics of light, God wraps himself in the radiance of a light that fills the world.[34] When God created the world, the latter sought to expand to infinity, until God set limits to its expansion.[35] In connection with the biblical idea of the upper and lower waters, Jewish Gnostics speculate on water as the primal matter of the world, and declare in thoroughly mythological fashion: "Three creations preceded the world: water, spirit, and fire; water conceived and gave birth to darkness, fire conceived and gave birth to light, the air conceived and gave birth to wisdom."[36] The continuation of these Gnostic doctrines can be found in post-Talmudic Jewish mysticism, but for the religious development of Judaism as a whole, they merely represent a sideline. Both in the Talmudic and post-Talmudic eras, they were cultivated only in small circles. Even if at times their influence was relatively great, they never determined the general religious scene.

Nothing so well indicates the limits of theological reflection in the Talmud as the absence of any dogmatic formulation of the substance of Jewish teaching. Attacks from the outside on certain doctrines, like the resurrection of the dead, are refuted, or those who deny them are excluded from the fellowship of Israel.[37] The Talmud nowhere systematically attempts to fix the contents of the Jewish faith; hence the impossibility of establishing with any precision the boundary between a generally valid doctrine and a teacher's individual opinion. This proved of far-reaching consequence for the later development of Judaism.[38] The flexible form in which the faith of Judaism was cast allowed the religious thought of later generations a great deal of freedom. Medieval Jewish philosophy was able to reinterpret traditional religious beliefs with a freedom that was denied to Christian scholasticism. Attempts were made in the Middle Ages to limit this freedom by formulating articles of faith, but since Jewish spiritual authorities could demand general recognition of their rulings only insofar as they acted as interpreters of the Talmud, such efforts could at best have limited success. Nevertheless, the freedom with regard to the tradition of faith had certain boundaries set to it from the beginning. The basic principles of the Jewish faith needed no dogmatic systematization in order to be clearly determined. The belief in the divine origin of the Bible as well as of the complementary oral tradition authoritatively bound the individual both in matters of belief and religious law.

Religious truth had been given once and for all in the Bible and the oral tradition, and it was the absolute norm for faith. All freedom was merely a freedom to interpret this truth, which by its very nature was valid for everybody. Also with regard to the material contents of faith, this freedom was bound to certain fixed principles. Thus the Jewish belief in revelation entailed a whole series of religious assumptions, sharing the authority of revelation and consequently not requiring explicit dogmatic emphasis in order to assert their authority over the faithful. The ideas of providence, retribution, and miracles were firmly established as elements of the Jewish faith through their connection with belief in revelation. Their factual truth was beyond doubt; only in regard to their precise understanding was there freedom for philosophical interpretation. Other religious ideas, though they lacked this close formal relationship to the notion of revelation, attained such prominence in liturgy and public worship that their authority was unquestioned. The whole complex of religious convictions that had grown up in the Talmudic period served as an incontestable, valid norm of faith for future Jewish generations and for their philosophies. Both facts—the existence of a norm of faith and the absence of a systematic formulation of dogma—are of equal importance for subsequent developments: both the freedom and constraint of medieval Jewish philosophy derive from them.

II

Jewish Religious Philosophy in the Middle Ages

1 The Rise of Jewish Philosophy in the Islamic World

WITH the disappearance of Hellenistic Jewish philosophy, a new philosophic movement within Judaism did not arise until the Middle Ages. But this movement was incomparably longer in duration than its ancient predecessor. Its beginnings lie in the early portions of the ninth century C.E. at the latest, and while undergoing continuous development it stretched to the end of the Middle Ages. Traces of its influence can be discerned at the beginning of the modern period as well.

Throughout this period philosophy profoundly influenced the spiritual life of Judaism. For those sections of the Jewish people whose spiritual life was not limited to the study of Bible and Talmud, but who strove for a universal ideal of intellectual culture, philosophy was the queen of the sciences, the central focus of their endeavor. Philosophic knowledge was not only the highest form of knowledge to which the secular sciences were subordinate, but as the highest form of religious knowledge it was also superior to the study of religious law. This central position of philosophy was not merely a theoretical program, but actually shaped the reality of spiritual life. All areas of religious literature were influenced by philosophy. Biblical exegesis searched for the deeper sense of the Bible in a philosophic spirit; religious poetry echoes the ideas of philosophy, and the philosophic preachers of the later Middle Ages sought to spread its ideas among the faithful. Out of this philosophic interpretation of Judaism there grew a philosophic form of religion which, although admitting the unquestionable authority of divine revelation, nevertheless represented a considerable transformation of biblical and Talmudic Judaism, and in the course of time reached a broad circle of educated Jews.

Jewish philosophy in the Middle Ages arose in the cultural world of Islam and was strongly influenced by Islamic philosophy. Its beginnings were deeply influenced by the religio-philosophic ideas

47

of the Islamic Kalam. Even after Jewish philosophy had come under the influence of Neoplatonism, and—subsequently—Aristotelianism, its connection with Islamic philosophy was maintained. Jewish Neoplatonists drew upon the Arabic translations of Neoplatonic sources as well as upon the Islamic Neoplatonist writers themselves (especially the Encyclopedia of the Pure Brethren of Basra). Jewish Aristotelians took up the interpretations of Aristotle as taught by the Arabic Aristotelians such as al-Farabi, Ibn Sina (Avicenna), and later on, Ibn Rushd (Averroës). In the later Middle Ages, Jewish philosophy spread to Jews living in Christian lands. Its major centers were the Christian parts of Spain and Provence; Italy too, took an active part in this work of philosophic labor. But even there, the influence of Islamic philosophy remained dominant, and in comparison with it the influences from Christian scholasticism were negligible; the latter gained in importance only towards the end of the Middle Ages. The measure of dependence on Islamic philosophy is illustrated by the manner in which Jewish philosophy passed to Christian lands. For among the Hebrew translations which opened up the world of philosophy to non-Arabic-speaking Jews, those of Islamic philosophers by far outnumber those made from original Greek sources. Aristotle, upon whom all later Jewish philosophy was based, was known mainly from the translation of the commentaries of Averroës, which, of course, incorporated large sections of the original text. This phenomenon was not limited to the sphere of philosophy alone, for the entire realm of Islamic culture made a tremendous impact upon the Jews at a time when Latin, the language of Christian scholars, was known to very few Jews. There was no such linguistic barrier in the Muslim world where the Arabic language reigned supreme in both life and literature. Moreover, the less rigidly religious character of Islamic culture made it possible for those of another faith to participate in it.

In the realm of science and especially in the cultivation of mathematics, astronomy, and medicine, the Jews took an active part. Other tendencies within Islamic culture become models for Jewish emulation. The resultant Judaeo-Arabic culture produced important and brilliant achievements, and counts among the most fruitful and influential phenomena in the history of Judaism.

The same cause which accounted for Jewish participation in all aspects of Islamic culture also explains the success of Islamic philosophy. But the origin of Jewish philosophy at this time cannot be accounted for by theoretical interest alone. The very existence of Judaism within an Islamic world demanded a philosophic justification. The religious enthusiasm of the first centuries of Islam also had an effect upon Judaism; as in the Islamic world, it manifested itself in the proliferation of religious sects. Most of these sects, of course, were merely ephemeral phenomena that left no permanent trace upon Judaism. Only Karaism, which arose in the middle of the eighth century and which acknowledged only the authority of Scripture, rejecting oral law and with it the Talmudic expansion of biblical law, succeeded in maintaining itself. By the eleventh century even Karaism had passed its peak, and as time went on lost more and more of its dynamism and propagandistic appeal, until it became a minor deviant sect. But in the first several hundred years of its existence it developed a fierce energy and threatened to become a serious rival to Talmudic Judaism. The major point of attack for the various religious sects was the Talmudic law. But occasionally religious polemics entered the field of beliefs and doctrines. This was especially true of the Karaites, who accused rabbinic Judaism, on the basis of the many anthropomorphic expressions in Talmudic and Midrashic literature, of perverting the biblical concept of God.

At the same time Judaism had to defend itself against violent external attacks. The rise of Islam and its spread throughout the Middle East and North Africa aroused stormy polemics, not only between Islam and the faiths it came to supplant, but also between those older faiths themselves. Judaism could not avoid being drawn into the controversy. The charges made against Judaism were not fundamentally new, but they were expressed with new energy, and the Jews by now were so involved in the cultural life of the time that traditional apologetic arguments and methods, based on the Talmud, were no longer adequate. It was necessary to meet the challenge by adapting apologetics to the modes of expression and thought of the times. The Christian side of the attack was not important at that time, although it is uncertain whether some of the thrusts parried by the Jews were originally Christian or Islamic. This applies, for example, to the two objections quoted by Saadia Gaon, which were already known in ancient Christian literature: first, that the dispersal of Israel among the nations proved that God had abandoned them; and second, that the Bible was an inferior revelation since it teaches retribution in this world only.[1]

These polemic charges were based on the assumption common to the two faiths that Judaism, although a revealed religion, had been superseded by later revelations. Islam especially emphasized this idea. It was the duty of Jews, as well as of members of all other faiths, to believe in God's absolute revelation as completed and "sealed" by Muhammad, who has abolished all earlier revelations. In addition, the Islamic polemic claimed that the text of the Bible had been falsified at a later time; consequently, it no longer represented the original divine revelation. Similarly, the Islamic theologians advanced the argument (or possibly borrowed it from the Karaites) that the Talmudic idea of God was anthropomorphic—in spite of the fact that even within Islam crudely anthropomorphic conceptions of the Godhead were current.[2] Jewish theology not only had to prove the factual untruth of these charges but also was forced to make a thorough examination of the problem of anthropomorphism, which became one of the main subjects of systematic thought both in Judaism and Islam. First, Jewish theology had to refute the doctrine that the revelation given to Israel had been abrogated by that granted to Muhammad. Beyond this, it had to disprove not only the superiority but also the truth of Muhammad's revelation. A few isolated Jewish sects admitted Muhammad to the rank of a prophet to the Gentiles; usually he was considered a false prophet, and the religion founded by him was thought of as the work of men.

In the battle concerning the truth of the Islamic revelation the two sides to the controversy did not restrict themselves to purely dogmatic affirmations. Islamic theology sought to bring proofs for the divine origin of Islam, and Jewish theology replied in kind. The proofs adduced were essentially historical, but the criticism that each side levelled at the other led to the fundamental question as to the proper criteria for estimating the reliability of historic traditions. Each side emphasized those elements which were useful for its own purposes. Nevertheless, there developed through this controversy the primitive beginnings of historical criticism as a court of appeal before which the religious tradition itself had to be judged. The Muslim argument that with the revelation of Muhammad all previous revelations, including that of Judaism, had been abrogated, was countered by transferring the entire issue into the sphere of philosophy. The notion of a series of revelations, the earlier of which were abrogated by later stages, seemed to presuppose that God could change his mind; the assumption that God at first commanded one thing and then another was thought to be incompatible with a pure and exalted conception of the divine. The same problem had already been faced by the early Christian Church, which had answered by saying that ancient Israel had not been ready for the fullness of God's truth and therefore received from him only that measure that fitted its capacities. Islamic philosophy treated the question from a more formal standpoint and sought to prove that God commanded different things at different times without there being any change in his will. As a result of what was originally an historical question, there arose a metaphysical problem which was discussed with all the dialectical subtleties of scholastic argument.[3]

Even more radical were the attacks made upon monotheism as such—Judaism, Christianity, and Islam together. They emanated mainly from the non-monotheistic Near Eastern religions. Even after the conquest of the Sassanid empire by the Arabs and the establishment of Islam in Persia, the Parsee religion continued a vigorous struggle for several hundred years. In its dualistic conception of existence it came very close to various Gnostic systems, one of which, Manicheism, attained considerable importance and influence during the first centuries of Islam. Finally, the young religion of Islam also encountered offshoots of Hinduism.

In themselves, these syncretistic movements had little or no effect upon Judaism, but their polemics against Judaism were of some significance. Whereas Christianity and Islam admitted the revealed basis of Judaism, these other religions denied the very fact of a biblical revelation, and criticized biblical teaching from the point of view of their own religious positions.

It is not clear to what degree the Indian religions participated in this controversy. In Islamic and Jewish literature from the end of the ninth century and thereafter, it is given as the opinion of the Brahmins that there is no necessity for prophecy, since man's reason is sufficient to guide him on the right path. It is quite clear, however, that this view is incompatible with the basic theological principles of Brahmanism, and therefore the theory has lately been advanced that a ninth century Islamic skeptic put his own skepticism into the mouth of the Brahmin—a literary device that could succeed if his readers were unfamiliar with the real nature of Brahmanism.[4] Occasionally the immense time units of Indian cosmology were contrasted with the biblical view that the world was created only a few thousand years ago. But whatever the extent of the controversy between the Indian faiths and monotheism, it was unimportant compared with the battle which was waged against the dualistic faiths, whose influence is attested by the continual anti-dualist polemics in Islamic and Jewish literature. In the first place, the basic principle of the dualistic religions was an emphatic denial of the biblical view that the world, both in its good and evil aspects, was the work of a good God. They also attempted to prove, by a detailed examination of Scripture, that the God of the Bible was not a God of truth and perfection but was deficient from both a spiritual and ethical stand-point. This, too, was merely a renewal of old ideas which Judaism had met and contended against in the past. The doctrine that there were "two powers" had already been countered by the post-exilic prophets, and the Gnostic denigration of the biblical idea of God had been combatted by the sages of the Talmud in the early centuries of the Christian era. The old Gnostic arguments were revived by the late Gnostic system known as Manicheism.

These attacks were renewed in the early centuries of Islam, when the Parsee teachers also joined in them.[5] A Parsee text of the ninth century sharply attacks the biblical account of creation, taking up and often literally copying arguments that had already been used in earlier Gnostic, and particularly Manichean literature. According to this author, God could not have created the world by his word, as in that case, creation would not have taken six days for its completion. Likewise, it was impossible that a God who created the world by his word alone, would need rest. As for Adam's sin, if God desired that men should heed his commandments, why then did he give them the opportunity to sin? God's question to Adam, "Where art thou?" seems to be an admission that God did not know the where-abouts of Adam; hence the Bible did not consider God to be omnis-cient. The biblical view of the wrath and vengeance of the Lord are taken as proof of the ethical inferiority of the Jewish notion of God.

The clash of the great religions and discord between the sects severely shook the naive faith in religious authority. Within the the ever-widening religious horizon, the rival religions were all seen on one level, and the opposing claims to exclusive truth seemed to cancel one another. Symptomatic of this mode of thought is the development in Islamic literature of the interest in comparative religion. Religion itself was made an object of theoretical inquiry, and the rich variety of its manifestations became a matter of scientific description and classification. This latent emancipation from naive faith in authority appears quite explicitly, most impressively perhaps in the well-known report from the end of the tenth century on the friendly discussions concerning religion held in Bagdad between members of various religions. The participants agreed upon absolute tolerance toward one another; when their various faiths were being discussed, any dogmatic appeal to authority was ruled out. The only source upon which one could rely in the search for the true religion was the "human intellect." Reason, instead of authority, thus became the criterion for religious truth.[6] We find the same mode of thought in a philosophic circle that flourished in Bagdad during this period and which was composed of adherents of different religions, including two Jews who, we are told, were very highly esteemed. In the discussions of this group, the question was raised whether philosophy could decide in favor of one of the competing faiths, or whether it permitted every individual philosopher to follow the faith in which he was nurtured. The answer has unfortunately not been preserved, but the very posing of the question is indicative of the spirit of the group.[7]

This new rationalism was in many cases definitely antagonistic to religion. Participants in the above-mentioned philosophic discussion included "materialists," and the polemics of Islamic and Jewish scholars mention the Dahriya, a sect which denied the existence of a divine Being, as taking part in the disputations. There were also religious rationalists who denied all positive revelation. The well-known report of the orthodox Muslim theologian, Ibn Hazm, who lived in Spain in the eleventh century, might be used to illustrate the spiritual condition of the Orient at a somewhat earlier period. His account shows the widespread and manifold forms of skepticism in regard to revealed religion. Next to the radical denial of all revealed religion, we find the relativistic notion of the equal value of the various faiths. According to this view, every man should follow some one religion, for without religion no moral life is possible. The essence of religions is in their common ethical demands; this is attested both by the area of agreement between the positive religions and by rational evidence. Compared to the common rational core of the positive religions, their differences are relatively insignificant; the idea of their equal value was expressed by the disappearance of conversion from one religion to another, as well as by the rule of the Bagdad circle that every man should follow the religion given to him by God.[8]

The Islamic fraternity of the Pure Brethren, which arose in the tenth century, believed in this common core of all religions, though they conceived it as a core of hidden metaphysical truth which every religion expressed in a different set of symbols. This truth and the practical ideals that follow from it are a popular version of Neo-platonic philosophy, and even the doctrine of the Brethren that the various religions concretize one truth in different symbols was derived from the Greek Neoplatonic view that all religions worshipped the same God, who differed only in name, and that the same truth under-lay all the various myths. A more negative attitude towards the positive religions comes to the fore in the view that the purpose of religion was to make the mass of the people obey the laws and maintain the political order. The most radical form of this view, which was directed against the teachings of several of the Greek Sophists, sees in religion merely a human invention designed to serve political ends. But even the more moderate form of this doctrine, which admitted that the founders of the positive historic religions were divinely inspired, insisted that they received their doctrines from God only for political purposes and that the beliefs which they had taught to mankind were intended to strengthen obedience to the laws they had given, but had no claim to truth.[9]

The influence of Greek philosophy, which is obvious in some of these doctrines, was undoubtedly also at work in other systems that were critical of revealed religions. Naturalism, which denies all belief in God; rationalism, which bases this belief on reason alone, and relativism, which views all positive historical religions on one level, all make use of arguments drawn from Greek philosophy and often appear in connection with Greek systems of thought. However, it is impossible to derive all the aforementioned doctrines from this one source alone. Even in their later forms they clearly show the extent to which they had been motivated by interreligious rivalry. The critical attitude toward religion as such was independent of philosophy, despite the attempt to find support and justification in Greek philosophy as it spread among the Arabs. Essentially this attitude consisted in a somewhat naive and elementary (but nonetheless powerful and self-assured) enlightenment which regarded historic and dogmatic differences between religions of secondary importance, as compared to their common ethical and religious principles. This enlightenment afterwards adopted from Greek philosophy the view that these basic common truths of all religions were rooted in reason; occasionally this notion was linked with the specifically Stoic doctrine according to which belief in God is innate in human nature. Although no definite concept of a natural religion was developed, as in the eighteenth-century Enlightenment, at least its elements seem to be present, and the general religious temper is not dissimilar.

Under the influence of these tendencies, the theology of Islam expanded into a philosophy of religion. Conceptual inquiry into the doctrine of the Kalam had its beginnings in the rationalistic school of the Mu'tazilites; other schools arose later which utilized the same methods (although for opposite purposes) and were consequently also considered as Kalam. The Mu'tazilites at first limited themselves to adapting traditional beliefs to the demands of theoretical and ethical reason, but the intellectual attacks on Islam forced them to go further and to justify the foundations and doctrines of religion. They thus crossed the boundary line from theology to the philosophy of religion. Against the denial of the belief in God they sought to prove his existence; against the belief in two powers, they sought to demonstrate his unity; against the critique of revealed religion they advanced both rational proof of the necessity of revelation, and historical proofs of the truth of Islam. To the critical rationalism which rejected revelation, they opposed a believing rationalism whose ultimate religious ideal was similar to that of its opponents, but which held the Islamic revelation to be the sole true realization of this ideal.

The same needs which brought about the development of the Muslim philosophy of religion produced its Jewish counterpart. This Islamic background determined the character of medieval Jewish philosophy from beginning to end. Even more than Islamic philosophy, it was definitely a philosophy of religion. Whereas the Islamic Neoplatonists and Aristotelians dealt with the full range of philosophy, Jewish thinkers relied for the most part on the work of their Islamic predecessors in regard to general philosophic questions, and concentrated on more specifically religio-philosophic problems. There were, of course, exceptions to this; among the Jewish Neoplatonists, Isaac Israeli and Solomon ibn Gabirol dealt with philosophy of nature and metaphysics independent of any specific religio-philosophic questions, and among the Aristotelians in the later Middle Ages, Levi ben Gerson and Moses Narboni, for example, commented very thoroughly on Averroës' treatises on logic and on the natural sciences. But the great majority of Jewish thinkers made the philosophic justification of Judaism their main subject, dealing with problems of metaphysics in a religio-philosophic context.

This limitation of Jewish philosophy does not detract from its historic significance. For it was in the philosophic explanation of religion that medieval philosophy was at its most original. Dependent in many respects upon ancient traditions, and productive only in so far as it reworked and continued traditional speculations, it found here a new sphere of problems for investigation. Its recasting of traditional metaphysical ideas was due to the necessity of adapting ancient metaphysics to the personalistic religion of the Bible. It was this central area of medieval philosophy to which the Jewish thinkers devoted themselves and in which they made their historic contribution.

First
Beginnings

The first extant writings of medieval Jewish philosophy were composed in the early tenth century C.E. At the earliest, the work of Isaac Israeli can be ascribed to the end of the ninth century, but the preceding philosophic development must have gone back at least to the beginnings of the ninth century. The little that we know, however, confirms the extreme importance of religious controversies for the beginnings of Jewish philosophy. The great work of Saadia Gaon, with its wealth of information concerning earlier Jewish philosophers, teaches us something of the degree of subtlety reached in the discussions between Jewish and Islamic theologians concerning the possibility of a plurality of mutually exclusive revelations.[10] Saadia mentions Jewish thinkers who sought to prove by logical concepts that a law once given by God could not be altered. They argued that a divine law was either eternal and hence could not be abrogated, or else was of limited validity from the very start and it would be meaningless to speak of "abrogation" in circumstances or at times and places for which it was never meant to apply. But once a law was given without the duration of its validity being specified, it was impossible that a later communication could legislate on its eternal or temporal validity, since the precision with which the sphere of application of laws was usually defined clearly intended to exclude all such ambiguities. From the counter-arguments quoted by Saadia, it appears that the Jewish case for the unalterability of the divine law rested mainly on the notion of the unalterability of the divine will. We are told that the Muslim theologians argued that the divine will ordained for man continuous alterations of life and death, riches and poverty, and that nature, too, was subject to eternal change. This surely implies that their Jewish opponents had deduced the immutability of revelation from the immutability of the divine will. Since Saadia advances these arguments in his own name, and without mentioning his predecessors, we cannot reconstruct the precise state of the controversy which he found. In all probability, however, he merely developed arguments that he had already found in existence. Not only the general philosophic treatment of the problem, but also the dialectical sharpness of his arguments, probably derived from earlier Jewish polemicists.

Just how severely Judaism was affected by the various forms of religious criticism in the first centuries of Islam can be seen quite clearly from the little that is known to us of the Jewish heretic Hiwi of Balkh (in what is now Afghanistan). His book, composed in the second half of the ninth century, and containing two hundred objections to the Bible, is no longer extant. We can, however, form a fairly accurate idea of its contents from its passionate refutation in later Jewish literature, and especially from the large fragment of Saadia's polemic against him discovered some years ago.[11]

Hiwi attacked the Bible from every angle. He pointed to the contradictions in the scriptural narratives and sought to explain miracles, such as the crossing of the Red Sea and the gift of manna, in a naturalistic fashion.[12] He was ruthlessly critical of the religious content of Scripture, particularly of its anthropomorphic idea of God. From the story of the Garden of Eden in which God asks man "Where art thou?" as well as from the reference to God "tempting" Abraham (Gen. 22:1) he concluded that the Bible did not conceive of God as omniscient.[13] Other objections to the biblical idea of God are that God prevented man out of fear from eating of the tree of life; that God "repented" he had made man (Gen. 6:6); that in the flood he destroyed not only the wicked, but also innocent creatures, and that he required animal sacrifices for his sustenance.[14] Monotheism as such was criticized by Hiwi with arguments such as: Why did God plant the evil impulse within the heart of man, and why does he bring upon him misery and suffering, and—finally—death?[15]

Hiwi gathered the material for his criticism from various sources. Some of his objections bring to mind questions that had already been raised by the Talmud. The decisive influence upon him was the dualistic Manichean polemic against Scripture—the same dualism that was the source of earlier Persian texts.[16] His assertion that the author of the biblical story of paradise did not conceive of God as omniscient, and his question of why God endowed man with the power to sin, are identical with those of the Parsee polemicists. Also the general tendency of polemic recalls the previous controversy.

As for Hiwi's own religious ideas, there are no clear indications in our sources. He is said to have inclined towards Persian dualism, and it seems that he interpreted the scriptural verse, "And the earth was void and empty, and there was darkness of the face of the abyss," in the sense of a fundamental dualism of light and darkness.[17] Saadia's observation that in his pamphlet against Hiwi he had given proofs for the creation of the world, seems to imply that Hiwi had denied creation.[18] (This is not absolutely certain, however; although Saadia contrasted the doctrine of creation with that of dualism, Hiwi may have reconciled both these positions in his own thought.) When, however, Saadia attributes to Hiwi belief in the Christian doctrine of the Eucharist, and another of his opponents charges him with denying the freedom of the will,[19] we must give up the possibility of combining such diverse doctrines into a coherent philosophy. This is not necessarily due to the distorted presentation of his heretical doctrines in our sources. It may rather be due to the very nature and purpose of Hiwi's polemic, which was essentially concerned with destroying the authority of Scripture. Hence he took his weapons from all sides, showing at one time that scriptural teachings logically led to dualism, at another time, that they led to Christian ideas; there is no deducing from this, however, that he was an adherent of such doctrines.[20] The destructive character of his work was also the reason for its influence. Perhaps we should be skeptical of the statement, reported in Saadia's name, that even elementary-school teachers were spreading Hiwi's doctrines. Even so, the many and violent attacks directed against Hiwi are ample evidence of the impression his work must have made.

There also appears in the ninth century the beginnings of Jewish metaphysical speculation. Benjamin b. Moses of Nahawend, a distinguished mid-century Karaite leader, is credited with the opinion that the world was not created immediately by God, but that God merely created an angel, who in turn created the world, and from whom the prophets received their prophecy. Similar doctrines are attributed to the sect of Magaria, also called Maqaria or Maqariba in some sources. Scholars have recognized in this doctrine traces of Philo's logos, and their identification has gained in probability by the discovery that the Jews of the Orient in the first centuries of Islam did have some knowledge—albeit superficial—of Philonic doctrines.[21] Judging from what we know of Benjamin of Nahawend, there is very little in him of the profounder meaning of Philo's doctrine of the logos. Not only is the characteristic Philonic notion of the relationship of the logos to God lost in Nahawend's concept of a created angel, but even Philo's main purpose, to mediate, by means of the concept of a logos, between God and man, gives way to Benjamin's entirely different interest of finding satisfactory explanations for those biblical statements concerning God that might be offensive to a pure monotheism.[22] Verses that at first sight seem to impugn the uniqueness of God—for example, "Who is like unto Thee, O Lord, among the Gods?"—refer not to God, but to that highest angel, at whose side there are other, though inferior, angelic beings. Similarly, the anthropomorphic expressions used in Scripture concerning God are understood as referring to this angel. Even the notion of the angel as a demiurge is founded upon the same reasoning. When Scripture says that God created man in his own likeness and image, this account refers not to God, of whom there is no image, but merely to this angel.[23] Likewise, the Islamic theologians interpreted all traditions concerning visions of God as relating not to God, but to a First Intellect created by him.[24] Their view that the sensual visions of the prophets did not relate to God, but to an essence created by him, was then taken over by later Jewish philosophers for whom, however, this essence had no creative function. The same idea holds a prominent place in Benjamin's thought, whereas the question of a mediator between God and the world has receded into the background.

However, a number of Jewish thinkers mentioned by Saadia were concerned with this problem of the origin of the world. In place of the traditional Jewish notion of *creatio ex nihilo*, they took the view that God created the world out of a pre-existent primary matter, and actually sought to read this idea into the biblical text. This basic theme appeared in several variations. The doctrine of Plato's *Timaeus* concerning the origin of the world is expressed in the bizarre form that God created the material world out of eternal spiritual substances.[25] Others connected the cosmological doctrines of the pre-Socratic philosophers with the biblical idea of God by assuming that God created the world from a primary element, either water or air. Proof of this was found in the account of creation in Genesis.

From the verse, "and the earth was void and empty," it could be deduced that before the creation the chaos of primeval waters existed in place of the earth, and that the spirit of God hovering upon the face of the waters was none other than the primeval element of air.[26] Saadia also reports another attempt to reconcile the ancient cosmologies and the story of creation: one of the elements, either water, fire, or air, was conceived to be the primary element created by God, and from it the other elements were derived. There is no way of telling whether the two last-mentioned theories are really different, or whether the difference is merely due to Saadia's presentation.[27] At any rate, none of these attempts, insofar as we can judge from Saadia's report, exhibits any originality. Greek cosmological theories, which ninth-century translators had made widely known, were indiscriminately taken up and combined insofar as possible with the biblical account of creation.

The rapidly rising philosophic culture soon discarded these primitive initial attempts; henceforth its points of reference were the mature forms of the Greek philosophical systems. Nevertheless, in spite of their crudeness these early attempts are significant as evidence of the ferment and struggle which the first contact with Greek philosophy produced among Jews.

With the end of the ninth century, the prehistory of Jewish philosophy came to an end and its true history began. Meanwhile, Islamic philosophy had made significant progress: in addition to the Kalam theology, Neoplatonism had evolved to a high degree, and Aristotelianism, whose first representative was al-Kindi, developed considerable power. The first of the great and creative Arab Aristotelians, al-Farabi, was active before the beginning of the tenth century. Jewish philosophy, to an even greater extent than Islamic, permits of no strict temporal division between alternating philosophic trends. The first Jewish philosopher, Isaac Israeli, was a Neoplatonist, whereas his younger contemporaries, Saadia and David al-Moqammes, are followers of the Kalam. Israeli's Neoplatonism found no followers in the East, where it first developed; it was continued only by the Spanish philosophers of the eleventh century. Our exposition begins with the Kalam since, generally speaking, it can be said to stand at the beginning of Jewish philosophy.

2 The Kalam

Saadia

SAADIA B. JOSEPH from Fayyum in Egypt (882-942) deserves to be considered the father of medieval Jewish philosophy of religion; his two older contemporaries, Isaac Israeli and David al-Moqammes, are inferior both as regards independence of philosophic thinking and depth and range of historical influence. Saadia was the first to develop the notions of Islamic theology and philosophy in an independent manner; he was also the first to undertake a systematic philosophical justification of Judaism. Saadia received his scientific training in Egypt, where he apparently spent the first thirty years of his life. Afterwards he resided in Palestine, Syria, and Babylonia; in 928 he was appointed Gaon (head) of the celebrated Academy of Sura, in Babylonia.

Saadia pioneered not only in philosophy, but in all other areas of medieval Jewish science. He was one of the fathers of Hebrew philology. His Arabic translation of the Bible and his commentaries laid the foundation of scientific biblical exegesis among rabbanite Jews. In Talmudic studies, too, he opened up new paths through his systematic presentation of certain subjects. His many-sided literary activity was, however, dominated by his polemic against Karaism, and he also wrote a refutation of Hiwi. His major philosophic work combines the exposition of his own system with criticism of opposing viewpoints; among the latter are Christian Trinitarianism, Zoroastrian dualism, the Muslim theory of biblical revelation, rationalistic attacks on the idea of revelation, as well as all cosmological, psychological, and philosophical doctrines opposed to the teachings of Judaism.

Saadia began to study philosophy in his youth. While still in Egypt he addressed a few philosophical letters to Isaac Israeli, which did not, apparently, meet with the approval of that Neoplatonist.[1] More important philosophic writings were composed in later years: in 931 a commentary on the mystical book, *Yetzirah* (*The Book of Creation*), and in 933 his major philosophic work, *The Book of Beliefs and Opinions* (the Arabic title is *Kitab al-Amanat w'al*

I'tiqadat; the Hebrew translation is entitled *Sefer Ha-Emunot we ha-Deóth*). His commentaries on the Bible also contain many philosophic passages. His system as a whole, however, is found only in *The Book of Beliefs and Opinions;* his other writings merely furnish details.

For his fundamental theses Saadia relied on the Kalam. Like other Jewish followers of the Kalam, he inclined towards its rationalist Mu'tazilite version which approximated the Jewish position both in its strict and uncompromising treatment of the concept of God's unity, and in its insistence on the doctrine of free will. Saadia followed Mu'tazilite convention even in the formal structure of his book by having the chapter on God's justice follow the chapter on the unity of God. But apart from this, he handled the traditional scholastic themes with great freedom. He denied the atomism of the Kalam and substituted Aristotelian views on natural science; in his psychology he combined Platonic and Aristotelian elements. Even where he agreed in principle with the tenets of Kalam, he frequently developed these notions in an independent fashion.[2]

His doctrine of the relationship between reason and revelation, accepted by most succeeding Jewish philosophers, formed the methodological foundation of Saadia's religious philosophy. It was in this form that medieval thinkers discussed the general problem of the relationship between religion and knowledge.[3] Religious truth is characterized by its origin in revelation, whereby it becomes a distinct form of truth. As a result of the exclusiveness of the concept of revelation, which dominated medieval thinking, the problem was not posed in terms of the relation of reason and religion as a general function of human consciousness, but rather in terms of the relation of reason to a specific religion claiming divine origin. Although we find medieval enlightenment speaking of a core of truth common to all religions, this core is not considered as an expression of a general and encompassing religious consciousness; it is reason that is supposed to provide the common foundation of the various religions. Only where the claim of exclusiveness is relinquished and a plurality of divine revelations conceded, do we find a more general formulation of the problem independent of particular religions.[4] But this broad formulation of the question is entirely foreign to Saadia. According to him, the Jewish religion, revealed by God, is radically different from all other religions which are merely the work of men and thus falsely claim divine origin. However, the content of this truly divine revelation is identical in Saadia's eyes with the content of reason. Negatively, this means that there is no contradiction between the two spheres; positively, it signifies that reason is capable of reaching through its own powers the content of the divine truth. This holds equally for the theoretical as well as the moral contents of revelation. Both fundamental metaphysical truth and the moral demands of revelation are evident to our unaided reason.

This view raises the almost inevitable question: What is the purpose of a revelation of truths, if reason can apprehend them through its own powers? In reply, Saadia propounded the idea of the pedagogic value of revelation. This idea, which became very influential in medieval thought, was developed in two directions. In the first place, revelation seeks to make the truth available to every man, even to those who are unable to think for themselves. Secondly, it seeks to protect the philosophers themselves from the uncertainties and inconstancies of thought, and to give them from the very beginning that absolute truth at which their thought would arrive only after sustained and protracted effort.[5] But reason must not rest satisfied with this form of the possession of truth. For Saadia, the acquisition of truth by rational means is a religious precept. This view of the purpose of revelation was taken over by the rationalistic trend in Jewish religious philosophy, which was dominant during the Middle Ages; it was adopted by philosophical systems that differed widely from Saadia in the content of their doctrines. The notion appears in Maimonides, from which it passed to Christian scholasticism, which had already been prepared for it by similar views in ancient Christian theology. Even the modern Enlightenment of the eighteenth century, insofar as it maintains the idea of revelation, views the relationship between religion and revelation in fundamentally the same manner.

Nevertheless, the tensions implicit in the ambiguous identification of reason and revelation are discernible in Saadia. In his systematic discussion of the problem he demands that the believer approach philosophy with the prior conviction of the truth of revelation. The task of philosophy was merely to provide rational proof of what was already known through revelation. Elsewhere, however, Saadia declares agreement with reason to be a necessary precondition for the acceptance of any doctrine claiming the status of revelation.[6] Although Saadia makes this statement explicitly only with regard to the ethical teaching of religion, its validity may justifiably be extended to the whole theoretical content of the Torah. The supremacy of reason becomes quite evident in the question of the interpretation of revelation. According to Saadia, one of the instances in which Scripture may be interpreted against its literal sense is precisely when the latter contradicts reason.[7] Although the truth of revelation is firmly established prior to any investigation by reason, yet reason is entitled to explain and interpret the truth of revelation. Saadia himself uses this principle sparingly, and sharply criticizes the excessive and uninhibited reinterpretation of Scripture by some philosophical commentators. For Saadia, the fundamental beliefs of the Bible and the Talmud remained unchanged, but his principles also admitted a more radical application; later Jewish thinkers with different philosophic attitudes appealed to Saadia's rule in order to justify their sometimes radical transformations of Jewish ideas.

The revealed character of any specific religion cannot command dogmatic assent of itself; according to Saadia, it must be proved by means of miracles. Every prophet is obliged to validate his divine mission by means of public and indubitable miracles. This theory of proof through miracles, though not new, gave rise to interesting developments in Saadia's doctrine of tradition. Miracles have force only for the witnesses to the event. Their relevance for future generations presupposes the acceptance of tradition as a legitimate source of knowledge. Saadia develops his doctrine of tradition within the rubric of a general theory of the sources of knowledge, which he divides into three: 1) sense perceptions; 2) rational self-evidence; and 3) rational conclusions from the data furnished by sense and reason.[8] His discussion of the third source of knowledge contains some penetrating comments, apparently derived from Greek sources, on the construction of scientific hypotheses, and their logical requirements.

To these three sources of knowledge, there must be added that of a reliable tradition. Although it is based upon the three elementary sources, nevertheless it has its own significance and value[9] which extend beyond the actual range of religion for whose sake Saadia had introduced it. Without reliance upon trustworthy reports, no orientation in reality would be possible. Everyday life in all its aspects— work, politics, and family life—presupposes our reliance upon information provided by others. Thoroughgoing doubt of everything that has been transmitted to us by others would lead to the result that only immediate sense perceptions could be considered real.[10]

The concept of religious tradition is thus only a particular instance of the general principle of tradition. The same kind of evidence that is required to prove the veracity of tradition in general also applies to religious tradition; the latter cannot be accepted except insofar as it satisfies the criteria for any reliable tradition. Saadia's reduction of the concept of religious tradition to the general notion of tradition is of permanent importance since religious faith, to the degree that it is a principle of knowledge, is thereby disclosed as merely a specialized form of historical knowledge. Revelation in itself, as the source of religious truth, has a supernatural origin; but the belief in revelation has the certitude of natural knowledge only. Revelation is a demonstrable fact, and it is upon its demonstrability that the validity of the content of revelation rests. The tendency to define religious certitude in terms of demonstrable knowledge is not limited to the realm of religious tradition alone. Even in regard to the prophets, Saadia maintains that some sensible sign to vouch for the divine origin of their revelation or vision was necessary.[11] This is not, as may appear at first glance, sheer hypertrophy of miracle-hunting, but rather is the result of the need to eliminate all purely subjective certitude and to base the prophet's own consciousness of a divine mission on tangible facts. Applying his theory of tradition to Judaism, Saadia proves the authority of the Mosaic revelation by pointing out that it was given publicly, before the eyes of all Israel. Such publicity rules out any conscious or unconscious deception, and in the transmission of such an event no mistake could have been made.[12] This proof of revelation, with its implicit critique of Islamic and Christian claims, was adopted and continually reiterated by Jewish religious philosophy.

In the theoretical realm, the congruence of reason and revelation is validated above all in regard to the problem of God. The existence of the one God, Creator of the world, is just as much a certainty of reason as it is a doctrine of revelation. Saadia's proof follows the usual arguments of the Kalam, which show that the world must have had a beginning in time, and therefore presupposes a Creator. He offers four proofs for the temporal beginning of the world:

1. The spatial finitude of the world requires that the force inherent in it also be finite. But a finite power can maintain the world in existence for a finite time only. Hence, it is impossible that the world existed from eternity.

2. Every composite thing must, of necessity, have been created by a Creator who fashioned a whole from different parts. Both the earth and all bodies found upon it, as well as the heavens, are compounded

of many parts. Hence the world, which is a composite of them all, was created.

3. All natural bodies in the world are the bearers of accidents, immersed in an unending stream of generation and corruption. These accidents are found throughout the world, from organic beings, subject to generation and corruption, to celestial bodies engaged in their various movements. All accidents originate in time. Substances in which such accidents inhere must also, of necessity, have originated in time.

4. If the world existed from eternity, then infinite time must have elapsed before every particular point in time. But this is not possible, since infinity cannot be traversed. Hence, the duration of the world must be conceived as finite, that is, the world must have had a beginning in time.[13]

The first of these proofs rests on Aristotelian premises. Both the notion of the spatial finitude of the world, and the assertion that the force residing in a finite body must be finite too, derive from Aristotle. The arguments by which Saadia demonstrates the spatial finiteness of the world and refutes the assumption of a plurality of worlds, show that he accepted the Aristotelian cosmology in its major outlines. In using these premises in a thoroughly un-Aristotelian manner to demonstrate the creation of the world in time, Saadia was following John Philoponus, under whose name that argument was current in Islamic literature.[14] The other arguments are drawn mainly from the Kalam, deviating from the latter only insofar as Saadia detached them from the atomistic view of the world, based on the traditional Kalam formulation of the second and third proofs.

From his rationalistic standpoint in which belief in creation is demonstrable, Saadia sees the main enemy of the faith in a Creator in the sensualistic materialism which recognizes no reality beyond sense. He finds the explicit expression of this doctrine in the teachings of the Dahriya school, according to which the world has never been any other than as perceived by our senses; questions regarding a transcendental principle underlying the world are therefore meaningless.[15] Saadia recognizes the same sensualist limitation to the empirically given in those cosmological theories which, though they seek an explanation for the world structure, conceive of the principles of their explanation in the manner of corporeal substances.[16] The idea that God created the world not *ex nihilo,* but from pre-existent eternal elements, springs from this same sensualist assumption. This theme occurs again and again in Saadia's polemics against the various theories of the origin of the world, and his argument aims at demonstrating the inner impossibility of a sensualistic cosmology.[17]

The apparently consistent sensualism of the Dahriya proves on closer inspection to go far beyond the boundaries of sense experience. Legitimately, sensualism can only affirm that neither the beginning nor the end of the corporeal world has ever been perceived. But the statement that the world has neither beginning nor an end is not a judgment of the senses but a rational conclusion which transcends the evidence of the senses just as much as the idea of creation does.[18] A consistent sensualism leads to skepticism and to inner contradictions, which Saadia proves mainly by arguments taken from Plato's *Theaetetus*.[19] Still greater inconsistency is exhibited by those cosmological theories which reject creation *ex nihilo* because of its alleged incompatibility with the experience of the senses, but propound their own cosmogonies with complete disregard of sense perception. Apart from the fact that the elements of their cosmology cannot be proved by means of sense perception, even the derivation of reality from these elements is completely arbitrary.[20]

Saadia rigorously marshals his objections to the doctrine that God made the world from a simple, pre-existent element. The assumption of such an element is based upon the notion that being can proceed only from being. But once we accept this assumption we must apply it also to the concrete determinations of things: simple things can derive only from simple things, composites from composites—heat from heat, and so on. An explanation of the origin of the world structure thus becomes meaningless. But if we assert that God has the power to produce the special determinations of things and can create something entirely new, then the assumption of a pre-existent element is unnecessary.[21] As Saadia explains elsewhere, in regard to the assumption that eternal matter produced of itself the plurality of existents, the dualism of God and matter faces still another difficulty: how is it possible that matter, which is independent of God, becomes subject to divine activity?[22] Of course, Saadia's extremely detailed criticism of the various cosmological theories does not always maintain this level of consideration of general principles. To increase the number of his proofs, he jumbles together valid and sham arguments, attacks opposing systems without doing them full justice or even making sure that he understands them correctly, and generally shows a passion for polemics characteristic of immature thinking. In order to do full justice to the real significance of Saadia's criticisms, we have to disregard his dialectics, which are characterized by breadth rather than by depth, and to extract the profounder core of his arguments from his repetitions. Saadia recognizes that even the idea of creation cannot explain the origin of the world from God, and he sees here an ultimate and impassable limit of human thought.[23] But this limit is inherent in the very nature of the concept of creation, and since it is necessary to think of the world as having come into being, only the doctrine of creation which takes the idea of an absolute beginning seriously, and forgoes sham explanations, can give a satisfactory answer to the question of the origin of the world.

The God thus arrived at is a Creator-God, who by his free will originates the world. Saadia's doctrine of God is an effort to formulate this concept of God with philosophical precision. From the idea of creation Saadia first deduces, with the customary arguments of the Kalam, the unity of God. Creation itself posits the existence of only one God; to assume more would be sheer arbitrariness. With special reference to the dualism of Persian religion, which he had already attacked in his discussion of the doctrines of creation, Saadia denies the possibility of two supreme powers participating in the work of creation. One work cannot be the product of two creators, especially if these creators are conceived as voluntary agents whose wills might possibly be opposed to each other. The dualistic doctrine must lead to the conclusion that one part of the world was created by one god and the second by the other. The variety and contradictions in the world do not preclude their origin from one common source; otherwise even dualism would be insufficient to account for the wealth of contradictions in the cosmos.[24]

The idea of creation requires three fundamental attributes in God —life, power, and wisdom—without which the act of creation would not be possible. (The formal attributes of unity and uniqueness should be added also.) These three fundamental attributes are not to be understood as separate elements within the essence of God; we can grasp them only as three aspects contained within the concept of a Creator; it is solely because of the impotence of human language that we must use three words for this one idea.[25] In his detailed polemic against the Christian doctrine of the Trinity, which in its speculative formulations views the divine attributes as relatively independent of one another, Saadia gives another turn to this notion by saying that God's attributes are identical with his essence.[26] Here, too, he follows the Mu'tazilite doctrine of God; its main concern was to define God in such fashion that the plurality of his attributes would not destroy his essential unity. We are not concerned here with the question of how far the Mu'tazilite thinking on the subject was stimulated by Christian attempts to find a philosophic formulation of the doctrine of the Trinity. The fundamental logical problem is already well known to us from Greek philosophy. The old question of the Cynics, of how one subject could have many predicates, is here asked of the Godhead. The problem led Neoplatonists to the conclusion that the divine One was devoid of all positive attributes and was therefore beyond the grasp of reason. The Mu'tazilites tried hard to avoid this radical conclusion. They upheld the idea of a personal God, predicating to him the necessary basic attributes; but they did not differentiate his attributes from his divine essence, claiming, rather, that the attributes were identical with the essence, which remained absolutely simple. Yet all the subleties of this argumentation could not resolve the inherent contradictions of their position. If they really meant to identify the attributes of God with his essence and thereby to insure the absolute simplicity of the latter, the attributes—now identical with one another—no longer had any meaning. In fact, the formula would be no more than a disguise for the negation of the attributes. If not, then it is difficult to see how the predication of a plurality of attributes could be avoided.

Saadia was also unable to overcome this difficulty, and his thesis that the three basic attributes merely illuminated the idea of a Creator from different angles is extremely instructive. The derivation of the attributes from the concept of creation implies no more than that they are necessary correlates. Saadia then turns this correlation into an identity and makes language responsible for our inability to view all three aspects as a unity. Occasionally the logic of his own thought forces Saadia to surrender the positive meaning of the attributes as determinations of the divine essence. The concept of a Creator, he once remarks, merely expresses the idea that there is a creation; accordingly the other attributes which qualify the concept of a Creator-God only contain the existence of created effects. In more scholastic language: attributes of essence are converted into statements concerning divine action.[27] Elsewhere Saadia makes the even more radical statement that if we wish to avoid loose expressions concerning God, all we may say is that *he exists*.[28] All this, however, does not permit us to attribute to Saadia the negation of all positive attributes. In many statements he clearly admits the fundamental attributes of God, and there is no doubt that he held fast to the concept of a personal God with his fundamental attributes. We must accept his doctrine as it stands, with all of the intrinsic contradictions which Saadia felt but could not resolve.[29]

This initially purely metaphysical concept of God receives a religious content through an investigation of the problem of divine providence. Its basis is that ethical rationalism of Saadia which we have emphasized above. The demands of ethics have their source not only in revelation, but also in dictates of reason. It is especially in the realm of ethics that Saadia maintains the superiority of reason to revelation; he demands that every prophetic doctrine be legitimized by its agreement with the rational claims of morality, even before its divine origin is further examined by reference to miracles. The fundamental rationality of the laws of ethics is not impugned by the fact that reason contains only the most general ethical norms, and that it needs concrete application and supplementation by revelation.[30] Similarly, in the Stoic system, the unwritten law must be specified in the positive law of the state. On the basis of this conception of ethics, Saadia introduces the distinction between the rational commandments which revelation merely reiterates, and the "commandments of obedience" which are exclusive to revelation and which include the cultic and ceremonial laws of the Bible.[31] The ethical commandments are, for Saadia, the center of the divine revelation. The fundamental elements of any revealed religion are its positive and negative precepts, announcements of reward and punishment for those who obey or transgress them, and historical narratives giving examples of divine reward and punishment.[32] The main purpose of revelation is thus not theoretical but practical, and even the theoretical truths taught by religion merely serve as presuppositions to the ethical content of revelation.

In its concrete application to details, Saadia's ethical rationalism remains somewhat superficial. Reason teaches us that creatures are obliged to give thanks to God for his mercies, and forbids us to blaspheme his name or to injure one another. From this latter rule Saadia derives most important ethical commandments in a somewhat primitive utilitarian manner.[33] No less primitive is the argument—used by many later Jewish thinkers—contending that these commandments need supplementing by means of revelation. The required supplements are mere legal technicalities and are not distinguished from the ethical commandments themselves. Whereas the ethical laws, in spite of utilitarian explanations of details, are fundamentally imperatives and commandments, Saadia develops elsewhere a eudaemonistic ideal: the correct mode of life is that which leads to the satisfaction of man's needs and to the development of all his powers.[34] The injunction to live a happy life, and the ethics of commandment and duty, stand side by side without any attempt at reconciliation.

It is true that even the idea of an ethical imperative can be interpreted within a eudaemonistic system, if it is conceived, not from the viewpoint of man, but from that of God. For God, ethics is not an end in itself, but a means for the attainment of human happiness. God has made man's happiness conditional upon the observance of his commandments, because man's pleasure in the happiness granted to him is increased by the recognition that he himself has earned it through his own deeds.[35] The ultimate aim of God's creation is the good of his creatures. God's self-sufficiency rules out any thought of his doing anything for his own good; creation, therefore, serves only the good of creatures, and especially the most perfect among them—man. The detailed elaboration of this idea lends to a theodicy which provides the framework within which Saadia, like the Mu'tazilites, discusses ethical and religious questions. No theodicy is possible without positing a hereafter, for this world always contains an admixture of pain and suffering. In fact, suffering, according to Saadia's pessimistic view of things, preponderates in this life.[36] Only the faith in a hereafter provides the possibility of a more positive evaluation of life. All innocent suffering in this life will be made good in a future life. Like some Mu'tazilite thinkers, Saadia applied this idea not only to the sufferings undergone by innocent infants, but also to the beasts, to whom amends will be made for their sufferings in this world.[37]

Despite all the suffering in it, the world has a positive value since it serves as a vestibule in which man renders himself worthy, through his own efforts, for the happiness of the world to come. In order to explain the evils of this present world, Saadia connects the idea of divine justice with that of divine mercy. Generally speaking, the sufferings of the righteous are their punishment for sins, which they too have committed. Saadia here simply follows the Talmudic view, which accounts for the sufferings of the righteous and the prosperity of the wicked by assuming that the former receive immediate punishment for their transgressions, even as the latter are immediately rewarded for their good deeds in this world; whereas final reward and punishment are meted out in the hereafter. Saadia's somewhat mechanistic distinction between righteous and wicked, in terms of the quantitative proportion of good and evil deeds, is similarly drawn from the Talmud.[38] But the idea of retribution is, by itself, insufficient to explain the whole range of evil. It fails to account for the sufferings of innocent children and beasts, or to justify the many sufferings and evils attendant on the physical constitution of man. A theodicy becomes feasible only if we add the notion of purification to that of retribution as an explanation of evil. The purpose of sickness is to make us humble; pain gives us an idea of the punishment awaiting sinners in the hereafter.[39] The ultimate purpose of the threat of punishment in the hereafter is not retribution, but to act as a deterrent from sin in this world.[40] In the last resort, the idea of God's justice is thus subordinate to that of his mercy, in spite of Saadia's strong emphasis on the former and his mechanistic elaboration of its details. It is the divine mercy that gave man the moral law, so as to enable him to attain supreme felicity; sufferings and punishment are visited upon him only as a means to this end.

This theodicy implies two metaphysical assumptions: freedom of the will, and belief in a hereafter. Together with belief in God, they form the three basic truths of religion: God, freedom and immortality—the same that were taught by the modern Enlightenment, whose religious attitude was akin to Saadia's. Saadia expounds and proves the two metaphysical doctrines in great detail. Against the Islamic doctrine of predestination, he argues that without freedom of the will, divine law would be meaningless, and that it would be a contradiction of divine justice to punish man for sins for which he was not responsible. Moreover, Saadia considered freedom of the will an immediate fact of consciousness which tells us that we determine our own acts.[41] The various difficulties implicit in the idea of freedom are envisaged by Saadia, as by most Jewish philosophers, only from the theological angle. The main difficulty, the contradiction between God's foreknowledge and man's free choice, is resolved by saying that divine omniscience is not the cause of human decisions but their result; the decisions themselves, although foreseen by God, are arrived at independently of him.[42]

The metaphysical foundation of the idea of immortality is provided by Saadia's psychology which seeks to establish the substantiality, incorporeality, and unity of the soul. Against the variously formulated theories of the soul as an accident of the body, he argues, among other things, that the power and wisdom inherent in the soul presuppose its independence. Attempts to identify the soul with one of the material elements, such as air or fire, are rejected on the ground that none of the characteristic qualities of these elements are exhibited by the soul. Its essential unity is proved by the connection between its various functions; such connection would be impossible if, for example, feeling and thinking belonged to two different substances. Nevertheless, its incorporeality is not conceived as absolute immateriality, and Saadia thinks of the soul as a luminous substance similar to that of the celestial spheres.[43]

The idea of immortality based on this psychology is subordinated to the idea of the resurrection of the dead. After the soul's separation from the body, it remains in a kind of intermediate state until it is joined again with the body at the resurrection, when both together will receive their proper reward in an eternal life.[44] All this is in accordance with Talmudic teaching, and similar views were also held in Islamic theology. In adopting this view, however, Saadia was not merely following the tradition, in spite of his close adherence to Talmudic sources in detailed and sometimes fantastic eschatological descriptions. His heart was as much with the Jewish hope of an historical future as with belief in a hereafter; hence he formulates the latter so as to fit into the former. This is strikingly illustrated by his insistence that the resurrection of the dead will take place in the days of the Messiah, and not in "the world to come," in order that past generations should share in the rebirth of Israel. Individual and collective hopes for the future are intimately related. Saadia's doctrine of retribution is thus deeply rooted in Jewish tradition, not a mere echo of certain Talmudic statements. The same holds true of the whole system. It adheres to the essential contents of traditional Jewish religious ideas. The ethical tendency of Saadia's rationalism corresponds to the biblical conception of a personal Creator-God, and of a personal and moral relationship between man and God, even though he one-sidedly stresses the rational elements of biblical religion.[45] Saadia attempted to describe and establish the religious ideas of Judaism in a rational manner without altering their content.

The Development of the Kalam
in Rabbanite and Karaite Judaism

The Mu'tazilite ideas, of which Saadia was the most distinguished and influential representative, were especially widespread among Oriental Jews. The more we learn about Saadia's contemporaries and successors, the greater the influence of these ideas appears to be.

Their hegemony was not restricted to philosophers, who developed them in systematic fashion; they penetrated all branches of theological literature and even determined the religious thinking of circles far removed from scholastic speculation. It must be admitted, though, that the same views were repeated again and again, and that the various forms in which they were stated are of interest to the history of religion rather than to that of philosophy.

David b. Merwan al-Moqammes, probably an older contemporary of Saadia, belongs to the history of philosophy proper. Since the Arabic original of his *Twenty Tractates* has not yet been published, we are dependent for our knowledge of him on Hebrew summaries of his teachings as given by Judah Barcelona in his commentary on *Yetzirah*.[46] These, however, are sufficient to acquaint us with the general drift and character of his doctrine.

Like Saadia, he combines views of the Kalam with Greek philosophic doctrines, which seem to have influenced him even more than they did Saadia. He teaches the Aristotelian division of the sciences and the Platonic cardinal virtues; his discussion of retribution closely follows the Kalam and shows many points of contact with the ideas of Saadia.[47] Especially instructive in the combination of these various elements is that part of his system which we happen to know best, the doctrine of God and his attributes. Starting with a discussion of the various definitions of the Kalam schools, he gradually approaches a Neoplatonic theology. Most of his investigations open with the well-known Kalam controversy: in speaking of God's knowledge or life, do we mean that God knows with a special attribute of knowledge, and lives with a special attribute of life, or do we mean that "He knows, but not with knowledge, and lives, but not with life"? Al-Moqammes emphasizes that in either case it is obvious that God cannot have "acquired" any of his perfections, never having lacked them. The statement that "God lives with life" can only mean that his life is as eternal as he is himself. Even so, the formula requires close analysis. If it is interpreted in the sense that God's life is distinct from his essence, logically we would posit a whole series of eternal attributes, all distinct from God. This would be tantamount to a heretical denial of God's unity, similar to the Christian doctrine of the Trinity. Hence, God's life (and similarly, all his attributes) and his essence, are, of necessity, one. The view that God lives with life is thus reduced to formula upheld by some masters of the Kalam: "God lives with a life which is identical with his essence." Al-Moqammes has nothing to object to in this formula, but rightly points out that it differs only in wording from the statement that "God lives, but not with life." Both formulas are merely different ways of saying that God lives, knows, and creates with his essence. At first glance this presents no difficulties, for the soul, which animates the body, also lives through its essence, and the same is true of the angels, in whom essence and life are identical.[48]

Despite occasional expressions to the contrary, al-Moqammes does not stop at this point. The identity of the attributes with the divine essence does not mean that the latter is a composite of the various attributes which we predicate of God. The absolutely simple essence cannot contain a plurality of distinct determinations; it is therefore one and the same divine essence with which the various attributes are identified. From this, al-Moqammes draws the explicit conclusion that the various divine attributes are identical among themselves; their differences are a matter of expression only, and not of substance. Here al-Moqammes explicitly states the doctrine that was already implicit in the Kalam formula: "God knows, lives and acts with his essence."

But he goes one step beyond this, by adding that the various positive attributes of God have different meanings only insofar as they negate different imperfections in God. The real significance of apparently positive attributes of God is thus negative, and al-Moqammes concurs with a saying attributed to Aristotle that negative statements about God are more adequate and true than positive ones. Similarly, he wholeheartedly endorses the demand of some philosophers that we should restrict ourselves to purely negative statements concerning God.[49] Al-Moqammes has thus taken the decisive step from the Kalam, which even in its most radical forms upheld the doctrine of positive divine attributes, to Neoplatonism. The significance of this step lies in the illustration it provides of the immanent logic which drives the Mu'tazilite position beyond itself to a rejection of all positive attributes. The radicalism of this conclusion is not dulled by the fact that apparently al-Moqammes continues to use Kalamic formulae, thereby creating the erroneous impression that he has returned to the basic tenets of the Kalam.

There was no further systematic development of the Kalam in rabbinic Judaism. Nevertheless the scope of its influence is sufficiently interesting to warrant illustration by a few examples. This influence is quite evident in the case of Samuel ben Hofni (d. 1013), who, like Saadia, stood at the head of the Academy of Sura. Of his main work, *The Abolition of the Law*, we know nothing except the title, but fragments of his commentary on the Bible which have been preserved contain considerable philosophical material, much of it stemming from Greek philosophy rather than from the Kalam. His division and hierarchy of the sciences is Aristotelian, whereas his psychology is Platonic.[50] In the main there is a preponderance of Kalam influence: he adopts the formula that God lives, is wise, and all-powerful with his essence, not with the attributes of life, knowledge, and power, which are separate from him,[51] he also gives a rationalistic interpretation of the Bible. He combats the belief in magic and astrology; for instance, he says that the witch of Endor could not possibly have raised someone from the dead, but merely deceived Saul. Like the Mu'tazilites, he ascribes to the prophets alone the power to work miracles, denying this capacity to the pious and the saints. He justifies this Mu'tazilite doctrine by arguing that miracles served to legitimate the prophets; their evidence would be inconclusive if saints who were not prophets were also to perform miracles. A corollary of this theory is that miracles happened only in the past and do not occur in the present. The point is argued very forcibly by Samuel b. Hofni, even with regard to those Talmudic saints of whom many miracles are reported.[52]

Another faithful follower of the Mu'tazilites was Samuel's younger contemporary, Nissim ben Jacob, from Kairuan, in North Africa. "The Praise of God," at the beginning of his introduction to his commentary on the Talmud, is full of Mu'tazilite formulae. Thus it is said that the wisdom, life, and power of God are not distinct from his essence but are one with it, and that God did not give his creatures any commandments without also giving them the power to obey them. He also applies his doctrine of God to Talmudic passages whose literal interpretation would involve a crudely anthropomorphic view of God, emphatically rejecting each and every form of anthropomorphism. The problem of retribution is treated in Mu'tazilite fashion by arguing that the divine wisdom may cause innocent children to suffer in this world in order to reward them more richly in the hereafter.[53] Like Saadia he considers the purpose of revelation to be the removal of all doubts that rational knowledge cannot fully dissipate, but he gives this idea an additional twist which is later significant in the thought of Judah Halevi: rational knowledge is not only uncertain in its initial stages, but permanently. Only the evidence of the senses is completely certain. The superiority of Israel to the other nations lies precisely in this sensory evidence provided by revelation.[54]

Hai Gaon (d. 1038), the son-in-law of Samuel b. Hofni and the last head of the Academy of Pumbeditha, has greater reserve with regard to Mu'tazilite doctrines. He accepts the Talmudic notion that the pious, too, can work miracles, just as the prophets did, and blames Samuel b. Hofni's opposite view on the excessive influence of non-Jewish notions. However, he, too, sharply objects to superstitious beliefs by which miraculous effects, like those produced by the prophets, are ascribed to mechanical means such as the manipulation of God's name. He shows acquaintance with the arguments of the Mu'tazilites and against them, and wants to defend the traditional teaching of the Talmud on the power of the pious to perform miracles. The fact that two queries were addressed to him on the subject shows how this kind of problem agitated contemporary Judaism.[55]

Some of his other responsa also deal with philosophic questions which clearly occupied the popular mind. The biblical story that Isaiah first announced the imminent death of King Hezekiah, whose life was then prolonged by fifteen years in response to Hezekiah's prayer, had raised the problem how to reconcile the omniscience of God with the nonfulfillment of a prophecy inspired by him. Hai solves this problem by means of an extremely subtle theory of the nature of divine knowledge. God knows not only that which is actually going to happen, but also the situation and the consequences that would have followed if men, exercising their freedom, had acted differently. Of course, God knows which decision man will, in fact, make in each and every instance; but since freedom admits of various possible decisions, divine omniscience should also be able to foresee all the consequences of each of these possibilities. Just as the divine promises of reward and threat of punishment are conditional upon man's acting in a certain way, so also the prophetic utterances merely foretell what would happen if certain conditions were fulfilled—in this case, if Hezekiah had not prayed to God.

A striking parallel to this line of thought was provided by the Spanish Jesuits at the beginning of the modern period. Referring to the same biblical example discussed by Hai, they developed a very similar theory and designated this particular form of divine knowledge, *scientia media*. This concept was still discussed by Leibniz in his *Théodicé*.[56] Hai also endorses the view that the beasts would be rewarded in the hereafter for their sufferings, and altogether shows himself familiar with the current doctrines of the Kalam.

A more unreserved and unconditional acceptance of the Mu'tazilite form of the Kalam was found among the Karaites. Their most important and original philosophical authorities in the eleventh century were Joseph b. Abraham al-Basir (early eleventh century) and his disciple, Joshua ben Judah (mid-century), who, because of the similarity of their thought, may be treated together. In their radical rationalism, they go far beyond Saadia. According to Joseph al-Basir, reason and revelation cannot be regarded as parallel principles, for the certainty of revelation presupposes a rational knowledge of God. The miracles of the prophets are no proofs of the doctrines they reveal unless we determine first that the Being which sent them desires our good, and is not a spirit of deception but a spirit of truth. Only reason can convince us of the veracity of God, by proving his existence, wisdom, and omnipotence, upon which the reliability of revelation depends. It is impossible to prove the truth of revelation, except insofar as it rests on a concept of God attained by reason.[57]

It is thus for theoretical reason to verify the concept of God. Nevertheless, the decisive argument for the primacy of reason also implies ethical considerations. We need rational knowledge of God in order to be assured of his veracity. But it is in the ethical sphere that the extreme rationalism of these two philosophers attains its full power. Although they share the belief in the essentially rational character of ethics with the majority of Jewish philosophers, yet nowhere is this conviction upheld with such energy and ethical fervor. Joseph al-Basir appeals, first of all, to the fact of our ethical consciousness, in which we apprehend with immediate evidence the value of good and the reprehensibility of evil. We experience an immediate impulse to bring those who stray back to the right path; we feel gratitude for favors received, and an immediate attraction to truth, whereas falsehood repels us. It is solely the inner evidence of our moral consciousness that is responsible for these sentiments. Eudaemonistic considerations are completely alien to this moral consciousness, which arouses us to do the good without any thought of heavenly or human reward.

The Karaite thinkers defended the autonomy of the moral consciousness not only against the claims of revelation, but also against those of a rational belief in God: Not only the Brahmins, who were supposed to deny all revelation, but also the Dahriya, who denied belief in God as such, recognized the distinction between justice and injustice; this was not in the least surprising since this distinction was self-evident.[58] As against the Ash'aria who, in the interests of an absolute conception of divine sovereignty, denied the rational character of ethics and based it upon the will of God alone, al-Basir and Joshua ben Judah not only appealed to the evidence of our ethical judgment but also attempted to demonstrate that the theological theory of ethics was self-contradictory. Unless ethics was independent of revelation, we could neither be sure of the veracity of God and his revelation, nor would there be any obligation on our part to ascertain whether an alleged "revelation" really originated from a divine source. This obligation, as well as the duty of gratitude toward God, must be assumed even by the Ash'arites if they are to justify the demand of submission of the divine commandment.[59]

Here we have practically the whole armory of arguments marshalled by the modern Enlightenment in order to establish the idea of an autonomous ethics. The basic conception of the rational nature of ethics possibly goes back to Greek, and particularly to Stoic, sources. But it was only through its defense and justification, in the face of the heteronomy of ethics as maintained by Islamic theologians, that this doctrine received its fully evolved and rigorous form at the hands of Joseph al-Basir, Joshua ben Judah, and their Mu'tazilite models.

Given the above assumption, it follows of necessity that the moral law is binding on God no less than on man. This immanent necessity, inherent in the distinction between good and evil, excludes the possibility of God's actions being beyond this distinction. The fact that God is the Lord, and men are his servants, makes no difference in this respect, since the ethical demand also exists in relation to the servant. Actually, this assumption is implicit in our praise of God's goodness, for it would be senseless to qualify God's acts as good, if good and bad depended solely on his will. That God acts in accordance with the moral law, follows, as Saadia had already pointed out, from his self-sufficiency. No one does evil unless impelled by a selfish motive. Since the self-sufficiency of God precludes any selfish motive, he cannot but act morally.[60]

Creation is necessarily an act of God's goodness, and this goodness must be manifest in everything. Joseph al-Basir criticizes, however, the extreme assertion of some Mu'tazilites, that since goodness was God's essence, he must, of necessity, do the good. To this, Joseph objects that in that case, creation, being a necessary consequence of the divine nature, would be co-eternal with the Creator himself. It is not an immanent necessity, but the freedom of the divine decision, which chooses the good and creates the world. This distinction is more than scholastic hairsplitting. By conceiving of creation as a necessary result of the divine goodness, the universe ceases *ipso facto* to be the product of a divine will, and becomes instead, a necessary consequence of the divine essence. The dialectical dissolution of the concept of a divine will ultimately substitutes for the idea of creation, that of a necessary emanation of the world from God. Against this, Joseph al-Basir maintained that although God, in his wisdom, only does the good, he chooses it freely. If the world did not exist, it would be meaningless to talk about God's obligations towards his creatures; but once God has freely created them in his goodness, he is under necessity to provide for them.[61]

The close dependence of Joseph al-Basir and Joshua b. Judah on their Mu'tazilite sources involves them in some of the abstruse complexities of this system. This is particularly apparent in their proofs for the creation of the world. Their principal proof (which was also accepted by Saadia) states that substances in which created accidents inhere, of necessity, must be thought of as themselves created. Whereas Saadia presents this proof in a simple and straightforward manner, the two Karaite philosophers develop it in an extremely complicated fashion and in many variations, which need not be reproduced here in detail, though their main motifs may be briefly indicated.

The reason for the excessive complications of the proof is that its assumptions are not justified merely empirically, as by Saadia, but are derived conceptually as well. Saadia was content to show empirically that all bodies were subjects of accidents and that all accidents were subject to generation and corruption. Joseph al-Basir and Joshua ben Judah want to show that this is so because of logical necessity. This is because, unlike Saadia, they hold the atomistic theory of reality, as taught by the Kalam. Saadia's empirical proofs apply only to composite bodies, not to the ultimate elements of reality, the atoms. For the proof to be conclusive, it would be necessary to show that accidents necessarily inhere also in atoms, and that these accidents came into being at some time. The first part of this statement can easily be demonstrated in regard to the principal determinations which are movement and rest, composition and separation, since atoms too are subject to these "modes of being" (in the terminology of the Kalam). Every atom must be either in motion or in rest, either compounded with other atoms or isolated. Stating this argument in an even more abstract form, Joshua ben Judah suggests that the fact that every atom occupies a determinate place in space must also be considered a mode or state of being; in fact, he seems to regard even existence as an accident, since everything may either be or not be.[62] The main difficulty of the argument here is that of proving that the principal determinants or modes of existence must, of necessity, come into being. At this point the argument becomes so involved that only the most general outline can be presented. First of all, it is impossible that the modes of existence follow from the essence of the atoms; for, in that case, since the essence of all atoms is the same, all substances ought to share the same modes of existence, and it would be unthinkable that certain atoms are in motion while others are at rest, or that certain atoms are joined, while others are isolated.

Joshua applies the same argument to the position of atoms in space. Since the atom stands in essentially the same relationship to every point of space, its position in space cannot be deduced from its essence, or else all atoms sharing the same essence must occupy the same space.[63] Hence the modes of existence of atoms are conditioned by external factors. However, these external factors cannot be eternal, since by definition that which is eternal cannot change. If, for example, rest were due to an eternal cause, then a body at rest could never acquire motion, and vice versa.[64] The simple fact that change is possible at all, proves that the causes of the modes of existence cannot be eternal. The causes, and hence the modes or states of being themselves, have come into being; hence, the atoms have come into being too.

The Kalam maintained its supremacy among the Karaites until the end of the Middle Ages. Karaite thinkers resisted the trend toward Neoplatonism and Aristotelianism which characterized Islamic and rabbinic philosophy. The last great work of Karaite religious philosophy, *The Tree of Life* of Aaron ben Elijah of Nicomedia (composed 1346), still treads the old paths. According to Aaron ben Elijah, the teaching of the Kalam was in full accord with that of the Bible, and was, in fact, of Jewish origin, whereas the Aristotelian system had grown on pagan soil and hence contradicted the doctrines of Judaism in many essential points.[65]

What distinguishes his work from earlier Karaite writings is the extraordinary simplicity of his argumentation, and his attempt to defend the doctrines of the Kalam against Aristotelian criticisms. Maimonides appears as the chief representative of this Aristotelian critique. Aaron continually refers to him, and his own treatise is evidently intended as a reply to the *Guide for the Perplexed*. Maimonides' main objections to the Kalam are refuted in great detail, and the accusation that the Kalam had adopted an atomistic conception of physical reality for purely theological reasons, in order to prove the creation of the world, is countered by the assertion that atomism was confirmed by any impartial scientific view of the world. In fact, it was the opponents of the idea of creation in ancient Greece who advocated atomism.[66] Whereas Maimonides thought it impossible to demonstrate that the world had a beginning in time, and therefore divorced the argument for the existence of God from the question of the origin of the world, Aaron not only reaffirms the Karaite proofs for a created world, but actually considers them as the sure and safe path for proving the existence of God.[67] He also criticizes Miamonides' rejection of positive divine attributes, by arguing that a careful examination of the negative attributes admitted by Maimonides actually reveals a positive content.[68] Maimonides' doctrine of providence—which admits a special providence only for human beings and posits a general providence for subhuman nature—is condemned as an inadmissible concession to Aristotelianism, to which Aaron uncompromisingly opposes the biblical doctrine of a particular divine providence over all existents.[69] Maimonides' attempt to justify the existence of evil by defining it as mere privation was a failure, since even on its own premises the doctrine presupposed a positive divine act, the annulment or suppression of some specific good.[70] The existence of the human soul, he holds, is not bound up with the body, as implied by the Aristotelian definition of the soul as the form of the organic body. Without rejecting this definition as such, he nevertheless draws a radical distinction between the soul on the one hand, and the form of natural substances on the other, the soul being an independent substance. It is also immortal in its own right, as against the doctrine held by many Aristotelians, of the immortality of the acquired intellect.[71]

In certain points of theological detail, Aaron accepts some of the views of Maimonides; for example, the distinction between the prophecy of Moses and that of other prophets.[72] Though a staunch upholder of the fundamental doctrines of the Kalam, he would admit criticism of points of detail. He abandons both the doctrine (still accepted by Joseph al-Basir) that the will of God was not of his essence, since the effects of that eternal will would then also be eternal, and the concomitant theory that God created the world by means of a created will. He similarly rejects the belief that animals will receive reward in the hereafter.[73] The moral laws are no longer considered as laws of reason (as in the Kalam); they are described, in the manner of the Aristotelians, as "conventional rules," but not as rational in the strict sense.[74]

Aaron's work is thus more than a mere compendium of earlier Karaite doctrines; its polemics against Aristotelianism, combined with an acceptance of some of its tenets, give it a character and value of its own. Aaron's originality resides less in his systematic development of earlier ideas than in his intelligent reduction of the Kalam doctrines to their basic principles, and their skilful adaptation to later theories. But even in his controversy with Aristotelianism, Aaron fails to grapple with its basic principles.

3 Neoplatonism

Isaac Israeli

THE Kalam scholasticism of Saadia and al-Moqammes already exhibited a strong admixture of Aristotelian and Platonic doctrines. An analysis of these Kalam systems clearly discloses Greek influence, both in their metaphysical and ethical rationalization of the idea of God, and in its scientific justification. Yet the Kalam was essentially a product of the religious and theological origins to which it owed its peculiar character. Whatever it accepted from Greek philosophy was adapted to the basic direction and tendency of its thinking. There may have been exceptions among some of the heads of the schools who overstepped the boundaries of the Kalam—but even Saadia and al-Moqammes did not allow the increasingly numerous Greek doctrines admitted into their systems to destroy their fundamental character.

As against this, the new relationship to Greek philosophy on the part of the Islamic and Jewish Neoplatonists and Aristotelians was different not only in degree, but also in kind. Greek philosophy was no longer the source of particular doctrines only, but the systematic foundation of their thought. Even where they modified Greek ideas for religious reasons, the change applied to the system as such, irrespective of the measure of depth to which this or that particular thinker had penetrated its principles, or of the particular aspects of it which he emphasized. In this respect, Jewish Neoplatonism, with which we shall deal first, exhibits a variety of forms of different worth. But even those Jewish Neoplatonists for whom Neoplatonism was a kind of popular theology referred to the system as a whole and expounded it as such.

The first Jewish Neoplatonist, Isaac b. Solomon Israeli (ca. 850-950), was an eclectic compiler and his fame rested mainly on his medical works, which were highly regarded in Islamic, Jewish, and Christian circles. His eminence as a medical writer helped to boost his philosophic reputation among Christian scholastics, whereas Jewish philosophers were rather contemptuous of him and only a few later writers care to quote him. His two philosophic works, *The Book of Definitions* and *The Book on the Elements,* survive only in Hebrew and Latin translations, and do not provide a systematic presentation of his basic doctrines. *The Book of Definitions* simply lists definitions of the most important philosophic concepts, though some are followed by a fuller discussion of their subject. *The Book on the Elements* is essentially an exposition of the Aristotelian doctrine of the elements, which the author identifies with that of Hippocrates and Galen, together with a criticism of differing conceptions regarding the idea of elements. Israeli's discussion does not lack critical acumen, though he merely develops ideas already found in Aristotle and Galen, and it is doubtful if even their dialectical application is entirely his own contribution. The course of the argument is continually interrupted by naive insertions of medical, logical, and metaphysical investigations. These investigations and the discussions in *The Book of Definitions* constitute the main source for his philosophic ideas. In addition to a few fragments of other works,[1] we have also a commentary on the *Sefer Yetzirah*, the substance of which certainly goes back to Israeli, though the text we possess has been edited or revised by his students.[2]

Despite his lack of originality, Israeli's was the first attempt to transplant Neoplatonism to Jewish soil, and consequently has all the interest attaching to the beginnings of all great historical processes. The problems which arise from the synthesis of Judaism and Neoplatonism, and which we shall find in the Jewish Neoplatontists (and Aristotelians), are already apparent in Israeli, although he was not clearly conscious of them. These appear in his definition of philosophy. Philosophy is essentially a drawing near to God, as far as is possible for human beings.[3] This ideal of the *imitatio dei,* which goes back to Plato's *Theaetetus* and which was used for the definition of philosophy in the Neoplatonic commentaries on Aristotle, was in fact also a demand of biblical and Talmudic religion. But the meaning of the religious ideal is completely changed when this communion with God is defined as the knowledge of the truth, understood as systematic theoretical knowledge. Of course, the Greek Neoplatonists also demanded that right knowledge should lead to right action, yet Israeli seems to regard right action as a mere by-product. Although the Neoplatonic formula lends itself to uniting the religious and philosophic ideals, Israeli's emphasis is always on the philosophic aspect.

In Israeli's world view there is a continual clash between Jewish elements. He emphatically reiterates the idea of creation and distinguishes clearly between the divine creation, which is *creatio ex nihilo*, and the natural generation of things, which clearly presupposes a material substratum.[4] The source of creation lies in the wisdom and goodness of God, which he wanted to make manifest. Here Israeli's idea of God is far removed from the abstract concept of the Neoplatonists.[5] At the same time, he combines the idea of creation with the Neoplatonic idea of emanation, according to which the plurality of things proceeds by degrees from ultimately simple, primary substances. The highest of these substances is the intellect, created by God himself; and from it there descends by degrees all the other substances, according to the usual Neoplatonic schema. The fullness of light of the higher essences is such that they can emanate the lower ones without being diminished or divided.[6]

This combination of the doctrine of emanation with that of creation was considered by Israeli and many later Jewish Neoplatonists as self-evident, without any attempt being made to justify it. He never explains why the direct creative activity of God should be limited to the creation of intellect, from which all other things proceed by emanations. There are also some obscurities in details. Concerning the supraterrestrial world, the idea of emanation is developed with great clarity. The soul with its various divisions emanates from intellect, and from the lowest part of the soul there emanates the heavenly sphere in which nature inheres as its active principle. The result is a slightly modified version of the Neoplatonic triad of soul, intellect, and nature.[7]

As regards the sublunar universe, however, his position is not so clear.[8] In *The Book on the Elements* the description of the formation of composite bodies from the elements stops at the elements themselves, for which, according to Israeli, there is no prior cause other than divine omnipotence.[9] It would thus appear that the terrestrial bodies were outside the process of emanation. However, Israeli makes similar statements about the soul,[10] which is explicitly included in the process of emanation. Hence, statements of this kind may not be construed as qualifying or limiting the doctrine of emanation expounded in *The Book of Definitions*. We are certainly not entitled to assume that *The Book on the Elements* completely denies the doctrine of emanation merely because it makes no mention of it. The somewhat misleading passages cited merely say that the elements and the soul did not come into being by natural generation, but have a metaphysical source which is not further explained.

In the main portions of *The Book of Definitions*, the process of emanation is discussed in detail only until the stage of the heavenly sphere is reached. Instead of proceeding with a description of the next step, the emanation of the terrestrial world from this sphere, Israeli merely describes the influence of the celestial sphere upon the process of generation and becoming within the already existing terrestrial world.[11] Only rarely does he give a detailed exposition of the complete process of emanation from beginning to end.[12] Similar inconsistencies in an exposition which glides cavalierly over the assumption of the origin of matter from spirit, and which then goes on to discuss the relationship between the sensual world and the suprasensual world in terms of a thoroughgoing dualism, can be found, of course, in the Greek Neoplatonists. Israeli's text provides no evidence at all for the assertion that the process of emanation broke off when it reached the heavenly sphere, and that the elements of the material world were directly created by God.[13]

Israeli fits a number of Aristotelian doctrines, like that of the elements, into his Neoplatonic philosophy. Even his doctrine of the soul contains Aristotelian elements. The three forms of the soul taught by Aristotle—the rational, the animal, and the vegetable—are ascribed by Israeli to the universal soul as well. In the process of emanation the intellect first produces the rational soul, followed by its two lower parts.[14] The individual human soul, in accordance with Neoplatonic principles, is regarded as a substance independent of the body, and he even tries to reinterpret Aristotle's doctrine of the soul in this sense. The purpose for which body and soul have been joined is that men should know the truth, and by it distinguish good and right, worship God and recognize his sovereign power, desist from every unworthy deed, and receive his heavenly reward.[15]

In the definition of the goal of human life, the moral element is emphasized to a far greater degree than was the case in the earlier definition of philosophy, and the notion of a hereafter is interpreted completely in terms of heavenly retribution. But the idea of retribution is comprehended in Neoplatonic fashion. Reward consists of the union of the individual human soul with the upper soul through which it attains the light of knowledge and elevates itself to the level of spirit, where it will be united with the light created directly by God himself.[16] This entrance into the world of spirit is a natural consequence of the purification of the soul effected by knowledge and a moral life, and hence does not require a specific, retributive act on the part of God.[17] The net result of this Neoplatonic conception coincides with that of the theological doctrine of retribution, in spite of the difference in the argument leading up to it. This convergence in particular makes it easy to understand how Neoplatonism could appear as merely another expression of religious ideas taught by Judaism.

The same applies to the doctrine of prophecy as expounded in *The Book on the Elements*. It seeks to explain why prophetic revelations present the truth, not in its conceptual purity, but clothed in a sensual garment. The answer, according to Israeli, lies in the nature of the faculties involved in the process of revelation. During sleep, when the intellect wishes to infuse its peculiar spiritual forms into the soul, these forms assume a shape halfway between spirituality and materiality, for only in this way can they impress themselves upon the common sense and be transmitted further to the imagination and memory. It depends on the capacities of the recipient of a revelation—the clarity or dimness of his perception, and his intellectual powers—whether he will be able to extract the spiritual core from its material husk, or will require the aid of an interpreter whose intellect has already been illuminated.[18] Here we have a psychological theory of vision and dreams, which regards the latter as communications of the intellect to the soul, and which accounts for their peculiarities in terms of the nature of these two faculties. Prophecy in the narrower sense is also expressly included in this theory, whose general tendency becomes even more evident if we disregard the statements, apparently added at a later date, attributing the prophetic act to God, who uses the intellect as mediator between himself and the soul. Essentially it is the same naturalistic explanation of prophecy as expounded, at about the same time, by al-Farabi—allowing for some differences due to al-Farabi's divergent psychological system—and whose major ideas turn up again and again in the doctrines of the Arabic and Jewish Aristotelians.[19]

But Israeli adds a completely different explanation in order to account for the fact that in the prophetic writings we find the truth at times in pure conceptual form, while at other times it is clothed in a sensual garb. Such devices are necessary because revelation, being intended for all classes of men, must perforce take a form that will satisfy the needs both of the enlightened and of those who are bound to the world of sense.[20] Here we have a teleological instead of a psychological-causal explanation for the material manner by which the prophetic writings convey the divine truth; but Israeli was apparently unaware of the difference between the two. While al-Farabi and his followers attempted to reconcile these two viewpoints, which they too accepted, Israeli's explanation is completely transformed in its application to the prophetic writing. Stating that the free spontaneity of the divine will accords the prophet a vision in the form best suited to the divine purpose, he no longer concerns himself with the psychological intermediaries in the act of revelation. From the dynamic causality of Neoplatonism, Israeli thus passes to the free action of God, but contents himself with a few general statements concerning the possibility of reconciling these two viewpoints.

Solomon ibn Gabirol

Israeli found no followers outside the inner circle of his disciples. It took one hundred years before Solomon ibn Gabirol inaugurated a new succession of Jewish Neoplatonists, who dominated the development of Jewish philosophy for another century. The Kalam was displaced by Neoplatonism, and only a few representatives of the latter retained elements of the older system. This shift of philosophic orientation coincided with a change in the geographic location of philosophic effort. With Solomon ibn Gabirol, Spain became the center of Jewish philosophy, which, like all other forms of Jewish cultural activity, passed from the East to Europe.

Solomon ibn Gabirol (b. 1026, d. 1050, or—according to some authorities—1070) was a religious poet of great though austere power. As a philosopher, his place is in the general history of metaphysics rather than in the history of Jewish philosophy. The original Arabic text of his major work, *The Fountain of Life* (Latin, *Fons Vitae*; Hebrew, *Mekor Hayyim*), is lost, and only the Latin translation and some Hebrew excerpts have come down to us. The *Fons Vitae* is a purely metaphysical work, presenting an essentially Neoplatonic system, without as much as one word about its relationship to Judaism. It is only from the few surviving remnants of Gabirol's allegorical commentary on the Bible[21] that we can form an idea of how he attempted to read his philosophic doctrine into Scripture. That there was a chasm in Gabirol's consciousness between his philosophical and religious convictions is shown by his famous and sublime liturgical poem "The Royal Crown," whose basic ideas are those of the metaphysical treatise, with the difference that the religious impulses which were only occasionally adumbrated in the *Fons Vitae* find full expression in the poem.[22] His minor and unimportant ethical treatise on the *Improvement of the Qualities of the Soul*[23] is only loosely related to the basic ideas of his system.

The character of the *Fons Vitae* may help to explain its extraordinary fate. Jewish Neoplatonists used it a great deal, but after the victory of the Aristotelian trend in Jewish philosophy, the treatise fell into oblivion even more than other books of the earlier period, because it paid no attention to the more specific problems of the philosophy of religion. Consequently, it was never translated into Hebrew during the entire Middle Ages. Here and there it drew some attention until the end of the Middle Ages; thereafter it was completely forgotten.[24] In Christian scholasticism the *Fons Vitae* played an important role, but its author, known as Avencebrol or Avicebrol, was thought to be a Muslim—occasionally even a Christian—philosopher. Until the middle of the nineteenth century, nobody knew that this name hid the identity of the famous Jewish poet, Solomon ibn Gabirol. Only when Solomon Munk discovered the Hebrew excerpts from the *Mekor Hayyim*, and proved their identity with the *Fons Vitae* of the scholastics, did Gabirol find his rightful place in the history of philosophy.

Most of the elements from which Gabirol's system is constructed are derived from the Neoplatonist tradition, and even where this does not appear to be the case, we must suspect lacunae in our knowledge of the Neoplatonic sources. Thus, although Gabirol teaches that both the intelligible and the material worlds were composed of an intelligible matter, it is not impossible that the Plotinian notion had already developed along similar lines. It is likewise possible that some earlier thinkers may have anticipated and approximated Gabirol's doctrine of the divine will to a far greater degree than those philosophers whose similar speculations we happen to know.

However, the question of Gabirol's originality is independent of these or similar possibilities. His originality does not lie in isolated details of his philosophy, but in the systematic energy with which he constructs and derives his Neoplatonic world view from its ultimate presuppositions. Unlike the other known Jewish Neoplatonists, he is not content with receiving the basic structure of his system, complete and ready-made, but seeks to strengthen its foundations and to justify its premises by means of an ever-renewed dialectic. This applies even to those parts of his system which do not go beyond traditional Neoplatonic ideas. But Gabirol's speculative independence shows itself especially in the thoroughgoing consistency with which he constructs his system on the basis of his specific interpretation of the concepts of matter and form, whereby the system as a whole is given an entirely new turn. Even if we assume that this particular conception of matter and form had been developed before Gabirol, the function of these concepts within his system, its complete construction through the categories of universal form and universal matter, and the unfolding, from all angles, of the problems connected with these concepts, are surely his own.[25]

His interest is focused upon the conceptual development of these problems. Neoplatonism in the *Fons Vitae* appears not as a religious world view, but as a metaphysical system, the proof of which is presented in sober, dry, and scholastically abstract fashion, and with ever-new variations of the same basic arguments. The strength of Gabirol's thinking does not lie in the clarity and correctness of his arguments; his dialectic wrestles with the concepts more often than it overcomes them. It is not in the compelling quality of his arguments, but in the intellectual energy with which he follows his basic concepts to their last consequences, that we shall find Gabirol's real philosophic strength.

A decisive factor in Gabirol's construction of his system is his way of defining and mutually delimiting the central concepts of matter and form. For Aristotle, these two concepts were determined by the problem of becoming, the latter understood as the transition from potentiality to actuality. Matter is the principle of potentiality, form that of actuality. In an aside, Aristotle applies the same language to the relationship between the concepts of genus and species, giving the relatively indeterminate genus the name of matter, whereas the species, which further determines the genus, is given the name of form.[26] This view had already attained considerable importance with Plotinus, who concluded that the intelligible substances, including *nous,* were composed of matter and form, since even in the case of *nous,* the plurality of its particular determinations is distinct from the general substance that is thus determined.[27]

Ibn Gabirol follows this view. But unlike Aristotle and Plotinus, he does not equate the general (as distinct from the particular) with matter primarily because of its indeterminacy, but rather because it is the subject. If substances of different kinds yet exhibit common traits, this similarity must be due to the identity of a common substrate underlying them all, while their differences are due to a differentiating principle. The principle of generality is matter, and the principle of differentiation or individuation is form. Since everything that exists exhibits both generality and differentiation, reality must be a composite of both factors. And since generality is prior to differentiation, and all particular determinations continue to share in its essence, matter must be the substratum which imparts their essence to the various substances. The differentiating form inheres in matter, and develops from it the multiplicity of separate particulars.[28]

This dualism of matter and form recurs on all levels of universality and particularity. Climbing the ladder from the lowest species to the most general all-embracing genus, we must necessarily find a corresponding series of forms and matters, the lower of which are always surrounded and contained by the preceding higher ones. It is, therefore, easy to see how this ladder rises from the plurality of earthly bodies, through the four main elements, to a general material substance, and that even the terrestrial world and celestial bodies must of necessity have a common foundation in the unity of the concept of matter.[29] The same holds true of the incorporeal intelligible substances. If we assume with the Neoplatonists the existence of a plurality of such substances, then we must assume they share a common essence whose particulars are the various separate immaterial substances; that is, even these are composed of matter and form.[30] But just as corporeal and spiritual substances are contained within the one concept of substance, so also they must have their root in a common matter.[31] One and the same matter thus underlies all reality. For Plotinus, on the other hand, intelligible and corporeal matter were two distinct substances, and only the similarity of their functions caused them to be referred to by the same name.[32]

This argument, simple and straightforward in itself, is complicated by the fact that Gabirol identifies the sequence of general and particular with that of higher and lower, thus comprehending the whole scale of being, from the lowest level of corporeality to the highest level of spirituality, as a uniform series of matters and forms, rising step by step from maximum particularity to maximum universality. Terrestrial and celestial matter are no longer conceived as two parallel epiphenomena of one and the same corporeal prime matter, but the matter of heavenly bodies is set above that of earthly bodies. Similarly, corporeal and spiritual matter are not considered as two parallel manifestations of one and the same prime matter, but material reality is conceived as subordinate to the spiritual. The relation of the higher, spiritual reality, to the lower, material one, is that of the universal to the particular.[33] Ibn Gabirol was forced to this conclusion by his determination to construct the whole Neoplatonic sequence of substances with his concepts of matter and form. However, the manner in which these two disparate sets of ideas are synthesized remains obscure, though a clue can be found in his analysis of the concept of a primary corporeal substance. The form of materiality inherent within it is what makes it matter. From this Gabirol deduces that matter as such, as the subject in which this form inheres, is essentially immaterial; only by union with the form of materiality does it acquire a material character.[34] The matter of corporeality thus stands on the boundary between corporeal and incorporeal existence. The conclusion, however, that this matter, therefore, forms part of the spiritual world is fallacious, since it presupposes the subordination of the material to the spiritual, and regards the incorporeal basis of the corporeal world as the lowest rung of the spiritual world, instead of as a neutral substratum which subsequently differentiates into spirituality and materiality.

The gap in this argument may perhaps be filled by a consideration which, it is true, Gabirol does not explicitly state in this connection. Concept and sense perception are related to one another as is the universal to the concrete. The object of conceptual knowledge is the universal; since Gabirol also holds the doctrine of the unity of thought with its object, he could easily contrast intelligible reality, as the universal, to material reality, as perceived by the senses. The lowest degree of spirit is thus in relation to the highest degree of corporeality; in this way it becomes possible to describe the sequence spirit-body in terms of universal and particular. Whatever Gabirol's method of combining these two sets of concepts, the result is beyond doubt: corresponding to universal matter and inhering in it, there is a universal form. Both together constitute the highest of all the emanated substances, intelligence. These two, universal matter and universal form, are the ultimate elements of all reality. They unfold and differentiate into separate, particular forms and separate, particular matters, whose mutual interaction produces the fullness of separate beings.

This reduction of the whole of reality to two primary elements—matter and form—emphasizes the unity of reality even more than in original Neoplatonism. It is no longer a mere postulate that reality, from its highest source even unto its lowest particulars, is one tightly knit structural whole, for this postulate is fulfilled by the reduction of all realms of existence to the same two primal elements. The ultimate dualism of primary matter and primary form permitted the construction of a consistent monistic world view. This appears very clearly when we consider the relationship between material and spiritual existence. Here the Neoplatonic system comes up against one of its major obstacles, and the struggle between opposing tendencies of the system appears most clearly. Sensual reality is, at one and the same time, the last link in a uniform series of emanations, and the absolute opposite of the suprasensual world. There is a manifest clash here between the monism of the metaphysical view of the world, and the dualism of its theory of values. Even apart from this difficulty, the attempt to bridge the gap between material and spiritual existence, and to convert this essential difference into one of degree, never gets further than vague and metaphorical language. In the last resort, Gabirol, too, could not solve this fundamental problem; nevertheless, the transition to corporeality is conceived by him with greater lucidity and precision than by others, and at least formally, the gap between these two worlds is closed. According to him, the corporeal world does not come into existence as a result of reality becoming increasingly materialized until spirit is finally transformed into matter. The corporeal world has its origin in the form of materiality which determines the corporeality of the underlying matter.[35]

This particular form of corporeality, in turn, is but one link in the chain of successive forms. Its connection with the higher forms appears even more clearly by its determination as quantity. If form on its highest levels is unity, then the form of quantity is unity that has differentiated and unfolded into plurality.[36] Its continuity notwithstanding, the form of quantity bears the same relation to unity as does the discrete plurality of numbers. With the emergence of space from the original unity of form, the transition from spiritual to material reality has also been effected.[37] Hence, the value opposition between sensual and suprasensual worlds is not absolute. The sensual world is admittedly lowest in the chain of value, but it is neither essentially evil, nor without value. The concept of matter exhibits the same reevaluation in even greater measure.[38] Since from its very beginnings the spiritual world contains within itself the same primary matter as the world of the senses, the concept of matter must necessarily be defined in a neutral fashion, relative to the distinction sense-spirit. Of course, this change in the conception of matter and the new evaluation of the sensual world are interlinked. The material world can no longer be placed in absolute opposition to the world of spirit, as there is no principle upon which such an opposition could be based.

The ontology of this system is clear. The sequence of beings corresponds to—or rather, is identical with—the order of concepts, descending from the highest generality to the lowest particularity. The concepts of matter and form are defined in such a way that they can serve as subjects of this particular order, and prime matter is specifically designated as the *genus generalissimum,* the highest genus.[39] The principles of universality and particularity are embodied in matter and form as two independent potencies. Following Aristotle, Gabirol teaches that the two can exist in combination only, and never in isolation. As elements of reality, however, they must be conceived as material potencies. The difficulties necessarily arising out of the fact that two correlative concepts, such as matter and form, become hypostasized into independent realities did not escape Gabirol's sagacity, and his logical depth is nowhere revealed more brilliantly than in his vain wrestling with the problems encountered at this point. Gabirol realized that by defining matter as subject, and form as predicate, the two were determined only in terms of their mutual relationship; and he emphasized the difficulty of escaping this correlative determination and defining matter and form not only by their mutual relationship, but according to their own essense.[40] He accounted for this embarrassment by the fact that the intellect, composed as it is of both elements, has difficulty in rising above itself to its own presuppositions; but even this metaphysical explanation merely expresses the logical difficulty of positing as independent entities concepts which have been derived from the objects of which they are constituent elements. His attempt to overcome these difficulties only led him to define matter and form, not according to their mutual interrelationship, but according to their relation to the things of which they are the constituent elements.

Gabirol also notes the further problem that we cannot think of matter and form as two separate things without immediately distinguishing in each of them, as in every object, between a material and a formal factor. In regard to matter, he asks whether matter itself should not be distinguished from its substantiality and its unity, which are its form. There are two possible answers: one, that unity is not something added to the essence of matter but is identical with it; the other, saying the opposite, that matter cannot be comprehended in isolation from form, and therefore can never be thought of, in itself, as a substratum for any determination such as unity. Both answers are impossible on Gabirol's own premises.[41] Nevertheless, it is the merit of Gabirol's analysis to have pressed forward to the point where the problems arising out of the hypostatization of the concepts of matter and form become clearly visible.

This "logism," which identifies the order of things with the order of concepts, is by itself insufficient to derive existence from its primary elements. In order to account for the emergence of the lower from the higher, it is necessary that the latter be conceived as dynamic: it must contain the power, or rather must itself be the power, which unfolds in the multiplicity of its effects. This dynamic aspect shows itself whenever Gabirol does not analytically reduce being into its elements, but attempts to derive the source of reality from given elements. Then he returns to the Neoplatonic account of the origin of the world, and he, too, teaches that the lower substances emanate from the higher ones. The more pure, simple, and spiritual a substance is, the greater is its active power.[42]

Hence, Gabirol arrives at an entirely new conception of matter and form. Dynamic activity, generally attributed to simple substances as such, is now especially predicated of form. Form had been thought of as the active principle in philosophical tradition, and hence everything said hitherto about the activity of simple substances as such, could now be referred in a more narrow and precise sense to their form.[43] Thus form as the principle of actuality is opposed to matter as the principle of potentiality.[44] This function of the two concepts is difficult to reconcile with that presented earlier, and the contradictions—in which Gabirol's conception of the relationship of these two principles involves itself—which have frequently been pointed out,[45] are ultimately due to this coupling of two distinct functions. Gabirol's assertion that matter is the primary substance underlying all things and bestowing their essence upon them, but that it is only through their form that they come into being, is a combination of incompatible definitions. It is contradictory to argue that the potential being of matter enables us to conceive it as the primary essence of things, and yet deny to it actual being. This contradiction is laid bare when matter, originally conceived as the uniform primary substance of all things, appears to be held together solely by means of the simple unity of form.[46]

The opposition of these tendencies becomes explicit in the account he gives of the process of emanation. Matter is logically the superior, and form the subordinate, principle. Hence Gabirol, in an incidental formulation, could describe every level of being as standing in the relation of form to the one preceding it, and of matter to the one immediately below it. But this original hierarchy is reversed, and form, owing to its dynamism and actuality, becomes superior to matter, which is now conceived as the passive substratum of becoming. The increasing imperfection and compositeness of things is attributed to the increasing grossness of this substratum of becoming, which robs form of its original unity and spirituality.[47] This account implies, in opposition to Gabirol's original presuppositions, an inner differentiation within matter itself. There emerges a new motive leading to contradictory definitions. One primary form and one primary matter are by themselves not sufficient to account for the manifold plurality of things. Consequently the inner differentiation of the one matter is derived from form, just as that of the one form is derived from matter, by attributing the plenitude of being to the activity of form, and the descent of things to the increasing grossness of matter. The various basic qualities ascribed to these two concepts make it possible to focus attention first on one side and then on the other.

The abstract concepts of matter and form are only the framework of Gabirol's world view, which is filled out by the concrete series of things. Between God and the corporeal world there are the intermediary substances—intellect, soul, and nature, successive products of the combination of the fundamental elements. Although in assuming these intermediary substances, Gabirol closely follows the Neoplatonic tradition, yet he is at pains to justify this assumption independently. In fact, on no other part of his system has Gabirol devoted so much care as on the proof of the existence and tripartite structure of the suprasensual world.

Between God and the material world there exists of necessity an intermediate suprasensual world. This is proved, first of all, with the decisive argument of the Neoplatonic doctrine of emanation, and Gabirol shows, in a great number of variations, the impossibility of direct emanation of the corporeal world from God. To this end he illustrates from all possible angles the absolute opposition between God and the corporeal world—an opposition which necessitates an intermediary link. The concept of unity requires that there intervene between the absolute unity of God and the multiplicity of the material world a relative unity, which could unfold into the multiplicity of forms of the material world, and enter into it as one of its elements.[48]

There must also be a level of existence between the finitude of the corporeal world and the infinity of God, which is neither simply finite nor simply infinite. Similarly, the being of the corporeal substances must serve as a bridge between the temporality of the corporeal world and the eternity of God.[49] God's creative activity obeys the general principles of all action, that like produces only like. Despite the repeated emphasis that the divine creativity as *creatio ex nihilo* was different in operation from that of all other substances, all the general categories of action are also applied to God. A closer determination of the supratemporal world is arrived at through the idea that as the material substance is passive by nature, all the moving and active forces must be imparted to it from outside. In this argument, corporeal substance is conceived as the passive substratum of becoming. All effects within the sensual world have their cause, not in matter *per se,* but in the forces of the form which it bears, and which act upon it. Since these forces cannot originate from matter itself, of necessity they must derive from incorporeal, active, and form-producing substances.[50]

Clearly, the suprasensual world is conceived in this argument less as the cause of the being of the corporeal world, than as the cause of the dynamic energies immanent in it. In keeping with this character, it is defined as the world of dynamic, active, and moving substances. It represents the unity of the principle of power, which unfolds in the material world into the multiplicity of its effects. The final definition of the suprasensual world and the proof of the existence in it of separate substances is obtained by a detailed elaboration of this argument. For in addition to the moving forces active in the inorganic world, we can discern a higher level of vegetative life within the vegetative realm, and above it, in the realm of animal life; finally, within ourselves we find the activity of thought. All of these must have their origin in cosmic suprasensual substances, and their gradation must correspond to a similar gradation among the suprasensual essences.[51] With particular reference to man, this idea is expressed by the statement that the structure of the macrocosm can be inferred from that of the microcosm. The suprasensual world, considered so far only in its dynamic aspects, can now also be defined from its spiritual side.

As with Israeli, the Neoplatonic sequence of the three spiritual substances—intellect, soul, and nature—is complicated by the fact that the soul is itself subdivided in the Aristotelian manner into a vegetative, an animal, and a rational soul. This entails many difficulties regarding the details of the relationship of the highest part of the soul, the rational soul, to the intellect. Gabirol's basic intent is to differentiate between the two by attributing to the intellect knowledge in its ultimate unity, whereas the rational soul embodies knowledge divided into the multiplicity of concepts.[52] Another, slightly differently oriented formulation defines the original knowledge of the intellect—which contains truth within itself and is identical with it— as intuitive, whereas the knowledge of the rational soul which is derived from the intellect is discursive.[53] Both formulations affirm the same principle, that the same cognitive content is present in the higher and lower level of knowledge, although in the latter only in its derivative and splintered form.

The same holds true of all the levels of existence. One and the same content is present in various gradations from intellect down to the corporeal world. Like matter and form, the elements of being themselves, so also the content of all being constituted by them is essentially the same in all spheres and degrees of existence, and differs only in its manifestations. This is also true of the relationship of created existence to God. The ultimate source of things lies in the divine knowledge which contains them all in a superior form of unity, beyond human thought and conception. But even this content of the divine knowledge is identical with the actual content of being in all essences. It is thus more than a pantheistic figure of speech when Ibn Gabirol says that the power of God fills everything, exists in everything, and works in everything.[54]

This doctrine of being also provides the basis of Gabirol's theory of knowledge. Its starting point is the notion that the intellect, as the highest degree of created being, contains within itself all lower degrees, and hence also the knowledge of all being emanating from it.[55] The explication of this doctrine is based upon Aristotle's dual notion of form as both the concept and the essential principle of things. The union of primary matter with primary form produces intellect, which is at once both the perfect, self-contained unity of truth, and the perfect self-contained unity of being. The element of form inherent in the intellect is on this supreme level, the form of all-encompassing knowledge. All separate forms are contained in its self-knowledge, even as they are contained in its being. The consistency of this viewpoint is disturbed only occasionally by the dualism of sensuality and concept, and is limited by the *a priori* conception of knowledge of the suprasensual world, said to represent the concept in its purity, since the intellect needs the help of the senses in order to know the sensual world. But this limitation of *a priori* knowledge is inevitable and in keeping with the spirit of the system, insofar as it refers to the individual human intellect. In regard to the latter, Gabirol maintains the aprioristic view. In order to explain its actual dependence on sense perceptions, he adopts the Platonic doctrine of recollection, according to which sense perception serves to arouse within the human spirit the remembrance of dormant conceptual knowledge, or—as Gabirol puts it in a characteristic change of the Platonic formula—to arouse the knowledge of suprasensual substance through knowledge of the sensuous. Here Gabirol combines with his Platonic argument the superficially similar doctrine of Aristotle, according to which human thought is brought from potentiality to actuality through sense perception.[56]

As a result of the specific changes which the fundamental ideas of Neoplatonism underwent in Gabirol's system, the question of the emanation of the world from the absolute unity of God has to be put in a different form. The difficulty is somewhat lessened by the fact that Gabirol's concept of God does not preserve the abstract unity of the Neoplatonic concept. Unlike ancient Neoplatonism, Gabirol does not hesitate to speak of God's knowledge, which is essentially different from all other knowledge, and to consider the being of all things contained in it, in a perfect, supraconceptual unity.[57] On the other hand, the problem is rendered even more acute since, for Gabirol, reality is already split in a fundamental dualism of matter and form at its highest level. Neoplatonism's original tendency was to mediate, insofar as possible, the transition from the one to the many, and to derive from the absolute divine unity only one essence, containing the minimum of multiplicity appropriate to an emanated form of being. Gabirol has the two essentially different principles of matter and form follow immediately from God. The Aristotelian dualism of these two principles is not resolved in the spirit of Greek Neoplatonism, but is applied with such thorough consistency even to supra-sensual reality, that Gabirol is forced to derive this duality immediately from God. Prima facie, the acceptance of the concept of creation may appear to resolve this question, but as has already been shown, in Gabirol's system even the divine activity is subordinate to the general categories of action.

To solve this problem, Gabirol puts forward his doctrine of the divine will. It is a profound though obscure and not easily penetrable conception; yet the intention is clear. Gabirol seeks to account for the duality in creation by discovering in God himself a duality of elements corresponding to the duality in his effects. To this is added another motive: Neoplatonism understood God as the self-contained One; thereby it deprived itself of the possibility of comprehending the causality of God. The expressions by which philosophers tried to formulate compromise solutions are hardly more than symbolic and metaphorical figures of speech. With his doctrine of the divine will, Gabirol attempts to introduce into the concept of God an element of activity which would serve to explain the causality of God. Besides these metaphysical reasons, there is a religious one: the doctrine of the divine will introduces a voluntaristic element into the system; it allows for the spontaneity of divine action, and raises the origin of the world, in God, above the compulsion of a necessary process of emanation.

However, the explication of the doctrine of will lacks essential clarity on many decisive points. Neither the derivation of the duality of matter and form from God, nor the relationship of will to the divine essence, are in any way rendered intelligible. With regard to the former, Gabirol seems to hesitate before different possibilities. He frequently states that both matter and form are derived from the divine will, suggesting occasionally that the possibility of this duality is found in the very nature of willing, since it was characteristic of the will to be able to produce opposites.[58] But generally speaking, he does not attribute to the will anything but the element of form.[59] This, of course, is a necessary consequence of his concept of the will, according to which will and form are essentially related and, in fact, embody the same principle in different phases of its development. The active, dynamic, and "formative" character of form has its ultimate source in the will, which is the ultimate principle of power, from which form is emanated and to which it owes its dynamic energy. It is the will that informs matter with form, and imparts to the latter the power to permeate this passive element.[60] The will is alive in all the effects produced by form, and hence it may truly be said of it that it fills everything and moves everything. According to this viewpoint, matter does not originate in the will; it apparently is Gabirol's intention to account for the duality of the divine action by deriving both form and matter from God, but the former only from God through the will. However, though the derivation of form from will is made clear, Gabirol does not succeed in explaining the origin of matter in God. His usual formulation is that matter, unlike form, does not flow from one of the divine attributes, but from the divine essence. This is justified by the argument that the will cannot act in opposition to the divine essence, but is dependent in its operation on the latter.[61]

This argument reveals the profound sense of Gabirol's derivation of form and matter from God. For the divine creativity is not unlimited in its freedom. The possibilities of creation are prescribed to God by the immanent laws of his essence, and are subsequently embodied in matter which, as the substratum of being, is rooted in the divine essence. However, once the possibilities of being are turned into the real principle of matter—which, moreover, is to be considered as created—there arises a double difficulty: we must assume an activity of the otiose, self-contained divine essence in addition to that of the active will, and we must imagine the pure actuality of the former to produce the potentiality of matter. This last difficulty clearly mirrors the inner contradiction in the conception of matter which is viewed as the essence of things, on one hand, and mere potentiality, on the other. In the main, Gabirol skates quickly over the question of the derivation of matter from God, but enlarges on the details of its fashioning by means of the form emanating from the divine will. All this may give the impression that Gabirol agreed with Aristotle in holding matter to be a primary, uncreated principle, though this was surely not his opinion, and would, moreover, have destroyed the ultimate intention of his system.[62]

No less difficult is the relationship of this will to the divine essence—in accordance with the simple unity of the latter; to be able to fulfill its specific function, it should be distinct from it. The description of the will as a quality of the divine is difficult to fit into the concept of God prevalent in the Middle Ages. Misgivings must increase when, in spite of its identity with God, the will is conceived as a mediating link between God and creation—no matter whether the latter is defined as form alone or as form and matter. Gabirol attempts to reconcile this contradiction by distinguishing between two aspects of the divine will. As pure being, independent of any activity, it is identified with God; but it becomes distinct from him as it begins to function.[63] The same distinction is made again under the aspect of infinity: by its essence the will is infinite like God himself, becoming finite only in its effects and actions.[64] The tendency of these formulations is easy to discern. In order to be able to conceive of God as an active principle, Gabirol must introduce an element of movement within God himself. Since he shrinks from the idea of the divine essence as self-moved, he allocates to the will, as the principle of divine activity, an impossible intermediate position between an aspect of the divine essence, on the one hand, and a full-fledged hypostasis emanating from God on the other.

Gabirol takes up some of the speculations of the Kalam and of Islamic Neoplatonism concerning the divine will, and his frequent identification of the will with wisdom and with the word of God places his doctrine of the will squarely in the broad stream of the history of the logos-idea. From our knowledge of Gabirol's Islamic predecessors, however, we should never have guessed the special function fulfilled by the concept of will, nor its specific difficulties in Gabirol's system. The notices of later authors concerning the concept of will, in the pseudo-Empedoclean writings, are much too confused to permit the attribution of Gabirol's doctrine to this particular source. No doubt Gabirol's will is reminiscent, in many ways, of the Philonic logos, and it is understandable that after the discovery that the earliest Jewish philosophers showed some acquaintance with Philo's teachings, scholars should have suspected some historic filiation. But the very crude conception of the logos, which is all that is attested, has nothing in common with Gabirol, and as long as we know of no Arabic translation of Philo, it remains extremely hazardous to attribute to the Spaniard Gabirol even that superficial knowledge of Philo which is attested only for the Orient. In point of fact, the similarity with Philo is in the final result of Gabirol's doctrine of the will, rather than in his argument or the specific functions predicated of the will.[65] In this, as in all other points, Gabirol has used and adapted traditional material, but the systematization of traditional elements, the specific form given to the concepts, and their integration within the system as a whole, are as much Gabirol's own as the basic constructive ideas of his system.

Bahya ibn Pakuda

Not one of the Jewish Neoplatonists who came after Gabirol could compare to him in speculative power or in the originality of his theoretical interests. For them, Neoplatonism was a fixed and inherited system, and even when they attempted to provide a theoretical justification of its doctrines, they remained content with repeating the traditional proofs. Even in harmonizing Neoplatonism with Judaism, they trod familiar paths. To begin with, they started out from a form of Neoplatonism that had been modified and weakened to the extent of absorbing the idea of creation. It was the religious rather than the metaphysical content of Neoplatonism that interested them, and hence it is not surprising that they could combine its tenets, in varying degrees, with those of the Kalam that also lent themselves to their religious interests.

The immediate successor of Gabirol, Bahya ben Joseph ibn Pakuda (ca. 1080),[66] can be considered a Neoplatonist—with the aforementioned restrictions—only in a qualified sense. His *Book of Guidance to the Duties of the Heart (Kitab al-Hidaya ila Faraid al-Qulub)* has no theoretical purpose, but seeks to intensify the devotional life. The book is not intended for philosophers, but for the religious congregation, to whom it wants to show the path towards the true worship of God. Very few Hebrew books became so popular as Bahya's *Duties of the Heart*. Its warm and simple piety made it a favorite of devotional reading, widely appreciated as the truest and purest expression of Jewish piety. No doubt the book would have been influential, especially among those that were completely innocent of any philosophical interest and were thoroughly steeped in Jewish tradition, even if it had not been written in a profoundly and originally Jewish spirit. It is, therefore, all the more instructive to note the extent to which the book bears the marks of the influence of alien religions. The specific religious coloring of the book places it in the neighborhood of Neoplatonism—though not in the narrow sense. Similar religious tendencies were also alive in Hermetic literature, whose influence upon Bahya has recently been stressed,[67] and the relationship between him and the ascetic literature of Islam, with its strong touch of Neoplatonic elements, is especially intimate.[68] Bahya mentions many more exemplars of piety than he does philosophic authorities, and the Jewish sage does not hesitate to appeal for the confirmation of his teachings to the great ascetics of

Islam who, though he does not mention them by name, seem so close to him in spirit.

The influence of non-Jewish trends of thought on Bahya's religious attitude is particularly manifest in his estimate of theoretical knowledge as a necessary prerequisite for the religious life. He only seeks to guide man toward the fulfillment of the duties of the heart, but holds such guidance impossible without theoretical knowledge. There is no right relationship to God without the knowledge of God, and complete fulfillment of our duties is impossible without previous insight into their ground and essence. Hence the deepening of the devotional life presupposes an intellectual grasp of the foundations of religion.[69] Every believer is thus duty bound to prove to himself the existence and unity of God. Bahya compares the great mass of believers in tradition to a company of blind men, each one of whom is led by his fellow, and who all must follow in good faith the one leader who can see.[70] Thus the value of philosophic knowledge is immeasurably greater than that of Talmudic learning, which deals only with the details of external duties. Bahya attributes to pride the casuistic preoccupation with religious law and the concomitant neglect of essential religious questions, pride, which attempts to dazzle the eyes of the multitude with a show of erudition, evading at the same time the real tasks of religious knowledge.[71]

In spite of the popular character of the book, Bahya, therefore, finds it necessary to justify scientifically that belief in God which is the basis of the religious life, and to develop the concept of God along strictly rational lines. His proof of the existence of God, which is set forth with scholastic precision, is borrowed from the Kalam, though the presentation is somewhat changed. Of the various proofs adduced by the Kalam for the creation of the world, Bahya chooses the one that proceeds from the composition of things. Every composite is composed of a multiplicity of essentially prior elements, and presupposes the existence of a composing substance, logically and temporarily prior to it.[72] The idea that a series without a beginning, an infinite series, is impossible—which serves as an independent proof in the Kalam—is used by Bahya to develop his own proof. He deduces from it the necessity of a first cause, since it is impossible that a series of causes should regress infinitely. However, Bahya does not differentiate sharply between the infinity of a causal series and that of a temporal series.[73] In his hands, the proof of the Kalam receives a teleological twist that was foreign to it in its original form. The compositeness of the world immediately becomes a teleological order in which one thing points to another. Bahya's proof of the existence of God is thus determined by his teleological view of nature, which is an essential element of his religious philosophy.[74]

Along with God's existence, he proves the wisdom of the Creator who fashioned this world according to plan. Although, from a strictly logical viewpoint, Bahya's proof does not necessarily entail the idea of *creatio ex nihilo*,[75] there can be no doubt that he intended to establish the notion of creation, and he conceived of God as the creator of the world. In his proofs of the unity and uniqueness of God, he mainly follows the Kalam; an individual trait appears only in his characteristic predilection for giving cosmological arguments a teleological turn; for example, when proving the unity of the Creator from the purposive unity of the world. However, with these proofs deriving from the Kalam, he combines reasons of an entirely different sort, which mark the transition of his argument to Neoplatonism. Thus he proves by purely conceptual deduction that unity necessarily precedes plurality, and that the ultimate source of things must, therefore, be in an absolute unity.[76] This leads to a thoroughly Neoplatonic idea of God. God is now defined as the absolute unity which logically precedes all things, just as the abstract unity of the number one precedes all numbers. Bahya carefully develops the concept of the absolute unity of God in the spirit of Neoplatonism, distinguishing it sharply from the merely relative unity applicable in the world of things. Whereas unity is found only accidentally in things, it is of the very essence of God.[77] Bahya's doctrine of attributes corresponds to this concept of God. Only the formal attributes of unity, being, and eternity are attributes of essence; all other attributes are merely assertions about God's actions.[78] But even the plurality of the three formal attributes is viewed as a danger to the simple unity of God. He therefore emphasizes—as Saadia had done before him in regard to the material attributes—that the formal attributes were three only in appearance; actually, they were alternative expressions for one and the same fact, since each predicate implied all of the others. In addition, Bahya demonstrates that unity, being, and eternity cannot be attributed to God *strictu sensu;* they merely serve to exclude the opposite determinations.[79] Bahya thus arrives at a completely Neoplatonic concept of God; but although, like other Jewish philosophers, he accepts this idea of God, he fails to draw from it the obvious religious conclusions. To be sure, Bahya did realize that he had made it impossible to know God. The nature of human knowledge permits us to deduce the existence of God from his effects, but precludes any knowledge of God himself.[80]

The Neoplatonic complexion of Bahya's religious ideals has already been noted. For the fundamental idea of his work, he had no need of philosophic influences. It is rooted deeply in Jewish tradition, and only the forms of its expression are borrowed from non-Jewish literature. The distinction between the duties of the heart and the duties of the limbs is of Mu'tazilite origin, but had acquired a particular importance in the ascetic literature of Islam which subordinated the observance of the external commandments to the inner devotion of the soul and its communion with God.[81] But this is only another expression of an "ethics of the heart" ideal which stands at the center of prophetic preaching, and which is also shared by the Talmud, despite its unconditional demand of conscientious observance of external religious commandments. On this point, Jewish tradition completely coincided with Bahya's Islamic sources. Philosophic literature only confirmed his Jewish piety, and biblical and Talmudic quotations could be placed peacefully at the side of the dicta of Muslim ascetics. Preaching a simple piety of the heart, Bahya became one of the most popular devotional authors. But the conceptual formulation of a contrast between the duties of the heart and the duties of the limbs tends to change the ideal of a religious "ethics of the heart" in a very specific way. It substitutes for the distinction between intention and act, a very differently oriented distinction between two kinds of duties. It is true that the duties of the heart also provide the basis for those duties of the limbs, since actions receive their ethical value from the underlying intention of the heart.[82] Nonetheless, the notion of duties of the heart also presents a distinct category of duties from the material point of view. For beyond the combination of the two types of duties, there is a definite sphere of pure inwardness which is the true region of the duties of the heart; it is essentially in this sphere that Bahya's thought moves.

The sphere occupied by the duties of the heart in their pure and restricted sense is that of the relationship between man and God. Bahya's real concern is to establish the correct sentiments in regard to God, and to produce the correct inward disposition of the soul; his *Duties of the Heart* strives to expound this religious disposition from every possible angle. Of course, he does not minimize the importance of the ethics of human relations; but this morality is only a

self-evident corollary of the correct religious attitude, and consequently remains somewhat outside the focus of Bahya's main interest.
A glance at the table of contents of the book makes this clear. The
first chapter deals with the recognition of the true unity of God; the
second is devoted to the study of creatures as witnesses to divine
wisdom; the third, to the duties of worshiping God; the fourth, to
trust in God; the fifth, to the purity of our actions in relation to God;
the sixth, to humility; the seventh, to repentance; the eighth, to self-
examination; the ninth, to abstinence; and the tenth, to the love of
God. Bahya's thought revolves around God and the soul. The devout
absorption in God is man's true end. The recognition of God's
sublime majesty and of the wisdom with which he provides for all his
creatures, as well as meditation on the smallness and frailty of man,
should develop that disposition of the soul which finds its highest
expression in the love of God. This absorption in God is not the same
as theoretical cognition, although the latter, of course, is the indispensable foundation of our inner knowledge of God; it is, rather, the
direction of the soul toward God, in whom it finds its sole happiness
and for whose sake it detaches itself from all external possessions.

This is accompanied by a strong emphasis on the notion of a hereafter. God created man together with the spiritual substances in
order to elevate man to the rank of his chosen creatures that are
closest to his light. To this end the human soul has been placed in
the terrestrial world, where it should achieve its purpose by laying
aside the veil of folly, proving itself in obedience to God's will, and
resignedly bearing the sufferings of this life.[83] At a first glance, this
does not seem to go beyond the Talmudic demand to consider this
world as merely the vestibule to the world to come, and Bahya may
sincerely and legitimately have believed that he only inculcated
traditional rabbinic doctrine concerning man's destiny in the hereafter. In point of fact, Bahya goes far beyond the clues provided by
the Talmud; for though the Talmud places man's ultimate aim in
the world to come, it does not view the moral and religious task of
this life exclusively from the viewpoint of the hereafter. According to
the Talmud, the observance of the divine commandments, by means
of which we prepare ourselves for the future world, has primarily an
intrinsic, positive value. The active character of biblical ethics is
preserved: man's task is the realization of the divine will; the world
to come constitutes the reward, but not the significance, of moral
action. This is not the case with Bahya. Submission to God, whereby

we attain the perfection of the world to come, has for him an entirely different meaning. It has the quality of a test in which man has to prove himself; the active aspect of ethics, without completely disappearing, thus recedes before the cathartic aspect. Ethics is essentially the purification of the soul, its liberation from the fetters of sensuality, its elevation to the purity of spirit, and its final exaltation to communion with God. The dualistic tension between soul and body, between spirit and sensuality, is far greater here than in the Talmud.

Bahya admits the relative rights of the senses. He recognizes in the body a work of the divine wisdom, and demands that we provide for its rightful needs, as otherwise the soul, too, would be weakened.[84] Radical asceticism would put an end to the continued existence of human society, and thus contradict the divine will which demands the preservation of life.[85] He asks the pious not to shun contact with the rest of humanity in order to devote themselves to the salvation of their own souls; they should rather teach mankind and lead them to the worship of God.[86] On the other hand, Bahya teaches a mitigated form of asceticism in accordance with both the will of the Torah and the Aristotelian principle of virtue, as a mean between two extremes. Bahya has in mind an ideal of life which combines outward participation in the activities of this world, with an inner detachment from them, which he considers as the true life desired by God.[87] The pious man is in duty bound to accept life in this world as a task, but he must remain inwardly detached from it, seeing the true goal of his life in communion with God, and in the preparation for the world to come, for which he is destined.

It is this ascetic trait of his ethical doctrine which brings Bahya close to Neoplatonism and related tendencies of late antiquity. What distinguishes him from the Neoplatonists, however, even more than his qualification and restriction of the ascetic ideal, is the significance which he attributes to the latter. It is not the purpose of asceticism to liberate the soul from the bonds of sense, and to enable it to elevate itself through theoretical knowledge to the world of spirit, or to unite itself with God in mystical ecstasy. The purpose of asceticism is to enable the soul to recollect itself for the devout worship of God. In spite of the considerable Neoplatonic influence on Bahya's theoretical construction of the concept of God, the religious relationship of the soul to God, as conceived by him, is absolutely different. The basic religious categories are trust, humility, and love, and Bahya's simple piety, rooted in these sentiments, is too profoundly aware of the exalted majesty of God to desire the vision of God, or even mystical union with him. Religious sentiment thus restored to God the personal, living character, of which the conceptual definition had deprived him. This sentiment is essentially the same as that pervading the Jewish tradition. Divergent traits in Bahya's system may lend it a special color, but they certainly do not affect its fundamental character.[88]

The Twelfth-Century Neoplatonists

Far more profoundly influenced by Neoplatonism than the *Duties of the Heart* is the little treatise, *On the Essence of the Soul* (*Kitab Ma'ani al-Nafs*), falsely ascribed to Bahya. The place and date of its composition are unknown to us; it was probably written sometime between the middle of the eleventh and twelfth centuries.[89] Even in this treatise, Neoplatonism serves as a religious world view rather than as a strictly metaphysical system, and it appears in the somewhat loose and popular form which the Pure Brethren in particular had introduced into Islamic literature.

For the author, true metaphysics is Neoplatonism and is identical with the teachings of the Torah; he is unaware of any contradiction between the two.[90] The same holds true of the doctrine of emanation, which is stated in the form common to Islamic Neoplatonism, and without any attempts at justifying it, though the author refers to a special work of his, *On the Gradation of Things*. According to his system, intellect, called the "active intellect" in Aristotelian fashion, is followed first by soul and nature; next, by matter, as the primary element underlying all corporeal substances; and finally, by the bodies of the spheres, the stars, and the four elements.[91] These essences descend one from another in a necessary sequence, and none could exist without the one preceding it.[92] The entire chain was created by God, whose will and wisdom gave these essences their active powers. The higher essences impart their divine active power to the lower ones, in order to manifest God's wisdom throughout the cosmos.[93] The ideas of emanation and creation are combined as a matter of course, and in a manner which suggests that, by the author's time, the distinctive features of the two concepts had been obliterated to such a degree that he was no longer aware of their essential difference. He is interested less in the origin of the world than in the gradation of things, and in the distinction between the pure world of spiritual essences and the sensual world. The dualism of a sensual world and a suprasensual world is central to his religious view of the world.

The same dualism also dominates his psychology, which is the main subject of his treatise. The soul belongs to the higher, suprasensual world, and the author attempts to prove, against the theories of materialistic psychology, that it is a spiritual substance, independent of the body.[94] The spirituality of the soul obviously implies, according to the author, its origin in the suprasensual world. Avicenna's views that the soul, though a spiritual essence, comes into being together with the body, is rejected out of hand as self-contradictory, without so much as an attempt to examine his cogent arguments.[95] The immortality of the soul is, therefore, considered a return to its spiritual origin. Employing ideas that go back to late antiquity, the fate of the soul is described in highly imaginative fashion as a descent to the world of the senses, and a subsequent return to the higher world. In its descent, the soul traverses all the heavenly spheres and the zones of the elements until it reaches the earth and is embodied; on the way, it is affected by the influence of all the substances through which it passes, so that the further it descends, the more gross are the impurities attaching themselves to its pure essence and enveloping it. These influences also account for the differences between individuals souls. For although in their spiritual essence souls are all equal to one another, yet during their descent they tarry for different lengths of time in the spheres of the various stars, and hence are exposed to these influences in varying degrees.[96] The soul is alienated still further from its spiritual source as it enters the body, and the lower—vegetative and animal—parts of the soul are joined to the rational soul, to which alone all that has been said so far applies. The soul then forgets its original, specific knowledge and succumbs to the influence of sensuality.[97] These vicissitudes are imposed on the soul in order that, by breaking the fetters of sensuality, it might reach a full awareness of its original perfection and true happiness, and raise the body and the two lower parts of the soul joined to it to a higher level.[98] The purification of the soul is achieved through virtue which, in Platonic fashion, the author defines as knowledge and the rule of the rational soul over its lower parts.[99]

The consequent doctrine of the fate of the soul after death elaborates in great detail the highly imaginative notions about a hereafter which Islamic and Jewish philosophers had developed from Platonic and Neoplatonic elements. The return to the world of the spirit is possible only for those souls that have regained their original intellectual and moral perfection. Those souls that have achieved moral perfection, but not the degree of knowledge necessary for their ascent, enter an earthly paradise, where they acquire the missing knowledge. According to the Greek Neoplatonists, the souls that have attached themselves to the sensual appetites must re-enter human or animal bodies. The Jewish Neoplatonists rejected the doctrine of transmigration. In its stead, Israeli had already advanced the doctrine (which ultimately goes back to Greece) that the souls of the wicked, since they are weighed down by sensual passions, vainly try to rise to the suprasensual world. In their vain longings they are driven hither and yon underneath the heavens; in fact, this is their punishment. The treatise describes this in great detail for the various classes of sinners, reserving a special form of punishment for every type of transgression.[100] In this way Neoplatonism became a doctrine of the future world, portrayed with an almost mythological concreteness.

Similar views, more restrained and sober, were presented by Abraham bar Hiyya of Barcelona (beginning of the twelfth century), renowned mainly as a mathematician and astronomer, and the first philosophic author to write in Hebrew. From the philosophical point of view his small treatise, *Reflections Concerning the Soul* (*Hegyon ha-Nefesh*), has little value, and even the interesting supplements found in his messianic treatise, *Scroll of the Revealer* (*Megillath ha-Megalleh*), are mainly of theological and cultural interest. For the Neoplatonic monism which includes matter in the process of emanation, he substitutes the Aristotelian dualism of matter and form. Both existed in the thought of God until God actualized them.[101] This must not be understood to mean, as with Gabirol, that spiritual substances are composed of matter and form. For Abraham b. Hiyya, the spiritual substances are pure forms, complete within themselves; only the corporeal world is a composite of matter and form. A sharp distinction therefore has to be drawn between the self-existent form of the suprasensual essences, and the form of the corporeal world which requires matter in order to exist *in actu*, and which emanates from pure form to matter.[102]

In his messianic treatise he expands the traditional Neoplatonic scheme of a tripartite intelligible world into a five-level model by superimposing above the intellect a world of light and a world of dominion—the world of the Godhead. The philosophic predecessors to whom he refers in this connection are unknown to us; from his own exposition of the doctrine of five levels, we can hardly elicit its philosophic meaning since he presents it with a theological slant, identifying the various intelligible substances with manifestations of divine light which correspond to various biblical theophanies, the world of the angels, and future blessedness.[103] On the whole, he is fond of giving theological interpretations of philosophic views. In *Reflections Concerning the Soul* he quotes with apparent assent a philosophic theory of retribution, which varies certain ideas of the Pseudo-Bahya treatise, *On the Essence of the Soul*. Four types of fate are in store for the soul after death, according to its intellectual and ethical level. Only those souls that unite within themselves intellectual and moral perfection will ascend to the intelligible world; souls that are intellectually perfect, but tainted by vice, are punished by being driven hither and yon underneath the sun, and are consumed by its heat; souls that have acquired piety, but no knowledge, are transmigrated to other bodies until they gain the requisite knowledge; finally, those souls which have neither knowledge nor piety are destroyed together with the body.[104] In his messianic treatise, the author changes this doctrine not only by completely rejecting metempsychosis, but also by substituting for the causal relation between earthly life and the future destiny of the soul, the notion of a divine justice determining the fate of the soul in the hereafter. Intellectual achievement is of relevance only for the punishment of sinners; their souls simply perish if they lack knowledge, but are preserved and receive their due punishment in the world to come if they have gained the requisite knowledge. In contrast, the reward of the righteous is determined by moral considerations only, and hence varies according to the soul's virtues.[105]

The gap between Abraham b. Hiyya and Neoplatonism becomes even wider in the meaning he attaches to history. History has no place at all in the world view of Neoplatonism, which is wholly focused on the timeless opposition between the sensual and the suprasensual worlds; man's salvation lies in his ascent to the eternal realm of spirit. But Abraham bar Hiyya is as much concerned with the essentially historical prophecies of Scripture as he is with the fate of the soul in the hereafter. In his philosophic work he has already discussed the messianic hopes of Judaism, but in his messianic treatise, he develops a comprehensive religious historical view. The purpose of his treatise is to determine the date of the advent of the Messiah. In order to do this, he attempts to find a religious explanation of the whole process of history, from creation to the end of days; to discover the divine plan of history; and to divide history into a series of periods which would find their realization and end in the messianic age.

This philosophy of history is founded upon the idea of an exact correspondence between world eras and the days of creation.[106] The division of the world into periods according to this analogy provides a basic pattern in which a vast number of detailed calculations and constructions can be fitted. The analogy has, of course, been found in the historical speculations of the Church Fathers, but this is the first instance of Christian speculation exerting a direct influence upon Jewish philosophy in the Middle Ages. In the elaboration of his historical view, Abraham bar Hiyya is fully aware that he opposes a Jewish view of history to the Christian one. The extent to which his philosophy of history is based on Christian models is shown by the fact that it even contains an analogy for the Christian doctrine of original sin. As a result of Adam's sin, the rational soul, upon whom not only knowledge but also morality depends, descended into the two lower parts of the soul, thus losing its power of independent development. After the flood, God again separated it from the lowest part, but still left it the power of the middle, animal part of the soul. Nevertheless, ever since Adam there have been in every generation members of the elect in whom the rational soul dwelt in all its purity. Transmitted by inheritance through a chain of the elect, this rational soul broke through with all its power in the patriarch Jacob, and hence all his descendants have a portion in it. From that time, the effects of original sin on Israel were broken, and the rational soul was restored to its original position.[107] The consequent limitation of morality to Israel alone is, however, only incidental to Abraham bar Hiyya's system; at any rate, the notion that outside of Israel there can be no morality is nowhere reaffirmed by him. He certainly does not doubt that piety and the fear of God are present in the Jewish people far more than among non-Jews, but he also teaches that there are pious men among the Gentiles, and that they, too, will receive their reward from God.[108]

In a more textbook-like fashion, Joseph ibn Saddiq (d. 1149) presents a clear and well-thought-out system in his treatise *Microcosm (Sefer ha-Olam ha-Qatan).* It is a basically Neoplatonic system, interspersed with Aristotelian and Mu'tazilite elements, and without claims to originality. The idea of a microcosm, which gives the book its title, provides the intended main subject rather than the actual argument of the treatise. According to the author's plan, introspection should be shown to lead to a knowledge of the cosmos, all the parts of which are represented in man. In point of fact, however, the book's discussion of natural philosophy, psychology, theology, ethics, and eschatology has only the most tenuous relation with the principle of a microcosm. In his philosophy of nature, Ibn Saddiq mainly follows Aristotle, the one important deviation being his definition of the concepts of matter and form. Matter, as that which bears everything else, is the one real substance; whereas form, which inheres in something else, has a status similar to that of the accidents.[109] All bodies share not only matter but also the form of corporeality, which is then differentiated into the separate forms of the individual bodies.[110] The similarity to Gabirol is evident, and becomes even more remarkable when Ibn Saddiq attributes matter to the spiritual essence, which is related to form as genus is related to species.[111]

Gabirol's main doctrine, however, is alluded to only in a cursory manner by Ibn Saddiq. Altogether, the intelligible substances are treated in very summary fashion. His psychology is almost exclusively a psychology of the individual soul, and the relationship between the individual soul and the world-soul is raised only at the end of his discussion. His essentially Neoplatonic arguments for the immateriality and substantiality of the soul are mainly those of Isaac Israeli and the author of *On the Essence of the Soul,* but they are worked out more clearly and systematically. The incorporeality of the soul follows from the fact that it lacks all specifically spatial qualities such as extension and shape; but the crucial proof is found in the fact that the body, of itself, is lifeless and receives its life only from the soul. Being the principle of life animating the body, the soul itself cannot be conceived as bodily, since in that case its own life would have to be derived from yet another soul, thus leading to an infinite regression.[112] Neither can the soul be considered an accident, since it is the very essence of man, and he cannot be thought of without it. It is distinct not only from the ordinary changeable accidents which come and go, while the underlying substance persists, but also from immutable accidents, such as the blackness of Negroes. The accidental nature of even immutable qualities is shown by the fact that they are permanent in certain objects only, whereas in others they are subject to change.[113] The soul, however, as the essence of man, is predicable of all human individuals. Ibn Saddiq even seeks to introduce the Aristotelian definition of the soul, against its original intention, into his concept of the soul as an independent, incorporeal substance.[114] The source of the individual soul is the world-soul. The transition from the one to the other is reminiscent of Gabirol in its hypostatization of logical categories. To begin with, the universal soul is defined as the genus of the individual soul, and its existence is proved by the existence of particulars which belong to it. Next, the relationship of the universal to particulars is identified, as so often in the history of metaphysics, with the relationship of the whole to the part; hence it is easy to arrive at the idea of a universal soul embracing all individual souls. The splitting of the world-soul into a plurality of separate souls with all their individual differences is due to the plurality of bodies absorbing the soul, just as the light of the sun is differently refracted by the plurality of bodies illuminated by it.[115] All this, however, is without essential detriment to the substantial character of the individual soul, as is shown by Ibn Saddiq's doctrine of immortality. The relationship of the individual soul to the world-soul is expounded with the vague haziness which is so characteristic of Neoplatonic psychology.

Ibn Saddiq's theology, like Bahya's, starts from the Kalam, but then gets on a Neoplatonic track. He, too, proves the existence of God from the creatureliness of the world. But unlike Bahya, Ibn Saddiq's proof does not proceed from the composite nature of bodies. Instead, he utilizes another Kalamic proof: since all substances are subject to accidents, they must have come into being like the accidents themselves.[116] This Kalam argument leads to the idea of creation; the origin of the world is in the divine will whose sole motive, considering God's absolute self-sufficiency, can only be his goodness.[117] The transition to the Neoplatonic concept of God is effected—as with Bahya—by the idea of the divine unity. The unity of God is postulated as the ground of the plurality of things; the relationship between the two is explained by means of the analogy of the relationship between unity (the one) and the numbers, with the difference that the simple unity of the divine is superior to the unity of the numerical one, which is, after all, capable of multiplication. God alone is absolute unity—or rather above unity, since the quantitative significance of the concept of unity, which is the only one meaningful to us, is inapplicable to him.[118] God's utter incomprehensibility is thus established as the most adequate expression for the divine majesty, for if God could be comprehended by our understanding he would, by definition, be finite and incomplete.[119] Even infinity can be predicated of God only metaphorically, since, strictly speaking, no quantitative concept, whether "finite" or "infinite," can apply to God.[120]

Ibn Saddiq is well aware of the difficulties which this concept of God presents for the theory of a divine will. He considers it self-evident that the will is identical with the divine essence, but fails to explain how the immutability of God can be squared with the fact of his willing. His hints on the subject seem to make most sense if interpreted in the spirit of Gabirol's doctrine of the divine will.[121] His discussion of the question of divine attributes is somewhat obscure. He explicitly rejects the view held by earlier philosophers—and apparently also implicit in his own concept of God—that no attributes whatsoever can be predicated of God. Divine attributes are possible, provided it is understood that they are as different from the attributes predicated of other existents as the divine essence is different from the essence of all other things. Moreover, the divine attributes must be conceived of as one with the divine essence. This viewpoint is expressed by the well-known formula of the Kalam, that the divine attributes of wisdom and power are identical with the essence of God. Ibn Saddiq here seems to mitigate the radicalism of his earlier statements, since the divine unity beyond all unity now appears, after all, as an essence bearing positive determinations.

The detailed elaboration of his doctrine of attributes, however, yields a different picture. Our knowledge of God's attributes derives mainly from his actions, and hence such attributes are no more than figurative expressions for his deeds. Thus we attribute wisdom to God on the grounds of the perfection of creation; but the sense of this predication is merely the rejection of his ignorance.[122] This leads to the significant result that all attributes can be viewed as attributes of action, on the one hand, and as attributes of essence, on the other. Whereas attributes of essence and of action had hitherto been distinguished as two separate categories, they are now viewed as two aspects of the same attribute, which may appear as positive insofar as it describes God's actions, or effects, and as negative insofar as it refers to the divine essence underlying these effects. The Neoplatonic concept of God has thus been completely restored, although in one somewhat allusive remark Ibn Saddiq seems to interpret the attributes in a manner leading in a very different direction. Calling God good or merciful on the basis of his actions serves to arouse within us the desire to imitate this divine mode of action. The divine attributes are thus converted into models of moral action, and their knowledge leads us from the theoretical to the ethical sphere.[123]

That this idea is of far greater importance to Ibn Saddiq than appears from his brief allusion to it is borne out by what he has to say regarding the end and destiny of man. He begins by saying that man was created for the sake of the knowledge of the suprasensual world, but then proceeds to regard this knowledge merely as a preliminary condition for the right conduct leading to eternal happiness. The same notion recurs in connection with the highest form of knowledge, the knowledge of God: it reaches perfection as we recognize God as the *summum bonum,* and attempt to walk in his ways and to imitate him as far as possible. From a metaphysical point of view, the ethical attributes of God describe not his essence, but his effects, yet they provide the real meaning of our knowledge of God.[124] We shall later find Maimonides giving the same ethical twist to what was originally a purely theoretical concept of the knowledge of God, in exactly the same context, and quoting the same biblical verses as Ibn Saddiq. As Maimonides explicitly states that he had never seen Ibn Saddiq's *Microcosm,* a direct historical relationship between the two is ruled out.[125] Nevertheless, the fact remains that Ibn Saddiq preceded Maimonides in a direction which the latter developed with far more impressive intellectual energy.

The last in the line of Jewish Neoplatonists, Abraham b. Meir ibn Ezra (ca. 1092-1167), was not a systematic thinker but a man stirred to the depths by philosophic thinking. His minor works on the names of God and on the commandments of the Torah (*Yesod Morah*), are of little philosophical value. His commentaries on the Bible, however, contain a great many philosophic digressions which clearly exhibit the basic pattern of his thought even if they do not add up to a fully elaborated philosophic system. In fact, any systematization of thoughts would be incompatible with the restless mobility of Ibn Ezra's spirit. The forms in which he expresses his thoughts may serve as an indication of their character. Particularly in the philosophical parts of his commentaries, he strives for enigmatic brevity, leaving it to the reader to guess rather than understand their playful allusiveness. Undoubtedly there is more to Ibn Ezra's manner of writing than preferences of style, or even fear of uttering the ultimate audacity of his thinking. In a way, his veiled language is the expression most adequate to the esoteric quality of his thought.

Ibn Ezra was moved more profoundly than most of his Jewish predecessors by the mysterious depths of Neoplatonism, approaching its metaphysical content more closely than any of the others except Gabirol. This is especially true of his doctrine of God. From a strictly conceptual standpoint, his idea of God is less markedly Neoplatonic than that of Bahya or Ibn Saddiq. But, whereas behind the Neoplatonic formulas of the latter there always lurks the transcendent Creator-God of the Bible, Ibn Ezra's theology is filled with a genuinely pantheistic spirit. "God is the One; he made all and he is all." "He is all and from him cometh all." "He is the One, and there is no being, but by cleaving to him."[126] As in Neoplatonism generally, this pantheism must be understood in an emanationist fashion; God is one with the totality of the world, because he is the primeval force from which all separate powers flow, and whose effects penetrate all things. This relationship is explicitly stated in regard to the supermundane world, which neither came into being nor will pass away, but which exists through God alone.[127] This world is also different from God in that it is not absolute unity as he is. Ibn Ezra also holds with Gabirol that the intelligible substances are composed of matter and form.[128] The biblical account of creation relates only to the terrestrial world, which has a temporal beginning, though even here Ibn Ezra combines the idea of creation with that of emanation by saying that it came into being through the mediation of the eternal intelligible substances.[129] In his account of the relationship of the human soul to the universal soul, he also shows himself more Neoplatonic than others. All Jewish Neoplatonists agree that the human soul has its origin in the universal soul. But Ibn Ezra understands the immortality of the soul not merely as its ascent to the intelligible world, but as its reunion with the world soul.[130] Similarly, he holds prophetic illumination to depend on the relationship of the prophet's soul to the universal soul.[131]

Contemporary Aristotelianism modified Neoplatonic ideas on essential points without affecting their fundamental character. Thus Ibn Ezra speaks of a divine knowledge, but agrees with the Islamic Aristotelians that this knowledge extended only to the general essence, to the formal laws, flowing from God, which govern all sub-

stances; the particular was included in this knowledge only insofar
as it was a link within this chain of formal causality. The same limitation applies to divine providence, which has—at least in the terrestrial
world—only a general character.[132] (The exceptions to the rule are
those men who enjoy a particular divine providence.)[133] These
Aristotelian theorems do not in any measure contradict Ibn Ezra's
fundamentally Neoplatonic tendencies, for this Aristotelianism itself
had undergone Neoplatonic transformation, which provided it with
its own formulation of the idea that God is the primary force from
which all other formal powers permeating the world are descended.
One fundamental difference, however, comes to the fore with the
further development of Islamic Aristotelianism, where matter is not
derived (as in Neoplatonic monism) from God, but is posited—in
dualistic fashion—next to him. God thus becomes merely the highest
principle of the law governing the forms. This entails the limitation
of divine knowledge and providence to the general causality of the
forms only. Ibn Ezra accepts this dualism and consequently understands the creation of the terrestrial world as the imparting of form to
uncreated matter.[134] At this point, however, the various elements of
his philosophy seem to clash. For a thinker who, like Gabirol, holds
even the intelligible substances to be composed of matter and form, it
is a strange inconsistency to maintain that the intelligible world
flowed from God both as to its matter and its form, and yet to regard—
at the same time—the matter of the terrestrial world as an uncreated
substratum of creation. Considering the aphoristic character of Ibn
Ezra's thought, we must not be surprised at finding that old and new
ideas are not yet harmonized.

Judah Halevi

The singular figure of Judah Halevi belongs to no philosophic
school. Only the fact that some strands of his thought link him
with the Neoplatonic tradition justify discussing him in this context.
He was born about 1085 in Toledo. After years of study and wandering, he settled in southern Spain, practicing the profession of a physician in his native city, and possibly later in Cordova. Around the
year 1140 he decided to go to Palestine. He was detained for some
time by his ardent admirers in Egypt, but then proceeded toward
his goal. Whether he ever reached it, we do not know; it is certain

that he died shortly after 1141. Except for Solomon ibn Gabirol, he is the most celebrated Hebrew poet of the Middle Ages, excelling both in the depth and fervor of his feeling, and in his perfect mastery of the Hebrew language. Reading his poetry one forgets that Hebrew was not at the time a living language. He was able to animate with genuine feeling the artificial forms of Arabic prosody, which the Judaeo-Spanish poets had transferred to the Hebrew language. His greatness lies mainly in his religious poetry; no other Jewish poet expresses with such depth of feeling and in such moving tones his pride of Israel's election, his grief at its sufferings, and his longing for redemption. The same emotions also permeate his philosophy, which seeks to show that Judaism was the sole carrier of religious truth and the sole source of religious life, and that the Jewish people was the core of humanity, capable of realizing the religious life.

The full title of the Arabic original of his philosophic work, al-Hazari (usually called Kuzari in Hebrew), is The Book of Argument and Proof in Defense of the Despised Faith. Halevi's apology, unlike that of his rationalist predecessors, does not attempt to identify Judaism with rational truth, but, elevating it above the rational sphere, claims for it exclusive possession of the full truth. He also created an extremely successful literary form to serve his apologetic purpose. In the tenth century the rumor reached Spain that the Khazars, a people living near the Caspian Sea, had embraced Judaism after one of their kings had examined the Islamic, Christian, and Jewish faiths, and had been convinced of the truth of Judaism. The story of this conversion provided the framework for Kuzari. After a brief introduction in which a philosopher, a Christian, and a Muslim unsuccessfully present their opinions, a dialogue ensues between the Khazar king and a Jewish sage; this soon leads to the king's conversion, and goes on to initiate him still further into Jewish doctrine. This framework also provided opportunities for the confrontation and criticism of rival religious and philosophic positions.

Basic to Halevi's own teaching is his criticism of philosophic knowledge of mathematics and logic, and the pseudo knowledge of philosophers, he denies the possibility of rational certainty in the metaphysical sphere. Both the claim of philosophy to provide knowledge of the ultimate grounds of being, and the fact that people admit this claim, are due to a failure to distinguish between the genuine knowledge of mathematics and logic, and the pseudo knowledge of metaphysics.[135] The legitimacy of the distinction is proved by the fact

that there are no opposing schools in mathematics, whereas the views
of the philosophical schools are in violent conflict with each other
and agreement exists only between adherents of the same school.[136]
In his challenge to philosophy, Judah Halevi follows the great Islamic
thinker, al-Ghazali, who had argued a similar position in his book,
The Destruction of Philosophy, in which he presented a thorough
criticism of the theories of the Islamic Aristotelians and a brilliant
refutation of their arguments.[137]

In demonstrating the arbitrariness of philosophic doctrine, Judah
Halevi contents himself with a few illustrations. He scores an interesting point by showing that the doctrine of four elements, then current in natural philosophy, has no basis in experience. We do, of
course, find in our experience the four fundamental qualities: heat,
cold, wetness, and dryness, but never their pure manifestation as
primary elements. Theoretically, we may reduce all bodies to these
elements, but we cannot ascribe real existence to them.[138] He discusses with a good deal of sarcasm the somewhat bizarre theory of
emanation of the Arab Aristotelians, according to whom every separate intellect emits another intellect when it thinks of God, but a
sphere when it thinks of itself.[139] He demonstrates the impossibility
of the doctrine of the immortality of the acquired intellect, by pointing to the absurd conclusions to which it must lead; for example,
immortality begins when a certain amount of knowledge has been
acquired.[140] The object of his criticism is Islamic Aristotelianism because its doctrines contradict his religious views. But even when he
assents to their propositions, he rejects their arguments, because he
desires to derive truth from revelation and not from philosophy.

It is clear that Halevi is striking at the conclusions of philosophy,
not at its foundations. He does not attempt to prove the impossibility
of metaphysics as such, but merely demonstrates the futility of previous metaphysical effort, and from it deduces the unscientific character of metaphysics. Although it has often been said that he is
criticizing basic principles, this is even less true of him than it is of
Ghazali; in fact, his rejection of metaphysics is far from absolute. He
admits that the reduction of the world to a divine principle is also
required by reason, and that philosophy, with its proof of the unity
of the divine cause of the world, is superior to all other explanations
of the world.[141] Thus, the existence and uniqueness of God are also
rational truths, even if they are not capable of stringent proof. Only
the precise determination of the relationship between God and the

world is beyond philosophic knowledge. Even philosophers who are far from the antirationalism of Judah Halevi will admit that the question of whether the world was created, or is an eternal action of God, cannot be decided on philosophical grounds. Halevi's assertion of its insolubility is not unique; a century later the same view was still maintained by so radical a rationalist as Maimonides.[142] Halevi also recognizes a rational truth in the sphere of ethics, affirming the existence of a rational—although clearly utilitarian—morality, independent of revelation.[143] His conception of a rational ethics and its reduction to those norms which make for honesty among thieves should not be construed as a devaluation of ethics. Many of the rationalistic Jewish philosophers followed the same line of reasoning. For Halevi there exists a lower level, wholly within the sphere of reason, and above there is the specific sphere of religious truth, but no clear demarcation of boundaries.

The source of religious truth is biblical revelation. Its authenticity is proved by Saadia's argument that the public nature of the act of revelation excludes the possibility of error.[144] Judah Halevi never wearies of opposing the historical certitude of the fact of revelation to the doubtfulness of philosophic arguments. The interpretation of faith, in revelation, as a kind of historical knowledge is common to him and the rationalist Jewish philosophers, and the concept of religious knowlege thus loses little of its intellectualism. Halevi would agree that if metaphysics were possible, it would embody religious truth just as revelation does. He differs from the rationalists merely in contending that no such metaphysics does in fact exist. The difference lies not so much in his concept of religious truth, as in his evaluation of metaphysics. As against illegitimate attempts at "modernizing" Halevi's doctrine, it must be emphasized that his antimetaphysical polemics do not serve the cause of an autonomous religious truth, but that of a strictly supernatural concept of revelation.

Halevi's interpretation of the phenomena of religious life is also developed in terms of antimetaphysical polemics. The metaphysics of the Arab peripatetics sought to be more than a mere knowledge of God. It claimed for itself the specific function of religion, of establishing communion between man and God. According to this doctrine, the human intellect, through metaphysical knowledge, comes into immediate contact with the "active intellect" of the cosmos, and through it with God. Prophecy, too, is explained in the same way. Halevi shares the view that genuine religious life is a matter of immediate communion between man and God, but he denies the power of the intellect to effect such a communion. His logical criticism of metaphysics indirectly refutes this claim of philosophy, whereas history contradicts it in more direct fashion, since philosophers are not known to have ever attained communion with God or to have risen to prophetic vision. On the contrary, history testifies that prophecy and communion with God are found exclusively outside the circles of philosophers.[145]

Halevi's final and decisive objection is based on the nature of the religious relationship itself. Philosophy claims that human reason is capable, by its own powers, of finding the way toward communion with God. This contradicts the nature of the religious relationship, which is initiated by God alone; only God can show the path whereby man achieves communion with him. Here lies the difference between genuine and pseudo religion. The yearning for communion with God is innate in man, and all men strive to attain it. Philosophy does, in its own way, what the various religions try to do. All of them seek to attain communion with God, but as long as they endeavor to discover the means thereto by themselves, they never get beyond the illusion of such a communion.[146] Only a God-given revelation can show man how to reach his goal. Revelation establishes not only the one true, but the one real religion. Halevi places this real historical religion in sharp contrast with the "intellectual religion" of the philosophers. It is noteworthy that in this context, though nowhere else, he introduces the idea of a religion of reason.[147]

The religious relationship is thus initiated by God and not by man. However, the conflict between Judah Halevi and the Aristotelians must not be reduced to the simple formula that for one the activity in the religious relationship lies with God, and for the other with man. The Aristotelians themselves thought that human thinking was not a purely active process. The human intellect passed from potentiality to actuality through the action of the active intellect, and its specific achievement consisted in acquiring the necessary disposition. On the other hand, Judah Halevi does not exclude all activity from man's religious life. Divine revelation furnishes only the means whereby man can attain communion with God; man himself must apply these means and with their aid acquire the special disposition which will enable him to receive divine influence. Nevertheless,

Judah Halevi felt this fundamental distinction between philosophy and religion more radically than appears from its somewhat formal presentation. The philosophers' god rests unmoved in himself; he knows nothing of man and does not care for him. Man, in his desire for knowledge, uses the laws governing the order of emanations in order to reach his proper goal.[148] Thus, even though from a purely logical viewpoint the act of knowing does not form part of human activity, nonetheless the initiative lies with man, and it is he who elevates himself to the self-sufficient divine world. The God of religion, on the other hand, desires to elevate man to himself. Though man must prepare himself for communion with God by means of the observance of divine commandments, yet it is God who draws him into this communion.

The full depth of the difference between religion and philosophy is revealed by another aspect of it to which Halevi draws attention. For the philosopher, God is merely an object of knowledge towards which he adopts the same theoretical attitude as he does towards other objects of knowledge. As the first cause of things, God is, no doubt, the most important object of knowledge; but it is a logical priority only, which this knowledge of God enjoys from a purely theoretical viewpoint.[149] As an historical account, this characterization of philosophy is decidedly one-sided. Halevi's Aristotelian opponents were far from thinking of God only as an object of knowledge. In fact, Halevi himself attributes to them the opposite tendency of endeavoring to attain communion with God through knowledge, thereby substituting a kind of pseudo religion for true religion. Although incorrect as an historical account, Halevi's view of the relationship of philosophy to God is eminently and profoundly true. It certainly applies to science as such, and correctly describes the attitude of science to its objects and its utter indifference to all non-theoretical distinctions of value. Indeed, such theoretical quiet and absence of passion is not foreign to the contemplative religiosity of Aristotelianism. Thus, Judah Halevi is enabled to place philosophy as mere knowledge of God, in fundamental opposition to religion, which is life with God. The pious man is driven to God not by desire for knowledge, but by his yearning for communion with him. He knows no greater bliss than the nearness of God, and no greater sorrow than separation from him. The yearning heart seeks the God of Abraham; the labor of the intellect is directed toward the God of Aristotle.[150]

The superiority of religion to knowledge finds its psychological expression in Halevi's assumption of a specifically religious faculty which mediates the relationship to God. Whereas man was generally held to be related to the suprasensual world by means of his rational soul, thought to be his highest faculty, Judah Halevi distinguishes from it a superior divine power, which functions as the psychological organon of divine revelation.[151] The ultimate intention of this assumption of a special religious disposition is, perhaps, best interpreted as an attempt to give psychological expression to the specific character of religious experience. Halevi's actual elaboration of his doctrine shows that his immediate purpose was not so much a theory of the principles of religion, as an explanation of the special supernatural status of Israel. The religious faculty was granted solely to the people of Israel. It inhered in the first man, but was inherited by only one chosen representative every generation (who thus formed the core of humanity), until it passed to the whole seed of Jacob. From that time on it has been the property, although in varying degrees, of the entire Jewish people, which is thus the core of humanity.[152] That which Abraham bar Hiyya had attributed to the rational soul, Judah Halevi predicates of the supraintellectual religious faculty; with regard to intellect and morality, on the other hand, he does not admit any distinction between Israel and other nations. However, this religious faculty is only a disposition which must be developed through the divine law. This is accomplished through the ceremonial and cultic parts of the biblical law.

For Judah Halevi the ceremonial law is not an end in itself. It does not minister to the moral or intellectual perfection of man, as the rationalist Jewish philosophers taught, but serves the suprarational purpose of developing man's disposition for communing with God. This has to be understood in a very concrete manner. The observance of the divine law does not of itself produce this result, which depends rather on the specific form of the actions commanded by God. It is true that we may not be able to understand the nature of their efficacy, yet we also know that the effects of certain medicaments depend on their specific composition without understanding the connection of the latter with its effects. Similarly, we know that the vitality of an organism is dependent on the specific structure of its parts, and can be destroyed by even minor changes.[153] Corresponding to these naturalistic analogies illustrating the efficacy of the ceremonial law, Halevi explains the religious superiority of the Holy Land in equally naturalistic fashion in terms of the nature of its climate, which was particularly suitable for the development of Israel's religious faculty. Judah Halevi illustrates the influence of these two factors by comparing Israel to a superior grapevine, which will produce superior grapes only if it is planted in the proper soil and tended in the proper way. The soil is the Holy Land, and the precepts of the ceremonial law are the appropriate cultivation.[154] These ideas are put forward as a theoretical explanation of the biblical doctrine of election. Israel is God's people by reason of its peculiar religious disposition; the Holy Land and its immediate environs, by virtue of its favorable climate, is the only place where prophecy manifests itself; the ceremonial and cultic law of the Torah, that part of the divine legislation which is added to the universal and rational moral law, and which was given to Israel alone, is not a preparatory stage for the universal part of the law, but rather, the means for the specific religious destiny of Israel.

This theoretical formulation of the idea of election has a strong particularistic edge that is foreign to the Bible. It intensifies the distinctiveness of Israel by ascribing to it a specific religious faculty lacking in all other nations. Halevi himself strives to mitigate the harshness of his conclusions. The moral law was given to all peoples; he who observes it may be sure of his heavenly reward.[155] No doubt a narrow and rigid interpretation of Halevi's doctrine of the religious faculty would mean that proselytes were excluded from religious communion with God, but this would be in blatant contradiction to the evident purpose of the main theme of the *Kuzari,* which is the conversion of a pagan king to Judaism. Hence, the notion is qualified in the sense that the highest form of communion, prophecy, is denied to non-Jews, but that everyone who submits to the influence of the Jewish way of life attains the lower forms of communion, which alone apply to the entire nation (the higher levels are reached by outstanding individuals only). In the messianic era this last barrier, too, will fall and Israel will assimilate to itself the other nations, even as the seed hidden in the earth absorbs its materials.[156]

Although undoubtedly Halevi's immediate purpose was solely to justify the special position of the Jewish people, yet the significance of his formulations is more extensive, since they include a description of the specific character of the religious life which, as we have seen, is accorded in its fullness to Israel only. Since the excellence of the Jewish people is due to its communion with God, a description of this excellence amounts to a description of the nature of this communion. One aspect of the latter is completely external: the special, supernatural providence governing the destinies of the Jewish people rests upon this communion between God and Israel. The rest of humanity is subject to the workings of the law of nature, and to it Judah Halevi applies the philosophic concept of "general providence," which he identifies with the teleological order of things.[157] A supernatural divine providence, manifesting itself in reward and punishment, exists only for Israel, not only in the biblical past, but continuing into the present and governing the scattered members of the Jewish people. In keeping with the basic intention of Judah Halevi's doctrine, however, greater significance attaches to the internal communion of the soul with God than to the merely external link. The former is the purpose of Israel's election, and it is this life with God that elevates the soul above the level of merely intellectual life.

The highest form of communion with God is granted to the prophets. They comprehend God through immediate experience, which is as distinct from the conceptual philosophic knowledge of God as the immediate certainty of intuition is distinct from the lifelessness of discursive thought. The God of the prophets is not the supreme abstract cause of the world, but a living presence permeating everything above and beyond the limitations of nature. He is not simply "God" but "their God."[158] Even prophets, however, cannot comprehend the presence of God without any mediation whatsoever. God reveals himself to them in sensual manifestations which serve as signs of his presence. This certitude of God based on immediate perception is the foundation for the love of God which distinguishes religion from philosophy. In this connection Judah Halevi develops his distinction between the God of Aristotle and the God of Abraham. On the lower level of religious life there is no difference between prophets and average believers, since religious life invariably means communion with God. The difference between prophecy and normal religious life is one of degree, not of essence. As communion with God, all religion transcends nature. Whereas the Aristotelian considers prophecy the expression of the natural powers of man raised to their highest pitch, Judah Halevi regards every religion as a lower degree of the supernatural and suprarational gift of prophecy.[159] This description of the life of the pious man is similar to that of the prophet. The pious man lacks only the specific prophetic revelations, mediated by means of sensual images. He too lives in the presence of God, although in a more indeterminate form of it, for the exact analysis of which Judah Halevi lacks the conceptual tools. The effect of this experience of God is that devotion of the soul to God which intellectual knowledge alone can never produce.[160] Prayer and worship are the climax of the pious man's life; through them he acquires the power which permeates his everyday life.

In accordance with his religious viewpoint, Judah Halevi explicitly denies the ideal of extreme asceticism and inward contemplation; in this he is closer to the fundamental attitude of Judaism than the Jewish Neoplatonists. In opposition to this ideal he portrays a religious life in which the active fulfillment of the divine will is held to be of equal value with the practice of recollection in prayer and devotion. The entire life of the pious man is sanctified by the performance of the religious acts commanded by divine law, and thus becomes a service of joyous obedience.[161] The description of this form of life develops into a complete religious ethic, in which Judah Halevi's moral ideal fully unfolds itself. Even the rational ethics of the *Kuzari* outgrows its initial utilitarianism, and absorbs such values as love of one's fellow man, humility, and perfection of the soul.[162]

It is here that Halevi fully develops his conception of the ideal moral personality. The pious man is portrayed as a ruler, in complete control of the powers of his soul, to each of which he appoints its specific functions, thus establishing a completely harmonious life. This viewpoint is easily recognized as Platonic, since it applies to the pious man what Plato had said about the philosopher. The Platonic origin is even more evident when we consider that the judge deciding the uses of the powers of the soul is none other than reason. Halevi deviates from Plato, however, in that he orients the entire order of life to the supraintellectual, religious destiny of man. The pious man rules over the powers of his soul in order to serve God through them, and to rise to the "angelic" heights of communion with God.[163] One of the principal elements of piety is joy in God. The pious man attains the full bliss of communion with God in this world, viewing it as an earnest of the future life of the soul in the hereafter. To him the bliss of the world-to-come is not some far-off event: he anticipates it in this life, and in his communion with God he feels assured of eternal life.[164]

Judah Halevi sees no contradiction between this inward conception of the religious life, and the natural, almost mechanical way in which it is brought about. For an historical understanding of his doctrine it is quite easy to see how these two sides of his concept of religion combined. His description of the religious life originated from his immediate observation of religious phenomena; their "reification" is due to their subsequent interpretation in terms of given metaphysical categories. Strange as it may seem at first glance, the influence of Neoplatonic metaphysics is most marked at this point. The assumption of a special faculty of soul mediating the communion of elect human beings is reminiscent of the old Greek idea of the *theios anthropos,* the "divine man." The precise formulation of this idea, to which Judah Halevi is indebted, is difficult to ascertain, though the special position which he accords the religious faculty brings to mind Proclus' notion of a suprarational faculty of the soul upon which our knowledge of the divine is founded.[165]

More important, however, is the connection between Halevi's general theory of the religious process and the basic categories of Neoplatonic metaphysics. Forms are continually streaming down from the higher to the lower world, and the beings of the lower world receive them as the disposition of their matter permits. Despite its underlying dualism of form and matter, this notion is less Aristotelian than Neoplatonic, since the idea of forms descending from the upper to the lower world is foreign to the original Aristotelian system, and appears only among those Aristotelians who had undergone Neoplatonic influence. Judah Halevi makes sweeping use of this principle of explanation. Provided it has the proper disposition, matter can receive the vegetative soul together with the corresponding form of life; at a higher level of perfection, it will receive the vital or animal soul; on the still higher level of the human organism, it will receive the rational soul. The notion of a religious faculty represents a new species in the chain of being. The same process which engenders the other levels of being produces this one. Just as the vegetative soul, to which Judah Halevi gives the Stoic-Neoplatonic name of *nature,* "chooses" the essences capable of receiving it, so also do the animal and the rational souls, and even the highest "angelic" soul-form.[166] The faculties belonging to each of these forms are at first only potential, and must be actualized. This process depends upon the conditions in which the development of the organism takes place. Mention has already been made of the simile of the vine, which requires the right kind of soil and cultivation if it is to yield fruit according to its capacity. The same idea, applied to individual men, is elaborated in great detail as a "philosophic" doctrine, though clearly approved of by Judah Halevi. The identical form of human essence is impressed on individual humans in varying degrees of perfection; in addition to inherited dispositions, it depends on such external circumstances as climate, food, and study.[167]

Following ancient sources, Judah Halevi develops a complete environmentalist theory, which he also applies to the evolution of the religious disposition of the Jewish people. This mere potentiality requires certain external conditions, such as the climatic effects of the Holy Land, and the actions prescribed by the divine law, in order to develop the capacity of absorbing the divine influx and realizing the communion with God. It thus happens that the very philosophy which Judah Halevi so strenuously opposes provides him with the principles by which he interprets religious phenomena. His theory of the almost "natural" effects of religious acts is based less on a sacramental conception of the religious commandments than on their metaphysical understanding as links in a cosmic order.

Judah Halevi's world view thus approaches that of the Neoplatonists and Aristotelians, and actually tends to obliterate the religious differences between them. The variety of form of the powers accorded to the different separate bodies depends on the disposition of their matter. Wherever the necessary disposition exists, the corresponding form is sure to realize itself. Divine activity produces form whenever the necessary conditions exist in matter. Attributing this to God's goodness, which denies to no being the perfection of which it is capable, this explanation is not very different from the philosophic explanation of the emanation of forms from God.[168] This necessity applies to the highest religious form and to communion with God, of which it is the condition. It is supernatural in that it is essentially different from all other spheres of natural process, but within its own sphere, as everywhere else, the same law operates. This would imply that although another, higher level of being is added, the basic conception of the cosmic process remains the same. The similarity to the philosophic world picture is strengthened by Halevi's declaration that, if necessary, religion could even come to terms with the assumption of an uncreated matter.[169]

All this, however, does not affect the central core of Halevi's teaching. In the first place, he deviates from the current philosophical doctrine of emanation by ascribing the production of forms directly to God, and denying the existence of mediating beings between God and the world.[170] There is, of course, causality inherent in all things, but it is completely natural and mechanical in character. Halevi considers the assumption of suprasensual essences producing forms, as a kind of polytheism and as a denial of the unique creative activity of God.[171] A parallel situation occurred at the beginning of the modern period when the development of creative principles of form from natural explanation and the preference for mechanical explanation were justified by the argument that no purposive forces were possible outside God. God thus becomes the sole principle of form.

All of this, however, does not alter the conception of divine causality itself. There still remains the possibility that the unity of the divine principle of form *necessarily* produces the plurality of individual forms according to the disposition of matter. But this is hardly a view to be held by Judah Halevi, who emphatically distinguishes the God of Israel, who works miracles and freely interferes in the course of the world which he created, from the god of philosophy, the first cause of the world, acting by an inner necessity. The contradictions are somewhat harmonized by the distinction between the original creative act of God and his continual influence upon the world. Creation was an act of free divine will, which brought the world into existence "when and how it listed," and of divine wisdom, which fixed the order of the world according to a plan.[172] All substances and their dispositions are ultimately derived from this spontaneous act of creation, and the permanent relation between form and matter is also regulated by this order, fixed at the creation of the world.

Events within this world thus take place according to a fixed order, which even includes divine causality. This is a special variation of the usual distinction between God's creative act and his continued action within nature. But the matter is complicated by the fact that the supernatural religious sphere is included in the natural nexus, while at the same time it is supposed to manifest the miraculous operation of God. No doubt Judah Halevi attributes God's immanent action in the world to spontaneous divine causality, and it is in earnest that he ascribes the bestowal of forms on adequately disposed matter to the grace of God. By interpreting the divine action in terms of the metaphysical nexus of matter and form, however, he arrives at a causal limitation of divine operation which is irreconcilable with his basic intention. Halevi attempts to relate the communion of man with God and the resultant determination of the destiny of the elect to certain conditions, yet at the same time he regards divine providence as a manifestation of the transcendent sovereignty of divine will, always free to irrupt into the course of the world. These two conceptions of the divine activity—God as the ultimate formal principle of things, and God as the omnipotent will governing the course of the world—are never synthesized into an organic unity.[173]

Contradictions are evident in other parts of Halevi's writings. In his doctrine of the essence of God, he follows the rationalist Jewish philosophers, holding that the unity of God excludes any positive statement concerning his essence. The attributes which we predicated of God, unless they merely denote his actions or our relationship to him, must be considered as negations.[174] At first glance it might appear that this concept was limited to the rationalist idea of God, whereas the notion of the divine conveyed by the biblical revelation, and expressed in the Tetragrammaton and its correlated attributes, had a positive content. Closer examination, however, shows that the idea of God is not changed by revelation;[175] a new aspect of God's *modus operandi* is merely made apparent. The rational concept of God understands him only from the viewpoint of his natural effects, while the prophetic notion of God, since it is the expression of the prophetic experience, knows him in the fullness and immediacy of his acts. But the same conception of the divine essence underlies both viewpoints. Judah Halevi's religious idea of God advances a new theory of divine action, not of divine essence. The God of Abraham, to whom the soul cleaves in yearning and longing, is conceived metaphysically in terms of the Neoplatonic idea of God.

4 Aristotelianism
and Its Opponents

The Concepts of God
and the World in Aristotelianism
and in Revealed Religion

IN THE middle of the twelfth century Aristotelianism displaced Neo-platonism as the dominating influence in Jewish philosophy of religion. This change was already noticeable in the thought of Abraham ibn Ezra, and Judah Halevi's polemic was directed against philosophy in an Aristotelian garb. It is true that the first work of Jewish Aristotelianism, Abraham ibn Daud's *The Exalted Faith* (*Emunah Ramah*), was not published until some decades after the *Kuzari*. Yet it stands to reason that Judah Halevi would not have directed his attacks at the Aristotelian system if it had not counted adherents among his contemporaries. Jewish Aristotelianism is surely older than its literary expression. It is certainly no complete innovation with regard to Neoplatonism. Islamic and Jewish Neoplatonism had absorbed many Aristotelian elements in addition to those already present in the original Neoplatonic system; conversely, Aristotelianism had undergone a Neoplatonic transformation in the hands of its Islamic adherents. Its metaphysical structure was radically transformed by the adoption of the doctrine of emanation. The world of conceptual forms now appeared as the unfolding of a unitary principle of form; to the extent that even matter was originally regarded as a link in the chain of emanations, Aristotelianism was displaced by a completely monistic world view.[1] Together with its metaphysics, the religious attitude of Neoplatonism invaded the Aristotelian system, and the Aristotelian ideal of the eudaemonism of knowledge received a religious interpretation, entirely foreign to its original intention. The true purpose of knowledge was now defined as the comprehension of the suprasensual world, and the self-sufficient bliss of knowledge became the blessedness of communion with God, mediated through knowledge.[2] This development, already adumbrated in antiquity by the Neoplatonic commentators on Aristotle, was fully elaborated in the Islamic Middle Ages.

In spite of this influence, however, the Aristotelian foundations of the system held its own; its fundamental ideas might be pushed aside, but they were never completely silenced. Not only were the Neoplatonic doctrines reformulated in a different terminology, but actual Aristotelian ideas were left intact beside them. A few brief hints concerning some points of particular importance to the philosophy of religion must suffice here. The extension of the doctrine of emanation to matter was discarded in due course, and the ancient dualism of form and matter re-established. God was consequently the source of the essence of forms only; the world came into being by God shaping or forming matter. As in Aristotle, God himself was defined, from the beginning, as the supreme thought thinking itself.[3] At first an unsuccessful compromise was made to combine this formula with the Neoplatonic idea of the divine One that is above all thinking. At any rate, the definition launched the problem which occupied interpreters of Aristotle until our own day, whether and to what extent the knowledge that God has of himself includes a knowledge of the world derived from him. No longer conceived in Neoplatonic fashion as an emanation from the universal soul, essentially independent of the body, the soul was now defined as the form of the body,[4] and as a result all the ancient difficulties about the Aristotelian doctrine of immortality were revived. The theory of knowledge, too, turned from the Platonic doctrine of recollection— the metaphysical aspects of which had been preserved in Neoplatonism—to the Aristotelian theory of abstraction.[5] Although this epistemology placed human thinking in a transcendental context by means of the doctrine of the illumination of the passive human intellect by the active cosmic intellect—a doctrine which remained ultimately incompatible with the Aristotelian theory of abstraction— it tied human thought more firmly to its sensual presuppositions than Neoplatonism ever could. This changed conception of knowledge also entailed a change in the structure of the system, which now re-emphasized the presuppositions of metaphysics in logic and the natural sciences, maintaining that the soul's ascent to metaphysical knowledge would have to start from the latter. To a greater or lesser degree, the intellectualist character of the Aristotelian ideal of life colored all religious formulations. In the last resort, even the blessedness of communion with God was, at least to some extent, conceived as a participation in the eudaemonism of divine knowledge.[6]

Most of these traits emphasize the characteristic differences of philosophical religion from the revealed religion. Although the tension between the two existed in Neoplatonism, it emerged more forcibly in the conceptual system of Arisotelianism, whose scholastic precision differed in this respect not only from Neoplatonism in general but from its attenuated, popular form so widespread in the Islamic world in particular. It is no surprise, therefore, that Avicenna's systematic presentation was immediately followed by Ghazali's attack on philosophy, and that Judah Halevi likewise attacked Aristotelian philosophy as the enemy of revealed religion. Both parties were thus clearly aware of the contrast between the philosophical and the religious views of the world. Islamic Aristotelianism found its champion in Averroës, who developed the Aristotelian system in a more radical fashion than ever before. Jewish Aristotelians attempted to reconcile the oppositions on the basis of the Aristotelian system. Previously, they had quietly attempted to reach a working compromise between religious and philosophic views; now the relationship between the two became the conscious focus and dominant problem of all philosophic inquiry. It may be useful, therefore, before proceeding with our account of philosophical developments, to present the problem in broad outline, and to take up again—in a more systematic context—a number of points previously mentioned only in passing.

This problem is extremely complex because these contrasting spiritual worlds show points of contact and of opposition in equally strong measure. These points of agreement and disagreement cannot simply be distributed over individual doctrines, as they relate to the two systems rather than to points of details. On the one hand, the Aristotelian and Neoplatonic philosophies appear as decisive confirmations of the fundamental tenet of religious monotheism by positing one God as the highest principle of reality. If the God of Aristotle as the prime mover still fell short of the fully developed idea of a highest cause of the world, Neoplatonism turned the divine One into the source of all being and was followed in this by the later, emanationist Aristotelianism. The spirits of the spheres of the Aristotelian system, as well as the forms of the terrestrial world—indeed, at first even matter—were derived from God, who was the source of all causality. Philosophic proofs of the existence of God thus appeared as scientific validation of the monotheistic idea. Arguments drawn from Greek philosophy were utilized in the Kalam; later, they were overtly taken over. A similar scientific confirmation was found for religious faith in the purposiveness of the created order. The

Aristotelian explanation of the world viewed everything teleologically. All changes were referred to the "forms" of things, conceived as purposive forces. This immanent teleological order of existence, transformed by both Neoplatonism and the later Aristotelianism influenced by it, turned this *immanent* teleology into a transcendental one. Since all forms are derived from God, the inner teleological nexus of all things becomes an effect of the supreme, divine, final cause, and the plurality of individual purposes is viewed as part of a wider teleological order pointing back to God. Both philosophy and religion find in the purposiveness of the world a manifestation of the perfection of its divine origin. In agreement with the religious belief in providence, scientific philosophy held that the order of the world, since it was grounded in God, realized the good of all creatures. There is one detail in this doctrine that brings it even closer to the religious idea of providence: the philosophical notion of a continual influx of forms into the world strengthens the permanent dependence of the teleological nexus upon God.[7]

When applied to man, the most important consequence—from the religious point of view—of this theory of reality is its conception of the relationship between body and soul. Both Neoplatonism and Aristotelianism subordinate the body to the soul. The idea of the independence of the soul is developed most clearly and simply by Neoplatonism, which considers the individual soul as an emanation of the universal soul, and holds the soul to be different in substance from the body. Though the Aristotelian doctrine of the soul as the "principle of form" of the body excludes such a fundamental dualism, it, too, asserts that the thinking spirit was independent of the body.

The idea of immortality implicit in the Neoplatonic concept of the soul could thus be adopted by Aristotelian psychology and applied to the highest thinking portion of the soul. The religious belief in immortality thus becomes a scientific idea, and—as in the case of the proofs of the existence of God—the proofs of the immortality and the immateriality of the soul appear as scientific confirmations of religious truth.

This doctrine of man has two other, no less important corollaries. The first bears on the metaphysical relation of the spirit to God. The general connection of the terrestrial world with the form-giving divine principle appears to the human spirit as illumination by the divine spirit.[8] All human knowledge is interpreted as the reception of conceptual forms coming from the higher world of the spirit; knowledge is the participation of human thought in the realm of truth, which is realized, in timeless permanence, in the pure world of spirit. The thinking spirit does not produce truth but receives it directly from the active intellect, and ultimately from God. The concept of knowledge easily finds its place within the general framework of this concept. The second corollary concerns the realm of ethics. The metaphysical conception of the nature of man provides the basis for an ideal of life which, both in its Neoplatonic and Aristotelian versions, of necessity, appeared close to that of a religious ethics. The ethics of Neoplatonism had, of itself, a religious character. It enjoined upon man the task of liberating himself from the chains of sensuality, and of striving to elevate himself through moral and spiritual purification to his celestial home. Though this trait is absent from Aristotelian ethics, the scientific idealism of the latter shares with religion the demand of disciplining the will and of dominating the passions by reason. The religious reinterpretation of this idealism yielded a result very similar to Neoplatonism. In this way, the moral demands of revealed religion were scientifically justified; traditional religion and philosophical ethics agreed in making man's happiness in the future world conditional upon his fulfilling ethical imperatives. Thus philosophy exhibited an exact parallel to the interconnected pattern of religious ideas.

The same interconnected pattern of ideas, however, revealed radical contradictions. The God of philosophy, whether in the Neoplatonic version of the highest unity or in the Aristotelian version of the highest thought, is radically different from that of the personal, willing, and ethical God of the monotheistic religions. Though medieval thinkers remained for a long time unaware of the profound difference in the conception of the essence of God, and though they thought that they could equate the transcendence of the Neoplatonic One, who is above and beyond all conceptual determinations, with the majesty of the biblical God, to whom nothing created can be compared, yet the gap between the respective conceptions of the divine causality was less easily bridged. According to a system of emanation, God is the highest principle of power, unfolding itself in the fullness of individual powers. He was the cause of the world, not in the sense of a creative will, but as the primeval power, which, of necessity, produced the multiplicity of separate powers.[9] The teleological order of reality was an expression of this interconnection of powers, the active forms being the forces realizing this order and the representatives of causal interrelation of all processes, extending in an unbroken continuum from God to the lowest level of the reality of the senses. The divine concern for things extends only as far as their general causal interconnectedness. Hence, a divine providence, if it is to mean anything at all, can only mean the purposive causality of all processes as grounded in God.

The doctrine of man is constructed within this context and in strict correspondence to its basic ideas. The soul of man, whether in Neoplatonic or Aristotelian versions, is conceived as a special type of active form flowing down from the higher world, and its destiny is determined by the laws corresponding to its essence. This is seen most clearly in the Aristotelian doctrine that the immortality of the acquired intellect is dependent upon the level of knowledge reached.[10] Here the ethical consequences, too, become evident. Immortality is a necessary consequence of the level of knowledge reached; it is thus intellectually and not morally determined. Moral perfection serves an ultimately intellectual end; it is a means and not an end in itself. This does not apply strictly to pure Neoplatonism, though even here the significance of moral action is essentially cathartic, since it enables the soul to return again to the intelligible world. The resultant interpretation of the nature of man's relationship to God is of particular importance, for the relationship loses its personal character, and becomes part of the general law of the cosmic order. The nexus of effects extending from God down to the terrestrial world operates to bind the duly qualified soul to God by elevating it to the spiritual world immediately emanating from him. The same nexus of effects also mediates the prophetic illumination. Instead of the conception of prophecy as a mission, we now have prophecy as the infusion of the light of knowledge into the prophet's spirit, according to fixed causal laws.[11] Of course, this is not just metaphysics; it is also religion. But it is the religion of mysticism or contemplation, not the personal religion of monotheism.

At the center of this system stands the idea of a dynamic nexus of effects, establishing a teleological as well as causal order of things, and combining the laws of nature and the laws of knowledge in a systematic unity. The main representative of this unity is the idea of form, which, since Aristotle, served both as a concept and as an active power. Once processes are viewed as realizations, then conceptual relations automatically become relations between effects.

Both viewpoints combine in the idea of emanation, which denotes at one and the same time the unfolding of concepts from an ultimate principle and the emergence of powers from an ultimate source of power. These two sets of ideas are brought into still closer relation by a third type of nexus which, like the preceding, also derived from the idea of form. A special, but very important variation of the idea of form defines form as thinking spirit. This conception of the intellect, which is evidently based on the doctrine of the identity of the act of thinking with the thought, permits interpretation of the merely ideal conceptual nexus as a real and actual thinking nexus. The process of emanation thus becomes a sequence of intellectual essences, in each of which the same conceptual content continues to unfold into a multiplicity of its elements. This is how the Islamic Aristotelians, in particular, interpreted the process of emanation. From another viewpoint these thinking essences are thought of as dynamic potencies. Thanks to their energy, by which one potency produces another, they communicate the powers of the active forms to the corporeal world—since these same forms are present in human thought as concepts.[12] In this way, all aspects of the interrelation of reality can be viewed as manifestations of the divine principle of form.

This dynamic regularity circumscribes and defines the natural order of cosmic processes. Unlike modern natural philosophy, which confines the concept of nature to immanent relationships within empirical reality, the medieval notion of a natural order includes the suprasensual reality right up to God. The boundary between the natural and the supernatural is marked by the opposition between the necessary interconnection of forces in the cosmos and the free, spontaneous providence of God. Hence, belief in magic and astrology is easily compatible with a naturalistic interpretation of the world, whereas miracles, in the strict sense, are excluded. This radical limitation to a naturalistic principle of explanation was considered as a kind of freethinking by the later Middle Ages. Atheists, such as the Dahriya, presented no problem to late medieval philosophy; atheism had been scientifically liquidated by the Aristotelian proofs of the existence of God. To be a freethinker now meant to deny the existence of a transcendental sphere beyond the divinely established natural order. The struggle by Judaism and Christianity in the last centuries of the Middle Ages against "unbelief" was really aimed at this kind of freethinking. In its most extreme form, this philosophy actually denied revealed religion as such. A more moderate version attempted to interpret revealed religion in a manner which kept it within the framework of a naturalistic world view. The parallelism between the religious and the philosophic world views outlined above marked out the lines along which such attempts would proceed. Ultimately, they represented an effort to transpose the teleology of a divine will into a teleology of the dynamic regularity of nature. The inner congeniality of these two views was felt so strongly that no one realized the arbitrariness involved. People thought they were interpreting the idea of revelation, not reinterpreting, let alone changing its validity, since this seemed to be guaranteed by the philosophical concept of a natural revelation. Historical revelation was recognized and accepted in these terms. The formal possibility of combining historical revelation with a philosophic world view was provided by the notion that the former was addressed to the masses, to whose conceptual reach it was matched. Behind the literal meaning was concealed the truer and deeper meaning, accessible to the aristocrats of thought, the philosophers. The personalist and supernaturalist conception of religion was its exoteric form, the dynamist-naturalist one enshrined its true esoteric significance.[13]

From the very beginning, though not with equal consistency, the Islamic Aristotelians had taken this path, adapting the doctrines of Islam to the Aristotelian system as they understood it. Thus they interpreted the Islamic notion of God in terms of their own, more Neoplatonic—or alternatively, more Aristotelian—concept of God; the doctrine of the creation of the world, in terms of their theory of an eternal emanation of the world from God; the omniscience of God, in terms of his knowledge of the regularity of active forms, ultimately founded in him; the belief in providence, in terms of the general purposiveness of all being. Similarly, the doctrines of revelation and immortality of the soul were adapted to corresponding philosophic ideas. At the same time, the Islamic doctors sought to come as close as possible to religious ideas, and to get the maximum for religion out of philosophy. Thus Avicenna explains in great detail that the limitation of divine knowledge to the general laws of the forms governing all things was not intended to exclude God's knowledge of individual things. The latter was implicit in his knowledge of the general causality of being, even if only as links in the chain of the whole natural nexus. Nevertheless, the philosophic theologians sought to broaden this notion so that not even a speck of dust would remain hidden from the knowledge of God.[14] Similar attempts were probably made to justify the doctrine of divine providence and we may, perhaps, assume that the Jewish philosophers who extended the doctrine of natural providence to apply to the individual human being were following the example of Islamic doctors.[15]

Even the concept of miracles was at least partially justified by Avicenna when he argued that outstanding men like the prophets, who stood in an immediate relationship with the world of spirit, could absorb special powers which would enable them to produce extraordinary effects beyond normal human capacities.[16] Avicenna even succeeded in interpreting Aristotle's concept of the soul in a way which safeguarded the substantial difference of the soul from the body; hence immortality could be ascribed to the soul as such and was no longer restricted to the acquired intellect alone.[17] Moreover, it appeared that the Aristotelians at times surrendered, or at least reinterpreted, fundamental axioms of philosophy in favor of the religious viewpoint. Al-Farabi defended Aristotle at great length against the charge of having taught the eternity of the world. Aristotle's denial of a temporal beginning of the world meant only that the universe as a whole, unlike individual things, could not have come into being in time, but that it was produced by a supratemporal act; only within such an already existing world was it possible to speak of temporal succession.[18]

In the light of this philosophic readiness to meet religion more than halfway, it is difficult to understand how Ghazali and Judah Halevi could accuse the Aristotelians of denying the fundamental doctrines of religion.[19] Even if we allow for a tendentious presentation of philosophy by its opponents, this answer would hardly do for the Jewish Aristotelians, who could have had no conceivable reason for broadening the gap between Aristotelianism and religion. Maimonides himself considered the doctrine of the eternity of the world as genuinely Aristotelian—on the authority of al-Farabi[20]—and this is only one of the points wherein his interpretation of Aristotelianism agrees with that of the anti-Aristotelians. His presentation of the Aristotelian doctrine of divine knowledge, and his account of the theory of the purely natural character of prophecy, are far more definite and unequivocal than those of the Islamic Aristotelians.[21] The reason can only be that Maimonides rejected all attempts to gloss over the philosophic attitude, and preferred to state what seemed to him the genuine Aristotelian position. That the Aristotelians themselves were not averse to accommodation and glossing over difficulties is evident. Even Averroës, the most extreme of the Aristotelians, did not disdain such tactics, although inside philosophic circles everybody knew what they were worth. Maimonides and subsequent Jewish Aristotelians, however, took Aristotelianism for what it was and understood perfectly how Islam had been reinterpreted in terms of it; they were simply not prepared to follow the Islamic example. Having no desire to conceal the opposition between philosophy and revealed religion, they undertook to formulate the problem in all its sharpness and to seek a solution that would overcome it from within.

Abraham ibn Daud

The first Jewish Aristotelian, Abraham ibn Daud of Toledo (d. ca. 1180 as a martyr), seems unaware of the above-mentioned problems in their acuteness. His work, *The Exalted Faith* (Hebrew, *Emunah Ramah*), gives an impression of complete harmony between Judaism and Aristotelian philosophy. An energetic rationalist, he teaches that true philosophy is in complete agreement with religion, and that only those who are too weak to hold the light of faith in one hand and the light of science in the other allow the former to be extinguished when they light the latter.[22] It is Judaism's greatest glory that the truth at which science arrived after long toil, had, from ancient times, been the common property of the entire Jewish people.[23] In concrete terms, this declaration of the principle of complete agreement between religious and scientific truth means for Ibn Daud the agreement of Judaism with Aristotelianism in the form the latter had been given by the Arabic Aristotelians, particularly Avicenna, whom he followed closely. For the most part, his philosophy is only a lucid and systematic presentation of the main lines of Avicenna's basic teaching. Avoiding all those aspects of the system which might conflict with monotheistic religion, Ibn Daud was especially careful to eliminate the doctrine of the emanation of the world from God, but he did not undertake a profound examination of his position. Like most Jewish Neoplatonists, he simply approximated or equated philosophic theories and religious ideas, circumventing rather than solving the problem of their difference. It is not surprising that once

Maimonides had placed the issues neglected by Ibn Daud at the center of philosophic discussion, the latter's work lost in importance. Maimonides may have drawn on it for some minor points, but it exerted no influence[24] upon the further development of philosophy. In fact, Ibn Daud's reputation rests mainly on his widely read historical work, *The Book of Tradition* (Hebrew, *Sefer ha-Kabbalah*). *The Exalted Faith,* whose Arabic original is now lost, though composed in 1161 was not translated into Hebrew until the end of the fourteenth century. Of the two translations, one entitled *Emunah Nissa'ah* is still unpublished; the other, entitled *Emunah Ramah* was first published in 1852. But even translations failed to arouse greater interest in the book.

At the beginning of his work, Ibn Daud states that he wrote it in order to solve the difficulties connected with the problem of the freedom of the will, since elucidation and discussion of these difficulties required a presentation of basic metaphysical and religio-philosophical truths.[25] The book itself gives no evidence of this supposed central importance of the problem of the freedom of the will, the latter being but one of many questions on the philosophy of religion, all of which are treated with equal attention. The actual discussion of the problems of the philosophy of religion is preceded by what is held to be a necessary and detailed account of the basic principles of Aristotelian physics and metaphysics. Thus the discussion of general principles of natural philosophy and the doctrine of matter, form, and motion provide material for the proof of the existence of God. Similarly, the lengthy presentation of Aristotelian psychology serves to prove the immortality of the soul and its relationship to immaterial essences.

The arguments for the existence of God are those of Islamic Aristotelianism beginning with the Aristotelian proof of the existence of a prime mover. Every movement presupposes the existence of a moving cause, distinct from the object moved; since an infinitely regressing series is impossible, we must of necessity posit the existence of a first principle of movement. This unmoved mover has infinite power, and since all bodies and their inherent powers are finite, his infinity of necessity entails his incorporeality.[26] To this is added another proof already developed by al-Farabi and Avicenna: the merely contingent being of all things must have its source in a being which necessarily exists. In the form in which Ibn Daud, like all subsequent Jewish philosophers, states this argument from his Islamic predeces-

sors, the purely conceptual deduction from possible to necessary existence is combined with the causal deduction relating to a first cause;
the nerve of the argument seems to be the idea that the series of
causes necessarily leads to a first cause. According to Ibn Daud's definition, something can be said to be a possible existent if its existence
is due to something else; its actual existence consequently implies
the existence of its cause. Exactly as in the original Aristotelian argument, the impossibility of an infinite regress is invoked at this point
in order to infer a being whose existence was uncaused.[27]

This proof differs from the original Aristotelian argument only
in that it wants to establish a first cause of existence instead of a first
cause of motion. Although the argument from possible to necessary
existence is not developed by Ibn Daud in a full and independent
form, it is nevertheless contained implicitly in his discussion. There
are, in fact, two meanings to the concept of possibility. According to
one, it is merely another way of saying that something is caused. But
something may also be said to have possible existence if its essence
alone does not determine whether or not it should in fact exist. As
against this, something can be said to be necessarily existent if its
essence implies its existence.[28] The formulation of both concepts is a
matter of purely conceptual deduction of necessity from contingency.
If all things had merely possible existence, there could be no reality.
Reality is possible only because there is a being whose essence implies
existence. This demand of a congruence of essence and existence in
the ultimate ground of the world clearly contains the main element
of the ontological proof of the existence of God, with the difference
that here we have as a mere postulate what the latter endeavors to
establish by deduction.

As stated, this development of the original Aristotelian argument
transformed the prime mover of the world into the cause of being of
reality. Whereas at the side of Aristotle's God there existed a world
which he merely set into motion; now, God causes the existence of
all things. Only this view permits a rigorous demonstration of the
unity of God too, for the proof of the existence of a prime mover
does not necessarily lead to a sole, ultimate and immaterial cause of
motion. If we assume an immaterial cause of movement for every
heavenly sphere, these immaterial essences might well coexist independently with God, with God supreme only in the sense of being
the highest of these causes of motion. From God's necessary existence,
however, his unity can be strictly deduced. Following Avicenna, Ibn

Daud shows that there can be only one existing essence; all other beings, whether material or immaterial, are derived from it.[29] Even the intelligences of the celestial spheres have essntially only a possible existence, which is realized by God. Hence plurality is of their very being, which combines possible existence—due to their essence—and necessary existence, which is due to God.[30] But only an absolutely necessary existent can be—in fact must be—utterly simple. Every multiplicity of determination within an essence implies that the elements which it contains were united by a higher cause, and hence it would cease to be a necessary existence.

But this transformation of the Aristotelian concept of God into the notion of a cause of the world by no means led the Islamic Aristotelians to the idea of a Creator-God as taught by Judaism and Islam. The adoption of the Neoplatonic theory of emanation by the Islamic Aristotelians has already been described. Their version, however, substituted for the Neoplatonic series of intellect, soul, and nature the sequence of the immaterial intelligences of the spheres; the last of these, the active intellect, also controlled the terrestrial world. Moreover, each of these intelligences was held to emanate not only the spirit of the following sphere, but also a new sphere together with its soul. These variations in details did not, however, affect the basic principle. Ibn Daud, while faithfully repeating this theory, finally rejects the attempt to explain the celestial spheres and the intelligences as emanations from God. Less objectionable is the view that the terrestrial world emanated from the supraterrestrial world and its controlling intelligences,[31] though elsewhere he regards heaven and earth as immediate creations of God; the divine activity is mediated by the intelligences of the spheres only in regard to the details of events in the world.[32]

But this rejection of the doctrine of universal emanation was not justified on grounds of principle; on the contrary, this crucial point clearly illustrated what we have seen as the lack of a firm attitude based on insight into the fundamental differences between Aristotelianism and the Jewish religion. Ibn Daud rejected the doctrine as "unproven"; he accused it of going beyond the limits of human knowledge, and losing itself in pure arbitrariness. As the spirit of man was unable to comprehend how the world proceeded from God, every attempt to penetrate this ultimate mystery of the origin of the world was a misuse of our powers. We can only determine the given order of things, and show how—within this order—terrestrial processes flow from supratemporal essences, but we must renounce all attempts to determine the origin of this order itself.[33] Nowhere does Ibn Daud seem to recognize that the real issue was the conception of the nature of divine activity: the whole point of the doctrine of the mediate emanation of the world from God was its conception of the relationship between the world and God as a necessary one, while the biblical notion, as stated by Ibn Daud, of an immediate production of the world by God, conceives of it as a free creative act. The boundary line between emanation and creation is blurred even further by Ibn Daud's view, which was also that of Ibn Ezra, that the intelligences of the spheres were eternal, and only the corporeal world had a beginning in time.[34] This effacement of the fundamental distinction between the concepts of emanation and creation permitted Ibn Daud to view the doctrine of emanation of the Arabic Aristotelians as no more than an attempt by philosophic rationalism to overstep its limits and to penetrate more deeply into the mystery of the origin of the world than is possible to human understanding. The corollary is that we have merely to rectify this overstepping of the boundaries of our thought in order to establish complete harmony between the biblical and the Aristotelian doctrine of the origin of the world.

Of Ibn Daud's very detailed psychology, only his view of the nature of the soul, for which he is also indebted to Avicenna, is of importance. He adopted, as did Avicenna, the Aristotelian definition of the soul as the entelechy of a natural organic body.[35] His argument proceeds by way of a criticism of the materialistic theories of the soul, according to which the soul was one of the accidents of the body, or, as in the more radical formulation of the physicians, a composite of the various elements combined in the body. The traditional polemical arguments current in Jewish religious philosophy since Isaac Israeli and Saadia were put forward far more forcibly by Ibn Daud than by his predecessors. Admitting that a specific mixture of the elements combined in a single body was a necessary presupposition of organic life, he contended that such life could never be derived from a simple mixture of inorganic substances.

The wonderful purposiveness manifest in the structure and order of organisms cannot possibly be the result of a mixture of elements obeying purely mechanical laws; it presupposes, on the contrary, the existence of an immaterial, purposively creative principle.[36] If organisms are only the result of a mixture, then they can exhibit only those qualities that were present in the original elements, although in different proportions. The fact that they reveal entirely new characteristics shows that an immaterial element, from whom these characteristics derive, has been added to these material elements. The soul is thus defined in Aristotelian fashion as the principle of organic life. The independence of man's rational soul from the body is proved in an even more precise manner. The objects of our thought (concepts) differ essentially, because of their universality, from all corporeal and hence individual being. Every concept covers an infinity of possible cases, and is, therefore, itself infinite, whereas every bodily existence is finite. Similarly, each is an indivisible unity, whereas all corporeal reality is divisible. Thus the knowledge of concepts cannot be brought about through the aid of our bodily organs but necessarily presupposes the existence of an incorporeal substratum.[37] The fact of our self-consciousness leads to the same result. The senses can know their objects, but not themselves. Therefore thought, which by its nature comprehends not only its objects but also itself, cannot possibly be dependent upon any bodily organ.[38]

Man's thinking soul is thus independent of the body not only in function but in essence. However, following Aristotle, who in this respect expressed a general tendency of Greek philosophy, this independence of the soul from the body was limited to the thinking consciousness only in the narrow sense of the term. It should be noted that this is very different from separation of consciousness *per se* from the body, a concept indigenous to modern philosophy since Descartes. There is no radical distinction between sensory consciousness, whose objects are corporeal things, and the other functions of organic life. The line of demarcation between corporeal and incorporeal is constituted by the direction of thought on nonsensual objects. The immortality of the thinking soul follows from its immateriality. Since it is essentially independent of the body, the death of the body does not affect it.[39] This strict separation, however, of the thinking soul from the body is hardly reconcilable with the Aristotelian concept of the soul as the form of the body. According to Aristotle, matter and form always go together. Since the thinking soul is a portion of the soul, which has been defined as the form of the human body, it is difficult to see how it could exist apart from the body.

This difficulty, which beset all versions of the Aristotelian doctrine of the intellect, was met by Avicenna (and, in his wake, by Ibn Daud). He argued that it was illegitimate to extend our experience, according to which no form could exist apart from the thing in which it inhered, beyond the circle of observed facts.[40] The Aristotelian principle of the necessary correlation of matter and form is thus degraded to the rank of an inductive truth, inapplicable to the soul in spite of the latter's character as form, and the substantial immortality of the individual soul is asserted on the basis of Aristotelian psychology. In opposition to the doctrine that only the acquired intellect is immortal, immortality is now attributed to the thinking portion of the soul as such, and philosophy rejoins religious faith in the immortality of the soul. The conception of the soul as an individual substance excludes the Neoplatonic doctrine according to which the individual soul is merely a part of the universal soul; hence Ibn Daud also rejects the doctrine of the pre-existence of the human soul current among Neoplatonists.[41]

Even Ibn Daud's psychology becomes the starting point for a proof of the existence of supraindividual spiritual substances. The human intellect originally had only the capacity to know. Of itself, it is merely potential, and only through the acquisition of knowledge does it change its potentiality into actuality. When our thought acquires the first principles of knowledge, it becomes an "active intellect"; by further knowledge it becomes an "acquired intellect." But the transition from potency to actuality presupposes the existence of a moving principle, which in this case must be an intellect already in actual possession of the knowledge that must still be realized in us. We thus arrive at the idea of an "active intellect" which effects the transition from potency to actuality of thought in all human beings.[42] Like the Arabian Aristotelians, Ibn Daud adopted the doctrine of Alexander of Aphrodisias, who removed Aristotle's "active intellect" from the individual soul and turned it into a cosmic intellect. He did not, however, accept Alexander's identification of the acquired intellect with the divine intellect; the former is merely the lowest in the series of immaterial essences, the one that takes place when concepts stream from the active intellect into the individual intellect. Knowledge is participation in the one world of truth, which is realized in the active intellect in a nontemporal actuality. The other immaterial essences are interpreted as the efficient causes of the motion of the spheres. By means of this combination of astronomical and psychological deductions, the Neoplatonic doctrine of mediating essences was integrated —although in a changed form—into the Aristotelian system.[43]

The Islamic Aristotelians had described prophecy as the highest form of the illumination of the human spirit by the active intellect.

Ibn Daud, too, adopted this natural explanation of prophecy, emphasizing that prophetic revelations did not come immediately from God, but from created intellectual substances, and especially from the active intellect.[44] Prophetic knowledge is unique in that, unlike scientific knowledge, it does not communicate the general, conceptual order of reality, but knowledge of the future. For Ibn Daud, the intellect is the exclusive organ of prophetic revelation. Whereas Maimonides was to declare, a few years later, that it was characteristic of prophetic revelation that it extended in equal measure to the imagination and the intellect, Ibn Daud saw in imagination only a disturbing element. The highest prophecy is that which is freest of the confusing admixtures of the imagination.[45] But neither Ibn Daud nor the Arabic Aristotelians, who hold similar views, are consistent in this matter. Ibn Daud speaks of the spiritual substances adapting to the capacities of the human mind and appearing in a sensual form; this seems to imply that even apart from the arbitrary additions of the human imagination, a sensual element was inherent in the very essence of the act of revelation.[46]

The distinction between the natural conception of prophecy, and the biblical notion of prophecy as a mission, is much obscured. The Islamic Aristotelians, in their discussion of the social and religious function of the prophets, had come close to the idea of the prophetic mission. But, whereas they regarded the appearance of prophets as a manifestation of general providence, providing the human race with the necessary prophetic lawgivers and teachers,[47] Ibn Daud translates the same idea into the language of prophetic mission by teaching that God, in his mercy for those of insufficient intellect, sends elect men who teach the unenlightened his divine precepts and guide them on the path to the perfect life.[48] Ibn Daud's departures from Aristotelianism are apparent in his discussion of the conditions of true prophecy; he describes the prophet as the messenger of God, and actually combines the thoroughly universal character of prophecy, implicit in the Aristotelian theory of revelation, with Judah Halevi's doctrine of prophecy *strictu sensu*, as limited to Israel and to the Holy Land.[49]

Even more radical is Ibn Daud's deviation from Islamic Aristotelianism in the question of freedom of the will. The Aristotelians had changed the Islamic doctrine of predestination into a philosophical theory of the absolute determination of human acts.[50] As against this, Ibn Daud clings to the traditional Jewish doctrine of the freedom of human action. Whereas the earlier Jewish philosophers had extended the omniscience of God to include the free acts of man, and had argued that human freedom of decision was not affected by God's foreknowledge of its results, Ibn Daud, evidently following Alexander of Aphrodisias, excludes human action from divine foreknowledge. God, he holds, limited his omniscience even as he limited his omnipotence in regard to human acts.[51]

Ibn Daud's somewhat fragmentary system of ethics merges Platonic and Aristotelian elements in the way many Islamic and Jewish philosophers had done before him. As in Aristotle, practical philosophy, conceived in its widest sense as instruction for attaining happiness, includes ethics, economics, and politics. Ethics is developed as the doctrine of virtues, combining the Platonic definition of virtue as the right relationship between the parts of the soul, with the Aristotelian doctrine of virtue as a mean between extremes. Ibn Daud thus interprets the Platonic cardinal virtues in an Aristotelian sense, as the mean between the extreme modes of behavior of the soul.[52] He identifies this ethics with that of the Torah. The Torah contains the whole "practical philosophy" in its most perfect form, and, in fact, this rational part predominates in biblical legislation. Ibn Daud explicitly appeals to the prophetic polemics against sacrificial worship, in order to demonstrate that the Bible itself attributes a much lesser value to cultic and ceremonial ordinances than to ethical laws. The former are mainly means toward the superior ethical demands of the Bible; they have intrinsic value only insofar as their irrationality provides an opportunity to demonstrate unconditional obedience to the divine law.[53] Ibn Daud's concrete demonstration of the identity of philosophic and biblical ethics leads him far from his original philosophic starting point, for the religious ethics of love of God and reverence for his majesty have only very tenuous connections with such a doctrine of virtues. Similar contradictions are discernible in Ibn Daud's social ethics, as contained in his economics and politics; philosophically, it is developed on a purely utilitarian basis, whereas its religious foundation is said to be in the commandment to love one's neighbor.[54]

Man's ultimate goal, however, is beyond ethics. Above man's practical reason, which is oriented downward to give moral guidance to the lower parts of his soul, there is his theoretical reason, directed upwards and receiving knowledge from the spiritual substances. It is in the latter that man's true end is to be found. But this Aristotelian ideal of knowledge, as the acme of human perfection, is a reinterpretation in a religious sense, by subordinating all knowledge to the ultimate ideal of the knowledge of God. The empirical sciences are only the preliminary steps to metaphysics, whose proper content is the knowledge of God. This knowledge of God, and the love of God which is based on it, are the vocation of man, in which he realizes his perfection and happiness.[55]

Moses Maimonides

Maimonides endeavored to effect an inner reconciliation between the spiritual worlds whose opposition had been blurred and obscured by Ibn Daud. The wide sweep and penetrating power of his philosophical thinking were bent to this task of planting Aristotelianism in the soil of Judaism. Whereas Ibn Daud's writings give the impression that the struggle of Ghazali and Judah Halevi with Aristotelianism had left no mark on him, Maimonides threw the opposition between Aristotelianism and biblical revelation into bold relief in order to overcome it by a genuine synthesis. This major achievement made Maimonides the leading philosophical figure of the late Jewish Middle Ages. The problems posed by him were taken up again and again by his successors, who were not always content with his solutions but sought to establish the unity of religion and philosophy along other lines, or else tried to overcome Aristotelianism itself. But this development, which continued for three centuries, was entirely dominated by Maimonides. His work not only laid the foundation for subsequent philosophic inquiries, but actually influenced them by its continued vitality and immediate relevance. Discussions of the problems that he raised continued beyond the Middle Ages, sometimes by critical development of his position, at other times by radical opposition to it, but always with reference to him. His influence extended beyond Judaism; the founders of Christian Aristotelianism, Albertus Magnus and Thomas Aquinas, found that he had shown the way to a system of theistic Aristotelianism, and the traces of his influence upon Christian philosophy can be followed right into the first centuries of the modern era.[56]

The greatness of Maimonides does not lie in his introduction of completely new motives into philosophical speculation.[57] In his understanding of the Aristotelian system, he followed the Islamic Aristotelians, al-Farabi and Avicenna. In his critique of Aristotelianism, he had been preceded by Ghazali and Judah Halevi. In his biblical exegesis, and even in his philosophic doctrines, he was indebted to the earlier Jewish rationalists for many details. He has been denied originality, as have other thinkers whose strength was the synthesis of traditional ideas. But there is also such a thing as originality of creative synthesis, and Maimonides had this to a very high degree. Between the emanationist system of the Arabic Aristotelians and the extreme voluntarism of Ghazali, he marked out his own path, the result of a mature and profound rethinking of earlier and current ideas. Others may have been seeking a similar path, but it was Maimonides who responded to the challenge of the intellectual situation of his time and found the classical formulation of its problems.

Maimonides (Moses ben Maimon, 1135-1204) was born in Cordova, where his famous father served as a judge in the rabbinic court. After the Almohad conquest of Cordova in 1148, Maimon and his family left the city, probably in order to escape the religious persecution of the fanatical conquerors. After living for a decade in several cities in southern Spain, the family settled, in 1159, in the city of Fez in North Africa. What determined this choice of domicile is unknown; Fez was also under Almohad dominion. Maimon and his household could practice their religion only in secret, and it is unlikely that they embraced Islam in outward appearance, despite later rumors to that effect. In 1165, they succeeded in escaping from Almohad dominion. Maimonides settled in Fostat, near Cairo, where at first he was in partnership with his brother, a jewel merchant. After his brother's death, he devoted himself to the vocation of medicine. His extraordinary Talmudic scholarship made him the spiritual leader of Egyptian Jewry even before he was formally appointed to public office. Later he was appointed to the office of Nagid, the chief justice and political head of Egyptian Jewry.

His universal spirit spanned the whole compass of contemporary science, and he composed important works in many fields. He was a prolific medical author, an investigator of critical and independent judgment, though he never departed from accepted medical traditions.[58] Of immeasurably greater significance are his Talmudic writings, in which he introduced contemporary scientific methods into Talmudic studies, and thereby gave the latter a completely new form. His *Commentary on the Mishnah*, written in Arabic, sets forth with great clarity everything necessary for an understanding of the text; in cases of more difficult and complicated subject matter, a concise summary of the relevant concepts and principles precedes the detailed interpretation. His mastery appears at its height in his rabbinic code, written in Hebrew, and entitled *Mishneh Torah (Repetition of the Law)*. Here, for the first time, the totality of Jewish religious law is systematically presented, and the vast material arising out of the discussions of the Talmud is exhaustively summarized and organized according to a plan worked out to its smallest details. The work met with enthusiastic recognition, but also, at first, with sharp opposition. The main criticisms were that it collected the laws without indicating their proper sources, decided Talmudic controversies without justifying the decisions by argument, and attempted, by its character of a comprehensive legal digest, to replace the Talmud. Despite all opposition, this monumental work quickly established itself; it became a standard authority, particularly among Spanish and Oriental Jews, and served as a basis for all later compilations of Jewish law up to and including the *Shulhan Arukh*.

Maimonides' first philosophic effort was a short explanation of the most important technical terms of logic. This small treatise, which survives in Hebrew translation, was written when the author was only sixteen years of age, and can claim no independent value. During the next decades, Maimonides composed no original philosophic works, though he touched on philosophic questions in his medical, and particularly in his Talmudic, writings. In his introduction to the *Commentary on the Mishnah*, where he discusses the historical and dogmatic presuppositions of Talmudic religious law, he frequently passes over into philosophy, and his commentary on *Ethics of the Fathers* (a collection of ethical sayings of the Talmudic sages) is prefaced by a systematic presentation of the foundations of ethics. In connection with a statement in the Mishnah (b. Sanhedrin X.1), denying eternal blessedness to the adherents of certain heretical notions, Maimonides gives a summary of the basic and obligatory doctrines of Judaism which proved to be of far-reaching importance since it provided the starting point for all subsequent attempts to develop a Jewish dogmatics. Similarly, his code of laws, the *Mishneh Torah*, opens with a popular exposition of the fundamentals of Jewish faith and ethics—an elementary presentation of his philosophy of religion, stated in a style that would render it intelligible, as far as possible, to the minds of ordinary believers. His philosophic *magnum opus*, the *Guide for the Perplexed (Dalalat al-Hairin*; Hebrew, *Moreh Nebukhim)*, was not published until 1190.

This work, as its title affirms, was meant to reconcile the apparent contradiction between philosophy and revelation, and to serve as a guide to those who, as a result of this contradiction, had come to doubt either religion or philosophy. But this endeavor to establish the unity of religion and philosophy was not envisaged as a reconciliation of two opposing powers. Despite Maimonides' keen awareness of the differences between Judaism and the Aristotelian schools, he does not consider philosophy as something alien or external to religion, something that needs some adjustments and adaptations in order to effect a reconciliation. On the contrary; the relationship between the two is essentially one of identity, and its demonstration is Maimonides' main concern. The conviction of the unity of these two forms of truth had dominated Jewish philosophy since Saadia, and here Maimonides fully agrees with his Jewish predecessors. But for Maimonides, this is not merely a matter of the congruence of the objective contents of revelation on the one hand, and of philosophic knowledge on the other. Philosophy is rather a means, in fact the sole means, for the internal appropriation of the content of revelation. Religious faith is a form of knowledge.[59] The historical knowledge of traditional faith seizes its objects in an external and indirect manner, but philosophical knowledge renders an immediate apprehension of the objects of faith possible. Here we have an intellectualist concept of faith, which, by equating the degrees of philosophic knowledge with those of religious certitude, makes religious inwardness dependent upon the deepening of philosophic understanding.[60] Philosophy not only has religion as its object, but it is the central element of religion itself, the royal road that leads to God. Maimonides thus conceived his philosophic task as a religious one, and the pathos of this religious rationalism set the characteristic tone of the *Guide for the Perplexed*.

With the same decisiveness with which he bases religious faith upon philosophic knowledge, however, Maimonides severely limits the scope of this knowledge. Not only the essence of God, but also that of the suprasensual world in general, is beyond our comprehension. The question of whether the world proceeds from God in an eternal emanation, or whether it has a temporal beginning, however important from a religious point of view, is incapable of a solution one way or another. Maimonides accounts for this incapacity of our intellect by arguing that reason enables us to know the terrestrial world surrounding us, but not that which is beyond. This seems to be the kind of agnosticism more becoming Judah Halevi than Maimonides.[61] In fact, however, it is not a simple, unsophisticated agnosticism. From the world of the senses we can clearly infer the existence of a suprasensual world, proceeding up to its ultimate divine cause. But whatever we say of this world is of necessity based on inferences from its relationship to the material world; we are incapable of penetrating its specific essence. Maimonides' subsequent statements concerning God, that all assertions about him refer only to his actions and are negative in character (merely denying imperfections in him), apply equally well to our knowledge of the suprasensual world. Of course, the knowledge of the prophets is superior to that of the philosophers. Yet it appears from Maimonides' discussion of prophecy that even prophets cannot transcend the limits of human knowledge.

Even within these limits, however, metaphysical knowledge has a special quality which sets it apart from the other sciences. Maimonides expounds his view of the nature of metaphysical knowledge in the introduction to the *Guide*. The objects of metaphysics and of the adjacent principles of the natural sciences are not known to us in continuous clarity, as the facts of empirical reality are. Metaphysical truth comes to us in flashes of momentary illumination; this characteristic is common both to philosophic and prophetic knowledge, and it determines the respective presentations of metaphysical truth. If the prophets spoke in parables and metaphors, this was due (even apart from their consideration for the masses who cannot comprehend truth in its pure form) to the very nature of truth itself, which does not lend itself to straightforward conceptual formulation. Philosophy had attempted such formulation, but merely became entangled in ambiguities and difficulties; the nature of its subject matter prevents it, as it does prophecy, from attaining the clarity of the other sciences.[62]

The peculiar nature of metaphysical knowledge also appears in the fact that it requires not only perfection of intellect, but also purgation and purification of the entire human personality. The conception of metaphysical knowledge as a momentary intuition, held in similar form by the Islamic Aristotelians, and especially by Ibn Tofail, accounts for Maimonides' identification of metaphysics and natural science with the two esoteric disciplines mentioned in the Talmud—the "mysteries of the chariot" and the "mysteries of creation."[63] This concept of metaphysical knowledge appears to derive ultimately from Neoplatonic mysticism and is strangely out of keeping with the lucidity of metaphysical deduction, which is the hallmark of the main part of Maimonides' work, and seems more in accord with the Aristotelian notion of metaphysics as a demonstrable science.

Maimonides seems to subscribe to this latter view, but he does not explain how he means to reconcile it with the doctrine of the intuitive nature of metaphysical knowledge as stated in his introduction. We may, perhaps, assume that he envisaged some kind of combination of conceptual and intuitive thinking, such as that required by Plato for a comprehension of ideas; but there are no detailed indications as to how these two act together, or at what point the concept passes into intuition. In any case, both aspects of knowledge are common to prophet and philosopher. The intuitive knowledge of the prophet includes the conceptual knowledge of the philosopher and cannot exist without it; the discursive thought of the philosopher passes suddenly into a flashing illumination of the intellect, which, admittedly, remains inferior to the illumination of the prophet. Since philosophy unites in itself these two elements, it is essentially identical with religion, and is our sole means of immediate access to the truths of faith.[64]

In order to demonstrate the unity of religious and philosophic truths, Maimonides had to reinterpret and transform Aristotelianism. Herein, no doubt, lay his most significant achievement. But until he reached the parting of the ways, he traveled a good distance with the traditional form of Aristotelianism. He proved the existence of God by purely Aristotelian arguments. Whereas the Kalam first proved the temporal beginning of the world, in order to deduce from it the existence of a creator, Maimonides endeavored to dissociate the proof of the existence of God from the controversial question of the eternal or temporal origin of the world. His proofs of the existence of God assume the eternity of the world, in order to demonstrate that even on this hypothetical assumption, God's existence is certain.[65] Taking his stand upon strict science—that is, the metaphysics of Aristotle—Maimonides repudiates the proof of the Kalam as superficial and tendentious. His arguments are more or less the same as Ibn Daud's, though presented in a much more refined and subtle fashion. Maimonides, too, starts from the Aristotelian proof of the existence of a prime mover, and adds the further argument of the Arabic Aristotelians to the effect that the existence of substances that are merely possible existents presupposes a being of absolutely necessary existence. Two more proofs add nothing fundamentally new.

One, Aristotelian in origin, argues that since, in addition to bodies which are both moving and moved, there are other bodies which are moved and yet are not causes of movement, there must also exist a being which moves without being moved. The second proof is based not on the movement of bodies, but on their transition from potency to act: the transition presupposes the existence of an actualizing principle which is external to the being thus changed. The impossibility of an infinite regression of causes, just as it led in the first proof to a prime mover, now serves to establish the existence of a first actualizing principle, free of all potentiality and hence also immaterial in nature.[66] Like Ibn Daud, Maimonides can prove the origin of the world as a whole, from God, only by deduction from the contingent existence of things. In this proof, therefore, the prime mover of the first argument becomes the cause of being of all things. As in the case of the world of bodies, the immaterial movers of the celestial spheres also have their origin in God, since there can be only one necessarily existent being, and because a plurality of immaterial beings is generally possible only if one is the cause of the entire multiplicity.[67]

Maimonides presents the argument from the merely possible being of things in a stricter and more specific form than Ibn Daud, who combines it with the idea that the series of causes must terminate in a first cause. Maimonides does not infer the existence of an essentially necessary cause of the world from the impossibility of an infinite series of causes, but demonstrates that the world could not exist unless there was a being whose essence excluded nonexistence. This positive concept of necessary existence finds its most frequent formulation in the idea, borrowed from Avicenna, that existence, which in all other substances is an accidental determination added to their essence, is in God's case identical with his essence.[68] This ultimate ground of being is absolutely simple; every essence with a plurality of determinations depends, for its existence, on these determinations and their combinations, and ceases to be an ultimate.[69]

Maimonides thus arrives at the concept of God as an absolutely simple essence from which all positive definition is excluded. In this central point he follows the Neoplatonic tradition as absorbed by Arabic Aristotelianism. His systematic account of the idea of God is identical with that of Neoplatonism in its formal structure, though he goes far beyond his Islamic predecessors in the consistency of his elaboration. His well-known inquiry into the doctrine of divine attributes is the most powerful and thorough presentation of this theory in Islamic or Jewish philosophy. Although essentially Maimonides teaches nothing that had not been said before by a number of earlier Jewish philosophers, yet the conceptual sharpness and the profound systematic consistency with which he developed these basic ideas make him their classical exponent in Jewish philosophy. It was evidently the apparently inescapable formal consistency with which Neoplatonism developed the idea of abstract unity, and applied it to God, which caused Maimonides to accept the Neoplatonic concept of God. This concept of unity excluded all plurality, whether of conceptual determinations or of actual parts. Whatever exhibits a plurality of conceptual elements is a composite of these elements, and hence no longer truly one. The religious demand to purge the concept of God of all sensual elements seemed to have found its most radical fulfillment in this philosophy. In the eyes of Maimonides, therefore, the philosophic transformation of the idea of God was by no means a concession to scientific thinking. On the contrary, the philosophic sublimation of the idea of God appeared to him as a genuinely religious demand, which alone rendered a true understanding of monotheism possible.

The critical portion of Maimonides' doctrine of attributes, his demonstration of the impossibility of predicating positive attributes of God, is essentially only an explication of the logical consequences implicit in his concept of God. Inasmuch as the dualism of subject and object in every proposition involves a plurality of conceptual determinations, the absolute simplicity of God excludes any predicative propositions. This basic idea is rendered fully evident by illustrating, with concrete examples, the various possibilities of positive statements about God. The properties which we predicate of God cannot be essentially different than his essence; if they were, the unification of essence and properties would imply plurality in God.[70] Neither can they be considered part of the divine essence, for then this essence itself would contain a plurality of determinations. A definition of the divine essence is impossible on two grounds: a strict definition, the reduction of the defined concept to its conditions, can apply only to a contingent being, which God is not; whereas a definition listing individual characteristics can apply only to a composite entity.[71] No positive statement about God can thus go beyond the mere tautology that God is God. The theory of the Kalam that God has attributes, but that these are identical with his essence, is rejected by Maimonides as a veiled attempt to attribute positive properties to the divine.[72] Even the formal determinations of unity and existence cannot be considered as positive attributes of God since, in God, both are one with his essence and not inseparable qualities added to it.[73]

Nor can God be defined by his relationship to other things. For although the assumption of such a relationship in no way affects the divine unity, yet the absolute difference of kind between the divine essence and that of all other things excludes any relation of comparison. Similarly, the self-sufficiency of his being, which is completely turned in upon itself, excludes any relationship of being between him and other things. The one positive statement that we can make of God concerns the effects proceeding from him. Since we know— and *can* know—God only as the highest cause of being, this last category of attributes must necessarily be possible.[74]

This denial of any positive knowledge of God gives rise to the need to interpret scriptural statements concerning God according to their true meaning. Here again, Maimonides followed the example of his Jewish and Muslim predecessors by understanding Scripture's positive statements about God as being partly positive expression of essentially negative propositions, and as statements concerning the effects and not the being of God. But it is in the development and application of this principle that the superior power of Maimonides' philosophical thinking becomes fully manifest and, in fact, reaches its climax. For the task which he took upon himself was not merely exegetical, as might appear at first sight, but eminently philosophical. The real problem was to determine what, in fact, could be known concerning God, in spite of the impossibility of making positive statements about him. The groundwork was already laid for the doctrine of the attributes of action. In order to complete this structure it was only necessary to add that the multiformity of divine actions in no wise implied plurality in the active divine principle itself; it remains the same, absolutely simple divine essence from which the infinite fullness of divine action proceeds. The various aspects of divine acts are indicated by the attributes of action. The anthropomorphic expressions of Scripture belong to the same category; not only anger, but also God's love and mercy are merely descriptions of his action.[75]

The doctrine of negative attributes seeks to demonstrate that statements concerning God's essence are negative in terms of their true logical significance; at the same time, it answers the question of the value of this negative knowledge. Maimonides shows that in the realm of empirical knowledge it is possible to know an object with increasing precision by excluding from it more and more positive determinations. In the empirical world which consists of a limited number of genera, a series of exclusions eventually leads to a positive definition. With God, a definition is impossible; yet our knowledge of him increases as we succeed in avoiding false and inappropriate determinations, and in understanding the absolute difference between him and any other category of being. The specific function of this general knowledge is the exclusion of any imperfection from the idea of God. We know God through the negation of privations; we distinguish him from the totality of the corporeal world by means of the attribute of immateriality. We distinguish between him and the totality of being by saying of him that he has no cause—this is the actual meaning of the positive attribute of eternity. This thoroughgoing reinterpretation of all statements concerning the divine essence is more than an exegesis of the specifically religious determinations of God given in the Bible, since even ultimate philosophic principles are subjected to reinterpretation. Thus, existence and unity, which in God are identical with his essence, cannot be attributed to him as separate positive qualities. When we say that God exists, we merely deny his nonexistence; and when we say that he is one, we merely exclude multiplicity from him.[76] The doctrine of attributes is rounded off perfectly as two aspects interlock: the attribute of action, and the doctrine of negative attributes. In order to arrive at the notion of God as the self-sufficient cause of all being, we must elevate his essence above all imperfections which might prejudice his action. Taken as an attribute of essence, the attribute of omnipotence means that we deny impotence in God; but it also expresses positively that the highest, most perfect effect may proceed from God. By reason of his absolute unity, God is the cause of the most perfect effects. The fact of divine operations can be ascertained, though its source in the divine essence can only be indicated by denying any imperfection of God's activity. Similarly, these two aspects are combined in the concept of divine omniscience, which excludes all ignorance from God and hence defines the divine essence in such a way that it must be conceived as the cause of significant and purposive action.[77] God thus appears as the essentially incomprehensible cause of the most perfect actions; and Maimonides tightly sums up the final result of his analysis in the statement that we can know nothing of God except the fact of his existence.

What we have here is apparently nothing but the Neoplatonic doctrine of God as the highest and incomprehensible One, of which we know only that it is beyond and above every known or knowable perfection. But even though Maimonides, from a purely formal point of view, accepts this Neoplatonic position and argues it with great acumen, the content of his own idea of God is very different. His God is the Creator-God of Scripture, and his doctrine of attributes remolds the Neoplatonic "One" to serve as an expression for the biblical God. This is quite evident in his doctrine of the attributes of action, according to which the divine activity is conceived as materially directed toward a predetermined goal. Only in this way can the attributes of grace and mercy on the one hand, and of anger and wrath on the other, be understood as attributes of action. For although God is above the effects of mercy or anger, he may nevertheless act mercifully because he desires the good of his creatures, or act angrily because he punishes wickedness.[78] The same applies to the doctrine of negative attributes; it negates all those privations which might affect the perfection of divine activity, and furthermore, this activity is explained as the creation and the providential government of the world in accordance with a predetermined purpose.[79]

As the creator of the world, God cannot be the subject of any defect or ignorance whatsoever. Maimonides, like Saadia, deduced the attributes of God from the concept of the Creator, thereby determining their nature. We have seen, however, that Maimonides would not predicate them positively of God, but merely used them to deny their opposites. The method of his argument follows the tradition of the Greek Neoplatonists, for whom negative statements concerning God served as means for expressing a positive content. Even their denial of the possibility of a logical definition of the divine essence was accompanied by a strong awareness that at the root of this negative form of our knowledge of God there lay hidden a superior positive content. This becomes particularly evident when even the existence and unity of God are interpreted in a negative way. When Plotinus (and in a somewhat different form, the Islamic philosophers) exalted God even above existence, they only intended to exclude from him the limitations of the concept of being. To state the same idea in the form in which Maimonides held it: The positive attribute of being cannot be predicated of God, because being and essence are not separate in him, as in all other being, since his essence includes existence. We must be satisfied with the negative statement, denying nonexistence to God precisely because the essence of God contains within itself, in a higher form, that which we usually call by the name of being or existence. Here Maimonides goes beyond Plotinus. We cannot attribute unity to God in a positive sense, because in his very essence he is One in an even more precise sense than that denoted by the positive attribute of unity.

The same holds true when Maimonides, in his negation of all weakness and ignorance in God, expresses the idea that God possesses power, will, and knowledge to a degree which positive attributes are insufficient to express. Thus even from a formal standpoint, Maimonides' use of the negative attributes is somewhat different from that of the Greek Neoplatonists. The latter especially emphasize that God is beyond even the highest perfections known to us, which cannot, therefore, be positively attributed to him. The point has already been illustrated by the concepts of existence and unity. Maimonides agrees that the essence of God transcends all perfections, and consequently, that they cannot be positively predicated of him. But like his predecessors in the Middle Ages, he constantly emphasizes the necessity of denying any imperfections in God. According to the Greek Neoplatonists, God is the supreme One, beyond all perfections know to us; Maimonides, on the other hand, when denying all privations to God, wants to say that the absolute perfection of God includes all those things which cannot be predicated of him as positive attributes. This has already been shown in regard to the formal attribute of existence. (In regard to the concept of unity, Plotinus himself maintains its positive significance.) While Plotinus and his followers emphasize that God is beyond being, Maimonides reiterates that we must negate the nonbeing of God. In regard to the formal attribute of existence, there is not much difference whether it is stated positively or negatively. It is another matter, though, with material attributes such as knowledge. The Greek Neoplatonists maintained that God was exalted beyond knowledge. Maimonides, however, in his negation of ignorance in God, intends to say that the absolute unity of God includes within itself a perfection corresponding to knowledge.

In the Middle Ages, Maimonides' doctrine of the negation of privations found objectors who argued that the doctrine led indirectly to the predication of those very attributes which, according to Maimonides, should not be directly predicated of God. By denying his ignorance, for example, we do in fact affirm his knowledge; by denying weakness, we do, in fact, affirm his power.[80] From a purely logical point of view, it is doubtful whether this objection really strikes at Miamonides' conception of privation, though from a material viewpoint there is no doubt that, according to him, the essence of God does contain, if not knowledge, will and power themselves— at least something corresponding to them. Many times he goes beyond this limitation. He presents in detail the Aristotelian notion of God as the supreme thought, and seeks to show that the identity of thought, thinker, and that which is thought, present in every active thought, permits us to attribute thought to God without injury to his unity.[81] He goes on to demonstrate that God's knowledge extends to all particular entities in the world. Although this knowledge is identical with the essence of God, and thus has nothing in common with our human knowledge other than an homonymous name, yet it does not, therefore, cease to be knowledge; despite the essential difference between it and our human knowledge, the nature of knowledge is common to both.[82] Similarly, Maimonides' argument that God's will acts in complete independence of external influences and causes, because it is not directed to any end external to God, assumes that this is a will, although of another kind, which cannot be compared to anything else.[83]

In these instances Maimonides oversteps the limits set by his own theory of attributes. His doctrine of the negation of privations merely enables us to say that the simple essence of God includes within itself perfections which correspond in one way or another to the qualities of knowledge, will, and power, but whose essence remains undetermined. The importance of these limits is more than merely logical.[84] For Maimonides, as for the Neoplatonists, God is incomprehensible and mysterious; in fact, he is God precisely because he is incomprehensible and mysterious. Also, as in Neoplatonism, his essence combines infinite perfection with absolute simplicity in a manner that is incomprehensible to us; it contains all the perfections necessary for planned and purposive action. But the nature of these perfections surpasses our understanding, even as the nature of the divine perfections in general remains veiled from us. The God of Maimonides is the Creator-God, and as such he is a personal God. But the concept of personality is hardly compatible with that of the divine One, and hence it must be taken to denote something hidden from us in God's essence. The same applies to God's ethical qualities. God acts morally with regard to man, and the presuppositions for such activity must of necessity be hidden within God's essence. But his ethical attributes express only the fact that hidden within the divine essence there lie the presuppositions for such activity; their value is thus merely symbolic.

The concept of a Creator-God, which serves as the presupposition for Maimonides' doctrine of attributes, is fully established in the doctrine of creation. It is here that Maimonides comes into fundamental disagreement with Aristotelianism. In his critique of the Aristotelian doctrine of the eternity of the world, he insists that its fundamental opposition to the Jewish doctrine of creation does not relate to the question of whether the world was eternal or had a temporal beginning, but to the question of whether the world emanated from God of necessity, or was freely created by him.[85] He links the concept of "free creation," however, with the temporal beginning of the world; the attempt to explain the eternal procession of the world from God as an eternal activity of the divine will is seen as hiding the opposition between a necessary consequence and a free creation.[86] Did God fashion the world as its sovereign master according to his will, or is he himself bound to obey its eternal laws? Maimonides' discussion of this problem is guided by the desire to replace the Aristotelian system of necessity by a system of freedom compatible with divine sovereignty, and in keeping with the voluntaristic character of the Jewish idea of God.

The doctrine of the eternity of the world had changed the original Aristotelian notion of a world eternally coexisting with God, into the idea of a world eternally proceeding from God. This view, to which Maimonides objected—unfortunately his presentation of it is somewhat obscure on this point—seems to have deviated from Aristotelian dualism by including matter in the sequence of emanations, instead of positing it as an independent principle alongside of God. Nonetheless, the same view advances arguments against a temporal beginning of the world—arguments based on the dualistic assumptions of Aristotle, which, in turn, are drawn from his concept of nature. According to Aristotle, we cannot conceive of motion as having come into being, for the origin of motion, a transition from potency to act, is itself a motion, and the allegedly first motion must have been preceded by another motion, and so on, *ad infinitum*. The idea of a temporal origin of matter leads to a similar infinite regression, because according to the Aristotelian doctrine of generation, all becoming presupposes matter, and hence the origin of primary matter would presuppose yet another primary matter, and so forth.[87] To this series of arguments, derived from the conditions of natural processes, the Islamic Aristotelians added another series of arguments going back to the Neoplatonist philosopher Proclus, concluding that divine action must be conceived as eternal. If God's action had a beginning, then it must have passed from potency to act. Only an eternal activity of God is compatible with his immutable actuality. Essentially, the proof is the same as the further argument: only a being whose activity is dependent on external conditions is at times active, and at other times inactive. God's activity, which is not caused by any external factors but whose causation lies solely in the necessity of his own essence, must, therefore, be as eternal as his essence. The tendency of this line of argument—the dialectical dissolution of the concept of divine will and its conversion into that of a necessary action—is even more evident in the suggestion that it is more in accordance with divine wisdom to bring forth the world in the highest possible perfection, which can be realized only in an eternal world.[88]

Maimonides contends that these arguments apply the laws and conditions valid within the world, to the relationship of the world to God, without first asking whether the claim of such absolute validity is justified. Aristotle's own proofs refute the temporal origin of the world by demonstrating that all becoming is dependent upon certain conditions, which, therefore, cannot themselves have come into being. This is undoubtedly correct, as far as becoming in our world is concerned; but it does not prove anything with regard to the origin of the entire universe. Whoever thinks that the world came into being does not conceive of its origin as similar to the natural generation of the things within it. It is merely begging the question to apply to the origin of the world as a whole the laws of generation operative *within* it, and which, of course, cannot be said to have had an absolute beginning in time. Maimonides somewhat blunts the edge of this critique with his formulation that the conditions obtaining in the case of being that has already come into existence, must not be applied to the process of its coming to be. The conditions of life of the embryo are very different from those of the adult man.[89] Maimonides' general intention is clear, however, in spite of its inadequate formulation. It is directed against a dogmatism which considers the immanent laws of nature as absolute, and applies them without further examination to the relationship of the entire universe to God. The same mistake is committed by those who attempt to infer the eternal emanation of the world from the concept of God. Such an inference subjects God's absolute will to the same laws of motivation that apply to our limited and conditional wills. Only a will which is aroused by external impulses and is directed towards external purposes can be said to be subject to temporal changes. As for the absolute will of God, which is unaffected by any external factor, the question of what causes him to act at certain times and not at others, is illegitimate. He remains the same being, even if in his spontaneity he chooses a determinate point of time to act. The necessary procession of the world from God can be proved only by extending the laws operative within the universe, also to God.[90]

Maimonides buttresses his criticism of his opponents' arguments with a penetrating analysis of the difficulties in which the theory of emanation involves itself. The pivot of his argument, which goes into details of the contemporary concept of nature, is his contention that the Aristotelian doctrine of emanation is unable to account, as it ought to do, for the cause of the concrete determination of reality. Maimonides admits that Aristotle succeeded in explaining the given order of the sublunar world by its dependence upon the world of celestial spheres. That the matter which is common to all bodies in the terrestrial world should take various forms, and that the bodies which come into being in such a way should follow one another in a certain order can be explained, together with all consequent complications, by the influence of the heavenly spheres. But an analogous multiplicity reigns within the heavenly spheres themselves. Although they, too, are composed of the same basic matter, they exhibit a great variety, both with regard to the stars belonging to the different spheres, and in regard to the direction and velocity of their motions. Here, too, there arises the question of what caused those different manifestations of one and the same matter, or—putting the question in more Aristotelian terminology—what made it take so many forms? The question is accentuated by the fact that this variety fails to exhibit any rational order; spheres of quicker and slower motion alternate without any recognizable order.[91] We are faced with a variety of ultimate data, for which no further cause can be discovered within the corporeal world. Maimonides goes on to show that this variety cannot be explained by reference to any preceding immaterial essence as posited by the Aristotelian series of emanations. If, as the doctrine of emanation teaches, a simple essence can produce only another simple essence, then the last link of such a series of emanations must be simple, too. The emanation of corporeal objects, such as the celestial spheres and, *a fortiori*, the emanation from simple intelligences not only of the spheres but even of the stars fixed in them, defies all explanation. It is even less comprehensible how such an emanation should have produced this rationally inexplicable variety in the structure of the celestial spheres. This given order of the heavens can be explained only as the work of the divine will.[92]

Maimonides himself shows the indebtedness of his argument to the Kalam proofs of creation. According to the Kalam, not one natural datum, from the color of a blossom to the structure of the stars, can be said to be necessarily determined. Everything could have been other than it happens to be. If it happens to possess a definite set of qualities, this must be due to the activity of a free will, which chose one particular possibility among many.[93] Ghazali illustrates this idea, especially with regard to the differences in motion among the stars. Similarly, Maimonides' point that the theory of emanation had not succeeded in accounting for the transition from the immaterial essences to the celestial bodies, had already been argued by Ghazali. This has led many scholars to deny the originality of Maimonides in this matter,[94] though a more conscientious comparison with the Kalam will demonstrate that the purpose and significance of Maimonides' arguments were of a different order altogether. The starting point of the argument, the concept of contingency, is essentially different from that of the Kalam. For Maimonides, the determination of individual objects is not accidental simply because we could imagine alternative determinations; on the contrary, he regards the world as an interconnected whole, bound together by certain laws. It is this uniformity of laws in the world, and not mere conceivability, which provides the criterion for what is possible or impossible. Maimonides' main problem concerns the ultimate conditions of the cosmic process, on which everything else depends according to fixed laws. Even in regard to these ultimate conditions, Maimonides does not argue from the fact of their contingency, as such, to their dependence upon a voluntary act of God. The fact that these conditions are not logically deducible serves, in the first instance, merely as a proof against the doctrine of emanation, since the latter demands that the world be logically deducible. If the corporeal world, or prior to that, its source in the celestial spheres, *necessarily* proceeds from the pure intellectual substances, then its structure, too, must be rationally deducible. The recognition that factual reality cannot be logically derived is, strictly speaking, only a refutation of the rationalism of the doctrine of emanation. It is only the further assumption that the origin of the world lies in God, which entails the conclusion that a free act of the divine will gave it the form it has.

Maimonides did not claim logical stringency for this argument. Though he considered the arguments for the creation of the world to be, on the whole, weightier than those in favor of its eternity, he nevertheless held a compelling logical decision—one way or the other —to be an impossibility.[95] Such being the case, the religious motive, which demands the existence of a supernatural God, may for once decide the issue. The purposive order of the divine will is superior to the natural dynamics of teleological causality. Maimonides did not deny a natural teleology or the dynamic interrelatedness of events, but he limited it to the intramundane sphere. Whatever occurs in our world is subject to this order. A permanent process of emanations binds the world together, from the immaterial essences to the terrestrial bodies, and provides the natural medium for the exercise of the divine government of the world. Even in regard to the origin of the world, the principle of emanation has only a limited application, since the incorporeal substances, whose differences must be due to their mutual interdependence, must, of necessity, have proceeded from one another. However, the creation of the world as a whole is an act of the free divine will and the natural, necessary teleology of the immanent world order remains eternally subordinate to the free determination of God.

In the present context it is impossible to do more than merely hint at the fact that this restored personalism of the idea of God explodes the definition of the concept of God implicit in the doctrine of attributes. It is more important to examine the consequences of the newly-won standpoint. It relieves Maimonides of the necessity of interpreting the religious ideas of God's activity and his relationship to the world in terms of an immanent, teleological, and largely impersonal dynamism. He can now reinvest these ideas with their original meaning, though he makes only sparing and very cautious use of this possibility. Wherever a natural interpretation of a religious event seems sufficient, and does not detract from the religious significance, Maimonides adopts it. Altogether, he is careful to prevent the affirmation of God's supernatural activity from becoming a means for the continued suspension of, or eruption into, the natural order. This tendency is clearly exhibited in Maimonides' attitude to miracles. By destroying the Aristotelian system of necessity, he had established the possibility of miracles; yet he was far from returning to the naive faith of popular religion. This can best be seen in his *Commentary on the Mishnah,* where he teaches that the disposition for miracles was implanted in nature at the time of creation. Both the regular processes of nature, and the extraordinary events which cannot be deduced from the natural order, derive from the immanent course of events, because of the disposition with which nature was endowed at its creation.[96] In the *Guide for the Perplexed,* Maimonides no longer seems to maintain this extreme position, which would exclude any interference by God with the course of nature, but admits the possible eruption of God into the order of nature. These eruptions, however, are not conceived as a subsequent suspension of the natural order, but as part of the original over-all divine plan for the world.[97] A great number of miraculous narratives of the Bible, especially those of a markedly mythological or fabulous character, such as the speeches of the serpent in the Garden of Eden, or of Balaam's ass, are explained away by means of an allegorical exegesis, or else by interpreting the stories as experiences and fantasies of the prophetic imagination.

His doctrine of God's knowledge is fully consonant with the religious faith in divine omniscience. Unlike the Islamic Aristotelians, Maimonides did not limit divine knowledge to the general laws of the forms of substances. God knows individual objects not merely as links in the general causality of forms, but directly and immediately. As the creator of the world, God knows it in all its details. The fact that we cannot conceive of a knowledge which encompasses an infinite multitude of beings, and which remains the same despite the change of its objects, does not contradict the possibility of such a knowledge in God.[98]

Maimonides did not draw all the consequences of this changed concept for the idea of providence. The latter had undergone great changes in Aristotelian philosophy. Aristotelianism, as has been pointed out, equated divine providence with the natural purposiveness of the world. The generic essences were the real subjects of providence, which was consequently limited to the general order of things. Maimonides realized that this idea of a general providence betrayed its religious meaning; yet he did not fully return to the original meaning of the idea of divine providence. For the subhuman world, general providence is sufficient; it is only in regard to man that he admits of an individual providence. He even tries to interpret this in a naturalistic way, as Ibn Ezra had before him, through the idea that man is able to establish through knowledge a link with the intellectual world, and ultimately with God. By means of this link of communion, man becomes worthy of that guidance in which God shapes his destiny. God warns him of the approach of external dangers, and thus extends his protection.[99] Divine providence does not, therefore, mean interference with the external course of nature, but is transferred to the inner life of man, where it is founded on the natural connection between the human and the divine spirit. This naturalistic interpretation of providence realizes its aim only imperfectly, since the intellectual character of the connection between man and God makes the strength of this link dependent on the level of knowledge of the individual human being. Intellectual and not ethical factors are decisive for the rule of divine providence.[100]

In his theory of prophecy, Maimonides adopts the Aristotelian position, severely limiting it on some essential points. He agrees that the phenomenon of prophecy is founded upon the natural connection between the human spirit and the active intellect.[101] Its character results from the fact that the influence of the active intellect on the prophet is of a more comprehensive and exalted nature than in the case of ordinary knowledge. Whereas in theoretical knowledge, the influence of the active intellect extends only to the intellect, and in the case of oracles, dreams, and the inspirations of statesmen it extends only to the imagination, it embraces both the imagination and the reason of the prophet, who must have a natural disposition in both directions.[102] Though Maimonides fails to give an adequate psychological account of the interlocking of these two sides of the concept of prophecy, there can be no mistaking the general significance of his theory. The intellectual side of the process is the same for the prophet and the philosopher, for it is the same truth which both are grasping. The identity of the truths of revelation and of reason is expressed psychologically by the fact that the prophet is, *ipso facto*, a philosopher, and that prophetic inspiration includes the philosophic inspiration. The imaginative side of the process accounts, first of all, for the specifically factual contents of prophecy, and secondly, for the picturesque and symbolic form in which prophetic speech announces conceptual truth.[103] The purpose of this form of prophetic speech is conformity to the intellectual capacity of the masses; its psychological cause lies in the peculiarity of prophetic genius. One is tempted to conclude that the speculative content of prophetic revelation is presented in an inadequate form, and that philosophy with its purely conceptual presentation of ultimate religious truth is superior to prophecy. This, however, was certainly not the opinion of Maimonides. The prophet is superior to the philosopher, even from a purely speculative point of view, because his knowledge reaches intuitive heights, far beyond the boundaries of discursive comprehension.[104] The difference between the two forms of presentation is further minimized by the view that philosophy, too, as has been pointed out before, merely hints at the ultimate metaphysical truth.

Maimonides limits this naturalistic theory of prophecy from two sides. In general, he teaches that the divine will can refuse inspiration even to individuals who have the necessary disposition and natural qualifications for prophecy.[105] This paradoxical doctrine which attributes not the occurrence, but the abeyance, of prophecy to an act of the divine will enables Maimonides to regain the notion of prophecy as a mission. The second restriction is even more important. The naturalistic explanation of prophecy is said to apply to all biblical prophets, with the exception of Moses. The scriptural expressions emphasizing the superiority of Moses above all other prophets, does not, according to Maimonides, indicate a difference in degree, but a difference in kind.[106] The prophecy of Moses is a phenomenon *sui generis*, transcending the natural order, and wholly due to a supernatural action of God. In this way, Maimonides also safeguards the uniqueness of biblical religion against the danger inherent in a naturalistic interpretation of prophecy. If prophecy can be interpreted naturalistically, it becomes a universal datum, and most historic religions could be said to share the same revelational character, as indeed the Islamic Aristotelians had taught. On these assumptions, the only difference between religions is the relative one of higher or lower degrees of revelation. In order to forestall any such conclusions, which are incompatible with the exclusive absoluteness claimed by biblical religion, Maimonides elevated the prophecy of Moses above all other prophetic phenomena. Just as the prophecy of Moses is not the highest representative of a certain type, but is an absolutely unique phenomenon, so also the religion which he revealed is more than the highest form among a variety of revealed religions; it is the one true revealed religion which—and here, the polemical reference to Islam is evident—will never be superseded by another revelation.[107]

By his changed concept of the divine creative act, Maimonides had set himself a problem which could never have arisen on strictly Aristotelian premises: the problem of the purpose of creation. Aristotelianism, too, understood the world from a teleological point of view, and considered all natural events as expressions of an immanent purposiveness. But it would never raise the question of an ultimate purpose of creation because, as Maimonides shows with great acumen, the Aristotelian world is not the creation of a will, but a necessary effect of God.[108] Given the doctrine of creation, this problem seems to be inescapable. A profounder analysis, however, shows that even granting the doctrine of creation, the problem, if developed to a certain point, ceases to exist. For if the existence of man, as is commonly supposed, were the end of creation, the world as a whole could be said to have a purpose only insofar as it was an indispensable condition for human existence. Since it is evident that humanity has no need of a great part of the cosmos, the latter cannot be said to have any purpose. The anthropocentric view of the world, which is contradicted by the fact that the essences of the celestial world are far superior to man, is emphatically rejected by Maimonides. If this argument disallows the elevation of a particular individual being, such as man, into the purpose of the universe as a whole, the more fundamental question of whether creation as such has an ultimate purpose can be answered by the consideration that it necessarily leads to an infinite regression. Assuming, for example, that the existence of man is the ultimate purpose of creation, we cannot help asking, what is the purpose of the creation of man? Even the answer that man exists in order to worship God, merely invites a similar question. There is no other answer except that such was the will of God, that is to say, that the world has no purpose outside the will of God, since the divine will cannot be determined by anything external to it.[109] The divine will, however, willed the world in its fullness; though it can be maintained that certain beings were created only for the service of others, it remains true, in a general way, that originally all parts of the world were equally intended by the divine will. They are ends in themselves, without being ultimate purposes. Here Maimonides approaches the voluntarism of the Ash'arites, who elevated the divine will above all purposes and criteria external to it—though

he is careful to demarcate his position from their extreme irrationalism. The masters of the Ash'aria not only denied an ultimate purpose
of the world, but rejected all and every immanent teleology as well.
They denied purposiveness even within an individual organism; the
various organs were not created in order to serve specific purposes,
but the nature of each had been separately ordained by an act of
the divine will.[110]

Maimonides considered this abolition of every immanent teleology an offence to the honor of God, whose actions would be completely senseless unless directed toward a purpose, and more especially, an intrinsically significant purpose. God's will must not be
conceived as completely arbitrary; it is guided by the divine wisdom,
which produced the world in its greatest possible perfection. Maimonides further elucidates this idea by saying that God had created
everything whose existence was possible, because existence was a good
in itself.[111] Though this conclusion agrees with his previous result in
recognizing an immanent teleology, and in assuming that God created
things for their own sake, yet the two lines of argument stand in an
almost irreconcilable opposition to each other. If it is true that God's
actions, if they are not to appear as senseless, must be directed toward some purpose, then we cannot stop at immanent ends. The
meaningfulness of divine action requires not only that the structure
of the world should be organized and arranged according to a purpose, but that its existence, too, should be purposive. Otherwise, the
paradoxical conclusion would impose itself, that the existence of the
world must be attributed solely to the will of God, whereas its particular determinations are due to the divine wisdom. Maimonides
himself is forced beyond this position when he describes being as a
good that was realized through the creation of the world, for thereby
he posits a value concept which enables him to attribute a purpose
to the divine creation. In doing so, however, he abandons the position according to which every alleged purpose of creation inevitably
leads to the further question about the purpose of this purpose—the
questioning coming to an end only in the divine will. The demand
that the divine activity must appear meaningful pushes us toward
the concept of an ultimate intrinsic value—the very concept that was
negated by the denial of an ultimate purpose of the world. It is possible that Maimonides meant to reconcile these two tendencies in
the idea of a principle of meaning which does not lie outside God,
but which is grounded in his essence; but he never succeeded in formulating this idea.[112]

From what has been said about the purpose of creation, it should be sufficiently clear that the conception of God does not entail anything as to his moral nature. Other considerations confirm that in his doctrine of religious values, Maimonides was far less successful in establishing contact with biblical Judaism than in his religious metaphysics. His views concerning the ultimate goals of human existence are very close to Aristotelianism, and for the ethical religiosity of the Bible, he substitutes a religiosity of inner contemplation. Ethical perfection, it is true, is rated higher than the perfections of the external conditions of life or of the body, yet it does not touch the essential core of man. The value of ethical perfection resides in its social utility, and consequently diminishes the more we think of man as detached from society. Only spiritual perfection belongs to the true essence of man, and ethics is of significance to him only insofar as it is necessary for the attainment of this spiritual perfection.[113] In characteristic contrast to Saadia, who had ascribed a purely moral purpose to revelation, for Maimonides the distinction between the divine law and human laws is that the former is not content with providing for the external welfare of men and regulating their mutual relations, but guides them to the knowledge of truth and illumines their spirit. Ethics is treated only in its social dimension.[114] In addition, it helps to emancipate man from the domination of the senses, which is the main obstacle to the full development of his intellect. Man needs ethics because he has to assert his true essence in a struggle against his passions.[115]

All this agrees with Aristotle's view of knowledge as man's highest perfection and bliss. In fact, Maimonides is even more extreme, for although Aristotle subordinated the ethical to the intellectual virtues, yet he conceded to the former some measure of intrinsic worth. However, as has already been shown, the Aristotelian doctrine of the eudaemonia of knowledge had acquired from Arabic Aristotelians, Neoplatonism, and some commentators close to that school—a religious content completely unknown to Aristotle himself, but in which, for Maimonides, lay the true significance of the whole doctrine. This religious content is seen, first, in the fact that our knowledge is ultimately directed toward God. The knowledge of nature is only a preliminary step toward metaphysical knowledge, whose highest and essential object is God. Moreover, since the knowledge of truth pours into the human intellect from the realm of purely spiritual substances, it also constitutes the bond between man and God.[116] This communion with God does not belong to the realm of subjective experience, but is a fact of metaphysical reality. Knowledge endows man with the bliss of this immediate communion with God, and gives rise to the emotion of the love of God, and to the happiness of communion. The eudaemonia of knowledge becomes transformed into the bliss of communion with God. For Maimonides, this communion with God never becomes a mystical union, and even the characteristic emotional emphasis of mysticism remains foreign to the sober restraint of his spirit. His piety, however, is of a markedly contemplative character. The highest bliss is the contemplation of God. The life of this world has only a relative value. Maimonides teaches no asceticism that would exempt man from his duties in this world, yet he seeks to limit man's participation in external things to the absolutely necessary. Like Bahya, he sees the highest ideal (realized only by Moses and the patriarchs) in the concentration of the mind on God in a permanent communion, which remains unaffected by outward activities or social intercourse.[117]

Knowledge is also the preliminary condition for the immortality of the soul. Maimonides accepts the doctrine of acquired immortality, according to which only the actualization through knowledge of man's intellectual power leads to immortality.[118] The immortality of the soul thus becomes the immortality of the knowing spirit. But this metaphysical idea also has a religious meaning; it is the communion with God, gained through knowledge which endows man with eternal life. Here Maimonides manifests the typically ethical character of Jewish religiosity, which we have already noted with other Jewish philosophers. The concluding chapter of the *Guide for the Perplexed*, enumerates the various levels of human perfection, of which the highest is the perfection of knowledge, and describes the supreme knowledge of God as that of understanding the ethical activity of God, by which we are made to imitate it in our own actions.[119] Ethics, though previously subordinate to knowlege, has now become the ultimate meaning and purpose of the knowledge of God. It is the same transition from theory to ethics that Maimonides made in his doctrine of the essence of God, where he argued that limiting the knowledge of God to his actions in no way detracts from the significance of this knowledge, since it provides us with the standard of morality.

This conception of the knowledge of God is more than a mere adaptation to Jewish tradition; it is a necessary consequence of Maimonides' concept of God. While the God of Aristotle is still the supreme thought, and that of the Neoplatonist is the highest self-indwelling being, the God of Maimonides is a God of moral action. This conception is clearly reflected in his ideas concerning the communion between God and man. The transformation of the eternal happiness flowing from the knowledge of God into the love of God would not, in itself, distinguish Maimonides from the Neoplatonic view. But it becomes a different thing altogether when it is conceived as a love for a God who governs the world according to moral purposes, and when humility and the fear of God are added to it.[120] The knowledge of God leads to the desire to imitate his moral activity. This morality, grounded in the knowledge of God, is completely distinct from the morality which is prior to knowledge. Originating in the knowledge of God, it is part of man's supreme perfection, even if the action itself is directed toward an external object. In spite of all this, however, the theoretical aspect remains central in the religious consciousness of Maimonides. The connection between man and God is established principally through knowledge, and all other aspects of the relationship to God depend upon this primary link. Knowledge is man's true happiness, and his highest perfection consists in having his thoughts rest in God, even when his outward actions are concerned with worldly duties. The contemplative character of Maimonides' religious thought has no doubt absorbed ethical elements, yet it is certainly inadmissible to define his system, as a whole, exclusively in terms of the latter.

In presenting the basic religious concepts of Talmudic literature, we have met with some ideas that could serve as starting points for Maimonides. His philosophic-intellectualistic conception of religion could make use of the fact that the Talmud assigns an intrinsic religious value to study of the Torah. In a more immediate way, the Talmudic descriptions of the beatific vision made it easier to absorb Neoplatonic and Aristotelian religious ideals. Nevertheless, this philosophically inspired intellectualist conception of religion, as well as the essentially contemplative character of its religious ideal, represents an innovation. Such changes in primary religious motives are possible because the inner attitude of a religion is something far less tangible than its expression in metaphysical doctrines. Maimonides, for example, clearly perceived the difference between the Creator-God of the Bible, and the God of Aristotelianism producing the world in a necessary process of emanation. Yet he was unable to distinguish between the meaning of moral communion with God, as taught but not dogmatically formulated by Judaism, and the idea of the communion of the knowing spirit with God, as held by Aristotelianism.

This intellectualization of religion restricts the full participation in religious values to a small elite. In Islam, this posed the problem of reconciling an exclusive concept of religion with the character of Islam as a religion of the people; and the result was a radical distinction between the exoteric and esoteric forms of religion. Averroës, a contemporary of Maimonides, held this position in its most extreme form, but it was not unknown also to Maimonides. The profounder sense of Scripture which was identical with philosophic truth was accessible only to an intellectual elite; like the Islamic philosopher, Maimonides held that it should not be revealed to the masses.[121] His view is not far from Averroës' trenchant formula, according to which religion was morality for the people, but for the chosen few, knowledge. Yet Maimonides was too well aware that Judaism addressed itself equally to all its adherents, to countenance the rigorous application of Averroës' distinction between the enlightened few and the masses. The masses are not simply excluded from religious truth. The Torah, which seeks to enlighten the spirit of all Israel, had established certain simple and basic truths of religion; in particular, the incorporeality of God, and the elimination of all sensual elements from the concept of God. These are within the grasp of everybody, and their propagation is not only permitted, but actually a duty. The metaphorical, figurative understanding of biblical anthropomorphisms which, according to Averroës, must be kept from the masses, should, according to Maimonides, be taught even to the lowest of the low.[122] Maimonides apparently seeks to avoid what is perhaps the harshest conclusion implied by his intellectualism—the restriction of immortality to philosophers. It is true that, strictly speaking, his system can hardly consider the conventional acceptance of religious truths sufficient to assure immortality to the intellect. But here Maimonides apparently bursts the bonds of his own system by suggesting that a certain minimum of knowledge, of which every adherent of Judaism was capable, was sufficient to make all Israel worthy of a portion in the world to come.

Maimonides summarized this minimum of knowledge in his *Commentary on the Mishnah*, in the thirteen articles of faith already mentioned.[123] These truths of religion, obligatory upon every Jew, are: 1) The existence of God; 2) His unity; 3) His incorporeality;

4) His eternity; 5) The obligation to worship Him alone. 6) There is prophecy; 7) Moses is the greatest of all prophets; 8) The Torah, delivered by him, is of divine origin; 9) The eternal validity of the Torah. 10) God knows all the deeds of man, and 11) metes out reward and punishment accordingly. 12) He will send a messianic redeemer, and 13) resurrect the dead.

This attempt at a dogmatic fixation of Jewish faith is fundamentally different from the summaries of the essential truths of Judaism occasionally preferred by earlier Jewish philosophers, in that it makes life in the world to come dependent upon the confession of these truths. Maimonides went far beyond his starting point in the Mishnah, which merely denied a share in the world to come to the followers of certain heretical doctrines. The reason for this "dogmatization" of Judaism evidently lay in Maimonides' conviction that these basic and generally binding truths—combined, of course, with their historical presuppositions—represented the minimum of knowledge which even the Jew without philosophical training must attain in order to participate in the truth of Judaism. Only the confession of these truths opens to the intellect the way to immortality. Unlike in the Mishnah, there is no question of reward for the faithful or punishment for the infidel, but solely of the intrinsically necessary conditions of immortality. Religious dogmatism is a necessary consequence of philosophic intellectualism.

This conception of religion is not altered by the fact that, according to Maimonides, the Torah is the divine law and Moses the lawgiver sent by God. In his concept of the Torah, Maimonides followed the doctrines of the Islamic Aristotelians concerning the nature of prophecy. The purpose of the prophetic mission was legislation, the establishment of political laws. This theory is based on the view that man can live only in society, and that a life in society requires laws which determine relationships between man and man. According to Maimonides, however, a perfect legislation requires prophetic inspiration. Legislation thus becomes the main function of the prophet, and all his other activities are subordinate to this. The prophet here fulfills the task which Plato had assigned to the philosopher, and the Islamic philosophers were, in fact, very much indebted to Plato's ideas concerning the foundation of the ideal state by philosophers. This conception of prophecy gained support from a peculiar characteristic shared by Islam and Judaism; both contained a divine law, which included political law as well.

Maimonides, too, adopted this doctrine. The purpose of the Torah is to order social life, and both its political laws and moral commandments are directed to this end, educating the individual and making him fit to live with the rest of society.[124] Maimonides did not regard the political law as the sole purpose of divine revelation, and in this, too, he was influenced by his Islamic predecessors. He held that the essential difference between divine law and human law was that the former not only sought to establish a social order, but also sought to illuminate the spirit of mankind by the revelation of truth. Its purpose is to lead man to both bodily and spiritual perfection. Legal and ethical laws serve the first purpose; the second is served by those general truths which in their simplest form are addressed to the entire people, endowing them with knowledge adapted to their intellectual capacities, but whose profounder content illumines the spirit of the wise as well.[125] The ultimate purpose of the Torah is the spiritual one, the first serving only as a preparation for it. It is clear however, that the second purpose no longer has the character of law or ordinance. Looking at the Torah in its external aspect, it appears that the proclamation of religious truth is a part of its political legislation; but looking at its inner structure, we find that the political law is a means to an end that is completely beyond the sphere of legislation. Only the latter conception leads us to a true understanding of Torah, and, hence, the fact that the Torah is a political law does not detract from its essential purpose as the means whereby man arrives at his ultimate perfection, communion with God.

The subordination of the ethical element of religion to its theoretical aspect necessarily appears even more strikingly with regard to the cultic and ceremonial laws of Judaism. Maimonides was rooted with the very core of his being in Talmudic Judaism; he was a Talmudist no less than a philosopher, and his rabbinic activity stood at the center of his practical work. But, however profound the influence of biblical and Talmudic law, or his religious life, on his consciousness, his theory of religion evaluates it in a very different way from that of naive Jewish piety. The study of Torah, which a thorough and integral Talmudism considered as the highest ideal of knowledge, is now said to be greatly inferior to philosophic knowledge. In his well-known allegory of the royal palace, the Talmudic scholars, whose knowledge rests on faith in tradition, get merely as far as the palace; the way into the palace is found only by those whose faith is founded upon a philosophic basis.[126] The ideal of a religious culture in which the Talmud constituted only a part of religious knowledge, whereas philosophy, the queen of sciences, was its summit, had been gaining ground in many Jewish circles, particularly among the Spanish Jews. Maimonides was not the first, though undoubtedly the most powerful, defender of this ideal.

The evaluation of Talmudic study corresponds to that of the various biblical laws and ordinances, and in particular of the ceremonial law. Maimonides' view of the legal aspect of the Bible has already been discussed; the cultic and ceremonial laws were a means to the twin ends of the Torah—the ordering of society and the proclamation of religious truth. The former end is served by those laws which educate the people toward moral behavior, the latter by laws which strengthen man's faith in specific religious truths.[127] Maimonides developed this idea, familiar to both Judaism and philosophy since ancient times, in an entirely new way. Not content with the general statement that there was such a purpose, he sought to demonstrate this purpose in individual laws. A number of biblical precepts, such as the observance of the Sabbath and holidays, the laws of the fringes (Numbers 15:37-41) and the phylacteries (Deuteronomy 6:8), easily lent themselves to interpretation in terms of a rational purpose.[128] Where such interpretations were not feasible, Maimonides used historical insight in order to reach his goal. Thus certain laws are interpreted as defenses against pagan beliefs and cults current in the biblical period. In regard to the sacrificial laws, Maimonides went even further by considering sacrifices as a concession to the mentality of ancient times when even Israel, under the influence of paganism, could not conceive of worship without animal sacrifices.[129] Within the limits of the belief in the divine origin of the Law, the way was open for an historical explanation of the biblical commandments. Applying his principles and using a strictly historical method, Maimonides attempted to discover the meaning of biblical laws by comparing them with the beliefs and ordinances recorded in Sabean literature, which he thought to be Arabic translations of pre-Mosaic writings.[130]

The value of his methodological principle is not impaired by the fact that this literature was composed in Islamic times, though undoubtedly drawing on older traditions. These turgid sources nevertheless helped him to hit the mark in many instances, and through the influence that his work exerted on the *De Legibus Hebraearum Ritualibus* of the seventeenth century English theologian, John

Spencer, his basic approach did much to shape the modern religio-historical interpretation of biblical laws.[131] But although this historical method of explanation was meant to prove the wisdom of the divine legislation, it tended in fact to detract from the immediate significance of many of the biblical laws. Like the sacrificial system which had fallen into disuse, considerable other parts of the laws that were still observed had lost their original meaning. Moreover, the relation—or rather distance—between the ultimate purpose of the divine revelation and the religious law is not the same for Maimonides as for those thinkers who thought of the ultimate purpose of the divine law as essentially moral in itself. The difference is fundamental, since the equality of means and end, so characteristic of the latter view, is lost in Maimonides' system, which considers morality only as a means to the theoretical or contemplative purpose of religion. The ceremonial law thus becomes, for the most part, only a means to a means, and moves somewhat to the periphery of religion —if not in the religious consciousness of Maimonides, at least for his theory.

This conclusion once more throws into relief the historical significance of Maimonides' achievement. His theory of religious law sought to reveal the spiritual content of biblical legislation. But this spiritualization of Judaism interpreted the law in terms of the religious values of Aristotelianism, and thereby gave it a different religious meaning in some essential points. Maimonides' theistic Aristotelianism established the place of the biblical Creator-God within the framework of philosophical cosmology, and thus achieved a true metaphysical synthesis between biblical religion and Aristotelianism. For this achievement he was revered by the later Middle Ages as the "great teacher" who had scientifically established the Jewish faith. Within the sphere of philosophical rationalism, even his interpretation of the Law was felt to provide a justification of Jewish religion. But the religious ideals of this theistic Aristotelianism were still Aristotelian, though they were introduced into historical Judaism without any awareness of basic religious discrepancies. It is not difficult to understand the opposition which the system of Maimonides aroused in circles which lived integrally and fully in the Jewish tradition. Genuine Judaism felt, long before it was able to give scientific expression to its feeling, that the scientific validation of the Jewish religion involved a profound transformation of its religious contents.

The Struggle Against Philosophy
in the Hundred Years After Maimonides;
the Philosophic Influence of
Maimonides and Averroës

Maimonides' *Guide for the Perplexed* made its way with amazing
rapidity. Undoubtedly, Maimonides' fame as a Talmudic author
facilitated the success of his philosophic work. But the enthusiastic
reception which the latter found immediately upon its publication
was primarily due to the fact that it answered those questions which
had agitated philosophically alert minds since the penetration of
Islamic Aristotelianism into Jewish circles. The book at once became
the focus of philosophic interest and set the course of further philosophic inquiry. Even during Maimonides' lifetime, his admirers in
Provence, who knew little or no Arabic, requested Samuel ibn Tibbon to translate the book into Hebrew. This translation was soon
followed by a second, more fluent, though less exact translation by the
poet Judah al-Harizi, and it brought the work to the attention of Jews
outside the cultural orbit of Islam. The influence was immeasurably
greater on Jews living in the Christian lands of southern Europe than
were the translations of older Jewish philosophical works, composed
several decades earlier. In northern Spain, which was under Christian
rule, in southern France, and to a lesser degree in Italy, there quickly
developed a philosophic literature in Hebrew, although at first it
produced few works of original value. In the realm of general philosophy it consisted mainly of compilations of the works of the Islamic
Aristotelians, and in the sphere of religious philosophy, it was completely dominated by Maimonides, assimilating his ideas and ex-
pounding them in various forms. Only here and there is it possible to
detect the influence of the last and most radical Islamic Aristotelian,
Averroës, whose influence grew only in the last decades of the century.

In the wake of Maimonides, a violent controversy raged among
Jews throughout the thirteenth century on the very right of philosophy to exist. The rationalistic transformation of Jewish religion in
the system of Maimonides aroused even greater opposition because,
in addition to the school philosophers, it was taken up by wider
circles of philosophically cultured people, among whom it produced
a kind of religion of philosophical enlightenment. In many cases the
quarrel was aggravated by certain radical tendencies which went far

beyond Maimonides' own teaching, but which were manifested by his followers, or at least attributed to them. The main object of the controversy, however, was not the radicalism of certain conclusions, but the philosophic rationalization of Judaism as such. A bitter quarrel raged between the followers of Maimonides and his opponents in the communities of Spain and southern France, flaring up again and again during the century and shaking Judaism to its depth. Acrimony on both sides reached a point at which the antagonists excommunicated each other, and at the height of the struggle the Christian Church intervened and burned the heretical work of Maimonides.

This is not the place to trace the course of this controversy. But the oppositions which it reflected throw so much light on the position of philosophy in the spiritual history of medieval Judaism that we cannot entirely ignore it. Maimonides himself had been forced to defend himself against the charge levelled against him in the East, that in the dogmatic parts of his great Code, he had given up belief in the resurrection of the dead and only taught the immortality of the soul. The same accusation had already been directed by orthodox Moslems against the Islamic Aristotelians. Maimonides, who in his *Commentary on the Mishnah* had included the resurrection of the dead among the basic Jewish dogmas, could easily rebut this charge,[132] yet it was significant that the accusation could be made at all. The fact that Maimonides did not mention the dogma of the resurrection of the dead, either in his Code or in the *Guide for the Perplexed*, is surely no evidence that he repudiated the idea propounded earlier in his *Commentary on the Mishnah*; yet it does show that it was merely an inherited dogma, to be believed on the ground of tradition, not an essential element of his own religious consciousness. Not only the belief in the resurrection of the dead, but also the Jewish historical hope for the future in general, was overshadowed by the idea of individual immortality; however strong his belief in the advent of the Messiah, it is obvious that it was not messianic redemption, but the eternal bliss of the individual soul, which was the main theme of his eschatology. The extent to which there were doubts about his belief in the resurrection of the dead can be seen from the fact that shortly before his death a prominent Spanish rabbi, who was also well versed in the sciences of his time, R. Meir b. Todros Abulafia, accused Maimonides of this heresy in an epistle to the Jewish sages of Provence, and completely unaware of similar reactions in the Orient, unsuccessfully tried to organize a countermovement against him.[133]

It was not until the thirties of the thirteenth century that a movement in which the conflicting views clashed with the utmost violence gathered strength in southern France.[134] The initiators of the controversy, Solomon b. Abraham of Montpellier, and two of his disciples, admired Maimonides as a Talmudist, but judged his philosophy in the light of a naive faith and rejected everything that seemed to deviate from traditional doctrine. Their philosophical training was insufficient to enable them to grasp and formulate the full depth of the opposition.

The extant remains of the polemical literature do not make clear exactly what they objected to in Maimonides' theology. In the course of the controversy, they denied that they had ever contested the pure spirituality of God, or that they had attacked Maimonides because of his rejection of all anthropomorphisms; nevertheless, they insisted that the idea that God was enthroned in the heavens should be taken literally.[135] Similarly, they imagined life in the hereafter in a material fashion, and considered Maimonides' allegorical interpretation of Talmudic expressions to that effect as heretical.[136] Finally, they objected to Maimonides' interpretations of the biblical laws.[137] They attacked even more vehemently the followers of Maimonides among their neighbors, in whose radicalism they detected the inevitable consequences of their master's doctrine. Samuel ibn Tibbon, the translator of the *Guide for the Perplexed,* was alleged to have considered all biblical narratives as allegories, and all commandments as mere aids to the moral life.[138] They apparently also accused the philosophic party of laxity in the observance of the ceremonial law. The latter had no difficulty in refuting these charges easily. They rejected accusations against themselves as false, and in reply to the objections raised against Maimonides, they could show that his views were shared by scholars of unimpeachable orthodoxy. But the rabbis of northern France, to whom the initiators of the controversy appealed, lived completely in the world of the Talmud, and unanimously condemned Maimonides. They even went so far as to pronounce a ban on his writings, and only after their allies in southern France had appealed for help to the Church, did some of them withdraw their signatures.

To those who were capable of looking objectively at the controversy, the superiority of Maimonides over his first opponents was obvious. These, however, succeeded in enlisting the help of writers, particularly in Spain, capable of fighting with philosophical weapons and of attacking the position of Maimonides on grounds of principle. Judah Alfagar, in particular, raised the controversy to a philosophic level. Maimonides' attempt to reconcile the Bible and philosophy, he argued, was tantamount to a subordination of the former to the authority of philosophy. After all, Maimonides himself had admitted that if the philosophical proofs of the eternity of the world had been conclusive, he would have reinterpreted Scripture accordingly. Such reinterpretations of the unequivocal meaning of Scripture in order to please philosophy were illegitimate. Deviation from the literal sense of Scripture was permissible only where other biblical doctrines justify such a course, as in the case of anthropomorphic statements about God; but the Torah must never be sacrificed to the dubious and uncertain proofs of philosophy. Alfagar regarded Maimonides' attempt at harmonization as a halfhearted one, which did justice neither to the Torah nor to philosophy. With great skill, he pointed up this halfheartedness in his analysis of Maimonides' attitude toward the miracles reported in the Bible. In Alfagar's view, Maimonides' attempt to explain away some of the biblical miracles was quite useless, unless all miracles were abandoned. The same halfheartedness is in evidence in Maimonides' assertion that the advanced age reported by the Bible of the first generation was not general, but exceptional in those individuals specifically mentioned in the biblical text. To this, Alfagar replies that it does not really matter whether many, or few only, lived to such an age, since the contradiction to our scientific knowledge concerning the natural length of life of human beings remains unaffected by the precise number of the alleged exceptions.[139] What was only sensed by Maimonides' first opponents, was here formulated for the first time in clear concepts. The fact that Alfagar's discussion shows more critical ability than positive originality, does not detract from the significance of his achievement.

The controversy revived in the first years of the fourteenth century. By that time, the philosophic enlightenment stemming from Maimonides had firmly established itself in the congregations of southern France and Spain. The popularization of philosophy had progressed tremendously since the beginning of the thirteenth century, and the philosophical orientation of contemporary preaching and biblical exegesis had contributed much to its dissemination in wider circles. The status of philosophy also profited from the undisputed Talmudic authority of Maimonides, which in the course of one century had elevated his name above the strife of parties. Even the opponents of philosophy did not wish to impugn Maimonides himself, but only the abuses to which his teaching had lent itself; they objected to the popularization of philosophy which bred confusion in the souls of the young, and wished to prohibit the study of philosophy and the sciences to those who had not yet reached a mature age. A more extreme group sought to deny science any place at all in Jewish life, and the fluid and constantly shifting fronts render a reliable account of the whole struggle extremely difficult.[140]

However, these difficulties affect the external chain of events, rather than the inner motives of the controversy. In examining the latter more closely, two things immediately strike one's attention. In the first place, the philosophic enlightenment was attacked for its unbridled allegorization of the Bible. This tendency had already been noted in the first disciples of Maimonides, but as time went on it extended further until it included the historical portions of the Bible. The allegorical interpretation of Abraham as the principle of form, and Sarah as that of matter, was often quoted as a warning example.[141] The philosophic allegorists, on their part, denied that their method dissolved the concrete reality of biblical persons and events. They did not want to substitute an allegorical interpretation for the primary historical meaning, but rather sought to discover a profounder dimension of meaning in these historical occurrences. However, the suspicion remained that they displaced the historical content of the Bible in order to juggle with abstract concepts.

Of even greater significance was the second point of the controversy. The opponents of philosophy imputed to the philosophic rationalists the hidden intention of destroying the belief in a supernatural divine activity, and of subordinating the whole of reality to the necessary operations of the laws of nature.[142] The objects of these attacks indignantly rejected such imputations, and, in fact, the writings of one of the most maligned of contemporary philosophers, Levi b. Abraham of Villefranche, show that he was very far from any such extremism—indeed, he never went beyond the position of Maimonides.[143] No doubt a good deal of the suspicion and mistrust was due to a kind of heresy-hunting mentality which attributed to the philosophic rationalists more radical views than they actually held; yet this mistrust is in itself an instructive testimony to the deep impression made by the philosophic rationalization of Judaism. Moreover, extreme tendencies were not altogether absent. The great achievement of Maimonides—his harmonization of Scripture and

Aristotle—had not won universal assent. The form of Aristotelianism which he combated also had, despite his efforts, Jewish followers. Particularly potent was the influence of Averroës, who had completed his philosophy at about the same time as Maimonides did, and who had given a new—and, from a religious point of view, more radical— form to tendencies which Maimonides had opposed.

The Jews of Christian Europe took the leading roles, not only in these controversies but also in the composition of philosophic works. Nevertheless, Jewish philosophy had representatives in the Islamic countries as well, both among Maimonides' younger contemporaries and in the following generation. We may mention in passing an earlier thinker, the physician Abu'l Barakat, who lived in the East, and who died in the sixties of the twelfth century, after having embraced Islam. It was most probably his conversion to Islam that caused his complete disappearance from Jewish literature; whereas, in certain schools of Islamic theology, his reputation has continued down to modern times. But it was not only his conversion that prevented his influencing Jewish philosophy. Islamic philosophy, too, so far as we know, did not pay much attention to him for the simple reason that he was a radical opponent of the dominant Aristotelian system. His still unpublished *Kitab al-Mutabar,* dealing with logic, natural philosophy, and metaphysics, contains a severe critique of Aristotelian philosophy. So far, only his criticism of Aristotle's philosophy has been investigated.[144] We find in it the same chief objections which Hasdai Crescas was to raise two hundred years later against the Aristotelian philosophy of nature, as well as a discussion of certain aspects of Aristotelianism which Crescas neglected. Crescas' criticism will be dealt with in detail later, and will enable us to arrive at a better understanding of the main intentions of Abu'l Barakat's critique.

Maimonides' younger contemporary, Joseph b. Judah ibn Aknin, who was born in Spain and settled afterwards in Morocco, where he may have made the acquaintance of Maimonides, had no permanent influence, in spite of his vast literary output. The reason for this may lie in the spiritual affinity between him and Maimonides. Like Maimonides, he composed a series of Talmudic and philosophical works, and sought to interpret Jewish religion in the spirit of Aristotelian philosophy. But his writings were completely cancelled out by the works of Maimonides. The little that has been published in recent years is insufficient for a detailed reconstruction of his philosophy, though the general tendency of his thought appears clear enough. In his Hebrew commentary on the *Ethics of the Fathers*, he gives a free Hebrew translation of almost the complete commentary of Maimonides, who had explained the sayings of the Mishnaic teachers in the spirit of Aristotelian ethics.[145] Ibn Aknin's own share in his commentary is limited to the attempt to do justice to the original meaning of the Talmudic sayings. He does this by adducing parallel statements from other Talmudic texts. Of his great work on moral philosophy, *Tab al-Nufus (The Medicine of the Soul)*, only a few chapters have so far been published, two of which have philosophic importance. A short chapter on the essence of the soul explains, in the wake of Avicenna's interpretation of Aristotelian psychology, that the human soul could exist independently of the body, even though it was the form of the latter, and that it was essentially immortal.[146] The detailed chapter on pedagogy contains a full and typical exposition of the cultural and spiritual ideal held by Jews who had come under the influence of Islamic science and philosophy. It was the ideal for which Maimonides had provided the profoundest justification.[147] Ibn Aknin demands that the study of Scripture and Talmud be combined with the study of the sciences, beginning with logic, and including mathematics, physics, and finally metaphysics. Drawing on the writings of Islamic philosophers, he sketches a brief outline of the various subjects belonging to these branches of science. Like Maimonides, he identifies physics and metaphysics with the "works of creation" and the "works of the chariot," mentioned in the Talmud.[148] Metaphysics, which is the goal and queen of all the sciences, is also the key to the true understanding of the Torah, which contains the whole of philosophic truth. All this is in complete agreement with Maimonides' views.

Nevertheless, Ibn Aknin adopts an entirely different position in regard to the relationship of science to revelation. This attitude is already apparent in his demand that study of the sciences must be preceded by a profound study of the Torah and Talmud. This condition is made not only with regard to metaphysics, as did Maimonides, but is also applied to logic, which is the introduction to the course of scientific studies. A premature occupation with logic might result in a perversion of its methods, and thereby, in grave dangers for faith.[149] Ibn Aknin places himself in opposition not only to Maimonides, but also to the dominant trend in Jewish philosophy generally, when he demands that the words of Scripture must be accepted even when they contradict the theses of philosophy. Such contradictions, it is true, are only apparent, and due to the weakness of the human intellect. The spirit of the prophets, illuminated by the divine light, penetrates to depths which are forever closed to reason, which can rely only on its own resources. The relationship of prophecy to intellect, even when the latter is fully developed, is analogous to that between the thought of an able and experienced scholar, and that of a tyro. What the highly developed intellect of the former recognizes as not only possible, but actually true, may seem impossible to the intellect of the latter. Our intellect can thus never be the criterion of prophetic truth.[150] This conception of the relation of reason to revelation was widespread in Christian scholasticism, but in the Jewish world it was held only by the opponents of philosophy. All his concession to philosophy notwithstanding, Ibn Aknin is an even more radical critic of philosophy than Judah Halevi. His doctrine is of fundamental importance, though he is said to have applied it with extreme caution.

Joseph b. Judah of Ceuta in Morocco (d. 1226), often confused with Joseph ibn Aknin because of the similarity of names, was the favorite disciple of Maimonides,[151] to whom he dedicated his *Guide for the Perplexed*. He is an excellent witness to the fact that philosophers who were well-acquainted with Aristotelianism and influenced by it, nevertheless followed the Kalam on central issues. His only extant philosophic work is a small volume in three chapters, dealing with that essence which is necessarily existent, the manner in which all other things proceeded from it, and the creation of the world.[152] Joseph b. Judah presents and contrasts the doctrines of Aristotelians and Mutakallimun (the Kalam), but in important details clearly sides with the latter. In the first chapter, this position does not yet appear. Following Avicenna, he argues that the contingent existence of all substances requires a necessarily existent cause, and emphasizes, against the view of many of the Mutakallimun, that this proof of a necessary first cause does not entail the temporal creation of the world, but leaves the question undecided whether the world is eternal, like its cause, or has a temporal beginning.[153] The last chapter, on the other hand, quotes the standard proofs of the Kalam for the temporal creation of the world, in a manner which leaves no doubt of the author's agreement with them.

He quotes two of the many proofs of the Kalam. One, which goes back to the beginnings of the Kalam and had already been used by Saadia, argues that since all bodies were subjected to accidents with a beginning in time, these bodies themselves must also have a beginning in time. Joseph's formulation of this argument is very similar to that of the Karaite Mutakallimun. That all bodies are subject to accidents is shown by the fact that every body is either in a state of motion or rest; neither state is of its essence. Rest and motion must have come into being, since a body can pass from one state to another. Joseph b. Judah gives us a glimpse of the controversies which raged between the later exponents of the Kalam and their Aristotelian opponents. For example, the Aristotelians countered the previous argument by saying that although the separate states of motion came into being, this did not apply to motion in general, since every particular motion was preceded by another motion as its cause. Similarly, each separate body had come into being, but not bodies as such. To this Aristotelian argument, which was also cited by Maimonides in a somewhat different form, the Kalam philosophers replied that that which applied to separate motions and to separate bodies also applied to motion in general, and to bodies in general, since the whole and its parts were necessarily joined together and were subject to the same determination.[154]

The second proof, which is similar to one of the Kalam arguments for the creation of the world quoted by Maimonides, is based upon the rationally inexplicable differences between substances. The four elements, from which all terrestrial bodies are compounded, are rooted in one material substrate. Why one part of this matter takes the form of one element, and another the form of a different element, remains a mystery to us, just as we cannot explain how entirely different compound substances are derived from these elements. The celestial substances also share one matter, yet the heavenly spheres differ from each other in the direction and velocity of their movements, and in the number of stars they contain. This variety of specific characteristics can only be due to the action of a free will. The rationally inexplicable variety of forms of the substances shows that the world is the work of a God who creates through his free will.[155]

The argument for the createdness of the world receives further support from the Aristotelian critique of the emanationist theory. Its basic contention, first stated by Ghazali and repeated by Maimonides, is that the doctrine of emanation does not succeed in showing how the many could have proceeded from the one, or the material world from the spiritual. Moreover, the differences that have been noted between bodies in the terrestrial as well as in the celestial worlds, which served as a decisive argument for the creation of the world, can also be used logically to refute the doctrine of emanation.[156] If Joseph b. Judah composed his work before he made the acquaintance of Maimonides, and there are indications that this was the case, it would appear that the turn which Maimonides gave to this proof had already been elaborated by his immediate predecessors. But it is precisely the comparison with Joseph b. Judah which also throws into relief the great advance made by Maimonides in his formulation of this argument. Only he clearly recognized that the difference between the substances did not establish their createdness, but merely furnished a negative proof against the doctrine of emanation. Moreover, his critique of the theory of emanation proceeds from the assumption that all facts of reality are connected by laws; hence, once we admit certain basic facts, the rest can be rationally explained. These basic facts, however, are essentially contingent, and therefore disprove the doctrine of emanation. Maimonides also realized that this argument did not absolutely refute the doctrine of emanation, but merely increased the difficulty of maintaining it.

Maimonides' only son, Abraham b. Moses b. Maimon (1186-1237), though hardly deviating from his father's teaching, nevertheless exhibited a very different religious spirit. His polemic against his father's opponents in southern France leaves the impression that he agreed with Maimonides on every point. Yet the recently published ethical section of his great work, *Kitab al-Kifayat al-Abidin (The Book which Satisfies the Servants of God)*, is pervaded by the ascetic ideals of Sufi piety, and is possibly closer to the Sufi spirit than even Bahya ibn Pakuda's *Duties of the Heart*.[157] He adopts their principal doctrine, that in addition to the commandments and precepts that are binding on all the members of the religious community, revelation also teaches ways to perfection; and he sets out to expound these "highways to perfection" which lead us to communion with God. All true believers can take the first steps on this road, though few can progress to its higher stages. The higher the way, the smaller the number of those that can walk it. The purpose of Abraham's book was to develop this vision of moral and religious perfection. In pursuing this aim, he followed the Sufis not only in their general conception of this ideal, but also in the enumeration and description of its various forms, and in his account of the various paths leading to communion with God.[158] The relation of these "highways" to the commandments of the Torah, which are obligatory upon all, is similar to the relationship in Bahya of the duties of the heart to the duties of the limbs. However, ethics in the narrow sense of the term, as the relation of man to his fellow, occupies a much larger place in Abraham's system than in Bahya's. Mercy, magnanimity, the readiness to forgive insults—all these are part of the road to perfection. Nevertheless, for Abraham too, the inner states of the soul and their immediate relation to God are the essential. Purity of intention, asceticism, mastery of the passions, subjugation of all of the powers of the soul to the service of God, abstention from human intercourse, and concentration of all thoughts upon God, are stages on the road that leads directly to communion with God.[159]

Yet in spite of his dependence on Sufi teaching, Abraham's ideals are not fundamentally different from those of Moses Maimonides. Maimonides would have accepted all the above demands, and the ultimate goal is not conceived by Abraham along the mystical and pantheistic lines of the more radical Sufis, but in full agreement with his father, in terms of communion with God.[160] The bliss of this communion is described by Maimonides in even warmer colors than by R. Abraham. The latter, too, considers the intellect as man's highest power by which he is linked to the suprasensual world. He, too, conceives the struggle between the higher and lower natures of man as a battle between reason and the sensual impulses, and considers that the means through which man apprehends the majesty and wisdom of God is the knowledge of nature, in which these attributes are manifested.[161]

But it is not only the concepts and terminology which Abraham shares with the Sufis, which separate him from his father. Despite the importance which he attaches to reason, Abraham was far removed from his father's rationalism. According to Maimonides, the link between man and God was constituted solely and exclusively by theoretical knowledge. Asceticism and mastery of the passions were only means conducive to the full development of knowledge; conversely, the love of God and humility are by-products of the theoretical knowledge of God. For R. Abraham, on the other hand, the former were not merely preparations for contemplation, nor were the latter only its by-products. The purification of the soul has an intrinsic value; it can link us to God. In this process, theoretical knowledge is only one among many factors. One example will suffice to make this point clear: the knowledge that the celestial spheres—and, *a fortiori*, the immaterial substances—are infinitely more perfect than men, may serve to crush our arrogance and render us more humble;[162] yet this is not the only way to humility. Here, as in similar instances, theoretical knowledge is not decisive for the fear of God. The highest religious perfection is impossible without intellectual perfection, but is not identical with it, for it contains other powers and qualities of the soul of equal value with theoretical knowledge. If R. Abraham says that reason is the highest power of the soul, for him "reason" is something greater and more important than theoretical knowledge.

Also, his treatment of metaphysical theses shows the extent to which Sufi influence leads him to modify—though not to reject—his father's teaching. Abraham keeps the Aristotelian definition of the soul as the form of the organic body,[163] but believes the human soul originated in a supraterrestrial world; its purpose on earth is to prepare itself to return to its source.[164] He thus clothes the Neoplatonic conception of the soul in Aristotelian garments, exactly as Isaac Israeli and Joseph ibn Saddiq had done. When Abraham discusses the relation between the prophet and the philosopher, he does not emphasize their similarities but their differences.[165] He defines prophecy as a divine illumination which floods the soul of the prophet and bestows upon it the gift of divine wisdom; but he says nothing about this divine influx being mediated by the active intellect, or about a necessary intellectual preparation for the reception of the prophetic light.[166] We must not conclude from all this, however, that R. Abraham rejected the doctrine of prophecy held by the Arabic and Jewish Aristotelians, particularly as it is precisely in his discussion of prophecy that he leans most heavily on the opinions of his father. We may simply infer that this doctrine no longer held a central place in his system, and that the theoretical conception of the bond between man and God was no longer essential.

The same holds true of his conception of the nature of the divine activity, which serves him as the basis of genuine trust in God. In complete agreement with Maimonides, he objects both to the Aristotelian denial of special providence which conceived of God only as the source of the causal order of things, and to the opposite doctrine which attributed everything directly and immediately to God, thereby denying, out of ignorance or piety, causality altogether.[167] According to biblical teaching, there exists a causal nexus between objects whose ultimate source is God, and which is governed—and can be suspended at any moment—by God's will. The true believer is allowed and even required to utilize natural causes for his own terrestrial ends. Only a prophet who has received an explicit promise of miracles may rely on the direct action of God. What distinguishes the believer from the nonbeliever is his attitude to natural causes which he utilizes. The believer knows, in the last resort, that it depends on God whether natural means will be effective or not, in any given case; he knows that without God's acquiescence, the best medicine will prove ineffective, and the best food will not give nourishment; but when God wills it, man can be healthy, even if his food is poor. Man must therefore do everything in his power to achieve his purposes, knowing, all the while, that success depends solely on God.[168]

In his conception of the divine action, R. Abraham deviates in a characteristic manner from his father's teaching. According to Maimonides, special providence depends on the link between the human spirit and God, and not—disregarding miracles—on interference with the external course of events in the world. According to R. Abraham, too, the external action of natural forces is under the providence of God; the difference between this providence and actual miracles does not become quite clear. With this notion, R. Abraham returns to the traditional viewpoint of individual providence, though this was not his conscious intention. The motive was not so much theological traditionalism as the character of his own religiosity, which led him to the faith that our destiny is completely within the hands of God, and that the realization of our ideals depends at every moment on his will.

In the Christian countries of southern Europe, Jewish philosophy adapted itself completely to the requirements of Aristolelianism. Averroism penetrated Jewish philosophy at the beginning of the thirteenth century, though Averroës' reinterpretation of Aristotelianism did not, at first, become the object of systematic studies. The translator of the *Guide for the Perplexed,* Samuel ibn Tibbon, also translated several of Averroës' minor treatises into Hebrew, and in his philosophic commentary on the Bible, always quotes Averroës together with the older philosophers. As his treatise on Genesis 1:9 with its discussions of cosmological problems amply shows, Ibn Tibbon applied philosophic interpretation to Scripture and Talmud in great detail. Unlike Maimonides, however, he held that the Bible was written primarily for the masses, and that it took philosophers into consideration only secondarily.

His son-in-law, Jacob Anatoli, translated the middle commentaries of Averroës on several books of Aristotle's logic into Hebrew at the court of Frederick II. There he also came into contact with Christian scholars, patronized by Frederick, especially with the translator Michael Scotus. Anatoli's *Malmad ha-Talmidim (The Instruction of Students)*, a collection of lectures on the Pentateuch, is of historical and cultural rather than philosophic importance. The allegorical interpretation of Scripture is already carried far, though it still moves within the range of ideas of Maimonides. The book illustrates the spiritual bond existing between the representatives of philosophic enlightenment in the different faiths. Anatoli not only shows acquaintance with Christianity, but also quotes a large number of remarks of Scotus, as well as several philosophic interpretations of Scripture advanced by Frederick II, and actually based on Maimonides.[169]

The extensive philosophic literature of the end of the thirteenth and the beginning of the fourteenth centuries remained, for the most part, on well-trodden ground. The voluminous writings of Shem Tob ibn Falaquera (d. 1290) testify to great philosophic erudition; but his originality did not measure up to his learning. In a dialogue between a lover and an enemy of philosophy, written in a popular style, he endeavored to refute religious misgivings about the study of philosophy; and in a series of smaller treatises, he offered a compendious survey of the various fields of philosophy. Some of these minor treatises follow the older Islamic Aristotelians rather closely; for example, his treatise *On the Soul* completely ignores Averroës' doctrine of the intellect, whereas a larger encyclopedic work (as yet unpublished) is based entirely upon Averroës.[170] He also wrote an extremely valuable commentary on the *Guide for the Perplexed*, in which he pointed out the differences between Maimonides and Averroës, limiting himself to the mere confrontation of the conflicting views.

Levi b. Hayyim of Villefranche (ca. 1250-1315), though he was violently attacked by the opponents of philosophy, did not, as a matter of fact, go very much beyond the basic position of Maimonides, nor did he add many ideas of his own to those of the *Guide*.

More extreme in his rationalism was Joseph Kaspi (1279-ca. 1340), the author of many philosophic and exegetical works. He, too, wrote a commentary on the *Guide* in which he repeatedly attempted to interpret Maimonides' deviations from Aristotelianism, especially his polemic against the doctrine of the eternity of the world, as a mere accommodation on the part of the master to conventional religious views.[171]

The Italian philosopher, Hillel b. Samuel (d. after 1291), did not exceed his contemporaries in philosophic originality. But his systematic attempt to treat the question of the immortality of the soul—which Maimonides had touched only incidentally—is of importance, as it opened the debate with Averroës' reinterpretation of Aristotle at a central point.[172] Avicenna's conception of the Aristotelian doctrine of the intellect and its immortality, which Ibn Daud had adopted without alteration, had been rejected by Western Islamic Aristotelians in favor of Averroës' audacious theory of the unity of the intellect. Not only Avicenna's doctrine of the substantial immortality of the soul, but even the form of individual immortality, permitted by the doctrine of the eternity of the acquired intellect, had been rendered problematic by Averroës. It was thus a pressing problem that Hillel b. Samuel took up in *Tagmuley ha-Nefesh (The Rewards of the Soul)*. But he waged the battle with borrowed weapons. His knowledge of Latin, from which he translated not only medical works, but also the Neoplatonic *liber de causis*, enabled him to make use of the refutation of Averroës by Thomas Aquinas. Hillel b. Samuel's own contribution is very poor by comparison, yet despite his somewhat insecure eclecticism, his is the merit of having introduced into Jewish philosophy the contemporary discussion of a central problem.

The proof of the existence and substantiality of the soul follows the conventional Aristotelian pattern. Organic life presupposes the existence of a special principle of life which, since it constitutes the essence of organic bodies, cannot be an accidental determination of those bodies, but must be their substantial form. Hillel developed this idea of the soul, common to all the Aristotelian schools, together with its corollaries on the immovability and indivisibility of the soul, in close dependence on Avicenna. At times this dependence is direct and even literal, at others it is mediated by Dominicus Gundalissmus' *De Anima*,[173] which, in its turn, was influenced by Avicenna. Even Hillel's definition of the soul, which combines the Aristotelian concept of the first entelechy of the natural organic body with that of an independent, form-like substance, as well as with that of an emanation from the pure spiritual substances, is not far removed from Avicenna's, despite the obvious touch of Neoplatonism.[174]

Hillel discusses two sides of the problem, now newly constructed in Averroistic terms. At one point he attributes to Averroës the opinion—in the latter's commentary on Aristotle's *De Anima*—that the souls of all men are one and the same, multiplying only accidentally, by being joined to different human bodies. Later, he discusses the well-known Averroistic doctrine of the unity of the intellect in all men. In both places, however, we are dealing with the same doctrine, for when Averroës speaks of the unity of the soul, he refers only to the rational part of the soul, while its animal and vegetative parts are bound up with the body and hence participate in the plurality of bodies.

According to the first section of Hillel's work, Averroës had demonstrated the unity of the soul, because form, the conceptual essence of all things, is the same in all individuals. Averroës had changed the idea of an essential form, common to all individuals, to that of a common soul. He argued against the idea of a plurality of individual souls, since these could not be understood either as eternal or as created. They could not be eternal, since the form of a substance could not exist independently of the body. Similarly, the soul could not have been created, since form *qua* form could not have a temporal beginning. Unless we resort to the idea of a miraculous *creatio ex nihilo,* form must either have been derived from another form, or have arisen out of matter. Both of these notions are contradictory to the very idea of form. Since Avicenna's idea that the individual soul came into existence contemporaneously with the body had been shown to be inacceptable, the multiplicity of individual souls becomes hardly tenable.[175] At first Hillel adopted this Averroistic proof, and along with it, its necessary corollary, the unity of soul in the human species; but he added that the plurality of individual souls had emanated from this universal soul.[176] Despite the fact that Averroës' argument had been aimed against the entire idea of emanations, Hillel claimed that Averroës' objection to the temporal origin of the soul did not apply to the process of emanation. Aside from the weak counterarguments which he advanced, it remains unclear why Hillel at first adopted the Averroistic position of the unity of the soul, and then by a simple change in formulation reverted to the contrary of Avicenna.

Hillel also provides a discussion, in its familiar form, of Averroës' theory of the possible or material intellect.[177] Averroës tried to answer the objections to the Aristotelian doctrine of the intellect by adopting the position already taken by Alexander of Aphrodisias and the whole school of Aristotelians who viewed the active intellect as a suprapersonal spiritual essence. However, he broadened its definition so as to include the potential intellect. According to this doctrine, there is only one suprapersonal mind, which is individuated only insofar as individual men of different dispositions participate in it (in different forms), according to their individual capacities. In opposition to Hillel's previous exposition, this doctrine assumes the individuality of the individual soul, but elevates the intellect above it. Since only the rational part of the soul is immortal, however, individual immortality is again in danger. In his polemics against this doctrine, Hillel refers to the arguments of the Christian opponents of Averroës, though he fails to say that he actually copies from statements of Thomas Aquinas' *De unitate intellectus contra Averroistas.*

The entire chapter, especially the detailed demonstration that Averroës' doctrine contradicts the meaning and text of Aristotle, is taken from Thomas. The more exegetical details of his argument need not detain us here. In his conclusion, Hillel deviates from Thomas insofar as he considers only the potential intellect a component of the individual soul, while continuing to assert the suprapersonal character of the active intellect. In regard to the potential intellect he uses the same argument that Thomas had advanced against Averroës, objecting to the inherence of the intellect in the individual soul. The Aristotelian definition of the intellect as the form of the body is incompatible with the notion that the intellect—which for Aristotle, is completely separate from the body—should nevertheless be a part of the soul. Averroës sought to overcome this internal contradiction in Aristotle's psychology by distinguishing the intellect from the soul which is bound up with the body, and by making the former a suprapersonal substance. For Hillel, this is not a compelling argument. The soul can be the form of the body, and nevertheless contain powers, which are independent of the body.[178] Thus, he can maintain the immortality of the rational part of the soul; since it is independent of the body both in function and being, it can outlast the destruction of the body.[179]

Thus, Hillel renews, within the limits of the complicated Thomistic conception, Avicenna's attempt to establish, on the basis of the Aristotelian psychology, the substantial independence and indestructibility of the rational soul.

There is no formal contradiction in the fact that Hillel views the destiny of the human intellect and the highest blessedness of man in the union with the active intellect.[180] Such a view is possible even if we assume the substantial independence of the individual soul. According to its original intent, this view considers the eternity of the human spirit to be due not to its own essence, but to its connection with the active intellect, and interprets the eternity of the spirit in terms of its absorption by the universal active intellect. In this part of his doctrine, Hillel follows Averroës, especially that version of the latter's theory according to which the potential intellect does not appear to be separate from the individual soul. Hillel, for the most part, reproduces verbatim the minor works of Averroës concerning the union of the separate intellect with man.[181] Although Hillel's combination of such diverse interpretations of Aristotelian psychology remains free of essential contradictions, the unity of these heterogeneous elements in his doctrine is only external.

Isaac Albalag, a contemporary of Hillel who resided in southern France or northern Spain, owes his niche in the history of Jewish philosophy to being the first, and for many years the only, Jewish philosopher to maintain the doctrine of the double truth. He developed this doctrine in remarks and excursuses appended to his Hebrew translation of Ghazali's treatise on the principal opinions of the philosophers.[182] Like the Christian Averroists, from whom he apparently borrowed this doctrine, he maintains that philosophic knowledge need not necessarily conform to the teaching of revelation. When a contradiction arises between the two, one may, from the standpoint of faith answer Yes, and from the standpoint of philosophy, answer No, without harming either knowledge or revelation.[183] In Christian Averroism this doctrine gave rise to the suspicion that it was meant to camouflage a philosophic radicalism which did not want to subordinate itself to the authority of revelation; in the case of Albalag, this suspicion became a certainty.

When men of good will have maintained the doctrine of the double truth, it was due to their opposition to a superficial harmony between faith and philosophy, whereby the simple meaning of the pronouncements of faith was twisted to suit philosophy, or where philosophic doctrines were blunted to accommodate the certainties of faith. In order not to subvert the independence of each sphere, the unity of truth was sacrificed. Albalag admits such to be the case; he seeks to free philosophic inquiry from the shackles of dependence upon revelation. He strongly objects to Maimonides' attempts to refute the proofs for the eternity of the world so as not to disturb the Pentateuchal version of creation or the conventional interpretation of this event.[184] On the other hand, he does not grant the same freedom to revelation as he does to philosophy. In opposition to the Christian Averroists, who were very cautious with regard to changing the literal meaning of Scripture, he proceeds to outdistance his rationalistic predecessors in his interpretation of Scripture, and introduces into the Torah his own philosophic opinions, which are, for the most part, Averroistic. He interprets the story of creation in accordance with the doctrine of the eternity of the world, and in the scriptural account of the temporal creation of the world, he sees an exoteric expression of the philosophic doctrine of the eternal derivation of the world from God. In his interpretation of the creation story, and in its accompanying Midrashic supplements, he develops with great skill every detail of the Aristotelian cosmology, which Averroës had expounded.[185] He also tries to introduce Averroës' doctrine of *God's knowledge* into Scripture and Talmudic *aggadah*.[186] Only in giving a philosophic reconstruction of scriptural text, does he admit, in an offhand manner, to a recognition of the literal text and a belief in its veracity.[187] It is clear what judgment we must make as to these assurances, and to Albalag's form of the doctrine of double truth!

But Albalag did not truly believe in philosophic interpretation of the Torah, despite his lack of faith in the literal meaning of Scripture. He really thought that the Torah did not intend to teach religion and metaphysical truths. As he explicitly states in his introduction to the translation, the various laws which were given by God, and the Torah generally, were a matter of political legislation with a view to ordering social life. The same purpose is served by the doctrines found in the divine Torah. Their principal content is the idea of heavenly reward and punishment, by which the Torah seeks to educate the masses towards obedience to the law; their value consists in their effect and not in their truth or falsehood.[188] Even when the precepts correspond to the truth, and one can apprehend them as a popular version of the truth, not their truth content, but their practical utility is decisive. Albalag thus separates himself from Maimonides and the Arabic Aristotelians who had claimed that, in addition to its practical value, the divine law had a further, superior purpose. According to the Arabic Aristotelians, the goal of the divine law was to show man the path to otherworldly salvation, while, according to Maimonides, it was to perfect the human spirit by dealing with religious truth.

The only thinker sharing this view with Albalag was Averroës. Though he emphasizes that the goal of revelation was otherworldly, occasionally Averroës underscored the political value of faith in revelation and its doctrines—an emphasis which lends weight to the judgment that this feature of revelation was actually the most important for him. What was hidden and esoteric in the doctrine of Averroës became explicit in Albalag. At the end of his introduction he approximates the older idea when he says that the divine law has a bearing on truth, even for those souls who are more perfect than the ordinary run of human beings. The Torah refers to those philosophic truths which are within the grasp of the human intellect, and to those prophetic truths which the unaided intellect cannot attain.[189] He is thus able to justify both the philosophic interpretation of the Torah and the doctrine of the existence of a double truth by making the prophetic truth, which cannot be comprehended by the unaided human intellect, into a truth which contradicts our reason.

Later, however, he says that only a prophet can realize the prophetic truth in Scripture and that other men, including philosophers, can do nothing more than accept it from the prophet's hands; since such a tradition becomes less and less clear and certain with the passage of time, such truth does not actually exist for us any longer.[190] The philosophic truth embedded in the Torah is not of much greater value. Although he declared in the introduction that the Torah clearly hints as to the content of this truth to the philosophic initiate, he later claims that we can never know with certainty if we have plumbed the true intention of the Torah. He labels the philosophic interpretation of Scripture as but an indirect support for truth by its linking of scriptural expression with truth, which is known to us from a different source. We must first prove the truth under discussion in a scientific way, and only afterward should we look for a hint of it in the scriptural writings. If this is not possible, we must look upon this truth as a philosophic truth and no more; if the Torah contradicts it, as philosopher, man must uphold this truth, but as believer, he must uphold its contrary, which is found in the Torah.[191]

The proposition that the object of the Torah is to guide us to the knowledge of philosophic truth, is not in agreement with the statement that the philosophic interpretation of Scripture is only a support for truths arrived at by other ways, subsequently linking them to a biblical verse. Such a statement is acceptable only if we look upon Scripture as a political law whose intent is not to reveal truth either to the masses or to the wise. Apparently, this is Albalag's genuine doctrine; with almost cynical frankness he admits that he believes neither in a profound philosophic meaning, nor in a prophetic truth of the Bible that would be beyond—or, *a fortiori*, opposed to—philosophical enquiry. Knowledge of truth is the business of philosophy alone, and the latter need pay no attention to divine revelation, whose proper ends are legal and political.[192]

We have no reason to doubt that Albalag believed in the divinity of the Torah. He did not consider it merely as a natural revelation which had been the position of philosophic doctrines, similar to his, at the beginning of Islamic and Jewish philosophy. His idea of the relation of philosophy to Scripture corresponds to the doctrine which was later advanced by Spinoza.

In the first half of the fourteenth century, the problem of free will became the object of lively discussion. Its origin lay in the attempt of Abner of Burgos (who, after his conversion to Christianity, adopted the name of Alfonso of Vallodolid) to introduce into the sphere of Jewish thought the determinist doctrine of Islamic Aristotelianism. The only exposition of his determinist doctrine extant, a treatise entitled *Minhat Kanaut (The Offering of Zealousness)*, was composed after his apostasy.[193] But Abner does mention two earlier works in which he expounded this doctrine, one of which was undoubtedly composed before his conversion. The source for his determinist theory was Ghazali's treatise on the prinicpal opinions of the philosophers, in particular, the exposition of the philosophy of Ibn Sina, who also was an exponent of determinism, and from whom Abner borrowed the doctrine. According to this theory, natural causality applies to man's voluntary acts as well as to natural events. But the type of causality applied to man is different from that involved in natural occurrences. The essence of the will is that it can choose between alternatives; it can choose between opposites. But the decision to choose is not arbitrary in nature; it is made in accordance with factors operative upon the act of decision, and in accordance with its nature.[194] Essentially, it can choose between alternatives, but its decision is made in accordance with necessary laws.

Corresponding to this principle of determinism is a theological thesis: God cannot know the actions of men in advance, if these actions are themselves unclear until the moment of choice—as a completely voluntaristic theory would require. A thoroughgoing voluntarism makes nonsense both of God's omniscience and omnipotence. Unless the actions of men can be set within the framework of natural causation, which is ultimately founded upon the nature of God, we cannot assert the omniscience or omnipotence of God.[195] With great logical discernment, Abner refutes the stock objections to determinism. The divine commandments are not abrogated by reason of causality operating on the actions of men, as is popularly claimed; it is rather the purpose of the commandments to motivate man's will and to arouse him to do a certain deed.[196] Similarly, it is wrong to claim that the reward of the righteous and the retribution of the wicked are unearned if their acts are determined. Reward and punishment are obligatory consequences of man's actions, and there is no perversion of justice if every action gives rise to necessary consequences.[197]

Abner maintained that this doctrine of determinism appeared in Judaism, Christianity, and Islam. The Islamic theory of predestination was already explicated by the Arabic Aristotelians, from whom Abner borrowed his theory of determinism. Abner transferred their interpretation to the Christian doctrine of original sin, which he identified with the causal determination of human action. While in most cases he is loyal to the elements of Christian doctrine, and introduces Christian ideas into philosophy, here he faces in a different direction. Although the Christian Church had but a short time previously declared the doctrine of determinism of Christian Averroists to be heretical, Abner, like some of the later Renaissance humanists, interprets this doctrine in the spirit of philosophic determinism, without any regard to its religious presuppositions.[198] With even greater audacity, he tries to associate this doctrine with Judaism. For Abner the emphasis upon the free will of men found in the Bible and the Talmud, and with which medieval Jewish philosophy agreed, was simply advanced for the benefit of the masses, because the theory of determinism could only undermine their determination to uphold the divine commandments.[199] The true doctrine of the Bible and the Talmud is found in those verses in which he ingeniously unearths a reference to the predestination of the acts of men.[200]

Abner's views aroused violent opposition among the Jewish Aristotelians. The latter had always maintained the Jewish view of man's freedom of choice, and that this doctrine corresponded to that of Aristotle, as they conceived it, in opposition to the Islamic commentators. Even so devoted a follower of Averroës as Albalag, contemptuously threw out the doctrine of determinism, although he knew that it was a constitutive element of Averroës' world view. The Jewish Aristotelians showed the same opposition to Abner, and it seems that his metaphysical reasons for adopting determinism made no impression upon them at all. In their view, the only difficulty was the dilemma of man's freedom and God's omniscience. God knew all of the acts of man in advance, although until the very moment of the act they sought to protect the freedom of man's choice by limiting God's foreknowledge in one way or another.

The first to take up this line was Isaac Poleqar, who in his youth had befriended Abner, and later became his fiercest antagonist. In his popular philosophic book, *The Helpmeet of Religion (Ezer la-dat),* the entire fifth chapter is devoted to a discussion of Abner's theory of determinism. He does not refer to Abner by name, although he treats his viewpoint from many angles. The relation of man's freedom of choice to God's omniscience and omnipotence is what primarily concerned him; he overcame this dilemma by a semi-pantheistic conception of the relation between God's will and man's will. The divine will is the power by which anything and everything is decided in the world, and the powers on which individual action depends are related to it in the same way that the powers which move any individual limb of man are related to the will which motivates his entire body. This analogy is then applied to man's acts. All of man's actions are founded upon the imitation of the divine will by the human. At the moment when actions are realized, their completion is ordained by the divine will, and at the very same moment they become objects of the human will, which thus imitates the divine will.[201] This decision of the divine will subsumes the knowledge with which God predicts the actions of man, and both are found within the divine essence at the same moment. Precisely because God's knowledge comes into being, it must, like the divine will, be contemporary with its subject. What God knows, must necessarily come to be, and it is thus impossible that God's foreknowledge of man's acts should precede those very actions. But one cannot conclude from this that God's knowledge changes; all knowledge of particulars stems from the eternal and all-embracing divine knowledge, which is identical with the divine essence.[202]

This line of thought leads to contradictions on essential points. The mutual co-operation of the divine and human wills raises the problem whether there is a pre-established harmony between the two, or complete identity of the human will with the divine. In either case, it is unclear how the substantial independence of the human will can be maintained under such conditions. But the primary difficulty lies in the fact that God does not know the actions of men until after they have been done, but that nevertheless, no change is predicated of his knowledge. It is clear that an example of this kind of thinking is found in Maimonides' concept that God appears to act at a specific time, but without changing his essence. But Maimonides speaks of actions which, as it were, occur outside of God, while Poleqar refers to the knowledge specific to God himself, and which is manifested only at a particular time, without there being implied any change in God's knowledge.[203] Despite the fact that Poleqar did not attain his goal, his purpose is clear. God's knowledge must be understood in such a way that it will be impossible to speak of a divine foreknowledge of man's deeds, and thus man's freedom of choice will be saved.

A more penetrating solution to this difficulty was made in the next generation by R. Levi ben Gerson, who, though he never mentioned them, clearly had Abner's ideas in mind. He adhered to the viewpoint of the Arabic Aristotelians (especially Avicenna) that the divine foreknowledge extended only to the external laws governing the forms of the world, and not to the separate mistakes subject to change. From this he concluded that the divine knowledge extended neither to separate objects nor to their changes, nor to the deeds of man in particular. As opposed to this, R. Moses Yosef of Narbonne (Moses Narboni), writing against Abner, upheld Averroës' viewpoint, which corresponded to the position taken in his commentary to the Eight Chapters of Maimonides: that this opposition between the general and the particular, although applicable to man's ever-changing consciousness, does not apply to the divine knowledge.[204] In this, too, Averroës deviates from Avicenna, or, at least, from the principal formulation which the latter gave to this doctrine: he derived the knowledge of those laws that determine forms based on God's essence from God's own self-knowledge; however, he identified the two. God is the supreme causality of the forms, and within his essence there is contained that order which repeats and reveals itself— although in progressively lower degrees of perfection and unity—at every level of existence. When God knows himself, he thereby knows the causality of form on every level of existence; he knows the whole of existence, not in its lower form, as it exists outside of him, but in its highest form, where the whole of existence is one with his essence.

From this concept of divine knowledge, Narboni deduced certain corollaries as to the relationship between this knowledge and man's freedom of choice. Many of his statements are identical with the position taken by Maimonides; he completely accepts it in commenting on the *Guide,* postulating that the knowledge of God extends to the free acts of man, just as it includes every other event in the universe, even if in a form different from empirical reality. If this statement were all, we could justifiably ask what possible contribution Averroës could make in solving the problem of how God's knowledge could extend to that which has not yet been decided. It seems likely, therefore, that Narboni's real opinion was that the divine knowledge, since it included the essence of all other things, also included the essence of man's will, which has the power freely to choose between alternatives. But as to which alternative man will choose at each and every turn, this is not included in the divine knowledge; God's knowledge does not actually know the individual *qua* individual. This is but a cautious statement of the position which Levi ben Gerson eventually adopted. It appears that this is Narboni's authentic conviction; his apparent agreement with the conventional position is unimportant.[205]

In his inquiry on freedom of the will, Narboni again took issue with Abner on whether the moral law and man's desire for happiness can keep their meaning within the framework of determination. For Narboni, this doctrine is riddled with internal and external contradictions, and he thought it unworthy of Abner's philosophic stature that he could agree to such a contradictory philosophic position. He suggests that Abner adopted this position only as a rationalization for his apostasy from Judaism, which he thereby converted into a necessary act without accepting any real responsibility for it.[206]

Narboni's treatise is of philosophic importance both for its content and for the light which it casts on the author's character. Narboni is a striking philosophic personality, but apart from a few brief treatises on the freedom of the will, he did not compose original works. Most of his works are commentaries, centering around Averroës. Only his commentary on the *Guide,* to which we have referred, has so far been published. The latter was composed toward the end of his life and was a labor of love; despite its form, it is of independent philosophic value. He mounted a more penetrating Averroistic criticism against Maimonides than any of his predecessors. It is directed primarily against the Neoplatonic interpretation of Aristotelian doctrines, which Maimonides had borrowed from al-Farabi and Avicenna, and against whom Averroës maintained the construction of Aristotle's meaning. This critique is applied to the whole series of proofs for the existence of God, as well as to Maimonides' concept of God.[207]

Narboni attacked Maimonides' doctrine of attributes, which ultimately referred back to the Neoplatonic idea of God from an Aristotelian viewpoint. He proved that Maimonides' conflict with the Aristotelians concerning the eternity of the world only applied to Avicenna's version of Aristotle, which had been demolished by Averroës. Despite all of the criticisms, however, Narboni held Maimonides in the highest regard, and in the deepest sense did not see himself as an opponent. He did not abandon his conviction that Maimonides was *the* philosophic interpreter of Judaism. Along with his contemporaries, Narboni was under the influence of Averroës, and tried to comply with the latter's interpretation of Aristotle. Like his predecessors, Narboni did not choose either of the alternatives which arose out of this situation—either to give Judaism an interpretation congruent with the philosophy of Averroës (as Maimonides had interpreted Judaism along the lines suggested to him by a study of al-Farabi and Avicenna), or else repeat the arguments of Maimonides against Averroës. Narboni's contemporary, Levi ben Gerson was the first who undertook this latter task.

Levi ben Gerson

Levi ben Gerson (Gersonides, 1288-1344), born in Bagnols in southern France, was familiar with every branch of medieval science, and made distinctive contributions to every field in which he labored.[208] In theology, aside from several Talmudic dissertations, he wrote a commentary on the Pentateuch, the earlier prophets, and on most of the Hagiographa. In mathematics, he wrote on arithmetic, geometry, and trigonometry; in his geometric essays he took particular pains to demonstrate the axioms of geometry.[209] He won wide acclaim as an astronomer; two astronomical instruments, the staff of Jacob, which was used for the measurement of light angles, and the camera obscura, were invented by him (the latter he perhaps merely perfected, having realized its true significance). The results of observations made with the aid of these instruments were summarized in his lunar tables. Finally, in his major religio-philosophic work, he propounded a new hypothesis to account for the movement of the stars, which differed both from the Ptolemaic theory and its emendation at the hands of Arabic astronomers. The observed movements of the heavenly spheres contradicted the principles of Aristotelian physics, leading to the doctrine that astronomy had only one task—to observe and tabulate the movements of the heavenly bodies—and to the abdication of any claim on its part to absolute truth as a science; Gersonides, by trying to harmonize physics and astronomy, attempted to establish a true theory of the heavenly phenomena. Since the comprehensive astronomical chapter of his book as yet has not been published, and thus has not been evaluated by experts, it is impossible to make a fair judgment of its worth.[210] The Christian astronomers of the Middle Ages, however, and even of early modern times, not only made full use of his instruments, but through the medium of a Latin translation of his work, also occupied themselves with his astronomic theories.

As a philosopher, Gersonides, like his contemporaries, did not limit himself merely to the field of religious philosophy. He wrote a supercommentary on Averroës commentary on Aristotle's *Organon, Metaphysics,* and scientific works, and also composed an original treatise on logic. Latin translations of only a few of these have been published.

But his magnum opus is the *Milhamot Adonai (The Wars of the Lord),* which sums up his religious philosophy. This book treats only a few central controversial questions, but a detailed analysis yields the picture of a complete and well-rounded religious philosophy. This picture can be filled in if we study his commentaries on the Bible, especially with regard to "practical" philosophy, which the *Milhamot* does not consider. There we come across deviations from positions outlined in the *Milhamot,* but we must not conclude that Gersonides' true doctrine is expounded in the commentaries; in these, he consciously or unconsciously adapted himself more to the traditional religious viewpoint, but it cannot be doubted that the proper source of his major views is the *Milhamot.* Structurally, his book is completely scholastic in character. In regard to every question discussed, ample citation of previous views bearing on the question is given: reasons pro and contra are minutely analyzed, and only afterward does the author put forward his own solution to the question under discussion. Only those philosophic doctrines which center around the interpretation of Aristotle are accounted of philosophic importance. The controversies between the various Aristotelian schools form the starting point of the analysis of every question, and provide the material through which Gersonides clarifies his own viewpoint.

Gersonides concentrated his attention on his differences with Averroës. On the basis of, and in opposition to, the latter's philosophy, Gersonides sought to harmonize revelation and philosophic truth in a new way. In his formulation of the idea of God he completely followed Averroës who, in this point as in many others, had reverted from the Neoplatonism of al-Farabi and Avicenna to the original Aristotelian position.

For Gersonides, God is not the One, beyond all definition, but rather, in the Aristotelian sense, the supreme thought. There had, of course, been earlier theological attempts to satisfy the demands of the Aristotelian position, but they found themselves involved in inescapable contradictions. Gersonides differed with Averroës only in the greater precision with which he expounded the Aristotelian viewpoint. As against the principal objection raised to the doctrine of positive attributes—that every positive attribution necessarily destroys the divine unity—Gersonides maintained that everything that may be conceptually analyzed does not necessarily posit a material plurality in re. We may, in any particular instance of "red," conceptually distinguish between "color" and "redness," though the two do not exist as distinct realities. Similarly, there is no distinction in God between his essence and his thought, although analytically we distinguish between them, and posit his essence as the subject of his thought. God is, according to his essence, the supreme thought, and the duality of these two aspects inheres in the form of our conceptualization, and not in re.[211]

This same viewpoint underlies his polemic against the idea that we cannot predicate positive attributes of God as separate determinations, but can only negate nonexistence, multiplicity, and imperfection, since God is the only being in which unity and existence are not accidentally added to an essence, but are one with it. As against this, Gersonides upheld the original Aristotelian position, revived by Averroës, that existence and unity are substantially identical with the essence of all beings, and showed that these formal determinations, which necessarily inhere in all essences, do not imply any plurality in them. It is precisely because unity and existence are one with the essence that we may attribute them positively to God without thereby affecting his unity. Although Maimonides and Avicenna asserted that the qualities of contingent things had nothing in common with the qualities attributed to God but their homonymous names, and that, strictly speaking, their positive content was essentially inapplicable to God, Gersonides maintained that the attributes which we predicate of things and God have one and the same meaning. The attribution to God is primary; that of all other beings is derivative. Both the formal attributes of existence and unity, and the material determinations of his essence, are originally applicable to God alone. All other beings participate in these attributions only through him; thus the incomparability of God to his creatures is guaranteed by the essentially different form in which these attributes are applied to God.[212] But this deviation from the Neoplatonic idea of God does not imply an acceptance of the personal God of Scripture. The entire structure of his system shows how far Geronides was willing to go to uphold the Aristotelian idea of God as the supreme thought, and as the highest formal principle of being.

The relationship of God to the world is defined in the discussion of the problem of creation, which for Gersonides, as for Maimonides, is the focal point for harmonizing the scriptural and Aristotelian world views. Like Maimonides, he rejects the idea of the eternity of the world, but he goes beyond Maimonides in maintaining that this doctrine can be positively disproved; his analysis is different both in its conclusions and in its point of view. The strongest positive argument for the created nature of the world is its teleology. The teleological structure of things proves that they are an effect of a final cause. This reasoning is further strengthened by the fact that this teleology is expressed not only in the inner dispositions, but in the interrelation of individual objects, which shows that each object exists for the sake of some other object.[213] Only in a secondary way does Gersonides cite the Maimonidean argument that one cannot rationally deduce the specific individuality of things; this is especially true of heavenly phenomena. Of course, the teleological structure of things only proves their direct origination by God, not their temporal creation. Gersonides held the doctrine of emanation, and its underlying idea of an eternal procession of things from God, to be self-contradictory. It is impossible to think of things as eternal and created at one and the same time. If one wishes to unite these two concepts, one must necessarily posit the constant re-creation of things by God, and thus abandon the substantial perseverance of things. Their being would be an eternal generation and destruction.[214]

This rejection of the continual emanation of things from God leaves us with a choice of but two alternatives: either the uncreatedness of the world is eternal, or it came to be in one unique event. The teleological proof of the origination of things by God also proves their temporal beginning. As against the eternity of the world, one can point to the fact that it is impossible to think of past time as infinite in duration. This argument, taken from the Kalam, was wielded in thoroughgoing fashion by Gersonides against the Aristotelian doctrine of the impossibility of a beginning to time. Aristotle himself had taught that an actual infinite was impossible; he admitted only the possibility of a potential infinite. His proof for the existence of a prime mover was founded on the impossibility of an infinite regress of causes. And if, in opposition to his own doctrines, Aristotle maintained the thesis of the eternity of the world, and thus necessarily admitted the existence of an infinite duration of past time, he could justify this only by claiming that the infinity of time was potential only because time, *per se*, in which the past is gone and the future is not yet, has no actual existence. Gersonides denied this artificial distinction. The being of past time cannot be regarded as simply potential, without doing violence to the meaning of the concept of potentiality. Despite the succession of its parts, the past is still an existent; if there were no beginning to the world, one would necessarily have to conceive of this magnitude as being infinite. The concept of infinity is only legitimate if it does not lead to a contradictory notion, such as that of an immeasurable, infinite quantity. But this is unavoidable if we posit the existence of an infinite past time. A quantity can be multiplied indefinitely without ever becoming an infinite quantity; the assumption of the eternity of the world, however, considers the past *ab initio* as a perfect infinite.[215]

Maimonides had objected to the Aristotelian doctrine of the eternity of the world, for it illegitimately transferred laws governing all becoming within the structure of the world to the generation of the world as a whole. That all beings have a material substrate, and that this substrate is not subject to becoming; that every motion presupposes a previous motion and that motion *per se* is eternal; these laws apply only to becoming within the framework of the world. It is illegitimate to transfer these conditions, which apply universally to objects within the world-frame to the world as a whole. Maimonides later formulated this argument by saying that the laws which apply to complete and perfected being, cannot be applied to a being that is still in the process of becoming.

Gersonides accepted this idea, but formulated it more precisely and strictly. He did not think that the becoming of the whole and the becoming of its parts should be treated in the same fashion. But although it is illegitimate to equate the two, one should not also deny, as Maimonides did, their common features. What should be investigated is whether the conditions of becoming of the parts apply only to themselves, or whether these laws apply to all becoming.[216] Gersonides claimed that those laws to which a thing is subordinate, because it is that particular thing, cannot be applied to it before it receives this particular determination. Those laws, however, which apply to a thing, not by a virtue of any particular determination, but by virtue of its being an existent at all, obviously apply to that which is in the process of becoming, as much as to that which had already come into being.[217] If Maimonides had attributed an empirical value to all conditions of becoming, without making distinctions, the final result of Gersonides' distinction was to differentiate between those laws which have only an empirical validity, and those whose necessity was transempirical. These latter govern the becoming of the world as a whole, and even the activity of God is subordinate to them.

The consequence of these considerations is that matter cannot possibly have come into being. God, considered as the highest principle of form, can have produced only the new total of forms. Matter, which is essentially different from any form, cannot be derived from God. Moreover, every becoming must be preceded by the possibility of becoming, as well as by its substrate, which is matter.[218] Gersonides, with the same sharpness which characterized the analysis of Averroës, maintained the primary, unbridgeable dualism of matter and form. The creation of the world by God is not a *creatio ex nihilo,* but presupposes a pre-existent matter upon which he exercised his creative act. Maimonides had declared that such an idea, which he thought one could find in Plato's *Timaeus,* was acceptable from a religious point of view; and Gersonides easily accommodated the scriptural account of creation to such an interpretation. He thus endeavored to limit the function of matter to the purely formal role of a substratum for becoming. Matter does not contain any determinate disposition, but is perfectly indifferent, has the possibility of becoming as such, and hence in no way constrains the divine creativity.[219] That the pre-existence of matter does not signify temporal pre-existence is self-evident. Time is found only within the world. Just as the being of God is supratemporal, the being of unformed matter (as Gersonides might say) is subtemporal.

Even in this limited form, divine creativity goes beyond that which is postulated of the Aristotelian God. No longer is God the completely self-contained, highest thought; moreover, Gersonides rejected the emanationist theory of God's creativity. The act of temporal creation can be interpreted only as an act of God's will, and Gersonides repeatedly affirmed this conclusion.[220] Nevertheless, the reasons which he advanced for rejecting *creatio ex nihilo* certainly emphasize how much he remained bound to the idea that God as the supreme form is also the highest thought, and we have already seen how Gersonides defended the legitimacy of this definition against his Neoplatonic predecessors. But the divine thought can only think genera, and cannot extend or separate individual beings. The dualism of matter and form, which lay at the base of his doctrine of creation, made this conclusion unavoidable. Since only the most general laws of form derive from God, his knowledge, of necessity, can only encompass the general order of forms; the manifold of individual forms, which comes into being only through the union of form and matter, must always lie beyond the scope of the divine knowledge. This is a necessary consequence of Gersonides' doctrine of creation, just as from Maimonides' doctrine of a *creatio ex nihilo* it necessarily follows that God, as the Creator of all, also knew all its details.[221]

He arrived at the same result by maintaining that God's knowledge was included in the same category as human knowledge, not alone in terms of their common names, but also in terms of their common contents. Maimonides was able to withstand all the objections to his doctrine that the divine knowledge extended to particulars, because he posited an absolute distinction between the modes of human and divine knowledge. That the divine knowledge was infinite, that God, in advance, knew the free decisions of man—this was no insoluble problem to Maimonides, since the impossible for human knowledge might well be possible for the divine knowledge (which is only homonymous with the former). According to Gersonides, however, the concept of knowledge applied equally to human and divine modes of apprehension, and anything that contradicts the concept of knowledge is impossible for the divine as well. With this position he returned to the opinion, against which Maimonides had fought, that the divine knowledge included only the generic traits, and he propounded this theory without any of the qualifications that his predecessors had given to it.[222] He did not even make his position easier to accept by saying that God does not know the individual *qua* individual, but only as a link in the general order of being. Even Averroës' profound idea, that the divine knowledge transcended the distinction between the general and the particular (because this distinction is limited to the sphere of finite consciousness), did not, for him, elevate the divine knowledge beyond the limitations set to it by this doctrine.[223] His analytic acuteness, far more developed than his speculative depth, imperturbably maintained this line of thought with all its consistent consequences. As we mentioned previously, this concept also served as the means for solving the dilemma of God's omniscience and man's freedom. Like Ibn Daud, he maintained that God does not know in advance the free acts of man. This latter position is merely a result of the fact that the individual *per se* is not an object of divine knowledge.

In knowing himself, God knows the general and unchanging world of forms, which proceeds from him. Following Averroës, Gersonides formulates this doctrine even more sharply: in the last resort, he says, there is no question of dualism. God is the new total of all formal causality; in him, the totality of form exists in ultimate unity, and only outside him does it fall away into multiplicity.[224] The meaning of God's creation of the world is that he allowed the unified form to be separated from him, and be split into a manifold. On Averroës' authority, Gersonides rejects the ancient doctrine that only the intelligence closest to the divine essence proceeded immediately and directly from God. Because he conceived of creation as an act of the divine will, it was easier for Gersonides than for Averroës to suggest that God had created a multiplicity of immaterial essences.[225] The divine order of creation had also established and determined, how, from these, the forms would stream into the material world. Almost in the spirit of modern deism, Gersonides limited the direct activity of God to the act of the creation of the world. The order of world events proceeds, if not mechanically, then teleologically from these separate intellects. Not only are these separate intelligences the source of the natural order, but they are also the cause of prophecy, providence, and miracles. If for Maimonides, the operation of the active intellect had been the work of God, for Gersonides there was a definite distinction between the creative original act of God, and the causality of those essences, which are produced by him.

In particular, the terrestrial world receives its forms from the active intellect, which governs it. The forms then stream to all earthly beings, and in this process we can locate the cause of the phenomena already mentioned. Just as God includes within himself the totality of form, so too, within the active intellect, there is subsumed the order of forms of the terrestrial world. It extends even beyond the earthly to the celestial world, since earthly happenings are subordinate to the influences of the stars; therefore, it stands to reason that intellect governing the terrestrial world should have a knowledge of the celestial order. Whereas the intellect of every particular sphere apprehends only that order which is subordinate to it, the active intellect must, in a certain sense, apprehend the general order of the cosmos.[226] It manifests once again the sum total of the general forms, although not with the same originality, absoluteness, and unity as is characteristic of the divine knowledge. But like God, the active intellect lacks knowledge of the particular. Prophecy, providence, and miracles, however, relate to the particular. Certain specific events are communicated to the spirit of the prophet. A miracle is the intervention in an actual specific situation, and the same is true of the doctrine of special providence.

Gersonides employs all of his dialectical keenness to the explanation of these facts. Even Averroës had concluded that since prophetic revelation occurs in connection with specific events, the divine knowledge must extend to particulars.[227] As in so many cases, it is not certain that this represents his final view of the matter. In other places he claims that the general knowledge contained in the separate intelligences is received by the human imagination in an individual form, just as form as a whole is particularized by its absorption into matter.[228] But it remains unclear whether Averroës wished to emphasize merely the difference of psychological forms, or the material difference between the theoretical knowledge of the separate intelligences, which is directed towards the general, and human knowledge which is directed towards the particular. Gersonides, who was evidently influenced in this matter by Averroës, developed this thought further in order to explain prophecy, without abandoning the purely general character of the knowledge of the active intellect. He, too, claimed that in prophetic revelation, a general knowledge of the active intellect appeared in an individual form; but he took this to mean that the prophetic spirit applied a general connection, communicated to it by the active intellect, to the illumination of a concrete instance. From the active intellect, there descends what in itself is only a general connection, but which can be applied to any number of separate and individual events. It is the prophet who supplies the knowledge of the particular event, and subsumes it under the general connection revealed to him.

Gersonides was able to amplify this view in detail because of his belief in astrology, which was founded on the metaphysical doctrine of the dependence of all earthly occurrences upon the heavenly world. The general connection imparted to the prophet by the active intellect is the general order of the astrological constellation. The constellation under which a man is born determines his nature and fate, and constellations as well determine the life span of nations. In order to understand this connection with absolute certainty, it is not sufficient to know only the general conditions of the various constellations, for each basic form contains within itself heterogeneous special forms; only a knowledge of their subtle differences permits a reliable application of the general law to the individual case. The active intellect knows the astrological order, from the most general form of the constellations to their last specification, which in turn contains all of the conditions of occurrence of a particular event. Thus, when a prophet deals with the destiny of a particular person or human group, he receives from the active intellect a knowledge of the order of the constellations, and with sufficient precision to enable him to predict its fate in full detail. Of course, there are variations in the grades of certainty; these are dependent upon the capacities of the individual prophets, but this does not affect the general principle involved.[229]

Even the profound differences between the prophet and the ordinary soothsayer do not, in principle, affect the explanation. Prophetic revelation is directed to the intellect of the prophet, and thus prophecy presupposes the fullest development of the intellectual capacity. Soothsaying works through the imagination, which cannot receive the influence of the active intellect, but only the emanations from the souls of the stars which stand on a lower level. Unlike prophecy, with its certainty and dependability, soothsaying is prone to error.[230] Despite these differences, however, the same principle of explanation applies to both cases. The naturalistic explanation of prophecy, which is here developed with extreme consistency, and the acceptance of astrology (which Maimonides had rejected), sheds a new light on the contrast between Maimonides and Gersonides. That which repelled Maimonides in astrology, even more than its fantastic conceits, was its naturalistic explanation of the cosmos. This naturalism became for Gersonides the means of freeing the religious belief in prophecy from any direct connection with God. Even the prophecy of Moses is included in this category. This astrological determinism has only one limitation. The free will of man could shatter the course of action ordained for him by the stars; prophecy could therefore predict the future on the basis of astrological determination only insofar as the free will of man does not break through the determined course of things.[231]

In order to interpret belief in providence on these bases, Gersonides had only to take over Maimonides' doctrine. Maimonides limited individual providence to mankind, and had indicated that the human spirit, linked with God, would be forewarned of any possible dangers. This aspect of providence was on a lower level than that of prophetic prescience, and for this reason, commended itself to Gersonides. Even more audacious is the introduction of miracles in this connection. For Gersonides, miracles are not the direct result of God's act, but are produced by the active intellect. They constitute an interference with the laws of the natural order, but this interference has been foreseen and provided for in the natural order established at creation. Maimonides had already agreed that miracles were provided for in God's plan for creation, but the doctrine is now given a new twist: it is not particular miracles which are included as part of the general plan of creation, but at the time of creation God set down general conditions in conformity with which miracles might occur. These conditions are part of the general order of forms, contained in the active intellect, and thus we conclude that there is a natural law of miracles, which incorporates miracles into the immanent order of the world![232]

Gersonides' doctrine of immortality, which has remained outside the area of the problems we have considered, is more closely interrelated with the controversies of the Aristotelian schools than any other part of his thought. In a detailed discussion, he contrasts the various interpretations provoked by Aristotle's obscure and contradictory doctrine of the intellect. But one point, and it is perhaps the decisive one, remains outside of the discussion. When Aristotle distinguished between two types of intellect, the active intellect and the passive or potential intellect, which is actualized by the former, it was self-evident for Gersonides that the active intellect was not a part of the individual human soul. For Gersonides, this interpretation, drawn from Alexander of Aphrodisias, was the true interpretation of Aristotle, and he attributed it even to those commentators who, in fact, denied it—partially because he was led astray by Averroës' report of their doctrines. But such a consequence was materially unavoidable if one meant by the term, active intellect, an intellect in the exact sense of the word. If human consciousness was endowed from the start with an actual intellect, it is difficult to see the possible meaning of a potential intellect, which is just beginning to develop the ability to think.

For Gersonides, the active intellect, which was so important for his system, denoted an immaterial substance (as it had for his Jewish and Arabic Aristotelian predecessors)—a substance from which forms proceed to the earthly world, and which lead the human intellect to the actuality of knowledge. The object of his explanation was the potential, or as it was called, the hylic intellect. The principally opposed interpretations were those offered by Alexander of Aphrodisias, and Themistius. According to Alexander, the hylic intellect was a capacity of the human soul, indissolubly bound up with its subject, man, that would perish with the death of the person. According to Themistius—as Gersonides understood him—the hylic intellect was an immaterial substance, existing from eternity and uniting with the human soul during its sojourn upon earth. To these primary interpretations, two more were added later. In order to escape the difficulties of these two views, Averroës accepted the assumption that the hylic intellect was also a substance completely independent of the individual human soul. In Gersonides' summing up of this theory, the hylic intellect is no more than the active intellect, insofar as it unites with man. While the active intellect *per se* can apprehend only itself, by reason of its union with man, it acquires the capacity of knowing particulars, and thus acquires—in this respect—a potentiality which is completely alien to its pure essence. Later philosophers, by whom Gersonides means the Christian scholastics, modified the theory of Themistius, so that the hylic intellect was considered an immaterial substance united with the soul, with no pre-existent status, which comes into being with the birth of an infant.[233] The primary opposition lies between the two original positions;

through the discussion of their assumptions, Gersonides arrived at the essentials of his own position.

Despite the dialectical subtlety with which he turned over reasons pro and contra, Gersonides operated essentially within the framework of the Aristotelian arguments. Aristotle strongly emphasized both the belonging of the intellect in the soul, and its immateriality. Because the soul, defined as the form of the body, was indissolubly linked with the body, there came into being an opposition between these two requirements, which Aristotle himself was unable to resolve. If his statements were applied to the hylic intellect, on the one hand there arose a contradiction to the position of Themistius, and on the other, a contradiction to the position of Alexander. Since Themistius conceived of the hylic intellect as an independent substance, joined to the human soul only during the latter's lifetime, it could no longer be the perfection of the soul, and its relationship to the human essense became problematic. An immaterial essence cannot at the same time be the form of man. Moreover, if it is an immaterial essence, the hylic intellect must be the same for all men; it cannot belong to the individual soul, and partake of its individual differentiation.[234] The immateriality of the intellect contradicts the position of Alexander. If the soul, with its sensual faculties, is the subject of the hylic intellect, how can the latter be conceived as totally independent of sensuality? That the intellect can know non-sensual objects, and that the aging of the body does not affect its powers—this must prove, according to Aristotle, that the function of the intellect is not tied to any bodily organ, and thus is independent of sensuality. But this can no longer be said of the hylic intellect, once we make of it, as Alexander did, a power of the soul.[235]

Both of these doctrines run headlong into the same difficulty—the Aristotelian notion of the pure potentiality of the hylic intellect. According to Aristotle, the essence of the potential intellect lay in its ability to absorb or to become all forms. Since form and concept were equivalent, the understanding of the concept was equivalent to the absorption of its form, and the intellect which comprehends all concepts must bear within itself the possibility of all forms, or be the possibility of all forms. But the intellect can serve as this pure medium for the comprehension of concepts, only if its own nature does not modify the forms which it receives. Aristotle, therefore, required that the intellect be perfectly simple in nature. This meant at first that the intellect cannot be compounded with the body, and must remain untainted by its sensual nature in order to apprehend all forms purely. But the commentators turned this idea in a different direction: the receiving intellect must have no formal determination peculiar to itself, because such a determination would, of necessity, prevent it from comprehending other forms.[236]

This is a necessary corollary if we identify the ideas of concept and form; but it leads to the impossible result that the intellect, in order that it might truly serve as the medium of knowing, becomes an almost suspended absolute possibility. On the one hand, it must be uncompounded with any matter whatsoever, and on the other, it must be free of any formal determination! The ultimate ground of all of these difficulties, which the (taken in themselves, correctly Aristotelian) assumption caused, was that the noetic relationship of thought to its object was treated as a material relation, and became subordinate to the material categories of matter and form.[237] This difficulty existed both for Themistius, for whom the hylic intellect was an immaterial substance and thus possessed a formal determination, and for Alexander, who saw in the hylic intellect a capacity of the human soul and thus questioned its noncomposition with matter.[238] From Alexander's viewpoint, it is possible to escape the difficulty by making the purely formal distinction that the soul, as the bearer of an intellectual capacity, was the condition only for the latter's existence, not of its function. The absorption of concepts by the intellect, is accomplished, as it were, independently of its substratum.[239] Now we can at least understand the idea of the intellect as pure potentiality. By means of this distinction, we have also turned the point of the objection made earlier to the doctrine of Alexander. Functionally, the intellect remains immaterial; materially, since it is dependent upon the soul which is the form of the body, it is bound up with the body. Gersonides, therefore, opted for Alexander, and against Themistius.

After this fundamental decision, the chronologically later theories were easily dispatched. The critique which Gersonides made of Themistius applied equally to those amendments made to the latter's doctrine which we mentioned as the fourth option. Averroës' doctrine of the unity of the hylic intellect stands in stark contradiction to the individualization of thought in the plurality of men. If the hylic intellect is the same for all men, it must possess and not possess the selfsame knowledge, since one man knows and another does not. In this conception, the human drive for knowledge loses all point, for the universal intellect *per se* has no need of it; but the connection between man and the universal intellect, by which knowledge is individualized, disappears at death, and with it, the individualization too.[240]

The end of this wide-ranging discussion thus becomes a return to the basic position of Alexander. Accordingly, Gersonides also accepted the eternity of the acquired intellect, which was implicit in his doctrine of the intellect. While the hylic intellect is borne by the soul, and thus cannot survive it, the concepts acquired by it are (as Gersonides had previously shown) independent of the soul. Since the soul has no part in the comprehension of concepts, they can exist independently of it. But this interpretation of immortality is in one essential point quite different from Alexander's position. According to him, those concepts whose objects are things of the world of sense have no permanence. Being pure forms, they have no existence outside the spirit; they cannot, therefore, as simple products of abstraction, have a duration in thought that would outlast their temporary actualization. Only when our thought comprehends those immaterial substances which exist independently of it, does it acquire a lasting content. The knowledge of the immaterial substances also implies unification with them, and when the intellect attains such unification, it also participates in their eternity.[241]

Gersonides denied both these assumptions of Alexander's view. He maintained that it was impossible that knowledge could bring about a union of the human intellect with the active intellect, because such a union presupposed an actual grasping of the content of the active intellect, to which our human intellect cannot attain. The essence of all of the individual forms, which on earth are separate, is unified in the active intellect. Thus we cannot know the active intellect unless we have grasped these forms as a whole, and comprehend their unitary interrelation. Since such knowledge is denied to man, it is impossible to grasp the essence of the active intellect.[242] The only possible form of immortality which Gersonides, in opposition to Alexander, could see lay in the lasting existence of the concepts men have acquired through sense perception. For Gersonides, these concepts are more than mere products of abstraction; since in them we grasp the permanent essence of things, we can attribute to them a permanent existence. This peculiar version of conceptual realism enabled Gersonides to maintain the permanence of the concepts in their psychological form as well. The concepts which we know, do not spring into existence at the moment we know them, but enter our consciousness in the specific form in which they are cognized.[243] The fact that they arise as contents of our thought does not prove that they must also pass out of existence, as Averroës had claimed. Even if we grant that these concepts came into being, Aristotle's principle that everything which comes into being must eventually be destroyed, does not apply to immaterial objects.[244]

The acquired intellect of man is the sum of the concepts which he has acquired. These can survive the death of the soul, since, according to Gersonides' previous proofs, the soul has no part in their acquisition. The concept has acquired an independent existence, unaffected by man's death and the perishing of his soul. In accordance with Aristotle's doctrine of the unity of thought and its object, this permanence of the concept serves as a guarantee of the permanence of thought. Should we hold that the human intellect is thus merely a sum of its separate concepts, Gersonides seeks to ground its unity by denying that the content of our thought is a mere aggregate. The concepts which we acquire in the process of thinking have a unitary interconnection, in which later thoughts subsume the earlier. The concepts of our knowledge, the highest and most encompassing of any particular time, constitute the form in which all the previous contents of our knowledge are comprehended.[245] This unitary interrelationship, which constitutes the acquired intellect, is immortal. We have thus returned to the notion of individual immortality, which had been uprooted, or at least veiled, in the union of our intellect with the active intellect. But the religious content of this doctrine has been lost. The individual intellect remained isolated. Just as Gersonides had previously separated the world from God, and had discarded the possibility of a continuous emanational interconnection between God and the world, there is now established an unbridgeable gap between the human intellect and the higher intelligence.[246]

If the religious content of the emanationist philosophy has thus been lost, very little of the religious life of biblical monotheism has replaced it. The way in which Gersonides justified the idea of creation showed little trace of its religious significance. God's act was limited to the unique act of creation; otherwise, Gersonides' God remained as distant from the world as Aristotle's "thought thinking itself." This impression is strengthened by his ingenious reconstruction of the concepts of prophecy, providence, and miracles. Whereas Maimonides had erected a true synthesis of Judaism and Aristotelianism, in Gersonides the Aristotelian element was of decisive importance. His rejection of the emended Neoplatonic doctrine only made clearer the theoretical sobriety of the essential Aristotelian doctrine. Judging by the final intentions of his thought, Gersonides may be the truest disciple of Aristotle whom medieval Jewish philosophy produced; but because of this, he was essentially alien to those biblical doctrines which in his formulation he seemed to approach.

Hasdai Crescas

Having failed, at the beginning of the fourteenth century, to restrain the philosophical enlightenment by external controls and overt suppression, the need to overcome it internally became all the more imperative. The polemical literature of the later thirteenth and early fourteenth centuries was only beginning to take this direction. Despite this, there were also attempts to establish another kind of Judaism, opposed to the rationalistic Judaism of philosophy.

R. Moses ben Nahman (Nahmanides) of Gerona, a Talmudic scholar and biblical exegete who adopted a mediating position in the polemical battle which raged around philosophy in the third decade of the thirteenth century, developed a unique and vigorous conception of Judaism which utilized some philosophic ideas in its details, but sought to escape philosophic rationalism. He glorified Maimonides for contending against the antireligious doctrines of non-Jewish philosophies, but was convinced that his views had a mystical strain which actually endangered the teachings of faith, and that it was necessary to be rid of Aristotelianism completely. His conception of Judaism stressed the uniquely supernatural character of the Torah. As in Judah Halevi's philosophy, it prized the historical character of the Jewish religious world view, a viewpoint which had receded in Neoplatonic and Aristotelian theories.[247]

Even when it is not outwardly apparent, these strands of his doctrine are rooted in his fundamental kabbalistic orientation, and they cannot be understood apart from the development of the Kabbala. He even shares his opposition to Aristotelianism with the Kabbala, which now becomes relevant to our own inquiries. The usual thesis that Kabbala (the Jewish mysteries which arose in the second half of the twelfth century in Provence, and came to full flowering there and in northern Spain in the thirteenth century) was only a reaction to philosophic rationalism, has been challenged recently for good and sufficient reasons. It was a positive religious movement, growing by reason of its own inner powers. Gnostic and mythological doctrines, which had lain dormant in Judaism for many centuries, were now awakened to new life under the influence of the religious tendencies which permeated Provence, where Kabbala had its birth.

To these mystical doctrines were added Neoplatonic ideas, which were drawn partially from earlier Jewish philosophy and partly from non-Jewish sources. Together these elements produced a rich and independent type of mystical and theosophical speculation[248] which, like mysticism generally, was completely opposed to rational philosophic thinking. It is true that many of the great rationalistic philosophic systems contain mystic elements, or lead up to mystical contemplation of God, and mysticism itself utilizes the concepts and methods of rationalistic philosophy in order to explicate its principal doctrines in a speculative way; kabbalistic speculation also did this to a great degree. Nevertheless, the relationship of Kabbala to rationalistic thought, especially to that form of it which was Jewish Aristotelianism, was for the most part one of opposition. This opposition was felt by the Kabbala from its very inception, and the more that speculative thought developed within it, the greater it became. But even on this level, Kabbala remained satisfied with opposing its own version of Judaism to the rationalistic one, and did not attempt to battle with philosophy in the latter's sphere or with its weapons. Even after Moses Narboni and Gersonides had recognized the acuteness of the conflict, it took a long time before a position of scientific and thoroughgoing criticism of the Aristotelian viewpoint was worked out.

A strong impulse in this direction was given by the famous Talmudic scholar Nissim ben Reuven of Serona, in the second half of the fourteenth century.[249] Judging by his sermons, however, he never went beyond providing encouragement. His philosophic importance lies in the fact that he aroused his pupil, Hasdai ben Abraham Crescas, to write a book which, for the first time since the days of Judah Halevi, offered a full-scale critique of Aristotelianism.

Hasdai Crescas (b. ca. 1340, d. 1410) was, due to his personal authority and his position as chief rabbi of the Aragonian Jewish communities, one of the most influential personalities of Spanish Jewry. After the terrible persecutions of 1391, in which his only son was murdered, he worked incessantly for the reconstruction of the decimated Jewish communities. His literary production is meager in scope. His plan for a great Talmudic work, designed as a continuation of his religio-philosophic work, was never realized. Aside from a short account of the persecutions of 1391, he wrote a *Refutation of the Principal Dogmas of the Christian Religion,* in Spanish, which is extant only in Hebrew translation. It criticized Christianity from a philosophic point of view, and was marked by calm objectivity and the logical sharpness of its argumentation. His philosophic magnum opus, *The Light of the Lord (Or Adonai),* completed in 1410, has, in terms of its formal structure, more of a dogmatic than a philosophic cast. It deals with the principal doctrines of Judaism not in terms of their systematic connection, but in the order of their dogmatic importance. First place is accorded to the basic dogma of the existence and unity of God. Second place is granted to those religious truths which constitute the presuppositions of the concept of revelation. Next come those doctrines which, although not logically deducible from the concept of revelation, nevertheless have a religious value and are binding upon all men; finally, there are a series of doctrines of no binding dogmatic character.

Crescas was by no means the great antagonist of philosophy that he appears to be from some of his statements. Although he brusquely enunciates his conviction that only the Torah and not philosophy has the power to lead man to truth, he does not content himself with a demonstration of the inadequacies and contradictions of philosophic theories, but seeks to establish the doctrines of Judaism in a positive manner in order to displace false philosophy by true philosophy. If his programmatic statements remind one of Judah Halevi's assertion that philosophy was powerless to grasp religious truth, he nevertheless stands on totally different ground. Not only does he attribute the power of grasping certain general metaphysical truths to reason, but he seeks to penetrate philosophically those questions which Halevi relinquished to faith. This same difference separates him from Ghazali's critique of philosophy, which has wrongly been considered a distinct influence on Crescas. His critique is not directed against philosophy as such, but against the dominant scholastic Aristotelian philosophy, especially its intellectualization of religion, which he considered Aristotelianism's greatest error. Although he undertook to prove the true meaning of religious concepts and the real essence of the religious life, his stance vis-à-vis Jewish tradition is much more liberal than his continued insistence upon living in accordance with the precepts of the Torah might lead one to suspect. Certainly the separation of Judaism from Aristotelianism entailed a return to the fundamentals of biblical religion, with the result that in applying this viewpoint to particulars, Crescas for the most part recaptured the original meaning of the individual concepts. But despite this harmonization with Jewish tradition, a profound difference still remained. He gave the voluntarism, which linked him with the Bible, a deterministic twist, and thus stamped it with an entirely new form.

Although independent of his basic religio-philosophic viewpoint, his critique of the fundamental concepts of Aristotelian physics—in many respects the forerunner of modern natural science and philosophy of nature—was in itself very important.[250] Of course, his originality may appear doubtful after the recent publication of Abul-Barakat's critique of the Aristotelian science of nature. But no possible connection could have existed between these two thinkers; so far as we know, Abu'l Barakat's book never reached Europe, and besides, Crescas did not know Arabic. Thus it is clear that he propounded independently those same questions which Abu'l Barakat had asked. Without dissolving the dualism of matter and form as such, Crescas gave these concepts a meaning which entailed an entirely new concept of substance. The common substratum of the four elements was prime matter, which did not need any form, but could exist independently *in re*. Thus matter became an independent primary material substance, concretized only through the forms of the individual elements.[251]

In the center of his analysis was Aristotle's doctrine of space and his concept of infinity. In opposition to Aristotle, Crescas maintained (it is possible that Kalamic physics first suggested this to him) the possibility of the vacuum. From his critique of Aristotle's arguments against the vacuum, it becomes apparent that his real objection was to the Aristotelian doctrine of space. Since his understanding of the concept of space was different from that of Aristotle, he also came to a different conclusion concerning the vacuum. For Aristotle, who did not differentiate between space and the place of a body, space is the limit between the enclosing and the enclosed body. It is self-evident that with this definition there can be no space without a body. Crescas showed the unreasonable consequences resulting from this concept of space; it would be impossible to say that the outer heavenly sphere, unbounded as it was by any other body, was in space in the literal meaning of the term. It would also be impossible to say that any complete body was in any specific space; one can say this only of its outermost sections.[252] Thus the natural meaning of space was dissolved. For Crescas, therefore, space was not a mere relationship of bodies, but must be prior to bodies. Everybody occupies a place, which is equivalent to its extension. This extension, by virtue of its containing the body, constitutes the true essence of space. Even in filled space, extension *per se*—that is, space free of bodies—is primary to the extended body. Conceptually, space is simply extension, and thus the noncontradictory existence of a vacuum is possible.[253]

The objections which Aristotle had made to such a viewpoint were founded on the observation that we attribute to space that which properly belongs to bodies. Once we distinguish between the two, it is no longer possible to say, as Aristotle did, that just as the body is found in space, space must be found in a further space; extension, as such, no longer needs a space in which to be located. The other Aristotelian argument, that the filling up of immaterial extension by an extended body would violate the impenetrability of bodies, is of even less significance. Impenetrability does not pertain to extension *per se*, but to material bodies; there is, therefore, no contradiction to impenetrability if a body enters pure extension.[254] From this formulation of the concept of space, which Crescas justified both conceptually and physically, he concluded that space was infinite. An absolute limit to space is impossible, because beyond such a limit there must lie further space (whether empty or full). Whereas Gersonides had thought this to be merely a limitation of the power of human imagination, which could not grasp the notion of an absolute limit to space, Crescas viewed this as an objective theoretical necessity.[255] He also saw no objection to the thesis that material existence extended infinitely, but nevertheless said that material existence was finite, and that beyond it there lay empty space.[256] As it was later for Newton, for Crescas space was the infinite receptacle of things. There is another similarity between the two, in that both thought of space as the archetype of God's omnipresence.[257]

This acknowledgment of infinity within the doctrine of space is fully explicated by Crescas. Just as he maintained the infinity of space, he upheld the infinity of time and number. In regard to infinity, he was at pains to refute Aristotle and his followers, and two of his arguments are of fundamental interest. Against the possibility of an infinite quantity it was argued, with many variations, that this would lead to the absurd conclusion of one infinite quantity being greater than another. For example, if we cut a section of an infinitely straight line drawn from a certain point, the remainder must also be infinite. To this, Crescas replied that the ideas of "equal to," "larger than," and "smaller than," apply only to finite quantities, and do not apply to the realm of the infinite. There is no measure to the infinite, and hence it is foolish to ask whether two infinite quantities are equal to or larger than each other.[258]

Of more importance is the second counterargument. The assumption of an infinite does not mean that a finite suddenly ceases to be finite after reaching a certain position and then becomes infinite, but that it transcends all possible limits. In order to prove that the circular motion of an infinite body was impossible, Aristotle argued that if the body's radii were infinite, the distance between them would necessarily be infinite, and could never be traversed. Against this, Crescas claims that there can never be one point at which the radii become infinite. Such a point could only be the end point of the radius. But the infinity of an extension means that it has no end point. Every point which we describe on one of the radii has a finite distance from the center, and the meaning of an infinite radius is that it stretches beyond any possible point drawn on its length. From any possible point we can draw further points transcending the sphere of the finite.[259]

Crescas applied this same point of view to the concept of number. Aristotle had claimed that there was no infinite number, since every number must be either odd or even, and in both cases must be finite. This was not a compelling argument to Crescas, since the distinction between odd and even numbers holds true only of finite numbers; infinite numbers would transcend such a distinction, because they have no final term.[260] This argument is not developed in rigorous detail. Logically speaking, instead of discussing infinite number, Crescas should have spoken of an infinite series of numbers which has no end, although every particular number in it is finite. In his concept of the infinite, Crescas followed Gersonides, who expressly stated that no matter how much one added to any magnitude, it remains forever finite; no addition can make a finite magnitude infinite.[261] Nevertheless there is an important difference between the two. Gersonides admitted only the possibility of magnifying a magnitude limitlessly, and objected to the existence of a real infinite *per se*. For Crescas, a real infinite exists, which, however, can only be conceived as an unfinished magnitude, and can never be reached by a limitless extension of the finite.

This difference between the two is sharpened in terms of the problem of time. From his concept of infinity, Gersonides deduced the impossibility of time without a beginning, since it would lead to the idea of a past infinite. But Crescas, who affirmed the existence of a real infinite, came to the opposite conclusion. Time was possible and conceivable without a beginning, and he did not affirm the conclusions which Gersonides drew. For past time, too, remains at a finite distance from the present, no matter how far back in the past we go. Infinite time simply means that prior to each section of time, there exists a preceding section, and for this reason alone we have no right to speak of a completed infinite.[262]

The application of this point of view to the notion of causality is of special significance for religio-philosophic problems. If an infinite series is possible, then the causal chain can also be infinite. Thus the Aristotelian proof for the existence of a prime mover is abolished.[263] The only proof left for the existence of God is the proof from the merely possible being of things. Since the essences of things have only a possible existence, there must be a necessarily existing substance, through whom things acquire existence.[264] Maimonides had already differentiated this argument from the question of the finite or infinite nature of the causal chain. On the basis of this distinction, we have now drawn the positive conclusion that even if there is an infinite series of causes, the existence of a being whose essence necessarily coincided with existence must be assumed as the first cause of the world.[265] This dependence of all existence upon God is also the principle meaning of the concept of creation. Gersonides' assumption, that the world had been fashioned from matter independent of the being of God, was therefore impossible. Since all beings derive from the necessary being of God, the existence of such an independent matter is impossible. Matter, too, comes into being, and whatever its conceptual status, it must have been originated by God.[266] Thus God is the absolute and sole cause of the world. But this has no bearing on the question of whether or not the world had a temporal beginning. Even if we assert the eternity of the world, Crescas maintains creatio ex nihilo in the same sense given to it in Christian Scholasticism by Thomas Aquinas; that is, the world in the fullness of its being stems from God and has no ground for being independent of him.[267]

In opposition to Gersonides, Crescas saw the significance of the idea of creation in the absolute derivation of the being of things from God, and the question of the temporal creation of the world became of purely secondary importance. The question of the origin of the world in the divine will was also minor. He emphatically asserted the possibility that an eternal world would also be the work of the divine will, a possibility which Maimonides had rejected. In line with this conception, the idea of the divine will was decisively changed. According to Maimonides, the world could not have been originated by the divine will unless this will was absolutely free. Voluntary causality and necessary causality are contradictory terms. For Crescas, this opposition did not exist, and it was possible to understand the world as the result of the necessary operation of the divine will. The essence of willing means only that it assents to that which is presented to it conceptually, and by this assent brings it into existence. This is also possible when the act of affirmation is a necessary consequence of the essence of the willing agent. Even if we say that God's goodness realizes the good because of the necessity of his nature, and permits it to proceed from him, the voluntary nature of God's creative act would not be prejudiced. Thus the emanationist doctrine of the Aristotelians was given a voluntaristic form. Crescas, like his teacher Nissim ben Reuven, thought that he could combine this idea of the eternity of the world with the biblical doctrine of miracles.[268] Despite his inclinations, since it was a doctrine of the Torah, the belief in the temporal creation of the world must be affirmed as true. Even if we accept the latter as his authentic opinion, it merely demonstrates his hesitancy in accepting completely the consequences of his own philosophic thought.

At the basis of this concept of divine creativity there lies a new concept of the essence of God. Before we present its content, however, we must elucidate the formal problem of the divine attributes. Like Gersonides and Averroës before him, Crescas recognized the possibility of positive attributes. He confirmed this recognition in a penetrating critique of the opposed Maimonidean doctrine. Maimonides attempted to give a negative connotation to the positive attributes of God. If we say that God is wise, we are only negating his lack of wisdom. But this attempted semantic displacement does not accomplish its purpose. The negation of ignorance is logically equivalent to the affirmation of knowledge. For Crescas, it was obvious that ignorance was something negative, and the negation of this negation yielded the positive assertion of knowledge; as he puts it, the lack of knowledge has no other contrary than knowledge, and the negation of one was equivalent to the affirmation of the other. Thus, the concept of knowledge has the same meaning for man and God; the uniqueness of God's knowledge lies only in its infinity and originality, all other knowledge being finite and derivative. The more negations, the more affirmations there must be, since it is obvious that the opposite of ignorance and the opposite of impotence are two different things.[269]

Whereas Maimonides' formulation was based on the idea that the absolute unity of God's essence contained all positivity, though we could know the latter only in the separate form of knowledge, power, and so forth, Crescas stated that we can literally apply these predicates, along with their variety, to God. Of course, this immediately raises the question of how these multiple predicates could be reconciled with the divine unity. The basic idea with which Crescas answered this objection—perhaps through a sharpening of the ideas of the Asharites, whose ideas admittedly were much simpler than his—gets to the heart of the matter. Multiple qualities do not imply a compound subject if these qualities are interconnected and bound to the subject by inner necessity. That the absolute necessity of God's nature excludes all composition is unconditionally correct, for he cannot be compounded of separate parts. There would otherwise be a plurality of determinations, each of which entailed the other, and which cannot exist in separation from each other. But Crescas did not develop this idea completely, for he remained bound to the conventional view which elevated the being of God above any kind of plurality and, therefore, beyond all cognition. He distinguished between essential attributes and the divine essence, in which there was no plurality, and which cannot be known. The essential qualities do not constitute the essence, but are added to it, although necessarily. Thus we have the strange idea that beneath the knowable essential attributes, there lies undefinable essence. The comparison to light, which necessarily belongs to the luminous body, does not clarify the obscurity of this conception.[270]

He gave special attention to the predicates of unity and existence, which Maimonides had claimed could not be positively attributed to God. Here Maimonides followed the opinions of Ibn Sina, for whom existence and unity were accidental qualities added to the essence; they could not be attributed to God, because in God, existence and unity were inseparable from and identical with his essence. As against this, Averroës and Gersonides accepted the Aristotelian doctrine that existence and unity are everywhere identical with essence, and can, therefore, be attributed to God as all other things. Crescas maintained that both these conceptions of existence and unity were inadequate. His critique consisted of playing off the arguments of one conception against the other. Existence cannot be identical with essence, for this would make every existential judgment a tautology; neither can it be accidental to essence, because substance as the carrier of accidents would then not be able to come into being except through one of its own accidents. He therefore conceived existence as the logical condition of essences. It does not follow upon essence, as do accidents, but is the precondition for essence.[271]

Here again he lacked the means to realize fully his significant intention. He correctly estimated that existence could not be located in the disjunction of substance and accident, but the very important concept of the precondition of an essence did not really clarify the nature of the relationship between essence and existence. If existence was the precondition for essence, then an existential judgment again becomes a tautology. Crescas tried in vain to establish the peculiar character of the determination implicit in the concept of existence. The inner uncertainty in which he found himself is evident in the fact that the concepts of existence and unity, whose positive character he attempted to demonstrate, are always referred to negatively in the course of his presentation. Existence is always spoken of as equivalent to the negation of nonbeing, and unity as the negation of plurality.[272] Even if we are dealing more with a semantic uncertainty than a material contradiction, the return to the negative wording of the concepts shows that he could not clearly explicate their positive content.

The admission of positive attributes led Crescas to give an entirely different content to the idea of God than did Gersonides and Averroës. For the Neoplatonic idea of God, they had substituted the Aristotelian one of God as supreme thought. But Crescas was original in making the primary content of the God-idea not thought but goodness. In his doctrine of attributes he made clear that goodness was the unitary ground which welded the plurality of the attributes into a whole.[273] Thinking was obviously one aspect of the God-idea, but was not its central feature. It was rather included within the all-encompassing principle of goodness. He placed his position clearly in sharp opposition to that of the Aristotelian. That divine bliss should lie in knowledge, as Aristotle had taught, was impossible on two grounds. The analogy to human beings, in accordance with which Aristotle had constructed this idea, showed that bliss was consequent not upon the possession but the continuous acquisition of knowledge, and thus did not apply to God, who had no need to acquire knowledge—it was his eternal possession. Above all, bliss could not be predicated of a God whose essence consisted only in thinking. Joy does not come from the intellect but from feeling, and therefore has no place in a God conceived as exclusively intellectual. We cannot speak of God as joyous unless we apprehend him not as a mere thinking substance, but as a willing one, and, therefore, subject to emotions.[274] Joy is related to the act of creation, which was the expression of the divine will. Because in his essence God is supreme goodness, he allows this goodness to overflow and create; in this creation, which is not a once-for-all occurrence, but which continually maintains the world in existence, lies the bliss of God. Love, which rejoices in acts of loving-kindness, is joy in the goodness brought forth by God. It is merely another way of saying the same thing when we attribute to God love for his creatures, a love that is infinitely greater than the love of creatures for God.[275]

In this light Crescas was able to answer the question of the ultimate purpose of the world (which Maimonides had rejected because, to every attempted answer, one could always ask: Why did God desire this?). For Crescas there was an ultimate purpose, in terms of which this question became meaningless. If the essence of God is ultimate goodness, doing good deeds is an ultimate purpose, and cannot be questioned further.[276] Gersonides' question, if God is the highest form, can matter emanate from him, can be answered in the same way. There is a community of essence between God as the highest good, and the world as emanated goodness, and this common essence extends to all of the elements of the world, form and matter. Emanated goodness obviously derives from ultimate goodness.[277] Undoubtedly the Aristotelian tradition provided certain starting points for such a conception. With the admission of the Neoplatonic doctrine of emanation, there also came into Aristotelianism the notion that, due to God's perfection, things emanate from him, and he actualizes in them the maximum perfection that they can attain. Plato's statement, that jealousy was not to be found in God, became for many Arabic and Jewish philosophers a fixed formula for the idea that God grants to every being the maximum amount of being that it can receive. Among the Aristotelians, Avicenna, especially, expounded a similar doctrine, which in regard to God as the ultimate perfection and ultimate goodness seems not far removed from Crescas. But if we consider the matter more exactly we shall detect a sharp difference between the two. For Avicenna, thinking was God's perfection. God's bliss lay in the self-enjoyment of his thinking, and when Avicenna spoke of the love of God, this was his love for himself as being ultimate perfection. It befits such perfection that its goodness should overflow, but Avicenna expressly rejected the idea that this occurred as a result of God's benevolence toward the world.[278] Goodness proceeds from God because it is grounded in his essence, but he does not will this. He approves it only because it is a necessary consequence of his being.

In opposition to this, Crescas shifted the essence of God to goodness, and conceived of the procession of the world from him as being completely voluntaristic. God is will, and his love is not confined to himself alone, but is directed to his creatures, and to the perfection realized by them. Whereas Avicenna, as well as the Jewish Neoplatonists and Aristotelians, considered God's love for his creatures an affect unworthy of his dignity, and interpreted the biblical verses which spoke of God's love as merely denoting the beneficence of his act, for Crescas this love was not an affect, but was grounded in God's spontaneity. He went far beyond the Platonic conception of God's goodness, especially since God's love was personally directed toward his creatures, and particularly to man.[279]

The same disengagement from Aristotelian intellectualism is involved in the conception of man and his destiny, as Crescas' treatment of the purpose of the Torah makes clear. If we seek the ultimate purpose toward which all of the individual goals of the Torah tend, it cannot lie in the transitory earthly happiness of men. Crescas thus denied that the moral perfection of man was the final goal of the Torah; here Crescas remained bound to the Aristotelian tradition, and viewed morality only in terms of its social effects, as the promotion of the common weal.[280] The final goal of the Torah could only be the supreme good of man, the attainment of eternal happiness. For the Aristotelians, this goal was reached through the intellectual perfection of man. The acquired intellect is that which survives man, and the bliss of the hereafter is the bliss of knowledge; here Crescas found the object of his polemic.

We can deal later with his attack on the doctrine of the eternity of acquired intellect. Along with it, however, he combined a rejection of the intellectualistic concept of human happiness, and utilized the same arguments brought forward in his treatment of the problem of God. The main argument is once again psychological; joy and happi-

ness, and also the joy of knowing, do not belong to the sphere of intellect, but to feeling. Even if the acquired intellect survived the
death of man, one still could say nothing concerning its happiness.
For Crescas, feeling and will were not merely concomitant phenomena of thought, but independent elements of consciousness; this
psychological independence of feeling made him seek the ultimate
purpose of man in something other than the purely intellectual
realm. He therefore added an argument which we have already met
in connection with the idea of God: that the mere possession of
knowledge does not in itself grant joy. Knowledge, which certainly
cannot be increased after death, cannot be that good toward which
our feelings are directed.[281] The highest good of man is, rather, the
love of God. Through it, and not through knowledge, man attains
communion with God, and eternal happiness. However, we should
not consider the love of God, which in itself is the supreme happiness,
as simply a means to future happiness. As man's highest good, it is
also his final end. Only when seen from God's viewpoint is it at the
same time a means toward future happiness. But since man's end
also lies in the happiness of the love of God, there is no opposition
between the two goals, and the eternal love of God completely contains the final goal of man.[282] This final goal is not like that of the
Aristotelians, limited only to philosophers. The love of God is not the
product of knowledge. It is attained not through philosophy, but
through the Torah, which aims at this goal in all its precepts.[283] Revealed religion thereby acquires an independent significance vis-à-vis
science. Here Crescas agrees completely with Judah Halevi, but he
reaches this goal by a simpler route, in the theory of the supernatural
efficacy of the ceremonial law. Of the many consequences of this
doctrine we shall mention only one. For Crescas, prophecy was a
natural phenomenon, the climax of man's communion with God,
which could exist without this final stage. Like this communion in
general, this highest stage does not rest upon the intellect. It is rooted
in the love of God, which is produced by the observance of the divine
commandments.[284]

The presupposition of this doctrine of eternal life is a changed
notion of the essence of the soul. The soul must be conceived as immortal, and its immortality is not to be limited to the acquired intellect alone. Crescas maintained the fundamental Aristotelian conception of the soul as the form of the body, but sought to define it in
such a way that it would conform to the substantial independence of

the soul. In his definition, therefore, he combined these two factors of the analysis—that the soul was both the form of the body, and a spiritual substance predisposed towards knowledge; it was then quite easy to deduce the soul's substantial immortality. This definition and its validation remind us of Avicenna and Thomas Aquinas: of the two, Thomas developed the idea with greater subtlety.[285] In Crescas, however, the character of the soul as form, and its spiritual substantiality, were joined together in a superficial manner. More important than his own position is his critique of the eternity of the acquired intellect. This doctrine equated intellect with the total of the concepts which it had acquired, but the unity of the thinking is thereby dissolved. If the concepts which constitute our intellects are plural, the understanding which results from their sum must be plural; it is then difficult to see wherein this unity resides.[286] The idea that the acquired intellect is separate from the soul and its predisposition for thinking, is equally difficult and full of contradictions. It is through thinking that the potential intellect becomes actualized; this actualization occurs through the act of thought, by which we acquire concepts. If we maintain this definition, the acquired intellect must result from the potential intellect. But it would be paradoxical if the acquired intellect continues to exist separately from the potential intellect, while the potential intellect perishes with the death of the individual soul.[287]

From a similar theoretical perspective, Crescas criticized the Aristotelian doctrine underlying the doctrine of the eternity of the intellect; namely, that in actual thinking, the thinking—that is, the intellect, that which thinks—and that which is thought, are identical. He saw this doctrine's basic error as mistaking the necessary interconnection of thinker and object of thought for an identity.[288] In spite of the fact that his critique had less as its object the presuppositions than the consequences of this theory, it did throw into relief all the difficult points which arose from the Aristotelian identification of thought with its conceptual objects, and it contained the point of departure for a fundamental revision of the entire Aristotelian standpoint.

While defending the substantial immortality of the soul, Crescas conceded immortality not only to the rational part of the soul, but to will and feeling as well. Eternal happiness depended upon them. The deepest meaning of his voluntarism, however, becomes clear only with the investigation of freedom of the will. Crescas' very formulation of the problem was essentially different from that found in any prior Jewish religious philosophy. From Saadia onwards, the dominant theological question had centered around the problem of reconciling the freedom of man with the omniscience and omnipotence of God. For Crescas, this retreated into the background in the face of the philosophic problem of reconciling free will with the law of causality. The arguments for freedom of the will are essentially the traditional ones: the possibility implanted in the essence of the will of choosing between alternatives, the senselessness of all human efforts if man's actions are predetermined, and the impossibility of understanding from a deterministic standpoint that man was given a divine law for the observance of which he was responsible. As against this, the arguments in favor of determinism are merely variations of the idea that every action in the world has a cause.[289]

Crescas introduces the omniscience of God only as additional support. He deviates even more decidedly from the unanimous doctrine of all previous Jewish religious philosophy by settling the conflict in favor of determinism. Outwardly, his solution of the problem appears as a compromise between the two extreme positions. He agrees with indeterminism insofar as he accepts its basic tenet concerning the possibility of events. An event can be said to be possible if looked at merely from the essence of the individual object. In accordance with its essence, the human will can decide one way or another, and in this sense the characterization of the nature of the human will is correct. Similarly, the fact of ethical commandments also presupposes that the nature of the human will would not prescribe its mode of action, that human choice is not predetermined. On the other hand, determinism is correct if we center our attention, not upon the essence of single individuals, but upon the causes which work upon them. The human will as such has the possibility of choosing between many alternatives, but the causes operating on the will plainly determine which course to choose at any given time. If two men were situated in identically similar inner and outer conditions, their decisions would also be the same. By comparison with the causes which determine events from all sides, the concept of possibility loses all validity.[290]

This compromise was really a complete capitulation to determinism, and can be defended only by a misunderstanding of this concept, which is the same concept we met with in Abner of Burgos. Abner had already alienated himself from Judaism long before his conversion, but Crescas was firmly rooted in Judaism, and looked upon himself as the defender of the teachings of the Torah in the face of its philosophic detractors, representing it in its purity against its perversion by the Aristotelians. That a man of such intellectual stature could accept determinism was something quite different for Jewish religious philosophy than the assent of Abner of Burgos. Crescas was not dependent upon Abner, but drew upon the same sources, the Islamic Aristotelians, who changed the Orthodox Islamic notion of predestination into that of a causal determination of human acts. He was especially close to Averroës, for whom human action consisted of the joint action of human will and that external causation which penetrated it. His view was described as a mediation between the thesis of extreme determinism and extreme indeterminism.[291] From Abner he took the changed deterministic interpretation of Judaism's belief in the freedom of the will. His proofs from Scripture and the Talmud, chosen to validate the deterministic position, essentially repeated Abner's contentions.[292]

Materially, Crescas was close to Abner's arguments when he tried to refute the ethical arguments against determinism. He, too, maintained that the meaning of the ethical command was not perverted by a properly conceived determinism, but rather helped to guide man towards the good. Just as determinism did not make nonsense of man's aspiration for his material welfare, but encouraged this striving, it also took nothing away from man's ethical aspiration and the commandments pertinent to it. Both were necessary means for bringing about the good, since good and evil were not caused by an eternal moral obligation implanted in human nature but were caused by the determinate motivation of the will.[293] This argument had been used by earlier philosophers, including Judah Halevi, to prove that the value of the moral law was not impugned by God's foreknowledge.[294] Halevi had begun his argument, presupposing freedom of the will; Abner and Crescas placed it in a predestinarian context and thus gave it a completely different meaning. Crescas justified reward for the righteous and retribution for the wicked by claiming that the content of true justice was contained in the divine goodness. God does not punish for the sake of revenge, but to deter man from wickedness. Reward and punishment are justifiable as means for strengthening the will to do good, and thereby producing it.[295] All the basic ideas of the modern deterministic argument of ethics are found here: the replacement of the indeterministic concept of freedom by a psychological concept which defines freedom of the will as the psychologically motivated choice which causes an action, the conception of ethical ideals as a psychological motivating factor, and the justification of reward on the basis of motivational power.

In addition to this teleological justification of punishment, there is another causal explanation. The fact that all human acts are conditioned does not invalidate the reward of the righteous or the punishment of the wicked, since both follow necessarily upon the behavior of humans, just as burning follows contact with fire.[296] Crescas used this idea, which Abner had expressed only in general terms, to demonstrate that true reward, attained only in the world to come, follows from man's conduct.

Eternal bliss consists of communion with God, which follows necessarily from the love of God. Genuine observance of the divine commandments presupposes joyful surrender of the soul to God, and in turn produces love of God; bliss must spring from it by inner necessity, and by the same necessity will be absent when its presuppositions are missing. Thus it is self-evident that only the freely willed, and not the compulsive action, can be rewarded or punished, although both actions are equally necessary. For it is only when necessity has penetrated the inner direction of the will that the actions of man can bring him closer to or drive him away from God.[297] Only in this formulation do we see the religious meaning of determinism. Just as God acts by reason of the goodness of his essence, so does the man whose actions are determined by the love of God. The essence of God is his goodness, and man's bliss is his participation in this goodness. The power of good rests in will and love, but their power to confer happiness does not presuppose absolute freedom; it is grounded necessarily in their essence. In this way, the value of freedom is removed both from the acts of God and from the communion of love between man and God. This diminution of the religious value of freedom poses the question of why Crescas felt impelled to draw upon the Islamic Aristotelians' metaphysical determinism, which even the most exterme Jewish Aristotelians had rejected.

As in his doctrine of the divine will, Crescas did make the qualification that the objectively possible deterministic theory would have to be abandoned if it contradicted the words of the Torah. He tried to understand the Torah in such a way that the freedom of man was not destroyed by the various motives which operated on his behavior, and that necessity existed only from the viewpoint of God's knowledge.[298] But this qualification is as weak as it was before, whatever

Crescas' sincerity. Inwardly, Crescas was on the side of determinism, even if at the end he did not want to admit it completely.

This attempt to overcome Aristotelianism stands in a very special relation to Maimonides' efforts to formulate a theistic Aristotelianism. The basic similarity of the two was in their explanation of God's creativity, where both upheld a voluntaristic rather than the Aristotelian position. Only in Crescas does voluntarism affect the entire system and thereby overcome Aristotelianism. Maimonides remained an Aristotelian in his theory of values, as well as in his doctrine of man and of man's relationship to God. In Maimonides' concept of God, voluntarism applied rather to God's activity than to his essence. Crescas was a voluntarist especially in his theory of religious values. The ultimate religious values were outside the sphere of reason. The concepts of God, man, and their relationship to each other are now entirely redefined. Whereas metaphysical freedom and spontaneity had been essential considerations for Maimonides, in the voluntarism of Crescas they become matters of indifferent concern. For Maimonides, will and necessity were incompatible; for Crescas they were essentially compatible. He transformed the doctrine of emanation into the necessary volition of the divine creativity. In the place of reason, the love of God, necessarily developing in the soul of man, served as the link between God and man. This conception was quite distant from historical Judaism, both metaphysically and religiously. Maimonides took the idea of freedom from the ethical monotheism of Judaism, while Crescas received from it the supremacy of the values of will and love; considered in the most general terms, it is difficult to say which of the two remained closer to the essence of historical Judaism.

5 The End and
Aftereffects of
Medieval Religious Philosophy

The End of Jewish
Philosophy in Spain

WITH Crescas the productive era of Jewish philosophy of the Middle Ages came to an end. What followed did not equal it either as continuation or as counterstatement. The philosophic work of the fifteenth century was primarily an eclectic utilization of the traditional theories. The thinkers of the period differed from each other principally in the way in which they made these combinations. Among them we find extremely erudite men, as we see from the various commentaries on Maimonides and Averroës. The frightful pressure under which Spanish Jewry, the foremost bearers of Jewish philosophy, lived during the fifteenth century precluded any productive or original philosophic work. To these persecutions and pressures we can at least partially attribute the more conservative bent of thought that became characteristic of the period. There was not a trace of that boldness which marked the spread of the philosophic enlightenment through the Jewish world in the period between Maimonides and Gersonides. Philosophy now displayed a definite tendency toward orthodoxy, and rejected the possibility of the more latitudinarian views of the older Jewish Aristotelians; it was marked by a fundamental change in the spiritual atmosphere in which it developed. The radical form of philosophic thought, which Jewish Aristotelians from Maimonides to Gersonides felt obliged to refute, more and more ceased to be a pressing reality, and was operative only as a literary factor. Crescas was the last philosopher whose thinking shows the awareness of facing a living and powerful enemy. More pressing than the philosophic justification of Judaism was the need of Jewish apologetics against Christianity, and this gave philosophic work an entirely different focus and direction.

This change of focus was already present in Crescas' younger contemporary, Simon ben Zemach Duran (1361-1444). His philosophy, although developed independently, was in many respects parallel to that of Crescas. He, too, turned away from the view of Maimonides that all attributes of the divine were only negative. He endeavored to preserve their positive character, but unlike Crescas, who developed an unfinished but extraordinarily penetrating theory, Duran returned to the idea common to earlier Jewish philosophers of religion that the attributes did not posit plurality in God because they are all identical with his essence. To the objection that any statements about God would, therefore, be tautological, he replied that the concept of attributes predicated of God does not of itself include an identification with the divine essence. Identification of these attributes with his essence can only be said to "occur" when we think of them as related to this essence.[1] This theory, which is very obscure in the form in which it is stated, will become somewhat clearer if we see it as a very laconic review of the doctrine of Thomas Aquinas. Aquinas held that the divine attributes were various aspects of God's essence which, taken in itself, is simple. The attributes are separated only in the form in which they are known to us by experience; in their highest form, free from all empirical defects with which they have been associated—that is, when applied to God—they are identical with each other and with the essence of God.[2]

Like Crescas, Duran rejects the immortality of the acquired intellect. In order to justify the essential immortality of the soul, he attributes to men, in addition to those parts of the soul which are bound to the human body, another, immaterial soul derived from God, the *neshame*, which is the bearer of the rational capacity. This idea, drawn from the Kabbala, is combined somewhat artificially with his version of Aristotelian psychology.[3] This enables him to prove that man's immortality does not depend on how much knowledge he has acquired, but on his ethical conduct, in obedience to the divine commandments. Divine providence was not limited to those men who, as Maimonides taught, by reason of their superior intellect were in communion with God; all men participated in it. Despite the apparent similarity of this position to the extensive critique which Crescas made of the significance of the intellect, it is far removed from the latter's principled critique of such intellectualism. When it came to matters of principle, Duran followed the lead of Maimonides and only modified the latter's intellectualism when it ran counter to Jewish tradition. Thus Duran also accepted Maimonides' theory of prophecy, but in addition to maintaining the natural presuppositions of prophecy, he emphasized its dependence upon divine grace even more than Maimonides did.[4]

Only Duran's concept of the dogmas of Judaism, developed in the introduction to his commentary on Job, is of independent value. There he allied himself with the Maimonidean formulation of the content of Jewish teaching in thirteen universally binding articles of faith. He characteristically deviated from Maimonides in his reasons for distinguishing dogmas. Maimonides had fixed the contents of Jewish faith in dogmas, because he considered the fundamental elements of a philosophic view of religion to be the indispensable presuppositions of right belief. Only a Jew can share life eternal, and that only if he has adopted at least the results of the philosophical knowledge of God, even if this be merely in the form of belief.

For Duran, however, this philosophical rationalizing of Judaism was subordinate to another interest. He intended to stabilize the concept of orthodoxy; one might be tempted to say that he wanted to establish the boundaries of the philosophical rationalization of Judaism. The development of Jewish philosophy had resulted in viewpoints far removed from the soil of Jewish tradition. To these, the traditionalists had answered with charges of heresy. What was the possibility of fixing the boundaries within which a thinker might still be considered Jewish? This standard question, which became more urgent in the course of Judaism's historical development, was answered by Duran in such a way that, while safeguarding the basic principles of Judaism through the establishment of boundaries, it still allowed freedom for philosophic speculation. His first answer was that any deliberate contradiction of one of the doctrines of revelation constituted a break with Judaism. Every Jew must profess that the Holy Scriptures, and especially the Pentateuch, were divinely revealed, which meant that its entire content must be accepted as absolute truth. For this viewpoint there is no distinction between the important and the significant. Whoever denies the minutest detail of the Torah's doctrines, while knowing it to be a teaching of the Torah, thereby becomes an unbeliever.[5]

Duran thus gives precise expression to the authoritarian concept of religion which governs the entire Jewish tradition, and with it, all Jewish philosophy of religion. The formal acknowledgment of the authority of revelation was also a self-evident assumption for the most radical thinkers of the Jewish Middle Ages, insofar as they wanted to be considered Jews. The few exceptions to this rule were those who advocated the well-known view of Albalag that the Torah was only a political document and did not purport to teach the truth. All of the other philosophers assented to the absolute truth of every word of the Torah. Truth was conclusively given in the Torah, and hence there was firm limit to the freedom of philosophical speculation. This freedom was that of interpreting the meaning of the Torah, harmonizing this with its own conclusions. Philosophic radicalism revealed itself only in the boldness and recklessness of such interpretation. Even such a thinker as Gersonides wanted nothing more than to establish the true meaning of the Torah with the aid of philosophy. The same was true of Averroës with regard to Islam.[6] He, too, did not merely pretend to recognize the authority of Islam; we have every reason to believe his statement, but we should also bear in mind that his naturalistic interpretation of revelation was not identical with that of revealed religion itself.

However, the fact that it was possible to transform the admittedly revealed contents of religion by means of interpretation shows that it is impossible to define the limits of orthodoxy merely by the belief in revelation. It was Averroës who, with programmatic sharpness, claimed orthodoxy for philosophy from the viewpoint of content. After first claiming for philosophy the sovereign right of finding the truth, and with it establishing the meaning of revelation, Averroës afterward emphasized that there was a limit to this freedom of philosophic inquiry and to the philosophic interpretation of revelation. These limitations are inherent in the basic principles of religion which philosophers, like simple believers, must affirm, without changing their literal meaning; to deviate from any one of them is equivalent to denying revelation *in toto*. Duran adapted this distinction between basic principles of the Torah, and the remainder of revelation, to his own purpose. Changing the meaning of any of the details of revealed religion did not make someone a heretic, even if he thereby departed from the true meaning of the doctrines. Whoever goes too far in his interpretation of details is considered in error, but not heretical.[7] In regard to details, there is complete freedom of philosophic inquiry. This is not true for the basic principles of the Torah; it is forbidden to change their meaning, and everyone must accept them as they are.

Duran felt obliged to prove that such principles were universally binding. The thirteen principles of faith could not have suited

Duran's purpose, since Maimonides gave no reasons for his selections. For the thirteen articles Duran substituted his own list of three dogmas: the existence of God, revelation, and retribution. All of these concepts were necessary entailments of the idea of revelation. Revelation would be impossible without a God who revealed himself, and the law thus revealed is secured by the thought of retribution.[8]

From Duran's own words we know that these three principles were not first laid down by him, but were well-known long before his time.[9] In all probability they originated with Averroës, who had said that these three truths were inherent in every revealed religion, although he did not specifically call them dogmas.[10] This idea, that the three basic principles which flow from the concept of revelation are shared by all revealed religions, is also found in Duran. But as the origin of this doctrine indicates, these three principles are insufficient to fulfill the purpose assigned to them in Duran's scheme. Whoever admits the authority of revelation must affirm these doctrines in some form. On the other hand, they were given such a broad definition that they left room for even the most radical reinterpretation of revelation. They did not exclude the possibility of replacing the idea of a personal God with that of an impersonal divine principle from whom the world proceeded by necessity, or that revelation would be interpreted as a natural fact, or that reward in the hereafter would consist of the bliss resulting from the perfection of the intellect. Thus Averroës could affirm these dogmas as universally binding, without contradicting his own views. In order to utilize these principles for his own purpose, Duran had to give them a more precise and concrete meaning. He did this by showing that they entailed unmistakable conclusions; if this had not been the case, they could not have served as principles. They were, therefore, universally binding, like the dogmas of the Torah themselves. Even if he did not express himself with complete clarity on these points, his conception of the notions of revelation and retribution indicated that for him their supernatural meaning was essential and faithful to the true content of these doctrines.[11]

Only that man is a believer who acknowledges revelation and reward to be the work of divine providence which knows and governs every particular thing. In line with this, Duran emphasized that *creatio ex nihilo* was not one of the fundamental doctrines of revelation, but that the Aristotelian doctrines of the eternity of the universe, which claimed that the world necessarily coexisted with God, could not be harmonized with the principles of revealed religion. Taken by themselves, Duran's three dogmas did not settle the question whether God created and ruled the world freely, or whether it proceeded from him necessarily, and was therefore subject to the unbreakable rule of natural law. But in stating the necessary corollaries of these dogmas, he took the opportunity to safeguard the supernatural meaning of religion, and to establish a barrier to an interpretive change of the contents of revelation which would impose the sense of natural necessity upon them.

This theory of dogmas is one of the most famous doctrines of medieval Jewish philosophy, but it is not entered under Duran's name, but that of Joseph Albo (d. 1444), one of Hasdai Crescas' students. He was well-known for his participation in the religious disputation held at Tortosa, and devoted his book *Ikkarim (Basic Principles)* to a discussion of the problem of dogmas. Albo's *Ikkarim* was widely circulated because of its fluent style, and its spirited and interesting exposition. Its important doctrines were drawn for the most part from Maimonides, Crescas, and Duran, and its dialectical structuring gives evidence of cleverness rather than profundity. The first main section of the book deals with the doctrine of the three dogmas of faith; then, a chapter is devoted to each dogma. In this way the entire field of religious philosophy is covered. His theory of dogmas was built completely upon Duran's, but he analyzed his ideas with greater precision, and thereby clarified the purpose of the doctrine.[12]

Like Duran, Albo taught that an erroneous conception of one of the truths of faith did not make one an heretic, and this enabled him to maintain the rights of philosophic inquiry. At first glance it appears that only the affirmation of the three basic dogmas was absolutely required by orthodoxy.[13] He also accepted from Duran the idea that one can deduce a series of corollaries from each of the basic principles. Denial of one of the corollaries implies a denial of its root-principle; only a believer who accepts these corollaries has a share in the world to come.[14] In making this requirement of acquiescence to the corollaries, his intention to maintain the supernatural character of religion became even more obvious than in the case of Duran. Since he believed that the dogma of revelation also included God's knowledge of particulars, and that of reward and punishment included God's special providence for the individual, any view which enclosed the action of God within the bounds of the natural was contradictory to revealed religion.[15] Similar considerations applied to belief in *creatio ex nihilo*; although as a basic principle it was not obligatory, yet the relationship of the world to God must of necessity be so understood that the free sovereignty of God over creation could not be in the least diminished. From a dogmatic standpoint, it was permitted to maintain the Platonic view that God created the world from pre-existent matter, although this belief was not congruent with the true meaning of the Torah; on the other hand, the Aristotelian doctrine of the eternity of the universe, since it uprooted the freedom of God, was declared false.[16]

All this agreed completely with Duran's view, but Albo's statements were so precisely phrased that one was able to delineate clearly the doctrinal status of the derived principles. Nevertheless, the corollaries deduced from the idea of revelation, and the conclusions which flow from them, were insufficient to comprehend the basic elements of the Jewish faith in their entirety. Albo was forced to admit that apart from the principles deduced from the concept of revelation— and which would, therefore, hold true for any revealed religion— there were other beliefs peculiar to Judaism, such as resurrection and the coming of the Messiah, which could be set within the framework of these principles, but which could not be logically deduced from them. They, too, were universally binding beliefs, even though he could not place them on the same level as the basic principles which were inherent in the concept of revelation.[17] One could direct the same question to these peculiarly Jewish dogmas that Duran and Albo had presented against the thirteen articles of Maimonides; Albo has no more of a criterion for the selection of these principles than Maimonides had for his thirteen articles of faith.

Albo's doctrine of derived principles had a further, no less essential, significance. He offered a criterion for the truth of those faiths which claimed to be divinely revealed. For Averroës, to whom we attributed the derivation of the three basic dogmas from the concept of revelation, this concept had no exclusive significance. Prophecy was found everywhere as a natural occurrence, and the many historic faiths were all equally of divine origin. In addition, the regulation of communal life, which was the function of the prophets, required that these prophetic lawgivers be present everywhere. The various religions are differentiated from each other only by the varying superiority of their founders, and accordingly by the perfection of their contents.

At first Albo accepted this idea. He, too, viewed the divine law as a necessary presupposition for well-regulated community life, and therefore concluded that God could not withhold from mankind law-givers enlightened by him.[18] On principle, he, too, posited the possibility of a plurality of revealed religions, and developed the idea that the difference between the laws of the various religions was grounded in the variant natures of the men for whom they were established, and to which they are appropriate.[19] But he is far from Averroës' idea of a universal revelation, and twists the latter's doctrine so as not to impugn the exclusive and overriding value of scriptural revelation. By multiple revelations, he means only those of which the Bible speaks—to Adam, Noah, and Abraham—and which preceded the Mosaic revelation. According to the Talmud, the seven commandments of the sons of Noah are universally applicable to mankind, and were perfected by the Mosaic revelation only for the sake of the children of Israel. There still exist many revealed religions, and the differences between their ordinances is explained in the manner suggested above.[20]

On the other hand, Albo refused to recognize extra-biblical faiths, and unconditionally maintained the exclusive character of the biblical revelation. Christianity and Islam, which arose after Judaism, unjustly claimed to be revealed religions. The polemic against Islam had no actual significance for Albo, but he was seriously and urgently concerned with the polemic against Christianity. The doctrine of the necessary principles of revealed religion and their consequences provided the springboard for this polemic. Only that religion was of divine origin which was not only in agreement with the basic principles but also with their consequences.[21] The differences between revealed religions always concern their legislative, never their dogmatic content. Theoretically it is possible that the Mosaic law could be abrogated by another, later prophet, but such a prophet would have to be publicly certified by God, as Moses had been.[22] But truth was one and the same for all religions, and its main features were set by the assumptions of the concept of revelation. Christianity contradicted these assumptions with its doctrine of God, since it dissolved the unity of the divine essence, which was entailed by the very idea of God. The philosophic critique of Christianity, which was at some points accompanied by an historical criticism, stressed the anti-rationalism of Christianity in its dogmatic expression.[23] Albo sharply differentiated between those matters which are contrary to nature and those which are contrary to reason: the boundaries of nature could be broken by the activity of God, but those of reason are inviolable.[24]

Albo defended the supernatural character of religion from every angle. Prophecy—which is the origin of religion—springs from the will of God. Albo admitted, however, that certain psychological requirements were necessary for the attainment of prophecy. But these requirements, which taken in themselves were beyond the capacity of ordinary human nature, provided only the possibility for prophecy.

To be invested with the divine spirit was always conditional upon the divine will, which could in exceptional instances disregard these psychological prerequisites.[25] The content of revelation, too, points beyond the natural sphere. This holds true even for the ethical precepts, which are aimed at this-world happiness, and which in principle belong to the sphere of natural reason. Indeed, reason can postulate a general ethical order, but it can never concretely establish what is actually good and helpful for man. With reference to Aristotle, who clearly stated that it was impossible to establish the correct mean—which in conceptual terms was the essence of virtue— Albo showed that only revelation could fix concretely the correct moral and political order, and thus he returned to one of the ideas of Saadia Gaon.[26] This applied with even greater truth to the attainment of eternal happiness, which could not be reached by natural means. Like Crescas, Albo rejected the philosophic doctrine that one could attain bliss through the perfection of the intellect; it was not knowledge, but the observance of the divine precepts which was required. If a man observed these precepts with the right intention, they operated on his soul so as to prepare it for everlasting life. But Albo did not try to overcome Aristotelian intellectualism in terms of its fundamental assumptions, as did Crescas; on the contrary, he admitted that the purpose of man's existence was to perfect his rational capacity. Such a perfection of the intellect, however, must not be understood in terms of theoretical understanding, but in man's conviction that his happiness lies in finding favor with God; to this Albo joined Judah Halevi's idea that only the Torah could give man full knowledge of the means for winning God's favor.[27] His previously mentioned doctrine of prophecy was similarly eclectic. He opposed the idea of prophecy as a natural phenomenon, and along with it, Maimonides' teaching that divine act was necessary to prevent the occurrence of natural revelation. On the contrary, prophecy was based on the divine will. He nevertheless persisted in the Maimonidean doctrine of the psychological conditions for prophecy, but weakened them into mere presuppositions. This was done repeatedly, especially when he tried to combine the doctrines of Crescas and Maimonides.

His doctrine of the divine attributes provides an excellent example of this eclecticism. He first treated the principle of the divine unity in the spirit of Maimonides, and concluded that it was forbidden to make positive attributions to God.[28] But later he cites Crescas' opinion as that of genuine Jewish theology: it is impossible to negate a negation without thereby making an affirmation; for example, the negation of ignorance implies knowledge. The acceptance of positive attributes, which follows from this proof, did not affect the unity of the divine essence, since these attributes are plural only in the imperfect form in which they are known to us empirically. However, in their pure and perfect form, where they are predicated of God, they are identical with each other and with the divine essence.[29]

The source of this doctrine—both in his case and in that of Duran —was Thomas Aquinas, and Albo's detailed exposition made its similarity to that of Aquinas strikingly evident. At first it appeared that Albo could not decide between two contradictory views, but only set them alongside each other as of equal value. But at the end, he expounded the position of Maimonides—which he labeled the position of the philosophers generally—an explication that brought it into harmony with the opposed position. If with Maimonides one had to deny all attributes in God, a fundamental distinction must still be made between the negation of the attributes of perfection and their privation. The latter, such as ignorance, are negated in God, but the former, such as knowledge, are not negated unless they point to a lack of perfection; one can therefore fully affirm them as a divine perfection. Instead of abandoning Maimonides' position, he thus reconciled it with its opposite, by changing its meaning and turning it upside down.[30] These compromises have neither material nor historical importance. Only in regard to the problem of dogmas did Albo exert strong influence upon later Jewish thought, although even here he was not an innovator.

This conservative tendency maintained itself throughout the fifteenth century, and again and again the concern was with the same two questions: the acknowledgment of the supernatural activity of

God, and the elimination of intellectualism from the doctrine of man and his otherworldly destiny. With vehement fanaticism, the kabbalist Shem Tob ben Joseph ibn Shem Tob (circa 1440) attacked philosophy in general from these two orientations, and criticized Maimonides with even greater sharpness than he did such extreme rationalists as Albalag. Precisely because of the former's moderate position, he saw him as the greater foe of religion. He repeatedly found within Maimonides' doctrines of providence, prophecy, and miracles the same tendency—the limitation of the supernatural activity of God. In Maimonides' doctrine of the immortality of the acquired intellect, and of knowledge as the link between God and man, he saw an attempt to make philosophy superior to the Torah, and to place the unbelieving philosopher on a higher level than the professing believer.[31]

Characteristic of the defensive stance which philosophy increasingly was forced to assume was the form in which Shem Tob's son, Joseph ben Shem Tob, found his way back to the discipline which his father had outlawed. He was more concerned to defend philosophy in the forum of orthodoxy than to promote the clarification of philosophic problems. He believed that the surest way of achieving this was to show that Aristotle did not maintain the erroneous doctrines attributed to him. In opposition to the conventional view that Aristotle had repudiated individual providence, he ingeniously cited the sentence of the *Nicomachean Ethics* that agreed with the conventional idea of the gods concerning themselves with man, and deduced from it that man became beloved of the gods through the cultivation of his intellectual powers. By a lucky stroke he was able to utilize this remnant of an older, more religious phase of Aristotle's thought in order to interpret his whole system.

By strangely tortuous ways, he also managed to remove the offensiveness from the Aristotelian doctrine of the eudaemonia of knowledge. It was true that Aristotle had thought man's happiness resulted from the development of reason, his highest power. But this applied only to this-worldly happiness. The idea that understanding could grant man otherworldly happiness and bliss could not be found in Aristotle; it was only his commentators who had introduced this assertion into his system. But their arguments were not really convincing, and one could not complete Aristotle's thought in their spirit. Since Aristotle had explained positively how man attained otherworldly happiness, we could rightly limit his declarations to happiness in this world, and thus they could be linked to the teachings of the Torah. Above the happiness of this world, which is attained by reason, is the bliss of the future world which one attains only through observance of the commandments of the Torah.[32] Thus Aristotle was pitted against the Aristotelians, including Maimonides, who had been influenced on essential points by the dominant interpretations of the Stagirite. From this perspective, which placed the goal of the Torah completely on the supernatural level, Joseph ben Shem Tob also rejected Maimonides' rationalistic interpretation of the divine commandments. His son, Shem Tob ben Joseph, returned to Maimonides on this point in a voluminous and substantial commentary to the *Guide* (written in 1488, four years before the expulsion of the Jews from Spain). A similar standpoint was represented by his contemporary, Abraham Shalom, who, after a penetrating analysis of the problems, vigorously defended Maimonides against the attacks of Crescas.

Jewish philosophy in Spain reached its end with Isaac Abrabanel (b. Lisbon, 1437, d. Venice, 1509), the last in the line of Spanish Jewish statesmen. For several years before the expulsion of the Jews from Spain, he served the Spanish royal house, and afterward, the King of Naples. In spite of his encyclopedic knowledge, which also encompassed Christian literature, and his dialectical skill, he was poor in original ideas, and the pursuit of philosophic inquiry as such was secondary for him to the dominant interest of so blunting the point of philosophic concepts and theories that they lose their religious debatability. In a work on the basic teachings of Judaism, he first rejected the objections which later thinkers had made against Maimonides' thirteen principles of faith, but afterwards concluded that such a list had absolutely no significance because every verse in the Torah was to be given unconditional credence; no distinction could be drawn between more important and less important verses.[33] He devoted his best energies to the discussion of creation, though here, too, he operated with essentially the traditional arguments. Against Gersonides' assumption of a pre-existent matter, he objected that the correlativity of matter and form precluded the existence of a formless matter.[34] Against Crescas, he inclined rather towards Maimonides' view that the eternity of the world could not be reconciled with the concept of the origination of the world by the divine will; Crescas' idea of a necessary will seemed to dissolve the concept of will.[35] For Maimonides, only the temporal creation of the world was congruent with the requirements of religion; Abrabanel accepted this position, although philosophically (as Maimonides had indicated) it could not be demonstrated, but was only possible. His only difficulty was the idea of God's creative act beginning at a determinate time; he, therefore, inclined to the view that, prior to the existence of our world, God had brought into existence countless worlds, each of which was created for a limited time.[36]

He tried to restore to miracles and prophecy their supernatural character, which even Maimonides had unconscionably weakened. Prophecy did not originate in the active intellect, but in God himself, and it was not dependent upon specific rational and imaginative powers; its only presupposition was the moral purity of the prophet, for without this precondition God would not have appointed prophets.[37] Similarly, Abrabanel maintained a special, supernatural, individual providence, exercised on behalf of Israel alone, while other nations stood under a divine providence mediated through natural processes. As was the case with his assumption that the Torah was the supernatural connection between man and God, he thus nearly returned to the standpoint of Judah Halevi. Whereas the latter's view served as a theoretical articulation of the consciousness of a religious communion between God and man that lay beyond the bounds of thought, for Abrabanel this was really an attempt to tear religion completely out of the natural order, and convert the living religious and historical intuition of Halevi into a sober, scholastic supernaturalism.

In contrast to his lack of originality in metaphysics, Abrabanel was both independent and full of substance in the sphere of philosophy of history and culture. He developed a critique of culture which was completely alien to earlier Jewish philosophy and to Jewish thought as a whole.[38] In his commentary on the opening chapters of Genesis, he maintained that God willed that men should be satisfied only with the possessions conferred by nature's bounty, without the benefit of man's labor. Such possessions would have fully satisfied the needs of men, and they then could have devoted their entire energies to their true destiny—the perfection of their spirits, and especially the knowledge of God.[39] From this viewpoint the sorrows and troubles of mankind stemmed from the fact that men were unsatisfied with natural existence, and had fashioned civilizations which only served to alienate them from their true goal. The earliest generations of men had already taken the first step in this direction. Abrabanel interpreted the prohibition of eating from the tree of knowledge of good and evil in the spirit of Maimonides, but gave it a significant twist when he said that God had prohibited men from pursuing unnecessary possessions, which could be gained only by creating civilization with its arts and crafts and its specific system of values. The first refusal of this command, brought other evils in its train, like the conflict between Cain and Abel. Further steps along this road resulted in the degradation of the human species, which in turn caused the flood. Even after this, men returned to their un-natural ways, as the story of the Tower of Babel proved.[40]

In connection with this story there came into the center of Abra-banel's investigation an idea which had long been known, but which only now was revealed in its full significance. His critique of culture also included a critique of political life. Man's natural state, to which he had been ordained by God, was apolitical. This state showed only the most primitive forms of human association, forms which had not required the existence of a political order. The state was a part, and the most dangerous part, of that civilization which deflected man from his true destiny. Insofar as the state was not brought into exist-ence by the division of labor made necessary by civilization, it was based on the lust for honor, and the desire to rule, which could only be satisfied by the mutuality of political life.[41] A temporary approxi-mation to man's natural state had been made by the Israelites in the desert, but God had not ordained the extinction of civilization and the state for the Israelites in their own land, since such a withdrawal was impossible in an imperfect world.

In his critique of the state, Abrabanel was more extreme than Christian theology, which looked upon the political order as a neces-sary means for coercing humanity, which had been infected by the sin of Adam, into the observance of morality. According to Abra-banel, however, this order was in itself sinful. Indeed, the criticism which he arraigned against luxurious living and its ruinous conse-quences was undoubtedly influenced by Stoic views. But he went further than the Stoics by including civilization as such, and espe-cially political life, in his criticism. Such a condemnation of the po-litical order was found in antiquity only among the Cynics, who demanded a complete return to nature. Abrabanel, who was an ad-herent of Seneca in many items of his cultural critique, affirmed these conclusions even more strongly than had the Roman philos-opher. (It is worth recalling that Seneca, despite his closeness to the Cynics, was mainly affiliated with Stoicism.)[42]

Abrabanel gave the Cynics' critique of culture an entirely different meaning when he claimed that the knowledge of God and the religious perfection of men were the true ends of the natural life. These were ascetic doctrines, found in earlier Jewish philosophy—in Bahya and to some extent in Maimonides—where, however, they had not been fully developed; now they were linked to a thorough-going critique of culture. Pointing out the sources of Abrabanel's thought does not account for his adoption of a view which was novel, not only in Jewish religious philosophy, but in Judaism as a whole. Although the Torah's account of the first human generations offers some evidence for his opinions, the essential relationship of Scripture to civilization and the state was completely positive, and it is more than straining a point if Abrabanel sees the Torah's political laws only as a concession to existing human depravity. From a literary-historical viewpoint, it is difficult to understand how he came to accept this Cynical doctrine, even with its religious change of dress, in opposition to the general viewpoint of Judaism. His position bespeaks an intense personal involvement—and as some modern scholars have claimed, it is possible that his experiences in statecraft, and the breakdown of Jewish life in Spain which he encountered in his lifetime, caused him to deny civilization and the state, and to exalt the simple, quiet life of the state of nature.

Jewish Philosophy
in Italy

After the expulsion from Spain, Jewish philosophy was for the most part cultivated in Italy. Abrabanel wrote his most important philosophic works in Italy, and together with him, other Spanish refugees transplanted their philosophic tradition to Italian soil. Yet even before this, Italian Jewry had taken part in philosophic studies. We have already come across the thirteenth century Hillel b. Samuel; since his time, philosophic interest among Italian Jews had not ceased, although they did not produce important and influential works. In Italy the relationship with Christian philosophy was stronger than had been the case with Spanish or Provencal Jewry. It is not impossible that some of the Spanish philosophers, too, were influenced to some extent by Christian thinkers; in later times there may have been at least a partial counterinfluence, like that exerted by Ibn Gabirol and Maimonides on Christian philosophy. In our chapter on Crescas, we referred more than once to the possibility of such influences. Although Crescas always cited the opinions of his Islamic and Jewish predecessors, he never mentioned any Christian scholastics in his *Or Adonai*; he evidently looked upon himself—and justifiably so—as completely within the continuity of Arabic and Jewish philosophy.[43]

In Italy, these ties with Christian doctrine were evident from the very start. Hillel ben Samuel used Thomas Aquinas a great deal, and though he did not always acknowledge them, he frequently referred to the Christian scholars to whom he was indebted. We come across this contact with Christian scholastics repeatedly. This is not to say that contact with Renaissance philosophy was lacking, but it was not sufficient to bring about a renewal of Jewish philosophy in the small Jewish community of Italy. Despite the lively participation of Italian Jewry in the cultural movements of the Renaissance, the flowering of philosophy in Italy did not fructify Jewish philosophy at all. Its participation in the philosophy of the Renaissance was limited to isolated occurrences; insofar as the philosophic interest was not ousted by the growing kabbalistic tendencies, it occupied itself mainly with traditional medieval themes. This remained unchanged, even when the Jews later found a new haven in Holland. They continued to live in the world of medieval problems, and perhaps contented themselves with decorating the older ideas with the embroidery of humanistic learning. A truly modern Jewish philosophy did not arise until the eighteenth century.

One Italian Jew, Judah Messer Leon, was active even before the beginning of Renaissance philosophy, and was obviously affected by the humanistic tendency of Italian culture. He was the author of a rhetoric, which drew upon Aristotle, Cicero, and Quintilian, and sought to apply their categories to Scripture. Philosophically, however, he belongs to the medieval period. Most of his writings were commentaries on Aristotle—or rather, supercommentaries on Averroës. The only one to be thoroughly investigated (none has so far been published) is his commentary on Porphyry's *Isagoge* and on the first books of Aristotle's *Logic,* composed in 1450. Both formally and materially, this work is clearly dependent upon Christian scholasticism. The many excursuses dealing with general logical problems, which interrupt the interpretation, are worked out in accordance with the schema of scholastic literature; in terms of contents, Leon for the most part follows the lead of the English scholastic, Walter

Burleigh, a disciple of Duns Scotus, and throughout the work he conducts a running campaign against Gersonides without once mentioning his name. His compendium of logic also seems to be based on Christian sources; one of its copyists thought it to be an abstract of the logic of Maestro Paulo (Paul of Venice), an early fifteenth-century philosopher.[43a]

Elijah del Medigo (ca. 1460-1493), a native of Crete, was in close personal contact with the leader of the Florentine Platonists, Count Pico della Mirandola. At the urging of Pico, who found medieval translations inadequate, he translated the writings of Averroës from Hebrew into Latin, and expounded them in several Latin monographs, several of which he reworked into Hebrew. Prior to this, he had lectured on philosophy at the University of Padua, and was in close touch with Christian scholars. But he remained completely within the circle of the older Arabic and Jewish philosophy, and conceived his task to be that of making available the doctrines of Averroës in their original form to the world of Christian scholarship, and interpreting them more lucidly. He was apparently unaffected by the newer Platonizing tendencies of his disciple, friend, and patron, Pico; and the examination of his books has so far shown no traces of such influence.

His minor religio-philosophic work, *Behinat ha-Dat (The Examination of Religion),* is based on Averroës. The book is a reworking of the Averroistic inquiry into the connection between religion and philosophy, but he changed the viewpoint of his master considerably. For Averroës, the deepest sense of the doctrines of revelation necessarily agreed with the ideas of philosophy, and the philosopher was justified in so interpreting the contents of revelation that they would harmonize with the results of philosophic reflection. He did not recognize any limits to this freedom, as long as the conclusions of philosophy showed that the concept of revelation was a genuine possibility. The masses were to be excluded from this esoteric meaning of religion, and were to remain bound to the literal meaning of revelation.[44] This distinction between philosophic religion and the religion of the masses was also taken over by Elijah del Medigo. He, too, maintained that the masses must uphold the literal meaning of Scripture, and only the philosopher was justified in reinterpreting the meaning of the text.[45] But he denied the right of a philosophic interpretation of religious truth with regard to the basic principles of religion, and demanded that the philosopher, like the others, accept them.[46] He singled out Maimonides' thirteen principles of faith as such fundamental doctrines, but like his predecessor Duran, grounded them on three major principles—the existence of God, revelation, and divine retribution.[47] If a contradiction arises between reason and revelation with regard to these principles, the philosopher, too, must defer to revelation. But he must steer clear of the attempt to harmonize philosophy *per se* with revelation, because philosophy and revelation are two different spheres, and operate under different laws.[48]

It is obvious that Elijah accepted the doctrine of the double truth, which reappears in some of his other works.[49] Although this doctrine was previously held by Isaac Albalag, everything points to the fact that Elijah borrowed it from Christian Averroism, whose acquaintance he made when he lived in Padua. He limited this theory by two considerations. First, one can resolve any controversy which does not affect the fundamentals of faith by reinterpreting revelation. With regard to the basic dogmas themselves, he maintained that it is unlikely that any teaching of true revelation will conflict with the first principles of reason, as the Christian dogmas do, and he narrowed the theory of the double truth in such a way that revelation could be used in opposition to the results of philosophic deduction.[50] From such ideas he built up a cautious and circumspect compromise between the doctrine of the double truth and the philosophic interpretation of religion. Nevertheless, he somewhat justified this popular doctrine, and thus approached the Averroistic tendency of Christian philosophy of his time.

The one truly Renaissance philosopher was Leone Ebreo. Born in Spain, he came under the influence of Italian culture only during his maturity. Judah Abrabanel, the son of Isaac Abrabanel, and known among Christians as Leone Ebreo (born circa 1460 and died after 1521), was thirty years old when the Jews were expelled from Spain, but he absorbed with youthful enthusiasm the spirit of Italian Platonism, which never achieved as immediate and personal an expression as it did in his gay and imaginative *Dialoghi d'Amore (Dialogues on Love)*. The very fact that Leone expressed his world view in Italian, demonstrates the new turn which his philosophizing took. He wrote, not as a Jew for other Jews, as had the Spanish Jewish philosophers, but for the members of an enlightened philosophic circle, who were superior to any particular religion; he was not content to use Latin, as Elijah del Medigo had, but as was customary among the first Italian philosophers, he used the living language of the new culture.[51] In place of the conceptual dryness and sobriety of the medievals, we meet here a vaulting imagination, an emotionally moving presentation of a world view based in the depths of feeling. He was so deeply influenced by contemporary movements of thought that he also offered philosophic interpretations of ancient pagan myths.[52] That pagan myths should be presented in an unprejudiced manner, and should indeed form the vehicles for the communication of philosophic truth—this had been unheard of in Jewish philosophy. Here the Renaissance faith in the unity of truth which had been given to all mankind, and which could also be found in pagan mythology, displaces the abrupt challenge to every expression of pagan polytheism.

Leone's Platonism, drawn from Plato and the Greek Neoplatonists, again gave emphasis to the esthetic direction of the Platonic form of thought which had almost been lost in Arabic and Jewish Neoplatonism, and which had been completely abandoned in the Aristotelian reworking of Platonism. For Leone, beauty is of the essence of the world, and it takes on a metaphysical meaning in his system. Like Plato, he makes the beauties of bodies dependent upon the ideas which they embody,[53] and although he refrains from subsuming God under the category of beauty, God is still the source of all beauty. God is superior to beauty, and to the world which is filled with beauty; he is the one who apportions beauty.[54] Closely related to this esthetic transfiguration of the world is its thoroughgoing animation. The universe is conceived as a living unity, animated and vitalized by the supreme power of love.[55]

Leone's concept of love, which is the central doctrine of his system, rests on Jewish foundations. If the world is conceived as the work of love which strives toward the highest perfection, and the love which fills the world is conceived as yearning for God, we have what appears to be an interpretation like the one Crescas gave of scriptural love. That which distinguishes Leone from Plato and Plotinus—his idea that love streams not only from creatures to God, but from God to his creatures—unites him with Crescas. The latter is close to Leone in his conception of the divine love as the will which seeks to make love proceed from the divine essence. Because of the cosmological extension of love, however, the term has a much different meaning for Leone than it had for Crescas. Crescas had mentioned in passing the doctrine of Empedocles, that love was the unifying principle of the world; but for Crescas, this was merely a metaphor, while for the Renaissance philosopher it is a reality. Because of this, Crescas was able to preserve the personal character of love, while for Leone, such a meaning, as far as the main direction of his thought is concerned, is submerged in the cosmological extension of the concept. The all-embracing principle of love loses its personal significance in Leone, and becomes a cosmic conatus toward the bringing forth of perfection or union with perfection.[56] Thus the ultimate communion with God does not rest upon love alone. Love is merely an expression of the conatus for God, which is only fulfilled by complete unity with him. Every part of the cosmos partakes of this conatus. The love which ensouls the universe is fully expressed in the striving of the cosmos to attain to God and to unite with him.[57]

The belief in the unitary life of the cosmos is alien to the Islamic and Jewish emanation theories of the Middle Ages, and it is evidently the cosmic feeling of the Renaissance that produced this belief in Leone. The medievals sharply distinguished between the animated heavenly world, and the lifeless earthly world which was ruled by blind necessity; the terrestrial bodies stood below the level of life, and the intelligible world transcended them. Especially in those systems which were deeply influenced by Aristotle, the spiritual substances were understood as self-subsistent intelligences. The Aristotelian concept of the unmoved mover was applied both to God and the intelligences dependent upon him. The emanation of the single forms from the intelligences was so conceived that the latter remained motionless. Despite its dynamic structure, such a picture of the world remained basically fixed and static. This fixity was abandoned by Leone; one stream of life pulsed through all the spheres of existence. The movement of love extends from God to the pure intelligences, and even to the earthly world below. With all of this supposed transformation, however, this world picture is basically no more than an emancipation of the traditional world view from its logical rigidity, and a freeing of its previously encysted dynamic elements. This dynamic conception of becoming made it quite easy to ensoul the world order, and Leone had no need to create a new theory of the interconnections of the cosmos, but had merely to interpret the conventional world view in terms of his principle of love. Not only Neoplatonism, but Aristotelianism, too, carried within itself elements for the animation of the world of terrestrial bodies, through its notions of matter striving towards the realization of essence-conferring form, and of bodies seeking their natural places.[58] The idea of higher essences which emanate lower essences from themselves by virtue of their perfection, an idea that underlies the doctrine of emanation, can easily be converted into the idea of their love for the inferior beings which derive from them.[59]

The community of ideas which links the older Renaissance philosophy with the Jewish and Islamic world view of the Middle Ages, was comprehended by Leone, who grew up in the traditions of both philosophies. Just as the philosophic tradition in which he was brought up was easily combined with Neoplatonism when he encountered it in Italy and easily absorbed its esthetic elements, this same tradition served as the basis for giving a soul to the world by the principle of love.

Of the concepts which he inherited from the Middle Ages, the most important is that of knowledge. He holds that the potential human intellect is not actualized and brought to real knowledge except by the suprapersonal illumination of the active intellect. Leone differs from the medievals only in his return to the doctrine of Alexander of Aphrodisias, who had identified the active intellect with God, and thus forged an immediate bond between God and man.[60] Leone's doctrine of unity of the human spirit with God corresponds to this position. At first it appears that he deviates from the doctrine of the community of knowledge between God and man, since he subordinates knowledge to love, and makes knowledge the precondition of love. But this holds true only of the initial preparatory form of knowledge, by means of which our souls become enflamed with love for the object known. In order for us to be united with it, love, if it is considered only as the desire for such unification, is insufficient. It reaches its goal only in the final and highest form of knowledge, the complete and unifying knowledge of God.[61] This separation of intuition, which unites us with God, from discursive knowledge, is a firm step toward mysticism. But the conception of knowledge as the bond between God and man remains essentially unchanged, and serves as the capstone to Leone's doctrine of the return of the world to God.

Leone's relation to Judaism was no different from that of medieval philosophy. Although his notion of love as the soul of the world was close to pantheism, the decisive step in this direction was never taken by him. For Leone, the world was fashioned by God, and in his well-known inquiry into the problem of whether the world is eternal or created in time (mainly taken from medieval Jewish sources), he decided in favor of temporal creation. But he also accepted the idea of preexistent matter, which came to him not only via medieval philosophic systems, but from Plato. This he combined with his father's theory of a multiplicity of worlds created before the appearance of our present world order, although his father had not invoked the assumption of pre-existent matter.[62] In terms of his basic intentions, these modifications did not affect the essence of the idea of creation. Like the Christian Platonists of his time, Leone saw himself in agreement with scriptural revelation. Firmly grounded in the soil of Judaism and the philosophic tradition, he combined both, just as his medieval predecessors had. The faith of Israel, the world view of the Middle Ages, and a new feeling for the world which had been aroused by renewed contact with the world of antiquity, in his consciousness, were brought into a unified whole.

The newly developing natural science of the seventeenth century only affected Judaism slightly. Joseph Solomon del Medigo (1591-1655), one of the descendants of Elijah del Medigo and, like him, a native of Crete, was a student of Galileo, and had absorbed the new astronomical theories. He adopted the heliocentric theory of the universe and recognized that this destroyed forever the supposedly essential difference between the heavenly and the earthly spheres. The heavenly bodies were not composed of a special substance, and their motions were not spherical.[63] He also abandoned the Aristotelian idea of bodily substance. His criticism was directed especially against Aristotle's concept of form, which he claimed could not account for natural processes. There was no need for form, either in order to transform the potential being of matter into actuality (such potential matter was itself a fiction), or to clarify the distinctions between the various kinds of natural objects which are the result of the various qualities and dispositions of matter itself. Finally, we do not need form as an efficient cause, because matter is not a passive substrate, as Aristotle had thought, but all change is caused by the qualitative determinations of matter. Empirically, we only know material substance with all of its qualities, and this data is quite sufficient to explicate natural events.[64]

This conception of matter is uninfluenced by Galileo's doctrine of the subjectivity of sensible qualities. Matter is fitted out with a multiplicity of sensible qualities by which the elements are differentiated from each other, but matter with all of its special qualities is an ultimate datum, and there is no need to go beyond it and make it dependent on the ambiguous concept of indeterminate matter. Like many other Renaissance natural philosophers, del Medigo diverged from the doctrine of the four elements. He listed only three elements, and did not exclude fire from his list, as was the custom, but air.[65] He was fully aware of the metaphysical conclusions entailed in this change of the concept of nature. In order to understand the motion of the stars, he noted, no recourse need be taken to the immaterial movers of Aristotle.[66] He also understood that his criticism of the Aristotelian doctrine of form could be extended to Aristotle's psychology, and he apparently tended to ground the souls of animals on the combination of material elements. When he came to the soul of man he recoiled from this conclusion, but adopted the Platonic position which viewed the soul, not as the form of the organic body, but as a substance connected with the body.[67] With regard to the details of psychology, having rejected the idea of immaterial movers, and the dominant Judaeo-Arabic philosophical theory of the active intellect as a spiritual supraindividual substance, he preferred the Christian scholastic doctrine which transformed the active intellect into an aspect of the individual soul.[68] These psychological doctrines are far removed from the certainty which del Medigo found in the natural sciences. Instead of constructing his own doctrine, he contented himself with a critique of the conventional theories, but came to no apodictic conclusions. He relied sometimes upon Platonic ideas, and sometimes upon Aristotelian notions, and concluded with possibilities instead of certainties.

Such is the nature of his inquiries whenever they deal with basic metaphysical and religio-philosophic problems. His hesitation is partially clarified by the fact that he was prevented from fully expressing his own views on these questions. In his major work he defended the Kabbala, against which his ancestor Elijah had fought, but in another place he bitterly mocks its superstition. When he gives vent to freethinking doctrines, he immediately blunts their sharpness by all sorts of qualifications. But it is doubtful whether his caution had anything more to hide than isolated latitudinarian ideas without systematic connection. The changes in the scientific world view, which he upheld, did not produce even a suggestion for the renewal of metaphysics, or harmonization of the religious and scientific viewpoints. He recognized the necessity of this task, but did not have the powers of concentration necessary for its realization. Like so many restless spirits of the Renaissance, the criticism which he directed against religious and philosophical traditions did not lead to any degree of emancipation from them. Perhaps the reason for his ambivalent attitude towards the Kabbala can be found here. He mocked the superstitious practices which were bound up with the coarsest and most external forms of Kabbala, but like others of his generation who had begun to doubt Aristotelian scholasticism, he was attracted by the Kabbala's platonizing viewpoint. His formulation for harmony between religion and reason—that one must follow reason wherever it presents positive and demonstrative proofs, but that in regard to probabilities one must hold fast to the religious tradition[69]— served not only to conceal his inner thoughts, but permitted him to remain loyal to religious convictions which had been shaken by the criticisms of science. Scientific enlightenment, attachment to tradition, and reliance upon mysticism did not, in his case, form a consistent whole.

The Influence of Jewish Philosophy on the System of Spinoza

Spinoza's system belongs more properly to the development of European thought than to a history of Jewish philosophy. The primary goal of Jewish philosophy until this time—to interpret and validate the religion of Judaism in philosophic terms—lost its meaning for Spinoza at the very beginning of his work. His philosophy stands in profound opposition to the Jewish religion, not only to its traditional dogmatic form, but also to its ultimate convictions. At the outset, Spinoza recognized this fact very clearly, and he abandoned the attempt to reconcile this opposition through harmonization. The critique presented in his *Tractatus Theologico-Politicus* is testimony to this inner recognition, which dominates all of his philosophic works. Separated from any connection to the Jewish religion, his philosophy is no longer directed to believers in Judaism, but to the community of European thinkers, who are united by the idea of an autonomous truth. Spinoza consciously placed himself within this European movement of thought, and sought to develop his system within it. His influence was exclusively beyond the boundaries of the world of Judaism, and found its place wholly within the history of modern philosophy. Only when Judaism became attached to the spiritual life of the European nations did his thought have any entry to, and influence upon, the world of Jewry.

Spinoza was involved with Jewish philosophy only insofar as the latter served as one of the formative causes of his thought. Older Jewish philosophers afforded him his first entry into the world of philosophy, and through diligent and continuous industry he acquired a detailed knowledge of their doctrines. His correspondence, and even more, the *Tractatus Theologico-Politicus,* show that even in his maturity has had a deep and thoroughgoing knowledge of their works. The *Tractatus Theologico-Politicus* proceeds mainly on the basis of medieval philosophers. Of course, from a philosophic point of view, this is not very important, because Spinoza did not use their theses to develop his own system, but to advance his polemics against the Bible. Their influence upon his system, although not apparent, was nevertheless significant. The world view erected by Jewish philosophers, which was a synthesis of Aristotelian and Neoplatonic elements, had a decisive effect upon Spinoza's thought and took on a new lease of life in his system, although in a changed form. Even when, as Spinoza maintained, the transfer of this world view to Jewish soil had weakened or completely destroyed its major objectives, the discussions and controversies of the Jewish philosophers often concerned the original form of those ideas, and they developed its arguments with thoroughness and clarity.

It was not difficult for Spinoza to purify this world view from its adaptations to Jewish teaching, and to introduce the fundamental elements of its doctrine into his own system. Of course, Jewish philosophers such as Maimonides, Gersonides, and Crescas, who exerted a strong and continuing influence on Spinoza, are quite distant from the latter's pantheism. It is also possible that other Jewish sources, such as the biblical commentaries of Abraham ibn Ezra and the literature of the Kabbala, played a part in the formation of his pantheism, but this is uncertain.[70]

The historic roots of Spinoza's philosophy, however, extended far beyond the Jewish sphere. To these Jewish sources, we must add the influence of the philosophy and science of his day. Taken together, these currents of thought produced the material which was finally embodied in Spinoza's system. The attempt to reveal the Jewish sources of his doctrine cannot completely disregard these other strands. The single most important philosophic system which came to complete expression in Spinoza's century was the mathematical science of nature. The ideal of this science—to comprehend nature as a mathematical-causal nexus—was also Spinoza's goal, and he transferred this ideal from the science of nature to the knowledge of the whole of reality. For him, the notion of law in the natural sciences became the axiom of metaphysical knowledge, and replaced the Aristotelian concept of substance. To understand reality no longer meant to look upon it as the realization of general essences in the indeterminate substrate of matter, but to view it as a network of causally connected elements. Causality was not the manifestation of dynamic powers (the doctrine of Aristotelianism), but was the logico-mathetical interconnection of conditions. This does away with the teleological structure of the Aristotelian world view, whose essence was made up of purposive creative forms, operating teleologically, and whose dynamic was the embodiment of teleological laws. For Spinoza, causality is logico-mathematical necessity. Because of its newly discovered method, the natural sciences had denied the dynamism of Aristotelianism and Neoplatonism, and Spinoza applied this view in the sphere of metaphysics. Although he maintained the world view of Aristotelianism, this was done only because he transferred it into the framework of modern natural law, and we shall see how the essentials of his doctrine followed from this.

In the sphere of philosophy Descartes had undertaken to comprehend the scientific method of the new sciences, and by its example, to establish the road toward true knowledge in general. Knowledge must first seek a fundamental and absolute certainty, which could firmly withstand all doubts, and must elicit the content of knowledge by way of analogy and strict deduction. Spinoza accepted this method of logical deduction. According to him, true knowledge was also rooted in a fundamental certainty, which grasped the ultimate principles of knowledge with immediate evidence. From this the entire corpus of knowledge could be explicated deductively (from the general to the particular) without any gaps or jumps.

Spinoza also applied this concept of knowledge to metaphysics. True metaphysics was not possible unless, from one clearly apprehended primary axiom, one is able to construct a deductive chain of reasoning that would embrace the fullness of existence.[71] This idea of a deductive metaphysics is again a departure from Aristotelianism. The empirical character of the Aristotelian system also characterizes its metaphysics, which infers from given existents to their presuppositions. The various Aristotelian proofs for the existence of God, for example, infer from the world to its primary and superior cause. The Neoplatonic elements which were absorbed in Arabic and Jewish Aristotelianism did not fundamentally change this systematic viewpoint, and even the argument from the contingency of the world to a necessary cause which brought it into being, despite its completely conceptual character, starts from the world and proceeds to God.

The metaphysics of Spinoza proceeds in an entirely opposite direction, and seeks to derive existence from its ultimate presuppositions.[72] This is only possible if existence itself is a logical nexus. In the natural mathematical-causal interconnection of being, which was elevated by Spinoza to the status of a nontemporal interconnection of logical continuity, the order of being indeed coincides with the order of logical understanding. But in order that this deductive grasp of existence be possible, the first cause of existence must be acknowledged as a conceptual necessity. Like his predecessor Descartes, but in terms of an intention which went far beyond his, Spinoza returns to the Christian scholastic ontological proof for the existence of God, in order to find the way from concept to reality. The concept of God contains within itself the idea of God's existence, for in this idea thought finds absolute certitude and a point of departure for future deduction, and with it the certitude that the interrelation of its definitions corresponds to the interrelation of things.[73] Spinoza's ideal of knowledge implies that in order to reach the idea of God he did not follow the Jewish philosophers, but the Christian scholastics, whose concept of the *ens realissimum* was better adapted, even in its details, to the formal construction of his idea of God than were the formulations found in Jewish theology.

Despite these radical differences both in content and in method, it is still possible to recognize a similarity to Jewish Aristotelianism in Spinoza's system. According to Aristotelianism, too, the world is ruled by a conceptual causality, and is built up into an ordered conceptual system. The general essences of Aristotle are hypostasized concepts of genera, which for him are the representatives of a conceptual conformity to law. At the peak of these conceptual forms there stands the highest divine form, in which the happenings of the world have their source. The adoption of the Neoplatonic idea of emanation by the Arabic Aristotelians was an attempt to derive the variety of individual forms from the primary divine form, and to understand the origin of the world in God as the unfolding of the fundamental divine conceptual essence into a manifold of single concepts. This viewpoint appears at its clearest in the emanation doctrines of al-Farabi and Avicenna, which Maimonides had discussed. They had derived from God a series of individual immaterial essences, which in their logical essence were pure conceptual forms, until the last of them had split into a multiplicity of separate forms which descended into matter. Even when Averroës deviated from the notion of the descending procession of immaterial substances, and derived the unified conceptual order of the world immediately from God, the principle of world explanation remained unchanged. As the development of a concept, the procession of the world from God was an eternal and necessary process. The parallelism and similarity to the system of Spinoza becomes quite apparent in one detail. Just as in Aristotelianism the immaterial substances underlying the entire world had first proceeded from God, and only afterwards do the separate forms of bodies come into being, so too, in his *Ethics* Spinoza derives immediately from God the infinite modes (or, as he calls them in his *Treatise on the Improvement of the Intellect,* the "firm and eternal things"). These are the common laws of existence, and from them derives the multiplicity of separate bodies.[74]

But his substitution of the concept of law for the concept of form gives this deduction an entirely new cast. Not only does Spinoza deny the Aristotelian reification of generic concepts, but he claims that these concepts in their empty abstractness are completely useless for an understanding of the concrete being of things.[75] His idea of law, like that of modern science, is designed for cognizing the concrete nexus of being of all things. General conceptual essences in the Aristotelian sense do not proceed from God, but from the concrete, causal order of actual being. The generality of this order is not a conceptual abstraction, but is the universality of the infinite whole in which every particular detail finds its place.[76]

Thus, God becomes the principle of the causal order in which all causal connections are rooted. But Spinoza is not completely free of this hypostasizing of concepts. God, the principle of law, is, *qua* substance, a material being. If the logical function of the concept of God is to establish the logical interconnection of bodies, God also serves as the material substratum of the being of individual things. This reification applies as much to the divine principle of law as to the fundamental laws of being deriving from God. These "firm and eternal things" include within themselves the laws, "according to which every particular thing happens and is ordered."[77] They constitute the concrete, infinite whole, in which every particular is contained. In this concept, the unlimited validity of a general law and the unlimited extension of an infinite being coincide.

The transition from one to the other is accomplished by the concept of space, which signifies both the law of space determining all individual parts of space, and the whole of space which includes them all. According to Spinoza's analogy, the unity of the law becomes identical with the material whole of being in the divine substance. As in the case of Aristotelian form, where the generic concepts were reified, here, too, the general law is turned into a reality. In both, the derivation of things from God is faced by the same limitations: the individuality of particular things remains a mere datum. The Aristotelian emanation can proceed only as far as the single forms, which are viewed as the conceptual essences of empirical things. The individuality of particulars must be accounted for by the new principle of matter, which absorbs the form in different materializations; despite all the attempts at the beginning of Arabic Aristotelianism to introduce the principle of matter into the sequence of emanations, the concreteness of the particular does not cease from being arbitrary. For Spinoza, only the infinite modes, the eternal laws of being, proceed from the infinite divine being. The finite modes, the totality of empirical things, cannot be derived from God; each of these modes presupposes another finite mode as its cause, and the series regresses to infinity.[78] This corresponds exactly to the logical function of law. The concrete particular can be explained in accordance with law. Law differs from the Aristotelian general concept in that it functions adequately for such explanation, but despite this, it is impossible ever to deduce a particular event from a general law. By extending the necessary dualism between causal law and the causally determined fact to the relationship between God and individual things, a limit is set to the derivation of things from God, a limit by which God ceases to be the efficient cause of all reality.

The change thus effected in the concept of God and in the derivation of things from God, by the formal change of the conceptual nexus, is paralleled by the changed relationship of God to things. Spinoza's special form of pantheism here becomes methodologically understandable. According to the doctrine of emanation, which Aristotelians had adopted from the Middle Ages, formal essences were derived from each other. Since the Aristotelians understood these concepts as existing essences, this derivation had to be not only a logical, but a real succession. Every one of these conceptual essences produces another essence by reason of its inherent power. Conceptual reality has become an operative power, from which a new being proceeds. This procession of things from each other, which was interpreted more as a metaphor than as a theory, could not easily be combined with Spinoza's concept of causally ordered interconnection. The concept of emanation, therefore, has no place in his system. Causality, conceived as a mathematical and lawfully ordered succession, has nothing in common with this obscure procession of things one from another. Causality is a network of conditions in which one determination follows from the other according to strict laws. Only in this way is it possible to explain the procession of things from God. God is not the primary substance from whom other substances emanate. He is the principle of the uniformity of law, upon which both the system of laws and the system of causally connected facts are founded. Just as this law inheres in facts, so God must of necessity inhere in separate particular things. The fact that the divine law of existence also serves as its material substratum does not affect this interconnection at all. From the divine substance, there proceed in lawful and ordered succession only those determinations which can be deduced from God, but not other substances. "One substance cannot yield another substance"; thus we find that the immanence of God in things, his sole substantiality, is the one possible way in which Spinoza's thought permits the derivation of things from God. Spinoza, of course, reached this conclusion by a complex path, starting from the traditional idea of substance.[79] But his argumentation is an afterthought, not the source of his conclusion. He affords us an insight into this concept, however, when he converts extension into a divine attribute, and objects in space become determinations of the divine essence, a conclusion required by his fundamental viewpoint.

The procession of material bodies from God caused notable difficulties for the doctrine of emanation. It was forced either to introduce matter into the process of emanation, and to derive it from the increasing coarseness of form, or it had to restrict the process of emanations to the sequence of forms alone, and make matter into another substantial principle independent of God. Neither of these alternatives can be reconciled with Spinoza, not only because these two opinions assume the dualistic splitting of the world into matter and form, but because it is impossible for there to be a substance independent of the all-encompassing divine causality, just as it is impossible that within an incorporeal world of spiritual essences there should exist a process which would eventuate in a corporeal world. The equality of cause and effect, which is implied in every true causal relationship, obligates us to predicate extension, the primary attribute of matter, to God, the primary source of the material world.[80] Just as the law of all beings must be included within God, so, too, the law of material being must be contained within him. From this example we can understand why the God of Spinoza is not the One of Neoplatonism, who has no positive determinations, but is rather the *ens realissimum* of Western Scholasticism. He cannot serve as the ground of individual bodies in the world unless he is the law of this ground. It is true that the infinity of this reality is no more than a function of the law, which fixes every individual happening, and the hypostasization of God to the level of material reality does not yield any content of being.

The necessary relationship between God and the world serves as the decisive locus for the treatment of the religious content of this God-idea which constitutes an unavoidable question. The uniqueness of Spinoza's doctrine is not contained in this necessity *per se*, but in its specific form. According to the emanation theory of Arabic Aristotelianism, the world proceeded necessarily from God, but this necessity was one of the system as a whole, that is, of dynamic causality. God, as the highest form, was the supreme teleological power, from whose fullness of being the world proceeded. His causality was the causality of teleological realization, the realization of the teleological unity of the whole that is implicitly contained within him. For Crescas, this idea was interpreted in voluntaristic terms. The divine goodness was determined by the divine essence to create. For Spinoza, the necessity of God's action was the only necessity which the system could recognize, that of logico-mathematical causal nexus, whose identification with pure logical entailment in connection with divine causality is sharply and fully expressed. Just as from the definition of each thing, a series of consequences follow, and these consequences are multiplied insofar as the definition expresses more of reality, so, too, from the necessity of the divine nature there must proceed infinite consequences in infinite ways.[81]

The activity of God is no more than another locution for the mathematical-causal law governing existence. Such a network would be impossible once we allow teleology to operate, whether a teleology of a will that fixes goals, or that of a power which creates in a purposeful way. Spinoza's polemic against the concept of final causation, given his world view, was simply a self-evident conclusion. Once the concept of teleology is discarded, the attribution of value to existence must also be abandoned. For the mathematically articulated necessary interconnection of things, there are no differences of value between the particular objects contained within it. The differences between good and evil, beautiful and ugly, are referred to the valuations of men, and do not inhere in the nature of objects.[82]

The hierarchy of the value of things, which lies at the basis of the emanation theory and is the foundation for its metaphysical construction of the world, becomes insignificant in Spinoza's system of mathematically ordered laws. Wherever he speaks of greater or lesser perfection, he means greater or lesser reality.[83] The value-free conception of existence in the natural sciences is here extended to the ultimate metaphysical explanation of the world, and the attraction which Spinoza's philosophy has always exerted on those who admire the scientific method lies in this rejection of all considerations of value from its conception of the whole. But for Spinoza this naturalistic mode of thought is unconsciously made into a religious relationship to the world. For him, the denial of all differences in value, which is implicit in the scientific world view, becomes a religious affirmation of existence, which by reason of God's activity is extended equally to all beings. The value of a perfection which is indifferent to all valuation becomes the bearer of religious affirmations of value, implanted in all beings. The same paradoxical combination of complete equanimity in the face of valuation, and absolute religious valuation of content, also characterizes his idea of God, who is no more than the sum of all the laws of existence. In the consciousness of Spinoza, however, God is the highest source of perfection.

This religious consciousness has nothing in common with the religion of Scripture and its belief in a good and gracious God. It can only be understood from the viewpoint of the religious foundations of the metaphysics of emanation, which understands the divine perfection to be the fullness of being, transcending all human comprehension. For emanationism, too, the fullness of being contains the greatest fullness of value, and is superior to any of the values found in the world. For Spinoza, the bare concept of being becomes the subject of religious appraisal. God, who in accord with his logical content can be labeled the concept of being of the natural sciences, becomes the object of a mystical divine feeling.

We find both similarity and opposition to Aristotelianism in Spinoza's doctrine of the human spirit. According to Arabic and Jewish Aristotelianism, the human intellect is a link within the cosmic process of emanation; just as all forms of the terrestrial world are conditioned, the human spirit is also conditioned as an essential form through the process of emanation. Man's knowledge, however, belongs to this emanation process in another sense as well. Man's reason, which considered *per se* is only potentially intellect, is brought to the actuality of knowledge by the influence of the supra-individual active intellect. The realization of knowledge is the incorporation of those conceptual forms which have proceeded from the active intellect into the human spirit. Aristotle interpreted human thought according to the analogy of perception—the effect of that which is thought, upon the inquiring mind. This was understood by the Arabic Aristotelians to mean that the object of thought has a separate existence in the active intellect, independent of the individual human mind, and from which it descends to the particular intellect. The real world, which is found in the active intellect and which is unchanging, is revealed to human thought according to the measure of the individual's capacity. In this form, the metaphysics of knowledge could not possibly be accepted by Spinoza, because of its dependence on the principle of emanation.

But in a youthful essay, *The Short Treatise*, where it is possible to recognize many connections between Spinoza's idea and this older mode of thought, he still upholds Aristotle's opinion that thought, like sense perception, is a passive act wherein mind is grasped by its object. That thought is grasped by its object also holds true of God's knowledge.[84] In later years, however, when Spinoza came under the influence of Descartes, he renounced entirely this view of the passivity of knowledge. Thought does not receive an idea from the external world, but produces it by reason of its own powers. The truth of thought is not caused externally, but is dependent only upon the nature and ability of the intellect itself.[85] The same holds true of that knowledge which relates to actual being. The correspondence between knowledge and its object is not due to the fact that knowledge is dependent upon its object. On the contrary, the inner truth of thought is a guarantee of the reality of its object, and the identity of logical order which dominates both knowledge and its object is surety for the correspondence between the inner connection of things and the inner connection of true knowledge.[86]

This doctrine of the logical correspondence between knowledge and its object is the basis for Spinoza's metaphysical theory of the parallelism between spiritual and corporeal being, according to which both are completely parallel to each other, although they never interact.[87] That the logical correspondence of knowledge and its object can be converted into the metaphysical parallelism of spiritual and material being is due to the fact that the all-embracing divine thought is nothing but the actualized connection of truth. Every thought is a part of the inner connection of the divine mind, and the causal connection of the contents of mind is identical with the logical connection of the order of thought which is rooted in the divine mind. Of necessity, this universal relation of truth must correspond point by point with the universal relation of material existence in space, which is the object of the former.[88]

In this way, human knowledge becomes a part of the content of the infinite divine knowledge. The axioms grasped by human minds are part of the universal interconnection of axioms whose source is the divine mind. The limited and incomplete complex of ideas comprehended by the human mind cannot, of course, express the fullness and purity of the interconnection of the divine mind. Whereas in the divine mind every content is articulated within a framework of logical interconnection, and the deduction of every particular determination is immediately and clearly comprehensible within the content of total knowledge, the limited complex of human axioms contains a multitude of separate elements, whose deductive grounds are not found within the mind itself; that which is deductively determined appears to men as something which is externally given.[89] Human reason achieves clear and adequate knowledge only insofar as the presuppositions of its knowledge lie within itself; or to put it differently, insofar as the deductive coherence of the divine knowledge becomes apparent within it. From this spontaneous and therefore adequate knowledge, our spirit grasps the basic order of existence which is common to all things, and which underlies the ideas constituting the human intellect as it does all other ideas. Since this order is rooted in the essence of God, it follows that this divine principle of order, through which all beings manifest the basic attributes of God, must be the highest and original object of adequate knowledge. When the human spirit reflexively questions the foundation of its own essence, there opens before it the completely certain knowledge of the eternal and infinite essence of God. The highest form of our knowledge is grounded in the fact that we are able to deduce the common essence of things, that is, the rational order of being, from God.[90]

We thus see renewed, though in a different form, the same interconnection of human and divine knowledge which first appeared in Aristotle. In both cases, man's knowledge is grounded in his participation in the divine knowledge. But Spinoza removes this idea from the language of images and transfers it to the terminology of an autonomous epistemology. In Aristotelianism, knowledge was defined as the absorption of the concept, a definition which resulted in the mutuality of divine and human knowledge: from the divine intellect, or from the active intellect deducible from it, conceptual forms proceed to the human mind. For Spinoza, however, it is precisely the spontaneity of knowledge which testifies to its divine origin. Rational knowledge is not the passive reception of an external object, but is the product of the interconnection of the mind. But within this self-productive orderliness of mind, God is at work. God is thus converted from an external object of our minds into the internal source of our power of knowledge, into the logical and primary cause of all rational human knowledge. This is the same basic thought articulated in Aristotelianism. There, all truth is realized in the active intellect; here, it is revealed in the divine mind. In both cases, human knowledge participates in the internal interconnection of ideas.

It is possible to demonstrate the continuity of this development in Spinoza's understanding of human consciousness. For him, the human spirit is an immanent idea within the divine mind, or better still—a complex of such ideas. For the particular consciousness there is no correlation between the act of thought and the contents of thought contained in it; consciousness is no more than the totality of the contents of thought. Spinoza undoubtedly arrived at this difficult conception because of internal necessity, as a consequence of his idea of substance, for which individual consciousness as a mode of the divine mind becomes a content of thought; but Spinoza found the exemplar for this idea of consciousness in Aristotle. Although the latter's doctrine of the rational soul, defined as the form of man, is constructed on other grounds, it comes close to Spinoza in its doctrine of the acquired intellect. The predisposition of the intellect, which is the essence of man, is actualized by the ideas produced within us under the influence of the active intellect. These fashion the acquired intellect of man, which constitutes the eternal part of the individual's soul. Human understanding again becomes the sum of the contents of thought. Concept and spirit are identical.

Spinoza's intellectualism treats human consciousness as the totality of its contents of thought, and the whole of the life of the soul is reduced to a theoretical process of representation. Willing, striving, and feeling are not independent phenomena, but the mechanical by-products of the life of representation. From the tendency of representations to self-preservation, all the drives of desire and will can be deduced.[91] Aristotelianism is far removed from such one-sided intellectualism. Theoretical knowledge is not the sole activity of consciousness. It is true, of course, that the psychology of Aristotelianism maintains the superiority of reason above all other powers of the soul. Reason is the highest power of the human soul, and all of the soul's other capacities are directed toward the embodiment and realization of reason. The highest activity of reason and the essential activity of man's soul is the activity of knowledge; ultimately, all the other functions of the soul are composites and are connected with material existence. Only in pure reason is the soul completely within its own realm, and is its essence fully realized.

The psychological intellectualism of both systems has as its most important consequence the intellectualism of their ethical and religious life-ideals. Here they are closer to each other than at any other point. According to Aristotle, whose ethic was designed to analyze human happiness, happiness results from that activity which fulfills man's essential nature; his highest and principal happiness is embodied in the development of his highest power, theoretical reflection. The eudaemonia of knowledge is the fulfillment of human life. The Arabic Jewish Aristotelians proceeded one step beyond this and made man's highest goal his only real purpose in life, but other forms of human perfection were also taken into account. As pure thought is the highest but not the only power of the spirit, theoretical eudaemonia is the highest but not the only perfection of man. All other human virtues are ordered toward making possible the free exercise of theoretical reason. Man's moral perfection does not have an absolute value, but serves as a handmaiden to the operation of thought, which is the purpose of human evolution and is conditioned by subordinate functions. Spinoza does not admit to this manifold of forms of psychological activity. He, therefore, cannot admit to a hierarchy of value. Since consciousness is a purely intellectual process, intellectual perfection is necessarily the sole perfection of man. The only possible difference of value among the contents of consciousness is the difference in their logical rank and order. The independence of pure knowledge which stems from the very essence of human thought is the sole possible form of all activity. Empirical knowledge, which is passive and dependent, stands in direct contrast to it. The true freedom of man is the freedom of pure reason; he is in bondage insofar as he is determined by unclear, externally given representations and phantasms.[92] The power of theoretical reason frees us from subjugation to the passions, just as our weakness makes us slaves to them. The free development of thought, which Aristotelianism had conceived to be the result of perfection, is for Spinoza the source of ethical freedom.[93]

Ethical understanding has no independent status in addition to theoretical understanding, but is contained within it, just as the will is contained within reason. Such a conclusion is required for methodological reasons, and also to harmonize with Spinoza's concept of consciousness. The denial of any differences in value eliminates the possibility of there being any independent ethical value. Spinoza quite consciously transfers the demand for a value-free knowledge to the realm of ethics, and gives himself the task of dealing with human passions and actions in the same way one would deal with lines, planes, and bodies.[94] The sole value is the distinction which exists for him in the logical difference between truth and error, between adequate knowledge and inadequate knowledge. From an ontological standpoint this is the same as the difference between strength and weakness; that is, between greater or lesser fullness of reality. Upon this basis he must erect ethical value distinctions, in order to bring them into line with the ultimate presuppositions of his system.

At first glance, the ideal of the free man who is determined by reason seems closer to Stoicism than to Aristotelianism; but this is more true of the formal analysis of the ideal than of its inner and principal content. For Spinoza, unlike the Stoa (at least in its original form), the primary and central value of reason is not shown in the freedom it grants to man but in theoretical knowledge alone. Despite all the differences in their methodologies, Spinoza agrees completely with the Aristotelian view which upholds the eudaemonia of knowledge as the final goal of human existence. This community of ideals is proved step by step in Spinoza's doctrine of the immortality of the soul, and in his idea of *amor dei intellectualis*, which constitutes the apogee and conclusion of his system.

Arabic Aristotelianism explained the Aristotelian idea of immortality of the reasoning part of the human soul as the conferring of immortality upon the intellect through the activity of knowledge. Man's capacity for thinking was linked with the fate of the body; only the reason acquired from knowledge, which is identical with the sum of knowledge that a man has acquired, is independent of the body, and therefore immortal. This conception is usually formulated in the statement that immortality is bound up with metaphysical knowledge because its object is eternal being. In metaphysical knowledge man's spirit is united with its object. This is the basis for Spinoza's position in his *Short Treatise*. There he demonstrates that the human soul must eventually disappear because it is united with perishable bodies; therefore, it cannot attain immortality except insofar as it is united with the imperishable essence of God.[95] In Spinoza's mature system, there is no longer any place for such an idea; neither the unity of the soul with God nor acquired immortality can be reconciled with his basic presuppositions. But the other form which the idea of immortality assumes in Spinoza's *Ethics* does not fundamentally alter this basic idea. The indestructible part of man is the eternal idea contained in the divine mind, and this idea is the nontemporal essence of the human spirit.[96]

The knowledge, which according to the Aristotelian doctrine of emanation streams from the divine to the human spirit, becomes for Spinoza the immanent idea in the divine mind, and constitutes the immortal part of man. Spinoza's doctrine of immortality is even closer to the later development of Aristotelianism. The eternity of the divine idea, which constitutes the human spirit, contains within itself the eternity of the sum of knowledge inherent in this idea. Empirical knowledge is inadequate because it deals with perishable things; adequate knowledge derives from the eternal essence of the spirit, and participates in its eternity. The more that spirit knows in this form, the more it participates in eternity, and the less fear it has of death.[97] As in Aristotelianism, here, too, metaphysical knowledge is the eternal part of consciousness, whose share of eternity increases as our spirit grows in the comprehension of such knowledge.

As a doctrine of the communion of knowledge between God and man, this is only a new mode of expression for ideas explained earlier. According to Aristotelianism, the basis of this communion lies in the fact that every bit of our conceptual knowledge flows from pure spiritual intelligences, all of which eventually derive from God. It is metaphysical knowledge especially which not only has the eternal world of spirit as its proper object, but also rests on a real union of our spirit with this realm, a union which becomes more profound as knowledge deepens. To know God is to be seized by him. The happiness of knowledge thus becomes the happiness of communion with God as realized in knowledge. The eternal life of the cognizing spirit is eternal communion with God, and constitutes the eternal happiness of this communion. Spinoza's *Short Treatise* sees this unification with God as the highest good of man; and in knowledge it sees the means of attaining this good, and thereby acquiring immortality.[98] The formula *amor dei intellectualis*, which is found in Spinoza's *Ethics*, expresses the same idea in the terminology of his changed epistemology. God is no longer the external object of our knowledge, but is rather its primary logical presupposition, the most basic inner element of our understanding.

For this reason intuitive knowledge, which grasps the idea of God as the primary certainty of knowledge, does not produce the communion of the spirit with God, but rather rests on it and raises it to consciousness within our spirit. Since it reveals to us the unity of our rational soul with God, it elevates us to the same happiness of communion with God, which is similar to the union with God already mentioned. For Spinoza, too, the joy of knowledge and the love of God coincide. The highest knowledge gives the highest joy to our spirit. Since the idea of God is at the root of this knowledge, the happiness of knowledge contains within itself a love for the divine cause of knowledge.[99]

The connection of these ideas with Aristotelianism is basic, and goes far beyond the sphere of metaphysical speculation. The primary religious feeling which pervades Spinoza's system brings him close to the Judaeo-Arabic Aristotelianism of the Middle Ages. The religious significance of Spinoza's pantheism is not that he experiences nature as an expression of the divine life. As the cause of nature, God is the mere principle of being, and the religious significance of this principle of being is latent rather than vital. The intense and immediate religious experience of Spinoza is first revealed in the consciousness of the communion of the human spirit with the divine. His pantheism comes to full religious expression as a pantheism of knowledge and not as a pantheism of nature. The joy of nature for Spinoza, as for Aristotelianism, is a basic religious affect, directed toward God as the source and totality of all truth.

Despite their profound inner connection, the two systems are separated by the difference between teleological and mechanistic metaphysics, and this accounts for their different relationships to the historically revealed religions. The teleological metaphysics of Aristotelianism could compromise with revealed religion; even for such a radical Aristotelian as Averroës, this compromise was founded upon sincere conviction.[100] Spinoza's mechanistic transformation of metaphysics led to a necessary break with revealed religion. The eternal procession of the teleological order of the world from God could easily be identified with belief in creation and providence, while the unification of the rational soul with God could be identified with belief in the immortality of the soul, making it appear that religious doctrines were but popular expressions of philosophic truth. Between Spinoza's doctrine of God as the foundation of mathematical necessity and the idea of God found in the monotheistic religions, or between his idea of the human spirit as a link in the necessary network of the divine mind and the belief of the revealed religions in the immortality of man's individual soul, there exists an abyss which cannot be bridged.

For Aristotelianism, revelation was an actual event, even if it was introduced and occurred within the necessary interconnection of the world. The universal transmission of knowledge from the divine spirit to the human could be so intensified and heightened as to explain the occurrence of prophecy. For Spinoza, however, there is no other relationship between the human spirit and the divine beyond the logically necessary procession from God of the coherence of ideas, which constitutes human knowledge. Together with the idea of revelation, Aristotelianism could affirm the concept of a divine legislation, because it admitted the existence of a moral law, despite the fact that this law was subordinate to the final end of man which was theoretical knowledge. For Spinoza there is no law that proceeds from God except the eternal law of nature. Of course, as the occasion warranted, Spinoza also utilized demonstrations in the same way that medieval philosophy had transformed the God concept of the historic religions. Just as those medieval philosophers who maintained the idea of the eternity of the world tried to demonstrate that the temporal creation of the world was not congruent with the eternal perfection of God, so Spinoza in his *Short Treatise* found that it would not be fitting for the divine goodness to fashion a finite instead of an infinite world, and quite in accord with the spirit of the Middle Ages, he identified divine providence with the natural law of things.[101] In his polemic against the idea of teleology, he utilized the very same proofs that Aristotelianism had employed against the idea that the activity of God was voluntaristically determined and directed towards the realization of fixed and specific ends.[102] For Spinoza, however, these proofs served only to destroy the traditional concept of God from within, not to change it so that it could be reconciled with his own.

The philosophical critique of revelation, only hinted at in Spinoza's strictly systematic philosophic works, is arranged in detail in his *Tractatus Theologico-Politicus,* but it is obscured by the deliberate ambiguity with which the book was written. Spinoza pretends to be a believer in the divine origin of Scripture, and proposes only to attack those distortions which Jewish and Christian theology have imposed on Scripture. He apparently identifies himself with the biblical doctrine, so that he might present, in the name of the Bible itself, his own critique of biblical ideas. But the reader finds little difficulty in understanding his intentional ambiguity and recognizing Spinoza's true doctrine. Spinoza's apparent consent to the divine origin of Scripture is so formulated that the philosophic impossibility of the concept of revelation is apparent. The supernatural illumination given to the prophets is posed in absolute opposition to the natural illumination of the human spirit. Instead of interpreting the prophetic illumination in the manner of medieval philosophy, in terms of the general conditions of human knowledge, Spinoza maintains that the possibility of prophecy is simply beyond the bounds of human reason. For the interpretation of prophecy we can rely only upon the words of Scripture itself.[103]

To assert the supernatural character of prophecy is to assert its philosophic impossibility; that this is the true meaning of Spinoza's words becomes quite clear from his critique of miracles, in which he draws a parallel between miracle and prophecy. In the critique of miracles he abandons his pretended agreement with the biblical viewpoint and argues purely on the assumptions of his own system. A miracle, insofar as it is an act which transcends the bounds of nature, is impossible, because the order of nature comes with absolute necessity from the divine essence. When he bases the order and causality of nature upon the eternal will of God, at first glance it seems that he is close to the biblical notion of God; he immediately unifies the divine will with the divine intellect, however, and clearly hints that this idea of a divine ordinance is no more than a metaphorical expression for the logical origination of the laws of nature in the divine essence. We can know God only from the determinate order of things; anything that happens contrary to this order necessarily conflicts with our certain knowledge of God. Even if it be an event whose causal explanation is impossible simply because of the limitations of our intellect, it cannot serve as a means for our knowledge of God.[104] This critique of miracles directly affects prophecy; the two presuppositions of revealed religion are uprooted by the philosophic concept of God. Spinoza maintains the fiction of complete agreement with the Bible only in order to demonstrate the impossibility of a lesion in the law of nature. This he sees as the proper doctrine of the Bible, and he can therefore disprove miracles from the Bible itself.[105] The material for such a demonstration was prepared for him by the rationalistic interpretation of the Bible by Maimonides and his followers, which in principle he rejects, but he does not hesitate to use it wherever it can help him undermine the doctrine of revelation.

Spinoza also refutes the idea of a divinely given legislation with the same proofs used to destroy the idea of miracle. The only thing that proceeds from God is not a commandment, which a man can obey or disobey, but an eternal and necessary truth. God is therefore the source of morality only insofar as the eternal order, which is rooted in him, contains within itself certain deeds which have benign consequences and other deeds which have evil consequences, and which can act as guides for our actions. Only a person who does not recognize this connection looks upon conduct, which is directed toward the realization of beneficial results, as a commandment. Only from such a lack of knowledge is it possible to make God, who is the ground of the laws of nature, into the lawgiver of the revealed religions.[106] Here again Spinoza maintains an outward connection with revealed religion. The true revelation of God is eternal truth. Only because of the ignorance of its recipients was this truth converted into a commandment ordaining specific acts. The imperfect understanding of Adam made the revealed truth of the consequences of his deeds into a commandment. According to Spinoza, it was from lack of knowledge that Israel—along with all of its prophets, including Moses—warped the truth that was revealed to them by making it into a statute and commandment.[107] But this so-called revelation, which apparently all of the prophets misunderstood, is simply a matter of the theological vocabulary of the *Tractatus*. The only thing that is of real importance is the criticism of the prophetic doctrine of a divine legislator. This idea originated in the inadequate understanding of the prophets, and along with revealed religion, which has as its fundamental doctrine the idea of divine law, must be consigned to the realm of popular fantasy. Spinoza's psychological portrait of the prophets corresponds to this judgment of revealed religion. Unlike Maimonides, who made prophetic inspiration dependent on the perfection of reason and imagination, Spinoza makes imagination alone the instrument of prophecy, and attributes to the prophets a one-sided imaginative proficiency.[108] In this way he gives prophets the same status which soothsayers occupied in Maimonides' system. For Spinoza, the power of imagination becomes the instrument through which the prophets receive their vision of God's revelation. His authentic doctrine is that the prophetic ideas concerning God are on the level of imaginative representation. Revealed religion stands in the same relationship to philosophy as imagination does to knowledge.

There can be no doubt as to the reason for the separation between religion and philosophy which is made by the *Tractatus Theologico-Politicus*. This has nothing at all in common with the attempt of modern philosophy to delimit the two separate spheres of religious and scientific consciousness. According to Spinoza, the religious need is most fully met in metaphysical knowledge; in the latter's complete and full truth, it finds its deepest satisfaction. His distinction between philosophy and faith is like that between philosophical and popular conceptions of God and morality. Faith in this sense does not include the entire content of revealed religion. It is limited to the ethical demands of the Scriptures, and to the representation of God and his relation to man which are necessary to establish its basis. Both the cultic and ceremonial laws of the Old Testament (to which Spinoza attributes only a political significance for the preservation of the Jewish state) and the dogmatic Christian ideas of the New Testament are really outside the domain of faith. Scripture is the word of God insofar as it contains this universal human religion. Religion, according to this conception, is a doctrine of obedience—that is, a doctrine for the maintenance of the ethical commandments insofar as they are divine laws, and not a doctrine of truth. Its primary goal is piety and not knowledge, and its primary religious representations are "pious" and not "true" doctrines. The criterion of the former is the extent to which it fulfills its purpose, which is education for piety.[109]

The relation of popular faith to philosophic knowledge of God is comparable to the relation of the esoteric and exoteric knowledge of revelation which was propounded by medieval philosophers, to which Spinoza gave an entirely new form. For the Arabic Aristotelians, and in a diluted form for Maimonides, the religion of the masses consists in the observance of the divine commandments. For the philosopher, however, it consists of the knowledge of God. The ethical concept of religion is the popular presupposition of the speculative. For the medievals, religion, and especially revelation (in which they believed wholeheartedly) contained both of these forms of religion. For Spinoza, however, the theoretical knowledge of God was the peculiar property of the philosopher. Scripture contains only the popular ethical idea of God. According to Spinoza, theoretical speculation is alien to Scripture because (and here again his thought is cloaked in the terminology of revealed religion) Scripture is the product of popular thought. In its doctrine of obedience, however, it contains the highest level of ethical and religious consciousness which the masses can possibly attain. Because of this religious kernel, it possesses intrinsic worth. Spinoza's system recognizes no other religion than the philosopher's intellectual love of God, and admits to no other ethic than the conquest of the passions by thought. It thereby excludes the masses, for whom philosophic inquiry, both in religion and ethics, is beyond their capacities. Popular religion and ethics have no logical place in this system.[110] Spinoza himself emphasizes that understanding alone cannot comprehend how men could acquire salvation simply by obedience. If we grant his presuppositions, morality is not only impossible but self-contradictory, unless it is grounded in knowledge. The transfer of popular religion and ethics to the sphere of revelation heals this gap in the system, and serves to patch up the contradiction between the system's consequences and Spinoza's recognition of a morality which has no philosophic grounding. Spinoza pursued the intellectualizing of the moral and religious consciousness to its logical extreme. The impossibility of grasping the nature of religion and ethics in terms of the presuppositions of a strict intellectualism necessarily became obvious in his system.

III

Jewish Philosophy of Religion in the Modern Era

Introduction

THE barrier which separated Judaism from the spiritual and social life of Europe was not breached until the middle of the eighteenth century. Until that time, the major European streams of thought came into only superficial contact with the world of Judaism. German and Polish Jews were not alone in rejecting any contact with foreign cultures, and occupied themselves exclusively with the Talmud and its problems. Even the broad and many-faceted culture of the Italian and Dutch Jews was rooted in the Jewish Middle Ages, and was only peripherally affected by modern culture. The eighteenth-century Enlightenment was the first movement to bring about a complete and concrete social and spiritual contact with modern Europe.

All this is especially true with regard to philosophy. Philosophic interests had been satisfied by the cultivation of the philosophic tradition of the Jewish Middle Ages; sporadic attempts at alliance with the dominant thought movements of the time, of which we have spoken, did not lead to any noteworthy results. In rejecting heretical tendencies which invaded Jewish circles in Holland many times throughout the seventeenth century, Jewish thinkers used the traditional arguments which they shared with Christian theology of that time. It is no accident, therefore, that the first representative personality of modern European Judaism was also the exemplar of the transition from medieval to modern philosophy. Moses Mendelssohn was, in his youth, a follower of Maimonides' school. But his first independent philosophic work stands firmly on the soil of modern philosophy. The orientation of Judaism in the new sphere of European culture made it necessary for Judaism to wrestle with the philosophic fundamentals of the European Enlightenment.

From this time onward, Jews played a vital role in the philosophic movement of thought in all lands of European culture; and especially in Germany, the birthplace of modern Judaism, they achieved important results. But the overwhelming part of this philosophic work had no connection with Judaism *per se*, and belongs rather to the general history of philosophy of the various European nations. During the course of the Middle Ages and the beginning of the modern period, Judaism was an independent and spiritually all-encompassing culture based completely on religious grounds, with the ability to absorb even those philosophic endeavors which lacked a direct relationship to Jewish religion. But modern European culture detached spiritual life from its anchorage in religious tradition, and thus destroyed the foundations of the traditional unity of Jewish culture. Henceforth, Judaism would be bounded by religious life in its narrowest and specific sense, and all other cultural spheres, including philosophy, would be outside its boundaries.

Even the most general questions of philosophy of religion would, for the most part, be treated independently of their connection with Judaism, and this would be true even of those thinkers who were in complete harmony with Judaism. These Jewish thinkers were merely conforming to the general tendency of modern philosophy—to demonstrate the truth of religion independently of any connection with a particular positive religion, and to develop the fundamental characteristics of a religious world view, without touching upon particular qualities of existing religions. This viewpoint yields different conclusions for Judaism than for Christianity. The fundamental religious doctrines of Judaism are completely identical—at least in their conceptual formulations—with the general ideas of monotheistic religion. Its religious notions do not go beyond these ideas, and unlike Christianity do not contradict them. Judaism was thus spared the conflict which resulted from the collision of rational criticism with Christian dogma.

On the other hand, Judaism was in danger of becoming simply identified with the idea of monotheistic religion and thereby losing its specific content. This identification continually recurred during the reign of the religion of reason, whether that of the Enlightenment or Kant's ethical religion of reason, and whenever that occurred, the need for a special philosophic presentation and grounding of Judaism seemed to disappear. But deeper analysis shattered this simple identity, and because the nature of the philosophic problem had changed, an independent philosophic grounding of Judaism became necessary. It is now clear why in the modern period, unlike medieval times, there was no continuous development of Jewish religious philosophy, and we meet only a series of isolated phenomena.

1 Moses Mendelssohn

THE first modern Jewish philosopher, Moses Mendelssohn (1729-
1786), occupies a position both in the history of philosophy and in
that of Judaism. By dint of his personality and work, he was able,
more than any other man, to shatter the spiritual and social barriers
which separated the Jews from the world, and open the way for the
Jews to enter modern Europe. But his place in Jewish history is not
due to his being a philosopher of Judaism. He had no thought of
constructing his own theory of Judaism, and if it were not for the
challenge of certain Christians, he probably would not have devoted
his efforts to making clear his own position vis-à-vis the faith of his
fathers. His philosophic bent was almost completely oriented toward
the general philosophic problems of his own time. His character as
a modern philosopher is indicated by the wide range of problems
which he considered in his philosophy. Religion no longer constitutes
the center of his philosophic concern, as would have been true in the
Middle Ages. His philosophic creativity was directed toward fields
such as psychology and esthetics, which are quite removed from religious interests; and although he claimed to interpret the phenomena of psychic and esthetic life in terms of his religio-metaphysical
presuppositions, his inquiry was really made for the sake of these
subjects. The autonomy of cultural life in all of its manifold rami-
fications is the self-evident presupposition of his philosophic activity.

As a philosopher of religion, too, he cannot be considered a philosopher of Judaism. Of his two religio-philosophic works, *Phaedon*
and *Morgenstunden (Morning Hours)*, the first attempts to demonstrate the immortality of the soul, and the second to establish the
belief in the existence of God, not so much as Jewish doctrines, but
as doctrines of rational religion and of general metaphysics. The
books themselves were written for an enlightened German audience,
and sought, successfully, to influence it.

Nevertheless, the content of these works was fully congruent with
Jewish doctrine. German Enlightenment, which was the soil in which
Mendelssohn flourished, did not achieve anything that could not
have been reconciled with Judaism. It was admirably fitted to the

Judaism of that particular hour, which strove with all its heart for reconciliation with the new Enlightenment, since it seemed to contain within it seeds of support for such a rapprochement. The belief in a wise and merciful God, and faith in the immortality of the human soul, were accepted as metaphysical truths, and were prized as the essential elements of a religion of reason. When Mendelssohn began his philosophic researches, German Enlightenment still seriously entertained belief in revelation and miracles, both of which were upheld, of course, by the historic religions. German Enlightenment saw in biblical revelation the divine disclosure of those truths, which were the essential content of the religion of reason as well. The mystery of Christian dogma, when it was not set aside completely, was interpreted in the spirit of rational belief in God. Nevertheless, the essence of religion did not lie in assent to certain dogmas, but was contained in the fundamental rational religious truth, and the universal moral law rooted in it. If Christianity was thereby required to surrender basic elements of its content, Judaism could find a home within such a perspective with little difficulty.

The idea of God outlined by Mendelssohn in his *Morning Hours* is basically similar to the biblical God-idea. In his prize essay, *Abhandlung über die Evidenz (On Evidence in the Metaphysical Sciences)*, he had already transformed the concept of the Supreme Being into that of a personal God, because he accepted as truly real only the faculties of the soul in their most comprehensive totality. All of these, in their most eminent sense, could be predicated of God, and thus we can arrive at a concept of the Supreme Being of Beings, who unites within himself the highest wisdom, intellect, righteousness, goodness, and loving-kindness.[1] The same conclusion is reached by the deduction of the contingent world from its necessary source. The contingent cannot proceed from the necessary except through an act of will which, since it is the act of the most perfect Being, must be directed towards the highest good. The divine creative reason is equivalent to the highest moral perfection.[2]

The proofs for the immortality of the soul found in the *Phaedon* likewise uphold the traditional idea of immortality. The soul must be immortal, for it is a simple substance. The latter must be a true doctrine, because consciousness presupposes a simple, uncompounded subject as the bearer of its operations.[3] This metaphysical demonstration, however, proves only the indestructibility of the soul. It does not decide whether, in its future existence, the soul will maintain its conscious status, or will sink to the level of unconscious being. But the goodness of God guarantees that the soul will lose nothing of its conscious being in its future life.[4] In all of these matters, Mendelssohn is more closely related to Jewish tradition than were his medieval Neoplatonic and Aristotelian predecessors. The personal attributes, which had been withdrawn by them from the idea of God, were preserved by Mendelssohn, and instead of the immortality of the active intellect—which was usually bound up with speculative contemplation, and for the most part balanced uncertainly between the eternity of the individual human soul, and absorption in the universal spirit—Mendelssohn stoutly and unconditionally maintained the immortality of the individual human soul.

In only one detail does he veer away from Jewish tradition. Like Leibniz, he curtailed the sphere of human freedom. Freedom, defined as an uncaused act, is impossible, either in relation to God or man. Every act of will has its motives. The will is free only in the sense that it is determined by a recognition of the good.[5] This doctrine differs from the determinism of Spinoza, because the necessity which binds the will is not a logical necessity, but one which is aroused by attraction to the good. Nevertheless, it is determinism, and it forces Mendelssohn to ask how it is possible to punish the sinner, since he has been forced to do evil against his own will! Mendelssohn answers by stating that divine retribution is not an end in itself, but rather comes to purge the sinner and thus make him ready for the life of the world to come. There is no eternal damnation in the future world. The punishment meted out by divine justice is subservient to God's goodness, which never excludes man eternally from the bliss of eternal life.[6]

Faith in God's goodness is the ultimate religious conviction of Mendelssohn. The knowledge attainable by reason totally satisfies his religious needs, in terms of which a life without God, providence, and the immortality of the soul (that is, without that divine order which leads all creatures to blessedness) would be empty and devoid of value.[7] Mendelssohn's piety is founded upon a secure and peaceful faith in a good God, who cares for man, and whom man obeys out of a sense of gratitude. Because it is far removed from passionate commitment, and lacks a recognition of the ambiguities and tensions of religious existence, Mendelssohn's piety finds its strength in the simple clarity of a quiet and trusting faith. Clarity of feeling and of thought are fused into one, and all the goals of life find their ordered place within this general religious framework. Despite their inner autonomy, the scientific knowledge of the world and its esthetic interpretation are both finally incorporated within the religious sphere, and serve to confirm it. Divine wisdom is manifest in the fullness of the world, and the more we recognize it, the more our faith in God's providence and goodness is strengthened.

This is the typical faith of the Enlightenment and is developed by Mendelssohn into a universal religion of reason. But this universal faith is identified by him with the faith of Judaism. When he was challenged by Lavater to either contradict Bonnet's proofs for the truth of Christianity, or accept the Christian religion, he publicly proclaimed this identity for the first time. With the proclamation that since the days of his youth, all his studies of the wisdom of the world had been designed to prepare him for an examination of his ancestral religion, he proudly averred that the results of this examination had merely confirmed his faith.[8] From that time forward, we find frequent reference in his letters to his agreement with biblical and rabbinic doctrines. In his conversation with his Jewish friends, he had already spoken in this vein for some time. In one of his letters he goes so far as to claim that his original intention was to publish his essay on immortality in Hebrew, in explicit agreement with rabbinic utterances on the subject, instead of placing his doctrines in the mouth of Socrates, with whom, as a believer in the true religion, he had nothing in common.[9] To all of this striving to fit himself into the thought pattern of Jewish tradition, there corresponds his announced intention to base himself completely on Jewish sources. Mendelssohn's deepest conviction and his continued affirmation of belief in revelation were undoubtedly true and genuine.

For him, reason and revelation were related in the same way that had been expounded by the medieval Jewish philosophers, and the conservative Enlightenment was so close to the latter in spirit that Mendelssohn was able to utilize and combine the formulae of both, in such a way as to make the medieval arguments relevant to the discussion of the problems of his own day. This becomes quite evident in his critique of miracles, which Bonnet and Lavater had used to substantiate the truth of Christianity. The main idea of this critique is that the fundamental criterion for the truth of any religion is found, not in any outward miracle, but in the inner truth of its doctrine. Thus religion is referred from the tribunal of history to that of reason.

No miracle can attest to the truth of any faith that is unable to withstand the probings of reason. Only after it has passed the test of reason can its divine origin be confirmed by wonders and miracles.
Mendelssohn is consistent in applying this criterion, not only in
regard to criticizing the essential doctrines of Christianity, that is, the
Trinity, original sin, and vicarious atonement, but also to the metaphysical doctrine of Judaism, which he does not accept on the basis
of revelation alone. Only after its rational truth had been demonstrated, is it possible, according to him, to accept biblical revelation.[10] This had been the classical doctrine of the Enlightenment
since the days of Leibniz and Locke, and even this strand, which
maintains the belief in divine revelation, assessed revelation in terms
of rational truth, and made assent to it dependent upon its agreement with reason. This same viewpoint, although not always accompanied by the same sharpness or awareness of consequences, had been
maintained by the medieval Jewish philosophers, to whom their
Islamic contemporaries, and later their Christian counterparts, might
have objected with the same question which Lavater placed so
squarely before Mendelssohn: How can you recognize as valid the
miracles of your own particular tradition and deny those of Islam
and Christianity? To the Islamic theologians, the fathers of Jewish
religious philosophy answered (while paying special attention to the
moral content of religion) that before examining the proof from
miracles, the content of revelation must first be tested in terms of
its agreement with the requirements of reason. The same answer is
given by Jewish apologists such as Joseph Albo (with whose work
Mendelssohn was well acquainted) to the Christian thinkers.[11]

The proof from miracles was overthrown by the critique of the
Deists, who pointed to the miracle stories of idolatrous religions,
and claimed that there was no basis for believing the miracle tales of
one religion more than those of another. Mendelssohn accepted this
objection. Although he believed in the metaphysical possibility of
miracles, he discards the proof from miracles because miracles can
rightfully be used as much for one religion as another.[12] It might
appear that here he differs from all of his Jewish predecessors. But
it is in this instance that he appeals to them quite explicitly, citing
their reasoning to show that Judaism is a faith rooted in a different
soil and is quite independent of miracles. Following those Jewish
thinkers who had attempted to ascribe a special character to biblical
miracles because of their public nature, Maimonides took an impor-

tant step further in his formulation. He refused to ascribe full probative worth to a prophetic miracle, even if performed in public. The certainty of the revelation on Mount Sinai was founded on the fact that God spoke face to face to the entire people; the fact of revelation is thus not dependent upon the veracity of a single prophet, but upon the trustworthiness of an entire people. This argument was fully endorsed by Mendelssohn. He, too, thought that the immediate divine revelation of the religion of Judaism was different in essence from the mediate authority of the other faiths, accredited only by the miracles of their prophets. The direct revelation of Judaism guarded it against those objections which could be made to the miracle stories of the other faiths.[13] The historical criticism of miracles by the Deists would, in the future, destroy this distinction, but within the circle of the conventional discussion of the Enlightenment concerning miracles, it still could be maintained. This distinction was so close in spirit to the rationalism of the Middle Ages that Mendelssohn could utilize medieval proofs to defend his belief in revelation, while still remaining within the Enlightenment movement of thought.[14]

There is, nevertheless, a difference between Mendelssohn and the Middle Ages, which at first glance is only a difference in form, but is actually a difference in essence and approach. For medieval rationalism, religious truths function both as religious and rational truths. Rational truth is revealed to man externally, in order that it might be transmitted to the common people for whom philosophic abstractions are too difficult to comprehend. The purpose of revelation is to publicize the essential doctrines of the philosophic view of God, together with their moral conclusions, and to make them accessible to everyone, to strengthen and validate them, by reason of their divine origin. This view—which was also accepted by Christian Scholasticism (although it was restricted to the rational aspects of faith)—maintained itself throughout and even beyond the period of the Enlightenment. Leibniz repeated it in the trenchant formula that Christianity had made the religion of the philosophers into the religion of the people.[15] Mendelssohn does not recognize such a repetition by revelation of the truths of reason. Rational truths fall completely and solely within the sphere of reason. The significance of the congruence between revelation and reason is that revelation presupposes rational truth. Of necessity, true revelation will be founded on the religion of reason and will see in the latter its true basis.

Mendelssohn first supports his theory by saying that the truths of reason are, by nature, impossible to transmit to mankind through the medium of divine revelation. It is impossible to prove to a man, through "the voice of thunder and the sound of trumpets" such eternal truths as the "existence of a necessary and independent being, which is omnipotent and omniscient and which rewards." Miraculous occurrences cannot infuse any concepts into the thoughtless mind of the "animal man" whose own thinking has not yet led him to the recognition of the existence of an invisible ruler of the universe. In other words, miracles cannot give birth to convictions. To the Sophists, who draw proofs from reason, miracles can point to the fact that there are mighty beings who can do extraordinary things, but miracles in no way afford a demonstration of the existence of the one, eternal and omnipotent God.[16]

The most profound reason for the exclusion of the truths of reason from the sphere of revelation, is independent of the above-mentioned formal considerations. Of necessity, eternal truths, which by definition are basic for the happiness and blessedness of man, should be equally available to all men. If revelation were truly necessary for making them known, it would contradict the goodness of God, for he would then be revealing them to only a portion of mankind and the rest of the human race would be left without such revelation. The particularity of revelation attests to the fact that it is not revelation, but reason which is the universal source of knowledge, and is the only path that God has provided towards the eternal blessedness of religion. Mendelssohn expounds these concepts in his book *Jerusalem,* and finds in them the "concepts of true Judaism," according to which "all the inhabitants of the earth are invited to partake of blessedness, and the means thereto are as extensive as the human race itself."[17] Mendelssohn undoubtedly here refers to the well-known Talmudic dictum that "the pious of all nations have a share in the world to come." But he goes further than the Talmud, both in the importance with which he invests this sentence, and the rationalistic cast which he gives to it. His real source lies in Deism, which, for similar reasons, had led Tyndal to proclaim that Christianity must be as old as the world itself, and that the truth of Christianity must be revealed in all countries and at all times. Mendelssohn draws the ultimate conclusion of these thoughts when he proceeds to divorce universal religious truth from revelation.

As against the particularity of the revealed religions, philosophy was no longer thought of (as was true, for the most part, during the Middle Ages) as a universal tribunal, adjudicating the claims of the different religious faiths. This function was now taken over by a universal religion of humanity. This religion of reason is also universal, by reason of the fact that it is not tied down to the particular methods of the sciences, but is open to the understanding of the natural, unspoiled intellect of every man. Only now do we see the importance which Mendelssohn attributes to the reasoning powers of the natural man. Within science, he has no intention of substituting common sense for exact investigation.[18] He continually required that scientific metaphysics be strict and rigorous in its reasoning. The immediate certainty of man's normal reason is not the distinguishing feature of metaphysics, but of the universal moral and religious human consciousness; rationalism, which specifies the logical place of religion in theoretical understanding, shatters the dependence of religion on scholastic subtlety and views religion as the legacy of all mankind.[19]

This view, which was soon to be accomplished more profoundly by Rousseau's doctrine of sentiment and Kant's doctrine of practical reason, was the goal of Mendelssohn's enlightened rationalism, and was attained through the concept of "natural reason." Even the questions which he directed against Lessing, concerning the education of the human race, can only be understood in terms of this basic view His objections are not directed against the belief in the progress of theoretical reason *per se*, but claim that one must not introduce into this process the ultimate moral and religious certainties. Of necessity, such must be the heritage of all generations; the portion allotted to earlier generations must be the same as that given to later ages. It is this interest in the universality of religious truth which is opposed to the idea of its evolution in the course of history.

With these ideas, Mendelssohn affirms the fundamental spirit of the western European civilization of his day. Medieval rationalism did not fully comprehend the universal consequences of the rational concepts of religious truth; in the reality of medieval life, the religious communities remained isolated in their exclusiveness. Those scientific interests which transcended the boundaries of the particular religions forged only loose and tenuous links between scholars, who remained, on the whole, within the exclusive domains of their particular religions. Modernity strove—first of all, in relation to the various Christian denominations—to reach an interconfessional com-

munity which would be founded on an all-embracing culture, independent of any ecclesiastical connection. The Enlightenment
justified this goal, with its idea of common moral and religious convictions founded upon the autonomy of reason, and transcending
the boundaries of particular religions. Mendelssohn asociated himself with this community; his religio-philosophic works served as a
kind of creed of such a projected future community, and exerted
a certain influence in that direction. His idea of the religion of reason
provided the theoretical justification of a new attitude, which seemed
to him about to recast the spiritual life of Europe.

But Mendelssohn now had the task of situating the revealed religion of Judaism next to the religion of reason, and to invest revelation with a content different than the basic religious truths, which
were already the property of the religion of reason. To this end, he
directed the well-known thesis of his book *Jerusalem*, that Judaism
was not a revealed religion but a revealed law. The eternal truths
of the religion of reason are, it is true, presupposed by Judaism, but,
as truths of reason, they apply to Jews as they do to all humanity.
The specifically Jewish element is found only in the observance of
the commandments, and in the belief in revelation on which they
are based.[20] This idea, so distant from metaphysics, thus allows
neither conflict nor competition between reason and Judaism, and
according to Mendelssohn gives the adherents of Judaism freedom
of thought, because Judaism only prescribes the deeds of man, but
frees his thoughts.

That Judaism was only law had already been propounded by
Spinoza's *Tractatus Theologico-Politicus*, which in many ways served
as a model for *Jerusalem*.[21] Spinoza, too, differentiates the general
religious content of Scripture from the specificities of Jewish law,
just as Mendelssohn divorces the truths of the religion of reason
from Jewish observance. Because it was intended only for Jews,
the *Tractatus* allots to Jewish law only a political goal and function.
The identification of Jewish law with Jewish political order was
intended to limit the scope of its applicability to the time when a
Jewish state existed, and to remove from it any possible value for
the present. For Mendelssohn, too, the law of the Torah is a political law. But his belief that biblical law has eternal value is contrary
to the political explanation of Spinoza. For Mendelssohn, the
uniqueness of the biblical legislation lies in its identification of
religion and the state, and that these two were not separated from

the outset.[22] Political law is merely one element of religion, and the latter remains in effect even when its political portion has lost its function. As religious law, it serves as a supplement to the religion of reason. The distinction drawn by Spinoza between the religio-political law of the Jewish state, on the one hand, and faith, on the other, is here replaced by the dichotomy between the particular religious law and the universal truth of religion.

We have seen the theoretical distinctions between the two worlds in which Mendelssohn lived. In his belief, he was a child of the universal religion of reason, and in his observance of the laws of religion he was a member of the Jewish community. He is fully devoted to both of these worlds, and there is no conflict or tension between them. The idealism of his religion of reason, and the priority of his Jewish sentiment, are both genuine parts of his spiritual essence. Just as his system was able to adapt the two to each other, his personal integrity was unaffected by their joint occupancy of his soul. Both aspects of his consciousness stand next to each other, although they do not stand over against one another. He was thus saved from inner turmoil, because he separated the two sides of his existence, the two bases of his consciousness.

This duality is clearly recognizable in his personal life. But despite their separation, the two elements strive to be reunited. The observance of Jewish law is not, for Mendelssohn, merely a matter of lip service or convention. By observing the commandments, he worships God, in whom his reason believes. The law, given by God, is a religious law, in which, because of his own personal piety, he feels at home. Because of this, it is impossible completely to separate the religious law from truth. It is impossible that the religious law should simply stand at the side of religious truth, which is itself constitutive of religion. Of necessity, the religious law must possess religious significance and meaning, and thus be joined to the heart of religion. His theory seeks to disclose this connection, a linkage which was self-evident to the religious feeling of Mendelssohn.

Mendelssohn seeks to re-establish the significance of the religious law by attributing to it the function, not of making known the eternal truths of the religion of reason, but of strengthening them. Scripture is not the revelation of the religion of reason, but all of its laws "relate to eternal truths, or are founded upon them, or remind man of them, and arouse mankind to be mindful of them." "The ceremonial law is in itself a kind of living Scripture, arousing the spirit and the soul, full of significance, continually stimulating man to take thought, and giving occasion and opportunity for oral instruction." Every custom and ceremony has a "sterling meaning" and dwells "in close relation to the theoretical understanding of religion and morality."[23]

The necessity of having such a guide to the knowledge of the eternal religious truths is all the more pressing when one realizes, that, due to the nature of the human spirit, there are many opportunities for falsifying these truths. The dominance of pagan errors for thousands of years would not have been possible, had there not been a deep tug of the human spirit towards the perversion of the pure truths of reason. Mendelssohn accounts for the origin of idolatry because mankind depicted the truths of reason in images, and afterwards mistook the images for realities. The Jewish people was guarded from this error. In the ceremonial law, it was given a representation of the truth, which led towards it and not away from it. The function of the ceremonial law was to guard the purity of the doctrines of the religion of reason, and thus, for Mendelssohn, the Jewish people was transformed into a kingdom of priests, in that it not only possessed "healthy and unfalsified concepts" of God, but that it also had the mission, "by its very existence, as it were, to proclaim them unceasingly unto the nations, to teach, call, preach, and seek to maintain them."[24]

It is clear that everything that Mendelssohn here gives to revelation he takes from reason. The belief in the victorious power, through which the basic and eternal truth of religion everywhere and at all times conquers and rules the unperverted human spirit, is now seriously qualified. The original clarity of the natural human spirit is obscured by this propensity of the human spirit toward error, and it is this which gives birth to idolatry, and makes necessary the revealed law, in order to preserve, within the life of the Jewish people, the pure belief in God. The theoretical clarity of religious truth has, during the course of history, disappeared from the majority of mankind. This is a variant of the theory of degradation according to which humanity originally possessed the truth in all of its fullness, but lost it during the course of history, making revelation necessary. This restriction of the original optimism of reason is not merely a theoretical construction.

The existence of the religious understanding in all men is a fundamental postulate of Mendelssohn's thought. He changes his mind as soon as he crosses over from theory to an evaluation of the facts of history. How thoroughgoing this transformation is, can be seen from a letter to his friend Herz Homberg, in which he seeks to demonstrate the necessity of the practical commandments even in modern times. Like Homberg, he pays scant attention to the revealed authority of the law or its symbolic meanings, and justifies it solely as a "bond of unity" which must remain in force, so long as "polytheism, anthropomorphism, and religious usurpation rule the world. As long as these evil spirits of reason remain united, genuine theists must maintain some kind of unity among themselves, so as to prevent these [forces of darkness] from treading everything underfoot."[25] The Jewish people must continue to exist as an association of genuine theists, and must, therefore, be bound by the unifying laws of the Torah.

Mendelssohn did not abandon the vision of a universal religion of reason, but for the foreseeable future he sees Judaism as the staunch guardian and firmest upholder of the true belief in God. The religion of reason cannot exist without such support, and without reliance upon the practical commandment. From Mendelssohn's words one can easily recognize the disappointment he suffered in his declining years, when the ideas of the Enlightenment retreated before the forces of the old dogmatic religion and the new irrationalism. Even prior to this, he was unable to justify theoretically the separate existence of Judaism, except in the manner outlined in the letter to Homberg, if he wanted to go beyond the mere formal duty of obedience to the law as law. The historical value of this association of theists lies in the fact that religious reason did not, in fact, enjoy the dominion due to it according to his theory.

The discord between these two tendencies is recognizable in Mendelssohn's interpretation of the history of religion. Here his doctrine of simple, natural reason as the organ of a universally present religious truth found in every man, finds its greatest support. The goodness of providence requires that the means of salvation be as widespread as mankind.[26] But there is no agreement between this meaning of providence with the actual course of history. The religious meaning of history expounded at the end of *Jerusalem* is completely different from these preceding explanations. Mendelssohn ends his work with an appeal for religious toleration, and contrasts this idea of religious toleration with that of the unification of the existing religions, a doctrine which had arisen from a misunderstanding of human nature. Every attempt to unify the religions of the world ultimately leads to the destruction of freedom of thought. Freedom of thought is impossible without equal respect being granted to different religious ideas and opinions, respect which allots to each man the right to call on God according to his lights and in the manner of his forebears. This freedom also corresponds to the intention of providence, which seeks, not a spurious unity, but diversity. No one feels and thinks exactly as his fellow, and it was not for nothing that God formed men with different faces.[27]

This divinely willed difference of human thought and experience became, for Mendelssohn, the basis for the multiplicity of religious faith. At first a consequence of human error, this diversity became incorporated into the divine plan, which is clearly recognizable from the course of history. With this profound and fruitful theory, Mendelssohn does not abandon religious rationalism as such, but does destroy the ground for his own doctrine of religion, which knew only ready-made rational truths, supported by a supernaturally revealed legislation. According to this doctrine, one cannot deduce any significant religious meaning from the multiplicity of the historic religions.

Thus the entire religious content of revelation is swallowed up by reason, and only when this doctrine is separated from its idea of reason, does it become possible for Mendelssohn to restore to Judaism that religious significance which it had for him personally. Mendelssohn sees in this congruence of Judaism to reason its most profound validation. But alongside the universal truth of reason, no place is left for the truth of historical revelation.

2 Post-Kantian Idealism in Jewish Philosophy of Religion

MENDELSSOHN'S astonishing thesis that Judaism was only revealed legislation did not attract many disciples. In its stead there once again grew up the customary form of rationalism, which made Scripture into a revelation of that truth which is also the portion of the religious understanding. Of course, many permutations occurred within this rationalism. By the end of the eighteenth century Kant's philosophy had penetrated to wide circles of Jewish readers, and had destroyed the belief in the power of metaphysics to demonstrate theoretically the basic truths of religion. Along with this, the belief in supernatural revelation waned, even among Mendelssohn's disciples. But despite these fundamental displacements, both in the ideas of reason and of Judaism, the relationship between the two remained basically unaltered. Kant's practical reason replaced theoretical reason as the logical locus of rational religious truth; just as congruence with religious reason had formerly served to justify supernatural revelation, it was now made to justify the historical religion of Judaism. The conviction that the Jewish religion represented the universal truth of the ethical religion of reason in its historically purest and most perfect form, and that it was the spiritual kernel of the religion of humanity, provided a firm basis for religious self-consciousness. When, in the twenties and thirties of the nineteenth century, the developmental hypotheses of the German historical school penetrated Jewish circles, it was easily combined with this earlier rationalism.

The evolutionary school now saw, in the universal ethical ideal and its religious presuppositions, the historically enduring essence of Judaism. Since its formation, Judaism had developed into ever-increasing clarity and fullness, and had become the permanent basis underlying the different forms of religious thought and life, despite some temporary and historically conditioned obscuring of its intent. This identification of Judaism with the simple, basic ideas of religious reason made all analysis or philosophic justification of the former unnecessary. The philosophic justification of the religion of reason was placed on the shoulders of general ethics and philosophy of religion. Jewish thought could simply accept the results of these disciplines, and merely had to add the proof that Judaism was, in fact, identical with the ethical religion of reason. The representatives of Jewish theology in the twenties and thirties of the nineteenth century contented themselves with this. In the whole field of Jewish studies, cultivated and developed at the time with such admirable energy, only a modest corner was reserved to the systematic philosophy of religion.

Those few solitary thinkers who, at the time of the beginning of Science of Judaism, sought to expound Judaism philosophically (although along totally different lines were not far from rationalism in their conclusions. They did not begin there, but found their methodology ready-made in post-Kantian German philosophy, which had developed—in various directions—far beyond the simple ideas of Enlightenment rationalism, as well as beyond Kant's practical religion of reason. On the one hand, the antirationalistic strand of the last part of the Enlightenment was adopted in a more mature form, and was developed into a theory of religion which sought to free the immediate certainties of religion from any rational mediation. On the other hand, speculative idealism sought to ground religion on reason in an entirely new way. Speculative idealism developed the transcendental philosophy of Kant into a metaphysics of the spirit, which derived the world-whole from the self-initiated movement of the ultimate spiritual principle, and demonstrated that this idealistic explication of existence was the true meaning of the religious world view, when the latter was fully and completely understood.

Now the notion developed that the central task of philosophy was to make spirit self-conscious. Spirit did not bear the truth ready-made in its bosom, as had been posited by the metaphysics of a bygone age, but gave birth to truth during the course of its own development. It was the task of dialectical philosophy to describe the dialectical law of spirit, which gives birth to all of its own content. The laws of spirit's concretion in history are dialectically organized and correspond to this dialectical correlation of truth. The task of the philosophy of history was to demonstrate that the historical process leads to a full development of the truth of the spirit, through a series of necessary stages. As with all of the departments of spirit, so too with the religious; it became necessary to have a philosophic elucidation of history, so as to complete the systematic self-consciousness of spirit, and to demonstrate religious truth deduced from it as a necessary concomitant of the historical development of the religious consciousness. Just as this method of historicophilosophic construction from the system of speculative idealism penetrated all the spheres of spirit, so it caused within Judaism attempts to interpret its own development in a philosophic way. Such an attempt was made, in a highly fantastic form, in an anonymous work, *The Biblical Orient,* published in 1821 in two fascicles and generally attributed to the chief rabbi of Hamburg, Isaac Bernays. Similarly, one of the pioneers of the historical study of Judaism, the great Galician scholar, Nachman Krochmal, opened his *Guide for the Perplexed of our Time* (published posthumously in 1851) with an historicophilosophic investigation of Judaism; this was influenced by German speculative idealism and was meant to serve as the basis for the detailed investigations of the book, and constituted its major contribution. His historicophilosophic doctrine had great influence on the religious philosophy which stemmed from this school of speculative idealism, of which we shall soon speak.

But however strong these influences of the speculative idealistic school were, Jewish thinkers rejected those elements of idealistic religious philosophy which, they felt, militated against the Jewish religion. The religious philosophy of idealism, was, in its most significant and influential achievements, a philosophic deduction from Christianity. If the older, rationalistic school had seen the essential content of rational religion to be belief in God, freedom, and immortality, the profound truths of religion were now located in the specifically Christian doctrines, which had previously been looked upon as superrational and supplementary to the above-mentioned rational principles. The dialectical concept of truth made it possible to interpret, as the profoundest depth of speculative truth, that which in the older rationalistic logic had been looked upon as antirational.

The most radical presentation of this thesis was given by Hegel, who found in the Christian doctrine of the Trinity the archetype of his own notion of the self-development of the spirit, and in the Christian idea of the incarnation, the immanence of the infinite spirit within the finite spirit. The philosophic structure of the history of religion was erected so as to lead up to Christianity as the final and most perfect form of religious truth, in which all previous religious aspirations were fulfilled. Judaism, with its "abstract" monotheism, was accorded a place in this developmental scheme, as one of the partial representations of truth, but it had been superseded by the universal truth of the absolute faith of Christianity. The relationship of Judaism to Christianity was, for Hegel, as the relationship of reflective thought, with its dichotomies between absolute and relative, finite and infinite, to speculative truth, which dialectically abolishes these distinctions.

From these formulations it is very apparent that the critique of Judaism in speculative philosophy was made from the viewpoint of a rational pantheism, which was taken as the proper content of Christian dogmas. According to this view, the one-sidedness of Judaism consisted in rigorously distinguishing between God and man, finite and infinite spirit, while in fact the infinite lives within the finite and is manifested by the latter.

Fichte's ethical idealism maintains the spontaneity of the human consciousness within the pantheism of spirit. But the esthetic pantheism of Schelling, which preceded his turning toward theosophy, and above all, the logical pantheism of Hegel, involves the finite spirit completely in the development of the infinite spirit. Reality is the unfolding of truth, and the finite spirit is a necessary element in this process. All spiritual life is under the necessary law of its dialectical self-unfolding. Even the ethical sphere is no exception. Freedom is nothing more than the rational determination of the will, and the moral law does not occupy itself with what ought to be, but with the self-unfolding of the objective spirit, which stems from the opposition between the concept of man and his reality as a finite substance conditioned by natural forces. Evil is the inevitable expression of this opposition, and is its unavoidable starting point.

This opposition between Hegel's philosophy of spirit, and Jewish religiosity, becomes even sharper if we consider that the sphere of ethical reason is subordinated to the sphere of logical understanding, where spirit returns from the activity of willing to a reflexive comprehension of its own essence. What was true of Aristotle and Spinoza is now reiterated in Hegel—thought becomes the essence of spirit; and the ultimate meaning of religion is that, in religion, spirit raises itself to consciousness of the eternal interconnection of truth, while conceiving of itself as a part of this greater whole.

Solomon Formstecher

One of the attempts to give Judaism a philosophic basis was *Die Religion des Geistes (The Religion of the Spirit)*, by Solomon Formstecher (1808-1889). The book, which was published in 1841, is indebted to Schelling, from whom it borrows, although in a very simplified form, its fundamental metaphysical presuppositions. The flux of phenomena points to an underlying uniform substance which necessarily lies beyond the sphere of sensation, and which is only manifested by the multiple forms of sensual perception. Thus the investigation of perceptible reality leads to the recognition of a divine world soul, whose manifestations are the forces of nature, and which is revealed to us in natural objects. Nature is a unified organism, which serves as the manifestation of the divine world soul through a hierarchy of powers and events.[1]

With Formstecher, as with Schelling, spirit stands beside nature as another manifestation of the divine, and only in this manifestation can the world soul underlying nature be recognized as God in the true sense. Spirit is disclosed to us only as human spirit, but human consciousness has a significance that reaches beyond man's separate existence. As the highest form of life on earth, it brings life to full self-consciousness. Only because spirit functions as the self-consciousness of the world, has it a knowledge of nature. Spirit can combine sensible occurrences into an objective unity, because it contains within itself the primary axioms of natural being.[2] This double function of spirit—to serve as the consciousness of the world and of itself —is basic for understanding its manifold aspects. The self-consciousness of the life of the world objectifies itself in physics, while the consciousness of the activity by which it knows nature objectifies itself in logic. With this knowledge of the two spheres of reality, there is combined in our spirit an understanding of the function which is inherent in each of them, a knowledge of the ideal which is to be realized by each. The ideas, which the various natural objects are destined to realize, are represented in the esthetic function of spirit. Spirit as the self-consciousness of the natural world bears the archetypes of natural objects within itself, and in its artistic creation nature attains a consciousness of the ideas which it embodies. The ideal as the principle of human life, the ideal of spirit itself, is the good. While nature embodies its essence necessarily, spirit fulfills its ideal in freedom. This freedom is the essence of spirit, and ethical life, as the life of freedom, is its proper destiny.[3]

By means of this absolute subordination of nature to spirit, and of the esthetic sphere to that of the ethical, this metaphysics renders possible the expression of ethical Jewish monotheism in the pantheistic forms of Schelling's nature philosophy and philosophy of ideas, the two phases of Schelling's philosophy which mainly influenced Formstecher. For such was its purpose, as can be seen in the description of the relationship between God and the world. Although the world is the manifestation of God, God in his being is not dependent upon the world. God is a free spirit, self-determining in essence, manifesting himself in the world by an act of his freedom. We can, therefore, recognize only the manifestation of God and not his essence. Our spirit, which is only the self-consciousness of earth, and which recognizes the whole of the cosmos in its relation to terrestrial existence, is unable to know God except in anthropomorphic similes. Every attempt to define the essence of God derives from the attempt to give these images absolute meaning and value; but whoever does this, commits the sin of anthropomorphism. This statement is specifically directed against the attempts of speculative idealism to constrict the absolute according to laws of thought which apply only to human consciousness, to introduce the distinction between subjective and objective into the absolute being of God, and to penetrate the mystery of the "why" and "how" of the divine manifestation in the world. This attempt at the absolutizing of human modes of thought can be characterized as a sublimated form of pagan gnosticism, as an attempt to apply the naturalistic world view of pagan philosophy to God, who can only be thought of as spirit. Thought, which recognizes its proper boundaries and limitations, will separate itself from all such attempts to derive the world from God in any form, and will accept the world as a given manifestation of God, resting satisfied with this manifestation alone.[4]

Formstecher's conception of religion, which constitutes the object of his book, flows from these metaphysical presuppositions. Religion is the knowledge of the ideal inherent in the spirit. Because spirit originally had a dual ideal, the esthetic ideal of the natural being, and the ethical being of its own life, two fundamental forms of religion result: the religion of nature and the religion of spirit—or, speaking historically, paganism and Judaism. To these two forms, in which the human spirit religiously expresses the *a priori* ideals found within it, there correspond opposing ideas of God. If spirit conceives itself only as the self-consciousness of nature, and sees in the natural life its own supreme ideal, of necessity God will be the highest principle of nature—that is, the world soul. Within the sphere of this basic world view it is possible to divinize nature in all of its various grades, from fetishism, which attributes divinity to natural objects, to physical monotheism, the hypostatizing the whole of nature as one God, without basically changing the primary outlook of paganism. In opposition to this, the self-conscious spirit recognizes its ideal in ethics, and will represent its God spiritually. According to the religion of spirit, God is the essence of ethics, and he does not depend on the world for his own existence, as the religion of nature's doctrine of the world soul had to assume, but freely creates the world as his manifestation.[5]

Formstecher pursues the basic opposition of these views through the entire series of religious concepts, without paying much attention to the esthetic source of the religion of nature. Natural religion cannot picture the origin of the world except as an emanation, and the human soul, which is part of nature, becomes removed from its divine source by its very entry into the world. Thus the destiny of man is to return to God, and his task is to become God. The religion of spirit elevates man above nature; it recognizes no idea of fate, which has been cosmically decreed for man, and no necessary descent of the human soul from God, but grants to the human soul the freedom of its ethical destiny. Moreover, it subordinates man absolutely to God, and in place of becoming God, it gives him the task of becoming like God. All the various types of natural religion are necessarily metaphysical, just as all the various types of spiritual religion are necessarily ethical.[6]

To this doctrine of the types of religion there corresponds a theory of the development of religion. This development proceeds according to the basic scheme of German idealistic philosophy of history, according to which, the destiny of spirit is to become self-conscious and apprehend its original essence. The two ideals of beauty and goodness are innate in spirit and in their absolute truth immanent to it. Formstecher calls this possession of ideals by the spirit, which is prior to all historical development, prehistorical revelation. But spirit bears its ideal content unconsciously. Only as man comes to recognize nature, and himself as its product, is there aroused within him the consciousness of the ideal of nature, and only then, when his own spirit begins to work, does he begin to be conscious of the ideal of his own spiritual life. This coming-to-consciousness of the ideal is historical revelation; it can be viewed as the conscious knowledge of the prehistorical revelation.[7]

From this beginning, historical revelation proceeds through a series of necessary stages. With the first consciousness of the ideal, spirit is unaware that it has grasped its content by its own powers, but believes that insight has been granted it by an external power. Thus the first step of the self-consciousness of spirit is in the form of prophecy. The prophet thinks his grasp of truth is the inspired spirit which has entered him from the outside, and he conceives truth itself to be objective. The continuation of this development goes through a series of intermediate stages, which displace the truth from the form of objectivity to that of subjectivity, and in which spirit becomes conscious of itself as the bearer of truth. The fixation of a prophetic revelation in Holy Scripture and in a religious tradition is, in reality, a preparation for the transition to subjectivity, despite the rigorous objectivity that is involved at the outset of such canonizing.[8]

Historical revelation, however, manifests the absolute content of the prehistorical revelation in a relativized and limited form only. Nevertheless, this relativity is essentially different in each of the two types of religion. The truth of natural religion is relative by necessity because it posits the inferior esthetic ideal in an absolute fashion. When it reaches its peak in physical monotheism, it reaches its own limit, for anything beyond this point is self-contradictory and becomes swallowed-up by the religion of spirit.

The religion of spirit is essentially identical with absolute religious truth. Although it is natural religion, because its principle is the spirit which elevates itself above nature, in its understanding of this principle it is independent of the impressions of a specific natural environment. But spiritual religion, too, is not free of relativity. First of all, absolute truth demands that even the inferior esthetic ideal must be manifested. It is not enough that the religion of spirit is apprised of its own opposition to natural religion; rather, it must interpenetrate the latter and make it its own in a harmonious unity. This is not a contradiction of its original principle, but is rather a fulfillment of it. Secondly, spiritual religion does not reach its absolute form until it has traversed the road from objectivity to subjectivity.[9]

This development can be seen under another aspect. At first, spiritual religion found its bearer in one people, the Jews, just as spirit, in every age and place, is bound to the concrete individuality of a people for its proper manifestation. Such embodiment in the concrete individuality of a people's life is a necessity for spirit, especially in its objective phase. The opposition to the pagan world which surrounded ancient Israel made necessary the maintenance of the identity of a separate people, and the protective shell of theocracy. The universal truth was known as universal, but was, nevertheless, particularized. Judaism, therefore, in its transition from objectivity to subjectivity, is bound up with the development by degrees toward a complete universalism. The first step in this direction was the destruction of the independent national life of the Jews, which caused the dispersion of the Jewish people among other peoples to whom it carried its faith. But the necessity to maintain its existence among hostile peoples brought about the reign of a theocracy of religious law which replaced the theocracy of the state: a separation from the nations by means of the system of religious precepts and mode of life. Despite this self-imposed isolation, which was strengthened by external persecution, the development of Judaism progressed, like that of the general spirit, from the subjection of feeling to the autonomy of reason, and more and more it apprehended its religious content in the form of the free subjectivity of thought. This process came to a conclusion in the modern era, and the liberation of the Jews from social oppression also set free the consciousness of the universal mission of Judaism, which had always been present in the messianic idea, and which now stood forth cleansed from the dross of a particularistic nationalistic hope for the future. The absolute truth of spiritual religion was now about to emerge in its full historical brilliance and clarity.[10]

Along with this progressive development of spiritual religion, a similar development took place in natural religion, its opponent. The bearers of such a development are the religions stemming from Judaism, the faiths of Christianity and Islam, which by their evolution win a place in the historical philosophy of religion. Islam, directed toward the spiritually enslaved peoples of the south, forcibly displaced the old religion with the new. Despite this forcible displacement, it maintained the content of the Jewish religion without substantial changes; but spiritual religion remained something external, without any foundation in the free consent of the spirit. To the contrary, Christianity sought to ground itself on the inner strength of truth, but because of this, had to accommodate itself to the modes of thought and life of the pagan nations which it attempted to influence and convert. It combined the spiritual religion of Judaism with the metaphysics of paganism; its conception of the ethical reconciliation of man with God, including the pagan concept

of the incarnation of God in human form, was joined with its concomitant apotheosis of the human spirit. Just as pagan ideas are
present in Christian dogma, so too in its cult, and especially in its
folk religion, do we find pagan elements which occasionally also
penetrated Judaism in the forms of Gnosis and Kabbala.

The history of Christianity is the history of a continuous struggle
between its Jewish and pagan elements, a struggle which gradually
eliminated the pagan elements. A decisive step in this direction was
taken with the Protestant Reformation, which in its later stages
emphasized ethical rationalism, but the speculative interpretation
of Christian dogma is still a stronghold of pagan metaphysical tendencies.[11] Until such time as the pure Jewish side of Christianity will
triumph, Judaism must remain isolated. But it is possible to see how
the development of both Judaism and Christianity tends toward one
goal, and both result in spiritual religion, which is now becoming a
universal phenomenon.

Judaism can prepare itself for that day by discarding its particularistic elements, and by gradually discarding its ceremonial laws.
This was the optimism of the Jewish Reform Movement, which is
given philosophic foundation by the historical construction of Formstecher.[12]

Samuel Hirsch

A view similar to this, but arising out of Hegelian postulates, was
expressed by Samuel Hirsch (1815-1889) in his book, *Die Religionsphilosophie der Juden (The Religious Philosophy of the Jews)*,
which was published in 1842 as the first and only volume of the projected *Das System der religiösen Anshauung der Juden (System of the
Religious Views of the Jews)*. Methodologically speaking, Hirsch was
dependent upon Hegel to a greater extent than Formstecher was
upon Schelling. Hirsch does not employ the dialectical method of
Hegel, but he conceives of the purpose and function of religious philosophy exactly in Hegel's spirit. Philosophy's task is to take the content contained in the immediacy of religious consciousness, and make
it the consciously known content of the spirit by conceiving it in its
intelligible necessity. Along with Schelling and Hegel, he conceives
the task of philosophy not as the discovering of new truth, but as
elevating the given content of consciousness to the level of conceptual

truth. The religious spirit is the bearer of truth, but only feels its necessity, without being able to recognize it. Hence its content must be viewed by the spirit, which does not recognize any truth which it cannot give to itself as something alien and therefore nonspiritual. Its opposition to such nonspiritual truth that is forced upon it leads it to deny religion *per se*. The spirit forgets that its opposition is not to the content, but to the form of the religious consciousness; by giving itself another content it involves itself in opposition to truth, and hence also in opposition to itself. Spirit's vain attempts to overcome this opposition eventually drive it to consider all knowledge contradictory, and to find truth in the immediacy of feeling which is free of all contradictions. This contradiction in the philosophies of feeling cannot be unified unless we consider the true character of the original dualism; we must understand that this dichotomy is not in the content, but in the form of the religious consciousness. Thus the task of religious philosophy is to overcome the opposition by showing the necessity with which the spirit gives itself content in religion, and by demonstrating that the content of religion is nothing but the content of the spirit itself.[13]

Although Hegel clearly recognized this methodological task, his own philosophy of religion did not fully live up to the demands which he made of it. The content, which he deduced philosophically, was not identical with the content of the religious consciousness. According to Hegel, religion contains the truth of absolute spirit only in the form of representation, and when philosophy grasps this truth in the form of a concept, it changes the content of the religious consciousness fundamentally. The religious consciousness and the philosophic consciousness are divided, not only in their form, but in their content. Thus Hirsch first poses to himself the task of showing the complete identity of religious and philosophic truth. Religion, according to him, contains the truth not in the inadequate form of representation, but the same truth is given to religious feeling which philosophy derives speculatively.[14] Moreover, the contents of religion and Scripture are identical. Scripture is the full and absolute embodiment of the religious consciousness, and thus is identical with philosophic truth. Because of this dogmatic spirit regarding the authority of Scripture, he rejects historical criticism of the Bible in his volume, *The Religious Philosophy of the Jews*.[15] In his later works, however, he concludes that the absolute truth-content of Scripture is entirely unaffected by historical questions concerning the origin of holy books.[16] His differences with Hegel bring him to another view concerning the structure of the system. He sees in philosophy of religion not a part, but the whole of the philosophy of spirit. The unwritten continuation of his work was to carry out this program.

But at the bottom of this methodological difference with Hegel, there lies a deeper difference in substance. To the Hegelian interpretation of the ethical life in terms of the necessary self-realization of reason, Hirsch opposes the idea of absolute freedom as the essential content of ethical consciousness. In order to develop the content of ethical consciousness, he opens with an analysis of the idea of man, and sees the peculiar property of man which elevates him above nature, as Hegel did, in his self-consciousness, in his ability to say "I" to himself, and thus to place himself over and against the world. This consciousness of oneself as an "I" is nothing more than the consciousness of freedom, which is, therefore, the essence of self-consciousness. But this primary freedom is only abstract freedom, and, therefore, empty of all content. It contains a double contradiction: first, because of its abstract emptiness, it has no concrete determination, and must grasp at any external content; and secondly, as a mere datum it is, again, something natural, and thus the opposite of true freedom.[17] The contradiction in the concept of an arbitrary freedom forces the consciousness to go beyond its initial starting point.

Up to this point, Hirsch agrees with Hegel, but he goes on to differ from Hegel in the way he makes consciousness overcome this contradiction. Hegel makes abstract freedom, which cannot exist because of its internal self-contradictions, necessarily pass into concrete freedom, and by means of this necessity he suspends the free self-determination of consciousness. This matter becomes clearer in another context, in which the fact of sin is deduced. Consciousness of sin is, for Hegel, only the consciousness of the inescapable split within man, who grasps himself, by reason of his emancipation, as being at once a creature with a natural will, and a creature destined for reason. When man sees his rational determination as the source of his development, and believes in the original innocence of his being, he attributes this split, which necessarily arises in the dialectical process, to his own split.

This derivation of sin substitutes the simple finitude of consciousness, which contains no sin at all, for the real sin which stems from the freedom of consciousness.[18] Progress beyond abstract freedom and its contradictions must, therefore, be sought in such a way

that freedom is not negated, as it is by Hegel, but is guarded and preserved. This is possible only if man is not compelled, in order to free
himself from contradictions, to walk one determined way, but is
given a choice among many alternatives. One possibility is that he
sacrifice his freedom to his nature, and this constitutes the essence
of sin; the other possibility is that he subordinate his nature to his
freedom, achieving by this constant subjection of sensuality to the activity of freedom a continually renewed and growing life. Not the
reality, but the possibility of sin is the presupposition for the transition from abstract to concrete freedom; and this is not interpreted in
the spirit of Hegel as the breakthrough of reason within man, but
in the spirit of Kant and Fichte, as the unending task of subjecting
the senses to reason.

The dialectical development of spirit is not a necessary process,
as is true of nature, for spirit is granted various possibilities.[19] Since
Hegel destroyed this distinction, he paid scant attention to the testi-
monies of the religious consciousness, and viewed them as inadequate
descriptions of philosophic truth. Thus he introduces into the biblical story of Adam and Eve his own notions concerning sin, which he
can find in the Scriptures only in the form of parable and allegory.
As opposed to this, Hirsch finds himself in complete agreement with
the biblical story. He does not hesitate to characterize the story as
mythical, but myth for him is not (as is true of rationalistic interpretations of myth) a poetic fabrication; it is the presentation of an inner event in the dress of an outer occurrence, which fully presents
this content free of all contingency.[20]

To the various forms of the ethical self-consciousness of men,
there corresponds, according to Hirsch, as many forms of the consciousness of God. He can now interpret the religious life of mankind.
The original abstract consciousness of freedom contained within itself
the feeling that freedom was something given to man; and it thus produced a representation of God, likewise abstract, as the donor of this
freedom, which in comparison to the same form of self-consciousness
was nothing more than a preparatory stage of religion reaching historical concretion. Its very embodiment was dependent upon the direction in which man transcends the empty freedom which stands at
the beginning of his own self-consciousness. If he sacrifices his freedom to his nature, he justifies it with the idea that the power of sensuality is irresistible. He attributes to nature an absolute dominion,
and elevates it to the status of a divine principle. Passive religion,

which arises from such an attitude, is the basis for paganism in all its forms. As opposed to this, if man rises to the level of concrete freedom, by dint of subordinating his nature to his freedom, the abstract image of God is filled with the content of the concrete freedom. God is not only the power which has given us the power of freedom, but he, too, desires the content of our material freedom. Human will and the divine will are one and the same.[21]

This active religiosity is the religion of Judaism. Man's self-consciousness, to which his consciousness of God corresponds, is always the primary datum. This conclusion, although differently derived, is very close to Formstecher's, and recalls his historical understanding of the two basic religious types, paganism and Judaism, with the same role of elevating paganism to Judaism being accorded to Christianity. But the details of Hirsch's historical construction are different, because of the difference in first principles involved. Paganism is not, as for Formstecher, a one-sided grasp of an essentially valid ideal which is immanent in the spirit, but is viewed as a consequence of the total perversion of human consciousness. Hence it cannot develop its partial truth to its highest limit, but must reveal itself in its inner emptiness. The fully-detailed explication of this development is made with the aid of Hegelian dialectic, according to which every stage in the process leads, through the force of its inherent contradictions, to the new stage, until at the end, paganism itself recognizes its own insufficiency. In these details Hirsch works with the full use of the Hegelian dialectic, but he changes its order to suit his own purpose. Moreover, Judaism is exempt from this type of development. Greek and Roman religion, which, according to Hegel, constitute together with Judaism the religions of the individual spirit, are given another position, for they are placed in the sphere of nature religions, even though anthropological nature religions. Their general development in no way leads toward a positive dialectical step in the direction of absolute religion, but has no other result than the disclosure of the emptiness of paganism.[22]

Judaism is part of this development only insofar as it proceeded from the liberation of the fundamental perversion of the ethical consciousness implicit in paganism. It did not require, therefore, the complete decay of paganism. Because ethical freedom is not totally lost to mankind, it is possible for man at any stage of his development to redirect himself toward concrete freedom, and hence toward the true consciousness of God. This turning point first occurred with

Abraham who, within the environment of paganism, attained and fully realized an active faith.

The further development of Judaism, like its origin, is not described along dialectical lines, for in Hirsch's mind the historical dialectic is directed toward the self-destruction of falsehood rather than to the self-unfolding of new truth. If man concentrates his mind on the essence of the religious truth, there can be no further development. Whoever has reached ethical freedom, is capable of grasping religious truth in its eternal content. Whoever seeks God in the right way, will find him always and everywhere. He reveals himself to men in the whole of their lives, in all of their flux and shifting circumstances, in good and evil. If we ask the reasons for our changing vicissitudes, these reasons cannot be sought in happiness or misfortune. We have no other destiny than to maintain ourselves both in happiness and in misfortune; the goal of our lives is freedom, and the natural conditions of our lives are pedagogic occasions which lead us onward to freedom. Thus we recognize God as the master of the universe, whom everything serves, and he has directed everything to serve us and to help us attain freedom. The relationship between creator and creature is changed into the relationship of father and son. This God of Judaism is not abstractly distant from the spirit of man, as Hegel thought, but is immediately present to him.[23]

God's historical revelation to the Jewish people corresponds to this perpetual revelation of God within the life of the individual. The two forms of revelation, miracles and prophecy, are directed to the recognition of God as the free sovereign of nature, who accepts man for his service. This supernatural form of revelation was necessary in order to uproot the idea of the omnipotence of nature—an idea which the Jews acquired in Egypt, and which persisted during their sojourn among the pagan peoples—and to demonstrate the vanity of such nature worship. When the Jewish people overcame these temptations, these means of revelation disappeared. Only the one miracle, inherent in the very fact of the existence of the Jewish people, permanently continues, and like the life of the individual, again and again it points to God.[24]

Thus, for the development of religious truth, there is substituted the ethical education of man by God, and his ever-deepening penetration by the content of true faith. Only in the spirit of such education is it possible to speak of the "development" of Judaism. Here we must distinguish two moments. The immediate vocation of the man who has attained ethical freedom and the knowledge of God is to renew and realize his ethical destiny in an ever fuller fashion. But whoever has found this destiny and grasped this truth, must of necessity strive to spread its truth among others. From a true knowledge of God, there must flow love toward mankind. Hirsch points to the Talmudic comment on the biblical verse, of how Abraham (who is in Hirsch's eyes the archetype of high religion) tries to convert people by speaking to them of the essence of his God. After this attempt came to nought, Abraham withdrew into himself, but he later realized that he could not bring men closer to God through words, but only through the example of his own life, and in this activity he discovered his proper vocation.[25] This vocation is the mission of the Jewish people. They did not receive truth only for itself, but for humanity as a whole; and the Jews must testify to this faith not by words alone, but through their existence, and must prove the power of their faith through its realization in their own lives. According to Hirsch, the sufferings of Israel also serve this purpose. Israel is the suffering servant of the Lord, through whose ordeals the impotence of evil becomes manifest.[26]

Only after this intensive religious feeling becomes part of the life of the Jewish people can there be extensive religiosity; that is, a time when this true faith is to be spread in the pagan world. In Rome, paganism came to an end. In this historical moment, Christianity, the embodiment of extensive religiosity, began to fulfill its mission. The first principle of Christianity, which is manifest in the life of Jesus, is based completely on Judaism. Jesus seeks the kingdom of heaven, but he has no intention of transcending Judaism. Conversely, he recognizes that the kingdom of heaven cannot come until every Jew becomes that which the people of Israel was destined to become, the "son of God," educated to overcome sin and ready to bear alone the destiny of Israel, the suffering of the servant of the Lord. He seeks to become the first to walk in this way, and to serve as an example for others. When Jesus refers to himself as the son of God, he is only directing attention to his mission to serve as the individual concretion of the mission of Israel, who is named by Scripture, the first-born of God.

The above is in complete agreement with Judaism, according to which every man can reach the height of ethical perfection. Jesus did not think that he would be the only person to reach such wholeness, but calls upon every man to follow him and be sons of God, and to accept the sufferings of the servant of the Lord.[27] Hirsch discovers the true representation of Jesus' feeling in the gospel of Matthew, while in Mark and Luke he finds traces of later anti-Semitism. In the gospel of John, the life of Jesus is not presented historically, but is philosophically explained; and in this "explanation" Jesus represents less the realization of the concept of Israel than the realization of the idea of free humanity, which as the final end of creation is prior to all reality. Despite this tendency, which runs through the entire gospel of John, and which purposely sought to weaken the connection between the Christian idea and its Jewish source, his interpretation of this idea and the Johannine Christianizing of the logos remains within the boundaries of Judaism, although it came close to crossing those boundaries.[28]

For Hirsch, the break with Judaism came only with Paul. The positive content of the latter's religious viewpoint did not necessarily lead to this break. Unmerited grace and atonement of sins were not foreign to Judaism, nor was the idea of the necessary priority of belief to the performance of the commandments. Judaism knows—and its history gives this knowledge its factual grounding—that the divine commandments could not be observed unless one is convinced that sin can be overcome. If Paul thought that with these ideas he was diverging himself from Judaism, it was because he had only a superficial acquaintance with Judaism.

But this misinterpretation of Judaism led to wide-ranging consequences. Paul saw the decay of paganism due to its own despair; because of his conception of Judaism he also concluded that since Judaism was only a series of laws, it could not give man the power to do good. Hence he proclaimed that until the advent of Jesus, mankind was totally under the dominion of sin, and he gave this idea dogmatic formulation in his doctrine of original sin. This doctrine included the total depravity of mankind and its redemption through Jesus, such redemption being considered the only way out of this depravity. A complete break was now made with Judaism, and its doctrine of freedom was completely reversed; only after the work of Paul is completely undone will it be possible once again to bridge the gap between Judaism and Christianity.[29]

Because of its doctrine of original sin and redemption, Christianity results in anti-rationalism, and gives rise to a conflict between faith and reason, a conflict that until now had never occurred. Christianity sharply distinguished between God and man, and Hegel's notion that Christianity is the concretization of the unity of the divine and the human, is mistaken. The contradictions which Hirsch finds in Paulinism give him the opportunity to construct dialectically the development of Christianity. He sees in the Catholic conception of the Church the corollary of Pauline doctrine, for it demands a mediator between God and man, and must also have an institution which gives access to this mediator. The Church thus becomes a mediator to the mediator.[30] Protestantism, with its idea of the universal priesthood of all believers, not only denies the Catholic idea of the Church, but Paulinism as well. Nevertheless, it was Luther who maintained Paulinism more strongly than Catholicism, and developed the contradiction inherent in Christianity to an even more rigid form than before. The Protestant principle causes a philosophic renewal, transcending the philosophic achievement of antiquity which had been buried in scholasticism; with Descartes, the philosophy of freedom begins. Despite its discovery of the true method, the contradictions between the religious consciousness and the dialectical philosophy of Hegel, which derives from it, still remain.[31]

Only after the contradictions in the religious consciousness have been overcome, when Christianity retreats from its Paulinian form, can it serve its mission of being an extensive religion, a religion for the entire world. When that time comes, Christianity will become materially identical with Judaism. Human development will reach its end-term in the days of the Messiah, in the era of absolute truth, which will see the unification of extensive and intensive religiosity. Hirsch still maintains the necessity of the separate existence of Judaism, even with regard to this future time, and advocates the return of the Jews to their own land. In its doctrine, Judaism will become one with all people, but it will nevertheless maintain its own special cult, in which its historic mission finds its permanent symbolic expression.[32]

Nachman Krochmal

Nachman Krochmal (1785-1840) was also one of the founders of modern Jewish studies (*Wissenschaft des Judentums*). His unification of historical inquiry with the philosophical interpretation of that historical process distinguished him from all his contemporaries. In his magnum opus, *Guide for the Perplexed of our Time* (issued posthumously in 1851),[33] the historical sections outnumber the philosophic. At first glance, the opening systematic-philosophic chapters seem to be nothing more than an introduction to the main body of the work, the historical chapters. But these introductory chapters constitute the foundation upon which the structure of the book rests. Even as an historian, Krochmal did not merely describe the course of Jewish history, but continually interpreted it in a philosophical-historical manner. He interpreted the outer history of the Jews as the outcome of the inner relation between the Jewish people and the absolute spirit. Because of this relationship, the existence of the Jewish people is not bounded by time, as is true of other nations, but after periods of decay and degeneration, the Jewish people again and again revive with the strength of youth. He sees a unitary process in the history of the Jewish spirit, in which the truth, present in Judaism from its inception, develops to ever greater clarity and higher forms of conceptual thought. This understanding of both the external destiny and internal development of the Jewish people is based completely on his philosophy, which he applies to the actual events of Jewish history, shedding a new light on them.

It is true that the philosophic interpretation of Jewish history was based on a thoroughgoing investigation of particular facts. Krochmal's book contains an abundance of enlightening critical inquiries, which are devoted partly to Scripture and partly to post-biblical literature, and some of them are of fundamental importance. But these inquiries are not included for their intrinsic value, but to provide a firm and solid factual basis for the philosophic interpretation of Jewish history. Despite all of this detailed factual spadework, Krochmal's historical construction—which he arranged, like those German historians who were his models, according to a scheme set up in advance—led to great difficulties.

These became obvious in his completely artificial construction of the outer course of Jewish history. But in the depiction of the inner development of Judaism, to which he devoted greater attention both in terms of scope and value, difficulties were also present. The assumption that the purpose of such development was only to reveal the truth granted to the Jews at the beginning of their history in progressively greater clarity and fullness, not only led to oversimplification, but to an intellectualizing of the historical scene, which did not do justice to the variety of spiritual forces which actually operate in history. But when it comes to the history of the Jewish spirit, all of these flaws may be disregarded—as with the German scholars who were his exemplars—in favor of the fruitful idea of development, which he borrowed from German philosophy. The attempt to establish the spiritual history of the Jewish people on unified factors and laws made possible a comprehensive survey of Jewish history, which otherwise would be nothing more than a series of particular opinions and viewpoints, whether of individuals or of groups. None of the founding fathers of the *Wissenschaft des Judentums* grasped this idea as fully as did Krochmal, and despite his rationalistic one-sidedness in the consideration of the operative forces in history, his ideas about the history of the Jewish spirit have a fundamental value for the development of Jewish studies.[34]

Although the book's introductory chapters state his philosphic views very cursorily, its basic elements can be detected with sufficient clarity both there and in the notes on the historical chapters. They leave no doubt that Krochmal viewed German idealistic metaphysics as identical with perfect truth. While both Formstecher and Hirsch adopted Schelling's and Hegel's systems only with qualifications, recognizing the opposition between the personal God-concept of Judaism and pantheism, Krochmal saw no opposition between idealistic philosophy and Judaism. He insisted that the doctrines of modern philosophy were in complete agreement with Judaism. Even in their philosophic form they were not new to Judaism; he viewed modern philosophy as the logical heir of the theses of medieval Jewish philosophy, especially of Maimonides and Ibn Ezra, whom he especially admired.[35]

There is a kernel of historical truth in this judgment, but it applies more to the Arabic sources of medieval philosophy, from which Maimonides and Ibn Ezra drew, than to their own doctrines. This is definitely the case with Maimonides. German philosophic idealism centered its attention—with new thought tools and in a modern framework—around the same emanationist pantheism which we found in the Arabic Neoplatonists and neo-Aristotelians, and to which Ibn Ezra was linked in certain ways. Maimonides, however, countered these notions with the idea of the personal God, as Formstecher and Hirsch did in the time of Krochmal.

Krochmal brought idealistic philosophy still closer to the Jewish philosophic tradition by stripping it of its dialectical character.[36] Only in that chapter, apparently written toward the close of his life, which deals with the assumptions of a religious philosophy embedded in logic (a typically Hegelian doctrine), did he develop Hegel's ideas in their dialectical form. From stray hints there, we can surmise that toward the end of his philosophic labors he was ready to accept the Hegelian dialectic. But this chapter stands completely isolated from the body of Krochmal's book. Outside it we find no dialectical method in the development of his ideas, and no dialectical understanding of the processes by which the world proceeds from God, and of how the separate spheres of existence develop and unfold from each other. The simple form in which Krochmal accepted the metaphysics of German philosophic idealism is closer in spirit to the metaphysics of the Middle Ages and that of the early modern period than to that of its founders, despite the fact that German philosophic idealism tried to divorce itself from those metaphysical views which approach the ideas of Krochmal. The differences between various adherents of German idealism are inconsequential in view of the common elements shared by all members of this school. Although couched in different formulations, they all maintained the same principles, and Krochmal was not inconsistent in accepting the opinions of one thinker on some points, and those of another thinker on others.[37]

His doctrine of the nature and essence of religion and its relation to philosophy was completely taken over from Hegel. That every religion, from the lowest to the highest, had its basis in the common direction of the human consciousness, and despite their differences, shared a single essence, was an opinion accepted by all schools of philosophy of religion in Germany since Schleiermacher. But the members of the school differed on the definition of the content of religion. Krochmal defined religion as the belief in spiritual powers. This belief could be found even in primitive animistic religions. The true subject of these primitive faiths was not the transitory natural object, but the power which maintained it in being—that is, the spiritual power (Krochmal speaks here of the "spiritual" in the most general sense) within it. This spirit was not only impervious to change, but unlike the body, which was an individual limited entity, the spiritual was essentially general and unlimited. This generality and lack of limitation of the spiritual powers inherent in natural objects are, however, only relative, for the multiplicity of forms of the spiritual powers stand opposed to each other.

As in the case of paganism, spiritual powers lose these qualities when they are viewed only in their connection with bodily exist-

ence.[38] Only in religion's highest stage, biblical religion, was the
spiritual revealed in its purity. There, faith was not directed toward
individual spiritual powers, but toward the absolute spirit, which is
their foundation. This absolute spirit, which Krochmal, like Hegel,
denoted the absolute truth, was the cause of all causes and the fundament of all true existence. Natural bodies which are subject to
continual becoming and destruction do not truly exist. Only spirit
actually exists, for unlike bodies, it is not subject to change. But the
individual spiritual powers exist by reason of the absolute spirit,
which bears and sustains them. Absolute spirit is the only universal
and infinite reality in the full sense of these terms. Only as faith in
the absolute spirit can religion express that which is fully embedded
in its essence. The adoration of God corresponds to this conception
of God. Such adoration depends on man's recognition that only by
reason of his spiritual essence can he grasp the love of God, and thus
assure himself of everlasting life. In a very careful formulation,
Krochmal here expressed the idea that the goal of the adoration of
God was the unification of the human spirit with the divine spirit.
Theoretically, religion was spiritual perception, and in its highest
reach it was the grasp of the absolute spirit; practically, it was the
striving towards unification with this spirit so as to become identical
with it.[39]

But philosophy, too, taught that spirit was the essence of all beings
—and this was a clear demonstration of the identity of religious philosophic truth. This identity, which can be found at all levels of religious and philosophic development, becomes clearest at the highest
level of religion and philosophy. Biblical religion, the highest form
of religion, contains the same faith in the absolute spirit which is
present in the ultimate truth of philosophy. Granted this postulate of
the identity of religion and philosophy, the only difference between
the two lies in the way in which they represent their common content. Philosophy conceives of spirit in the form of a concept, and religion in the form of a representation, to which Krochmal occasionally added the dimension of feeling. The representation is a form of
consciousness higher than that of sensation and observation, but lower
than that of concept. While in matters of principle only the elite
can reach the heights of speculative thought, imagination is common
to all men. Thus religion, which grasps the spiritual in the guise of
representation, makes it the legacy of all men. Every man is destined
for this belief in the spiritual; although it needs education and train-

ing in order to be actualized, the religious consciousness is native to man at birth.[40]

It was not only the faith of the religious congregation, rooted as it was on tradition, which was dependent on representation, but all religious geniuses including the prophets, and the greatest of them all, Moses, grasped the truth only through representation. The religion of the Torah was in terms of its content infinitely superior to the religions of paganism, but it comprehended its superior truth in the same form as these had grasped their flawed, inferior truth.[41] According to this doctrine, the source of religion lay in the human spirit. On the other hand, Krochmal not only considered the Torah to be divinely revealed, but explicitly said that prophecy was an incontrovertible fact; and he was especially outspoken about the wondrous nature of the theophany at Mount Sinai.[42] The opportunity to unify these two approaches was presented in his doctrine of prophecy, which we shall consider later. According to this doctrine, revelation depended on the inner connection between the divine spirit and the human spirit. By reason of this connection, the human spirit participates in the divine truth; through man's consciousness, with which it is linked, the divine spirit is made manifest, but its truth is always given in a form appropriate to man's power of apprehension. In the knowledge of God, the human and the divine are bound together in an indissoluable unity.

For Krochmal, the value of religion was not lowered because it comprehended truth only under the aspect of representation, for its primary object was the truth shared by philosophy and religion.

The final and complete truth was contained in biblical religion and was essentially present in the Jewish patriarchs. The later development of the spirit of Judaism—and more than this, of the spirit of humanity—did not add anything to this truth, but merely brought into clearer conceptual focus that which had always been present. The value of the Torah, therefore, was not solely historical. As Krochmal once put it in the terminology of medieval philosophy, it was the source of truth for all generations, and all the insights of philosophy were contained within it; by means of correct interpretation, one could find them there.[43]

For Krochmal, as for Hegel, the form with which truth was given to consciousness was not an outer husk without effect upon its contents, but at times stamped the contents of knowledge with its own character. It was impossible, therefore, that this identity of religious and philosophic truth should be an absolute one. Truth adopted and discarded various forms, according to the manner in which it was grasped, whether as representation or as concept. Truth was not to be grasped firmly except as a concept, and representation which stood midway between sensation and thought gave its object a distinct character, which was not essential to it, but belonged only to the sensual description of the object. The truth of philosophy was the truth of religion on a higher plane. The proof for the argument that religion cannot attain a perfect understanding of its object, lay in the various contradictions which characterize religious faith, of which Krochmal cited many examples from Scripture and Talmud. He made these paradoxes, which are contained in the religious consciousness, dependent on the imaginative form to which religion was limited, and he thought that they would disappear once conceptual knowledge replaced knowledge by representation.[44] His statement, therefore, that Scripture contained all of the insights of philosophy, meant only that they were there potentially. If we cleanse scriptural doctrines of their dross of representation, and change them into their pure conceptual form, and deduce from them all the conclusions that thought can derive, they are present in acts.

Moreover, such interpretations do not introduce anything extraneous into the text, but develop only what is already there. With all of the differences between truth as understood through representation, and truth understood through concepts, it is still the same truth in both contexts. The interpretation of Scripture which changes its content into a conceptual form does not affect the essence of the scriptural truths, although it is opposed to the representative form in which these are to be found in Scripture. Such an interpretation of Scripture was the task of religious philosophy. It could not fulfill this task unless it was given complete freedom to transfer the scriptural content to a conceptual form, and it should not hesitate to oppose particular scriptural doctrines which are only an expression of this content. Complete freedom of biblical interpretation was a necessity not only for philosophy, but for religion as well.

The goal of the religious ideal was the communion of the human spirit with the divine, which could not be reached without a knowledge of God. The greater the degree of knowledge, the stronger was this communion. This ideal, therefore, could be realized only by the free development of knowledge. This was, *in toto,* the same approach to religious perfection which we found in medieval Jewish philosophy of religion, and Krochmal, therefore, sharply rejected Luzzato's objections to Maimonides' and Ibn Ezra's rationalistic theory of religion. They had not substituted the ideals of Greek philosophy for those of Judaism, as Luzzato had accused them, but only separated themselves from the ideals of popular religion, which Luzzato had mistakenly identified with the ideals of Judaism as a whole. Similarly, Krochmal accounted it the great merit of the medieval scholars that even with regard to metaphysics they did not consider themselves as bound by particular scriptural doctrines. Their opposition to biblical religion in its imaginative form was not limited to those matters mentioned by Luzzato, but included all of the religious opinions of Scripture. Nevertheless, those scholars never ceased being faithful to the essence of biblical religion, and if it continued to walk in the path of the great leaders of medieval thought, modern religious philosophy would not renounce the truth of Scripture.[45]

The actual use which Krochmal here made of his fundamental insight—that the basic unity of religious and philosophic truth was unaffected by the oppositions arising out of the distinction between representation and concept—proved how deeply this distinction cut into the very content of the religious world view, and how doubtful is the task of setting boundaries between the form and the content of religious truth. The absolute opposition between the metaphysics of the medieval scholars, and the outer form of biblical religion, was essentially between the doctrine of emanation, which Krochmal attributed to Maimonides and Ibn Ezra, and the biblical view of God and his relationship to the world. It was this doctrine of emanation which modern philosophy tried to develop by other means. Despite this opposition, the metaphysics of medieval philosophers and that of modern times could be identified with biblical religion because both posited the highest spiritual principle as the source of the world. The difference between the scriptural faith in a personal Creator-God and the emanationist pantheism of medieval and modern metaphysics was no longer in the content of religious truth, but was inherent in their different forms of expression of that truth.

Krochmal's doctrine, although not identical with this pantheism, was very close to it. The few, brief occasions where he presented his own views give the most general outline only, but they leave no doubt that he thought the world dwells within God. He interpreted biblical monotheism in such a way that true existence could be attributed only to the absolute spirit, and all other beings exist only insofar as they participate in the being of this spirit; from these positions, however, one cannot as yet deduce the immanence of the world in God. Yet this is stated expressly in his assertion that God is both the cause and the totality of the world. In one context he designates God as the "general cause which comprises in its unity all causes and the being of all existents"; in another place, God is "the source and goal of all spiritual being," . . . "the existence of all spiritual beings in their absolute truth." The created spiritual powers are thought to be contained within the being of God.[46] They are connected with him and with material bodies, and insofar as they are joined to bodies in the material world, they participate in his true existence. Only they can be said to be immanent immediately in God. But since through their power they maintain all material substances, and since to every class of material substance there corresponds a spiritual power, which is related to the individuals in that class as the general is related to the particular, through these spiritual powers the immanence in the divine is mediated to the material world as well.

This limited and sporadic metaphysics is all that can be gleaned from the systematic chapters of Krochmal's work; moreover, all argumentation to prove his view is missing. The most important source for both the content of his doctrine and its supporting arguments can be found in his detailed explication of the philosophy of Ibn Ezra. For Krochmal, the philosophy of the medieval thinkers, although incomplete, was in principle the same as that of modern philosophy. He thus interprets Ibn Ezra, wherever he finds warrant, in the spirit of modern philosophy. Several times he explicitly agrees with ideas which he found in Ibn Ezra, but which rather refer to his own metaphysical doctrines. They must be developed and grounded in terms of a very wide context in understanding his thought. It is important to bear in mind this groundwork, and see how he finds his way from the given sensual world to the supersensual world of his metaphysics.[47]

This justification of Ibn Ezra's philosophy (and hence of his own position) is based on his epistemology. By analyzing the act of knowing, he finds his way from the sensual to the supersensual world. This analysis is quite similar to that of critical epistemology, according to which the knowledge of empirical reality arises by a conceptualization of the original data of sensual phenomena, thereby replacing the sensuous knowledge of things by a scientific knowledge of reality.

The details of brute existence are ordered within a network of laws. The singular occurrence cannot be understood unless it is seen as part of a law-abiding order. The purpose of science is to discover the principles and general laws on the basis of which individual events occur, and to ground individual phenomena on their general essence. Science, therefore, begins with individual laws, which are close to sensual experience, and rises from these, step by step, to the most general laws, until it finally comprehends all existence as one system.

But this process has still another aspect. By the time that consciousness has comprehended sense data under the form of a law, the empirical experience of these natural objects has already changed. The sensual qualities of things as given to us in perception are understood as the results of certain causes, which truly bring objects into being. In place of the sensual qualities such as color, sound, or smell, we now have their objective causes which cannot be grasped by the senses, but only by abstract thought. But the transition from sense experience to understanding is a gradual one, where the given sense data are slowly displaced by conceptual categories, and at the end we discover that at the base of many-faceted material existence the concept was already present. Moreover, thought seeks to go further and strives to shed all sensuous qualities and convert them into concepts. Thus, the concept is not a subjective approach to existence, as the theory of sensualism maintains, but rather it is only through the concept that existence can be understood objectively.[48]

In terms of this description of the knowledge of empirical existence, Krochmal reached metaphysics by attributing a special supersensual type of being to the general laws which determine the interconnections of reality. These laws are not merely connectives between different phenomena, dependent upon them for their existence, but they constitute the general essence of things, and have a separate existence independent of that which they connect.

This view of the laws of being as independent existents is also expressed by their relation to time. As opposed to the individual events, which are continually in flux, the laws of nature are unchangeable. But for Krochmal their supratemporal validity became a supratemporal being, and acquired a metaphysical reality beyond time. Krochmal himself was aware of the similarity of these general substances to the Platonic ideas. But unlike the Platonic ideas, they not only are patterns for material events, to which one can refer, but they constitute the source from which material bodies derive. One cannot judge these general substances to be lifeless, because they are dynamic forces. They have their own inner life, in which the most general essences are slowly detached and individualized, and from the most general concepts there always proceed more particular concepts. The "general" not only contains the particular within itself, but is the source from which the particular develops. This logical procession of the individual from the general is also a material differentiation, in which the individual essences come into being. The last stage of this descent is the step from nonmaterial to material existence.

Moreover, the relation of the separate fact to the general substance, which serves as its base, is as the relation of the particular to the general. Thus, when the lower and most particularized spiritual substances continue to develop in their particularization, they produce the facts of material existence.[49] But how is it possible for the particular to come from the universal, even if that universal is limited? More to the point, how can the universal suprasensual substances which are beyond time and place be transformed into empirical objects, into sensual existence, subject to change, bound to time and place? Krochmal could not explain this, just as the German philosophers for whom this problem has always arisen, although in different forms for the various adherents of the idealistic school, were unable to account for it, and which became, therefore, one of the chief difficulties of their theory.[50] But when at last Krochmal found a way to return to the material world, whose conception he had reached by his description of the knowledge process, he ordered the understanding of this world in terms of his metaphysics. He first denoted natural laws as "the general substances of things," and afterwards attributed a special type of existence to them. Nevertheless, in order to explain how these transcendental substances could order the natural course of events, he then showed that they not only produce individual existents, but that these were inherent within them. The transcendental substances enter the world of nature, and are the powers which preserve it, and determine its combinations. In agreement with Schelling, to whose metaphysics his chapter on Ibn Ezra is very close, he points out that nature bears spirit at all times, although at different stages of development. In inanimate nature, spirit is not at all self-conscious; in animate nature, self-consciousness first begins to be aroused; while in man, it reaches full self-consciousness and afterward returns and finds itself even in the lower levels of nature.[51]

But from these spiritual substances we must take another step upward. As substances they need a subject, within which they exist; as ideas they need spirit, in which they are gathered. There must exist, therefore, a supreme being which is their subject, a supreme spiritual principle to which they belong as ideas. Krochmal likened his spiritual substances to the Platonic ideas, but he understood them in the same way as has often been the case in the history of Platonism: namely, as the contents of the divine mind. Since they were God's thoughts, they were not silent and lifeless, but were vital forces, able to operate in the natural world. Thus we arrive, though with a different set of terms, at the previously mentioned doctrine of Krochmal; that is, that God contains within himself all of the powers and spiritual substances, despite the fact that they support the being of the bodily substances and preserve their existence. But God is not only their subject; he is their source as well. The chapter on Ibn Ezra also reveals in more explicit fashion how their source is in God.

From Schelling, Krochmal accepts the idea (which he again attributes to Ibn Ezra, this time because of a terminological misunderstanding) that all beings—whether they exist in the spiritual or the material world—are complexes of substances and forms, and that only God is above such duality.[52] The same substance is common to all things; their differences arise from the various forms this substance takes. Despite the intrinsic substantial unity of all things, the multiplicity of forms is the reason for its differentiation into a multiplicity of phenomena. From this, two additional definitions follow: substance is always the principle subject in which form exists. In its own right, it is completely unlimited, and only form makes it limited and finite. By reason of its union with form, the substance is deprived of its concrete infinity, which continues to exist in things only potentially.

From all that has been said concerning the substance common to all things, the conclusion must be drawn that it is identical with God. The infinity of God permeates all beings, and only because of the multiplicity of forms is it enclosed by set boundaries. Thus, the process by which things proceed from God is one of divine self-limitation. But God also contains within himself an emanationist aspect, because his substance remains absolute, and whether outside of form or within it, is unaffected by form and exists absolutely.[53] But the unlimited substance of God cannot be comprehended by our consciousness, which can only grasp limited and conditioned things; and we cannot even define it as being and existing, because everything that exists is a compound of substance and form. We know him only as the mysterious source of existence, and everything which in individual beings is fragmented and separate, combines, within him, into an inseparable unity.

The descent of things from God is also continuous and unending. It begins with the creation of the hylic form, which Krochmal also denotes as the "form of forms" or the "idea of ideas," because all forms and all ideas are included in it. It comes into being because of God's self-consciousness and self-knowledge. This self-knowledge of God is the first act of a progressive divine self-limitation, for as the idea of God slowly and progressively develops, the separate ideas contained within it also develop, and from this primary form all of the separate forms unfold. The path from the general to the particular (of which we have spoken previously) originates in this primary form, and from it descends through the hierarchy of the spiritual substances, until it reaches the existence of the individual, natural thing.[54]

In this idea of the descent of the world from God, Krochmal sees the true meaning of the scriptural belief in creation. It is impossible that God could have created a world from something independent of him, or that the world could come into being without any ground whatsoever. The coming into being of the world is possible only by God himself being its source, and by his substance permeating it. Krochmal took from the Kabbala the idea that "Nothingness" was the only name predicable to God, to whom it is forbidden even to attribute existence, and, therefore, he appears to human thought as nothingness. While the world descends from this divine substance, "Nothingness" is the source of its descent.[55]

Of the biblical idea of creation, only the notion that the self-limitation of God is a spontaneous act of divine freedom remains. In order to make the transition from the self-contained to the world, Fichte and Schelling needed this act; only Hegel was able to do without it, because for him the absolute does not precede the dialectical process, which develops existence, but exists only within it. For Krochmal the divine essence stands outside the developmental process. Thus it, too, needs a spontaneous act for its substantial self-limitation and its entrance into form; and despite hints as to other possible approaches, he upholds the idea of a spontaneous act, and by this representation comes closer to the scriptural idea of divine freedom of action.[56]

Krochmal saw clearly that a change in the form of this notion demands a corresponding change in all the other scriptural notions. But he did not systematically develop the conclusions which flow from his fundamental view, and he reinterpreted only a few of the scriptural teachings in terms of his metaphysics. We have already mentioned his theory of prophecy in connection with his views concerning religion: the basis for prophetic revelation is found in the intrinsic connection of the human spirit with the divine; it is prevalent in all men, but is stronger and more vital in the prophet. The spirit of man radiates those spiritual powers which inhere to God, and is thus, finally, the radiation of God himself. Thus these spiritual powers can illumine man, but he can only appropriate their influences in accordance with his powers of comprehension. Krochmal concluded, therefore, that the prophetic spirit had not yet reached the stage of conceptual understanding, and can receive divine revelation only under the form of representation.

He was similarly able to deal with the predictive powers of the prophets in terms of his doctrine of revelation. Because of his philosophic assumptions, he was able to consider them positively, but the ability of the prophet to accurately predict the future was dependent on the strength of his faculties. For the near future, directly connected with the present that is well-known to the prophet, a detailed knowledge is possible. Beyond this, however, the prophet can foresee only the general outlines of what is to happen. This limitation of the prophetic knowledge of the future is extremely important for Krochmal's critical exegesis of Scripture. Thus he denies that the second portion of the Book of Isaiah was written by the prophet Isaiah, and upholds the opinions of those who claim that this section should be assigned to a second Isaiah because the first Isaiah could in no way have spoken of the return of Israel from Babylonian exile as a *fait accompli*, or have specifically mentioned the name of Cyrus.[57]

The only time that Krochmal speaks clearly of the problem of providence is in one of his letters. Providence is mediated by those powers which proceed from God, which in the language of Scripture and Talmud are called "messengers of God." As Maimonides had already taught, whatever is said concerning the powers active in nature merely reflects the widespread opinion of the identity of providence with the laws of nature, whose source is God. But Krochmal takes a further step, in that he attributes an effect on the workings of nature not only to the immanent forces of nature, but also to those potencies and spiritual substances which are at their root and which are directly related to God. These can operate in a way which cannot be ascribed to the natural forces themselves, and which therefore appear to be miraculous. That this explanation of providence and miracles is close to that of the medieval philosophers was already felt by Krochmal. It was in this way that Maimonides had explained providence, and Ibn Ezra, miracles. Krochmal also postulates that there was a higher class of miracles, accomplished by God's interference in the course of the world, but he does not explain how this could be reconciled with his fundamental metaphysical principles.[58]

On the basis of his metaphysics, Krochmal also builds a philosophy of history in which historical events are first explained in terms of empirical factors, but afterward are treated in terms of metaphysical causation, their empirical causes being considered as manifestations of these active metaphysical causes. This is done especially with regard to the central concept of his philosophy of history, the concept of the spirit of a people. He defines it as the "sum total of the spiritual portion and heritage" which a nation creates in all the spheres of spirit, in jurisprudence, in ethics, and in science. These add up to the "spiritual treasure" of the nation; "they are gathered to form in their totality a holy spiritual treasure in every nation." The national creations in all these fields and disciplines share certain common characteristics because, although the spirit of a nation has a unique character, different for each, there is reciprocal relationship between all spheres of the spiritual life by which the specific characteristics of one area are transferred to the others.[59]

Krochmal attributes to each nation a "spirituality" which is present in the people from the beginning of its national existence, and which stamps all of its spiritual creations. The unity of the objective spirit of the different nations is no longer a consequence of the interrelationship and reciprocal relationship between different spheres of spirit, but is explained as the subjective unity of the national spirit, the unity of the power to create in all of the various spheres of the spirit, which is prior to all of the individual cultural creations of the nation. In this "spirituality" all members of the nation participate; by means of it they become members of that nation.[60] This spirituality contains potentially everything that is to be accomplished in the cultural development of the nations and brought to slow fruition. The idea of the spiritual ability of nations also provides the transition to metaphysics. Spirituality, which is inherent in all peoples at the time of their coming into existence, has its source in the spiritual substances which are generally revealed in the empirical world.

The process which leads upward from inanimate nature to its revelation in the spirit of man does not cease with individual men, but reaches its apogee in the spirit of nations. The transition from the empirical to metaphysical explanation is not accomplished without leaps and contradictions, which become sharp and clear when it comes to an accounting for the special characteristics of nations. The religious representations of a people are part of the spirit of that nation, and they express its peculiar spirit along with its other cultural achievements. But they do this in a very special manner. The gods, in which each of the nations believe, are embodiments of the nation's spiritual aptitude and essence. Everything is in accord with the nation's aptitude—whether it be for war, the fashioning of legal systems, art, or science—and these same characteristics and abilities are attached to its gods, and their manifestations are viewed as a natural occurrence, for the impression they give corresponds to these characteristics.

This is a positivistic explanation of the representation of God, which at first glance is a complete denial of the validity of religion.[61] But immediately following it one finds the opinion that religion is belief in the spiritual, and that polytheistic faiths are also directed toward spiritual substances which are contained within the absolute spirit, even though these faiths cannot grasp them except as they are connected with bodily substances.[62] The reconciliation of these two views, at which Krochmal only hints, is found in the doctrine that the spiritual aptitudes of the nations have their supersensual source in spiritual substances, and that in every nation either particular substances or specific aspects of those essences are embodied. What may be considered, from the psychological standpoint, to be the embodiment of the spiritual aptitudes of the nation, is, from the metaphysical viewpoint, a faith in the actual spiritual powers concretized in that ability.

In similar fashion, Krochmal describes the development of the nation, at first empirically, and then in terms of the metaphysical basis of his thought. He adheres to the popular doctrine that each nation goes through three periods of development: growth, maturity, and degeneration. He considers these stages absolutely necessary, and draws the conclusion that the life of each nation is of finite duration. All nations will eventually sink into decay and death

because of the destructive power of culture, which becomes prevalent in their mature periods. The development of the spirit causes
a luxurious refinement of life, which in its turn saps the vital powers
of the nation. The continuous accumulation of wealth leads to a
craving for pleasure, which destroys the purity of artistic creation.
The lust for power and prestige brings about social divisions within
the nation, and the passion for novelty causes imitation of foreign
customs, of thought, forms, and styles of life. All this erodes the
power of the nation to withstand its external enemies, and instead of
trusting to its own powers, it begins to believe in all kinds of superstitions, and slowly begins to degenerate and die.[63]

In addition to the empirical-causative explanation for the extinction and disappearance of nations, there is a metaphysical explanation: once the spiritual goal of the nation is realized, it must die. The
origin of the spirit of nations is found in one of the finite spiritual
substances, which are grounded in the Absolute Spirit. Because of
their individual specificity, these powers are themselves finite and are
thus unable to confer upon the nations which possess them more
than temporary existence.[64] Hegel had shown in detail how to combine the empirical and the metaphysical explanations; Krochmal,
who does not devote more than a few lines to this problem, does not
look for such a combination. Nevertheless, like Hegel, he stressed
that nations with intrinsically important spiritual accomplishments
would overcome their own physical destruction. Their achievements
would be absorbed and further developed by other nations; every nation finds its place, makes its own contribution, and is integrally related to this whole development.[65]

These general philosophicohistorical theories, which Krochmal
develops in the most cursory way, function as the basis for the philosophic explanation of Jewish history. It is easy to see that his idea of
the spirit of the nation is based on scriptural ideas. The national idea
of German philosophic idealism appears as a kind of generalization
of the Jewish view of the essence and role of the Jewish people. This
view, which was accepted by Krochmal, made the spirit of the nations the basis for their existence; each nation became united in its
task of developing its spirit to perfection. All this was simply a philosophic change in terminology for what Scripture says about Israel.
According to Scripture, Israel exists as a people only by virtue of its
faith and for the sake of its faith; for Krochmal, every people exists
solely by virtue of its spiritual power. Its role is to create those spir-

itual legacies which can only come into existence by reason of its
unique spirituality. With the aid of this idea of peoplehood, it was
easy to give a philosophic justification for the scriptural belief in the
mission of Israel—for Krochmal's faith in this mission of Israel was
not the vestige of a theological mode of thought, but the result of his
philosophic system.

He was the first of the modern Jewish philosophers to make not
only the Jewish religion, but also the Jewish people, a subject for
philosophic investigation. In doing this, however, he merely broadened the boundaries of Jewish religious philosophy. The Jewish people exists only by virtue of its spirituality, a religious spirituality,
and can only be understood through it. What differentiates him—and
Judah Halevi, his medieval predecessor—from the tradition of Jewish religious philosophy, is that he deals with Judaism not only in
terms of a consideration of its doctrines, but embraces within his enquiry the living Jewish people, and seeks to comprehend its whole
history in terms of its religious foundation. The danger of this attempt is that it deprives Israel of its unique place in history, attributing to it a mission only in the sense in which all great nations have a
mission. Krochmal's thought, however, is quite distant from this conclusion. The fact that, from the beginning of its national existence,
only Israel had faith in the absolute spirit and recognized the ultimate religious truth, elevates it above the fate of other nations and
distinguishes it from them not only in degree, but in kind. Its mission, therefore, is *sui generis*: it does not aim only at developing and
manifesting Israel's spiritual content at its highest, but includes the
task of proclaiming the word of its faith to other nations, and by so
doing, becomes the teacher of mankind.[66]

Krochmal sees in this essential difference between the content of
the Jewish spirit and that of other nations a proof for their different
metaphysical origins. Judaism's spirit did not originate in one of
the special spiritual substances which are grounded in the Absolute
Spirit, but flows from the very source of the Absolute Spirit itself. The
distinction between the polytheism of the other peoples, and Judaism's belief in divine unity, is thus given a metaphysical explication.
Every nation believes in the spiritual powers revealed to it. The
nations, the source of whose spirit is one of the special spiritual substances, believe in these powers; but Israel, whose spirit comes directly from the Absolute Spirit, believes only in it. This connection
between Israel and the Absolute Spirit is what the scriptural writings

and the Talmud refer to when they say that God dwells in Israel, that his spirit rests on the Jewish people, and that this indwelling spirit even accompanies the people in their exile.[67] This relationship must be represented in much the same manner as the special spiritual substances are related to the various other peoples. According to Krochmal's metaphysics, after spirit has produced nature, it is then absorbed by it, and is contained within it in different degrees and levels. At its highest level, it becomes the indwelling spirit of a people. All that is said concerning the special spiritual substances is applicable to the Absolute Spirit, which also produces a spiritual power that infuses the Jewish people and brings into being its historical essence.

Krochmal does not inform us how this direct derivation of spiritual power from the Absolute Spirit can be reconciled with his metaphysics, which postulates a transition by degrees from the absolute to the particular, from God to empirical reality.[68] He withdraws himself from these considerations, as Hegel had done—and even more, the right-wing Hegelians, who utilized the Hegelian doctrine of the unity of finite and infinite spirit (according to which the latter becomes concrete historical reality in the human spirit) to justify Christology, teaching that the infinite spirit manifested itself absolutely in Jesus Christ.

This grounding of the Jewish nation on the Absolute Spirit is put forward not only to explain Jewish monotheism, but also to elevate the Jewish people above the destruction which is the common lot of all other peoples. Nevertheless, the historical law that all nations must grow, mature, and decay also applies to Israel. Krochmal combines this assumption with belief in the eternity of Israel by means of the somewhat artificial doctrine that Israel's degenerative period never leads to destruction, but at its very nadir, its spiritual power is renewed.[69] Thus the cycle of three stages, which with other nations constitutes their whole, repeats itself in the case of Israel again and again. Israel's history is a series of such cycles. The first cycle began in the days of the patriarchs and ended with the Babylonian exile; in this cycle the period of growth extends to the conquest of Palestine, the period of maturity extends to the death of King Solomon, and all the succeeding years belong to a period of decline. The second cycle includes the era from the Babylonian exile until the revolt of Bar Kochba; the period of growth ended with Alexander the Great, the period of maturity with the death of Queen

Salome Alexandra, and once again a decline sets in. The third cycle, which Krochmal does not analyze in detail, ended with the seventeenth century; the fourth cycle is still going on.

Despite this cyclical process, a uniform tendency marks the spiritual development of Israel, which from cycle to cycle is elevated to a higher plane of conceptual consciousness. The first cycle, which in terms of its content was truly creative, remained, nevertheless, on the plane of unreflective faith. With the second cycle, reflection begins; its beginnings can be found among the postexilic Babylonian prophets, who first considered the problem of theodicy (the evil which befalls the righteous) and the responsibility of sons for the sins of their fathers. The level of intellectual reflection rises from cycle to cycle.[70] The detailed analyses of the first two cycles are rich in historical insights, and the critical and perceptive inquiries made by Krochmal into the matters that come up for treatment are extremely valuable. But the ordering of Jewish history according to such cycles is rather farfetched, which one can readily see from the schematizing of historic periods, and its influence on later investigation was minute.

In the later part of his work, in which he deals with the inner development of the Jewish spirit, Krochmal rarely uses this scheme; he tends to describe the gradual and continuous rise of the truth that is stamped on the Jewish spirit to greater and greater heights of conceptual thought, and he dispenses entirely with the notion of degeneration and renewal. When Krochmal first used this device in the actual investigation of the history of the Jewish spirit, he wanted to limit its application to certain portions of Jewish history, but even there he used it only intermittently. But what remains of his work proves his diligence in trying to comprehend the many aspects of the spiritual life of the Jews in terms of his principle of development.

In addition to the fundamentals of the faith, he also considered the development of the corpus of Jewish law as found in the *halakhah*, and Jewish ethics as found in the *aggadah*, and devoted a complete chapter to each of these topics. At the beginning of his book he describes the relationship of the *halakhah* to the laws of the Torah, in terms analogous to that of religious philosophy to the basic beliefs of Scripture. The halakhic midrash determined the principles implicit in the laws of the Torah, and abstracted from them the primary concept from which the derivative positive commandments of the Torah evolved.[71] But in the chapter on the *halakhah* he does not mention this hypothesis again. Here his thesis is that the halakhic midrash deduces the consequences of the biblical commandments, and on the basis of these laws, orders the various circumstances of life. These consequences are potentially contained in the biblical legislation, and as is true of the philosophic explanation of Scripture, the halakhic midrash does not add anything new; it merely reveals what had been concealed, but was present all the time. The laws derived in this fashion are, therefore, of Sinaitic origin, despite the fact that they are not based on a specific oral tradition. The Oral Law does not stand alongside the written Torah, but is included within it by way of logical implication.[72]

The same applies in a wider sense to the rabbinic ordinances, which have no explicit scriptural warrant, but which are based on the general character of the biblical law. The derivation of conclusions from the biblical commandments is a process which goes through a number of stages and involves complicated and obscure hermeneutics. Krochmal traces this process from the period of the scribes in postexilic Babylonia until the generation of the teachers of the Mishnah. He explicates the hermeneutics utilized by the halakhic midrash in its various stages of development, as well as the form of *halakhah* itself; he also deals with attempts to arrange the midrash before the time of the Mishnah of R. Judah the Prince, and thus lays the foundation for the critical investigation of the Talmud, where his influence is recognizable to this day.

His investigation of the *aggadah* does not trace its evolution through its various stages; here he attempts only to fix its essential relationship to Scripture and to distinguish between its various elements. Together with Zunz, he assumes that the *aggadah* developed from sermons which were intended to inspire the masses, teaching them piety and morality. The *aggadah* therefore leaves Scripture in its representative form, and seeks only to bring these metaphors, in an impressive form, closer to the understanding of the common man, to direct the moral demands of Holy Writ to the needs of the time. The transformation of scriptural faith into conceptual form never went beyond an elite few, for the masses it will necessarily remain in the form of faith for a long time. However, for the purpose of adapting Scripture to the understanding of the masses, the aggadic midrash served admirably; in this context, such exegesis, which can border on the ridiculous, becomes intelligible. The *aggadah* does not attempt to determine the literal meaning of Scripture, but tries to clothe religious ideas in a form which will ensnare the soul by discovering these ideas in the text, which is then explained in an ingenious and acute fashion that may be far removed from its actual, literal meaning. Aggadic parables, whose different types Krochmal analyzes, also serve this purpose of interpretation.[73] While this important section of the *aggadah* allows the content of Scripture to remain in the form of faith, there are two other elements, one of which is conceptually superior, and the other inferior to it. The former is its philosophic element. From the philosophic explanation of Scripture by the talmudic rabbis (which in the case of the esoteric doctrines of the "Work of the Chariot" and the "Work of Creation," were taught only to the inner circle of initiates), individual rays of philosophic thought penetrated the *aggadah* and were preserved. Below such heights there are representations of superstitions, such as the belief in demons and magic, which were popular among the masses and even upheld by some rabbis.[74] Although this distinction between the various strata of the *aggadah* was changed in many item by later historians, the central hypothesis remained fruitful.

Krochmal deals in greater detail with the history of philosophic reflection in Judaism, which transforms faith into conceptual understanding and thus progresses continually. As we said, he located the beginnings of this advance in the postexilic prophets. In later antiquity this progress was continued by Hellenistic Jewish philosophy, the effects of which can be seen in the philosophic explanations of the Talmudic sages of Palestinian Judaism. It was afterward succeeded by medieval Jewish philosophy and the early Kabbala, which paralleled it and which continued to the time of Nahmanides.[75] Krochmal's last epoch begins with Moses Mendelssohn. Krochmal was well aware that Jewish philosophy had always been strongly influenced from the outside by other peoples, yet this did not affect the continuity of its inner development because at every stage its content was the same scriptural faith, and it borrowed from the outside only those tools which aided it in interpreting that faith. Even when it was influenced by current philosophy as regards content, this content was composed of basically the same ideas which Judaism had bequeathed to ancient philosophy. Neoplatonism, which had a great influence upon medieval Jewish philosophy, is an outstanding example of philosophy being influenced by Judaism, and here Krochmal refers to the presumptive connection maintained by many scholars between Neoplatonism and Philo. He speculates on similar connections with regard to Christian and Islamic philosophy, whose re-

ligious elements came chiefly from Judaism.[76] His fundamental
conception of the history of general philosophy as a steady unfolding
of basic elements enables him to view the development of Jewish
thought as a linear process in which one content evolves through
higher and higher planes of conceptual maturity.

Krochmal never intended to present a complete history of
Jewish philosophy. Even the exposition of parts of that history
which he formulated was inadequate. His presentation of Alexandrian Jewish philosophy is nothing more than an abstract from
the works of contemporary Christian scholars, adapted to his own
special purposes; nevertheless, it has intrinsic value, as a chrestomathy
of those sayings from the Talmud and the midrashim, which, according to him, had been influenced by Alexandrian philosophy, and
whose origin could be traced to Essene communities.

Of the philosophers of the Middle Ages, he investigates only Ibn
Ezra with any thoroughness. The chapters which he had intended to
write on Maimonides' doctrine of attributes, and the doctrines of
the spheres of the early Kabbala, were never realized.[77] Although
printed afterward, his lengthy chapter on Ibn Ezra was written
before the first monographs of Munk. It was the first attempt to
expound the doctrines of a medieval Jewish philosopher historically.
He proposed a very difficult task for himself, because Ibn Ezra's
doctrines were scattered throughout his scriptural commentaries.
Krochmal collected them all together and tried to combine them
into a systematic unity. His wide-ranging inquiry into Ibn Ezra,
conducted in the spirit of his own time, gives us not only an insight
into Krochmal's own metaphysical doctrines but also possesses independent historical and philosophical value. Krochmal's recognition
of his proximity to the doctrines of Ibn Ezra has a definite basis in
fact. They expounded similar views, but in different modes of
thought. Indeed, Krochmal gave Ibn Ezra's ideas a different conceptual form, but he nevertheless remained true to their basic
tendency.

That Jewish religious thought always remained loyal to the
faith of Scripture, simply changing it into conceptual form, could
only be said of the principal line of development. Beside it we find
other tendencies which deviated from this norm, and which contradicted the fundamentals of scriptural Judaism. To this category
belongs the Gnosticism of the first centuries after the rise of Christianity, on which Krochmal wrote in detail, relying on contemporary

Christian scholarship as well as the later Kabbala (he considered that it was the degenerate form of the early Kabbala, which had been in agreement with philosophy, and that its nadir was reached in the doctrines of Sabbateanism). The mistakes made by Gnosticism and the later Kabbala appeared to him the result of the triumph of the imaginative faculty over conceptual thought.

It is characteristic of his rationalistic viewpoint, and illustrative also of his acute historical understanding, that he recognized the similarity of Gnosticism to Sabbateanism.[78] Although he attacked these tendencies very sharply, he admitted that a comprehension of them was essential to the complete understanding of Judaism. Krochmal was also convinced that, in order to evaluate Judaism properly, attention must be paid to the religions of Islam and Christianity, which came from Judaism and were influenced by it.[79] But these are no more than accessory trends in which we discover the development of the Jewish spirit; yet we must not disregard them, if we wish to understand it truly.

As the purpose of this comprehensive history of the Jewish spirit, Krochmal adumbrates "the recognition of our existence and essence, which constitutes the common soul of Israel," and he adds that by means of this we will be able to discern our future.[80] All of this is said in the spirit of the historical mode of thought of his own time, which saw in historical consciousness the means for grasping the nature and essence of the community, and which, on the basis of this consciousness, tried to determine the future task of the community. This historical mode of thought was shared by Krochmal with other founders of the *Wissenschaft des Judentums*. Only one thing separated him from them: the faith that the self-consciousness of the spirit is possible only on the basis of philosophy.

Solomon Ludwig Steinheim

Solomon Ludwig Steinheim (1789-1866), whose book *Offenbarung nach dem Lehrbegriff der Synagoge (Revelation according to the Doctrine of the Synagogue)* was issued in four volumes between 1835 and 1865, was opposed in principle to all philosophic rationalism. In a broad attack against rationalistic religious philosophy in all its forms, he developed the doctrine that religious truth was given exclusively in revelation. In his antirationalism Steinheim went much further than Judah Halevi had in the Middle Ages: not only was reason impotent to grasp religious truth, but there was essential opposition between reason and revelation. Reason must abandon itself in order to find the truth which is in revelation.

The source of this antirationalism was Jacobi; Steinheim also appeals to Bayle in asserting the dichotomy between reason and faith, though Bayle was quite distant from the specific form and methodical basis of Steinheim's antirationalism. Nevertheless, Steinheim reproaches Jacobi for counterposing to science nothing more than our spirit's immediate knowledge of God. If we seek the root of our faith in the human spirit, we destroy the distinction between this knowledge and philosophic dogmatism, and thus lose the possibility of opposing the arrogance of the latter. We cannot discard science unless we can oppose it not with a truth immanent in our spirit, but one which has been revealed to us. We should not weaken this concept of revelation by making it the true unmediated possession of our consciousness, but we should appropriate it in its strictest meaning as a message from God given to mankind in a unique deed at a specific time.[81]

Steinheim does not seek to base the actuality of this revelation on external evidence, as was customary during the Middle Ages. The content of the revelation was sufficient proof that it could not have originated in the human spirit. Human reason was bound to admit, once it compared its content to that of revelation, that the teachings of faith have clearly an extrahuman origin, and reason must subordinate itself to it. The proof for the impossibility of the revealed doctrines originating in man is the fact that these doctrines teach something which human reason, by its very nature, could never attain. Reason can acknowledge this revealed teaching, which is basically alien to it, only because revelation corresponds to our human needs more than the deliverances of reason itself. Critical reason compares the teachings of faith to the propositions of dogmatic reason, and freely admits the superiority of the former.[82]

The necessity for reason's self-renunciation is not limited to the religious sphere. An irreconcilable opposition exists not only between religious revelation and reason, but also between reason and empirical knowledge. It is not only impossible to derive empirical reality from the a priori laws of human reason, but empirical reality itself dissolves if we attempt to construct it according to the dictates of reason. To the intrinsic antinomies of reason, which Kant had pointed out, Steinheim adds the antinomy of rational and empirical knowledge, between the mathematical bases and the empirical content of experience.[83] Reason introduces its own self-contradictions into reality. Once reason recognizes this, it must admit to a knowledge of existence which is free of contradictions and submit to its testimony. The conceptual necessity of rational knowledge already contains the contradiction to experience. This conceptual necessity of rational knowledge must be everywhere and always the same; hence, it excludes the difference between here and there, earlier and later. Temporal change is especially uncongenial to this conceptual necessity. A conceptually necessary world would be an Eleatic denial of all becoming.[84]

Steinheim interprets Kant's second antinomy as meaning that the laws of space and time are inapplicable to the actual spatial and temporal order because they would destroy them. Space and time are infinitely extensive and have no limit. But the physical object would disappear if it were infinitely divisible or constructed out of indivisible elements. In analyzing the material world, natural science assumes the existence of ultimately extensive particles, and pays no attention to this contradiction of the demands of mathematics.[85] Following Kant, Steinheim attributes this contradiction between the rational construction of reality and the empirical knowledge of reality to the fact that reason hypostatizes its laws.[86] He does not attempt to reduce this contradiction to an illegitimate use of the principles of reason, or solve it by means of laying bare its origin. The dialectic of reason does not first appear, as was true for Kant, only when it advances from the conditioned to the unconditioned. For Steinheim, experience and reason are in profound and insoluble opposition. The only way out lies in a decision for experience and against reason. Steinheim gives decisive weight to the complete identity of this problem in the spheres of empirical knowledge and religious faith. Just as critical reason is aware of the contradictions between constructive reason and the sciences of experience, so it is aware of the contradictions between it and revelation; in both cases, it is critical reason itself which demands that we give up constructive reason.[87] However, Steinheim's antirationalism is quite distant from irrationalism. He claims the strict character of knowledge for the truths of faith, and the second part of his work bears the paradoxical title of "The Faith of the Synagogue Considered as an Exact Science."

In the detailed comparison which he makes between the basic

principles of Judaism and those of reason, Steinheim tries to demonstrate their complete opposition to each other and maintains that the truth lies entirely with revelation. The crucial part of his argument, brought forth by this opposition, is the contradiction between reason's idea of necessity and revelation's idea of freedom, which is apparent in their respective doctrines of God and of man. Reason cannot conceive of anything except in terms of necessity. All of its inferences are based on the principle that every effect must have a cause. By means of this principle it concludes that God, the supreme or first cause of the world, exists. Reason's God is subordinate to the principle of necessity, from which his existence is derived. His actions are possible only in accord with the law of necessity. When added to this, another rational principle—that of *ex nihilo nihil fit*—excludes the possibility that material reality, as it is given to us, should have had a temporal beginning. Thus it is impossible that the God of reason should be a creator. At most, he can be the world's organizer. Despite their different forms of expression, both pagan mythology, in its various forms, and the philosophic doctrines of God concur, for they are grounded upon the same basic assumptions of reason.

Natural religion—that is, religion without revelation—cannot proceed in any other direction. For it, God is doubly conditioned: by the necessity which determines his actions, and by the matter upon which he acts in making forms. The world that is fashioned by him, therefore, can only be as perfect as these conditions permit. It is not a good world, but merely the best possible one. Natural religion necessarily results in a theodicy, which excuses God by claiming that despite all the imperfections of his creation, this is still the best possible world. In contrast, the teaching of revelation denies the principle of *ex nihilo nihil fit*, and speaks of the free creative activity of God by which something is created from nothing—not the best possible world is created, but a good world.[88]

This contradiction between the idea of creation and the axioms of our reason demonstrates that the former is not a product of our reason, but is given to it from the outside. Its superiority to the doctrines of reason does not simply rest upon the fact that it is more satisfactory from a religious point of view. The two principles supporting mythology and speculation are mutually contradictory. If we assert *ex nihilo nihil fit*, it is senseless to search for a cause for material existence; and if we uphold the proposition that every effect must have a cause, we cannot exclude matter from this principle and we must therefore throw overboard the principle of *ex nihilo nihil fit*. The reconciliation of these two principles, by the representation of a God who fashions the form of matter, ignores the consequences of this compromise solution. In terms of these consequences we must either take matter as an absolute, and thus abandon the causal principle, or together with idealism deny the actual existence of matter in order to satisfy the causal principle of causation.[89]

Only the revealed doctrine of creation can free us from these contradictions. Reason, because of its principle of necessity, must equally deny the freedom of God and man. In opposition to this, man's self-consciousness offers clear testimony in favor of his freedom, so much so that it is impossible for thought to utterly disregard these depositions. Reason must either remain caught in the contradiction between the postulate of necessity and the fact of freedom, or so assimilate the idea of freedom that it removes its true significance and makes the free spontaneous act one which is devoid of external conditioning, but is bound to an inner necessity which flows from the essence of man. Freedom finds its true place only in the teachings of revelation, which breaks with reason's belief in necessity, and thereby demonstrates that it originates from a source other than reason.[90]

Thus, Steinheim's antirationalism led to the same contents of faith that ethical rationalism had taught. In content, his faith corresponds completely to the Kantian postulates of God: freedom and immortality. Steinheim differs from Kant only in that he locates the source of these doctrines not in ethical reason but in revelation. This same material agreement concerning the meaning of Judaism aligns Steinheim with his contemporaries, Formstecher and Hirsch. They differ only in terms of the philosophic presuppositions upon which they ground the doctrines of Judaism. The content of this teaching and its opposition to paganism is understood by them in the same way. For all three, the essence of Judaism consists of belief in a free and spontaneously creative God who transcends the world; in the moral freedom of man; and in the moral communion of God and man, a communion which outlasts man's death. They all firmly maintain these basic principles of ethical personalist religion. Neither Hirsch nor Formstecher allow themselves to be influenced by speculative idealism in their understanding of the concept of God or in their doctrines of ultimate religious values, in the way the medieval Jewish Neoplatonists and Aristotelians were influenced by the corresponding theories of those systems. Despite the fact that the medieval thinkers were, in their total personalities, far more deeply rooted in the tradition and substance of Jewish life, and that belief in the divine authority of revelation was self-evident to them, the modern thinkers, in their theoretical explanation of Judaism, upheld with greater staunchness the true meaning of its central religious doctrines.

3 The Renewal of
Jewish Religious Philosophy
at the End of the
Nineteenth Century

THE promising beginning of a modern Jewish philosophy of religion was tied too narrowly to the assumptions of German idealism, and, with the decay of the latter, its powers, too, declined. But at the end of the nineteenth century there was an efflorescence of philosophic work independent of these assumptions, this time under the auspices of a comprehensive movement toward the systematic understanding of Judaism. It originally arose as a reaction to the misunderstanding of Judaism current in the so-called scientific anti-Semitic literature, as well as to Christian theology; from the very beginning, however, it did not content itself with apologetics, but strove for the inner clarification of the Jewish consciousness as well. It accepted as its first and most urgent task the presentation of a correct and convincing portrait of the actual teachings of Judaism. Thus, in the majority of such portrayals, the philosophic analysis of Judaism was deferred in favor of historical description, so that Judaism itself, as it were, might be allowed to speak in its own behalf. This is not the place to discuss in detail these mainly historical descriptions of Judaism. In terms of its program, *Die Ethik des Judentums (Ethics of Judaism)* of Moritz Lazarus also belongs in this series. Because this statement of the Jewish ethic was vigorously determined by philosophical points of view, however, it requires a brief characterization.

Moritz Lazarus

Moritz Lazarus (1824-1903) was able to publish only the first volume of his *Ethics of Judaism* in his lifetime. His materials for the second volume were published posthumously in 1911. The work explicitly states as its major purpose the reproduction of the given content of the Jewish ethical teaching, principally in terms of Talmudic sources, the concepts of philosophical ethics to be employed only to give form to the presentation. This position is modified in the second volume, where only the judgments of philosophical ethics make possible a complete evaluation of the unsystematic ideas of the Talmud.[1] In reality, however, philosophy is of much greater significance throughout the work. It not only gives outer form to Jewish ethical teaching, but is of methodological significance—individual ethical teachings are referred back to a basic ethical theory which is exhibited by them. This theory is then judged in terms of the essence of ethics, and thus receives its justification.

The content of Jewish ethics is also interpreted in terms of the philosophic doctrine of ethics to such an extent that its major principle appears to be the Kantian notion of autonomy. Of course, this is possible only because Lazarus conceives the principle of autonomy somewhat loosely. He makes the notion of autonomy the principle of Jewish ethics because, taken as a religious ethical sentiment, it demands the fulfillment of the divinely given ethical statutes from pure love of God alone, and out of an aspiration to imitate God, and because—as he clearly recognizes—this principle is endowed with an intense awareness of that inner certitude which is implicit in the idea of the ethical good. For him, ethical sentiment is the ethics of autonomy, and the methodological meaning of the Kantian principle of autonomy is completely blurred in the demand for purity of intention.[2] This conceptual laxity allows Lazarus to consider the difference between Kant's imperative of practical reason, Herbart's value judgments, and Rümelin's ethical impulse, to be merely psychological.[3]

But this identification of Jewish ethics with Kant's ethics of autonomy has, in terms of subject matter, still another, more profound reason. Lazarus feels the essence of religion to be the ideality of ethical sentiment, to which religion only adds the awareness that God is the source of ethics. He therefore sees in the religious relationship of man to God only the ethical motive, and neglects to consider the specifically religious motive of the scriptural idea of the holiness of God and the fundamental religious sentiments of reverence and love.[4] Within the ethical sphere itself, he is at the same time more susceptible to the emotional warmth of Talmudic ethics than the passionate energy of prophetic ethics. In keeping with his own character and personality, the qualities of a balanced ethical harmony are more in evidence than the inexorable seriousness of the ethical demand.

Although his analysis does not exhaust the content of Jewish ethics, it does catch hold of certain of its essential aspects with great sensitivity, and also shows fine psychological insight, which is Lazarus' greatest talent. This is clear in the basic chapters of the book. That the ethical commandments, according to the Bible and the Talmud, have an immediate inner certainty is a most correct and informative statement, whose value is not at all lessened by unjustified consequences drawn in terms of ideas of autonomy. Of lesser importance is Lazarus' demonstration of how, formally, Jewish ethics is an ethics of duty, but materially its supreme ideal is one of love and the inner harmony of man, and that the natural ethical impulses of man are not displaced by religious ethics, but are reduced to their ultimate cause, and that Jewish ethics is an ethics both of the individual and the society.[5] Also, the continuity of the ethical development of Judaism, and the unfolding of the basic biblical elements in the interpretations of the Talmud are illuminatingly described.[6] But the real wealth of the book is in the concrete explication of these general insights. The idea of ethical community is not simply expressed in abstract formulations; Lazarus demonstrates how it is realized in the ethical life of the Jews, and how it has stamped their styles of life and institutions.[7]

From the importance of the "Study of the Law," and its significance for Jewish life, he shows how Judaism conceives of the connection between the moral and intellectual life, and what ethical significance is given to this idealism of the intellect.[8] We can already see, from these examples alone, that Lazarus not only tries to present the ethical doctrines of Judaism, but their concretization in the actual life of the Jewish community. Even as a theoretician of Jewish ethics, he remains a social psychologist who seeks to grasp the general spirit of the Jews and to understand the ethics which lies as much at the basis of formulated ethical norms as of actual moral behavior. This overlapping of systematic ethics and the psychology of morals certainly impairs the methodological unity of the book, but methodology is not its primary merit. Its value lies in the wealth of concrete insights which, to be sure, Lazarus could not master conceptually.

Hermann Cohen

Jewish religious philosophy was renewed by Hermann Cohen (1842-1918), the leader of the Marburg School of Neo-Kantianism.

In his work the tendency to base Judaism philosophically on the ethical and theological ideas of Kant (which could be found in Jewish circles in the nineteenth century and became widespread, particularly after the return to Kant of German philosophy) finally found its systematic realization. Cohen accomplishes this task in connection with his own philosophic system: from his substantiation of ethics, the concept of the religion of reason, whose historical materialization he sees in Judaism, grows and continually develops. Thus, his understanding of the basic principles of religion is unconditionally dependent upon the fundamental extension which he gives to the Kantian transcendental philosophy. That these principles acquire a new form can be seen even in his early works which are devoted to the interpretation of Kant, and in which he understands critical reason completely in terms of absolute idealism and excludes from it any notion of a transcendental reality. For him, the world of experience is not a manifestation of a metaphysical reality which is beyond knowledge, as it is for Kant, but consists simply of that which is. There is no reality beyond and exclusive of the being of experienced objects which are grounded in the objectivity of knowledge. One cannot speak of the thing-in-itself in terms of a contradiction-ridden absolute reality. Rather, this concept symbolizes the unending task of knowledge, for which any materialization of the ideal of knowledge, any level of knowledge already reached, must be understood only as an "appearance" of the true reality which is still to be constructed.

This critique of transcendental concepts strikes deeply into religious representations. According to Kant, the belief of practical reason has the power to make accessible that absolute reality which is beyond the grasp of our knowledge. While theoretical reason is forever bound to the sphere of appearances, practical reason can elevate us to the sphere of intelligible being; it can affirm the absolute reality of the existence of God, freedom, and immortality. But from Cohen's standpoint, this metaphysical significance can no longer be allowed to religious representations. They, too, must find their logical place in the fixed postulates of consciousness.

Kant had already pointed the way to this with his doctrine of the ideas of theoretical reason. He had shown that hypostatizing the ideas of soul, world, and God into absolute objects was a dialectical illusion, and had recognized their true significance in their attempt to subordinate our knowledge of experience to the absolute ideas. The demand of reason to bind together the data of experience into systematic unity, and the assumption that phenomena were amenable to such a connection—that all particulars can be conceived as specifications of a general principle, and experience grasped as a thoroughly systematic and, hence, teleological whole—was stamped on those ideas in various ways. At its most comprehensive, this can be seen in the idea of God, which teaches us to look upon the actual world as if it were the result of a unified rational plan, and which as a regulative principle therefore has a necessary and abiding function in the construction of theoretical knowledge.

Cohen transfers this interpretation of the idea of God from the sphere of epistemology to that of ethics in his book, *Kants Begründung der Ethik (Kant's Principles of Ethics* [1877]). In neither place does God exist as a metaphysical reality, but in epistemology as well as in ethics he has the same value as an idea. The ethical significance of the idea of God is exhibited in Cohen's critique of Kant's doctrine of the postulates of practical reason, which contains Kant's moral grounding of the belief in God and immortality. For Kant, the existence of God and the immortality of the soul were postulates of the practical reason, because only they can guarantee the unity of virtue and happiness which are required by ethics, but which are not exemplified in the world of our everyday experience. Cohen sees in this doctrine of postulates a concession to eudaemonia, which conflicts with principles of the Kantian ethics. He denies the immortality of the soul as a sensual, and hence mythical, falsification of the idea of ethical personality.[9] But the idea of God exhibits a deeper and more inward connection with the problem of ethics.

The selfsame idea of unitary purpose, which had already led to the idea of God in the theoretical sphere, recurs in ethics as the idea of a realm of ethical purposiveness, and is expressed there by the concept of the head of all moral beings. In this meaning, which is immanent to ethics, the idea of God is still no more than the symbol for the unity of the ethical world; its independent function is to connect the teleological realms with each other and bind them into a unity. It is impossible that the ethical and the natural world should be separate from each other, and there must be a necessary congruence of natural and moral teleology.[10] As the ground of this congruence "the idea of God is absolutely necessary according to the critical method; if these intelligible ideas appear as unconditional, this (the idea of God) is their unconditional ground—and is consequently a principle of superior rank and of greater comprehensiveness."[11] Ethics, which is basically autonomous, is crowned by the idea of God because, in forgoing every metaphysical claim, it achieves organic interrelation with the principles of ethics, which Kant's system never offered.

This definition of the idea of God, produced by his presentation of Kant's system, was constructed systematically in *Ethik des reinem Willens (The Ethics of the Pure Will)*, where its full import first appears. Precisely because Cohen distinguishes as completely as Kant did between theoretical and moral evidence, between the laws of nature and of moral will, he is able to ascribe a decisive weight to the endeavor to maintain the unification of these two realms. This unity is founded upon the community of their methodological character. The evidence of morals is not one of uncontrollable emotions. Within ethics there reigns the same legitimate productive reason as in logic; both are unified in the principle of purity, or—if we use Kant's terminology—in the principle of the autonomy of value. Thus the distinction between logical and ethical validity can never lead to opposition, and at its summit Cohen's ethics must list, as the basic law of truth, the methodological principle of the correlation of logical and ethical knowledge.[12]

But this correlation between nature and ethics has a meaning which goes beyond the sphere of formal method. It contains the problem of realization of the ethical. The being of ethics is that of a task, which is essentially different from the being of nature; but it is of the essence of ethics to demand realization; this realization, however, is possible only in the realm of nature. Despite its independence of the realm of nature, the realm of moral principles can be realized only in the concrete reality of nature. If nature does not make possible the feasibility of ethical ideals, they will lose, if not their validity, then at least their applicability.[13] That their realization be possible within nature is the indispensable assumption for the realization of morals. The unity of nature and morality, so understood, is guaranteed by the idea of God.

With regard to its contents, the meaning of this idea of the unity of nature and ethics is first presented in a very abstract way. The being of ethics is the being of an infinite task. Ethical consciousness is by nature directed toward the future, and the infinity of the ethical task implies an infinite continuation of ethical action. This direction toward the future is immanent in every moment of ethical activity. There is no ethics without the idea of eternity, which distinguishes the character of ethical consciousness. But this eternal character of ethics presupposes the permanence of nature. Because the continuity of ethical activity must not be interrupted, of necessity the future of nature must also be assured. The continuation of this line of thought shows what Cohen really meant when he required the permanence of nature on ethical grounds. For the eternity of ethics it is not enough that nature simply exist. Of necessity, humanity, the subject of ethical action, must exist and maintain itself in nature, and the preservation of its existence must not be impeded by entropy or by other forms of the natural process.[14] All this, however, assumes only the natural conditions for the possibility of ethical life. The meaning of all these assumptions is that they make possible the progressive realization of ethics. The ethical activity of humankind is keynoted by the realization of ethical ideals. And this is the true significance of the idea of God—that genuine ethics can and must be realized. The idea of God is the guarantor of that historical humanity which unfolds and develops under natural conditions and realizes this goal.[15]

Thus an immediate connection is made to the Jewish idea of God. What Cohen formulated here within the context of his system is the Jewish faith in the divinely-grounded moral order of being. Cohen posits as the essence of the Jewish faith in God the messianic futurism of the prophets, which he interprets in the spirit of modern liberalism as a continual progress toward the messianic kingdom of ethics. He injects this messianic concept into his ideal of the eternity of ethics and binds them together. But the messianic era, which was to end all moral development, now becomes an unending work of ethical perfecting. Ethical struggles do not end in a messianic kingdom of peace. The prophetic picture of the messianic end-time is only an esthetic symbol. Ethics conceives of it as an infinitely distant goal which directs all ethical action, but which is never reached, and just because of this is continually present to us.[16]

The meaning of Cohen's God-concept is fully presented when he discusses the transcendence of God. God is the basis for the unity of nature and ethics, and thus cannot be absorbed by the world of ethics or that of nature. He stands outside both of them, just as every ground is outside that which is grounded in it. Cohen is especially careful to deny any pantheistic identification of God with nature. Cohen was not insensitive to the esthetic appeal of pantheism, and in his youth was attracted by it, but in his maturity he strongly opposed it because he viewed it as a species of ethical naturalism. The identification of God and nature would entail the identity of nature and ethics. Spinoza reveals this corollary of his *deus sive natura* when he speaks of the actions of men as being as natural as lines and planes, and he thinks it legitimate to base ethics on such a description. The metaphysics of pantheism shatters the autonomy of ethics, which critical idealism erects. Because nature and ethics are not identified, but correlated, it must follow that God, as principle of this correlation, must stand outside both spheres. The God of ethics is not the God of pantheism, but the God of monotheism.[17]

But the introduction of the monotheistic God into ethical doctrine entails his reconstruction into an idea, involving the denial of his metaphysical claims and personal character. The transcendence of God can only be the transcendence of an idea, which can of course transcend the particular separate spheres of methodical consciousness, but can never go beyond the boundaries of the latter. Cohen saw a corrective to his doctrine of God in the efforts made by medieval Jewish philosophers to strip away anthropomorphic elements from God, and especially in Maimonides' doctrine of attributes, to whose metaphysical presuppositions Cohen failed to do justice.

The meaning of God as an idea does not seek to strip from the concept of God any of the fullness of its contents, or its validity. The ethical faith in God can be directed in its full glow and enthusiasm toward God understood as an idea, to the God who maintains the moral order of existence; in place of the material existence which bodies have, he receives the status of the being of principles which underlie the material existence of things.[18] This accommodation of God to the status of the productive principles of idealism is, as can easily be seen, only a relative comparison. Though Cohen introduces the idea of God into the core of his ethical doctrine far more deeply than Kant had done, this idea never goes beyond the character of a postulate. That ethics is realized in nature is never deduced, but postulated, since the concept of nature is constituted independently of the laws of ethics, all the more so since the actual flow of natural events must correspond to the necessities of ethical consciousness. This postulate is merely pushed one step further if we ascribe to the idea of God the function of guarantor for the realization of ethics. In this connection there arises another question, which cannot be discussed except by a systematic analysis of Cohen's concept of reality: whether this function does not lead beyond character as an idea, whether we should not rather think of him as the supreme existent in order that he might, as determining power, guarantee the realization of the ethical ideal in the framework of natural happenings.

The incorporation of the idea of God with the doctrine of ethics necessarily arouses the question of the relationship of ethics to religion, which was the historical origin of the idea of God. This relationship appears in two different principal forms, depending upon whether we treat it historically or systematically. Historically, religion is the source of ethical idealism, and philosophy, which seeks to develop and confirm its principles in continuity with the historical forces of culture, cannot ignore religion as one of the sources of ethics.[19] Cohen understands religion as religion in general, but nevertheless sees the primal power of morality expressed in its purest and profoundest form in Jewish monotheism. Only in the Jewish prophets does religion disengage itself from the entanglements of myth, and the ethical interest motivates this religion from beginning to end.[20]

The prophets are the creators of the most important ethical concepts upon which the ethic of pure will is based—that is, the ideas of humanity, messianism, and God. To what degree ethics is indebted to them can be seen in Cohen's essay on the social ideal of Plato and the prophets, in which he characterizes these as "the two most important sources of modern culture." According to Cohen, ethics received its methodical fundament from Plato's theory of ideas, but the depth of its content from the prophets. In his social ideal Plato is bounded by Greek reality; his intellectual acuity and exclusiveness perpetuate the divisions of the classes, and the genuine ethics which is bound up with Plato's view is limited to the private domain of the philosophic class; his concept of the ethical community does not go beyond the boundaries of Greece. He is lacking the idea of Man, which is contained in the concept of humanity of the prophets. As opposed to this, the prophets, in their ethical thought, soar beyond their given historical station; socially and politically, they burst the bonds of class and nation, and by reason of their orientation towards the future, attain to the idea of universal history.[21]

From the 1890's onward, Cohen continued to explicate this ethical content of Judaism in lectures and in many essays, not from the stance of a cold objectivity, but with the enthusiasm of commitment.

The ethical pathos of the prophets lived in him, and from this empathy of spirit he was able to interpret their ethical motives as no other man was capable of doing.

But for systematic ethics, religion only serves, despite all of its ethical content and passion, as an historical presupposition. Ethics accepts the ideas, which are the product of the innocence of the creative religious consciousness, and elevates them one step above religion by basing them upon the certainty of autonomous ethical knowledge.[22] This relationship also applies to the idea of God, which similarly passes from the sphere of religion to that of ethics where it has its true place.[23] After the religious idea of God has been reconstructed into the ethical idea of God, religion must be dissolved in ethics. Religion thus returns to its true ethical source and finds there "not its termination, but its perfection."[24]

Cohen's mature historical consciousness prevented him from claiming that such a transformation was imminent. He knew too well that the present is quite different from the systematic perfection of culture, wherein ethics would be able to direct the moral behavior of social life. Until this goal is reached, religion is indispensable to the advancement of ethical development. A popular ethical enlightenment unfounded in methodical knowledge, which at present seeks to replace religion, is unprepared for the task of direction of the ethical consciousness, and the religious duty of maintaining the ethical truth of the concept of God in the face of materialistic interpretations of nature and history is still necessary. Given our present historical circumstances, we are in duty bound to uphold our ancestral faith, not out of a sense of reverence for the past, but from a sense of responsibility toward the moral future. But this loyalty requires that the historical religion be idealized; that is, developed further in the direction of ethical idealism. This ethical idealism is the final goal to which all of the various religions should converge.[25]

Cohen's attitude toward Judaism is that of a complete Jew, both in the originality of his feeling and the consciousness of his philosophic knowledge. In him the power of faith in Jewish messianism lives on, and this power is embodied within his system in philosophic form. He viewed his philosophic work as a justification of Judaism, and became for his generation a philosophic herald for religious loyalty. But he encloses and enfolds Judaism within the systematic verdict concerning all religions, seeking to idealize it so that it might be ripe for the transition to philosophic ethics.

From this standpoint, Cohen wished to write a religious philosophy of Judaism which was to be a systematic summary of his work on the philosophy of religion. But before he had a chance to work out his plan, his religious viewpoint underwent a decisive change. He concluded that the religion which lived within him had been only partially explained by his prior theoretical analyses. He formulated the methodical basis for his new orientation toward religion in his *Der Begriff der Religion im System der Philosophie* (*The Concept of Religion in the System of Philosophy* [1915]), and gave a full-fledged presentation of religious philosophy on this new foundation in *Religion der Vernunft aus den Quellen des Judentums* (*The Religion of Reason Drawn from the Sources of Judaism*), which was published posthumously in 1919.

The names of these two books plainly demonstrate that his new concept of religion was founded also upon elements of his system. His methodical rationalism recognizes no other religion than the religion of reason, and his systematic concept of philosophy demands that the former find its place in a philosophic system. Faithful to the foundations of his system, he does not add religion to the system as a new element. If such methodical independence were granted to religion, it might endanger the autonomy of culture. The religious consciousness should not be added as a new dimension of consciousness, but must remain within the basic dimensions of consciousness, and especially within the realm of ethical consciousness, where it manifests itself merely as a novel aspect. Cohen puts this in the methodical formula that religion has independence, though it has an individual quality.[26] In regard to ethics, in which religion has a central place, this individuality stems from the one-sidedness of the ethical concept of God. The God of ethics is the God of humanity and not of the individual.

No other course is possible for Cohen's ethical doctrine, which is completely subordinate to the universality of the ethical principle, and under whose tutelage the ethical concept of mankind is considered. For ethics, man is not the individual, subject to all the contingencies of his natural and social life, nor the aggregate of such individuals in all of their interconnections and relationships, but the bearer of the ethical idea. Only the idea of human universality can do justice to this concept. Thus ethics must define man as a link in this chain of human universality, and it determines his destiny by saying that he must elevate himself to this idea of universality.

Ethics, according to Cohen, finds its realization primarily in the state, which serves as the primary representation of universality, and the multiplicity of individual states demand their unification in the universal idea of mankind. The necessary correlative to the idea of mankind is, of course, the individual bearer of ethical reason as the source of moral activity. But this concept of the individual is purely formal and external. The ethical individual is always and everywhere a rational construct of general ethics, and the ethical interrelationships of individuals are looked upon from a purely formal viewpoint. My neighbor is merely the "other," who is an ethical subject just as I am.[27]

Among the members of the ethical community, primary place is given to the rational relationships which derive from the concept of ethical personality, in contrast to which the more intimate moments of moral feeling are of relevance only as psychological vehicles and aids. Because of this decisive importance of the idea of ethical universality, the desire for the realization of the moral ideal is satisfied by the faith in the historic victory of goodness. Ethics has no consolation to offer for the moral distress of the individual, or his struggle with his own guilt. From a religious standpoint, Cohen's whole ethics is oriented toward a prophetic stance, in which political and world-historical interest occupy the central position. Judaism becomes the religion of ethical sublimity.

The correction of this partiality, which is attempted in Cohen's last works, affects both ethics and religion. The idea of the individual is emphasized both in relation to one's fellow man and in relation to the ego. Community with one's fellow man is accomplished out of sympathetic feeling for the need or distress of the other, and becomes an individual ethical communion in which the other becomes my neighbor, to whom I am immediately bound. This sympathy immediately becomes—and this is typical of Cohen's ethic—social sympathy. The psychological fact of sympathy is ethically legitimized by being denoted sympathy with the poor, whose social need demands our help. In finding a place for feeling in his ethics, Cohen proceeds not phenomenologically, but deductively, legitimizing the significance of feeling by means of its ethical achievements. His activism finds this achievement in the ethical deed, which flows from feeling; it recognizes that the intimacy of ethical community only arises from the sense of oneness with one's fellow man, which also derives from feeling.[28] While ethics itself only recognizes the reverence that we owe to the ethical dignity of our fellow men, pity is transformed into love toward one's fellow. The fundamental concept of ethical esteem thus is not displaced, but becomes the presupposition rendering love possible as ethical love. This new moral relationship is, for Cohen, a religious relationship, as distinct from the purely ethical.[29] At first sight it appears that the religious interpretation is not required by the phenomenon itself. The community of feeling is also possible within the sphere of pure ethics, but nevertheless Cohen asserts the profound insight that the human community of love and religious communion are essentially related.

It is clear, however, that ethics alone is insufficient for the human need for moral redemption. The soul which is burdened with guilt —and no one is free of guilt—is not satisfied by the prospect of the future historical victory of goodness over evil; the soul demands release from its guilt and restoration to ethical freedom. The moral commandment cannot free man from the bonds of sin, and the God of ethics is of no help to man in these straits. Purification from sin requires a God who is not merely the God of humanity, but of the individual. From the depths of his guilt feelings "the lonely man" becomes a religious individual and finds God, who grants him forgiveness.[30] But the ethical activity of man is not thereby abbreviated. Man himself must undertake the purification, he himself must win the battle over sin by means of remorse and repentance. But he finds the power to do this only by means of that trust which the faith in a forgiving and pardoning God can grant. The redemption of the individual is possible only because of the correlation of man and God, but in this correlation man is the active factor, and God is the goal, to which the power of man is directed. Moral activity is the duty of man, but such activity can only take place in the sight of God, only out of trust in the power of goodness, and only with the certainty of God's forgiveness.[31]

Here Judaism differs from Christianity, and although Cohen knew that modern Protestant Christian theology gave rise to the analysis of this problem, he can honestly contend that his solution of the problem is more congruent with the Jewish point of view. Christianity conceives the idea of redemption in a manner which transfers activity from man to God. Judaism strictly differentiates between the purification of oneself, an obligation which is laid upon man, and redemption, which is granted by God. Cohen finds the perfect expression of this doctrine in the Talmudic saying which is placed at the head of his *Religion of Reason*: "Blessed are ye, O Israel, for who purifies you and before whom are ye purified? Before your Father in Heaven!"[32]

The two starting points of religion, which we have until now been discussing separately, come together in the full development of the religious element of love. It was first given to us in the idea of the love of man, but now it is possible to establish a relationship of love between man and God, whether it be the love of God for man or the love of man for God. The God of the individual has become the God of love, and the religious relationship of man to God is expressed by the love of God. The concept of love has been invested with ethical meaning from two sides, which is made possible only because of the ethical significance of God. The love of God for man is bound up with the love of one's fellow man. Because of the social love of one's fellow men, I know at once that God loves man; as Cohen paradoxically expresses it, I must think of God as loving, because I too must love mankind. The love of God, like the love of one's fellow, is extended to human sufferings, which from a religious viewpoint can be explained only as the sufferings of love.[33] The love of man for God is also directed toward God as the archetype of morality, but with this religious change: that he has become the God of love.[34] All aspects of the human personality are swallowed up in the love of God, as expressed in the biblical commandments to "love the Lord, Thy God, with all Thy heart and with all Thy soul and with all Thy might."[35]

Cohen portrays religion in its relationships to all aspects of human consciousness from a psychological and systematic standpoint. The religious viewpoint is not limited to the sphere of its origin, but expands to all areas of culture and transforms them. This is first said of ethics, whose two methodically distinguishable sides—the ethical *per se,* and its religious derivation—are nevertheless unified. The union of these two methodically distinct factors is worked out in detail in the *Religion of Reason.* The ethical and religious concepts of man—and a fortiori the ethical and religious ideas of God—are presented as a unified whole. This means that the entire content of ethics has now been illuminated and transformed by religion: the ideas of humanity, of messianism, and of world history are bound together by their religious tie, freeing them of the severity imparted by a strictly rationalistic interpretation. Although religion at first seemed replete with the ideas of sin and suffering, the luminous and positive motives of religious consciousness, which are so strong in Judaism, have now been fully restored. Religion is both the original consciousness of closeness to God, and the yearning to bridge the gap between God and man, which has been caused by sin; religion rejoices in the light of God's face, and now has the courage to bear life's adversities.

From this ethical center, the immanence of religion is perceived in all the other realms of the spirit. The programmatic work, *The Concept of Religion in the System of Philosophy*, deals in detail with the relation of religion to logic, esthetics, and psychology, as well as ethics. The most important chapter, on logic, is especially concerned with ideas already mentioned in connection with the pure will. God is conceived as guarantor for the realization of morality, and thus is related to both morals and nature. In order for God to make possible the unification of the two realms, Cohen utilizes his transcendence vis-à-vis both nature and ethics. That which was intentionally transferred from religious terminology to the language of method is now restored to the language of religion. Cohen no longer speaks of the transcendence of God, but of his uniqueness; he does not contrast unity with the plurality of polytheistic gods, but speaks rather of God as incomparable to any other being. This uniqueness becomes the principal content of monotheism, and knowledge of it is testimony to the logical power which is inherent in monotheism from its beginning. But with the restoration of religious concepts, the content of monotheism also receives a new religious meaning. The methodical postulate of transcendence is converted into the religious idea of the incomparability of God, and his superiority to every other being.[36]

This same thought is brought into sharper focus when his being is made to denote the absolute "otherness" of God from all things in the world. When God revealed himself in the burning bush and said, "I am that which I am," Cohen sees in this "greatest of all the stylistic miracles of the Mosaic books" the recognition of God as the God of Being; corresponding to the Eleatic notion of being, there is "in religion the concept of the one God as the sole being." The knowledge of God as Being reveals the religious concept of being.[37] But here also, although formulated in logical terms, there is an originally religious fact at the bottom of the matter. Whatever the aseptic value of this interpretation of Scripture, it is certainly a primordial religious idea that only God is true Being, and that the world of things is nothing and insubstantial by comparison. It is self-explanatory that Cohen did not think the sole being of God nihilistically negates the being of the world. But the meaning of being which we attribute to God is that he is the source of the being of things. This corresponds completely to the articulation of concepts within Cohen's logic, which defines substance as the principle of existence and understands the basic concepts of knowledge as principles of origin in which nature comes into being. Thus God, too, has the character of a principle or origin, which is the logical motive of the idea of creation. But from the other side, this concept of beginning, although conceived as the concept of creation, proceeds from the realm of logic to the sphere of religion and becomes the bearer of all those religious motives which are contained in the concept of a Creator-God. Of course, Cohen eliminates the idea of a temporal beginning of the world from the concept of creation, and in agreement with the formula in the daily (morning) service, that God "renews the work of creation continually every day," he interprets creation as the continuous preservation of the world and its continuous renewal.[38]

In relation to man, the concept of origin begets the idea of revelation, not in the fixed historical sense, but as the source of human understanding within God. In opposition to all religious heteronomy, the religious character of religion is upheld, but the autonomous reason of man stands in a religious correlation with God, and may thus be described as a creation of God.[39] In this way, theoretic concepts of religion find their place within the system. The posthumous *Religion of Reason* unfolds the implicit ethical consequences of these concepts and arrives at a complete exposition of the Jewish religion. Whereas Cohen's ethics had only grasped the ethical content of Judaism, religious inwardness now comes into its own and the interpenetration of religion and ethics is demonstrated with profound understanding.

But the religious philosophy of Judaism is also understood as the presentation of the Religion of Reason in the Kantian sense, according to which the task of philosophy is not only to integrate religion into the system of reason, but also to derive it from reason. Cohen wishes to construct the true religion as the religion of reason, and discover the teachings of the religion of reason simply by an analysis of the historical religion of Judaism. Just as ethics in its narrowest sense depends upon reason, so too, its religious derivation depends upon reason; Cohen not only makes the ethical concept of the dignity of man depend upon reason, but also the idea of individual ethical community, which is founded on love and sympathy. We have already seen, with regard to sympathy, that what is deduced is social sympathy, even though this deduction is based only on the clarification of its ethical operations. This idea is repeated in relation to the other concepts of religious ethics, and with regard to religion itself. But we clearly recognize that the rational derivation of these concepts includes within itself a rationalistic interpretation and limitation of their contents. Not only is there a narrowing of the psychological fact of sympathy, but also a narrowing of the whole of ethical consciousness, if it is legitimized only as social sympathy.

This is repeated even more clearly if the faith in the love of God for man, which lived profoundly and naturally in the depths of Cohen's soul, is legitimized because we are obligated to love God due to our belief in the love of God for man. But there is still another reason. Even in this, the final reach of Cohen's thought, God remains an idea. Although he introduces into the idea of God the living substance of the religious imagination, and no longer holds back from speaking of God as a person,[40] the methodological bases of this thought restrain him from the possibility of interpreting God as a Reality, even in the spirit of post-Kantian idealism which interpreted God as the active principle of consciousness. The turning towards religion has changed the content of the idea of God, but not its methodological character.

But the new content of the God-representation and its given methodological form do not fit together. The principle of the ethical world order (that is, the way the concept of God is understood by ethics) can be interpreted without difficulty as the idea of an ethical world order, but this kind of explanation is incomparably harder with regard to the God of love. This brings about, as Cohen's critics have repeatedly emphasized, an unconscious leap into the realm of metaphysics; it also limits the free and broad development of the content of the God-representation. The love of God is understood as love for a moral ideal, and the concept of the love of God for man is only an archetype upon which the pure moral deed can model itself. We have previously emphasized that Cohen's doctrine of atonement, which demands that man purify himself, corresponds completely to Judaism's view. But along with this purification of man, Judaism posits the grace of God, and within Cohen's system the idea of the forgiving God can only hint at that faith which provides man with the power of moral renewal. Cohen, himself, continually transcended these weaknesses. His book is full of the spirit of living religion, and he bends all of his conceptual, form-giving power to the task of integrating religion within the circle of his concepts; but in his most characteristic formulations he is still bound to this limitation. In his wonderfully religious structure, there remains an unbridgeable gap between the content of religion and the philosophic creation of concepts.

Franz Rosenzweig

The great achievement of Hermann Cohen will long remain in the center of Jewish religious philosophy, despite many adverse criticisms. His influence is felt in every aspect of philosophic work carried on within Judaism since his day, despite the shifting of philosophic interests brought about by time and the inward life of the Jewish people. It is not our intention here to present a full-fledged discussion of the new tendency, which began to appear just a few years after the publication of Cohen's *Religion of Reason*. Many of its leading proponents are still alive and in the midst of their philosophic work. We shall only deal with one of the members of this philosophic circle, Franz Rosenzweig (1886-1929), who died in the prime of his life and whose magnum opus, *Der Stern der Erlösung* (*The Star of Redemption* [1921]), was further elucidated but not basically altered in his few later essays.[41]

Among the members of this philosophic circle, all of whom differ among themselves, Rosenzweig holds a special place, and on no account can he be designated as the leader of a school with views held in common. Only general themes connect him with other attempts made in our time to understand Judaism along new philosophic lines, and he stands as an independent and unique phenomenon, both in his conception of Judaism and his general philosophic orientation. He grew up with very tenuous connections to Judaism, and like many other members of his generation, he found his way back to it by dint of his own efforts. It was not the nationalistic aspect of Judaism which attracted him, but its religious side, and this he discovered in a special way. The return to religion, which arose at the beginning of the twentieth century in the spiritual life of many circles in Germany, also affected some of the younger German Jews who, though few in number, stood on a very high spiritual plane. Some of them, including some of Rosenzweig's friends, were strongly influenced by the religious tendencies among the younger German Christian groups, and converted to that faith. Rosenzweig was also for some time attracted to Christianity, but afterwards found in Judaism a fit expression for his faith and satisfaction for his religious needs; and the influence of Hermann Cohen strengthened him in his attachment to Judaism. After working out his own relationship to Judaism, he became adept in the ways of the Jewish spirit and way of life. But traces of the problems which gave rise to his religious development still characterize his version of Judaism. Both in *The Star of Redemption* and in his later writings it is evident that he is clearing his own road to Judaism and determining the nature of the road which he is traveling.

For him there is nothing in Judaism that is self-explanatory. He discovers ideas in it which scholars who were raised within the framework of Jewish tradition had passed over or ignored; but he also over-emphasized that portion of it which affected his own personal development, and because of this saw facts from a one-sided and partial point of view. From a philosophic standpoint, Rosenzweig was one of the first representatives of the tendency which later found systematic expression in the existentialist philosophy that attracted many of the younger German philosophers and that in recent years has had a great influence beyond the borders of Germany, especially in France. Not only did Rosenzweig clearly articulate the principles of existentialism, but there could be found in his work a whole series of ideas which became of central importance for Heidegger, although the latter reached different conclusions. When Heidegger's *Being and Time* was published, Rosenzweig greeted the book as a confirmation of his own views, and the close relation of his philosophy to existentialism was also admitted by partisans of the new "school."[42] Existentialist philosophy, however, had developed independently of Rosenzweig, since *The Star of Redemption* was thought of as a purely Jewish book and for many years was hardly noticed beyond the circle of Jewish readers.

Both in his introduction to the book and in one of his later essays, *The New Thinking*, Rosenzweig characterizes this philosophy as standing in stark contrast to the entire philosophic tradition which began with Thales and culminated in Hegel. For traditional philos-

ophy, it is self-evident that the world is a unity and can be derived
from a single principle. From the time of Thales, who viewed water
as the principle of being, to Hegel, who viewed Spirit as the one true
reality, no one challenged this assumption, which goes on to deduce
from this principle all of the modes of being. Philosophy maintains
that this view is self-evident, that the three elements which we encounter in experience—God, the world, and man—have one essence,
one of these being essential and the other two being looked on as its
manifestations. Philosophy only asks which of these three is the essential being, and which are derivative from it. Ancient philosophy, and
many of the tendencies of later naturalism, derive God and man
from the world; the theology of the Middle Ages, and mysticism
generally, derive man and the world from God; and modern idealism
establishes both God and the world upon consciousness—and therefore ultimately upon man. Necessarily correlative to this presupposition of primal unity is the assumption of the unity of thought, whose
power extends to all the realms of being, and can, therefore, base all
these realms on their common essence. Thought is assured that it has
the power to grasp all of being, without exception.

This, of course, is possible only if all of being is based upon
thought.[43] If anyone pursues traditional monism to its final conclusion, he must end up in idealism in order to establish reality upon
a single principle; even the traditional realistic schools must recognize the decisive power of thought, which leads to idealism as the
most consistent form of monism. Extreme idealistic monism has one
further consequence: the true reality of all individual beings is contained in the universal, in which all particular existents are swallowed up. This applies not only to the facts, which can be derived
from a general principle, but also to the principle itself. When
modern philosophy bases God and the world upon the consciousness
of man, it is not speaking of the individual human consciousness but
"consciousness in general," which is the ground of all separate human
consciousness.[44]

As Rosenzweig understands it, the "new thinking" is opposed to
traditional philosophy. He is especially vehement in denying what
he considers its monistic assumptions. The new thinking does not
seek to perfect or amend experiences which manifest God, the world,
and man as three separate fundamental entities; they are to be taken
as given. It recognizes that every attempt to found two of these elements upon the third is an illusionary deduction, for each of them

has its own special essence which thought must recognize as being inseparable from it.[45] Thought can describe and analyze these three elements, which experience brings before it, but cannot add anything to their essence. Since thought recognizes these three elements as given, it also recognizes that existence stands within its own separate realm as well. Thought does not seek to bring existence into being, but to understand existence as it exists apart from it. The authority and right of existence must not be distorted, as it had been by those irrationalisms which oppose reason and which were then current. Thought is the correct means for understanding things, and it has no substitute. But thought does not precede existence, but serves as one of its elements.[46] For such a viewpoint, the unity of thought is not a primary principle which produces the multiplicity of knowledge. That which is given to us is knowledge in all of its forms and many facets. Only after we know the connection between the fundamental elements of existence can the idea be validated that behind the diversity of knowledge there stands a unity of thought, beyond which our glance cannot penetrate.[47] This realism is in principle different from the realism mentioned previously, because it completely supports the originality of the personal and the material, and rejects any attempt to isolate it and establish it simply on an abstract essence.

The dichotomy between these two modes of thought is not only theoretical. It applies to the very content of existence, and especially to human existence. Traditional philosophy was not satisfied with transposing the true being of man into a general essence, which is the same for all particular men, but also asserted that the goal of human life is contained in the manifestation of this general idea of human being. In moral laws it saw primarily the task which is given to man as man, and the value of the individual man consisted simply in his being the bearer of this moral law. The new thinking protests against this derogation of the dignity of the individual. It attributes value to the individual man, not only originality of being, but primary value; it maintains that the value of the individual's life is found in that life, and not in a general principle which transcends him. This does not imply the denial of the moral law. This law maintains its absoluteness, but man does not exist for the sake of the moral law; the law exists for the sake of man.[48]

The first to attribute philosophic worth to the individual was Schopenhauer, who in raising the question of the value of the world, viewed the world from the viewpoint of the particular. Nietzsche later followed in his footsteps. His entire thought centers on the significance of human existence; vehemently upholding the value of the individual, he attacks all norms and laws that are outside the individual. His violent opposition to all previous philosophy is a sharp expression of the basic motive of his atheism. He does not deny God because of theoretical reasons, but because he cannot endure the thought that above him there is a God. The exact opposite of his justification of atheism is Kierkegaard's justification of faith. The knowledge that he is himself overburdened with sin, and needs redemption, brings him to faith. Only faith can grant him assurance, because it attaches great importance to the individual and to his sin, and redeems him from it. For Kierkegaard, Hegel's interpretation of Christianity substitutes man in general for the individual, paying no attention to that which is of prime importance—the individual. He sees this as proof of the failure of the entire philosophic enterprise because philosophy gives no answer to the life-questions of the individual man.[49]

Rosenzweig, too, began to have doubts about traditional philosophy, not because of theoretical speculation, but because of a lack of personal satisfaction. In the events and catastrophes of the First World War he saw the downfall of philosophy, because the outstanding fact about knowledge of the world was the fact of death. Philosophy seeks to free man from the fear of death, which is the prime force of his life, by teaching him to look upon himself as a part of the world process, or as the bearer of eternal values which are exempt from extinction. But man does not want to be free of the fear of death, at least not in these ways. He revolts against these attempts which totally neglect his individuality in order to quiet his fear of death.[50] This emotion caused Rosenzweig and many of his young contemporaries to demand of thought that it take account of the individual in his particularity, and not turn its face away from his sufferings. In the problem of death it becomes clear to man that he is not just a part of the natural world, but stands apart from it as a peculiar being. When man escapes the net of philosophical terminology, it becomes clear to him that this framework is also theoretically insufficient to comprehend the concrete "thusness" of existence.[51] The new thought, therefore, which had begun to form in the minds of certain nineteenth-century philosophers from the days of Schopenhauer onward, can be seen as truly revolutionary and new, in opposition to the form of philosophy current until then.[52]

This new thought is distinct from the old not only in content, but especially in method. The concrete thusness of existence cannot be grasped except through experience, and experience must therefore be the starting point for our thought. But the "experience" here intended is quite distinct from the experience encountered in the special sciences, and the empiricism of this philosophy is quite different from the usual meaning of this term. The special sciences analyze and separate specific sections of existence, and seek to impose a general law upon them. The meaning intended here is to contact and grasp existence precisely in its concreteness. Moreover, while the special sciences describe the being of phenomena completely devoid of quality and value, the experience we seek here relates both to the being and to the significance and value of things. The subject of such experience, therefore, can only be man in the fullness of his being, and not merely his epistemological organ; moreover, this is said of the actual individual man, who is both the subject and the object of philosophy. The insight of Schopenhauer is not that he only measured the world according to man, but that he made his own personal experience the source and beginning point of philosophy; with him, the philosopher becomes part of philosophy. The same is true of the other philosophers just mentioned, and it is the right of the philosopher to make his personal experience the starting point for philosophy; this is what Rosenzweig points to as the distinctive contribution of the new thinking.

From experience as so defined, Rosenzweig attempts to discover all existence. First, he seeks to demonstrate what this existence says concerning God, the world, and man, each taken separately, and how the relationships between the three are drawn. *The Star of Redemption* claims to be a philosophic system dealing with all the parts of philosophy, though on a different basis and with a different order.[53] This system validates and upholds the Jewish view of God and the world. But it is not a philosophy of Judaism. It does not intend—at least in the important sections of the work—to evaluate Judaism; the Jewish religion does not serve as the presupposition for Rosenzweig's thought—rather, it is thought, born out of Rosenzweig's own experience, which concludes in the confirmation of that religion. His relationship to Judaism is thus roughly equivalent to the relation of Jewish rationalistic religious philosophy, differing only insofar as the latter validated Judaism upon the basis of thought, while Rosenzweig seeks to found it upon the basis of his personal experience. In order to emphasize his independence of all Jewish dogmatic presuppositions, he makes the extreme statement that he expresses his personal experience in the language of Judaism, but that a Christian thinker or a freethinker would express this experience in another terminology.

With all of his declared opposition to traditional philosophy, both in regard to the content of its doctrines and its ultimate principle of certainty, he is nevertheless dependent upon it in many instances when it comes to the presentation of his own thoughts. His concept of reality, founded upon experience, is not expressed in the doctrine which experiences supposedly teach, but in the form of a theoretical construction. His meditations do not develop conclusions from basic facts which belong to experience alone, but theory constructs and creates facts themselves. The paradoxical attempt to clothe the content of experience in the form of a conceptual structure can be explained historically as due to the influence of German idealism, with which Rosenzweig occupied himself in his earliest researches, and from which he could not entirely free himself even after he proclaimed complete theoretical opposition to it. But his constructive method, although quite different from the dialectical method of German idealism, is nevertheless clearly dependent upon it. In his attempt to combine a philosophy of experience with conceptual construction, Rosenzweig walks in the footsteps of later Schellingian philosophy, which fiercely opposed the idealism of the early Schelling and its continuation by Hegel, although in certain areas it maintained the dialectical method. From a theoretical viewpoint, the goal of the dialectical method is to understand the facts, which are laid out before it by experience, in terms of their inner necessity.

This does not mean that one can prove them by formal demonstration. That God, the world, and man exist—and are related to one another in certain ways—does not have to be and cannot be demonstrated. The nature of God, the world, and man is disclosed to us through experience, but theoretical construction can show us that their various aspects, discovered by experience, do not stand next to one another disparately, but face each other. The essence of each of them is grasped according to their inward structure, and likewise, their relationships derive from their individual essences. The path of this construction begins with one of the ideas of Hermann Cohen's logic, but utilizes it in a way that Cohen could hardly have approved. Each one of these three elements of existence must be derived from its negation. This negation must be understood as meaning the negation wrought by knowing. Our knowledge of existence is destroyed in thought. We cast doubt upon it by conjecture, in order thereby to negate the negation and once more find our way toward being.[54]

Various aspects of being are thus revealed to our thought in their inner connection. This genetic method is made constructive because, in thought, the negation is made the source from which being develops. The deduction of being from nothing is accomplished for each of the three elements of existence in two forms. The first way is that against nothingness (the specific nothingness of which we speak in every case, whether it be that of God, the world, or man) there appears the positive assertion of being. The second way is that the negation *per se* is destroyed and denied by thought. In the first, the essence of each of the three elements, which is continuous and self-subsistent, is revealed as static; in the second, there is disclosed the dynamic, voluntaristic aspect of these three elements. These two sides pertain to the essence of each of the three elements, and in each one of them these two aspects interact continually, and only from this mutual interaction does the essence become that which it is.[55]

From this description of the deduction we can already see what Rosenzweig himself later admits: that this must be said not only of a conceptual construction, but of more important things as well. Not only does our cognition of God, the world, and man occur in a constructive way, but we find that the process of self-birth is attributed to existence itself.[56]

After each one of the three elements has been interpreted in itself, they are brought into relation with each other. If we relate God to the world, we cognize this relationship as creation; if we relate God to man, we cognize this relationship as the fact of revelation, and we cognize the relation of man to the world as redemption—which in its first step, at least, is viewed as the redemption of the world by man. At the ground of each of these conclusions there lies the essence of each of the three elements, as explained before, and according to it we can define the relationship between the two given causes. But the intention here is not to construct, just for the sake of understanding, the concepts of creation, revelation, and redemption. Construction only discloses how, from this meeting of God, the world, and man in existence, there arise the facts of creation, revelation, and redemption. Even the order of the succession of these three elements applies both to actuality and to thought. Creation is the foundation of revelation, and the latter is the foundation of redemption.

The second of the three books of *The Star of Redemption* relates, to use Rosenzweig's own words, the transition from creation to revelation, and it sees as the distinctive novelty of the new thought the depiction of existence as temporal, while traditional philosophy seeks only to cognize the eternal interrelations of concepts. But Rosenzweig's thought, too, does not rest completely within the temporal, but rises toward the eternal. The third book, which is the apex of *The Star of Redemption,* shows first how temporal life can take on the aspect of eternity, and concludes with the idea that the final goal of the evolution of the world is the unification of the world and man with God, when they will participate in his absolute eternity. The unity of existence, with which traditional philosophy began, is no longer the beginning point of thought, but its end; it is not an ultimate given, but is the purpose of the development of existence. According to its external structure, the third book united the three facts of the second book—creation, revelation, and redemption. When these two triads (God, the world, and man; creation, revelation, and redemption) are combined, we have the figure of a six-pointed star, after which the book is named.

The three steps of becoming, the elements of existence, their unification in creation, revelation, and redemption, the ascent to eternity and to the unification of existence—all of these are also important for the historical evolution of world consciousness. For the Greeks, who formulated the highest expression of the thought of the pagan world, each of the three elements is a perfect and complete entity, and each one of them is totally independent of the other two elements. The world for the Greeks was a plastic cosmos, self-subsistent, independent of both the gods and man, insofar as the latter is more than just a link in the chain of natural causation. Similarly, man in his human life maintains the same posture when he is dependent only upon himself. Thus Greek tragedy portrays its heroes, whose greatness consists in existing in their special nature, and whose fate is the isolation in which they are shut up. The Greek gods also live separate lives, except for occasional interference to assert their dominion over the destiny of the world and men.[57]

The manner in which Rosenzweig conceives their relation to the world is similar to that of Epicurus, for whom the gods exist in the spaces between the worlds and have no connection with the world. Only biblical faith binds the three elements together, makes the world into a creation of God, brings God and man in encounter in the act of revelation, and man and the world into a redemptive relationship. This viewpoint is common to both Judaism and Christianity; the difference between them lies in the differing ways in which they realize eternity in time. The first book of *The Star of Redemption* describes Greek thought; the second discusses the bases of biblical religion; and the third—in its opening two chapters—Judaism and Christianity as historical wholes. The concluding chapter paints the vision of the supreme eternity, before which the quarrels and differences between the two faiths will disappear in a mysterious manner which escapes both of them.

This current of thought, just outlined in general form, is explicated with great constructive energy, and from this central point Rosenzweig draws inferences and consequences for every area of philosophy, and produces a host of new and important insights. Nevertheless, this attempt to deduce, or just to construct a description of existence whose roots are in human experience, is still farfetched. On the one hand, the constructive deductions lack decisive logical weight. It is logically impossible, as regards the two ways in which thought makes the transition from nothing to something (that is, by the positing of Yes in the face of negation, and the destruction of nothingness), to clarify the fact that, of necessity, there must be posited two corresponding aspects resident in the basic elements; what these are must be explicated. And on the other hand—and this is even more important—the elements of experience in Rosenzweig's world view are never clearly delineated. They disappear behind the curtain of the constructively developed ideas, and thus it seems that on more than one occasion the ideas have been established dogmatically, and not inferred from experience.

One of the more important examples of this is that we are never told on the basis of which experiences our knowledge of the world and God as specific, independent, separate substances is founded. Moreover, it is not clear how one can have any idea of them at all without encountering man. With regard to the world, the problem is alleviated somewhat, because man, in one aspect of his existence, belongs to the world, and in this way he can know the world. But with regard to God, the question is left unanswered. According to the structure of *The Star of Redemption*, it seems as if the existence of God—that is, of the personal God—is a self-evident fact that needs no proofs. Rosenzweig openly says that it needs no proofs, and taking into consideration his basic point of view, it is clear why this must be so. But he still does not give us the experience, on the basis of which we cognize the existence of God and his personal character.[58] It is possible that this experience is hidden in the encounter between God and man, which Rosenzweig calls revelation, despite the fact that due to the structure of his book, he limits this denotation to one specific, though central, aspect of this encounter. If one exhausts its content, it seems that man's faith in God is dependent upon this encounter, and it must serve as the starting point of all the statements made concerning God in relation to himself and to the world. The constructive structure in Rosenzweig's doctrine, in which revelation later appears in terms of value, conceals the relationships between the various aspects of his viewpoint concerning God and his element of experience. This is also true of the other central concepts of Rosenzweig's doctrine. For his book to be fully effective, and in order that his work may be debated seriously, one must free his ideas from the framework of construction and return them to their natural relationship. This can be done now only in a general review, in which we will treat only those topics which are important from the viewpoint of Judaism.

In order to comprehend his doctrine in this way, we must attribute to the experience which man has of himself and the world a characteristic difference from the experience of knowledge that he acquires of God. From the latter experience, there flows a new understanding of the world and man, granted by faith in man and the world. But there is another understanding, independent of faith. This is described in the first two chapters of the first book, and they deal with the world and man. Later, there occur many clarifying statements on the various areas of human culture which are independent of one's knowledge of God. To systematize them in the spirit of Rosenzweig, we must label them as philosophy, in distinction from theology, which is founded on the experience of faith.

As we have seen, the experience in which the world is given to us is not the experience of empirical science, but the primary experience of the world, with which science begins. Rosenzweig finds two causes in the world, just as he finds them in all spheres of existence—one static and passive, the other dynamic and spontaneous. The passive element in the world is its theoretical and universal law, its immanent logos which constitutes, as it were, its framework; the active and spontaneous cause is the stream of the particular and the individual, which must continually go forth into existence.[59] The position which is given to thought expresses Rosenzweig's opposition both to irrationalism and to idealism. As opposed to the former, he sees in thought, which includes within itself the universal laws of things, one of the primary causes for the being of the world. And in opposition to idealism, he does not give to thought priority over the world, and does not allot it the function of confirming and maintaining the existence of the world. On the contrary, the existence of the world is primary; thought is contained within existence, and especially in the existence of the world.[60]

In order to express this idea clearly, let us read the chapter on the world which is called "Metalogic," and is analogous to the word metaphysics. The thought which is implanted in the existence of the world contains within itself, according to its essence, a relationship to all the various aspects of phenomena in the world. Thought is applicable to the multiplicity of things, its universality is of a general validity that essentially applies to the manifold of nature. In his conception of the relation between the general and the particular, there is an essential difference from idealism. For the idealism of Kant and the schools which stem from him, experience provides the particular content which the general form of knowledge articulates into a unity of experience. Rosenzweig does exactly the opposite: he places all dynamism and activity in the particular, and the universal serves the function of absorbing the particular; in union with the latter, it has no function but that of drawing the particular to itself and causing it to rest within the universal. Only with the entrance of the particular into the universal can the facts be combined into species, and the species into classes of higher and higher generality.

This viewpoint, which attributes a real, concrete character to the logical connection between the individual and the general, is dependent upon his view of the world which conceives of it, inanimate as well as animate, as a living process. The dead "given" of philosophic idealism has become full of living power. Everything that becomes, bursts into existence and seeks therein its place, both in terms of space and in terms of logic. On the other hand, the universal law of the world becomes an indwelling logos, and from the two there is built up a ladder of species and genera, each of which is a complete entity in itself: a cosmos arises before our eyes, in which a very neat hierarchy leads from the particular to the principle of the world as a whole.[61] This is a position exactly opposite to that of Aristotle, who attributes to matter the striving for form and general lawfulness. All of this applies equally well to man insofar as he is part of the world, but at a certain time in his life, man's essence is aroused within him, which places him beyond the world. Until then, he is a part of the world, and afterwards he is part of it by virtue of his natural existence, which includes both his body and his soul. Human forms of association, and especially the state, are creatures within the world, and are essentially of the same type as all other creatures of the world. The relation of the particular to the universal which includes it, is here given clearer meaning. Even the laws of ethics, which form and bind men together in associations, are part of the order of law which reigns in the world.[62]

This picture of the world in which the individual is serenely integrated into the harmonious order of the universal does not apply to his theory of man, which is dark and serious. In man there are found two causes, the static and continuous, which is his character, and movement and activity, which is his freedom. The freedom of man is not at first directed toward the outside world; his first activity is directed toward strengthening his own individuality. And what was true of the world, is true of man. These two aspects must interact, in order that man might attain his true essence.[63] Only the act of self-assertion makes man into man; only in it does he become a self, to use Rosenzweig's language, and thus he stands forth against the world as a being with his own essence. As an "ego" he is also differentiated from other men, and he is completely independent. Insofar as men belong to the world, they are particulars of a single type. In their individuality, they are not different from each other, just as the individuals of other classes are not different from each other; their individuality is that special way in which the common essence of man is manifested in each of them, an essence which binds them together. Between one self and another, this connection does not exist. Individuality can have a plural form; for the "self," only the singular exists. The proud selfhood of the "self" also determines its fate, which is solitude. The relations between men always remain in the sphere of the world's existence, but between one self and another there is no bridge. Every self is alone insofar as it is an ego.[64]

This complete isolation is the plight of the hero of Greek tragedy. It expresses in a specific way what the hero does and what happens to him. His character and self are not given to man at birth. At birth, the infant is merely part of the world. Character comes only at later stages of development, and does not develop slowly, but springs into being at a certain time. The awakening of man's character coincides with the arousal of eros. The sexual urge, which swallows man up in sexuality, also brings about the birth of the self which stands outside of sex; and the closest and most intimate relationship which is possible for humans, the act of love, reveals the final loneliness and isolation of the self, which takes no part in it and remains enclosed in its shell. After the state of old age, in which the sense of isolation has been further strengthened, death brings isolation to its apogee. In the face of death, everything disappears that had connected man as an essence to the world, and nothing remains but the temporary insubstantial isolation of the self.[65] The fear of death precedes this characteristic of death, with which the existentialism of Rosenzweig begins. The fear of death is the ego's fear, and the attempts made by philosophy to conquer it betray their purpose, for they do not envisage man as an ego but as a part of the natural world, or as part of a general spiritual network. It is possible for man, thus understood, to continue to live for the sake of the world, for humanity, for the development of spirit. But all of this evaporates in the face of the ego's fear of death. The ego needs redemption from its isolation and from its fear of death, which hold it in bondage as an ego.

Thus the analysis of human being, founded on itself, leads to the point where that communion with God, which Rosenzweig calls revelation, becomes possible. The revelation of God to man, which is the foundation of all communion with him, is a work of God's love, which turns toward man. This redeems man from his isolation and elevates him above the conflicts of his existence. A decisive importance is attached to this relation of man to God, which arises in such a way that the love of God is not experienced as a quiescent quality, but as a spontaneous act of love, which seizes man at a certain time, and always turns toward him anew. This act of love is not directed toward mankind generally, but is directed toward the individual, and not to all individuals in the same measure, but to him whom the will of God chooses.[66]

Rosenzweig disregarded the misgivings of our consciousness at the fact that the love of God chooses one, and rejects others. But our experience of the love of God is testimony to this fact, and teaches us that the love of God is acquired during the passage of time, and that there is a moment for every man in which it will rest on him. To the man who knows this love of God, there comes the knowledge—which replaces that ego independence which is self-subsistent—that he is dependent upon God. Thus faith and trust replace the isolation in which he previously existed, and to the love of God there now corresponds the love of man for God. This relation between God and man is a pure and absolute love relation, and in this character remains as product and derivative of this primary revelation of God. Of course, God is also thought of as a commanding and demanding God. That man, the beloved of God, should return him love for love —this is not left to man's free will, but he is commanded to do this by God. But this commandment rests upon the mutuality of love. According to its essence, love demands love in return, and the commandment of God to man to love him only expresses something which flows from the essence of the love relation. Thus, while the essence of God's love is personal, his commandment to love is also personal. It is directed toward the individual, to whom the love of God is directed, and is, therefore, different in essence from law, which is eternal and directed toward all creatures.[67]

Rosenzweig saw the moral law, which is binding upon all creatures, as part of the order of the world, or at least as analogous to it. This does not affect the ethic of faith, and since the order of the cosmic law is in the end dependent upon God, the same is true of the moral law. But the moral law does not enter the realm of the ethics of faith, and is totally separate from the commandment whose root is in the love of God. The purpose of such a separation between commandment and law is to answer the question, which many have asked, of how it is possible to command love.

But this distinction not only applies to the biblical commandment of loving one's neighbor as oneself, but applies equally to all the commandments in the Pentateuch. Although outwardly they have the form of a commandment, they are nevertheless "present" commandments given by the Lord this day, directly to the individual, and their source is in the actual relationship of the individual to God.[68] They are not arbitrary *obiter dicta* of God's will, but demands made by God of those who love him.

When Rosenzweig goes on to discuss Judaism, he again revives the idea of law. He explains it as a fundamental condition of Jewish life, and must therefore accept the idea of a commanding, lawgiving God. But here again, Rosenzweig upholds the idea that the divine commandment, as the content of revelation and as that which is demanded of the individual, is a *commandment*; and only because it is the social foundation of Jewish life—insofar as its activity relates to "the world," and must give this life consistency, order and cohesiveness—does it turn into a law.[69] Thus God does not cease being a God of love in his relationship to man, and only within the social context does his commandment turn into law. If Rosenzweig occasionally deviates from this view and distinguishes between the God who is a lawgiver and the God of love, he drew this from the religious tradition, not from his fundamental religious experience, which did not recognize the dualism of the gracious God and the vengeful God.

When it comes to the relation of man to God, the experiential element, upon which Rosenzweig builds his doctrine, is quite obvious, but it is more difficult to summarize his "constructive" presentation of the relation of God to the world, and his conception of the divine substance. Here we will see the broad, all-encompassing significance of the encounter of man with God, whose central focus—as has been said—is the experience of the divine love, but which nevertheless is still only a portion of the experience. In regard to the relation of God to the world, this problem is easily solved if we pay attention to the specific meanings which Rosenzweig attributes to the idea of creation. For him, creation is not a single, singular event, but a continuous creation of the world by God, or as it is expressed in the well-known prayer—the "renewal of the works of creation every day."[70]

This is not to be understood as an eternal procession of emanations of the world from God, as many who have defended this doctrine have claimed. God is not the impersonal cause from which all beings flow, and the world is not renewed at each and every separate moment of time. Although the world is in continuous existence, it is not an independent existence, but finds its stay and support in God. Just as revelation is the proper relation between God and man, so creation is the proper relation between God and the world. On the one hand, its ground lies in the creative power of God, which is the active cause, and on the other, in the contingency of the world, which is the passive cause. The world which appeared to the ancients as a self-subsistent cosmos, in Rosenzweig's language wakes to an awareness of its creatureliness; it is precisely the general causality governing the universe—that is, the logos which is its framework—which finds such support necessary. The world exists only by reason of its unity with the particular, and is therefore destroyed in its flux. If the world is disclosed as a creature, it must exchange, on the one hand, its perfect completeness for mere becoming; on the other hand, it must surrender its self-subsistence, and needs an external actuality to maintain it in being.[71]

All that is said here of the world as a whole holds for every particular existent within the world order, and of man as well, who in his natural existence is a part of the world. He sees himself as a creature, and from this shattering knowledge he infers that the world to which he belongs is also a creature, and its existence is given to it by God. Man views himself both as a creature and as a son of God; it is made known to him that his existence, as with all contingent beings, is completely dependent upon God, and that the God upon whom he is dependent directs his love towards him. Out of this dual experience, he apprehends God as the omnipotent creator and as a loving father.[72]

To the idea of creation and of man's self-knowledge of creatureliness, which was also invoked by the Christian theology of Rosenzweig's time, he gives an entirely different character than that of Christian theology. Although man knows himself as a creature, and is thus dependent upon God, he is not nothing; he does not look upon himself as "dust and ashes," and the God before whom he acknowledges his creatureliness, though a God of infinite creative power, is not a God before whom man appears in fear and trembling, but is a God who supports him in his existence. The activity of creation, which is constantly renewed, is identified with God's providence. In his relation to the world, God is the God of providence, and in his relation to man, he is the God of love. Rosenzweig sees in the eternal creative activity of God an expression of the voluntarism of God, which is nonarbitrary in its nature. The divine power is such that it must express itself in creation, but in this power there is contained the divine freedom. The activity of God is one with his essence, but does not flow from him of necessity from the tendency to make himself known, but is the product of free will.[73]

From what has been said, we can understand how the facts of creation and revelation, and the corresponding belief in the work of creation and in revelation, are mutually dependent upon each other. Creation is completed by revelation, and revelation is grounded in creation. The fact that God is the creator does not connect him with his creatures; this does not happen until he turns toward man in love. At first this happens between God and the individual, and then it fans out in ever-widening circles. The experience of divine love would be nothing more than the experience of an isolated individual if it were not for the fact that God, whose love is made known to us, is also the creator, in whom our existence inheres.[74] Rosenzweig demands a relationship of completion similar to that between philosophy and theology, which for him must first be combined with the idea of creation, and secondly, with the idea of revelation. Theology, that is, knowledge whose source lies in faith, must not limit itself to the sphere of feeling and become merely a theology of experience. On the basis of faith it must seek to understand all of existence, and to wrestle with all facts. In order to be true, it needs philosophy. And philosophy, which—as Rosenzweig understands it—is rooted in personal experience, needs revelation in order to escape the pitfalls of subjectivism. Only by its completion through theology, does it attain the objectivity of science.[75]

In the knowledge of creation and revelation, that is, in our double knowledge that we are creatures of God and the objects of his love, there is contained the knowledge of the essence of God. And this knowledge does not flow from the former but is part and parcel of it. These two aspects, the cognizance of God's relation to us, and the knowledge of his essence, are given together in every religious knowledge, and are one and inseparable. Rosenzweig posits this, first of all—and no further proofs are necessary—in regard to the personal character of God, which is included in his dual relation to man. He then goes on to distinguish between the infinite streaming of the divine substance, and his freedom which breaks forth anew at every instant. This dualism, which he seeks to deduce constructively, and of which we have made mention before, is based upon the essence of personal faith. For it, too, God is the infinite being, self-subsistent, in no less measure than for such impersonal faith as that of mysticism; but together with this, God is also free will. Faith requires the maintenance of both these phases of the divine essence, and sees no contradiction between them. For the philosophy of religion, the possibility of uniting these two forms is a central problem, and it must seek to understand the concept of divine freedom in such a way that it does not distort the unchanging stasis of the divine. Rosenzweig upholds —undoubtedly under the influence of Schelling—this primary dualism in the essence of God, and seeks to understand this essence in terms of its interaction. He begins by a formal inquiry concerning the essence of God, and returns to it in his treatment of the manifestations of God in the works of creation and revelation. In this form he becomes aware of the mystery of the divine essence, and his conception of God goes far beyond the boundaries of human experience or feeling.

The starting point for the concepts to be treated next, lies in the activity which the knowledge of the divine love works upon men.

Not only does it redeem man's ego from its isolation and loneliness, but it also breaks down the barrier of man's selfhood by arousing within him the desire to love God. Thus the primary religious experience brings about a fundamental change in the nature of man. The man of faith is different from what he was before the encounter of faith. Despite the apparent similarity, the nature of this change in man, by reason of his encounter with God, is totally different from the conversion process of Pauline Christianity. The change does not lie in the freeing of man from the bondage of sin; and it does not demand that man fight continually against the grain of his natural impulses. The selfhood of man, the rigorous obligation that man's ego determine his character—are not sins; and the change in man does not include the fact that he must battle against the tendencies and impulses of his nature, but that he direct them toward new goals. The rebellion of man's ego is transformed by divine love into faithfulness, which man gives as a response to God, and he maintains his love of God with all his strength.[76] These are the same natural powers which were directed inward, but now face outward, and they thus reach their full development and completion.

But this change is not limited to the love of God. In relation to other men and to the world, the isolation of the human essence has been overcome. The love for God is continued and prolonged through the love of one's fellow man, who is also a creation of God, and similar to the ego of man. Previously, the love of God was no more than the response to the divine love which rested on man; now the power of love has been set free, and spontaneously seizes his fellow man. The love of God had been directed inward towards him; now the love of one's fellow man can be manifested in works of love, and thus achieves its necessary expression. The love of neighbor and the works of love which derive from it are the relationships which arise from the experience of the divine love.[77]

Thus we have a religious ethic which is completely based on love. We have already explained how this ethic is formally different from the ethic of law, which is independent of faith. Man is commanded in regard to the love of his fellow, just as he is commanded to love God, but here, too, the commandment functions only as an expression for the demand which arises from the experience of divine love, and it is essentially different from law, which is universally binding. No less profound is the difference between the ethic of love and the ethic of law, in terms of their content. The ethic of law is directed toward fixed rational ends. Out of the ethic of law we derive specific tasks for man, which he must perform; it tells him for whose good he has to care at times; it directs his way toward these fixed goals, and appoints the correct means for their realization. This character of rational purposefulness is completely missing from the love ethic. The work of love does not seek its purpose by rational deliberation, but flows from the necessity of love's being made explicit and known, and occurs whenever opportunity offers.[78] Man walks in the way that love obliges him, and never seeks to calculate the promises of success that occur to him. His fellow man, to whom he is obligated, is not the one who is closest to him because of internal reason, but simply that person with whom he comes in contact at that time, and whom God prepares for him to love. He does not prize him because of his special characteristics, but he is obligated toward him as he is to any other man whom God prepares for him, and the relationship of love is personal in its profoundest sense, even though it has nothing to do with the personality of our fellow man.[79]

This conception of love is very reminiscent of the idea of love found in Christian mysticism, but differs from it because of the influence which Rosenzweig attributes to the work of love. In terms of its immediate success, this work is much less than that of the end-directed action which is commanded by reason. Because neither its end nor its means are determined by rational considerations, it is always in danger of never realizing anything. But perhaps in opposition to the end-directed act, practical realization is not a decisive consideration in relation to an evaluation of love's activity. Even if success be denied it, the power of love, which is actualized in the work of love, is not lost or destroyed, but blooms in another area. Precisely because practical aims serve only as a cause for the manifestation of the work of love, it can continue its activity even if it does not reach its goal. The power of love which is implanted in the deed finds fallow ground in unexpected places, and exerts an unforeseen influence.[80] Because of this abundant potency of the work of love, Rosenzweig assigns it the most elevated of all possible tasks—to bring about the redemption of the world.

We have already mentioned that, according to Rosenzweig, the redemption of the world rests upon—or reaches its first stage with—the binding together of man and God, and that here the initiating power comes from man. This dynamism is the power of love, which is aroused in man, the beloved of God, and bursts forth and influences the entire world. Its redemptive power is easily understood in relation to the existence of man in the world, and in relation to human associations, such as the family and the state, which are also products of the world. These are not the creations of love, but can be watered and fructified by it.

An example of this, to which Rosenzweig attaches great importance, is marriage. According to its biological basis as a sexual relation, as well as its legal form, marriage is first of all an association completely within the world, but it can be filled with love and become a human relationship of an entirely different type. As long as he is untouched by the divine love, man becomes aware of his isolation precisely through the *eros*. But after the birth of such love, this natural association can be joined with the communion of love and will become a complete unity, bringing about the greatest degree of closeness that is possible for human beings. Similarly, love can penetrate into the obligatory relationships between people, in the midst of their larger associations, and although the original character of these relationships remains in force, love can forge relations of the type specific to love between people, and can arouse new powers within men. Human redemption is the strengthening of these powers to their highest degree, the expansion and extension of the power of love to every realm of human life.[81] But when Rosenzweig speaks of the redemption of the world, he refers not only to the redemption of the human world, but to the world as a whole, whose redemption, too, will come about through love. The primary presupposition of such a redemption is his vitalistic conception of the world. The world is not alive at every place *in actu,* but it is everywhere the bearer of the possibility of life, and it is the task of love to make this possibility into an actuality. By it, the sleeping life of the world is aroused, and in contrast to its beginning, when there were only isolated islands of life, the world becomes more and more alive.[82]

But the vitalistic conception, taken in itself, is not enough to explain the redemption of the world. In order that the world might be aroused to life through the activity of love, the world must not only be alive, but ensouled, or at least contain the possibility for such ensoulment. That Rosenzweig thinks of some such possibility, without explicitly stating it, can be determined from his description of the world (insofar as we cognize it without involving a relation of faith) where he labels the reign of law in the world as its inner logos. Thus the world as a whole has a spiritual cause which is open to the influence of the activity of love, just as was true for Schelling and Hegel, for whom spirit lay asleep in nature, and slowly developed into self-consciousness. But the way in which the redemption of the world is realized also points up Rosenzweig's fundamental opposition to the monistic idealism of Schelling and Hegel. The growth of life in the world is not achieved by spirit's slow growth of self-consciousness through its becoming human consciousness, and finally becoming (as in Hegel) the Absolute Spirit. In order that the world be awakened to life and ensoulment, there is a necessity for the work of man, who is different from the world and who stands against it. That the world and man can influence one another is possible only because both originate in God, and the love which God caused to grow in the heart of man still operates in the world, and brings the dormant life of the world into development.[83]

Thus Rosenzweig's idea of redemption is founded completely on his faith in a personal God, Creator of the world, and God of love. But this personal religiosity has a distinctive coloration in that the world has an impersonal spiritual content from its very beginning, and this gives it the possibility of being activated by love, and thereby being brought to redemption. For the Scriptures and for the Talmud, the world was created only for the sake of man, and redemption of the world takes place solely for his sake, and only for him is the world renewed. For Rosenzweig, the world has an independent relationship to God, which stands next to the love relation of God to man. This matter becomes plainer when we reach the second stage of redemption, which is directly caused by God, and whose purpose it is to bind the world and man together into unity. Here, too, the world and man attain unity with God through the same path. Rosenzweig's religiosity, which is ultimately completely theistic, is joined to this feeling for the world, which in itself would lead to pantheism, and his religious metaphysics seeks to give the world a place in theistic religion.

Up to this point, the doctrine of Rosenzweig is truly, as he claims, independent of the authority of historical religion and of previous philosophy. His religion is based upon the personal experience of faith, and not on historical evidence. When he reinforces his words by quoting Scripture, he does this only to show that his judgment agrees with that of Holy Writ, and not in order thereby to validate his doctrine. Only one chapter in the last book of *The Star of Redemption* deals specifically with Judaism, and is formulated explicitly within its realm. But in this transition to historical religion, he does not limit himself to a consideration of Judaism alone. Next to the chapter on Judaism, there stands, as was mentioned previously, a chapter on Christianity, and although he is in complete agreement with Judaism, he conceives of both of them as twin forms of religious life, with equal merit and stature. They rest on the same foundations. For his doctrine of God and his relation to man and the world, he relies on both Christian and Jewish sources. He thinks of his doctrine as the shared truth of both religions, and only after this foundation has been laid do the two faiths part company. Because he is not interested in presenting the doctrinal content of Judaism and Christianity, but in viewing them as the two forms of religious life and of religious community—and thus to understand the differences between the two—is it possible that within *The Star of Redemption* there is one truth, which is merely expressed in different forms of life and thus can be expressed adequately in other ideas of faith as well. But his real opinion, which is clearly emphasized in his essay *The New Thinking*, is that the differences between the two faiths extend also to the content of their truth.[84] But still he regards them as of equal merit, and takes it as an ultimate fact that truth is given to man only in its divided form; only before the face of God, is truth one.

These statements do not imply a general religious relativism which looks upon the various religions as mere symbols of equal truth-value, truth in its pure content being unattainable by man. He emphatically negates the great religions of India and China, and also that of mysticism; and among the monotheistic religions, he criticizes Islam in a most unfair manner. He grants equal rights only to Judaism and Christianity because they share the ultimate elements of truth, and because through them one can understand that the truth, of necessity, is twofold. In this transition to a consideration of the historical religions, he makes a number of nonphilosophical assumptions, beginning with the concept of historical revelation. Instead of explaining revelation, as he did before, as the experience of divine love which is continually renewed in the soul of the individual, it now becomes the source of Judaism and Christianity. For Judaism, this is plainly evident because the commandment of love—which, according to its definition by Rosenzweig, is completely rooted in the concrete experience of divine love—is later transposed into the law which binds the generations to each other. Similarly, the belief in redemption absorbs the traditional faith in the Messiah, and thus the dogmatic difference between Judaism and Christianity can be explained in the usual fashion—according to the doctrine of the Jews, the Messiah is still to come, and according to Christianity, the Messiah has already come, and will only return in the future.[85] These doctrines, drawn from tradition, do not contradict Rosenzweig's views, which are demonstrated by human faith experiences. But it is impossible to deduce the former from the latter, and they are connected only insofar as they fulfill specific demands arising from Rosenzweig's presuppositions.

As the fulfillment of one of these tasks, we can point to the existence of the Jewish people, and to the Christian church. In order that love, which is the fruit of the individual's experience of God's love, and love for one's neighbor, might have the opportunity of penetrating not only into the existing associations of men, but of bringing into being a community of love, it is necessary that the singular experience of the divine love be extended to the experience of the social group. Judaism and Christianity are both communities of love, based upon the experience of God's love, and they can thus fulfill the other task which flows from the fundamental viewpoint of Rosenzweig, that eternity must enter into the stream of time. The necessary dualism of the two communities is shown by the fact that this task is to be fulfilled in different ways. The eternity of Judaism is the eternity of eternal life, and the eternity of Christianity is the eternity of the eternal way.

The eternal life of the Jews is the life of a people of faith, whose natural basis as a people serves as the carrier for a shared faith and for its embodiment, and the natural connection between the generations is the ground of its eternity.[86] For every community which is not founded on blood ties, eternity can only be a matter of will and of hope; but in the Jews we can see eternity in existence, in the present. But the blood tie, taken in itself, is insufficient. The existence of all peoples is maintained by the order of the generations, but is under the sway of temporality and the permutations of time; the life of the people is continually changing, and its way of life as embodied in custom and in law is renewed in every generation. The peoples of the world live in time, and are thus liable, despite the length of time that they have existed, to cease to be.[87] The length of time that a people has existed cannot be converted into eternity until its existence is lifted above and separated from time. This is true of Israel because along with its "self," its style of life, the Torah, which is binding upon all generations and times, came into being. By means of this, the past, present, and future of the people is one, and Jews exist beyond the changes wrought by time. Israel abandons the vitality which is continually renewed by temporality for the sake of the eternity of its life, which is above time. Israel does not increase with time, but always looks forward in constancy toward the promised redemption.[88]

As opposed to this, the Christian community is not linked to any natural tie, but exists on the basis of faith alone. The Christian church is an association of persons who are bound together by faith in the birth and return of Jesus. Its eternity lies in the fact which is the source of the Christian association—that the Messiah became flesh; and in the fact which forms the end-point of this faith—that the Messiah will return. Both have their source in the eternal existence of a transtemporal God. The Christian brotherhood is spread between these two extreme points. Its way leads it into time, but since its beginning and end are transtemporal, it is an eternal way. It is the same way in every one of its parts, because only the beginning and the end have any value for it. The Christian brotherhood knows at each moment that it walks this path, and thus, it consciously recognizes its own eternity. All that occurs in time is valueless for the Christian; he walks through time without being a part of time or being subject to its changes.[89] Along this path Christianity penetrates the nations of the world, but because of its being a community of faith without any natural ties, it can include them all. The Jewish people of God can live its eternal life when it is separate from the nations of the world; only the influences which emanate from it can penetrate into the peoples of the world. Christianity is not only prepared to absorb the nations, but as a church to which has been given the eternal way, it also has the mission to penetrate and enter the entire world of paganism and convert it into a Christian world.

Proselytizing is of the essence of Christianity, just as it is of no importance, and foreign to Judaism.[90] This transformation from paganism to Christianity, through which the pagan world has passed, is true of each and every Christian. He is not a Christian through birth, but a pagan, who must be renewed in order to become a Christian; and he can reach his goal only through battling against his natural essence. The reverse is true of the Jew: he is a Jew at birth. Whoever belongs to the people of God at birth, is thus confirmed as a Jew, and has the ability to take part in the eternal life of the divine people. The Jew betrays his own essence when he denies his faith, his life, and his doctrine of being a part of a Chosen People.[91] This contrast is developed with regard to the opposing views of Judaism and Christianity concerning the nature of man and the way which leads to union with God. According to Judaism, man is ready for union with God by reason of his human essence; he needs no renewal in order to participate in eternal life, which God has planted in his people. According to Christianity, the nature of man, which was depraved by original sin, must be changed by the grace of God so that man may be able to be united with God. According to Rosenzweig, the Jewish view is congenial to the Jew, the Christian to the Christian. If we compare this to his doctrine of the conversion which man undergoes under the influence of divine love, we see that this change occurs with the election of Israel once and forever, and that no individual Jew need undergo it again.[92] On the other hand, for the Christian this constitutes a break with human nature, a much deeper separation than appears at first glance from Rosenzweig's previous doctrine.

In other places and other ways, there are also obvious differences between Judaism and Christianity, which stem from the different essences of the two communities. Rosenzweig sees a characteristic difference between the two in the different ways they relate themselves to aspects of God, man, and the world. For both Judaism and Christianity, God is the God of love and justice, the God of creation to whom we are subject, and the God of revelation to whom we are thankful. But in Judaism, these various aspects of God are not distinct from each other. As the God of justice and the God of love, he is the same God; the Jew turns at the same moment to both aspects of his essence and calls upon him as King and Father.[93] This is impossible for the Christian; when he turns toward the justice of God, there is no longer any place in his consciousness for the idea of the divine love, and vice versa, he has, as Rosenzweig expresses it in a different context, one relationship to God as Father, and another relation to him as "son."[94] The same difference is true of similar aspects which are rooted in the essence of man and the essence of the world. Rosenzweig sees the root of this difference in that Judaism, defined as the community of eternal life which has all of its substance locked up within itself, intermixes in its inwardness all of these various aspects, while Christianity, insofar as it is the community of the eternal way, orients itself toward the love and justice of God in distinct ways; thus its path into the world is split in two: the way of the state and the way of the church.[95]

This dichotomy is, of course, correct, and leads quite deeply into the very heart of the two religions; but the explanation of Rosenzweig is not decisive. The differing ways in which the faiths orient themselves toward aspects of God's essence cannot be explained sociologically, but the roots lie in the primary differences of the life of faith. Of necessity, one must distinguish the two faiths, just as Rosenzweig tried to do, in relation to the other high religions, and there is no reason for the unwarranted assumption of a necessary primary split in fundamental truth. In this decisive matter of the relation of the two faiths, we cannot agree with him. His view allows him to conceive Christianity in a more positive way than any in Jewish religious traditional literature, and to turn toward it in inner love without any apologetic tendencies. The value of his conclusions remains unimpaired, even if we conceive of the relationship between the two faiths differently. After Rosenzweig, it is no longer sufficient simply to line up the doctrines of Judaism against those of Christianity; one must search out their sources in religious experience and in the religious life.

Because Rosenzweig places at the center of his attention not the doctrines of Israel, but the life of Israel (he is not interested in portraying the faith of Israel *per se*, except in terms of its embodiment in life-forms that are unique), he reaches novel and insightful conclusions. The novelty of his contribution does not consist in the discovery of new facts, but in the interpretation of the significance of what was already known. An important example of this is the description he gives of the uniqueness of *Knesseth Yisrael*, the ecclesia of Israel. For the Jewish consciousness, as already expressed in Scripture, the nation is independent of all external causality, such as land and language. According to the chronicles of the people, its progenitors did not live in the land of Israel from the beginning, such as other peoples deem to be true of themselves, but wandered and reached the land by reason of the commandment of the Lord, and became a people not in its own land, but in Egypt. Even in its own land, it must look upon itself as a sojourner. It is clear to Israel when it settles upon the land, that God will exile it from there, but that, nevertheless, he will continue to be its God even in exile. In all this it is clear that the people is a people only by reason of its blood ties, and that these ties are also the basis for its communion with God. Thus, its will to survive is directed toward the people as such, and this peoplehood does not cease even when the nation loses its ancestral homelands and is forced to speak a foreign language in a strange land.[96]

Unlike other nations, the Jewish nation was able to exist without a common land and a common language, because from its very beginning as a people, it did not make the peoplehood of Israel dependent upon these external factors. But this conception of the uniqueness of the Jewish people can also account for the profound relation of Israel to its land and to its language. Although, in order to be a people, Israel is not dependent upon these concrete binding factors, it can never cease thinking of the land as its land, and of the language as its language, without becoming untrue to itself. They continue to be the people's possession as a *holy* land and a *holy* tongue, and thus they become more truly the possession of the people than if they were the concrete, binding factors. The continuance of their status as a holy tongue and a holy land is essential for the continuance of the existence of the people Israel in a strange land. Because the language is in principle its language, and the land is in principle its land, no other land can ever be its homeland, no other tongue can be its tongue. The Jewish people is bound by other tongues and lands in its secular life, but not in its inner life. This dualism between its true life and its everyday secular life is felt especially in regard to language, and traces of it are evident in the spiritual conduct of the entire Jewish people. Since no other language can embrace the whole of his existence, since no other language which he speaks day by day can be in principle his tongue, the Jew no longer has the simplicity and wholeness of soul which characterizes others. The language exists outside his everyday life, and that which is the essence of his true existence fills only a circumscribed area of his being.[97]

Rosenzweig relates these facts to his conception of the eternal people. That Israel is independent in the chosenness of its land and language springs from its character as a world people. Israel cannot affirm its eternity without concomitant lack of ties to any external conditions. But Rosenzweig takes one step beyond this. Israel will be a completely eternal people only when it will be free of the ever-changing conditions of political life, and when its language shall be free of the temporal developments which are the heritage of other languages. Only as a holy land and a holy language, can land and language be included in the eternal existence of the people. Instead of losing its distinctiveness as an eternal people in exile, its existence is there brought to its highest point.

That exilic Judaism embodies the idea of the eternal people in all of its purity is the conclusion of his view of the relation of Israel to history. As an eternal people, Israel is beyond history, and the comings and goings of the historical peoples, their battles, their rise and fall, do not affect Israel. Despite the great influence which these latter have upon the external conditions of life of the Jewish people, despite the damage which the flux of political circumstance exerts on the Jewish people, in its inmost heart, Israel has no part in them. The world is not its world, and what occurs in the world is of little value for Israel's inner life. It is all the same to Israel whether nations appear or disappear; for Judaism, it is always the same world in which nothing basically changes from the day it was created even unto the days of the Messiah. Within this world it has but one task, one mission to fulfill: to transmit, from one generation to the next, the *style* of life that was given to it at the time of its birth, and to look forward with hope and confidence toward the messianic redemption.[98]

This description is quite correct for pre-emancipation Judaism, and Rosenzweig grasps this stance of Judaism toward history and political life with great acuteness. The Judaism of those times looked upon itself as outside the world of the nations; it was not responsible for that world, which had to arrange its affairs as best it could. In the emancipation period, however, a change was effected as Jews became citizens of the states in which they lived. But for Rosenzweig, the above description is true not only of a specific period of Jewish history—the pre-emancipation period—but of Judaism in general, for according to its essence as an eternal people, Judaism lives outside the sphere of history. The participation of the Jews in the political life of European states from emancipation times onward, which Rosenzweig does not protest against, has no effect on the proper relation of Judaism toward history. Even when the Jews do take part in the political life of other people, they essentially, as Jews, belong to an eternal people, the ecclesia of Israel, which continues to stand outside the circle of the nations and their history.

Still more important, Rosenzweig's description also applies to ancient Israel. Even in the days of its political flourishing, Israel was a nation that "dwelt alone," separate from the nations, though at the height of its political life, this distance was small.[99] Future times can only embody in greater purity that which was concealed in the life of Israel from its very beginning. Rosenzweig relegates the battles which Israel fought in order to conquer its land to the legendary past.[100] In his perspective, one clearly sees Israel differentiate itself more and more from the history of the nations, and especially from their political history, in accordance with its essence as an eternal people.

Rosenzweig's view, that the essence of Judaism as an eternal people is to be separate from state and history, flows from his fundamental attitude toward the state. The state attempts, through its laws and ordinances, to mold peoples over a long period of time, but insofar as the nations are in the stream of development, it must fashion them again and again in the image of its laws. The laws of the state change continually, just as does the life which they attempt to subdue. The state attempts to materialize its law through sovereignty and a monopoly of force; war and revolution are the only things which it recognizes.[101] These ordinances of the state, which continually wrestle with the stream of life, stand opposed to the true eternity of the eternal people, just as the life of the state, which is based on brute force, is opposed to the life of the eternal people, which is based on love. Like the world, the state can absorb the deeds of love, but in itself it is essentially foreign to such works. Similarly, the state is foreign to the eternal people, whose bond of association is love and a transtemporal life. Even at the height of its political affluence, the political existence of Israel was only externally bound to its character as an eternal people. Although the Torah contains political and legal regulations, the state does not serve as the proper area in which Israel can maintain its existence as an eternal people. Israel cannot enter this sphere accompanied by its essence, even though for external historical conditions it must have a temporary political life.

Rosenzweig differs here from the usual conception, according to which it is precisely this connection between the ethic of law and the ethic of love that defines the character of Judaism. In his doctrine of Israel as an eternal people, emphasizing the popular character of the community of Israel but denying any political connotation to this term, he is far removed from the tendency of contemporary Judaism. Nevertheless, and perhaps because of this, he had a decisive influence in many Jewish circles. His original and striking

conception of Judaism, which grasped the spirit of Judaism as exemplified in the entire range of Jewish life as a single whole, offered
a new way to look at Judaism. Although he left no school behind
him, in the formal sense of the term, he found great response from
Jews in the most diverse circles, who learned from him not only
theory, but rallied around him in his desire to renew Jewish life.
As against this, his ideas have not received systematic clarification,
either from a general philosophical or from a Jewish viewpoint,
because, with the Nazi destruction of European—and especially German—Jewry (which since the days of Mendelssohn had been the
focal point of Jewish religious philosophy), no new generation remained to work out the philosophy. There are some thinkers of the
past generation who are occupied with it, but they have no disciples. Jewish philosophy, which had been renewed in the last decades of the nineteenth century, has now reached its nadir. If it once
more arises to continue its work, it will develop under entirely new
conditions.

Jewish existence, which has undergone a fundamental change,
today places before Jewish philosophy a completely new set of problems. In addition, the philosophy of our generation is not what it
once was; indeed, from its present ambiguous situation, one cannot
discern in what direction it will turn. But no matter what course it
takes, there will still exist a connection with the tradition of Jewish
philosophy. In opposition to the progress and continual developmental change of the sciences, the history of philosophy is replete with
crises and controversies in which new ideas are constantly opposing
the thought of past ages. Even within modern philosophy, the major
doctrines of previous generations continue to play their role and
have an effect, and it remains true that the "revolutionaries" are
consciously or unconsciously continuing lines of thought of the tradition of philosophy, which now are grasped more profoundly or
have new conclusions drawn from them.

Philosophy maintains, through crises and polemics, a unique type
of continuity. A striking testimony to this is the development of
Jewish philosophy, which maintains its linkage with the past despite
the abyss which divides the Middle Ages from modern times. The
selfsame problems are reformulated in the thought of the Middle
Ages and in the thought of modernity; and the new Jewish philosophy has, in all its trends, learned from the solutions offered to these
problems by the great philosophers of our past, from Maimonides

on the one hand, to Judah Halevi on the other. This connection is felt no less in the development of modern Jewish philosophy itself, despite the differences and oppositions among the various schools and trends. Nor will the results of this great effort of thought be wasted for the Jewish philosophy of the future.

Bibliography

ABBREVIATIONS

HUCA	Hebrew Union College Annual, Cincinnati
JQR	Jewish Quarterly Review, Philadelphia
MGWJ	Monatsschrift für Geschichte und Wissenschaft des Judentums
PAAJR	Proceedings of the American Academy for Jewish Research
RÉJ	Revue des Études Juives

I have attempted to expand and correct the bibliographies contained in the original German and later Hebrew versions. Without the invaluable aid of Fritz Rothschild, of The Jewish Theological Seminary of America, the listing of new editions of the sources and secondary materials would have remained incomplete.

I FUNDAMENTALS AND FIRST INFLUENCES

BAER, YITZHAK. *Yisrael ba-amim: eeyoonim b'toledot y'mai ha-bayit hasheni oo-t'koofat ha-mishna, oo-v'yesod ha-halaka v'ha-emunah.* Jerusalem, 1947.

BONSIRVEN, J. *Exégèse rabbinique et exégèse paulinienne.* Paris, 1938.

———. *Le judaïsme palestinien au temps du Jesus Christ. Sa théologie.* 2 vols. Paris, 1935.

———.*Palestinian Judaism in the Time of Jesus Christ.* New York: Holt, Rinehart and Winston, Inc., 1964.

BREHIER, E. *Les idées philosophiques et religieuses de Philon d'Alexandrie.* 2ème ed. Paris, 1925.

CHAJES, Z. H. *The Student's Guide through the Talmud.* Translated by J. Schachter. 2d ed. New York, 1960.

EFROS, ISRAEL. *Ha-pilosofia ha-yehudit ha-atika.* Jerusalem, 1959.

FINKELSTEIN, LOUIS. (ed.). *The Jews: Their History, Culture and Religion.* 3d ed. New York: Harper & Row, Publishers, 1960.

———. *The Pharisees, the Sociological Background of their Faith.* Philadelphia, 1938.

FREUDENTHAL, J. *Hellenistische Studien.* 2 vols. Breslau, 1874-1875.

GINZBERG, LOUIS. *Legends of the Bible.* Introduction by Shalom Spiegel. New York, 1956.

———. *On Jewish Law and Lore.* Philadelphia, 1955.

GUTTMANN, JACOB. *Ha-safrut ha-yehudit ha-hellenisteet: ha-yahadut v'ha-helleneeyut leefnai tekoofat ha-hashmonaim.* Jerusalem, 1958.

HEINEMANN, I. *Philons griechische und jüdische Bildung.* Breslau, 1932.

HEINISCH, P. *Griechische Philosophie im Alten Testament.* Münster, 1913–1914.

HESCHEL, A. J. *Torah min ha-shamayim b'espekoolaria shel ha-yahadut.* 2 vols. London, 1962.

———. *Die Prophetie.* Cracow, 1936.

HÖLSCHER, G. *Geschichte der israelitischen und jüdischen Religion.* Giessen, 1922.

JOËL, M. *Blicke in die Religionsgeschichte zu Anfang des zweiten christlichen Jahrhunderts.* 2 vols. Breslau, 1932.

KADUSHIN, MAX. *The Rabbinic Mind.* New York, 1952.

———. *The Theology of Seder Eliahu: A Study in Organic Thinking.* New York, 1932.

KAUFMANN, YEHEZKEL. *The Religion of Israel: From its Beginnings to the Babylonian Exile.* Translated and abridged by Moshe Greenberg. Chicago, 1959.

———. *Toledot ha-emunah ha-yisraelit me-y'mai kedem ad sof bayit sheni.* 8 vols. Tel Aviv, 1937–1958.

LEISEGANG, H. *Der heilige Geist, das Wesen und Werden der mystisch-intuitiven Erkenntnis in der Philosophie der Griechen.* Leipzig, 1959.

LEWY, HANS (ed.). *Philo.* Philosophia Judaica. Oxford, 1946.

MEYER, R. *Hellenistisches in der rabbinischen Anthropologie.* Stuttgart, 1937.

MONTEFIORE, C. G., and H. LOEWE. *A Rabbinic Anthology.* London, 1938.

MOORE, G. F. *Judaism in the First Centuries of the Christian Era.* 3 vols. Cambridge (Mass.), 1927.

SCHECHTER, S. *Some Aspects of Rabbinic Theology.* London, 1909. Reprinted, paperback, Meridian-Jewish Publication Society, 1961.

SCHOLEM, G. *Jewish Gnosticism, Merkabah Mysticism and Talmudic Tradition.* New York, 1960.

SCHURER, E. *A History of the Jewish People in the Time of Jesus.* Edited and introduced by N. N. Glatzer. New York, 1961.

SCHWARZ, LEO (ed.). *Great Ages and Ideas of the Jewish People.* New York, 1956.

TCHERIKOVER, V. *Hellenistic Civilization and the Jews.* Philadelphia, Jerusalem, 1959.

WEBER, M. *Gesammelte Aufsätze zur Religions-soziologie.* Vol. III: *Das antike Judentum.* Translated into English under the title *Ancient Judaism.* Glencoe, Illinois: The Free Press of Glencoe, 1952.

WOLFSON, H. A. *Philo, Foundations of Religious Philosophy in Judaism, Christianity, and Islam.* Cambridge (Mass.), 1947.

ZELLER, E. *Die Philosophie der Griechen.* Vol. III. Leipzig, 1903.

II JEWISH RELIGIOUS PHILOSOPHY IN THE MIDDLE AGES

1 The Rise of Jewish Philosophy in the Islamic World

SOURCES

HEINEMANN, I. *Ta-amai ha-mitzvot b'safrut yisrael.* 2 vols. Jerusalem, 1954–1956.

KLATZKIN, J. *Otsar ha-munahim ha-pilosofeyeem v'antologia pilosofit.* 5 vols. Berlin, 1926–1934.

NEUMARK, D. *Toledot ha-pilosofia b'yisrael.* Vol. I: Warsaw, 1921. Vol. II: Philadelphia, 1928.

SCHOLEM, G. *Reshit ha-kabbala.* Jerusalem, 1948.

LITERATURE

ALTMANN, ALEXANDER. "The Delphic Maxim in Medieval Islam and Judaism," *Biblical and Other Studies.* Edited by A. Altmann. Cambridge (Mass.), 1963. Pp. 196–233.

BACHER, W. *Die Bibelexegese der jüdischen Religionsphilosophie des Mittelalters vor Maimuni.* Budapest, 1892.

BLOCH, PH. *Die Geschichte der Entwicklung der Kabbala und der jüdischen Religionsphilosophie.* Trier, 1895.

EFROS, I. "The Problem of Space in Jewish Medieval Philosophy," *JQR*, n.s., VI (1916), 495–554; VII (1916), 61–87, 223–251.

EISLER, M. *Vorlesungen über jüdische Philosophie des Mittelalters.* 3 Teile. Vienna, 1870–1884.

GUTTMANN, JACOB. *Die Scholastik des 13. Jahrhunderts in ihren Beziehungen zum Judentum und jüdischer Literatur.* Breslau, 1902.

GUTTMANN, JULIUS. *Dat oo-mada.* Jerusalem, 1956.

———. *Die Philosophie des Judentums.* Munich, 1933.

———. "Religion und Wissenschaft im mittelalterlichen und modernen Denken." *Festschrift zum 50jährigen Bestehen der Hochschule für die Wissenschaft des Judentums in Berlin.* Berlin, 1922.

HEINEMANN, I. *Die Lehre von der Zweckbestimmung des Menschen im griechisch-römischen Altertum und im jüdischen Mittelalter.* Breslau, 1926.

HOROVITZ, S. *Die Psychologie der jüdischen Religionsphilosophie des Mittelalters von Saadia bis Maimuni.* 4 Teile. Breslau, 1898–1912.

HUSIK, I. *A History of Medieval Jewish Philosophy.* 2 vols. New York, 1930.

———. *Philosophical Essays.* Edited by M. C. Nahm and L. Strauss. Oxford, 1952.

KAUFMANN, D. *Geschichte der Attributenlehre in der jüdischen Religionsphilosophie von Saadja bis Maimuni.* Gotha, 1877.

———. *Die Sinne, Beiträge zur Geschichte der Psychologie im Mittelalter.* Budapest, 1884.

KRAUS, P. "Beiträge zur Islamischen Ketzergeschichte," *Rivista degli studi orientali,* XIV.

LEWY, HANS (ed.), *et al. Three Jewish Philosophers.* (Selections from Philo, Saadya, Jehuda Halevi.) Philadelphia, 1960. New York: Meridian Books, 1960.

MUNK, S. *Mélanges de philosophie juive et arabe.* Paris, 1859.

NEMOY, L. "Al Quirquisani's Account of the Jewish Sects and Christianity." *HUCA,* VII (1930).

NEUMARK, D. *Geschichte der jüdischen Philosophie des Mittelalters nach Problemen dargestellt.* Vols. I; II, 1; II, 2. Berlin, 1907–1928.

SCHOLEM, G. *Major Trends in Jewish Mysticism.* New York, 1946.

STEINSCHNEIDER, M. *Die arabische Literatur der Juden.* Frankfurt a. M., 1902.

———. *Die hebräischen Übersetzungen des Mittelalters.* Berlin, 1893.

VAJDA, G. *Introduction à la pensée juive du moyen age.* Paris, 1947.

WOLFSON, H. A. "The Double Faith Theory in Clement, Saadia, Averroës and St. Thomas, and its Origin in Aristotle and the Stoics," *JQR*, n.s., XXXIII (1942–1943), 213–261.

———. "The Internal Sense in Latin, Arabic and Hebrew Philosophical Texts," *Harvard Theological Review,* XXVIII (1935), 69–133.

———. "The Meaning of ex nihilo in the Church Fathers, Arabic and Hebrew Philosophy, and St. Thomas," *Medieval Studies in honor of J. D. M. Ford.* Cambridge (Mass.), 1948. Pp. 355–370.

———. "Notes on Proofs of the Existence of God in Jewish Philosophy," *HUCA,* I (1924), 575–596.

———. "The Problem of the Origin of Matter in Medieval Philosophy," *Proceedings of the Sixth International Congress of Philosophy for 1926.* Pp. 602–608.

2   The Kalam

SOURCES

JUDAH B. BARZILLAI OF BARCELONA. *Commentary on Sefer Yetzirah.* Edited by Solomon Joachim Halberstam, with notes by David Kaufmann. Berlin, 1885.

SAADIA B. JOSEPH (Gaon). *The Book of Beliefs and Opinions.* Translated by S. Rosenblatt. New Haven, 1948.

———. *The Book of Doctrines and Beliefs.* Selections edited by A. Altmann. Oxford, 1946.

———. *Commentaire sur le Sefer Yesira ou livre de la creation par Gaon Saadja de Fayyoum.* Edited and translated by M. Lambert. Paris, 1891.

———. *Kitab al-Amanat w'al I'tiqadat.* Edited by S. Landauer. Leiden, 1880.

———. *Polemics against Hiwi al-Balkhi. . . .* Edited by Israel Davidson. New York, 1915.

———. *Sefer ha-emunot v'hadeot asher hiber R. Saadia b'lishon arav v'he-eteko R. Yehuda ibn Tibbon el lashon ha-kodesh.* Constantinople, 1861.

———. *Sifrei R. Saadia Gaon.* Edited by J. Derenbourg and M. Lambert. 5 vols. Paris, 1849–1893.

———. *Teshuvot R. Saadia Gaon al sh'elot Hiwi ha-balki.* Introduction and notes by Abraham Poznanski. Warsaw, 1916.

LITERATURE

ALTMANN, A. "Saadya's Conception of the Law," *Bulletin of the John Rylands Library,* XXVIII (Manchester, 1944), 320–329.

———. "Saadya's Theory of Revelation, its Origin and Background," *Saadya Studies* (Manchester, 1953), pp. 4–25.

DIESENDRUCK, Z. "Saadya's Formulation of the Time Argument for Creation," *Jewish Studies in Memory of G. A. Kohut.* New York, 1935.

EFROS, I. "Saadya's Second Theory of Creation in its Relation to Pythagoreanism and Platonism," *Louis Ginzberg Memorial Volume.* New York, 1945. English section, pp. 133–142.

———. "Saadya's Theory of Knowledge," *JQR,* n.s., XXXIII (1942–1943), 133–170.

FRANKL, P. F. *Ein mu'tazilitischer Kalam aus dem 10. Jahrhundert.* Vienna, 1872.

GUTTMANN, JACOB. *Die Religionsphilosophie des Saadia.* Göttingen, 1882.

HELLER, O. "La version arabe et le commentaire des Proverbes du Gaon Saadia." *RÉJ,* XXXVII (1898), 72–85, 226–251.

HESCHEL, A. J. "The Quest for Certainty in Saadia's Philosophy," *JQR,* n.s. XXXIII (1942–1943), 213-264.

———. "Reason and Revelation in Saadia's Philosophy," *JQR,* n.s. XXXIV (1944), 391–408.

HOROVITZ, S. "Über die Bekanntschaft Saadias mit der griechischen Skepsis," *Judaica, Festschrift zu Hermann Cohens 70. Geburtstag.* Berlin, 1912. Pp. 235–252.

MALTER, H. *Saadia Gaon, His Life and Works.* Philadelphia, 1921.

MARMORSTEIN, A. "The Doctrine of Redemption in Saadya's Theological System," *Saadya Studies* (Manchester, 1943), pp. 4–25.

NEUMARK, D. "Saadya's Philosophy," in Neumark's *Essays in Jewish Philosophy* (1929), pp. 145–218.

POZNANSKI, S. A. "Hiwi ha-Balkhi," *Ha-goren,* VII (1908).

RAU, D. "Die Ethik R Saadja's," *MGWJ*, LV (1911), 385–399, 513–530; LVI (1912), 65–79, 181–198.

RAWIDOWICZ, S. "Saadya's Purification of the Idea of God," *Saadya Studies* (Manchester, 1943), pp. 139–165.

ROSENTHAL, E. "Saadya's Exegesis of the Book of Job," *Saadya Studies* (Manchester, 1943), pp. 177–205.

ROSENTHAL, J. "Hiwi al-Balkhi," *JQR*, n.s., XXXVIII (1938), 317–342, 419–430; XXXIX (1939), 79–94.

SCHREINER, M. *Jeshu'a ben Jehuda.* Berlin, 1900.

———. *Der Kalaam in der jüdischen Literatur.* Berlin, 1895.

———. "Zur Geschichte der Polemik zwischen Juden und Mohammedanern," *Zeitschrift der deutsch-morgenl ändischen Gesellschaft*, XLII (Leipzig, 1888).

VAJDA, G. "Le commentaire de Saadia sur le Sefer Yecira," *REJ*, CVI (1941–1945), 64–86.

———. "À propos de l'attitude Religieuse de Hivi al-Balkhi," *RÉJ*, XCIX (1935), 81–91.

———. "Une source arabe de Saadia, le Kitab az-zahra d'Abou Bakr Ibn Dawoud," *RÉJ*, XCII (1932), 146–150.

VENTURA, M. *Le kalam et le peripatisme d'aprés la Kuzari.* Paris, 1934.

———. *La philosophie de Saadia Gaon.* Paris, 1934.

WOLFSON, H. A. "Arabic and Hebrew Terms for Matter and Element with Especial Reference to Saadia," *JQR*, n.s. (1947), pp. 47–61.

———. "Atomism in Saadia," *JQR*, n.s. XXXVII (1946), 107–124.

———. "The Kalam Arguments for Creation in Saadia, Averroës, Maimonides, and St. Thomas," *American Academy for Jewish Research*, II, Saadia Anniversary Volume (New York, 1943), 197–245.

ZUCKER, MOSES (ed.). *Saadia al ha-Torah.* New York, 1961.

3 Neoplatonism

SOURCES

ABRAHAM BAR HIYYA. *Hegyon ha-Nefesh o sefer ha-Musar.* Edited by Yitzak Isaac Freimann. Leipzig, 1860.

———. *Megillath ha-Megalleh.* Edited by A. S. Poznanski. Introduction by Julius Guttmann. Berlin, 1924.

BAHYA IBN PAKUDA. *Kitab al-Hidaya ila Faraid al-Qulub* (Book of the Duties of the Heart). Edited by A. S. Yahuda. Leiden, 1912.

———. *Sefer Torat Hovat ha-levavot.* Translated by Mendel Stern into German, according to the version of Ibn Tibbon. Vienna, 1856.

———. *Sefer Torat hovat ha-levavot.* Edited by A. Zifroni. Jerusalem, 1928.

HEINEMANN, I. (ed.). *Jehuda Halevi.* Philosophia Judaica. Oxford, 1947.

IBN EZRA, ABRAHAM B. MEIR. *Sefer ha-Shem.* Edited by Gabriel Hirsch Lippman. Furth, 1834.

———. *Yesod Morah v'sod Torah.* Edited by Samuel Waxman. Jerusalem, 1931.

IBN GABIROL, SOLOMON (Avencebrol). *Fons vitae, ex Arabico in Latinum translatus.* Edited by C. L. Baumker. Munster, 1895.

———. *Lekutim min ha-sefer Mekor Hayyim.* Collected by R. Shem Tob ibn Falaquera. Edited by S. Moloch. Paris, 1857.

———. *Mekor Hayyim.* Translated from the Latin by Jacob Blubstein. Introduction by Joseph Klausner. Tel Aviv, 1926.

IBN SADDIQ, JOSEPH. *Sefer ha-Olam ha-Qatan.* Edited by Sh. Horovitz. Breslau, 1903.

ISRAELI, ISAAC. *Sefer ha-Yesodot.* Edited by S. Fried. Drohobycz, 1900.

————. *Works.* Translated with comments and an outline of his philosophy by A. Altmann and S. M. Stern. Oxford, 1958.

JUDAH HALEVI. *Le livre du Kuzari par Juda Hallevi.* Translated by M. Ventura. Paris, 1932.

————. *Sefer ha-Kuzari.* Edited by H. Hirschfeld. Leipzig, 1887.

————. *Sefer ha-Kuzari.* Edited by M. Zifronovitz. Warsaw, 1911.

PSEUDO-BAHYA. *Kitab Ma'ani al-Nafs.* Arabic version edited by I. Goldziher. Berlin, 1902.

————. *Sefer Torat ha-nefesh.* Edited by Isaac David Broydé. Paris, 1896.

LITERATURE

ALTMANN, A. "The Climatological Factor in Judas Halevi's Theory of Prophecy," *Melilah,* Vol. I (Manchester, 1944).

BANETH, D. H. "Jehuda Hallewi und Gazali," *Korrespondenzblatt der Akademie für die Wissenschaft des Judentums* (Berlin, 1923–1924), pp. 27–45.

BERGER, E. *Das Problem der Erkenntnis in der Religionsphilosophie Jehuda Hallewis.* Berlin, 1916.

BORISOV, A. "Pseudo-Bahja," *Bulletin de l'academie des sciences de l'U.R.S.S.,* classe des humanités (1929).

DOCTOR, M. *Die Philosophie des Josef (Ibn) Zaddik.* Münster, 1895.

DREYER, K. *Die Religiöse Gedankenwelt des Salomo ibn Gabirol.* Leipzig, 1929.

EPSTEIN, I. "Judah Halevi as Philosopher," *JQR,* n.s., XXV (1935).

EFROS, I. "Some Aspects of Judah Halevi's Mysticism," *PAAJR,* XI (1941).

GUTTMANN, JACOB. *Die Philosophie des Salomon ibn Gabirol.* Göttingen, 1889.

————. *Die philosophischen Lehren des Isaak ben Salomon Israëli.* Münster, 1911.

GUTTMANN, JULIUS. "Das Verhältnis von Religion und Philosophie bei Jehuda Halewi," *Festschrift zu Israel Lewys 70. Geburtstag.* Breslau, 1911. Pp. 327–358.

————. "Zu Gabirols allegorischer Deutung der Erzählung vom Paradies," *MGWJ,* LXXX (1936), 180–184.

————. "Zur Kritik der Offenbarungsreligion in der islamischen und jüdischen Philosophie," *MGWJ,* LXXVIII (1934), 456–464.

HEINEMANN, I. "Temunat ha-historia shel Yehuda Ha-levi," *Tzion,* VII (1944).

HESCHEL, A. J. "Der Begriff der Einheit in der Philosophie Gabirols," *MGWJ,* LXXXII (1938), 89–111.

————. "Der Begriff des Seins in der Philosophie Gabirols," *Festschrift Jakob Freimann.* Berlin, 1937. Pp. 68–77.

————. "Das Wesen der Dinge nach der Lehre Gabirols," *HUCA,* XIV (1939), 359–385.

JOËL, M. "Ibn Gebirols (Avicebrons) Bedeutung für die Geschichte der Philosophie," *MGWJ,* VI (1857); VII (1858).

KAUFMANN, D. *Studien über Salomon ibn Gabirol.* Budapest, 1899.

————. *Die Theologie des Bachja ibn Pakuda.* Vienna, 1874. Also in *Gesammelte Schriften.* Vol. II (Frankfurt, 1910).

MILLAS, J. M. *Selomo ibn Gebirol como poeta y filosofo.* Madrid, Barcelona, 1945.

NEUMARK, D. "Jehuda Hallevi's Philosophy in its Principles," in *Essays in Jewish Philosophy* (1929), pp. 219–300.

ROSIN, D. "The Ethics of Solomon Ibn Gabirol, *JQR*, n.s., (1891), pp. 159–181.

———. "Die Religionsphilosophie Abraham ibn Esras," *MGWJ*, XLII (1898); XLIII (1899).

STITSKIN, L. D. *Judaism as a Philosophy: The Philosophy of Abraham bar Hiyya.* New York, 1961.

STRAUSS, L. "The Law of Reason in the Kuzari," *PAAJR*, XIII (1943).

VAJDA, G. "Les idées théologiques et philosophiques d'Abraham ben Hiyya," *Archives d'histoire doctrinale et litteraire du moyen age*, XV (1946).

———. "La philosophie et la théologie de Joseph ibn Zaddiq," *Archives d'histoire doctrinale et litteraire du moyen age* (1949).

WITTMANN, M. *Zur Stellung Avencebrols (Ibn Gebirols) im Entwicklungsgang der arabischen Philosophie.* Münster, 1905.

WOLFSON, H. A. "Halevi and Maimonides on Design, Chance and Necessity," *PAAJR*, XI (1941), 105–163.

———. "Halevi and Maimonides on Prophecy," *JQR*, n.s., XXXII (1942), 345–370; XXXIII (1942), 49–82.

———. "The Platonic, Aristotelian, and Stoic Theories of Creation in Halevi and Maimonides," *Essays in honor of J. H. Hertz.* London, 1942. Pp. 427–442.

ZAMORA, I. R. *Judah Halevi; Kovetz mehkarim v'ha-arakhot.* Tel Aviv, 1950.

4 Aristotelianism and Its Opponents

SOURCES

BEN GERSON, LEVI (Gersonides). *Sefer Milhamot Adonai.* Leipzig, 1866.

CRESCAS, HASDAI. *Or Adonai.* Johannesburg, 1861.

HILLEL BEN SAMUEL. *Tagmuley ha-Nefesh oo-perush 25 hakdamot shel ha-Moreh.* Edited by Halberstam. Leiden, 1888.

IBN DAUD, ABRAHAM. *Sefer ha-Emunah ha-Ramah.* Edited by Samson Weill. Frankfurt a. M., 1852.

KASPI, JOSEPH. *Amooday kesef oo-maskiyot kesef.* Two commentaries on Maimonides' Guide. Edited by Sh. Werbluner. Frankfurt a. M., 1848.

KELLERMANN, B. *Die Kämpfe Gottes.* German translation of Maimonides' treatises 1-4. 2 vols. Berlin, 1914–1916.

MAIMONIDES, MOSES. *Guide for the Perplexed.* An abridged edition with introduction and commentary by Julius Guttmann. London, 1952.

———. *Iggeret Teman. Epistle to Yemen.* Edited with introduction and notes by Abraham Halkin. English translation by Boaz Cohen. New York: American Academy for Jewish Research, 1952.

———. *Iggrot ha-Rambam* (Maimonides' Letters). Edited by D. H. Baneth. Jerusalem, 1950.

———. *Ma-amar Tehiyyat ha-Maytim.* Maimonides' Treatise on Resurrection. Original Arabic and Samuel ibn Tibbon's Hebrew translation. Edited by Joshua Finkel. New York, 1938.

———. *Milot ha-Higayyon.* Maimonides' Treatise on Logic. Original Arabic and three Hebrew translations. Edited by Israel Efros. New York, 1938.

———. *Moreh Nebukhim.* with two commentaries, one by R. Moses Narboni, the other entitled "Givat ha-Moreh." Vienna, 1828.

———. *Moreh Nebukhim (Dalalat al-Hairin).* Arabic original with French translation and notes. 3 vols. Edited by S. Munk. Paris, 1856-1866.

———. *Moreh Nebukhim.* With three commentaries: Efodi, Shem Tob, and Crescas, and a fourth by the noble Don Isaac Abrabanel. Vilna, 1904.

———. *Moreh Nebukhim*. According to Munk's edition, with variants and indices, edited by I. Joel. Jerusalem, 1931.

———. *Moreh Nebukhim*. With vowel points and a commentary by Yehuda ibn Shmuel. 2 vols. Part I. Tel Aviv, 1935–1938.

———. *Moreh Nebukhim*. Text with vowel points. Edited by Yehuda ibn Shmuel. Jerusalem, 1947.

LITERATURE

ADLERBAUM, N. *A study of Gersonides in his Proper Perspective*. New York, 1926.

ALTMANN, A. "Das Verhältnis Maimunis zur jüdischen Mystik," *MGWJ*, LXXX (1936).

BACHER, W. *Die Bibelexegese Moses Maimunis*. Budapest, 1896.

BACHER, W., M. BRANN, *et al. Moses ben Maimon, sein Leben, seine Werke und sein Einfluss*. Leipzig, 1908, 1914. In this volume the following essays appear: Ph. Bloch. "Charakteristik und Inhaltsangabe des Moreh Nebuchim"; H. Cohen. "Charakteristik der Ethik Maimonis"; Jacob Guttmann. "Der Einfluss der maimonidischen Philosophie auf das christliche Abendland"; Jacob Guttmann. "Die Beziehungen der Religionsphilosophie des Maimonides zu den Lehren seiner jüdischen Vorgänger."

BAECK, L. "Zur Charakteristik des Levi ben Abraham ben Chajiim," *MGWJ*, XLIV (1900).

BAER, Y. "Sefer Minhat Kanaut shel Abner mi-Burgos, v'hash-paato al Hasdai Crescas," *Tarbiz*, XI (1940).

BAMBERGER, F. *Das System des Maimonides: eine Analyse des More Nebuchim vom Gottesbegriffe aus*. Berlin, 1935.

BECKER, J. *Mishnato ha-pilosofit shel ha-Rambam*. Tel Aviv, 1956.

BLOCH, PH. *Die Willensfreiheit von Chasdai Kreskas*. Munich, 1879.

BOKSER, B. Z. *The Legacy of Maimonides*. New York, 1950.

BRÜLL, N. "Die Polemik für und gegen Maimuni im dreizehnten Jahrhundert," *Jahrbücher für jüdische Geschichte und Literatur*, IV (1879), 1–33.

DIESENDRUCK, Z. "Maimonides' Lehre von der Prophetie," *Jewish Studies in Memory of Israel Abrahams*. New York, 1927.

———. "Die Teleologie bei Maimonides," *HUCA*, V (Cincinnati, 1928).

EFROS, I. *Philosophical Terms in the Moreh Nebukhim*. New York, 1924.

FACKENHEIM, E. "The Possibility of the Universe in al-Farab, Ibn Sina and Maimonides," *PAAJR*, XVI (1947), 39–70.

GOLDBERG, D. *Maimonides' Kritik einer Glaubenslehre*. Vienna, 1935.

GUTTMANN, JACOB. *Die Religionsphilosophie des Abraham ibn Daud*. Göttingen, 1879.

GUTTMANN, JULIUS. "Chasdai Creskas als Kritiker der aristotelischen Physik," *Festschrift zum 70. Geburtstag Jacob Guttmanns*. Leipzig, 1915. Pp. 28–54.

———. "Levi ben Gersons Theorie des Begriffs." *Festschrift zum 75. jährigen Bestehung des Jüd. Theol. Seminars*, II (Breslau, 1929), 131–149.

———. "Das Problem der Willensfreiheit bei Hasdai Creskas und den islamischen Aristoteliker," *Jewish Studies in Memory of G. A. Kohut*. New York, 1935. Pp. 326–349.

———. *Die religiösen Motive in der Philosophie des Maimonides, Entwicklungsstufen der jüdischen Religion*. Giessen, 1927.

HEINEMANN, I. "Maimuni und die arabischen Einheitslehrer," *MGWJ*, LXXIX (1939).

HESCHEL, A. J. "Ha-he-emeen ha-Rambam sh'zakha l'nvuah?" *Louis Ginzberg Jubilee Volume.* Hebrew section. New York, 1945.

———. *Maimonides Eine Biographie.* Berlin, 1935.

HOFFMANN, E. *Die Liebe zu Gott bei Mose ben Maimon, ein Beitrag zur Geschichte der Religionsphilosophie.* Breslau, 1937.

JOËL, M. *Don Chasdai Creskas' religionsphilosophische Lehren,* Breslau, 1866.

———. "Lewi ben Gerson als religionsphilosoph," *MGWJ,* X (1860), XI (1861).

KARO, J. *Kritische Untersuchungen zu Levi ben Gersons Widerlegung des aristotelischen Zeitbegriffs.* Leipzig, 1935.

LEVY, L. G. *Maimonide.* Paris, 1911.

MAIMON, Y. L. R. *Moshe ben Maimon.* Jerusalem, 1960.

MARX, A. "Texts about Maimonides," *JQR, n.s.* (1935).

NEUBERGER, CH. *Das Wesen des Gesetzes in der Philosophie des Maimonides.* Danzig, 1933.

PINES, S. "Etudes sur Awhad al Zaman Abu'l Barakat al Baghdadi," *RÉJ,* CIII, CIV (1938).

RENAN, ERNEST, and ADOLPH NEUBAUER. *Les écrivains juifs français du XIVᵉ siècle.* Paris, 1893.

———. *Les rabbins français du commencement du quatorzième siècle.* Paris, 1877.

ROHNER, A. *Das Schöpfungsproblem bei Moses Maimonides, Albertus Magnus und Thomas von Aquino.* Münster, 1913.

ROSENBLATT, S. *The Highways to Perfection of Abraham Maimonides.* New York, 1927; Baltimore, 1938.

ROSIN, D. *Die Ethik des Maimonides.* Breslau, 1876.

SARACHEK, I. *Faith and Reason. The Conflict over the Rationalism of Maimonides.* Williamsport, 1935.

SCHEYER, S. B. *Das psychologische System des Maimonides.* Frankfurt a. M., 1945.

SCHORR, O. H. "R. Yitzhak Albalag," *Hehalutz* (1859–1865).

SILVERMAN, D. W. "The Treatment of Biblical Terms in the Philosophies of Maimonides and Spinoza." Unpublished Master's Thesis, The University of Chicago, 1948.

STRAUSS, L. "The Literary Character of the Guide for the Perplexed," *Essays on Maimonides.* Edited by S. Baron. New York, 1941.

———. *Persecution and the Art of Writing.* Glencoe, Illinois, 1952.

———. *Philosophie und Gesetz.* Berlin, 1935.

———. "Quelques remarques sur la science politique de Maimonide et de Farabi," *RÉJ,* C (1936), 1–37.

WAXMAN, M. *The Philosophy of Don Hasdai Crescas.* New York, 1920.

WOLFSON, H. A. "The Amphibolous Terms in Aristotle, Arabic Philosophy and Maimonides," *Harvard Theological Review,* XXXI (1938).

———. "The Aristotelian Predicables and Maimonides' Division of the Attributes," *Essays and Studies in Memory of Linda R. Miller.* New York, 1938. Pp. 201–234.

———. "Crescas on the Problem of Divine Attributes," *JQR, n.s.,* VII (1916), 1–44, 175–221.

———. *Crescas' Critique of Aristotle.* Cambridge (Mass.), 1929.

———. "Maimonides on Negative Attributes," *Louis Ginzberg Jubilee Volume.* New York, 1945.

5 The End and Aftereffects of Medieval Religious Philosophy

SOURCES

ABRABANEL, ISAAC. *Perush l'Moreh Nebukhim.* Vilna, 1904.
————. *Sefer Mif-alot Elohim.* Venezia, 1592.
————. *Sefer Rosh Amanah.* Constantinople, 1505.
ALBO, JOSEPH. *Sefer ha-Ikkarim.* Edited and translated into English by Isaac Husik. Philadelphia, 1930.
————. *Sefer ha-Ikkarim.* Together with commentary *Sharashim v'anafim* of R. Gedaliah ben R. Shlomo. Berlin, 1928.
DEL MEDIGO, ELIJAH. *Sefer Behinat ha-Dat.* Commentary and notes by Isaac Samuel Reggio. Vienna, 1833.
DEL MEDIGO, JOSEPH SOLOMON. *Sefer Elim oo-mayayn ganim.* Amsterdam, 1629.
————. *Sefer Novlot Hokhma.* Basel, 1631.
————. *Sefer Ta-aloomot Hokhma.* Basel, 1629.
DURAN, SIMON BEN ZEMACH. *Ohev Mishpat v'sefer Mishpat Zedek.* Commentaries on the Book of Job. Venezia, 1589.
————. *Sefer Magen Avot.* Livorno, 1763.
EBREO, LEONE. *Dialoghi d'Amore.* Edited by Carl Gebhardt. Heidelberg, 1929.
JOSEPH BEN SHEM TOB. *K'vod Elohim.* Ferrara, 1552.
SHEM TOB BEN JOSEPH (ibn Falaquera). *Reshit Hokhmah. Schemtob ben Josef ibn Falaqueras: Propadeutik der Wissenschaften Reshith Chokmah.* Translated by Moritz David. Berlin, 1902.
————. *Sefer ha-emunot.* Ferrara, 1552.
SPINOZA, B. *Opera.* Edited by Gebhardt. Heidelberg, 1925.
————. *Torat ha-middot.* Translated from the Latin by Jacob Klatzkin. Leipzig, 1924.
————. *Works.* Unabridged Elwes translation. Reprinted New York, 1955.

LITERATURE

BACK, J. *Josef Albos Bedeutung in der Geschichte der jüdischen Religionsphilosophie.* Breslau, 1869.
DE BOER, TJ. *Maimonides en Spinoza, Mededeelingen der Koninglijke Akademie van Wetenschappen.* Amsterdam, 1927.
FEUER, L. S. *Spinoza and the Rise of Liberalism.* Boston, 1958.
FISCHER, K. *Spinozas Leben, Lehre und Werke.* Heidelberg, 1909.
FREUDENTHAL, J. *Spinoza, Leben und Lehre.* Edited by C. Gebhardt. Heidelberg. 1927.
GEBHARDT, C. "Spinoza und der Platonismus," *Chronicon Spinozanarum* I. (The Hague, 1922).
GEIGER, A. *Josef Salomo del Medigo.* Berlin, 1840, 1876.
GUTTMANN, JACOB. "Die Familie Shemtob in ihren Beziehungen zur Philosophie," *MGWJ,* LVII (1913).
————. *Die religionsphilosophichen Lehren des Isaak Abravanel.* Breslau, 1916.
————. "Die Stellung des Simon ben Zemach Duran in der jüdischen Religionsphilosophie," *MGWJ,* LII (1908), LIII (1909).
GUTTMANN, JULIUS. "Elia del Medigos Verhältnis zu Averroës in seinem Bechinat ha-dat," *Jewish Studies in Memory of Israel Abrahams.* New York, 1927.
————. "Spinozas Zusammenhang mit dem Aristotelismus," *Judaica, Festschrift zu Hermann Cohens 70. Geburtstag.* Berlin, 1912.

HEINEMANN, I. "Abravanels Lehre vom Niedergang der Menschheit," *MGWJ*, LXXXII (1938).

HUSIK, I. "Joseph Albo, the Last of the Jewish Medieval Philosophers," *PAAJR* (1930), pp. 61–72.

———. *Juda Messer Leons Commentary on the "vetus logica."* Leyden, 1906.

HYMAN, ARTHUR. "Spinoza's Dogmas of Universal Faith in the Light of Their Medieval Jewish Background," *Biblical and Other Studies.* Edited by A. Altmann. Cambridge, (Mass.), 1963. Pp. 183–196.

JOËL, M. *Spinozas theologisch-politischer Traktat.* Breslau, 1907.

———. *Zur Genesis der Lehre Spinozas.* Breslau, 1871.

KLATZKIN, J. *Barukh Spinoza.* Leipzig, 1923.

MALTER, H. "Shem Tob ben Joseph Palquera," *JQR*, n.s. (1935).

MISSES, J. "Spinoza und die Kabbala," *Zeitschrift für exacte Philosophie*, VIII (1869).

PFLAUM, H. *Die Idee der Liebe; Leone Ebreo, zwei Abhandlungen zur Philosophie der Renaissance.* Heidelberg, 1926.

ROTH, L. *Spinoza, Descartes, Maimonides.* Oxford, 1924.

STEINSCHNEIDER, M. "Josef ben Shemtob's Kommentar zu Averroës' grösserer Abhandlung über die Möglichkeit der Konjunktion," *MGWJ*, XXXII (1883).

STRAUSS, L. "On Abravanel's Philosophical Tendency and Political Teaching." In *Isaac Abravanel.* Edited by J. B. Trend and H. Loewe. Cambridge, 1937.

———. *Die Religionskritik Spinozas als Grundlage seiner Bibelwissenschaft.* Berlin, 1930.

TAENZER, A. *Die Religionsphilosophie Josef Albos nach seinem Werk 'Ikarim' systematisch dargestellt und erläutert.* Frankfurt a. M., 1896.

WIENER, M. "Der Dekalog in Josef Albos dogmatischen System," *Festschrift für Leo Baeck.* Berlin, 1938. Pp. 107–118.

WOLFSON, H. A. *The Philosophy of Spinoza.* Cambridge (Mass.), 1934.

III JEWISH PHILOSOPHY OF RELIGION IN THE MODERN ERA

SOURCES

COHEN, HERMANN. *Der Begriff der Religion im System der Philosophie.* Giessen, 1915.

———. *Ethik des reinen Willens.* 2d ed. Berlin, 1921.

———. *Jüdische Schriften.* Edited by B. Strauss. Introduction by Franz Rosenzweig. Berlin, 1924.

———. *Ketavim al ha-yahadut.* Translated into Hebrew by Zvi Wisilowski. Jerusalem, 1935.

———. *Religion der Vernunft aus den Quellen des Judentums.* 2d ed. Frankfurt a. M., 1929.

FORMSTECHER, S. *Die Religion des Geistes.* Frankfurt a. M., 1841.

HIRSCH, S. *Das System der religiösen Anschauung der Juden und sein Verhältnis zum Heidentum, Christentum und zur absoluten Philosophie.* Vol. I: *Die Religionsphilosophie der Juden.* Leipzig, 1842.

KROCHMAL, NACHMAN. *Kitvai Nahman Krokhmal.* Edited by Sh. Rawidowicz. 2d ed. London, 1961.

LAZARUS, M. *Die Ethik des Judentums.* 2 vols. Frankfurt a. M., 1898, 1911.

MENDELSSOHN, MOSES. *Gesammelte Schriften*. Edited by G. B. Mendelssohn. 7 vols. Leipzig, 1843–1845.
——. *Gesammelte Schriften*. New Edition. 5 vols. Berlin, 1929.
——. *Yerushalayim: Ketavim K'tanim b'inyanai yehudim v'yahadut*. Introduction by N. Rotenstreich. Tel Aviv, 1947.
ROSENZWEIG, FRANZ. *Briefe*. Berlin, 1935.
——. *Kleinere Schriften*. Berlin, 1937.
——. *Naharayim: mivhar ketavim*. Jerusalem, 1960.
——. *On Jewish Learning*. Introduction by N. N. Glatzer. Appendices by M. Buber. New York, 1955.
——. *Der Stern der Erlösung*. Frankfurt, 1921. 2d ed., 1930. 3d ed., 1954.
——. *Understanding the Sick and the Healthy*. New York, 1954.
STEINHEIM, L. *Die Offenbarung nach dem Lehrbegriff der Synagoge*. 4 vols. Frankfurt a. M., Leipzig, Altona, 1835–1865.

LITERATURE

AGUS, J. B. *The Evolution of Jewish Thought*. Vol. I. New York, 1959.
——. *Modern Philosophies of Judaism*. New York, 1941.
ALTMANN, A. "Franz Rosenzweig and Eugen Rosenstock-Huessy: An Introduction to their 'Letters on Judaism and Christianity,' " *Journal of Religion*, XXIV, 4 (1944).
——. "Franz Rosenzweig on History," *Between East and West*. London, 1958.
BAMBERGER, F. *Die geistige Gestalt Mendelssohns*, Frankfurt a. M., 1929.
BERGMAN, SH. H. *Faith and Reason: An Introduction to Modern Jewish Thought*. Washington, D. C., 1961.
——. *Hogay Ha-dor*. Tel Aviv, 1935. Cf. chapters on Cohen and Rosenzweig.
——. "Shlomo Maimon v'Hermann Cohen," *Jubilee volume in honor of Y. N. Epstein*. Jerusalem, 1950.
BUBER, M. "Goyim v'elohav" (Krochmal's system), *K'nesset* (1940).
——. *Die Schriften über das Dialogische Prinzip*. Heidelberg, 1954.
COHEN, CARL. "Franz Rosenzweig," *Conservative Judaism*, VIII, 1 (1951).
EMMET, D. M. "The Letters of Franz Rosenzweig and Eugen Rosenstock-Huessy on Judaism and Christianity," *Journal of Religion*, XXV, 4 (1945).
FREUND, ELSE. *Die Existenzphilosophie Franz Rosenzweigs*. 2d ed., Leipzig, 1933.
FRIEDMAN, M. S. "Martin Buber and Judaism," *Central Conference of American Rabbis Journal*, XI (October, 1955), 13–19, 51.
——. *Martin Buber. The Life of Dialogue*. Chicago, 1955.
GLATZER, N. N. (ed.). *Franz Rosenzweig, His Life and Thought*. New York, 1953.
——. "Theory and Practice: A Note of Franz Rosenzweig," *Central Conference of American Rabbis Journal*, XI (October, 1955), 9–12, 34.
GUTTMANN, JULIUS. "Mendelssohns Jerusalem und Spinozas theologisch-politischer Traktat," *Achtundvierzigster Bericht der Hochschule für die Wissenschaft des Judentums* (Berlin, 1931).
——. "The Principles of Judaism." Translated from the Hebrew by D. W. Silverman. *Conservative Judaism*, XIV, 1 (Fall, 1959), 1–24.
——. "Yesodot ha-mahshava shel R. Nachman Krochmal," *K'nesset* (1941).
HALPERIN, YEHIEL. *Ha-mahpekha ha-yehudit; ma-avakim ruhaneyeem b'et ha-hadasha*. 2 vols. Tel Aviv, 1961.
KAPLAN, M. M. *The Greater Judaism in the Making: A Study of the Modern Evolution of Judaism*. New York, 1960.
KINKEL, W. *Hermann Cohen*. Stuttgart, 1924.

KLATZKIN, J. *Hermann Cohen*. Berlin, 1926.

LANDAU, J. L. *Nachman Krochmal, ein Hegelianer*. Berlin, 1904.

LEWKOWITZ, A. *Das Judentum und die geistige Strömungen des 19. Jahrhunderts*. Breslau, 1935.

LÖWITH, K. "Martin Heidegger and Franz Rosenzweig or Temporality and Eternity," *Philosophy and Phenomenological Research*, III (1942).

ROTENSTREICH, N. *Ha-mahshava ha-yehudit b'et ha-hadasha*. 2 vols. Tel Aviv, 1945–1950.

————. "Muhlat v'hitrahshut b'meesh'nato shel Ranak," *K'nesset* (1941).

————. "Solomon Ludwig Steinheim: Philosopher of Revelation," *Judaism*, II (1953), 4.

————. "T'fessato ha-historit shel Ranak," *Tzion*, VII (1942).

SCHWARZSCHILD, S. *Franz Rosenzweig: Guide of Reversioners*. London, 1960.

SIMON, E., SH. H. BERGMAN, et al. *Al Franz Rosenzweig*. Lectures presented at Hillel House, Jerusalem. Jerusalem, 1957.

UCKO, S. *Der Gottesbegriff in der Philosophie Hermann Cohens*. Berlin, 1929.

WIENER, M. *Jüdische Religion im Zeitalter der Emanzipation*. Berlin, 1933. English translation now in preparation.

Notes

The Basic Ideas of Biblical Religion

1. It is not part of our task to inquire how much of the groundwork for the religious ideas of the literary prophets was laid down by preceding developments. In contradiction to the Wellhausen school, which posited a break between the prophets and the Israelite religion of their day, it has been demonstrated recently that many "prophetic" ideas are to be found in older sources and that in the main the prophets drew upon ideas already current. Cf. Max Wiener's *Die Anschauungen der Propheten von der Sittlichkeit*, pp. 33 ff.; also M. Weber, *Gesammelte Aufsätze zur Religionssozologie*, III, 231-235, 250-255. In the details of the development of monotheism, there still remains much room for differing interpretations. Historical investigation of the Bible during the past two decades has tended to give an early date to the monotheistic conception of God, and some investigators locate its inception at the very beginning of biblical religion. I cannot accept these hypotheses, and I have, therefore, retained the text of my original German edition. For my purpose, which relates to the explication of the Jewish idea of God, it is unimportant whether this idea is first found in the literary prophets or is chronologically prior to them.

2. It may be said that the "mysticism" of which I speak in the text is merely that phenomenon which Heiler (*Das Gebet*, 3d ed., p. 248) and Söderblom refer to as the "negation of personality"—a mysticism which destroys any religious relationship to the Godhead. In what is described as mysticism that affirms personality, the mystical tendency functions as only one aspect of the religious consciousness. See Wobbermin's treatment of this point in *Das Wegen der Religion*, pp. 299 ff.

3. The powerlessness of all magical arts before the spontaneous acts of God is the theme of the story of Balaam. The difference between prophetic revelation and all forms of soothsaying can be found in Numbers 23:23 and also in Deuteronomy 18:14–16. On the distinction between miracles and magic, cf. Weber, *op. cit.*, p. 237, and many other instances cited in his book.

4. Despite all prohibitions, magical practices were quite common in biblical times. In relation to the Talmud, cf. Blau, *Das altjüdische Zauberwesen*. For material on the Middle Ages, cf. Güdemann, *Geschichte des Erziehungswesens und der Cultur der abendländischen Juden*, I, 199 ff.; III, 128 ff.

5. Compare Troeltsch, *Glaube und Ethos der hebräischen Propheten, Gesammelte Schriften*, IV, 48 f.

6. Ezekiel 18.

7. Cf. Wiener, *op. cit.*, pp. 23 ff.

8. Genesis 18:25.

Jewish Hellenistic Philosophy

1. This is the opinion of many scholars, such as Tyler, *Ecclesiastes*, 2d ed., pp. 8 ff.; Pfleiderer, *Die Philosophie des Heraklit von Ephesus*, pp. 255 ff; and to a lesser degree, Zeller, *Die Philosophie der Griechen*, III, 304 ff. Further literature on this subject can be found in Heinisch, *Griechische Philosophie im Alten Testament*, I, 45, who denies the fundamental thesis and summarizes the contrary argument with insight and erudition.

2. Ecclesiastes, 1:5-9; 3:14, 15.

3. *Ibid.*, 3:1-11.

4. *Ibid.*, 9:11; 2:15-17; 9:1-5; 4:1; 8:14; 6:7.

5. *Ibid.*, 7:23 f.; 8:16 f.

6. *Ibid.*, 2:13 f.; 10:2 f.

7. *Ibid.*, 1:18.

8. *Ibid.*, 9:1-7; 6:10.

9. *Ibid.*, 8:14.

10. *Ibid.*, 1:17; 2:1, 12; 8:16; and others.

11. Cf. Reinach, *Textes d'auteurs grecs*

et romains relatifs au judaïsme, pp. 7–12, 16, 99. H. Levy ("Aristotle and the Jewish Sage According to Clearchus of Soli," *Harvard Theological Review,* XXXI, 206–235) has most reasonably suggested that although Clearchus calls the Jewish sage a "philosopher," he attributes supernatural and magic wisdom to him. According to Clearchus, it was Aristotle who labeled the Jew a philosopher, not only in his speech but in his soul. The description which Theophrastus gives of the Jewish sacrificial cult stands in stark opposition to known facts, and what he reports of the religious controversies of the Jews and their scanning of the stars was apparently composed with Greek models in mind, as Joshua Guttmann has shown in an essay entitled, "Theophrastus on the knowledge of God in Israel" (*Tarbiz,* XVIII, 157–165). We can therefore assume that both Theophrastus and Clearchus had only a superficial knowledge of the high spiritual character of Judaism. According to all scholars, Posidonius is thought to be the source of Strabo. Cf. Heinemann, "Poseidonios über die Entwicklung der jüdischen Religion," *MGWJ,* LXIII, 113 f.; Reinhardt, *Poseidonios über Ursprung und Entartung.*

12. Cf. *Letter of Aristeas,* par. 129–171; Josephus, *Contra Apionem,* II, 22 ff.

13. Cf. Heinisch, *Die griechische Philosophie im Buch der Weisheit.*

14. Cf. Wisdom 3:5 ff; 4:10 ff; 7:15 ff; 11:1 ff.

15. *Ibid.,* 8:7.

16. *Ibid.,* 13 and 14. For the relationship to Posidonius, cf. Heinemann, *Poseidonios' metaphysische Schriften,* I, 136 ff.

17. *Ibid.,* 7:22 ff.; 8:1.

18. *Ibid.,* 8:1 ff.; 10:11 ff.

19. *Ibid.,* 7:27 ff.; 8:5 ff.

20. *Ibid.,* 8:7.

21. *Ibid.,* 1–3. Also 9:9 f.; 10:3; etc.

22. *Ibid.,* 11:17.

23. *Ibid.,* 8:19; 9:15.

24. Concerning the form of the book, cf. Freudenthal, *Die dem Flavius Josephus beigelegte Schrift über die Herrschaft der Vernunft,* pp. 18 ff. On its philosophic content, pp. 37–72.

25. 4 Maccabees 5:25; 9:32; cf. Freudenthal, *op. cit.,* pp. 43 ff.

26. *Ibid.,* 18:23; 6:29; 17:20–22.

27. *Ibid.,* 5:23 ff.

28. Freudenthal, *op. cit.,* pp. 59 ff.; Heinemann, *Poseidonios,* I, 156 ff. Cf.

Heinemann, Sec. IV., "The Fourth Book of Maccabees," *Pauly-Wissowa,* 109.

29. 4 Maccabees 5:22: 7:18; 6:31; 7:16; 13:1; cf. Freudenthal, *op. cit.,* 63.

30. *Ibid.,* 7:17 ff.

31. Philo, *De opificio mundi,* par. 7–9.

32. Philo, *De posteritate Caini,* par. 1 ff.; *Quod Deus sit immutabilis,* par. 52 ff.; *De opificio mundi,* par. 8; *De praemiis et poenis,* par. 40; *Legum allegorianum libri,* I, par. 36.

33. Philo, *Quod Deus sit immutabilis,* par. 62; *Quod deterius potiori insidiari soleat,* par. 160; *De vita Mosis,* I, 75.

34. Philo, *De opificio mundi,* par. 10; *De ebrietate,* par. 32; *Legum allegorianum,* I, 34.

35. Cf. L. Cohn, "Zur Lehre von Logos bei Philo," *Judaica, Festschrift zu Hermann Cohens 70. Geburtstag,* pp. 303–331; Hans Meyer, *Geschichte der Lehre von den Keimkräften von der Stoa bis zum Ausgang der Patristik,* pp. 26–46; G. Kafka and H. Eibl, *Der Ausklang der antiken Philosophie,* pp. 176 ff.

36. Philo, *De opificio mundi,* par. 23.

37. Philo, *De migratione Abrahami,* par. 9; *Quis rerum divinarum heres sit,* par. 68.

38. Philo, *Legum allegorianum,* III, par. 129, 134.

39. Philo, on freedom of choice: *Quod deus sit immutabilis,* par. 47 ff.; *Quaestiones in Genesim et Exodum,* IV, 64. On the necessity of God's help: *Legum allegorianum,* I, par. 86–89; III, 213 ff.

40. Philo, *De migratione Abrahami,* par. 47; *De opificio mundi,* par. 54.

41. Philo, *De cherubim,* par. 3–7; *De gigantibus,* par. 60 ff.

42. Philo, *Legum allegorianum,* III, 100; *Quis rerum divinarum heres sit,* par. 68 ff.

43. Philo, *Quis rerum divinarum heres sit,* par. 258–265.

44. Philo, *De opificio mundi,* par. 144.

45. Philo, *De migratione Abrahami,* par. 268 f.; *Quis rerum divinarum heres sit,* par. 22–31.

46. Philo, *De sacrificiis Abelis et Caini,* par. 59; *Quis rerum divinarum heres sit,* par. 166; *De migratione Abrahami,* par. 124.

47. Philo, *De vita Mosis,* II, 1–11, 187–191; *De praemis et poenis,* par. 52–56; *De opificio mundi,* par. 1–8.

48. H. A. Wolfson, in his important book, *Philo, Foundations of Religious*

Philosophy in Judaism, Christianity and Islam, has attributed to Philo theoretical independence and historical influence far beyond what is reasonable. According to Wolfson, Philo magisterially established the rule of revelation over his philosophy. In thus forcing philosophy to accommodate itself to revelation, Philo revolutionized his sources and gave them an entirely new character. Wolfson asserts that Philo was vastly influential both in his idea of the relationship between revelation and philosophy and through the basic change he effected in the impact of the content of Greek philosophic views on the philosophy and theology of medieval Judaism, Christianity, and Islam. For Wolfson, Philo was the creator of that philosophic form of thought which remained dominant until the beginning of the modern period. Spinoza alone rebelled against its dominion. To demonstrate this philosophic importance of Philo, Wolfson has promised to devote a whole series of additional volumes to it. In regard to his judgment concerning Philo, I am not convinced that he has proved either of his major contentions: Philo did not, as a matter of principle, subordinate philosophy to revelation; and he was not as independent of Greek philosophic positions as Wolfson seems to imply. Because of this, I have let my position on Philo stand unaltered.

The Religious Ideas of Talmudic Judaism

1. Cf. *Talmud Yerushalmi,* edited by Krotoschin, Berakhot 13 a, b; *Midrash Tehillim,* edited by Buber, p. 314. Further material in R. Travers Herford, *The Pharisees,* and G. F. Moore, *Judaism in the First Centuries,* etc., I, 439 ff. On the subject of God's hearkening to prayer and present-day miracles, cf. Büchler, *Some Types of Jewish Palestinian Piety,* pp. 196–264.

2. Babylonian Talmud: Abodah Zarah 3 b; *Sifre Numbers,* par. 84; Berakhot 9b.

3. *Mekilta to Exodus,* 15:3; Hagigah 13b.; *Pesikta,* ed. Buber, p. 109b, 110a.

4. *Sifra to Leviticus,* 19:1; *Sifre Deuteronomy,* 49; cf. *Mekilta to Exodus,* 15:2.

5. Sanhedrin 56a, b.

6. In general, the commandments were given to man only in order to purify his character. In detail, many ceremonial and cultic regulations were given ethical interpretations.

7. Shabbat 152b; Hagigah 12b; Sanhedrin 91a, b.

8. *Sifre Deuteronomy,* 307; Berakhot 28b; Shabbat 153a; Berakhot 17a.

9. Pirke Abot 4:16.

10. Berakhot 17a.

11. *Bereshit Rabbah,* 9:3.

12. *Sifre Deuteronomy,* 309, edited by Friedmann, p. 132a; *Bereshit Rabbah,* 8:11. Berakhot 10a.

13. Hagigah 12b; Niddah 30b.

14. *Sifre Deuteronomy, loc. cit.*

15. Berakhot 61a.

16. *Sifre Deuteronomy,* 32; cf. *Bereshit Rabbah,* 9:7.

17. *Sifra to Leviticus,* 19:18; Shabbat 31a.

18. *Sifra to Leviticus,* 18:4.

19. *Sifre Deuteronomy,* 32, p. 73a; Pesahim 50b.

20. Mishnah Peah, 1:1; Abot 1:17; Kiddushin 40b.

21. Berakhot 33b.

22. Abot 3:15.

23. Kiddushin 39b; Rosh Hashanah 17a.

24. Berakhot 5ab; Sanhedrin 101a, etc.

25. Kiddushin 39b; *Bereshit Rabbah,* 33:1.

26. Cf. Bergmann, "Die stoische Philosophie und die jüdische Frömmigkeit," *Judaica, Festschrift zu Hermann Cohens 70. Geburtstag,* pp. 145–166.

27. Berakhot 10a; cf. Seneca, *Epistolae Morales,* 65:24.

28. Niddah 30b (cf. Plato, *Phaedo,* 76D, and *Responsa of the Geonim,* X, 621A); *Bereshit Rabbah,* 1:1 (cf. *Timaeus,* 29a); Hullin 59b (*Responsa,* VII, 514 ff). According to Freudenthal (*Hellenist. Studien,* I, 69) and other scholars, the ideas of Plato were transmitted to the rabbis through the media of Jewish-Hellenistic writings, and especially through Philo, where these doctrines are also found. But despite all the exegetical parallels between Philo and Talmudic literature, it is very questionable if he was known to the Talmudic rabbis. Their knowledge of philosophic ideas, which, in general, was quite limited, was probably drawn from

wandering Greek philosophic preachers or through personal contact with Hellenistic Jews, who were also probably mediators of Alexandrian exegesis. Neumark (*History of Jewish Philosophy*, German edition, II, 89–91) claims that Platonic ideas had a decisive influence upon Talmudic Judaism, but very few of his arguments can withstand close scrutiny.

29. Abot 2:3.

30. Mishnah Hagigah 2:1.

31. Berakhot 33b; Hagigah 15a; *Sifre Deuteronomy*, 329.

32. Mishnah Hagigah, *loc. cit.*

33. Hagigah 14b; cf. Grätz, *Gnostizismus und Judentum*, p. 56 ff.; Bousset, "Die Himmelsreise der Seele," *Archiv für Religionswissenschaft*, IV, 145 ff.

34. *Bereshit Rabbah*, 3:4; *Tanhuma*, edited by Buber, on Exodus 37:1. Cf.

Freudenthal, *Die dem Flavius Josephus*, p. 71, who brings a parallel from Philo, *De fuga*, 110; Aptowitzer, *MGWJ*, LXXII, 363 ff; Ginzberg, *The Legends of the Jews*, V, 8, 9. For detailed treatment of the light metaphysics of ancient mysticism, *vide* Baeumkers, *Witelo*, pp. 361 ff.

35. Hagigah 12a; cf. Grätz, *op. cit.*, p. 39; Joël, *Blicke in die Religionsgeschichte*, I, 147. With reference to the preceding, it is worth while to consult Joël, *op. cit.*, pp. 114–170.

36. *Exodus Rabbah*, 15:22; cf. Freudenthal, *op. cit.*, p. 71. This saying is undoubtedly ancient, despite its recent context.

37. Mishnah Sanhedrin 10 (11): 1.

38. Cf. my essay: "Die Normierung des Glaubeninhalts in Judentum," *MGWJ*, LXXI, 241–255.

The Rise of Jewish Philosophy in the Islamic World

1. Cf. M. Schreiner, "Zur Geschichte der Polemik zwischen Juden und Mohammedanern," *Zeitschrift der deutsch-morgenländischen Gesellschaft*, XXXIV (Leipzig), 592 ff.

2. During the course of his critique of Rabbinic Judaism, Al-Qirqisani quotes such a collection of anthropomorphisms. Cf. L. Nemoy, "Al-Qirqisani's account of the Jewish sects and Christianity," *HUCA*, VII, 350 ff.

3. Cf. Paul Kraus, "Beitrage zur Islamischen Ketzergeschichte," *Revista degli studii orientali*, XIV, 64 ff.

4. *Ibid.*, pp. 341 ff., 356 ff.

5. Darmstedter summarizes the third chapter of the Persian book which attacks Judaism in his essay, "Textes Pehlvis relatifs au judaïsme," *RÉJ*, XVIII, 1–15. The very same strictures brought against Judaism by the Manichaeans are found in Augustine's anti-Manichaean writings.

6. Kremer, *Geschichte der herrschenden Ideen des Islams*, p. 241 f.

7. Goldziher, "Mélanges judéo-arabes," *RÉJ*, XVI; "Le Moutakallim Juif Abou-l-Kheyr," *RÉJ*, XLVII, 41 ff.; S. D. Gotein, "New Hypotheses on Jewish Philosophy in the Time of Saadia", *Sefer R. Saadia Gaon*, edited by J. L. Fishman, pp. 567–570.

8. Schreiner, "Zur Geschichte der Polemik zwischen Juden und Mohammedanern," *Zeitschrift der deutsch-morgenländischen Gesellschaft*, XLII (Leipzig, 1888), 615–618. On the concept of universal religion which lies at the base of these conceptions, cf. J. Guttmann, "Religion und Wissenschaft in mittelalterlichen und in modernen Denken," *Festschrift zum 50jährigen Bestehen der Berlin Hochschule für die Wissenschaft des Judentums in Berlin.*

9. J. Guttmann, "Zur Kritik der Offenbarungsreligion in der arabischen und jüdischen Philosophie," *MGWJ*, LXXVIII, 465 ff.

10. Saadia ben Joseph, *Kitab al-Amanat w'al I'tiqadat (Book of Beliefs and Opinions)*, chap. 3, pp. 128–131; edited by S. Landauer (Arabic), in the Hebrew translation, pp. 80–82. Further proofs were added from biblical exegesis on the problem of the abrogation of the Mosaic Law.

11. The remnant of Saadia's responsum was discovered and published by Israel Davidson, *Polemics against Hiwi al-Balkhi* (New York, 1915). All of the material on this issue known prior to Davidson's discovery was ordered and evaluated by Poznanski in his essay on Hiwi in the chrestomathy *Ha-goren*, VII, 112–137.

12. Poznanski, *op. cit.*, pp. 118, 124 ff.

13. *Ibid.*, p. 118; Davidson, *op. cit.*, p. 74.

14. Davidson, *op. cit.*, pp. 38, 48, 52, 68; Poznanski, *op. cit.*, pp. 121 ff.

15. Davidson, *op. cit.*, pp. 42–46.

16. On the similarity to the questions propounded in the Talmudic literature, cf. Jacob Guttmann, *MGWJ*, XXVIII, 260–270; on its dependence on Persian polemic, cf. D. Kaufmann *RÉJ*, XXII, 287–289. Cf. Poznanski, *op. cit.*, pp. 130 ff. and Davidson, *op. cit.*, pp. 80–82. Marmorstein's "The Background of the Haggadah," *HUCA*, VI, 157, 158, 161, points out that some of the objections of Hiwi appear in Marcion's writings and are also quoted in the Talmud as examples of anti-Jewish arguments. He ventures the hypothesis that Hiwi borrowed these arguments either from the Talmud or from the remnants of the Marcionite sect, which still existed in his day, but that he did see that these arguments were equivalent to those found in the Persian book. It was apparently unnoticed by all previous investigators that the very same arguments appear in Manichaean literature, which, probably, was the primary source for the Persian book and for Hiwi. The Manichaean sources were, of course, indebted to Marcion.

17. Poznanski, *op. cit.*, pp. 116 f.

18. Saadia ben Joseph, *Book of Beliefs and Opinions*, Arabic original, p. 37; Hebrew translation, p. 23.

19. Davidson, *op. cit.*, p. 68; Poznanski, *op. cit.*, pp. 117–118.

20. The matter is clear in regard to what one might call the "Christian notions" of Hiwi. A short time before Saadia demonstrated that the Last Supper was contrary to reason, he mentions that Hiwi "divides God into three." In context, this is apparently directed against Hiwi's opinion that the Old Testament story of the visit of three angels to Abraham (Gen. 18) includes the doctrine of the Trinity. This supposition, which exceeds the evidence for Hiwi's belief in the Trinity, apparently caused Saadia to call him a Christian. The same holds true for Hiwi's supposed belief in dualism.

21. Poznanski, "Philon dans l'ancienne littérature judéo-arabe," *REJ*, L, 10–31.

22. *Ibid.*, p. 15.

23. Cf. Poznanski's essay, "Benjamin son of Moses", *Otzar Yisroel*, III, 127 ff. According to Philo, too (*Quis rerum divinarum heres sit*, par. 231), man was created in the image and form of the Logos, and perhaps it is here that we should look for the source of Nahawend's view. But in terms of the reconstruction of the doctrine, it is typical that for Philo the logos too is made in the image and form of God.

24. Schahrastani, *Religionsparteien und Philosophenschulen* (German translation), I, 64.

25. Saadia ben Joseph, *Book of Beliefs and Opinions*, Chaps. 1, 2: Arabic, pp. 43 ff.; Hebrew, pp. 27 ff. The verses quoted from the Bible by the Jewish exponents of this doctrine correspond in greater measure to the depiction of the logos; and the form of some of Saadia's statements during the course of the polemic illustrate that something like this was the subject of debate. But the exposition he gives of this doctrine and the context in which the verses are quoted exclude any possible relation to the Logos doctrine. In the second chapter (Arabic, p. 89; Hebrew, p. 56), he mentions the scriptural explanations of the logos, but only as an explanation advanced by Christian scholars. One cannot establish conclusively if the idea of the logos was known to him from Jewish informants, or in what form he knew it.

26. Saadia ben Joseph, *Book of Beliefs and Opinions*, Chap. 1, Sec. 6, "On the Creation of Things": Arabic, p. 57; Hebrew, pp. 35 ff.

27. Saadia Gaon, *Commentaire sur le Sefer Yesira*, pp. 7 f. Neumark (in "The Philosophy of Saadia," published in a collection of Neumark's English essays, *Jewish Philosophy*, 1929, pp. 177 ff., 187) proved that Saadia speaks here of doctrines which look upon hylic matter as the creation of God.

The Kalam

1. Cf. the commentary of Dunash ben Tamin to *Sefer Yetzirah*, published by Grossberg, pp. 17 ff.

2. For further details, cf. Guttmann, *Die Religionsphilosophie des Saadia*, p. 30 ff.; and S. Horovitz, *Die Psychologie*

der jüdischen Religionsphilosophen des Mittelalters von Saadia bis Maimuni, pp. 1–10.

3. Cf. H. A. Wolfson, "The Double Faith Theory in Clement, Saadia, Averroës, and St. Thomas and its Origin in Aristotle and the Stoics," *JQR*, n.s., XXXIII, 213–264; A. Heschel, "The Quest for Certainty in Saadia's Philosophy," 265–303; "Reason and Revelation in Saadia's Philosophy," *JQR*, n.s., XXXIV, 291–408.

4. J. Guttmann, "Religion und Wissenschaft im mittelalterlichen und modernen Denken" in *Festschrift zum 50-jährigen Bestehen der Hochschule für die Wissenschaft des Judentums in Berlin*, pp. 148 ff., 173 ff.

5. Saadia ben Joseph, *Book of Beliefs and Opinions*, Introduction: Arabic, pp. 24 ff.; Hebrew, pp. 15 ff.

6. *Ibid.*, Arabic, pp. 21 ff.; Hebrew, pp. 13 ff.; Chap. 3: Arabic, pp. 132 ff.; Hebrew pp. 82 ff.

7. *Ibid.*, Chap. 7: Arabic, p. 212; Hebrew, pp. 135 ff.

8. *Ibid.*, Introduction: Arabic, pp. 12–20; Hebrew, pp. 8–13. On Saadia's epistemology, cf. I. Efros, "Saadia's Theory of Knowledge," *JQR*, n.s., XXXIII, 133–170.

9. *Ibid.*, Introduction: Arabic, p. 14; Hebrew, p. 9.

10. *Ibid.*, Chap. 3: Arabic, pp. 126 ff; Hebrew, pp. 79 ff.

11. *Ibid.*, Chap. 3: Arabic, p. 123; Hebrew, p. 77.

12. *Ibid.*, Introduction: Arabic, pp. 23 f.; Hebrew, p. 15; Chap. 3: Arabic, p. 127; Hebrew, p. 80.

13. *Ibid.*, Chap. 1: Arabic, pp. 32–37; Hebrew, pp. 20–23.

14. Cf. Steinschneider, *Al-farabi*, p. 122; R. Levi ben Gerson, *Milhamot Adonai*, Chap. 6, sections 1 and 3, pp. 295 ff. Both John Philoponus and Saadia assume the necessity of a power which would maintain and preserve existence in things. For Aristotle, this assumption applies only to those substances compounded of matter and form, which come into being and pass away, but not to the basic elements of existence, i.e., matter and form. It is thus impossible for Aristotle to establish a demonstration for the creation of the world in the strict meaning of this term. Although for him the heavenly elements are compounds of matter and form, essentially they stand above generation and destruction; the proof of their suscepti-

bility to change, which Wolfson presents in "The Kalam Arguments for Creation in Saadia, Averroës, Maimonides and St. Thomas," *American Academy for Jewish Research:Saadia, Anniversary Volume*, p. 203 is not to be found in Aristotle. For Aristotle, a cause is necessary only to account for that which occurs within the world, and the finiteness of the immanent efficient cause forces him to posit the existence of an unmoved mover. It is always surprising to me that his opinions on this matter have invariably been reconstructed in favor of the doctrine of creation!

15. Saadia ben Joseph, *Book of Beliefs and Opinions*, Chap. 1, Sec. 10, "On the Creation of Things," Chap. 1: Arabic, p. 63; Hebrew, p. 39 f.

16. *Ibid.*, Chap. I, Sec. 6: Arabic, p. 55; Hebrew, p. 35.

17. *Ibid.*, Chap. 1, Sec. 2: Arabic, p. 41; Hebrew, p. 26.

18. *Ibid.*, Chap. 1, Sec. 10: Arabic, p. 63; Hebrew, p. 40.

19. Cf. essay of Horovitz, "Über die Bekanntschaft Saadia mit der griechischen Skepsis," *Judaica*, pp. 235–252. *Festschrift zu Hermann Cohens 70. Geburtstag*.

20. Cf. Saadia ben Joseph, *Book of Beliefs and Opinions*, Chap. 1, Sec. 2: Arabic, p. 42; Hebrew, p. 27.

21. Saadia ben Joseph, *Commentaire sur le Sefer Yesira*, p. 4. Cf. also Saadia's *Book of Beliefs and Opinions*, Chap. 1: Arabic, p. 40; Hebrew, p. 25.

22. Saadia ben Joseph, *Book of Beliefs and Opinions*, Chap. 1: Arabic, p. 39; Hebrew, p. 25.

23. *Ibid.*, Chap. 1: Arabic, p. 70 ff; Hebrew, p. 44 ff.

24. *Ibid.*, Chap. 2: Arabic, p. 80 ff. Hebrew, p. 50 ff.; cf. Chap. 1, Sec. 5: Arabic, p. 48 ff. Hebrew, p. 30 ff.

25. *Ibid.*, Chap. 2: Arabic, p. 84 ff.; Hebrew, p. 53.

26. *Ibid.*, Chap. 2: Arabic, p. 86 ff.; Hebrew, p. 54.

27. *Ibid.*, Chap. 2: Arabic, p. 85; Hebrew, p. 53.

28. *Ibid.*, Chap. 2: Arabic, p. 97; Hebrew, p. 61.

29. Kaufmann, *Geschichte der Attributenlehre . . .*, pp. 1–77, attempts to interpret Saadia as being opposed in principle to attributes, and Neumark, *Geschichte der jüdischen Philosopie . . .*, II, 181–214, interprets Saadia as strongly

favoring the three elementary attributions, but his view is as partial and one-sided as that of Kaufmann.

30. Saadia ben Joseph, *Book of Beliefs and Opinions*, Chap. 3: Arabic, p. 118; Hebrew, p. 74 ff.

31. *Ibid.*, Arabic, p. 114 ff.; Hebrew, p. 71.

32. *Ibid.*, Arabic, p. 125 ff.; Hebrew, p. 78 ff.

33. *Ibid.*, Arabic, p. 133 ff.; Hebrew, p. 71 ff.

34. *Ibid.*, Chap. 10; cf. particularly the Arabic original, pp. 281–285, and the Hebrew translation, pp. 178–180. A detailed explication of Saadia's ethical doctrine may be found in Rau, "Die Ethik R. Saadjas," *MGWJ*, LV, 56.

35. Saadia ben Joseph, *Book of Beliefs and Opinions*, Chap. 3: Arabic, p. 112 ff.; Hebrew p. 70 ff.

36. *Ibid.*, Chap. 9: Arabic, p. 255 ff.; Hebrew, p. 162 ff.

37. *Ibid.*, Chap. 5: Arabic, p. 173; Hebrew p. 107. Chap. 9: Arabic, p. 260; Hebrew, p. 165. Chap. 3: Arabic, p. 141 ff.; Hebrew, p. 88.

38. *Ibid.*, Chap. 5: Arabic, p. 169 ff.; Hebrew, p. 105.

39. *Ibid.*, Chap. 4: Arabic, p. 149; Hebrew, p. 93.

40. *Ibid.*, Chap. 9: Arabic, p. 271 ff.; Hebrew, p. 172 ff.

41. *Ibid.*, Chap. 4: Arabic, p. 151 ff.; Hebrew p. 94 ff.

42. *Ibid.*, Chap. 4: Arabic, p. 154; Hebrew, p. 96.

43. *Ibid.*, Chap. 6: Arabic, pp. 188–194; Hebrew, pp. 117–120. Cf. Horovitz, *Die Psychologie der jüdischen Religionsphilosophen* . . . , pp. 12–26.

44. *Ibid.*, Chap. 6: Arabic, p. 206 f.; Hebrew, p. 128 f.

45. A sketch of Saadia's rationalistic mode of thought is given by Wiener in his unfinished essay, "The Primitive Rationalism of Rabbenu Saadia," *Dvir*, II (1923), 176–197. Cf. also J. Heinemann, "The Rationalism of Saadia Gaon," in *Sefer R. Saadia Gaon*, edited by J. L. Fishman, pp. 191–140.

46. J. Ginzberg, "Variantes arabe et hebraïque du traité de philosophie de Daud Ibn Mervan al Makonis," *Zapiski kollegii vostokovedenya*, V (1930), 481–507. The primary place which Judah of Barcelona occupies in the commentary on *Sefer Yetzirah* can be found on pp. 77–83.

Marmorstein (*MGWJ*, LXVI, p. 48 ff.) thought that, in one of the writings edited and published by him, he had found the introduction to al-Moqammes' book, but Mann (*JQR*, n.s., XVI, 90) demonstrated that al-Moqammes was not the author of that particular section.

47. Judah b. Barzillai of Barcelona, *Commentary on Sefer Yetzirah*, pp. 65, 151 ff. Goldziher published the selections on the virtues in his introduction to Pseudo-Bahya; *Kitab Ma'ani al-Nafs;* Hebrew translation by J. Broydé: *Torat hanefesh*, p. 18 ff.

48. Judah of Barcelona, *op. cit.*, pp. 78 ff.

49. *Ibid.*, p. 80 ff.

50. Cf. Bacher, "Le commentaire de Samuel ibn Hofni sur le Pentateuque, *RÉJ*, XVI, 117 f.

51. *Ibid.*, p. 118.

52. Cf. Schreiner, "Zur Charakeristik R. Samuel b. Chofni's und R. Hai's," *MGWJ*, XXXV, 31 ff. The responsum on the witch of Endor was published in its original form by L. Ginzberg in *Ginze Schechter*, I, 304 ff.

53. Cf. I. Goldziher, "R. Nissim b. Yacob Moutazilite," *RÉJ*, XLVII, 179 ff.

54. D. Kaufmann, *Geschichte der Attributenlehre* . . . , p. 167, n. 121.

55. Schreiner, *op. cit.* Cf. also, D. Joël, *Der Aberglaube und die Stellung des Judentums zu demselben*, II, 29 ff. Even R. Hai admits that supernatural conjurings, which are limited in scope and not miraculous, are, nevertheless, possible, but he is very skeptical of testimony relating to the occurrence of such events.

56. Kaufmann, "Ein Responsum des Gaons Haja über Gottes Vorherwissen und die Dauer des menschlichen Lebens," *Zeitschrift der deutsch-morgenländischen Gesellschaft*, XLIX, 73 ff. Kaufmann also notes here the parallel ideas in the *Théodicée* of Leibniz (I, 40).

57. P. F. Frankl, *Ein mu'tazilitischer Kalam aus dem 10. Jahrhundert*, p. 18. Frankl's essay deals with Joseph al-Basir. Harkavy later proved that Joseph lived in the eleventh century; Harkavy, *Studien und Mitteilungen aus der kais. off. Bibliothek zu St. Petersburg*, III, 7, 44.

58. M. Schreiner, *Jeschu'a ben Jehuda*, pp. 55–57.

59. Frankl, *op. cit.*, pp. 18, 37; Schreiner, *op. cit.*, p. 65 ff.

60. Schreiner, *op. cit.*, p. 65 ff.

61. Frankl, *op. cit.*, pp. 33, 48.

62. Schreiner, *op. cit.*, pp. 29, 31.

63. *Ibid.*, pp. 29, 32.

64. *Ibid.*, pp. 29; 3d proof, p. 30; p. 33 (IV); p. 35. The exposition in the text follows sections of Joshua ben Judah's book, as edited and translated by Schreiner. As is evident from his book *Kitab al-Muktabi*, edited by M. Klein and A. Morgenstern (Budapest, 1913), al-Basir's proof is essentially the same.

65. *Etz Hayyim* (Tree of Life), edited by Delitzsch, p. 3 ff.

66. *Ibid.*, p. 15.

67. *Ibid.*, p. 28 ff.

68. *Ibid.*, p. 86 ff.

69. *Ibid.*, p. 123 ff.

70. *Ibid.*, p. 120 ff.

71. *Ibid.*, p. 188 ff., p. 194 ff.

72. *Ibid.*, p. 173 ff.

73. *Ibid.*, p. 93 ff., p. 135 ff.

74. *Ibid.*, p. 155.

Neoplatonism

1. A. Borisov, *Some New Fragments of Isaak Israeli's Works*.

2. Cf. "Le commentaire: Nayda sur le livre de la creation," *RÉJ*, CVII, 5–62.

3. Isaac Israeli, *Hibbur* (Book of Definitions), p. 132. For the origin of the definition, which was built on the basis of that found in the *Theatetus*, cf. Joseph ibn Saddiq *Sefer ha-olam ha-katan*, p. XIII, n. 55; Jacob Guttmann, *Die philosophischen Lehren des Isaak ben Salomon Israëli*, p. 21, n. 1.

4. Isaac Israeli, *Sefer ha-Jesodot* (Book of Elements), p. 69; *Book of Definitions*, p. 140.

5. *Book of Elements*, p. 57.

6. *Ibid.*, p. 136 ff.

7. *Ibid.*

8. Borisov says, in the book mentioned previously: "The book tells us at length and repetitiously, that in the beginning two simple elements were created, form and matter, and reason, which is the first link in the chain of emanation, is compounded of these two simple elements."

9. Isaac Israeli, *Book of Elements*, pp. 7, 10.

10. *Ibid.*, p. 68.

11. Isaac Israeli, *Book of Definitions*, pp. 136–138; cf. especially p. 137, lines 14 ff. Cf. also p. 138, lines 25 ff., and bottom p. 140.

12. *Ibid.*, p. 136, lines 10 ff. Cf. especially the section of "The Book of the Spirit of Life and the Soul," published in *Ha-Carmel*, I, 403. Neumark's attempt (in *Geschichte der jüdischen Philosophen . . .*, II, 169 ff., 177 ff.) to deny the relevance of any of these quotations for the doctrine of the emanation of earthly bodies from the heavenly sphere distorts the meaning of these sentences. Neumark rightly perceived, however, with regard to the quotations

cited in the previous note, that they do not assert that the earthly bodies emanated from the heavenly sphere, but that even without these citations we have abundant evidence for this doctrine. Jacob Guttmann's *Die philosophischen Lehren des Isaak ben Salomon Israëli*, p. 30 f., is undoubtedly correct on the major issues involved, although some of Neumark's objections to his detailed interpretations do have a foundation in fact. Neumark is completely mistaken, however, in his claim that Israeli systematically rejected the introduction of earthly bodies into the emanation process and, instead, supported the idea of a special creation for these bodies. The *Book of Definitions*, which is the major source of Israeli's doctrine of emanation, knows nothing of such a creation. It is improper to insert the statements of the *Book of Elements*, concerning the direct creation of the elements, into the *Book of Definitions*, as I have previously demonstrated in the body of my text; and, a fortiori, it would be improper with regard to an author such as Israeli, who was by nature eclectic.

13. Borisov, *op. cit.*, "After nature come the elements . . . which are complete shadows, which receive their light from material nature."

14. Isaac Israeli, *Book of Definitions*, p. 136.

15. *Ibid.*, p. 132 (at bottom) f.

16. *Ibid.*, p. 133.

17. Heinemann, *Die Lehre von der Zweckbestimmung des Menschen im griechischen-römischen Alterum und im jüdischen Mittelalter*, p. 36.

18. Isaac Israeli, *Book of Elements*, pp. 52–57.

19. Al-Farabi, *Der Musterstaat*, German translation by Dieterici, pp. 80–84. Al-

though for Israeli the theory of prophecy is founded on the categories of Neoplatonic psychology, while for al-Farabi it is based on the categories of Aristotle, the common elements are quite obvious. It was very important in the historical development of this doctrine that Israeli should have given it a Neoplatonic coloring. The relationship of this doctrine to the theories of inspiration in antiquity is still unclear, although, with regard to particular components, such as Israeli's conclusion concerning dreams and their interpretation, the theories can easily be traced back to ancient beliefs, as has been proved by a comparative study of the materials made by Hans Lewy (*Sobria Ebrietas*, p. 95, n. 2).

20. Isaac Israeli, *Book of Elements*, pp. 57–60.

21. Contained in the Pentateuchal commentary of Abraham ibn Ezra, explained by Bacher, *Die Bibelexegese der jüdischen Religionsphilosophen des Mittelalters vor Maimuni*, p. 46 ff., and by Kaufmann, *Studien über Salomon ibn Gabirol*, p. 63 ff.

22. For a philosophic interpretation of the "Royal Crown," cf. M. Sachs, *Die religiöse Poesie der Juden in Spanien*, p. 224 ff.; Jacob Guttmann, *Die Philosophie des Salomon ibn Gabirol*, p. 20 ff.

23. Its contents are reviewed by D. Rosin, "The ethics of Salomon ibn Gabirol," *JQR*, III, 159 ff.

24. Outside of the sphere of Neoplatonism, Ibn Gabirol had a strong effect only on certain kabbalistic writings of the thirteenth century and on Isaac ben Latif, who stood midway between philosophy and the Kabbala. His doctrine of the will, of universal matter and universal form, and of the composition of spiritual substances from matter and form influenced early Kabbalism. But of the philosophic elements of his doctrine of the will, only a few have left traces. For the most part, their place was taken by completely different elements, drawn from the Kabbala. One can conjecture that after its publication, interest had been aroused in the doctrine of matter and form, and that both Gabirol and the kabbalistic writers utilized these or related sources, although along with these, Gabirol's own influence can undoubtedly be felt. A detailed investigation of this question can be found in G. Scholem's

"Traces of Gabirol in the Kabbala," *Collection of Israeli Authors* (1940), pp. 160–178. On Gabirol's influence on Jewish literature as a whole, cf. Munk, *Mélanges de philosophie juive et arabe*, p. 274 ff.; Jacob Guttmann, *Die Philosophie des Salomon ibn Gabirol*, p. 39 ff.; Kaufmann, *Studien über Salomon ibn Gabirol*, p. 108 ff. These latter inquiries have been outdated and obsolete since the publication of Scholem's work.

25. The reason that M. Joël asserts in his essay, "Ibn Gebirols (Avicebrons) Bedeutung für die Geschichte der Philosophie," *MGWJ*, VI, 7, that the *Mekor Hayyim* is nothing more "than a handbook of Neoplatonic philosophy" is due to the fact that Joël does nothing more than trace individual theses of the book back to ancient Neoplatonic sources. Wittmann, in his book *Zur Stellung Avencebrols (Ibn Gebirols) im Entwicklungsgang der arabischen Philosophie*, is also not free from this tendency.

26. Aristotle, *Metaphysics*, H, 2, p. 1043, a, 19; H, 6, p. 1045, a, 33 ff.

27. Plotinus, *Enneads*, II, 4, 1–5.

28. Solomon ibn Gabirol, *Fons vitae* . . . , I, 10, p. 13 f.; I, 12, 13, p. 15 ff. Cf. V, 22, p. 238 ff.

29. *Ibid.*, I, 17, p. 21; II, 1, p. 23 ff.

30. *Ibid.*, IV, 1, 2, pp. 211–215; IV, p. 6, p. 222.

31. *Ibid.*, I, 6, p. 8; IV, 10, p. 231 ff.

32. It is possible, as we have mentioned, that Gabirol knew of Plotinus' mature thought in the same form that we know it. Shem Tob ibn Falaquera, in his introduction to the *Mekor Hayyim*, asserts that Ibn Gabirol follows in the footsteps of Empedocles, who had attributed a spiritual matter to spiritual substances. In those pseudo-Empedoclean fragments, writings on the five senses published by Kaufmann (Budapest, 1899), we do find it said (p. 19 and p. 25) that the first creation of God was matter, in which all the forms are contained in their highest simplicity and from which all of the levels of being emanated. But here matter is only the first stage in the series of emanations from which all other things are derived. The characteristic notion of Gabirol is that all things are compounded of prime universal matter and prime universal form, which is quite different. As opposed to this, in the treatise on substances, which is attributed to Israeli and

which was recently brought to light by investigators, there was found, as we have time and again stressed, the doctrine of Gabirol, i.e., that matter and form were the first creations of God, and reason is a compound of these two. Complete elements of Gabirol's doctrine are undoubtedly here, already formulated. But insofar as we can judge from the fragmentary theses of this treatise, the systematic, detailed explication of his doctrine, i.e., the idea that underlying the corporeal and spiritual worlds is one matter, the investigation of how the many-sidedness of the corporeal world can be derived from the universal form and the universal matter, and, especially, how one effects the transition from the spiritual to the corporeal world—all of these are peculiarly Gabirol's. Nearer to Gabirol is the pseudo-Aristotelian fragment of the thirteenth-century Kabbala cited by Scholem in his catalogue (p. 4, par. 4) of the kabbalistic manuscripts of the Hebrew University. As long as the *Book of Substances* remained unknown, the originality of the first portion of this fragment, where we find the closest resemblance to Gabirol, can be doubted. The same reservation holds true of this same section, minus the introduction, which can be found in Israeli's *Book of the Spirit of Life and the Soul*. Now there can be no question of the temporal primacy of Israeli's statement.

33. Solomon ibn Gabirol, *Fons vitae*, II, 2, p. 26.

34. *Ibid.*, II, 1, p. 23 ff; iII, 16, p. 112; I, 9, p. 12.

35. *Ibid.*, II, 1, pp. 23 ff.; IV, 8, p. 228 ff.

36. *Ibid.*, II, 8, p. 37 ff; II, 22, p. 64 ff.

37. From this it is ·fully apparent how Gabirol, true to his systematic purposes, penetrates to the heart of Neoplatonic ideas. Plotinus already had been convinced that sensuous matter per se was immaterial and that bodies come into existence only through the combination of matter with the form of materiality, whose basic attribute for him was quantity (*Enneads*, II, 4, 8, and 9). This "immaterial" matter is devoid of qualities, and quite ambiguous. It acquires qualities only through its union with form. It is the principle of sensing, and serves as the transition from the spiritual to the material world because form, which in essence is spiritual and one, cannot be grasped in its unique unity and is, therefore, scattered and becomes material extension. Islamic Neoplatonism, and especially that of the Brethren of Purity, marks a great advance beyond these categories. This has been pointed out by M. Wittmann in his volume, *Zur Stellung Avencebrols im Entwicklungsgang der arabischen Philosophie*, p. 63. The Sufis assert that matter, which lies at the root of a natural body, is a spiritual principle, and claim that the body comes into being by a union of matter with the formal principle of matter (Dieterici, *Die Naturanschauung und die Naturphilosophie der Araber im 10. Jahrhundert*, p. 2 f., p. 25). Cf. also his *Die Lehre von der Weltseele bei den Arabern im 10. Jahrhundert*, p. 11 ff. But if we disregard for the moment their statement that matter comes into being only at the point of transition from the spiritual world to that of the material, they maintain that the formal principle of matter, like matter itself, is an ideal principle in its own right, and they state that a body is generated only by the combination of these principles. Thus materiality is not evolved (*Die Lehre von der Weltseele*, p. 11). Because Gabirol posits, first, the source of materiality in form, and, second, derives the form of q·antity by reason of the multiplication of the primal form of unity, we have as a result an evolving material universe whose like cannot be duplicated in the reasoning of any other medieval thinker. But this deviation from the then current discussions of the relation of matter to form, of which we will speak later, did lead in this instance to a return to the older concepts.

38. D. Kaufmann, *Die Geschichte der Attributenlehre in der jüdischen Religionsphilosophie* . . . , p. 109, n. 19; Wittmann, *Zur Stellung Avencebrols im Entwicklungsgang der arabischen Philosophie*, p. 65.

39. Solomon ibn Gabirol, *Fons vitae*, V, 8, p. 270. (Hebrew translation by Y. Blubstein; edited by A. Zifroni; Tel-Aviv, Tarpav, Ta-sh-y.)

40. *Ibid.*, V, 4, p. 263.

41. *Ibid.*, V, 8, p. 270 ff.

42. *Ibid.*, III, 15, p. 109 ff.

43. *Ibid.*, III, 13, p. 106 ff.; V, 41, p. 331.

44. *Ibid.*, I, 13, p. 16; V, 10, p. 274.

45. Cf. Jacob Guttmann, *Die Philosophie des Salomon ibn Gabirol*, p. 185, n. 2.

46. Solomon ibn Gabirol, *Fons vitae*, II, 23, p. 67 ff.; V, 9, p. 272.

47. *Ibid.*, IV, 14, p. 242 ff.; III, 28, p. 144. Heschel attempts to answer the difficulties in his essay, "Der Begriff der Einheit in der Philosophie Gabirols," pp. 99–107.

48. *Ibid.*, III, 2, par. 3, p. 76.

49. *Ibid.*, III, 3, par. 19, p. 80; par. 13, pp. 78 ff.

50. *Ibid.*, III, 43, p. 175 ff.; III, 44, p. 176 ff.

51. *Ibid.*, III, 45, 46, p. 180 ff.

52. *Ibid.*, III, 41, p. 172.

53. *Ibid.*, III, 48, p. 187; II, 3, p. 29.

54. *Ibid.*, V, 30, p. 312 ff.; III, 15, p. 111.

55. *Ibid.*, V, 13, 14, p. 279 ff.

56. *Ibid.*, II, 6, p. 35 ff.

57. *Ibid.*, V, 19, p. 293.

58. *Ibid.*, V, 36, p. 323; V, 37, p. 325; V, 25, p. 304.

59. *Ibid.*, V, 40, 41, p. 328 ff.; III, 42, p. 173.

60. *Ibid.*, V, 37–39, pp. 324 ff.

61. *Ibid.*, V, 23, p. 300; V, 42, p. 333 ff.; cf. especially p. 335. The idea found here, that the divine will is necessarily limited by that law which is enshrined in the divine essence, reminds us of Leibniz who thought that the eternal truths, contained in the divine mind, limit the sphere of the divine will. According to Leibniz himself, his doctrine was foreshadowed by the outlook of the ancients, according to whom God and nature are mutually involved in the creative act. Gabirol is one step closer to this viewpoint, notwithstanding the fact that he specifically sets the ultimate cause for the law, which limits the divine will, in the divine essence.

62. Neumark attempts to interpret Gabirol in terms of such a primary dualism of God and matter (*Geschichte der jüdischen Philosophie* . . . , II, 2, pp. 311 ff., 355 ff).

63. Solomon ibn Gabirol, *Fons vitae*, V, 37, p. 325; IV, 19, p. 253.

64. *Ibid.*, III, 57, p. 205.

65. The question of the origin of Gabirol's voluntarism has occupied students of Gabirol's thought from the very beginning. Munk, in *Mélanges de philosophie juive et arabe*, argued—on the basis of the Latin translation of the *The Theology of Aristotle*, which was the only text available in Gabirol's days—that the doctrine of this text was the seed from which

Gabirol's voluntarism flowered. When Dieterici later published the Arabic text of the *Theology*, Jacob Guttmann pointed out (*Die Philosophie des Salomon ibn Gabirol*, p. 31 ff.) that all of the sections dealing with the Word of God were absent in this text, and that, consequently, Munk's argument was unfounded. More recently, however, Borisov found another Arabic version of the *Theology*, containing the passages concerning the Word of God, and restored Munk's hypothesis to evidentially warranted status (A. Borisov, "Sur le point de départ de la philosophie de Salomon ibn Gabirol," *Bulletin de l'academie des sciences de l'U.R.S.S., classe des sciences sociales*, 1933, pp. 757–768). His assumption, however, that this particular version was the original text and that Dieterici's text deliberately excluded the sections on the Word of God, has no reliable evidence to support it. It is, of course, well known that *The Theology of Aristotle* is nothing more than an abbreviated version of Plotinus' *Enneads*. In the main, Dieterici's text adheres to Plotinus, while the additional material in Borisov seeks to adapt Plotinus' emanationist theory to the monotheistic idea of creation, and introduces, for this purpose, the doctrine of the Word of God. Nevertheless, it was not impossible that Gabirol was acquainted with this revised text. If such was the case, it becomes possible to look upon the doctrine of the Word of God (which was also called the "Will of God"), found in the *Theology*, as the point of departure for Gabirol. But as we have emphasized in our text, it can be reckoned only as a point of departure and no more, because it lacks Gabirol's unique conception of the relation of God's will to his essence. This latter was pointed out by G. Vajda (*RÉJ*, XCVII, 100–103). Guttmann's, *Die Philosophie des Salomon ibn Gabirol*, p. 251, n. 3, was the first to emphasize that, from this viewpoint, Gabirol's outlook was very close to that of the Philonic Logos. But Guttmann did not establish an historic linkage between the two. As against this, Wittmann's, *Zur Stellung Avencebrols im Entwicklungsgang der arabischen Philosophie*, p. 29 ff., and Poznanski's "Philon dan l'ancienne littérature judéo-arabe," *RÉJ*, L, p. 31, both maintain the existence of an historic connection, and Poznanski relies upon the proof adduced by him of the fact that several Jewish philosophers of the East knew Philo's doctrine. But Poznanski's proofs have no bearing upon the alleged connection with Gabirol. We must unquestioningly accept the assumption that, aside from stray and isolated pieces of Philo, Gabirol did not know Philo's system directly, as can be seen from the abbreviated Arabic version of Philo's essay on "The Ten Commandments" (Cf. Hirschfeld, "The Arabic Portion of the Cairo Genizah at Cambridge," *JQR*, XVII, 1905, 65–66). But Poznanski's thesis does seem to hold true of certain Eastern thinkers, among whom Philo's logos doctrine was adopted in such a primitive fashion that it could not have served as an agent of transmission between Philo and Gabirol. From what we have stated previously, it also seems to be the case that *The Theology of Aristotle* was directly or indirectly affected by the logos doctrine of Philo. Only insofar as the idea of the Logos penetrated these volumes could they have possibly reached Gabirol. On the connection between Gabirol and the Islamic investigators of logos and will, both Horovitz (*Die Psychologie der jüdischen Religionsphilosophen* . . . , p. 95, n. 34) and Wittmann (*Zur Stellung Avencebrols im Entwicklungsgang*, p. 15 ff.) offer sufficient testimony. We must, in speaking of these topics, completely exclude any reference to the kalamic discussion concerning the eternity or createdness of the Word of God. In Islamic theology of the eternity of the Word of God, the logos idea becomes completely theologized. The Word becomes identical with the Koran and is more divine law than divine wisdom. For Gabirol, only Islamic doctrines concerning the will, in which the kalam, too, participated, have any relevance. The Islamic doctrines were vexed by the problem of describing God as a willing being, since this would mean that God is subject to change. This difficulty forced the Islamic doctors and, among the Jews, Joseph al-Basir, to claim that God operated through his will, which was his creation. In these controversies one position was that God's will stands midway between his essence and his act. Afterwards, this gave rise to the astonishing idea of Mu-amar that God's will is, in relation to any particular substance, something mysterious, since it is not identical either with God or with the createdness of the particular substance. The proximity of this doctrine to that of Gabirol, which was underscored by Horovitz, is worthy of the greatest attention, because Mu-amar was very close to Neoplatonic tendencies. But Mu-amar's thesis, which rests upon a series of negative arguments, is essentially different from Gabirol's idea, which, from one standpoint, identifies the will with God, and from another standpoint differentiates between the two. Similarly Mu-amar lacks any concept of the dual causality of God and of the likeness of the will to form, both of which are maintained by Gabirol. Nevertheless, it is almost certain that these voluntaristic doctrines did influence Gabirol. Even the most recent investigations, however, have found it impossible to determine precisely which sources lay before him as he wrote. Suffice it to say that the doctrines of the will and the logos utilized by him were transformed quite freely by him, in accordance with the necessities of his own system. Duhem's attempt (*Le système du monde*, V, pp. 38–75), to prove that Gabirol's entire system is based upon that of Johannus Scotus Erigena, has absolutely no evidence to warrant it.

66. The controversy regarding the date of composition of Pakuda's *Book of the Duties of the Heart* has at last been settled by Kokowzoff ("The date of the life of Bahya ibn Pakuda," *Poznanski-Gedenkbuch*, p. 8 ff.). It can be determined on the basis of one of the statements of Moses ibn Ezra, which Kokowzoff discovered, that the book was written in the last third of the eleventh century.

67. Heinemann, *Die Lehre von der Zweckbestimmung des Menschen* . . . , p. 37 ff.

68. A. S. Yahuda has demonstrated, in his introduction to the Arabic edition of the *Book of the Duties of the Heart* that many of the doctrines and isolated statements of Bahya are borrowed from the ascetic literature of Islam. Cf. Bahya ben Joseph ibn Pakuda, *Kitab al-Hidaya ila Faraid al-Qulub*, edited by A. S. Yahuda (Leiden, 1912). A systematic comparison of the ethical and religious doctrines of Bahya with the ascetic literature of Islam can be found in G. Vajda, *La théologie ascétique de Bahja ibn Paquda* (Paris, 1947), who proved quite recently how

dependent Bahya really was upon this literature.

69. Introduction to the *Book of the Duties of the Heart*: Arabic, p. 4, p. 15 ff; Hebrew (edited by Stern), p. 2, p. 12 ff; I, 3: Arabic, p. 41 ff; Hebrew, p. 37 ff.

70. Bahya ibn Pakuda, *Book of the Duties of the Heart*: Arabic, p. 13 ff.; Hebrew, p. 36. This same comparison is made by the Brethren of Purity; cf. Dieterici, *Die Philosophie der Araber im 10. Jahrhundert*, I, 90.

71. Introduction to the *Book of the Duties of the Heart*: Arabic, p. 13 ff.; Hebrew, p. 10 ff.; III, 4: Arabic, p. 145; Hebrew, p. 147.

72. Bahya ibn Pakuda, *Book of the Duties of the Heart*, I, 5: Arabic, p. 45; Hebrew, p. 41; I, 6: Arabic, p. 46 ff.; Hebrew, p. 43 ff.

73. *Ibid.*, I, 5: Arabic, p. 44 ff.; Hebrew, p. 40 ff.; I, 6: Arabic, p. 48; Hebrew, p. 45.

74. *Ibid.*, I, 6: Arabic, p. 48 ff.; Hebrew, p. 45 ff.

75. Cf. D. Kaufmann, *Die Theologie des Bachja ibn Pakuda*, p. 48, n. 1.

76. Bahya ibn Pakuda, *Book of the Duties of the Heart*, I, 7, proof 5: Arabic, p. 55 ff.; Hebrew, p. 53.

77. *Ibid.*, I, 9: Arabic, p. 63 ff; Hebrew, p. 58 ff.

78. *Ibid.*, I, 10: Arabic, p. 68; Hebrew, p. 62.

79. *Ibid.*, I, 10: Arabic, p. 69 ff.; Hebrew, p. 63 ff.

80. *Ibid.*, I, 10: Arabic, p. 85 ff.; Hebrew, p. 77 ff.

81. Cf. Introduction of A. S. Yahuda to the Arabic original.

82. Bahya ibn Pakuda, *Book of the Duties of the Heart*, Introduction: Arabic, p. 9 ff.; Hebrew, p. 6 ff.

83. *Ibid.*, III, 9: Arabic, p. 167; Hebrew, p. 177.

84. *Ibid.*, VIII, 3: Arabic, p. 342; Hebrew, p. 391.

85. *Ibid.*, IX, 3: Arabic, p. 360 ff.; Hebrew, p. 414 ff.

86. *Ibid.*, cf. also IX, 2: Arabic, p. 359 ff; Hebrew, p. 413, where ethical doctrine instruction is presented as the task of him who truly lives an ascetic life.

87. *Ibid.*, IX, 3: Arabic, p. 361 ff.; Hebrew, p. 415 ff. Bahya, however, does not fully plumb the consequences of this view. While he states here that inner separation from the world while externally remaining within it is the true form of asceticism, which is most defensible, and completely rejects the idea of absolute separation from the physical life of the community, in Chapter IX, 1, he merely objects to the general application of this radical asceticism and asserts that it is, however, entirely proper for an elite. There he views it as one of the necessary forms of human social life, which like all vocations, is open to only a portion of humanity. An attenuation of this opposition is evident, in that according to Chapter IX, 1, the elite may not withdraw completely from organized society, but must direct the moral life of the community. But the implied contradiction is not resolved by this compromise, and even in the later chapters of the book, Bahya still hesitates between the two views.

88. Vajda, *op cit.*, p. 140 ff., comes to the same conclusion as I did in the original German edition of this book.

89. In a Parsee manuscript which recently came to light, the treatise is ascribed to Bahya ibn Pakuda. Jacob Guttmann ("Eine bisher unbekannte, dem Bachja Ibn Pakuda zugeeignete Schrift," *MGWJ*, XLI, p. 241 ff.) was the first to dispute Bahya's authorship of this text, and Goldziher concurred with his opinion in the introduction to his Arabic edition (p. 5). Now Borisov has established ("Pseudo-Bahja," *Bulletin de l'academie des sciences de l'U.R.S.S., classe des humanités*, 1929, p. 786) that the Leningrad manuscript of this text has no reference to Bahya as its author. Since the manuscript makes mention of such authors as Ibn Sina and Nissim ben Jacob, who lived in the first half of the eleventh century, it could not have been written before the middle of the eleventh century, and since it was uninfluenced by the further development of Islamic and Jewish philosophy, it is doubtful if it could have been composed later than the middle of the twelfth century.

90. Pseudo-Bahya, *Kitab Ma'ani al-Nafs*, Chap. 3: Arabic, p. 17 ff; Hebrew, p. 21 ff.

91. *Ibid.*, XVI: Arabic, p. 54 ff.; Hebrew, p. 71 ff. There is nothing unique in this hierarchy of levels, other than the idea of there being ten levels in all, which cannot be found in any other text known to us.

92. *Ibid.*, XVI: Arabic, p. 53; Hebrew, p. 70.

93. *Ibid.*, XVI: Arabic, p. 54; Hebrew, p. 72.

94. *Ibid.*, I, II: Arabic, p. 3 ff.; Hebrew, p. 3 ff.

95. *Ibid.*, I: Arabic, p. 4; Hebrew, p. 5.

96. *Ibid.*, XVI: Arabic, p. 56; Hebrew, p. 74; XVII: Arabic, p. 57 ff.; Hebrew, p. 75 ff. On late antiquity's doctrine of the descent of the soul and the determination of its character and qualities by the constellations through which it passes in its descent, cf. Bousset, *Die Himmelreise der Seele,* Archiv für Religionswissenschaft, IV, 268; Wendland, *Die hellenistisch-römische Kultur in ihrer Beziehungen zum Judentum und Christentum,* 2d and 3d eds. pp. 170; 172, n. 1. Even the metaphor of the clothing and disrobing of the soul's garments, mentioned by Wendland, can be found in Pseudo-Bahya.

97. Pseudo-Bahya, *op. cit.*, XVI: Arabic, p. 56; Hebrew, p. 74; XII: Arabic, p. 42; Hebrew, p. 56.

98. *Ibid.*, XIX: Arabic, p. 62 ff.; Hebrew, p. 82 ff.

99. *Ibid.*, XXI: Arabic, p. 67; Hebrew, p. 88; XIX: Arabic, p. 62; Hebrew, p. 82; for the concept of the virtues, cf. XVIII: Arabic, p. 60; Hebrew, p. 79; and further, IX: Arabic, p. 34 ff.; Hebrew, pp. 44 ff., where the Platonic cardinal virtues are merged with the Aristotelian idea of the golden mean.

100. *Ibid.*, XXI: Arabic, p. 64 ff.; Hebrew, p. 85 ff.; for Israeli, cf. *Book of Elements,* p. 133. The idea that wicked souls strive in vain to ascend to the upper world and receive their punishment below the heavens has its source in Plutarch's description of Hades as being beneath the moon and in his notion that the wicked souls are repudiated by the moon; Zeller, *Die Philosophie der Griechen,* III, p. 200, n. 1; Bousset, *op. cit.*, p. 252 ff.

101. Abraham bar Hiyya, *Hegyon ha-Nefesh,* p. 2a.

102. *Ibid.*, 2a, b.

103. Abraham bar Hiyya, *Megillath ha-Megalleh,* p. 22. According to another version, the second level is called "the world of speech," instead of "the world of dominion," and we would then be able to relate it to the logos. Cf. my introduction to this text, p. 16, and the detailed *"explication de la texte"* of G. Scholem, *MGWJ,* LXXV, 180 ff.

104. Abraham bar Hiyya, *Hegyon ha-Nefesh,* p. 5a, b.

105. Abraham bar Hiyya, *Megillath ha-Megalleh,* p. 109 ff. On the relationship of the two forms of retribution, cf. my introduction.

106. *Ibid.*, pp. 14–47. On the Christian source of this doctrine, cf., Introduction, p. XIII.

107. *Ibid.*, p. 72 ff. Baer has luminously explained this theory of history (*MGWJ,* LXX, 120, n.) as a protest against the Christian doctrine of original sin and redemption. It is paradoxical that, in his doctrine of the fall of man, Abraham did not utilize the well-known Talmudic dictum that the serpent injected moral impurity into Eve and all her descendants, and that this taint was removed from the children of Israel when they stood at the foot of Sinai, while the nations of the world, who were not present, remain befouled.

108. Abraham bar Hiyya, *Hegyon ha-Nefesh,* p. 8a. Of course, the messianic treatise has a much stronger exclusively Jewish attitude than that of the *Meditations on the Soul,* but in it, too, it is not stated that morality is the portion of Israel alone.

109. Joseph ibn Saddiq, *Sefer ha-Olam ha-Qatan,* p. 8 ff. The question of the substantiality of form was also treated by medieval Aristotelians (cf. H. A. Wolfson, *Crescas' Critique of Aristotle,* pp. 573–576), but they are more thorough in their treatment than is Ibn Saddiq.

110. *Ibid.*, p. 13; cf. Wolfson, p. 588.

111. *Ibid.*, p. 7 ff.

112. *Ibid.*, p. 33.

113. *Ibid.*, p. 34.

114. *Ibid.*, p. 37.

115. *Ibid.*, p. 40.

116. *Ibid.*, p. 48 ff.

117. *Ibid.*, p. 52 ff.

118. *Ibid.*, p. 50 ff.

119. *Ibid.*, p. 57 ff.

120. *Ibid.*, p. 54.

121. *Ibid.*, p. 53 ff.

122. *Ibid.*, p. 57.

123. *Ibid.*, p. 58.

124. *Ibid.*, p. 66 ff. Cf Heinemann, *Die Lehre der Zweckbestimmung des Menschen . . . ,* pp. 57 ff.

125. Maimonides, *Guide for the Perplexed,* I, 54; III, 54. That the *Microcosm* was unknown to him was stated by Maimonides in a letter to Samuel ibn

Tibbon (*Letters of Maimonides* [Leipzig] II, 28b). It might be mentioned in passing that the redirection of the doctrine of the knowledge of God towards the ethical dimension can also be found in Abraham ibn Daud (*Sefer ha-Emunah ha-Ramah*, p. 46), where reference is made to Jeremiah 9:23, as is also done by Ibn Saddiq and Maimonides.

126. Commentary on Genesis 1:26; Exodus, 23:21; *Yesod Morah*, edited by Stern, p. 34b. Additional evidence is cited in D. Rosin, "Die Religionsphilosophie Abraham ibn Esras;" *MGWJ*, XLII, 43, 61 ff.

127. Commentary on Exodus 3:15; Daniel 11:12; Cf. Rosin, *op. cit.*, p. 66 ff.

128. Commentary on Exodus 26:1; excursus on the shorter commentary to Exodus, 3:13. See also Rosin, *op. cit.*, pp. 29, 161.

129. The citations adduced by Rosin, *op. cit.*, p. 69, testify to this.

130. Commentary on Genesis 25:8; Psalm 49:16.

131. Commentary on Psalm 139:18.

132. Commentary on Genesis 18:21; Psalm 73:12.

133. Commentary on Exodus; excursus on 33:17.

134. Commentary on Genesis 1:1.

135. Judah Halevi, *Sefer ha-Kuzari* (edited by Hirschfeld), V, 14, p. 322.

136. *Ibid.*, V, 14, p. 328.

137. D. Kaufmann, *Geschichte der Attributenlehre in der jüdischen Philosophie . . . .*, pp. 119–140, was the first to prove Halevi's dependence on Ghazali. For Halevi's critique of metaphysics and the consequent rejection of rationalistic theories of religion of the Islamic and Jewish philosophers, his demonstration is adequate. But he unjustly juxtaposes Halevi's view of religion to that of Ghazali. For a comparative analysis of the doctrines of these two thinkers, which evaluates both their differences and similarities, see J. Guttmann's "Religion und Wissenschaft im mittelalterlichen und im modernen Denken," pp. 166–173, and from a different viewpoint, D. H. Baneth, "Jehuda Hallewi und Gazali."

138. Judah Halevi, *Sefer ha-Kuzari*, V, 14, pp. 322f.

139. *Ibid.*, IV, 25, p. 280 ff.

140. *Ibid.*, V, 14, p. 326.

141. *Ibid.*, IV, 15, pp. 256 ff.; II, 6, p. 74; I, 97, p. 46.; also IV, 3, p. 288 which emphasizes the inadequacy of speculation and sees in this characteristic the source of such false doctrines as dualism and polytheism. Halevi does admit the superiority of philosophic arguments over these popular modes of thought and cavils against the latter because it denies to God knowledge of singulars and upholds the eternity of the universe.

142. Judah Halevi, *op. cit.*, I, 65, 67, p. 28; cf. Maimonides, *Guide for the Perplexed*, II, 15, 16; in II, 15, Maimonides seeks to prove that Aristotle did not believe that he could demonstrate the eternity of the world. On the basis of the statement made in the *Topics*, I, 11, and also on the basis of a skeptical statement of Galen, it can be seen that, among Islamic circles, prior to the time of Judah Halevi, this issue was still not completely settled.

143. *Ibid.*, III, 7, p. 148; II, 48, p. 106 ff. The introduction of the necessity for worshiping God as one of the demands of rational ethics is surprising, because it assumes that the personal character of God can be grasped and established by reason. Leo Strauss, in his essay "The Law of Reason in the Kuzari" (*PAAJR*, XIII, 47–96) pointed out the difficulties of Halevi's conception of rational ethics. It is impossible to enter here into a discussion of the merits of Strauss' attempts to settle these difficulties.

144. *Ibid.*, I, 84 ff., p. 36 ff.

145. *Ibid.*, I, 4, p. 8.

146. *Ibid.*, I, 79, p. 32; I, 98, p. 52; I, 109, p. 60; II, 32, p. 100.

147. *Ibid.*, I, 13, p. 16, "speculative religion"; I, 1, p. 6; I, 81, p. 34, "the rational laws."

148. *Ibid.*, I, 1, p. 4 ff.

149. *Ibid.*, IV, 13, p. 252 ff.; IV, 15, 16, p. 260. That Judah Halevi's characterization of the philosopher's task, despite its one-sidedness, has a kernel of historic truth, can be seen by the interesting parallel in Maimonides' *Guide for the Perplexed*, I, 36.

150. *Ibid.*, IV, 15, 16, pp. 258 f.

151. *Ibid.*, I, 95, p. 44. For the most part (cf. I, 42, p. 20; II, 14, p. 80) this stage is called the level of the divine word, or the divine itself. For Halevi, this means at times the power, specific to man, which prepares him for communion with God, and at times the divine essence, with which man comes into communion. It is this shift of meaning which has caused so much confusion.

152. *Ibid.*, I, 47, p. 22; I, 95, p. 42 ff.

153. *Ibid.*, I, 99, p. 52; II, 12, p. 76; II, 26, p. 94 ff.

154. *Ibid.*, II, 12, p. 76.

155. *Ibid.*, I, 111, p. 62.

156. *Ibid.*, I, 115, p. 64; IV, 23, p. 264 f.

157. *Ibid.*, I, 109, p. 58; II, 32, p. 100; IV, 3, p. 230.

158. *Ibid.*, IV, 5, 6, p. 246 ff.; IV, 15, p. 258 ff.; IV, 3, pp. 232, 238 ff.

159. *Ibid.*, V, 20, 4, introduction, p. 348; cf. also I, 103, p. 56; I, 109, p. 58 ff.; II, 34, p. 102.

160. *Ibid.*, III, 11, p. 156; III, 17, p. 166; V, 23, p. 356.

161. *Ibid.*, II, 50, p. 108 ff.; III, 11–17, p. 152 ff.

162. *Ibid.*, III, 7, p. 148 ff.

163. *Ibid.*, III, 5, p. 142 ff.

164. *Ibid.*, I, 103, p. 56; III, 20, p. 172.

165. Cf. Zeller, *Die Philosophie der Griechen*, III, 2, p. 879. Other analogies from Greek and Islamic literature are brought forward by Wolfson in his essay "Halevi and Maimonides on Prophecy" (*JQR*, XXXIII, 64–66), and Heinemann in the essay mentioned in n. 171, pp. 162–163.

166. Judah Halevi, *op. cit.*, II, 14, p. 80; II, 26, p. 94. On the Neoplatonic origin of these doctrines, cf. Pseudo-Bahya, *Kitab Ma'ami al-Nafs*, edited by Goldziher. D. Neumark in "Jahuda Hallevi's Philosophy in its Principles," 1908, Chap. II, *Essays in Jewish Philosophy* (1929), p. 231 ff., was the first to illuminate the importance of this doctrine for Halevi's system, but in many instances I cannot agree with his interpretation.

167. Judah Halevi, *op cit.*, I, p. 4.

168. *Ibid.*, II, 26, p. 94; V, 10, p. 308. The Neoplatonic analogies can be found in Pseudo-Bahya, *op. cit.*, p. 40. Cf. also Maimonides, *Guide for the Perplexed*, II, 14, the seventh argument, which derives the eternity of the world from the eternal perfection of God.

169. Judah Halevi, *op. cit.*, I, 67, p. 28.

170. *Ibid.*, V, 21, p. 354 ff.

171. I have already emphasized in n. 151 that the concept *imar ilahi* (divine word) has varied meanings—sometimes psychological, sometimes metaphysical. Goldziher was the first to investigate the significance and origin of this concept in his essay, "Le Amr ilahi chez Juda Halevi," *RÉJ*, L, p. 323 and *passim*. He concluded that it was drawn from Neopla-

tonic sources, among which he underscores the logos idea. He assumes that traces of the influence of this latter idea can be seen in Halevi. In the German edition of this book (see n. 151), I pointed out that Halevi does not recognize a logos, which is separate from the divine being, and used it only as a figurative equivalent for the divine essence. Recently Wolfson ("Halevi and Maimonides on Prophecy," *JQR*, XXXI, 353 ff.) contradicted Goldziher's hypothesis and concluded that Halevi's *imar* and the philosophic concept of the logos have nothing in common. Heinemann, too, in his essay, "Temunat ha-historia shel Yehuda Ha-levi" (*Tzion*, VII, 147–177), assumes that Halevi does not recognize a logos as a metaphysical essence separate from God. Nevertheless, he maintains Goldziher's hypothesis that the *imar* is connected with the philosophic concept of the logos and seeks the source of the *imar* in the logos doctrine of the Stoics. He points out that not only did Judah Halevi call the highest power, given only to Israel, by the name of *imar,* but he also differentiates the specific powers by means of which plants, organic entities, and man are distinguished from all other animate objects and from each other by the name of *imar*—by means of a special *imar* that each one possesses. He compares this to the Stoic doctrine, according to which the pneuma, of which the logos is the highest stage, is found in men, animals, and plants, and the difference between human souls and animal souls, and the souls of plants lies only in their different degree of absorption of this pneuma. He claims that the pantheism of the Stoics, according to which the pneuma serves as the principle of the divine life which fills and animates the world, is changed by Halevi, just as it was reinterpreted by the Church Fathers, who accepted the Stoic doctrine in the monotheistic sense of a transcendental God. He looks upon the pneuma, which at each of its stages is called logos, as the workings of the divine. The Stoic conception, however, is left undisturbed (i.e., that all stages of life are informed with pneumatic power, which is made manifest in greater or lesser degree at each stage). That Halevi has a terminological tie to the logos concept is undoubted. Nevertheless, from the viewpoint of content, there is an essential difference.

For Halevi (as is emphasized in chapters I, 39; V, 20, 3rd and 4th introductions, p. 348), there lies between the various levels of the *imar* not a difference in degree, but one of kind and essence. God allocates to each level of existence specific and local powers. This doctrine is close to that of the Neoplatonists and the Islamic and Jewish Aristotelians, according to whom those forms are apportioned to every category and type of being by the supersensual substances in accord with the power of absorption of each level and type of existence. But for Halevi, God himself apportions to the various levels of being the forms appropriate to them.

172. Judah Halevi, *op. cit.,* I, 67, p. 28; V, 14, p. 324.

173. Baneth came to a similar conclusion in "Jehuda Hallewi and Gazali," p. 33 ff. Heinemann, in the essay mentioned in n. 171, attempted to reconcile the oppositions by assuming that all of the instances relate to the joint action of the free divine will and the conditions of the laws of nature.

174. Judah Halevi, *op. cit.,* II, 2–6, pp. 70 ff. The formal contradictions in chapter II, 2, are of little pertinence to the central thesis of Judah Halevi. Concerning the possibilities of resolving these contradictions, cf. D. Kaufmann, *Geschichte der Attributenlehre in der jüdischen Reli-* *gionsphilosophie . . . ,* p. 157, n. 101; Horovitz, "Zur Textkritik des Kusari," *MGWJ,* X, 271, n. 1. On the contrary, it is difficult to reconcile the statement made at the end of chap. II, 2, that reason is not an attribute of God, but that God is the essence of reason and is, therefore, called wise, with the central thesis of Judah Halevi. Because of the laconic form of these statements, it is impossible to determine precisely how Halevi himself would have resolved this contradiction. Horovitz ("Zur Textkritik des Kusari," p. 272, n. 1) rightly points out that the Aristotelians, including both Ibn Sina and Maimonides, also rejected any attribution of essential qualities to God but nevertheless did characterize him as wise, without seeing any contradiction therein. Thus Judah Halevi was following the school tradition of Aristotelianism. I will return to this question when I discuss the doctrine of attributes of Maimonides. At any rate, there is absolutely no justification in completely overhauling the interpretation of Judah Halevi's doctrine of attributes so as to admit attributes of essence, as was done by Neumark on the strength of this isolated example ("Jehuda Hallevi's Philosophy in its Principles," Chap. IV; in *Essays in Jewish Philosophy,* pp. 265 ff.).

175. Judah Halevi, *op. cit.,* IV, 3, pp. 228 ff.

Aristotelianism and Its Opponents

1. All of these statements are applicable to al-Farabi (cf. his emanation doctrine in his *Musterstaat,* German translation of *Hamedinah l'mofait* by Dieterici, p. 29 ff.). There al-Farabi states that the heavenly spheres were emanated from the pure intelligences, and he makes no distinction between their matter and form. According to what he says on p. 44, the matter of sublunar bodies are emanations of the heavenly spheres, and thus there is no doubt that he introduces matter into the process of emanation. This same doctrine is repeated by Ibn Sina (Avicenna; cf., for example, Schahrastani, *Religionsparteien und Philosophenschulen,* II, 264 ff.; German translation by Haarbrücker), but out of his involved and complicated inquiries into the generation of the heavenly bodies, it appears that the process of emanation does lead to the existence of matter, and its function is only to bring it from potency to act. With Ibn Rushd, the Aristotelian dualism of matter and form is re-established in its pristine strength.

2. Al-Farabi, *Musterstaat,* p. 73; *Philosophische Abhandlungen,* p. 123, translated by Dieterici; on Ibn Sina, cf. Schahrastani, *op. cit.,* II, p. 278.

3. Al-Farabi, p. 13; on Ibn Sina, cf. Schahrastani, *op. cit.,* II, pp. 255 f.

4. Schahrastani, *op. cit.,* II, pp. 310 ff.

5. Al-Farabi, *Philosophische Abhandlungen,* pp. 68 f; on Ibn Sina, cf. Schahrastani, *op. cit.,* II, p. 316.

6. This characteristic is unique to all of the citations mentioned in n. 2.

7. Schahrastani, *op. cit.,* II, p. 273.

8. Al-Farabi, *Musterstaat,* p. 69 ff.; Schahrastani, *op. cit.,* II, p. 328.

9. Al-Farabi, *Musterstaat,* p. 23 f.; Schahrastani, *op. cit.,* II, pp. 258 ff.

10. Al-Farabi, *Musterstaat,* p. 73.

11. Al-Farabi, *Philosophische Abhand-lungen*, pp. 125–127; *Musterstaat*, p. 80 ff.; Schahrastani, *op. cit.*, II, p. 281 ff., 317 f., 329 ff. In both of these thinkers we find next to this explication of proph-ecy, the interpretation that the occur-rence of prophetic lawgivers is a necessity for the existence of the human social order, and, therefore, God provides such prophets. It seems, therefore, that these thinkers accepted the idea of missionary prophets, thus implicitly rejecting the naturalistic explanation of prophecy. But this admission of missionary prophecy is not that of the religious tradition, for the occurrence of prophets who are necessary for the existence of the social order is assured by the natural teleolog-ical order of things. Providence, which combines with this teleological order, certifies in advance that prophets will appear. Cf. al-Farabi, *Musterstaat*, p. 84 ff., p. 90 ff.; and especially Schahrastani, *op. cit.*, II, p. 282.

12. Al-Farabi, *Philosophische Abhadlun-gen*, p. 71 ff.; *Musterstaat*, p. 13; Schahras-tani, *op. cit.*, p. 255.

13. The most detailed and radical devel-opment of this view can be found in the writings of Ibn Rushd, translated into German and edited by M. J. Müller, un-der the title of *Philosophie und Theologie*. The citations assembled by Stöckl (*Ges-chichte der Philosophie des Mittelalters*, II, 25) prove that Ibn Sina, too, upholds the major portion of this view.

14. Schahrastani, *op. cit.*, II, p. 257.

15. Cf. Maimonides, *Moreh Nebukhim*, III, 18, for his reliance on the words of al-Farabi.

16. Schahrastani, *op. cit.*, II, p. 331.

17. Schahrastani, *op. cit.*, II, p. 324 ff.

18. Al-Farabi, *Philosophische Abhand-lungen*, p. 37 ff.

19. Cf. the exposition of the false doc-trines of the philosophers in the penetrat-ing essay of Ghazali (Schmölders' *Essai sur les écoles philosophiques chez les arabes*, p. 36 f.) and the presentation of philosophy made in Halevi's *Sefer Ha-Kuzari*, I, 1; IV, 19.

20. Maimonides, *Moreh Nebukhim*, II, 15.

21. *Ibid.*, III, 16; II, 32.

22. Abraham ibn Daud. *Sefer ha-Emu-nah ha-Ramah*, translated and edited by Samson Weil, p. 2.

23. *Ibid.*, p. 4.

24. *Ibid.;* cf. Jacob Guttmann in the book *Moses ben Maimon . . .* , edited by Bacher, Brown, *et al.* II, 233 ff.

25. Abraham ibn Daud, *op. cit.*, pp. 1–4.

26. *Ibid.*, p. 18 ff., p. 47.

27. *Ibid.*, p. 47 ff.

28. *Ibid.*, p. 48. Cf. Jacob Guttmann, *Die Religionsphilosophie des Abraham ibn Daud*, p. 121. On the contrary, Wolfson ("Notes of Proofs of the Existence of God in Jewish Philosophy," *Hebrew Union College Annual*, I, 583f.) states that, ac-cording to Ibn Daud's view, a necessarily existent entity is one which is, from its very beginning, uncaused and that the identity of essence and existence arises only from this state of being uncaused. But since Ibn Daud seeks to prove, in the citation mentioned, that a necessary exist-ent is uncaused, since its essence includes its own existence, it is impossible that the expression "a necessarily existent entity" should mean an *uncaused* entity.

29. Abraham ibn Daud, *op. cit.*, pp. 49 f.

30. *Ibid.*, p. 63 ff.

31. *Ibid.*, p. 67.

32. *Ibid.*, p. 86.

33. *Ibid.*, p. 67.

34. *Ibid.*, p. 47.

35. *Ibid.*, p. 21.

36. *Ibid.*, p. 22.

37. *Ibid.*, p. 34 f.

38. *Ibid.*, p. 35.

39. *Ibid.*, p. 37.

40. *Ibid.*, p. 38 ff.

41. *Ibid.*, p. 36.

42. *Ibid.*, p. 57 ff.

43. *Ibid.*, p. 58 ff.

44. *Ibid.*, p. 70 ff., p. 86 ff.

45. *Ibid.*, p. 70 ff.

46. *Ibid.*, p. 89 ff. Ibn Daud does not here explicitly say that the sense data are manifested to the power of imagination, but in terms of his psychological theory, extra-intellectual power must intervene. Al-Farabi also notes in the statement, quoted by Disendruck—"Maimonides' Lehre von der Prophetie," *Jewish Studies in Memory of Israel Abrahams*, p. 84— from the book *Hathalot ha-nimtzaim* (*The Origin of Things*), Ha-asif, p. 40, that prophecy is indigenous to the intel-lectual power alone, and the imagination which is spoken of in *Hamedinah l'mofait* (*Musterstaat* p. 81 ff., p. 93), is viewed only as a necessary condition of prophecy. *Hamedinah l'mofait* also speaks of the dis-turbances due to imagination, as does

Ibn Daud; cf. pp. 76 ff., 84. Thus, the apparent dismissal of the imagination from prophecy by Ibn Daud, found on p. 70, can be laid to the brevity of the exposition there. Besides this, one finds in all the various authors who discuss prophecy, that the word "imagination" includes not only phantasms but also the creative power of conceptualization, which is separate from the former. If we pay attention to this linguistic usage, we can clear away many ambiguities.

47. Cf. n. 11.

48. Abraham ibn Daud, *op. cit.,* p. 73.

49. *Ibid.,* p. 74 ff.

50. Al-Farabi, *Philosophische Abhandlungen,* p. 128.

51. Abraham ibn Daud, *op. cit.,* p. 96; Alexander of Aphrodisias, *De Fato,* chap. 30.

52. Abraham ibn Daud, *op. cit.,* p. 98. Proofs for the combination of Platonic and Aristotelian theories of truth in the Islamic and Jewish Aristotelians can be found in the introduction to Goldziher's edition of Pseudo-Bahya, p. 20.

53. *Ibid.,* p. 102 ff.

54. *Ibid.,* p. 100 ff.

55. *Ibid.,* p. 45 ff.

56. Concerning the influence of Maimonides on Christian philosophy, cf. essay of Jacob Guttmann in the chrestomathy of Bacher and Braun: *"Moses ben Maimon* . . . ,* Vol. I. Joseph Koch proved that Meister Eckhart, too, followed Maimonides in important aspects of his theology.

57. For the following exposition, I have utilized Julius Guttmann, *Die religiösen Motive in der Philosophie des Maimonides.* . . .

58. Cf. the essay, "Maimuni als medizinischer Schriftstellar," in the previously mentioned collection of Bacher and Braun, I, 1.

59. Maimonides, *Guide for the Perplexed* (hereafter referred to as *Guide*), I, 50. [In the pagination used below, Munk's Arabic edition is the source, and the Hebrew edition referred to is that translated by Jehuda ibn Shmuel (Jerusalem, 1946). In the Arabic edition, there is a separate pagination for each of the three basic divisions of the book.]

60. *Ibid.,* III, 51.

61. *Ibid.,* I, 31–32; II, 24.

62. *Ibid.,* I, Introduction: Arabic, p. 4, ff., Hebrew, pp. 6–7.

63. *Ibid.*

64. The three elements of Maimonides' theory of knowledge (epistemology), i.e., metaphysical rationalism, emphasis on those categories which are apprehensible by human cognition, and the intuitive grasp of metaphysical knowledge, are undoubtedly to be found in different sources. But here, and in similar instances, it is not sufficient to prove that he was influenced by various sources, but one must ask, in each instance, how far he was able to go in shaping from these various sources a unified and consistent view. In the actual text I have attempted to deal with this question, and not by means of hints alone. But it is proper to add that the reconciliation and construction is not a complete one and that contradiction still remains between the various viewpoints. The metaphysical rationalism of Maimonides is fully realized in the statement that thought can elevate us to the supersensual world. This is ambiguous, if the inner essence of the supersensual world is unknowable to us, if our knowledge of this world is purely a negative one. Similarly, it is unclear, as I have already remarked in the text, how the discursive element and the intuitive are united in metaphysical cognition, despite the fact that the dependence of human knowledge upon the active intellect introduces an element of intuition into discursive thought and thus bridges the gap between the two.

65. Maimonides, *Guide,* I, 76: Arabic, p. 127b; Hebrew, p. 202. *Critique of the Kalaam,* I, 73–76.

66. *Ibid.,* II, 1: Arabic, p. 5b–9a; Hebrew, pp. 212–217.

67. *Ibid.,* II, 1: Arabic, p. 7; Hebrew, p. 241; II, 4: Arabic, p. 14b; Hebrew p. 225.

68. *Ibid.,* I, 57.

69. *Ibid.,* II, Preface, 21.

70. *Ibid.,* I, 51: Arabic, 57b; Hebrew, pp. 25 f.

71. *Ibid.,* I, 52: Arabic, p. 59; Hebrew, p. 97.

72. *Ibid.,* I, 50: Arabic, p. 57a; Hebrew, p. 94.

73. *Ibid.,* I, 57, 430.

74. *Ibid.,* I, 52, Arabic, p. 60 ff; Hebrew, pp. 99–100.

75. *Ibid.,* I, 54.

76. *Ibid.,* I, 58.

77. *Ibid.,* I, 58: Arabic, p. 71; Hebrew, p. 116.

78. *Ibid.,* I, 54: Arabic, p. 65; Hebrew, p. 105.

79. *Ibid.*, I, 58, Arabic, p. 71; Hebrew, p. 116.

80. This question was specifically harped on by Hasdai Crescas; cf. below, pp. 245–246.

81. Maimonides, *op. cit.*, I, 68.

82. *Ibid.*, III, 21, 22.

83. *Ibid.*, II, 18, the second way.

84. Compare here my essay, "Maimonides' Theology" in the Festschrift in honor of Y. H. Hertz, the Hebrew section, pp. 53–69. From a more logico-formal viewpoint, Wolfson deals with the doctrine of attributes in his older essay: "Crescas on the Problem of Divine Attributes" (*JQR*, n.s., VII, 19); and in his newer essay, "Maimonides on Negative Attributes" (*Ginzberg Jubilee Volume*, English section, pp. 411–466). Among other things, in the older essay he says that in the statement "God exists," despite its negative interpretation, the implied positive attribution is of equal worth. All such statements are tautologies, for existence, unity, and knowledge are, in the case of God, identical with his essence. But even if the statement "God exists," upon analysis is tautological, i.e., "God is God," there is still some content to the statement because, first it denies lack of existence in regard to God and, secondly, it claims that God exists in a way unique to him: that his existence is one with his essence and has nothing in common with our mode of existence other than a common linguistic name. In this second sense of the statement, there is implicit the essential value of the positive form of attribution (Wolfson, *op. cit.*, *JQR* n.s., VII, 20). Against the proposition that one can attribute positive attributions to God, I listed in the German edition of this book a whole series of objections. In a more recent essay, Wolfson attempts to justify his previous view by giving a more detailed analysis of it. But if I fully comprehend his presentation, he demolishes the thesis to which I had objected. He now sees the significance of the statement "God exists" as being tautological only to the extent that it denies the lack of existence to God (Wolfson, *op. cit.*, pp. 420–421). Only in this roundabout way can God's existence be affirmed, and this is in agreement with my view. But this undercuts the essential value of the positive form of attribution, and my previous objections disappear before this formula-

tion of the theory. For the comprehension of the theory of negative attribution, the essay is rich in new materials and insights, a discussion of which would involve me in too detailed a discourse.

85. Maimonides, *Guide*, II, 25.

86. *Ibid.*, II, 21.

87. *Ibid.*, II, 14: Arabic, p. 30a; Hebrew, p. 249.

88. *Ibid.*, Arabic, p. 31; Hebrew, p. 250. Kaufmann (*Geschichte der Attributenlehre in der jüdischen Religionsphilosophie . . .*, p. 302, n. 139; p. 304, n. 145) had already pointed out that the same proofs had been educed by Schahrastani in the name of Proclus.

89. *Ibid.*, II, 17.

90. *Ibid.*, II, 18.

91. *Ibid.*, II, 19.

92. *Ibid.*, II, 22.

93. *Ibid.*, I, 74, the fifth proof: Arabic, p. 119b ff.; Hebrew, p. 190 ff.; II, 19. Arabic, p. 40a; Hebrew, p. 264. In the last mentioned place, Maimonides points out the similarities and differences of his proof from that of the Kalam.

94. Duhem, *Le système du monde*, V, 191 ff.

95. A detailed analysis, both of the opposed proofs to the eternity of the world, and those dealing with the origin of the world from the will of God, is given by Bamberger in his book, *Das System des Maimonides, eine Analyse des More Newuchim vom Gottesbegriff aus*, Chap. 2, "Die Kosmologie." I have dealt with several related problems in my essay, "Das Problem der Kontingenz in der Philosophie des Maimonides," which is scheduled to appear in the last volume of *MGWJ*. The volume was printed but has not yet been published.

96. Commentary on *Ethics of the Fathers*, V, 6.

97. Maimonides, *Guide*, II, 29: Arabic, p. 64b; Hebrew, pp. 302–303. From the tenor of the statements, which were carefully edited, it is difficult to determine with certainty whether Maimonides maintains his previous view or changes it in the manner suggested in the text.

98. *Ibid.*, III, 20.

99. *Ibid.*, III, 17, Arabic, pp. 35b ff.; Hebrew, p. 427. The similarity to the opinion of Ibn Ezra is not limited to this concept alone. He interprets the operation of divine providence, which guards the man who is attached to God through in-

tellectual activity by warning him of impending dangers, by means of an example which is entirely comparable to that given by Maimonides. Our explanation of Maimonides' doctrine of providence follows that given by most modern scholars, who rely upon chapter 17 of the third section, where the problem of providence is systematically set forth. But Samuel ibn Tibbon, translator of the *Guide*, had already noted in his letter to Maimonides that in chapter III, 23 (Arabic, pp. 48–49; Hebrew, pp. 449 ff.) and in chapter III, 51 (Arabic, pp. 127–128; Hebrew 585–587) there are locutions which yield an exactly contrary theory to that indicated in chapter 17 (cf. Diesendruck, "Samuel and Moses ibn Tibbon on Maimonides' Theory of Providence," *HUCA*, XI, 341–366). It is clear that these contradictions were not unintended. Maimonides did not propose a full-scale exposition of his final thoughts on this matter, and therefore—in agreement with the position he adopted at the end of the introduction to *Guide*—he allowed opinions which were contradictory to each other to stand in various places in the book, thereby arousing the informed reader to discover his true doctrine. The medieval commentators, however, when it came to a discussion of this problem of his esoteric doctrine, were of various opinions concerning its seriousness and application, and so long as there is no convincing and probative hypothesis otherwise, we have no course but to uphold the statements of chapter 17.

100. Maimonides does try, however subtly, to apply the intellectual hierarchy to morality; cf. *Guide*, II, 18: Arabic, p. 37b ff.; Hebrew, pp. 432–433.

101. Maimonides, *Guide*, II, 32, especially: Arabic, p. 73b; Hebrew, pp. 317–318; II, 36, especially: Arabic, p. 78; Hebrew, pp. 326–327. Diesendruck attempts to explain this theory in his "Maimonides' Lehre von der Prophetie" (*Jewish Studies in Memory of Israel Abrahams*, pp. 74–134).

102. Maimonides, *Guide*, II, 37. The doctrine of augury and its comparison to the inspiration of the statesman has its ultimate source in Plato; cf. *Meno*, 99.

103. On the prophetic foretelling of the future, cf. Maimonides, *Guide*, II, 38: Arabic, p. 82; Hebrew, pp. 331–333. On the metaphorical form of the prophetic Holy Spirit, cf. II, 47, especially at the end of

the chapter. We shall discuss later the political function of the prophets, to which we have paid no attention here.

104. *Ibid.*, II, 38: Arabic, pp. 82b–83; Hebrew, pp. 333–334.

105. *Ibid.*, II, 32: Arabic, pp. 73a ff.; Hebrew, pp. 317–318.

106. *Ibid*, II, 35: *Mishneh Torah, Hilkot Yesodei ha-Torah*, VII, 6.

107. *Ibid.*, II, 39: *Hilkot Yesodei ha-Torah*, VIII, IX.

108. *Ibid.*, III, 13: Arabic, p. 22b; Hebrew, pp. 406–407.

109. *Ibid.*, Arabic, pp. 23b f.; Hebrew, pp. 407–408.

110. *Ibid.*, III, 25: Arabic, pp. 55b ff; Hebrew, pp. 462 f.

111. *Ibid.*: Arabic, pp. 56 ff.; Hebrew, pp. 463–464.

112. An attempt to smooth out the contradictory statements in Maimonides' work and to construct a systematic whole of his system was attempted by Diesendruck, "Die Teleologie bei Maimonides," but many of his constructions are farfetched.

113. *Ibid.*, III, 54: Arabic, p. 132b ff.; Hebrew, p. 596.

114. *Ibid.*, II, 40: Arabic, p. 86b ff.; Hebrew, p. 339; III, 27.

115. Introduction to the *Commentary on the Mishnah* (Hamburg ed., p. 53); Maimonides, *Guide*, II, 36: Arabic, p. 79; Hebrew, pp. 327–328; III, 33.

116. Maimonides, *Guide*, III, 51: Arabic, pp. 125 ff.; Hebrew, pp. 581–582.

117. *Ibid.*: Arabic, pp. 126b ff.; Hebrew, pp. 583–584.

118. *Ibid.*: I, 70: Arabic, p. 92b; Hebrew, pp. 149–150; III, 27: Arabic, p. 60a; Hebrew, pp. 470–471.

119. *Ibid.*, III, 54: Arabic, p. 134b ff.; Hebrew, pp. 598–599.

120. *Ibid.*, III, 51: Arabic, pp. 125a, 129a; Hebrew, pp. 581, 588; III, 52. As we have said in the text, the value which Maimonides assigns to the love of God does not have any bearing on the moral-personal aspect of his religiosity, because the love of God can also be found in contemplative and traditional religiosity, and only the character (manner) of the love of God differentiates between these two forms of religion. When Maimonides derives the love of God from the knowledge of God, one finds a hint of the contemplative love of God. Nevertheless, it is easy to demonstrate how this contemplative love of God is given an increasingly

personal cast. His remarks concerning the connection between knowledge of God and love of God, and on the relations between the love of God and the fear of God, are replete with contradictions, which Hoffman has adumbrated in his essay, "Die Liebe zu Gott bei Mose ben Maimon." Maimonides' statements, however, can be interpreted either as being incomplete formulations of his position, or the presentation of different (various) aspects of one subject matter.

121. Maimonides, *Guide,* I, Introduction: Arabic, pp. 3b ff.; Hebrew, pp. 5, 6; I, 33: Arabic, p. 36b ff.; Hebrew, pp. 61–62.

122. *Ibid.,* I, 35.

123. *Commentary on the Mishnah,* Sanhedrin 10 (11), a.

124. Maimonides, *Guide,* II, 40; III, 27.

125. Leo Strauss, in his book *Philosophie und Gesetz,* was the first to treat of the value of the doctrines of the Islamic Aristotelians concerning the political function and goal of prophecy, the dependence of this doctrine upon Plato, and its influence upon Maimonides. But, for reasons at which I can only hint in the text of my book, it seems to me incorrect to interpret in a fundamental fashion the revelation of God, especially in regard to Maimonides, as the disclosure of laws and statutes. Even less can I agree with Strauss' hypothesis that one must set the political interpretation of prophecy as the foundation stone for the understanding of the whole of medieval philosophy. Just as in revelation, the laws and statutes set forth are means to an end which belongs not to the practical but to the theoretical sphere, so we find that in philosophy in general, for Plato and Aristotle and their medieval disciples, politics and statecraft are based upon the doctrine of the final end of man and, therefore, ultimately on metaphysics. This hierarchy is also applicable to the philosophic interpretation of revelation. Therefore, the relation of reason to revelation also cannot be understood from this "political" viewpoint. In a later essay ("On Abravanel's Philosophy and Political Teaching," pp. 99–100), Strauss advances his thesis that the relation of revelation to philosophy is settled or fixed by politics, insofar as the adjudication of philosophic truth to the understanding of the masses serves the need of political regulations. Truth to tell, Maimonides (*Guide,* III, 25) does explicitly say that many statements about God made in Scripture were put down only to arouse fear of the Lord in the hearts of the masses. But it certainly is not the major import of his doctrine that the adjustment of philosophic truth to the understanding of the masses serves only the purpose of law and statute! Such would be the case if it is true that the final goal of the Law, the enlightenment of the human spirit, is impossible for the masses—and such is certainly not the opinion of Maimonides. On the contrary, he upholds the necessity of teaching truth to the masses, insofar as they are able to apprehend it, in the form they are able to understand.

Moreover, if Strauss is correct, it would be impossible to analyze and settle the essential relationship between reason and revelation by means of the differentiation of the esoteric and exoteric meanings of revelation itself. Admitting the importance of this problem, nevertheless, from a methodological point of view, it is not the primary problem in terms of the general understanding of the philosophy of the Middle Ages. In his later essays, Strauss sets down the thesis that for medieval philosophers there is an abyss between the exoteric and esoteric interpretations of their own doctrines, an abyss far deeper than has been realized heretofore. Concerning their esoteric doctrines, he has not yet expressed himself in a systematic way, and thus it is impossible to form a decisive estimate of his position. But at present, it is clear, that for him, philosophy in its esoteric sense has no connection with revelation, as had been surmised in his earlier essays, but is completely autonomous.

126. *Guide,* III, 51: Arabic, p. 123; Hebrew, pp. 578–579.

127. *Ibid.,* III, 27.

128. *Ibid.,* III, 43, 44.

129. *Ibid.,* III, 29; especially, cf. end of chapter. There are many detailed explanations in Section III, Chaps. 37 and 46. The interpretation of the sacrificial cultus in Section III, 32: Arabic, p. 69b ff.; Hebrew, pp. 485–487.

130. *Ibid.,* III, 29.

131. Cf. my essay, "John Spencers Erklärung der biblischen Gesetze in ihrer Beziehung zu Maimonides," *Festschrift für Simonsen,* pp. 259 ff.

132. Essay on the resurrection of the

dead, in *Responsen und Briefen des Maimonides* (Leipzig edition), II, p. 7b ff. Ghazali characterizes the Aristotelian Muslims as those who disbelieve the resurrection of the dead. Cf. Schmölders, *Essai*, p. 36; Horten, *Die Hauptlehren des Averroës*, p. 278.

133. Meir ben Todros Abulafia, *Kitab al-rasil* (Brill edition), p. 14 ff.

134. Grätz, *Geschichte der Juden* (German edition), VII, 34 ff.; N. Brüll, *Die Polemik für und gegen Maimuni im 13. Jahrhundert*, *Jahrbücher für jüdische Geschichte und Litteratur*, IV, 1–33. I. Sarachek, *Faith and Reason, The Conflict over the Rationalism of Maimonides*.

135. *Responsen und Briefen des Maimonides* (Leipzig), III, 19b.

136. *Ibid.*, p. 18a.

137. Koback, *Jeshurun* (Hebrew section), VIII, 146 ff.

138. *Ibid.*, p. 100. N. Brüll, *op. cit.*, p. 9, interprets this section in the light of Ibn Tibbon's calling the commandments "conventional rules." But the Hebrew word "rule" really means "guide." The proper interpretation is, therefore, that just as the biblical narratives are popular parables, the commandments, too, seek to guide the masses along ethical paths. But, cf. this expression in Judah Halevi, *Sefer Ha-Kuzari*, IV, 19.

139. *Responsen des Maimonides*, III, 1b ff.

140. Grätz, *op. cit.*, p. 222 ff.; Geiger, *Wissenschaftliche Zeitschrift für jüdische Theologie*, V., 123–198; Perles, *R. Salomo ben Abraham Adereth*, pp. 12–54; E. Renan and A. Neubauer, *Les rabbins français du commencement du quatorzième siècle*, pp. 647 and *passim*.

141. Kaufmann presents a listing of similar allegorical interpretations in the collection, *Zunzfestschrift*, p. 143 ff.

142. Abba Mari, *Minhat Kanaot* (a collection of letters written during the epoch of the controversy), edited by Bisliches, no. 7, p. 40 ff.; no. 14, p. 49 ff.; no. 25, p. 69.

143. Cf. L. Baeck, "Zur Charakteristik des Levi ben Abraham ben Chajim, *MGWJ*, LXIV, 28, 343 ff.

144. Cf. Pines, "Études sur Awhad al Zamma Abu'l Barakat al-Baghdadi," *RÉJ*, CIV, 1–95.

145. Joseph ben Judah, *Sefer Ha-musar* (edited by Bacher, 1910); cf. Introduction, pp. xiv–xv.

146. *Responsen und Briefen des Maimonides* (Leipzig), II, 44–46.

147. This chapter was printed in Güdemann's book, *Das jüdische Unterrichtswesen während der spanisch-arabischen Periode*, both in the Arabic original and in German translation. Most recently, A. S. Halkin published an additional chapter of the book under the title, "Classical and Arabic Material in Ibn Aknin's Hygiene of the Soul" (*PAAJR*, XIV, 26–147), which includes ethical apothegms of Greek and Islamic sages in the Arabic original and in English translation; Halkin traces the material to their proper sources. But from this chrestomathy it is impossible to determine what was Ibn Aknin's philosophical viewpoint.

148. Güdemann, *op. cit.*: Arabic, p. 45; German, p. 114.

149. *Ibid.*: Arabic, p. 16; German, p. 67.

150. *Ibid.*: Arabic, pp. 14–15; German, pp. 64–67.

151. Baneth has recently contested this identification; *Letters of Maimonides* (Jerusalem, 1946), I, 6.

152. Joseph ibn Aknin, *A Treatise as to: Necessary Existence; The Procedure of Things from the Necessary Existence; The Creation of the World*, edited by Judah L. Magnes in his inaugural dissertation (Berlin, 1904).

153. Cf. Güdemann, *op. cit.*, Hebrew text p. 12; cf. also p. 5.

154. *Ibid.*, pp. 17–18.

155. *Ibid.*, pp. 19–20.

156. *Ibid.*, pp. 15–16.

157. Samuel Rosenblatt, *The High Way to Perfection of Abraham Maimonides*, Vol. I, 1927; Vol. II, 1938 (the major portion of the Arabic text together with an English translation). The first volume also contains a detailed introduction by the editor, which analyzes the book and demonstrates that the doctrines are of limited worth.

158. *Ibid.*, Introduction, I, 48–53.

159. Cf. *Ibid.*; the listing of Table of Contents in I, 130–131; II, 382–383.

160. This conception of the final end arises from the description of the complete union between man and God (*ibid.*, Introduction, I, 96–99, 52 and *passim*).

161. *Ibid.*, II, p. 312, 374, 376–380. Cf. Introduction, I, 42–44.

162. *Ibid.*, II, 60.

163. *Ibid.*, II, 58–60.

164. *Ibid.*, II, 306–308.

165. *Ibid.*, II, 54.

166. Cf. *ibid.*, Introduction, I, 65, and the citations found therein. Only once (II, 58) is it said there that the union of man with God is affected through the agency of the angels, but it is impossible to determine whether these angels are identical with the separate intelligences of the Aristotelians; this is but a theological presentation of the philosophic theory of prophecy.

167. *Ibid.*, II, 126–132.

168. *Ibid.*, II, 148–150, 132–138.

169. C. F. Güdemann: *Geschichte des Erziehungswesens und der Kultur der Juden in Italien*, p. 161 ff.

170. Steinschneider, *Die hebräischen Übersetzungen* . . . , par. 2, p. 5 ff.

171. A series of such radical interpretations of Maimonides' doctrines are listed in the Werbluner edition of the *Commentary on the Guide.*

172. For the exposition of the psychology of Hillel, I have utilized an unpublished essay of my father.

173. Hillel ben Samuel, *The Rewards of the Soul*, edited by S. Halberstam, pp.1–7. In p. 2a of the book, Hillel buttresses his arguments by invoking arguments presented in the sixth book of the physics of Ibn Sina and from the first book of his primary medical textbook, the *Canon*, of which he utilized the first-mentioned text to a great degree. Parallels to the Latin *De anima* of *Gundissalinus* (edited by Lewinthal) can be found, especially on pp. 2a, 3, 4a. It is possible that both utilized a common source (besides Ibn Sina) but this is rather unreasonable.

174. Hillel ben Samuel, *Tagmuley ha-Nefesh* (Rewards of the Soul), from Chap. 4 on pp. 3b ff. Ibn Sina also thought of the individual soul, which, according to him, was generated together with the body, as being an emanation of immaterial substances—this can be proven from Schahrastani's statements in II, 325 ff. On Hillel's definition, cf. I. Husik, *A History of Medieval Jewish Philosophy*, p. 317.

175. *Ibid.*, Chap. 5, p. 8.

176. *Ibid.*, pp. 9b ff.

177. *Ibid.*, Chap. 7, pp. 13b ff.

178. *Ibid.*, p. 17a.

179. *Ibid.*, p. 17b.

180. *Ibid.*, Chap. 6, p. 10 ff.

181. Published in a Hebrew edition by Hercz. In any case, the writings do not utilize the assumption that the potential intellect has a superhuman character. Despite this, it seems that they think of it as a positive portion of the individual soul. A proof for this, if we neglect certain isolated cases for a moment, can be seen in the posing of the question of how the union of the potential and active intellects is possible. If the former is also thought of as a supernatural substance, which ultimately is identical with the active intellect, the question put in this form is, therefore, obviated, and one can only ask how the human intellect is able, through the potential intellect, to attain unification with the active intellect. These various ways of putting the questions are intermingled with each other many times by Ibn Rushd.

182. Published in abbreviated form by Schorr in *Hehalutz*, IV–VII.

183. Schorr, *op. cit.*, VI, 93. The parallel doctrine of Latin Averroism can be seen in Mandonnet's book, *Siger de Brabant et l'avverroïsme latin au XIII siècle*, II, 154, 157, 167. Because Albalag was well versed in Christian books (cf. Steinschneider, *Die hebraischen Ubersetzungen des Mittelalters*, p. 305), his dependence upon Latin Averroism, some of whose definitions are identical with his, can be taken as certain.

184. Schorr, *op. cit.*, VI, 93; cf VII, 160.

185. *Ibid.*, VI, 85–94, VII, 157. Concerning his dependence upon Ibn Rushd, cf. my essay, "The Doctrine of Isaac Albalag," *Levi Ginzberg Jubilee Volume*, Hebrew section, p. 75 ff.

186. *Ibid.*, VII, 164 ff.

187. *Ibid.*, VII, 160.

188. *Ibid.*, IV, 92–93.

189. *Ibid.*, IV, 93–94.

190. *Ibid.*, IV, 94. Cf. VI, 90.

191. *Ibid.*, VI, 90–93.

192. My essay presents a more precise basis for this view of Albalag's doctrine.

193. The Hebrew version of the treatise has been lost. All that we have is the Spanish translation, done by Abner himself, and to this date, unpublished. For our knowledge of this treatise we must tender acknowledgment to Y. Baer, "Sefer Minhat Kanaut shel Abner mi-Burgos, v'hashpaato al Hasda Crescas" (*Tarbiz*, XI, 188–206), who gives an abbreviated Hebrew translation, analyzes its contents, and demonstrates its undoubted influence upon Crescas.

194. Schorr, *op. cit.*, pp. 190, 197; cf. also p. 103.

195. *Ibid.*, p. 192.
196. *Ibid.*, pp. 193–195.
197. *Ibid.*, pp. 193–195.
198. *Ibid.*, p. 196. In this small matter, I cannot agree with Baer who seeks to amalgamate Abner's doctrine of determinism to the Christian doctrine of predestination.
199. *Ibid.*, pp. 201–203.
200. *Ibid.*, pp. 191–196, 198.
201. Cf. Poleqar, *The Helpmeet of Religion (Ezer la-dat)*, edited by Blaskov (London, 1906), p. 57 ff.
202. *Ibid.*, pp. 69–70. Abner argues against an opinion similar to this in Poleqar, *op. cit.*, p. 190.
203. Several of Poleqar's statements make reasonable the interpretation that the atemporal knowledge of God has no temporal relation to the deeds of man and cannot, therefore, precede them in time. Only those matters which relate to God's knowledge have a temporal locus, and these have no prior place in God's knowledge than they do in actual existence. But, aside from the fact that such an interpretation contradicts certain other hypotheses of Poleqar, it leads to an illusionary solution of the problem, whose sophistic character can be seen upon immediate inspection.
204. Cf. Moses Narboni, "Essay on Freedom of Choice," in *Words of the Wise*, edited by Eliezer Ashkenazi (Metz, 1849).
205. *Ibid.*, pp. 39 ff. Cf. also Narboni's *Commentary to the Guide*, III, 20, p. 58a.
206. *Ibid.*, pp. 37–39, 41.
207. Moses Narboni, *Commentary to the Guide for the Perplexed*, edited by Goldenthal (Vienna, 1852), I, 57; II, 1.
208. For a quick summary of his writings, cf. Renan, *Les écrivains juifs du XIV siècle*, pp. 250–298; Steinschneider, *Gesammelte Schriften*, I, 233–258.
209. Cf. Carlebach, *Lewi ben Gerson als Mathematiker*. Here one can find a listing of the rest of the literature.
210. A brief listing of the contents of the chapter in Hebrew and in Latin can be found in Renan, *op. cit.*, pp. 178 ff.; *ibid.*, p. 278, for an explanation of the goal of the theory which can be found in the text. Cf. also Carlebach, *op. cit.*, p. 41; Duhem, *Le système du monde*, p. 201.
211. Levi ben Gerson, *Sefer Milhamot Adonai*, III, 3, p. 135 ff. A somewhat different understanding of the proof can be found in Wolfson, "Crescas on the Prob-

lem of Divine Attributes," p. 38, where he also cites the parallel doctrines of Averroës.
212. Levi ben Gerson, *op. cit.*, III, 3, 136 ff.
213. *Ibid.*, VI, 1, 6, p. 308 ff.
214. *Ibid.*, VI, 1, 7, p. 312 ff.
215. *Ibid.*, VI, 1, 11, pp. 336 ff., 344 ff.
216. *Ibid.*, VI, 1, 4, p. 306.
217. *Ibid.*, VI, 1, 17, p. 366.
218. *Ibid.*, p. 364 ff.
219. *Ibid.*, p. 367 ff.; VI, 1, 18, pp. 373 ff. Although Gersonides speaks of an eternal substance (body), the context intends only the undefined background of existence. This very conception of the generation of the world, can be seen explicity stated in Ibn Rushd's interpretation of Aristotelian physics. Cf. Duhem, *op. cit.*, p. 216 ff. The statement quoted there (p. 218), according to which Gersonides considered that the creation of matter is possible, is merely an exposition of Maimonides, as can be seen from the context.
220. Levi ben Gerson, *op. cit.*, VI, 1, 8, p. 320; VI, 1, 16, p. 359; III, 3, p. 137.
221. Cf. M. Joël, "Lewi ben Gerson als Religionsphilosoph" *MGWJ*, X, pp. 307 ff.
222. Levi ben Gerson, *op. cit.*, III, 2, p. 126 ff.; III, 4, p. 137 ff.
223. Cf. Horten, *Die Hauptlehren des Averroës*, p. 241; *Philosophie und Religion von Averroës*, p. 11.
224. Levi ben Gerson, *op. cit.*, V, 3c, p. 240 ff.; V, 3e, p. 257 ff.
225. *Ibid.*, V, 3h, p. 269 ff.
226. *Ibid.*, V, 3m, pp. 285 ff., 288 f.
227. *Philosophie und Theologie von Averroës (translated by Müller)*, p. 122.
228. Paraphrase to Aristotle's *"De divinatione,"* from which Gersonides quotes in his *Milhamot*, II, 6, p. 106.
229. Levi ben Gerson, *op. cit.*, II, 6, pp. 105 ff., 108 ff.
230. *Ibid.*, p. 111 ff.
231. *Ibid.*, p. 111.
232. *Ibid.*, VI, 2, 10, pp. 445 ff., 450 ff.
233. *Ibid.*, I, 1, p. 12 ff.
234. *Ibid.*, I, 2, pp., 14–16; I, 3, p. 21.
235. *Ibid.*, I, 2, p. 16 ff.
236. *Ibid.*, p. 13 ff.
237. The valid element of the Aristotelian conception is the striving to account for cognitive errors by the nature of the intellect. The notion that cognition is an abstraction from the concept or an objectification of the cognized concept constitutes a decisive step towards materializ-

ing the cognitive process. The identification of the concept with the formal essence of objects leads to the absorption of essence in thought. Thus, it is unnecessary for thought to have any constitutive structure or to be bound up with matter in order to be able to receive the forms clearly or to become one with them.

238. Levi ben Gerson, *op. cit.*, I, 3, p. 19 ff.

239. *Ibid.*, pp. 20 f., 23 ff. For Themistius, who thinks of the active intellect as an independent substance, this result is, of course, impossible. For it is the nature of a thinking substance to think. Therefore, it cannot be prevented from receiving concepts (I, 4, p. 34 ff.).

240. *Ibid.*, I, 4, p. 25 ff.

241. *Ibid.*, I, 8, p. 52; I, 9, p. 53 ff.

242. *Ibid.*, I, 12, p. 85 ff.

243. *Ibid.*, I, 10, p. 61 ff. My essay, "Levi ben Gersons Theorie des Begriffs," explains the very interesting theory of concepts of Gersonides, which forms the background for the matters discussed in the text.

244. Levi ben Gerson, *op. cit.*, I, 11, p. 82 ff.

245. Hillel ben Samuel, *Rewards of the Soul*, I, 13, p. 89 ff.

246. That the human spirit receives its terrestrial knowledge from the active intellect, which in turn is influenced by the intelligences of the spheres, does not affect what is said here.

247. Cf. Perles, "Über den Geist des Kommentars des R. Moses ben Nachman zum Pentateuch," *MGWJ*, VII, 81, 117 ff.

248. Cf. G. Scholem, "Hathalot ha-kabala," *Knesset*, X (Tel-Aviv, 1946), pp. 181–228, Scholem's previous view, embodied in "Zur Frage der Entstehung der Kabbala," *Korrespondenzblatt der Akademie für die Wissenschaft des Judentums*, IX, 4–26, progressed and was revised in many respects, under the impact of his new inquiries.

249. Cf. Rosenmann, "Das Lehrhaus des Rabbi Nissim Gerundi in Barcelona," *Schwarzfestschrift*, p. 489 ff.

250. The principal ideas of this investigation were set forth in my essay, "Chasdai Crescas als Kritiker der aristotelischen physik." Crescas' magisterial work (Wolfson, *Crescas' Critique of Aristotle*) presents a detailed explication of this view, and in the appropriate notes, which he cites together with an English translation of the *Or Adonai*, Wolfson gives a precise demonstration of the connection between Crescas and the medieval interpretation of Aristotelian natural philosophy. Already, Joël, in *Don Chasdai Creskas' religionsphilosophische Lehren*, p. 82 ff., had proved that the young Pico della Mirandola cited Crescas at many points in his essay "Examen doctrine vanitatis gentium" in connection with objections made by Crescas against Aristotle. Concerning the parallels between Crescas and Galileo Galilei and Giordano Bruno, which are somewhat startling, cf. my essay, "Chasdai Crescas," and the book by Wolfson.

251. Hasdai Crescas ben Abraham, *Or Adonai*, I, 2, 7, p. 12d.

252. *Ibid.*, I, 2, 1, p. 10c.

253. *Ibid.*, p. 10b, c.

254. *Ibid.*, p. 9d.

255. *Ibid.*, pp. 9d. ff.

256. *Ibid.*, p. 11d.

257. *Ibid.*, p. 10d.

258. *Ibid.*, p. 10a. The very same words are used as an objection to a similar argument drawn from temporality; III, 1, 4, p. 51a.

259. *Ibid.*, I, 2, 1, pp. 11b, c.

260. *Ibid.*, I, 1, 3, p. 4c; I, 2, 2, p. 11d ff.

261. *Ibid.*, VI, 1, 11, p. 345.

262. *Ibid.*, III, 1, 4, p. 51b.

263. *Ibid.*, I, 2, 3, p. 12a.

264. *Ibid.*, I, 3, 2, pp. 15c, d.

265. The Aristotelian proponents of the doctrine of the eternity of the world only seemingly believe that, together with the infinity of time, they are forced to admit an infinite causal series. They limit the recognition of such a series in making any portion of it only accidentally the cause of its proximate next term. The major causal series they take to be finite. Cf. Horten, *Die Metaphysik Avicennas*, p. 382, p. 479 ff.; Wolfson, *Crescas' Critique of Aristotle*, p. 494 ff.

266. Hasdai Crescas, *op. cit.*, III, 1, 4, p. 51c; III, 1, 5, p. 52a.

267. *Ibid.*, III, 1, 5, pp. 52a, b, d.; Concerning Thomas, cf. Rohner, *Das Schöfungsproblem bei Moses Maimonides, Albertus Magnus und Thomas von Aquino*, pp. 94 ff., 107 ff. The detailed agreement between the two suggests the dependence of Crescas upon Thomas. As I later learned, the essay of Y. Epstein, "Das Problem des göttlichen Willens in der Schöpfung nach Maimonides, Gersonides und Crescas," *MGWJ*, LXXV, 337, also

deals with the question of contact with Thomas.

268. Hasdai Crescas, op. cit., III, 1, 5, pp. 52b, c. 53a.

269. Ibid., I, 3, 3, pp. 17d ff.

270. Ibid., p. 17c, ff. On the inadequacy of his detailed explication, which Crescas was charged with by later philosophers, cf. Wolfson, "Crescas on the Problem of Divine Attributes." Nevertheless, the basic intention and thrust of Crescas' thought is not thereby affected.

271. Hasdai Crescas, op. cit., I, 3, 1, pp. 15b, c.

272. Ibid., p. 15c; I, 3, 3, pp. 15d, 17d. Despite the negative formulation, the middle of p. 17d indicates that Crescas understands the existence and unity of God to be positive attributes.

273. Ibid., I, 3, 3, pp. 17c, 18b.

274. Ibid., I, 3, 5, pp. 19b, c.

275. Ibid., pp. 19c, d; II, 6, 1, p. 40d ff.

276. Ibid., II, 6, 5, p. 44d; III, Introduction, p. 45d. The last mentioned citation actually belongs to Chap. II, 6, 5, but because of a printer's error in the first edition, it was moved and placed after Chap. III. Cf. Bloch, Die Willensfreiheit von Chasdai Kreskas.

277. Hasdai Crascas, op. cit., III, 1, 5, 53a.

278. Cf. Horten, Die Metaphysik Avicennas, p. 595 ff. According to the Rambam (Maimonides) Moreh Nebukhim, II, 19, 21, many of the moderns, i.e., the Islamic Aristotelians, proposed that the world is drawn from the womb of eternity by the will of God. It is possible that Crescas relies upon this opinion. Or it may be that the characteristic voluntaristic God-idea is Crescas' alone.

279. Hasdai Crascas. op. cit., II, 6, 1, p. 41a; II, 6, 3, p. 43d.

280. Ibid, II, 6, 1, p. 39a.

281. Ibid., pp. 41c, d. In terms of their basic direction, this order of concepts is quite close to the voluntaristic notions found in Christian scholasticism. Nevertheless, I have not been able to unearth sufficiently close parallels to justify an historic linkage.

282. Ibid., II, 6, 1, pp. 40a, b, 42b.

283. Ibid., II, 6, 2, p. 41b ff.

284. Ibid., II, 4, 4, p. 34a, b.

285. Ibid., II, 6, 1, p. 40b.

286. Ibid., p. 39d.

287. Ibid., pp. 39c, d. The basic question is already asked by R. Levi ben Gerson, Sefer Milhamot Adonai, I, 2, p. 17. But his answer (ibid., I, 3, p. 24), does not affect the more detailed formulation of Crescas.

288. Ibid., IV, 11, p. 70a.

289. Ibid., II, 5, 1, p. 34c ff.

290. Ibid., II, 5, 3, p. 35b ff.

291. Renan's Averroës et l'averroisme, p. 159 and passim; Philosophie und Theologie von Averroës (translated by Müller); my essay, "Das Problem des Willensfreiheit bei Hasdai Crescas und den islamischen Aristotelikers," deals specifically with the relationship of Crescas to the Islamic Aristotelians and especially to Ibn Rushd.

292. Cf. the essay by Y. Baer on the book Minhat Kanaut, Tarbiz, I, pp. 194 ff., 204.

293. Hasdai Crescas, op. cit., II, 5, 3, p. 35c.

294. Judah Halevi, Sefer ha-Kuzari, V, 20, p. 346. It is possible that Judah Halevi borrowed this idea from an Islamic source which utilized it to buttress the doctrine of necessitarianism. But it did not appear in this particular form prior to the era of the Islamic Aristotelians.

295. Hasdai Crescas, op. cit., II, 5, 5, p. 37a; II, 5, 3, p. 35d.

296. Ibid., II, 5, 3, p. 35d.

297. Ibid., II, 5, 5, p. 37a, p. 37c.

298. Ibid., II, 5, 3, p. 36a. Bloch explains in the German section of his book, Die Willensfreiheit von Chasdai Kreskas (pp. 37–38), Crescas' doctrine of the freedom of the will, by stating that Crescas explicitly admits that the principal view of the Torah is indeterminism and that, therefore, Crescas deviates from his own philosophic position of determinism. But Crescas really only states that if the indeterministic interpretation of the Torah is correct, we should have to abandon determinism; that he does not believe such an interpretation to be the true interpretation can be seen from his attempts at a deterministic exegesis of the Pentateuch. He only admits the possibility that this interpretation, which is completely contrary to the weight of Jewish tradition, might be incorrect, and if such should be the case, he is prepared to abandon his own philosophic position. Cf. my essay, "Das Problem des Willensfreiheit . . . ," p. 342, n. 22.

The End and Aftereffects of Medieval Religious Philosophy

1. R. Simon ben Zemach Duran, *Sefer Magen Avot*, p. 7b.

2. *Ibid.*

3. *Ibid.*, p. 83b.

4. *Ibid.*, p. 74b.

5. Simon ben Zemach Duran, *Commentaries on the Book of Job*, Introduction, 9, p. 14b.

6. *Philosophie und Theologie von Averroës*, pp. 14–15. I have given further, detailed substantiation to my thesis of Ibn Rushd's influence on the doctrine of *Ikkarim* (principles) of both Duran and Albo in my essay "Towards the Investigation of the Sources of the *Book of Ikkarim*" (*Memorial Volume in honor of Asher Gulak and Samuel Klein*, pp. 57–75).

7. Simon ben Zemach Duran, *Sefer Magen Avot*: Arabic, p. 14b; German trans. pp. 13–14.

8. Simon ben Zemach Duran, *Commentaries on the Book of Job*, VIII, p. 13b.

9. Simon ben Zemach Duran, *Sefer Magen Avot*, p. 2b.

10. *Philosophie und Theologie des Averroës*, p. 120, German translation, p. 110. For parallel instances, cf. my essay "Towards the Investigation of the Sources . . . ," p. 61, n. 1.

11. Cf. Simon ben Zemach Duran, *Sefer Magen Avot*, p. 2b; *Commentaries on the Book of Job*, Introduction, 8, pp. 14a, b.

12. On the relationship of Albo to Duran, cf. Jacob Guttmann, *Die Stellung des Simon ben Zemach Duran in der Geschichte der jüdischen Religionsphilosophie*," pp. 56 ff.

13. Joseph Albo, *Sefer ha-Ikkarim*, I, 15.

14. *Ibid.*, I, 2.

15. *Ibid.*, I, 13.

16. *Ibid.*, I, 5. Cf. also, Chap. IV, 7.

17. *Ibid.*, I, 23.

18. *Ibid.*, I, 6.

19. *Ibid.*, I, 25.

20. *Ibid.*, I, 25; III, 13, 14.

21. *Ibid.*, I, 13, 18.

22. *Ibid.*, I, 25; III, 18, 19.

23. *Ibid.*, I, 26; Cf. III, 25, Husik's edition, pp. 224 ff., 231 ff. The detailed critique of Christianity included in this chapter, which is related to that made by Duran, was suppressed by the censor and, since that time, has been missing from the more popular editions of the book.

24. *Ibid.*, I, 22.

25. *Ibid.*, III, 8, 10, 11.

26. *Ibid.*, I, 8.

27. *Ibid.*, III, 2, 5–7.

28. *Ibid.*, II, 10, 23.

29. *Ibid.*, II, 21.

30. *Ibid.*, II, 30.

31. Cf. Jacob Guttmann, "Die Familie Shemtob in ihren Beziehungen zur Philosophie," pp. 188 ff, 326 ff.

32. *Ibid.*, pp. 419 ff. Wolfson, in his essay, "Isaak ibn ShemTob's unknown commentaries on the physics and his other unknown works" (*Freidus Memorial Volume*, pp. 279 ff.), has clearly elucidated the ideas of Isaac ben Shem Tob, Joseph's hitherto unknown brother. In his supercommentary on the middle commentaries of Ibn Rushd on Aristotle's *Physics*, Isaac refutes Crescas' critique of Aristotelian natural philosophy in the same manner as did his brother, Shem Tob ben Joseph. In his commentary on the *Moreh Nebukhim* he tries to prove that the inquiries of Maimonides are in agreement with the Torah. Cf. Jacob Buttmann, "Die Familie Shemtob . . . ," p. 336.

33. Isaac Abrabanel *Sefer Rosh Amanah*, p. 29 ff. Simon ben Zemach Duran (*Commentaries on the Book of Job*, p. 14, 2) had already interpreted the idea that objection to any of the statements of Scripture constituted heresy, in the sense that every scriptural proposition is to be accounted a principle of faith, but he was not consistent in working out this formative viewpoint.

34. Isaac Abrabanel, *Sefer Mif-alot Elohim*, II, 4, p. 13b.

35. *Ibid.*, I, 3, p. 6 ff.

36. *Ibid.*, VII, 3, p. 45 ff.; VII, 5, p. 49a.

37. *Ibid.*, X, 8, p. 79 ff; *Perush l'Moreh Nebukhim* (*Commentary on the Moreh Nebukhim*), II, 36.

38. I. Baer was the first who discussed Abrabanel's critique of culture; cf. his essay, "Don Isaak Abravanel and His Relationship to Political and Historical Problems" (*Tarbiz*, VIII, 241–259). His lead was followed by Finkelshrer ("Quellen und Motive der Staats- und Gesellschaftsauffassung des Don Isaak Abrava-

nel," *MGWJ*, LXXXII, 406–508), and by Isaac Heinemann ("Abravanels Lehre vom Niedergang der Menschheit," *MGWJ*, LXXXII, 381–400), who discussed this question quite thoroughly. Leo Strauss criticized Abrabanel's political ideas from a different point of view in his essay "On Abrabanel's Philosophical Tendency and Political Teaching" (*Isaak Abravanel*, edited by Trend and Loewe, pp. 93–129). Abrabanel's critique of monarchy, which Baer in his essay, and A. Auerbach in the quarterly *MGWJ* (LXXXI, 2, 257–270) discuss, is of little interest from a philosophic standpoint.

39. Abrabanel, *Commentary on the Torah*, Genesis, II, 5.

40. *Ibid.*, Genesis, III, 22; IV, 11.

41. Compare to this the commentary on Genesis, 11.

42. Concerning his dependence on the Cynics, cf. Baer.

43. Similarly, Albalag. A greater involvement with Christian philosophy begins in the fifteenth century, without vitally affecting the course of philosophic inquiry. On Hebrew translations of scholastic works, cf. Steinschneider, *Die hebraischen Übersetzungen des Mittelalters, par.* 274–305.

43a. Husik, *Juda Messer Leon's Commentary on the Vetus logica* (Leyden, 1906), p. 64 and *passim.*

44. *Philosophie und Theologie von Averroës*: Arabic, pp. 2–6, 14–16, 17, 20–21; German, pp. 3–6, 14, 17, 20.

45. Elijah del Medigo, *Sefer Behinat ha-Dat*, pp. 6, 7.

46. *Ibid.*, p. 4 ff.

47. *Ibid.*, p. 23 ff.

48. *Ibid.*, pp. 8, 11, 17 ff.

49. Cf. my essay, "Elia del Medigos Verhältnis zu Averroës in seinem *Behinat ha-Dat*," pp. 197 and *passim;* 208, n. 58.

50. Elijah del Medigo, *op. cit.*, p. 12 ff.

51. Whether the dialogue was originally written in Spanish, as Gebhardt claims in his new edition of Leone Ebreo's (Judah Abrabanel) *Dialoghi d'Amore*, does not in any way affect Leone's primary intention.

52. Leone, *op. cit.*, II, p. 26 ff.

53. *Ibid.*, III, pp. 101 ff, 110 ff.

54. *Ibid.*, III, pp. 99 f., 124 ff.

55. *Ibid.*, I, p. 37; p. 73 ff.

56. *Ibid.*, I, p. 6; III, p. 58 ff., p. 76b ff.

57. *Ibid.*, III, pp. 140b, 144b ff.

58. Both serve as principal points of departure for Leone's proof of the existence of love in earthly bodies (*Ibid.*, II, pp. 5b, 11a). The striving of matter towards form was already explicated by Ibn Gabirol (*Fons vitae*, V, p. 316 ff.) as meaning the love of the good. Jacob Guttmann (*Die Philosophie des Salomon ibn Gabirols*, p. 52 ff.), Pflaum (*Die Idee der Liebe: Leone Ebreo* . . . , p. 100) and also Klausner (*Tarbiz*, III, 1, p. 79) see in him the source of Ebreo's doctrine. But the truth of the matter is that Gabirol never advanced beyond the bounds of the doctrine which was also common to Aristotelianism. The comparison which Leone draws between matter which aspires towards form and the lustful woman (II, 11) demonstrates that he also is dependent upon Maimonides (cf. *Moreh Nebukhim*, I, Introduction: Arabic 7b; Hebrew, 8b; III, 8).

59. An explanation, congruent with the Aristotelian doctrine of the movement of the heavenly bodies by pure intelligences, which is based upon Islamic interpreters of Aristotle, can be found in the *Dialogue on Love*, II, 69 ff.

60. Leone, *op. cit.*, I, 22, p. 25 ff.; cf. also, III, p. 76.

61. *Ibid.*, I, p. 28b ff; III, p. 141.

62. *Ibid.*, III, p. 48 ff.

63. Joseph Solomon del Medigo, *Sefer Elim oo-mayayn ganim*, p. 33, p. 147 ff.

64. *Ibid.*, pp. 33–36. The detailed discussion on the creation of matter in *Sefer Novlot Hokhma*, pp. 44–78, expounds the concepts in the customary manner, because Del Medigo intentionally bases himself upon tradition and does not give his own views. Cf. 66b, 67b.

65. *Ibid.*, p. 33. (On atomism in Renaissance philosophy, cf. Lasswitz, *Geschichte der Atomistik*, I, p. 306 ff.)

66. Joseph del Medigo, *Sefer Elim* . . ., pp. 39, 41.

67. *Ibid.*, pp. 35 ff., 41.

68. Joseph del Medigo, *Sefer Novlot Hokhma*, p. 18 ff.

69. Joseph del Medigo, *Sefer Elim* . . . , pp. 62 ff.

70. We cannot treat of the various and contradictory theories as to the precise relationship of Spinoza to Judaism. Of necessity, we must content ourselves with but a few observations and notations, i.e., a general orientation. M. Joël was the first to demonstrate scientifically Spinoza's dependence upon Jewish religious philoso-

phy, an hypothesis which had already been advanced by others. He began his investigations in his book on Crescas (*Don Chasdai Creskas' religionsphilosophische Lehren*), and continued it in his inquiry into the origins of Spinoza's doctrines (*Zur Genesis der Lehre Spinozas*), in which he maintained that the Jewish religio-philosophic background to Spinoza's metaphysical doctrines, i.e., such doctrines as the problem of the creation of the world and man's freedom of will—which Descartes had removed from the scope of philosophy, by classifying under the heading of miracles—pushed Spinoza beyond Descartes to the formulation of his own philosophic views. Moreover, in his essay on *Spinozas theologisch-politischer Traktat,* Joël maintained that Spinoza borrowed the major portion of his material for the understanding and criticism of the Bible from Jewish thinkers. While all scholars were willing to admit this, some questioned Joël's conception of Spinoza's philosophic development, and he was vigorously attacked on this point by Kuno Fischer, who in line with his own hypothesis maintained that Spinoza's views could only be understood against the immanent Cartesian background. More recently, L. Roth (*Spinoza, Descartes, Maimonides*) supported Joël's thesis in a different form, while Tj. de Boer, in his counterargument (*Maimonides, en Spinoza . . .*), comes to the same negative conclusion as that reached by Fischer. But most scholars accept Joël's hypothesis that Jewish religious philosophy was one of the weighty philosophic influences which formed the metaphysics and ethics of Spinoza. So Freudenthal maintains, in the second portion of his book on Spinoza, published posthumously, *Spinoza, Leben und Lehre . . .,* p. 84 ff. This is in fundamental agreement with the views expressed by me in "Spinozas zusammenhang mit der Aristotelismus." I merely established the place of Jewish religious philosophy in the development of Spinoza's philosophy in a more unified and specific fashion by demonstrating that he took from Jewish tradition a well-worked-out metaphysical conception, which he changed through the influence of his different conception of nature and epistemology. Thus, I justified the essential insight of Joël, which—so supplemented— is basically correct. But even for the metaphysical structure of Spinoza's thought, the Jewish Aristotelian world view is only one factor, with which the mathematical view of nature and the epistemology of Descartes must be considered as of equal importance. A *weltanschauung* quite similar to that of Jewish Aristotelianism can be found in the Italian philosophy of the Renaissance. But there is absolutely no basis for seeking any other source for the mutually convergent tendencies than that of the Jewish thinkers, with whose works Spinoza was deeply and intimately acquainted. This judgment applies to Gebhardt's attempt ("Spinoza und der Platonismus") to attribute to Leone Ebreo a determinative influence on Spinoza, because in the latter there can be found nothing— aside from some petty details—which had not already been said by previous Jewish philosophers.

Spinoza's relationship to medieval philosophy has recently been the subject of a comprehensive inquiry by Wolfson in *The Philosophy of Spinoza Unfolding the Latent Process of His Reasoning.* He analyzes Spinoza's system into its various components in order to determine whether he borrowed ideas from the medievalists, or whether he is opposed to the traditional notions, by arraigning a silent critique of the medievalists' leading ideas, in the development of his own characteristic doctrines. Although the scope of his inquiry includes all of medieval philosophy, its center is Spinoza's relationship to the Arabic and Jewish philosophy of the Middle Ages. Regretfully, this book has not yet been analyzed in terms of what is refutable and what is irrefutable. But it is undoubted that, after discarding what is incorrect in the volume, many new and valuable insights remain, and the incontrovertible worth of the book is its explication of the connection between Spinoza and medieval thought—a comprehensive and detailed analysis beyond any attempted to date. But the essential point of this relationship is not at all changed by any of these detailed inquiries. Insofar as Spinoza accepted medieval ideas, those ideas are of major importance for the formation of his thought, which are recounted in my text previously mentioned, and they are clothed in a new, characteristically Spinozian form under the impact of the new idea of nature and the new epistemology, which taken together with the tradition of the Middle Ages fashioned the thought of Spinoza.

71. Spinoza, *Tractatus de intellectus emendatione*, par. 38, 42, 97–99 (the numbering of the paragraphs is according to the Bruder edition).

72. Cf. the critique of the Aristotelian syllogism, *Short Treatise* I, 1 end; I, 7.

73. *Ibid.*, I, 1; *Ethica*, I, 11; *Tractatus de intellectus emendatione*, par. 97.

74. Spinoza, *Ethica*, I, 21–23; *Tractatus de intellectus*, par. 101.

75. Spinoza, *Ethica*, II, 40, 1, scholium.

76. Spinoza, *Tractatus de intellectus emendatione*, par. 93, 101.

77. *Ibid.*

78. Spinoza, *Ethica*, I, 28.

79. Wolfson's volume, *op. cit.*, explains Spinoza's proof for the exclusive substantiality of God as a critical opposition to the viewpoint of Jewish philosophy.

80. Spinoza, *Ethica*, I, 5th definition, 4th and 5th axioms: II, 2. Joël (*Zur Genesis der Lehre Spinozas*, p. 41) justifiably refers to Gersonides' idea that nothing can come from God that is not already included in his essence. But the essential Spinozian point is missing in Gersonides, i.e., that with the knowledge of the effect, there is necessarily given a knowledge of the cause.

81. Spinoza, *Ethica*, I, 16.

82. *Ibid.*, I, Appendix.

83. *Ibid.*, I, 11, scholium; I, 33, scholium 2.

84. Spinoza, *Short Treatise*, II, 15, 16, 22.

85. Spinoza, *Tractatus de intellectus emendatione*, par. 71.

86. *Ibid.*, par. 35, 38, 41 ff.

87. Spinoza, *Ethica*, II, 7. There the metaphysical theory is directly derived from the logical.

88. *Ibid.*, II, 8.

89. *Ibid.*, II, 11, 23 ff.

90. *Ibid.*, II, 38 ff., 45 ff. Spinoza's assertion that the human mind has an adequate comprehension of the essence of God is in radical opposition to the Neoplatonic doctrine of the absolute incomprehensibility of the divine essence. These doctrines are directly connected with the theories of differing conceptions of the derivation of the world from God. The emanationist theory of the world can accept an unknown divine One. In opposi-

tion to this, if we think of God as the principle of order from which all of existence is derived by logico-mathematical necessity, his essence, too, must be open to logical comprehension.

91. *Ibid.*, II, 49; III, 9–11.

92. *Ibid.*, III, 1–3.

93. *Ibid.*, IV, 23–26, 16 ff.; cf. especially 66, scholium.

94. *Ibid.*, III, Introduction.

95. Spinoza, *Short Treatise*, II, 23; cf. Joël, *Zur Genesis der Lehre Spinozas*, p. 65 ff.

96. Spinoza, *Ethica*, II, 23.

97. *Ibid.*, V, 31, 38 ff.

98. Spinoza, *Short Treatise*, II, 22 ff.

99. *Ethica*, V, 32–36. Cf. Joël, *Spinozas theologisch-politischer Traktat*, pp. 44 ff., and Introduction, p. ix ff. Gebhardt's "Spinoza und der Platonismus," pp. 21–29, maintains that Leone Ebreo's dialogue is the source of the doctrine of *amor dei intellectualis*. But Wolfson, *op. cit.*, p. 305, section II, proves that this concept is already found in Thomas Aquinas.

100. Cf. in addition to this and what follows, what is said at the beginning of the chapter on "Aristotelianism and its Opponents."

101. Spinoza, *Short Treatise*, I, 2; I, 5. Cf. Joël, *Zur Genesis der Lehre Spinozas*, pp. 35, 58 ff. At the beginning of I, 2, Spinoza uses the typical expression of medieval Neoplatonism and Aristotelianism, that God is never jealous. Cf. end of chapter on Judah Halevi and n. 168.

102. Spinoza, *Ethica*, I, Appendix, p. 219 (Bruder edition).

103. Spinoza, *Tractatus theologico-politicus*, I, par. 7, 44 (paragraphs are numbered in accordance with German edition of Bruder).

104. *Ibid.*, I, par. 7–26.

105. *Ibid.*, par. 59 ff. Cf. Joël, *Spinozas theologisch-politischer Trakat*, pp. 12 ff., 57 ff.; L. Strauss, *Die Religionskritik Spinozas als Grundlage seiner Bibelwissenschaft*, pp. 173 ff.

106. Spinoza, *Tractatus theologico-politicus*, IV, par. 23 ff.

107. *Ibid.*, par. 26 ff.

108. *Ibid.*, I, 23 ff.; II, par. 17.

109. *Ibid.*, XII, par 32–38; XIV, par. 13–31.

110. *Ibid.*, par. 22, 26 ff. Cf. J. Guttmann, "Religion und Wissenschaft im mittelalterlichen und modernen Denken,"

p. 200. Strauss (cf. *Die Religionskritik* . . ., p. 241 ff.) attempts to harmonize Spinoza's conception of religion with his philosophical principles. In my essay, "Mendelssohns Jerusalem und Spinozas theologisch-politischer Traktat," n. 42. I briefly referred to why I cannot agree with him in this endeavor.

Moses Mendelssohn

1. Mendelssohn, *Abhandlung über die Evidenz,* Part III (new edition), II, 310. All of Mendelssohn's writings have not yet been published in the new edition, and my quotations are cited according to the edition of G. B. Mendelssohn (*Gesammelte Schriften*).

2. *Ibid.,* pp. 103 ff.; *Morgenstunden* XII (*Gesammelte Schriften*), II, 333 ff.

3. Mendelssohn, *Phaedon,* second dialogue (*Gesammelte Schriften*), II, 152 ff.

4. Mendelssohn, *Phaedon,* third dialogue (*Gesammelte Schriften*), II, 164 ff.

5. On the determinism of divine acts, cf. *Morgenstunden* XII (*Gesammelte Schriften*), II, 334; *Sache Gottes,* par. 21 (*Gesammelte Schriften*), II, 417. On human acts, cf. *Gedanken vor der Wahrscheinlichkeit* (new edition), I, 162 ff.; *Abhandlung über die Evidenz,* Part III (new edition), II, 304 ff.; *Sache Gottes,* par. 44 (*Gesammelte Schriften*), II, 423 f.; *Über Freiheit und Notwendigkeit* (*Gesammelte Schriften*), III, 370 ff.

6. Mendelssohn, *Sache Gottes,* par. 77 ff., pp. 441 ff.; *Jerusalem,* Part 2 (*Gesammelte Schriften*), III, 345 ff. In the Hebrew edition, cf. *Yerushalayim: Ketavim K'tanim* . . . , translated by Sh. Herberg, pp. 33–143.

7. Mendelssohn, *Morgenstunden* VIII (*Gesammelte Schriften*), II, 303. *Jerusalem,* Part I, III, 287; Hebrew edition, pp. 33–143.

8. Mendelssohn, *Schreiben an Lavater* (new edition), VII, 8 ff.; Hebrew edition, pp. 172–213.

9. Mendelssohn, *Hebräischer Brief an Hartwig Wessely* (new edition), XIV, 119.

10. Mendelssohn, *Gegenbetrachtungen über Bonnets Paligenesie* (new edition), VII, 91 ff.; *Brief an den Erbprinzen von Barunschweig. Wolfenbuttel* (new edition), VII, 300; Hebrew edition pp. 214–221.

11. Cf. in relation to Saadia, pp. 62 ff.; on Joseph Albo, pp. 248 ff.; cf. also *Ikkarim* I, 18, 22.

12. Mendelssohn, *Schreiben an Lavater* (new edition), VII, p. 16; Hebrew edition, pp. 177–213. *Gegenbetrachtungen über Bonnets Paligenesie,* p. 84 ff.; *Brief an Bonnet, Feb. 8, 1770,* p. 321 ff.

13. Mendelssohn's rejoinder to Lavater's answer (new edition), pp. 43 ff., in reference to Maimonides' *Hilkot Yesode ha-Torah,* chaps. 8, 9, 10, and to the *Ikkarim* of Albo, I, 18. Cf. also, *Gegenbetrachtungen,* p. 86 ff.; *Brief an Bonnet,* p. 324. According to these references, miracles cannot be accounted as "a certain testimony to the divine mission of any of the prophets," even if they are historically validated, because they might be founded upon magical arts or upon an evil distortion of supernatural gifts. Such allegations are refuted by public revelation. The Enlightenment's crucial question of miracles, i.e., whether they have historical attestation, applies to him as well, but is answered by the undoubted, conclusive, and public character of the miracles.

14. Cf. Bamberger, "Mendelssohns Begriff vom Judentum" *Korrespondenzblatt der Akademie für die Wissenschaft des Judentums,* X, 12 ff.

15. Leibnitz, *Théodicée,* Introduction, par. 3.

16. Mendelssohn, *Jerusalem,* Part 2 (*Gesammelte Schriften*), III, p. 319 ff.; Hebrew edition, *loc. cit.* On the source of process of thought in Spinoza's *Tractatus theologico-politicus,* cf., my essay, "Mendelssohns Jerusalem und Spinozas theologisch-politischer Traktat," p. 38 ff. This essay may be profitably compared with what will follow in the footnotes.

17. Mendelssohn, *Jerusalem,* Part 2 (new edition, p. 315 ff.; Hebrew edition, *loc. cit.*) Similarly, *Gegenbetrachtungen* (new edition), VII, 73 ff.

18. Mendelssohn, *Abhandlung über die Evidenz,* Part 3 (new edition), II, 313; Part 4, p. 328; *Morgenstunden* VIII (*Gesammelte Schriften*), II, 306 ff.

19. Mendelssohn, *Abhandlung über die Evidenz,* Part 3 (new edition), II, p. 311 ff.; *Jerusalem,* Part 2 (*Gesammelte Schriften*), III, pp. 316 ff.; (Hebrew edition, *loc. cit.*)

20. *Jerusalem,* Part 2 *(Gesammelte Schriften),* III, pp. 311 ff., 319 ff., 348 ff.; (Hebrew edition, *loc. cit.*)

21. Cf. my essay, "Mendelssohns Jerusalem und Spinozas theologisch-politischer Traktat," p. 36 ff.

22. Mendelssohn, *Jerusalem,* Part 2, *loc. cit.,* pp. 350 ff.; (Hebrew edition, *loc. cit*).

23. *Ibid.,* p. 321, p. 324, p. 341; (Hebrew edition, *loc. cit.*)

24. *Ibid.,* p. 332 ff., p. 338 ff.; (Hebrew edition, *loc. cit.*)

25. Mendelssohn, *Brief an Homberg, Sept. 22, 1783 (Gesammelte Schriften),* V, 699.

26. Mendelssohn, *Jerusalem,* Part 2, *loc. cit.,* p. 316; (Hebrew edition, pp. 226–228). *Gegenbetrachtungen über Bonnets Palingenesie* (new edition), VII, 74 ff.

27. Mendelssohn, *Jerusalem,* Part 2, *loc. cit.,* p. 358 ff.; (Hebrew edition, *loc. cit.*)

Post-Kantian Idealism in Jewish Philosophy of Religion

1. Formstecher, *Die Religion des Geistes,* pp. 17–22.

2. *Ibid.,* pp. 22–29.

3. *Ibid.,* pp. 29–34.

4. *Ibid.,* pp. 21 ff., 358.

5. *Ibid.,* pp. 63–72.

6. *Ibid.,* pp. 100–195.

7. *Ibid.,* pp. 53–56.

8. *Ibid.,* pp. 87–100.

9. *Ibid.,* pp. 56–63, 195-202.

10. *Ibid.,* pp. 202-359.

11. *Ibid.,* pp. 365-413.

12. *Ibid.,* pp. 351–353, 421–452.

13. S. Hirsch, *Das System der religiösen Anschauung der Juden und sein Verhältnis zum Heidentum, Christentum und zur absoluten Philosophie,* I, XVIII–XXIII.

14. *Ibid.,* pp. XVI–XVIII, 30–34.

15. *Ibid.,* p. 79, n. 507 ff.

16. Steinthal, *Über Juden und Judentum,* p. 208.

17. Hirsch, *op. cit.,* pp. 11–25.

18. *Ibid.,* pp. 43–45.

19. *Ibid.,* pp. 38–42, 62–64.

20. The doctrine of myth, *ibid.,* pp. 53–58; interpretation of Adam's sin, *ibid.,* pp. 62–104.

21. *Ibid.,* pp. 25–30, 48–53, 97 f., 110–116.

22. Description of idolatry, *ibid.,* pp. 116–385. The basic viewpoint summarized at the end, pp. 383–385.

23. *Ibid.,* pp. 445–457.

24. *Ibid.,* pp. 537–620.

25. *Ibid.,* pp. 457–528.

26. *Ibid.,* pp. 617–620, 627–631.

27. *Ibid.,* pp. 646–690.

28. *Ibid.,* pp. 701–722.

29. *Ibid.,* pp. 722–767.

30. *Ibid.,* pp. 775–786.

31. *Ibid.,* pp. 786–832.

32. *Ibid.,* pp. 832–884.

33. Krochmal never completed the book. Certain chapters are missing, which he intended to write, and, with regard to the final sections, he never made a complete determination of their proper order. Zunz arranged the extant chapters according to his idea of what Krochmal had intended the order to be, and he was undoubtedly correct in his estimate. Citations from the book are drawn from the Rawidowicz edition (Berlin, 1924), which includes the inquiries and letters of Krochmal.

34. My own view of Krochmal is given in greater detail in my essay, "The Bases of the Thought of R. Nachman Krochmal" (*K'nesset,* VI, 250–286). I shall make use of this essay many times.

35. Krochmal, *Guide for the Perplexed of the Time,* Chap. 16, pp. 273, 274.

36. Rawidowicz dealt with this in connection with Krochmal's theory of history, both in the introduction to the edition of his letter and in his essay, "Was Krochmal an Hegelian–" *(Hebrew Union College Annual,* pp. 563–566). But from this topic, which is, in itself, quite important, he draws conclusions, which in terms of his basic purpose are unwarranted.

37. The only one of the post–Kantian philosophers who is alluded to in the *Guide for the Perplexed of our Time,* without, however, mentioning his name, although he is specifically named in one of Krochmal's letters, is Hegel. Since Krochmal included the essence of Hegel's logic in his book, and in many places, where the connection between the two thinkers is quite obvious, the point of the question concerning the relationship between the two men centered around whether Krochmal was or was not Hegelian. A positive answer to this question was

given by Y. L. Landau in his book, *Nachman Krochmal—ein Hegelianer*. A negative answer was advanced by Rawidowicz in the two inquiries cited in the previous note. Klausner maintains that Krochmal was dependent upon Hegel, both in his essay "The Influence of Hegel on Nachman Krochmal," and in his book, *The History of Modern Hebrew Literature*, II, 201–208. If one thus propounds the question, one must, in my opinion, answer it negatively, Of course Krochmal was indebted to Hegel for many important ideas, but in his basic metaphysical positions he is closer to Schelling than to Hegel, and in some matters he is more influenced by Fichte. But the entire matter of determining just how far and how much he was influenced by each of the representatives of German idealism is ambiguous. It is categorical that German idealism was the ground for his thought. The extension of the dialectic and the consequences derived from it do not suffice to differentiate Krochmal from the main stream of idealism. It is unwarranted to contend, as Rawidowicz did, that philosophy holds only a secondary position in Krochmal's thought, and to one-sidedly emphasize, when treating his historical doctrine, his dependence upon the historical school and its forerunners, thus playing down Krochmal's dependence upon the idealistic philosophy of history. Klausner, in his book, *op. cit.*, p. 196, emphasizes that besides Hegel, other leading German idealists affected Krochmal, and with this judgment he comes close to ours.

38. Krochmal, *Guide for the Perplexed of our Time*, VI, p. 29.

39. *Ibid.*, pp. 29, 30; cf. also Chap. VII, p. 38.

40. *Ibid.*, pp. 30, 38; cf., on the relation of the representation to the concept, II, pp. 11, 12.

41. *Ibid.*, p. 30; XVI, p. 272.

42. *Ibid.*, VIII, pp. 43 f.

43. *Ibid.*, XVI, p. 273.

44. *Ibid.*, III, p. 14.

45. Krochmal's polemic essay against Luzzato is printed in Rawidowicz's edition, pp. 432–443. Cf. especially, pp. 435–437.

46. Krochmal, p. 29, p. 38.

47. The proof for Krochmal's interpretation of Ibn Ezra in terms of his own principles can be found in my essay on Krochmal, *op. cit.*, Sec. 2. Cf. especially, pp. 270, 273, 274, 276, 277.

48. Krochmal, *op. cit.*, XVII, pp. 285–287.

49. *Ibid.*, p. 287, Sec. 2, p. 288.

50. The same problem appears in Krochmal as in Schelling, for Krochmal's metaphysics is quite close to that of Schelling, as we shall prove presently. On the abyss between the ideal world and the temporal-empirical world for Schelling, cf. Cassirer, *Das Erkenntnisproblem in der Philosophie und Wissenschaft der neueren Zeit*, III, p. 276.

51. Krochmal, *op. cit.*, p. 289.

52. Ibn Ezra agrees with Gabirol's doctrine, that all beings, with the exception of God, are compounds of matter and form. He names matter as "substance" and thus deviates from the usual usage of the term, which became fixed and traditional after his demise. Krochmal utilizes this term in its traditional connotation and attributes to Ibn Ezra the doctrine that all beings are compounded of substance and form.

53. Krochmal, op. cit., pp. 296–298.

54. *Ibid*, pp. 308, 318. As I have demonstrated in my essay on Krochmal, his basic metaphysical doctrines, expressed in the chapter on Ibn Ezra, are drawn entirely from Schelling, and he is especially dependent on Schelling's estimate of Bruno. Krochmal's God is the "absolute" of Schelling. In the systematic introductory sections of his book, Krochmal clothes this metaphysic in Hegelian terminology. He designates God as absolute spirit, but does not intend by this denotation the Hegelian Absolute Spirit, but rather, the Schellingian absolute. Rawidowicz correctly understood that Krochmal's absolute spirit is not identical with that of Hegel, but he himself wrongly identifies it with the first cause of the medievals. Klausner, *History of Modern Hebrew Literature*, II, 198, emphasizes that, in his essay on Ibn Ezra, Krochmal injected the ideas of modern philosophy, but he does not see that chapter as being especially dependent on Schelling.

55. Krochmal, *op. cit.*, pp. 306, 307.

56. Krochmal never speaks unambiguously on the first divine act of concentration and self-limitation, whereby God achieves self-consciousness and the power of will. But if this act is understood as a true act of self-limitation on the part of

God, and if the divine substance which, heretofore, was beyond all form, has now been clothed in form, one can understand it as being an expression of the spontaneous free will of God. Only when the prior form already exists can we strip away from it—by logical reasoning—the other forms.

57. Krochmal, *op. cit.*, XI, p. 117.

58. The letter is printed in Rawidowicz's edition, pp. 443–447; cf. especially p. 447.

59. Krochmal, *op. cit.*, VII, p. 35.

60. *Ibid.*, p. 36.

61. *Ibid.*, p. 37.

62. *Ibid.*, p. 38, Sec. 2.

63. *Ibid.*, VIII, p. 40; VII, pp. 35, 36.

64. *Ibid.*, VIII, p. 40.

65. *Ibid.*, VII, p. 37.

66. *Ibid.*, VII, p. 38.

67. *Ibid.*, pp. 38, 40.

68. N. Rotenstreich has devoted several of his essays dealing with Krochmal to the difficulties involved in the relationship between the spirit of the Jewish people and the Absolute Spirit. In his opinion, the difficulty lies in the fact that the Absolute Spirit, which is the supreme metaphysical entity existing independently of the world and unsusceptible to any change, nevertheless descends to the historical arena ("Absolute and Temporal in Ranak's Doctrine," *K'nesset*, VI, 339; "Ranak's Concept of History," *Zion*, VII, 30–31; *Jewish Thought in Modern Times*, I, 53–57). But this difficulty does not exist unless we identify the Absolute Spirit with the spirit of the Jewish people, and, therefore, it would be subject to the vicissitudes of history. It seems to me that Krochmal's views, both with regard to the spirit of other nations and that of Israel, is that they are manifestations—the one of specific metaphysical powers, and the other of the Absolute Spirit. Both of these are possible only if there is a bridge between the ideal world and the empirical world. For us, such must be the case, although we have not been able to prove it conclusively. With regard to the relation of the spirit of Israel to the Absolute Spirit, we have no other problem than the one treated in the body of our text, i.e., that there must exist an immediate transition from ultimate metaphysical existence to one of the strands of empirical existence. In this assumption we see evidence for specific personal elements in Krochmal's conception of God, despite his basically different conception of the divine.

69. Krochmal, *op. cit.*, VIII, 41; IX, pp. 51, 52.

70. A description of the cyclical theory of history can be found in chapters 9–10.

71. Krochmal, *op. cit.*, III, p. 13.

72. *Ibid.*, XIII, pp. 215–216.

73. *Aggadah* is treated in chapter XIV. On *Aggadic* exegesis of the Bible, cf. pp. 240–241; on parables, p. 242 ff.

74. On the philosophic elements incorporated in the *Aggadah*, cf. p. 244 ff. The philosophic materials of the Talmud are arranged and discussed in chapter XII, pp. 168 ff. On superstitions, cf. pp. 246 ff., 250 ff.

75. Krochmal comments more than once on the parallels between the ancient Kabbala and medieval philosophy. Lachover lists the various statements pertinent to this subject in his essay, "Kabbala and the Mysterious in the Doctrine of Ranak," *K'nesset*, X, 300–302. Concerning the development of ancient Kabbala, cf. Chap. XVI, p. 258. In regard to Neoplatonism, cf. Chap. XIV, p. 273; also Chap. XII, p. 167.

76. Krochmal himself thought that it was possible that the very beginnings of Greek philosophy had already been influenced by Judaism. He grounds this thesis, which was popular in antiquity and the Middle Ages, by an historical proof. He reminds us of the fact that the molders and originators of Greek philosophy lived in Asia Minor, where it was possible for them to come into contact with Jewish religion.

77. On his intention to speak of these two subjects, cf. Chap. XVI, p. 274.

78. Both can be found at the end of Chap. XV, p. 271, which deals with Gnosticism.

79. Krochmal, *op. cit.*, XII, p. 167.

80. *Ibid.*, p. 167.

81. L. Steinheim, *Die Offenbarung nach dem Lehrbegriff der Synagoge*, I, 150 ff.

82. *Ibid.*, I, 66–74, 96 ff; II, 17 ff. and *passim*.

83. *Ibid.*, II, 45 ff., 78 ff.

84. *Ibid.*, I, 246–253.

85. *Ibid.*, II, 48 ff., 78 ff.

86. *Ibid.*, II, 48.

87. *Ibid.*, II, 57–75.

88. *Ibid.*, I, 310–325; cf. pp. 214–227, 230 ff., 258 ff.

89. *Ibid.*, II, 143 ff.

90. *Ibid.*, I, 325–341; cf. pp. 263–285.

The Renewal of Jewish Religious Philosophy at the End of the Nineteenth Century

1. M. Lazarus, *Die Ethik des Judentums*, I, 82; II, p. xiv. (The second volume was published in collaboration with Y. Vinter and A. Vinshe.)

2. *Ibid.*, I, 89–106; cf. especially pp. 99 ff., 104 ff.

3. *Ibid.*, I, 116.

4. *Ibid.*, I, 187–206, 127; II, 100.

5. *Ibid.*, I, 351–361, 236 ff., 321 ff.

6. *Ibid.*, I, 289–310.

7. *Ibid.*, II, 257–360.

8. *Ibid.*, I, 76 ff.; II, 185 ff.

9. Kant, *Begründung der Ethik* (2d ed., 1910), pp. 350 ff., 360 ff.

10. *Ibid.*, p. 364 ff.

11. *Ibid.*, p. 365 ff.

12. H. Cohen, *Ethik des reinen Willens*, p. 83 ff.

13. *Ibid.*, pp. 391 ff., 436 ff.

14. *Ibid.*, p. 438 ff.

15. *Ibid.*, p. 449 ff.

16. H. Cohen, *Jüdische Schriften*, pp. 402–410.

17. H. Cohen, *Ethik des reinen Willens*, pp. 456–466; cf. pp. 15 ff., 55.

18. *Ibid.*, p. 452 ff.

19. *Ibid.*, p. 53 ff. Cohen, "Einleitung zu langes Geschichte des Materialismus," *Schriften zur Philosophie und Zeitgeschichte*, II, 275 ff.; "Religion und Sittlichkeit," *Jüdische Schriften*, III, 100 ff., 155.

20. H. Cohen, *Ethik des reinen Willens*, p. 402 ff.; *Jüdische Schriften* p. 122 ff.

21. H. Cohen, *Jüdische Schriften*, I, 306–330. Hebrew translation by T. Wislowski (Jerusalem, 1935).

22. H. Cohen, *Ethik des reinen Willens*, p. 60 ff.

23. *Ibid.*, p. 454 ff.; *Jüdische Schriften*, III, 147 ff.

24. *Ibid.*, 158.

25. H. Cohen, *Ethik des reinen Willens*, p. 586 ff.; *Jüdische Schriften*, pp. 158 ff.

26. H. Cohen, *Der Begriff der Religion im System der Philosophie*, pp. 15 f., 108 ff.

27. H. Cohen, *Religion der Vernunft aus den Quellen des Judentums*, p. 15; *Der Begriff der Religion*, p. 52 ff.

28. H. Cohen, *Religion der Vernunft*, pp. 131–166; *Der Begriff der Religion*, pp. 53 f., 70ff.

29. H. Cohen, *Religion der Vernunft*, p. 167 ff.; *Der Begriff der Religion*, p. 75 ff.

30. H. Cohen, *Religion der Vernunft*, pp. 208–251; *Der Begriff der Religion*, p. 61 ff.

31. H. Cohen, *Religion der Vernunft*, p. 220 ff.; *Der Begriff der Religion*, p. 63 ff.

32. H. Cohen, *Religion der Vernunft*, p. 260.

33. H. Cohen, *Der Begriff der Religion*, p. 80 ff.; *Religion der Vernunft*, pp. 167–184.

34. H. Cohen, *Religion der Vernunft*, pp. 184–191.

35. *Ibid.*, p. 184 ff.

36. H. Cohen, *Der Begriff der Religion* p. 26 ff.; *Religion der Vernunft*, pp. 41–57.

37. H. Cohen, *Religion der Vernunft*, p. 46 ff.; *Der Begriff der Religion*, p. 20 ff.

38. H. Cohen, *Religion der Vernunft*, pp. 68–81.

39. *Ibid.*, pp. 82–98, and especially, p. 95 ff.

40. *Ibid.*, pp. 48 ff., 243 ff.

41. References to the text of the *Der Stern der Erlösung* (Star of Redemption) are to the second edition, published in 1930. This is a reprint of the first edition, with, however, the three sections of the first edition now published in three separate volumes, each with its own pagination. Rosenzweig's essays are reprinted in *Kleinere Schriften* (1937) and references are given for this edition.

42. Rosenzweig's testimony that Heidegger's philosophic position is comparable to his own can be found in the essay: "Vertauschte Fronten" (Reversed Battlefronts) in *Kleinere Schriften*, pp. 355–356. Substantiation of this claim by members of the existentialist school can be found in Karl Löwith's essay, "M. Heidegger and F. Rosenzweig or Temporality and Eternity," *Philosophy and Phenomenological Research*, III, 53–77. Löwith demonstrates in detail that the methodological starting point of both philosophers is the same, although from the viewpoint of content, they arrive at exactly opposite conclusions. Löwith sets the atheistic existentialism of Heidegger against the believing existentialism of Rosenzweig and proves that Heidegger remains within the sphere of temporality, while Rosenzweig transcends it and points toward eternity.

43. Rosenzweig, *Star of Redemption*, I,

introduction, especially, p. 10 ff.; II, p. 21 ff. "The New Thinking," *Kleinere Schriften*, pp. 378–379.

44. Rosenzweig, *Star of Redemption*, II, pp. 63–64, 67 f., 73 ff.

45. *Ibid.*, I. p. 17 ff.; *Kleinere Schriften*, pp. 378–79.

46. Rosenzweig, *Star of Redemption*, I, pp. 21 ff., 57 ff.

47. *Ibid.*, I., p. 19, 57–58.

48. *Ibid.*, I, p. 17, 21.

49. *Ibid.*, I, pp. 12–15; from a methodological standpoint, the novelty of the new thinking is attributed to Feuerbach elsewhere (*Kleinere Schriften*, p. 388).

50. Rosenzweig, *Star of Redemption*, I, p. 7 ff.

51. *Ibid.*, pp. 17–18.

52. Rosenzweig, *Kleinere Schriften*, p. 388.

53. *Ibid.*, pp. 374–375.

54. Rosenzweig, *Star of Redemption*, I, pp. 30 ff.

55. *Ibid.*, I, pp. 30 ff., 34 ff.

56. *Ibid.*, I, pp. 115 ff., 218.

57. *Ibid.*, I, pp. 46 ff., 70 ff., 96 ff., 101 ff.; *Kleinere Schriften*, p. 381 ff.

58. Rosenzweig says: "with the aid of the sensual knowledge of experience" we are enabled to know precisely the meaning of God, of man, and of the world in themselves, and, with regard to this knowledge of the essence of the three primary givens, there is no distinction between God, man, and the world (*Kleinere Schriften*, p. 380). But knowledge of essence is dependent on the experience of factuality, which establishes the essence. Without a knowledge of the existence of God by reason of experience, there can be no knowledge of his essence. But the knowledge so gained is not that of God in his own self-limitation, but of God as he stands in relation with man. Even in those religions which affirm a God completely self-contained, who stands aloof and isolated from everything, man's knowledge of God is of his communion with man, which stems not from God, but from man.

59. Rosenzweig, *Star of Redemption*, I, pp. 57–61.

60. *Ibid.*, I, pp. 58–59. With this connection of thought to one of the three elements of existence, it is difficult to see how philosophy can make God and man into objects of cognition and, moreover, seek to comprehend their essence via a constructive method. Philosophy establishes itself—necessarily, by reason of its nature—outside of the boundaries which she attributes to the bearers of thought, and this objection is not answered by saying that thought, originally only within the world, is later on made dependent on God and is thus elevated beyond the limits of the world.

61. *Ibid.*, I, pp. 62–65.

62. *Ibid.*, pp. 72–75.

63. *Ibid.*, I, pp. 83–88.

64. *Ibid.*, I, pp. 88–90, 95.

65. *Ibid.*, I, pp. 94–95.

66. *Ibid.*, II, pp. 92–99.

67. *Ibid.*, II, pp. 114–115.

68. *Ibid.*, II, p. 115.

69. *Ibid.*, III, pp. 187–188.

70. *Ibid.*, II, pp. 41 ff.

71. *Ibid.*, II, pp. 42 ff., 58.

72. *Ibid.*, II, p. 46.

73. *Ibid.*, II, pp. 32–41.

74. *Ibid.*, II, pp. 20, 30, 85 ff., 121 ff.

75. *Ibid.*, II, pp. 18 ff., 22 ff. Rosenzweig reiterates the idea that philosophy and theology should be supplementary but does not explicate this idea, nor does he deal with the problems implicit in his concept of philosophy and of theology. For him, philosophy, because of its subjectivity, must be completed by theology, and because of such completion it attains the objective character of science. With this he undoubtedly intends to say that theology has an objective foundation in the datum of revelation, and thus can help philosophy reach objectivity. But the certainty of revelation is itself only founded on the certainty of human experience of revelation and as such has the same "subjective" character as philosophy. From the other side, theology needs philosophy, so that it may become not only a theology of feeling but may stand in the face of actual existence. But how can we support this notion of philosophy, which, viewed in itself is nothing more than "Standpunkt-philosophie," and cannot lead to a connection with actual existence? Philosophy can actualize this connection only if it "realizes within itself the knowledge of the world in the fullness of its systematic wholeness," as Rosenzweig expresses it (II, p. 19). It is clear that it is Rosenzweig's idea that philosophy, despite its beginnings in human experience, does not have to remain in the sphere of aphorisms alone, but can

attain a systematic unity. This is borne out by the fact that he considered his own treatise to be a philosophic system (*Kleinere Schriften*, pp. 374–375). Similarly, philosophy must have the character of knowledge, in order that it may independently give theology the connection of knowledge of the world, or, as Rosenzweig puts it in another place (*Star of Redemption*, III, p. 47), the objectivity of the philosophers hovers over objects." But if he thinks that philosophy which is founded upon human experience has the ability to attain systematization and scientific objectivity, then it no longer has any need to receive its scientific character from the hands of theology. With this, the central idea of the mutual supplementation of philosophy and theology is not refuted. The question of the relation of philosophy to faith and to theology, which is rooted in faith, is also present in existentialist philosophy, although there it takes on a special form. The various possibilities of settling this question, advanced by tradition, are apparent and are repeated in the framework of existentialist philosophy. Within its framework, Rosenzweig upholds the idea that there is no opposition between these two disciplines, and one cannot be subordinated to the other. But each, starting from its own principles, strives to reach the unitary truth. Thus, of necessity the problems of faith must be seen from the viewpoint of philosophy

and the problems of philosophy must be grasped from the stance of faith—and his inquiries of this type, scattered throughout the book, are very fruitful.

76. Rosenzweig, *Star of Redemption*, II, p. 105 ff.

77. *Ibid.*, II, pp. 152 ff., 163 ff.

78. *Ibid.*, II, pp. 164 ff.

79. *Ibid.*, II, p. 168

80. *Ibid.*, III, pp. 11–13; cf. also II, p. 197.

81. *Ibid.*, II, pp. 197–199.

82. *Ibid.*, II, pp. 173 ff.

83. *Ibid.*, pp. 220 ff.

84. *Ibid.*, III, p. 201; *Kleinere Schriften*, p. 396.

85. Rosenzweig, *Kleinere Schriften*, p. 396.

86. Rosenzweig, *Star of Redemption*, III, pp. 49 ff.

87. *Ibid.*, III, pp. 49 ff., 54, 56.

88. *Ibid.*, III, pp. 55, 87.

89. *Ibid.*, III, pp. 100–102.

90. *Ibid.*, III, pp. 103–104.

91. *Ibid.*, III, pp. 175 ff.

92. *Ibid.*, III, p. 175.

93. *Ibid.*, III, pp. 57–61.

94. *Ibid.*, III, pp. 112–119.

95. *Ibid.*, III, pp. 112–113; cf. III, p. 58.

96. *Ibid.*, III, pp. 50–51.

97. *Ibid.*, III, pp. 51, 53–54.

98. *Ibid.*, III, pp. 87 ff., 91 ff., 95 ff.

99. *Ibid.*, III, pp. 57 ff., 87 ff.

100. *Ibid.*, III, p. 90.

101. *Ibid.*, III, pp. 92–95.

Index